I TATTI STUDIES IN
ITALIAN RENAISSANCE HISTORY

Published in collaboration with I Tatti
The Harvard University Center for Italian Renaissance Studies
Florence, Italy

GENERAL EDITOR
Kate Lowe

MILAN UNDONE

Contested Sovereignties in the Italian Wars

JOHN GAGNÉ

Harvard University Press

Cambridge, Massachusetts

London, England

2021

For Elena Brambilla
(1942–2018)

First printing

Library of Congress Cataloging-in-Publication Data

Names: Gagné, John, 1977– author.
Title: Milan undone : contested sovereignties in the Italian Wars / John Gagné.
Other titles: I Tatti studies in Italian Renaissance history.
Description: Cambridge, Massachusetts : Harvard University Press, 2021. | Series: I Tatti studies in Italian renaissance history | Includes bibliographical references and index.
Identifiers: LCCN 2020020448 | ISBN 9780674248724 (cloth)
Subjects: LCSH: Sovereignty. | Milan (Italy)—History—To 1535. | Milan (Italy)—Politics and government. | Italy—History—1492–1559.
Classification: LCC DG657.8 .G34 2021 | DDC 945/.206—dc23
LC record available at https://lccn.loc.gov/2020020448

CONTENTS

MILAN UNDONE

TIMELINE

YEAR	DATE	EVENT
1388		Giangaleazzo Visconti's testament bequeaths Milan to his sons or—if they should all die—to his daughter Valentina
1395	11 May	Emperor Wenceslaus creates Duchy of Milan for Giangaleazzo
1396	13 October	Emperor Wenceslaus extends Duchy of Milan in second investiture
1447	18 August	Ambrosian Republic declared
1450	26 February	Francesco I Sforza assumes control of Duchy of Milan
1466	8 March	Francesco I Sforza dies; his son Galeazzo Maria becomes duke
1476	26 December	Galeazzo Maria Sforza assassinated
1480	7 October	Ludovico Sforza assumes nominal control of duchy
1494	September	King Charles VIII invades Italy
1495	26 March	Maximilian I invests Ludovico Sforza with Duchy of Milan
	6 July	Battle of Fornovo
1499	2 September	Ludovico flees Milan; city and duchy surrender to France
1500	27 January	Pro-Sforza insurrection; Ludovico's restoration
	10 April	Battle of Novara; Ludovico captured; Milan returns to French control
1502	July-August	Louis XII visits Lombardy

1505	7 April	Haguenau Conference—Maximilian I invests Louis XII with Duchy of Milan
1506	June	Genoa revolts against French rule
1507	April-May	Louis XII puts down Genoese revolt; visits Milan
1509	14 May	Battle of Agnadello
	14 June	Maximilian I re-invests Louis XII with Duchy of Milan
1511	2 November	Council of Pisa-Milan against Julius II opens
1512	11 April	Battle of Ravenna; French rule of Milan begins to crumble
	21 April	Council of Pisa-Milan declares Julius II deposed; Julius opens Fifth Lateran Council
	12 August	Massimiliano Sforza created Duke of Milan
1513	6 June	Battle of Ariotta (Novara)
	19 November	French garrison in castle of Milan surrenders
1515	1 January	Louis XII dies; François I assumes crown
	13 September	Battle of Marignano; Massimiliano Sforza ousted; François I assumes control of Milan
1521	20 November	French withdraw from Milan (except castle); Morone assumes governorship in name of Francesco II Sforza
1522	27 April	Battle of Bicocca
1523	14 April	French garrison in castle of Milan surrenders
1524	23 October	French recapture Milan
1525	24 February	Battle of Pavia; French lose Milan; François I taken prisoner
	27 July	Charles V invests Francesco II Sforza with Duchy of Milan
	30 July	Marquis of Pescara writes Charles V of Morone's plot
	14 October	Marquis of Pescara arrests Girolamo Morone for treason

1526	24 July	Francesco II exits Milan's castle after several months under imperial siege; flees to Como
1527	January	Spanish troops depart Milan; replaced by Swiss and Italian forces
1528		Milan governed by Leyva; city assaulted by Sforza, Venetian, and French forces
1529	6 August	Peace of Cambrai; France renounces Lombard claims
	29 November	Charles V re-invests Francesco II Sforza with Duchy of Milan
1530	14 January	Francesco II's forces assume control of Milan
1531	15 February	Spanish garrison in castle of Milan departs peacefully
1533	13 October	Duchess Christina of Denmark enters Milan
1535	2 November	Francesco II Sforza dies; Leyva named governor of Milan

Introduction

Investments

What is the nature of a state as it falls apart? The problem at the core of this book is Milan's sovereignty in the early sixteenth century. It examines how warring contenders for the city and its duchy constructed and defended their claims to sovereign power in a period that brought constant change to Lombardy. Sovereignty, after all, was—and still is—not an object to be passed from hand to hand like a scepter. It is not a thing but an argument, an investment. Or even better: it is an idea that aspires to be a practice. The early Italian Wars (1494–1535) describe a period in which the peninsula faced a chaotic repositioning of authority through violence, as the major European monarchies competed for mastery south of the Alps.[1] During these wars, disputants supported their clashing cases for sovereign rule with history, lineage, law, force: all of those justifications were locked into a deadly contest for preeminence in the dukedom between 1499 and 1535. By 1499, Milan had known the rule of Visconti and Sforza dukes for a century; in 1535, it came under a Spanish dominion that lasted over 170 years. But the three decades at the dawn of the century witnessed a tug of war over Milan between

French and Sforza claimants that entailed its undoing as an independent duchy.

The specific predicament in Milan's sovereignty to which the book devotes itself is the way that these clashes had a polarizing effect. Professed concurrently by multiple claimants, the idea of sovereignty—and the geopolitical community to which it pertained—sustained unusual pressure. It was not that princes or people stopped lending credence to the notion of sovereign rule itself; if anything, social and political destabilization actually stimulated greater desire for efficient authority. Rather, conflict pulled the idea in many directions at the same time. Competing aspirants to legitimation and its pursuant authority produced, if such a thing can exist, a surfeit of sovereignty. Too many ambitions ran up against too many defensible reasons to rule. Unable to resolve this opposition, these claims extinguished each other, or guttered. Like a flame, sovereignty could flicker: it could exist in scorching reality and vanish into nothingness at the same time.

This condition of flickering sovereignty—engendered by contest for total dominance—occurred along at least two chronologies. First, the quandary could present itself at a single juncture in time, when observers confronted the conflicting impingements of more than one sovereign. This muddle opens Chapter 4, at the instant in 1504 when a Milanese gentleman who has served both the Duke of Milan and the king of France decides that he can no longer obey either of them. In this moment, the very multiplicity of lordships dissolved them both from his affinities. Similar scenarios from 1513–1514 will concern us in the next few pages. Second, the phenomenon could also manifest across several years or decades, as assault after assault serially overturned Milanese regimes, producing a long-form shudder as the state spun between different rulers. Between 1499 and 1535, Milan endured nine changes of government as a result of ongoing wars for dominion. To pull in opposite directions with enough strength is ultimately to break the desired object, whether it is loyalty, territory, or a state itself.

Listen now to an articulation of this situation as voiced by a contemporary Venetian chronicler. All we need to know for the moment is that it describes Milan in the year 1500. French King Louis XII (1462–1515) has just ousted Duke Ludovico Sforza (1452–1508), often known as "il Moro," for a second time in less than a year (fig. I.1). France ruled

Fig. I.1 Ludovico Sforza, marble medallion attributed to Benedetto Briosco, before 1500. Musée Jacquemart-André, R.F. 615.

Photo by author.

Milan for five months in 1499–1500, then Ludovico—supported by a widespread uprising across the duchy—returned to power for just over eight weeks. (Ludovico's fleeting restoration and ultimate capture in April 1500 begin Chapter 3 of this book.) In eight months, Milan's rulership had violently changed three times. Watching from Venice, Girolamo Priuli remarked:

> Almost all the nobles and citizens of Milan were uprooted and mistreated. This was because when Lord Ludovico entered Milan most recently, all those citizens who had shown favor to the French crown were taken, imprisoned, and killed by him, and some were mistreated and had their goods confiscated. Then when the King of France returned to Milan, all those citizens who had shown favor to Lord Ludovico were scattered, imprisoned, mistreated, and killed, and their property made public. So, one way or another, the poor Milanese were treated very badly in this year, and only

> very few were left with any prominence or renown, either
> from the French faction or from Lord Ludovico's. And the
> French began to practice trades in Milan; no one could
> sell anything aside from them because the French pur-
> chased from their own, and so the Milanese could no
> longer sell anything.[2]

Today's persecuted were tomorrow's persecutors, and vice versa. In pointing to the apparent lack of Milanese winners in this rotation of re-gimes, Priuli describes the phenomenon of flickering sovereignty and its negative effects. The fluctuation of rulership made everyone a target for state recriminations.[3] He then hints at the new economic challenges that foreign domination brought to the usually bustling merchant city. The French regime unsurprisingly fostered the wares of its own mer-chants in Milan. In 1510, for instance, it prohibited the sale of any for-eign hats other than French ones.[4] Investments in sovereign rule, these small details remind us, were as much economic and corporeal as ideo-logical. Merchants—like urban governments, religious communities, and feudal lords—saw their own privileges in terms of agreements with the ruling authority. When a change of regime appeared to alter or usurp them, it posed a question: Do our rights still exist?

That doubt stimulated a culture of perennial petitioning, negoti-ating, and securing endangered or suspended privileges. Individuals or corporations worked to confirm their entitlements not only vertically (with the ruling authority itself, as did Pavia's sailors, millers, and fish-ermen with the French crown in 1502), but also laterally (with other polities whose agreements with ousted regimes now seemed imperiled; an effort along these lines entailed tetchy negotiations between Milan's merchant corporation and the senate of Venice in 1503)[5]. The formal language on such occasions leaned on conservative ideals, insisting that all parties should shun any novelties. But the circumstances them-selves were novel; the very reason to negotiate was the shock of some new dispensation. Novelty had already arrived—now came the necessity to deal with it. High tides of contract renewals act as social indices of shifts in sovereign power, as a fleet of actors sought to anchor their hi-erarchical standing in a world that war had inundated.

Fig. I.2 Massimiliano Sforza, fresco lunette attributed to workshop of Bernardino Luini, 1522–1526.

Raccolte d'Arte Antica, Pinacoteca del Castello Sforzesco, Milan. © Comune di Milano.

Evidence of profoundly hollow authority in this era could even manifest in ceremonial moments designed to broadcast majesty in its fullest form.[6] In late 1512, a Sforza duke reclaimed titular power over Milan after more than a decade of French dominion. Ludovico's eldest son, Massimiliano (1493–1530), a child of exile, had still not celebrated his twentieth birthday (fig. I.2).[7] The league of forces that had driven France from Milan, led by the Holy Roman Empire and a coalition of Swiss cantons, acceded to a Sforza restoration, and the Imperial Diet of Mantua elected Massimiliano as duke in 1512.[8] In the chill of a Milanese winter, three men oversaw the festive rites in which Massimiliano accepted the ducal mantle: Matthäus Lang, Matthäus Schiner, and Ramón de Cardona. Lang, bishop of Gurk, represented Emperor Maximilian I as imperial legate. Schiner, metropolitan of Sion, led the Swiss fighters in the campaign that dislodged French rule from the Lombard dukedom. He was also papal legate to Italy and the German lands. Cardona, Spanish viceroy of Naples, captained the troops opposing France at the Battle of

Ravenna in April. These stern warriors embodied the force that propelled Sforza fortunes back to prominence.

Observing the celebration in the December rain, the Venetian envoy reported that it "was very solemn with respect to the Viceroy, the legate of Gurk, and the other foreigners, but as for the Milanese and the feudatories of the duchy of Milan, it could not have been simpler or more naked."[9] Personages the diplomat expected to see had instead made themselves scarce. Turning to Massimiliano, the ambassador recognized that "the *Ducheto* is like a symbol (*tamquam signum*): these three men rule together with the Milanese senate. It can be said that Milan is governed by Germans, Swiss, and Spanish—all of them greedy for money. [. . .] The Milanese are all unhappy and desperate," he continued, noting the residents would be hard-pressed to pay the required exactions to one of the three powers, let alone all of them.[10] Purse-strings would be tugged in many directions.

An unresolved problem haunted the ceremony: the fact that a vacuum presided at its center. Not only did the young duke function— at least in the Venetian's cutting appraisal—as a cipher, but more pressingly, no agreement existed between the other players over the nature and extent of their power collaboration. This truth became blindingly clear at the moment of princely consecration. The Venetian continued:

> Some contention arose between the Viceroy, Gurk, and the Legate about which one of them should invest the Duke with the ducal mantle. The Legate, speaking on behalf of the Swiss, said it was up to them since they had expelled the French from Italy. A Spanish orator said that the Viceroy ought to have the honor since he had presided at the Battle of Ravenna. And Gurk said it pertained to him because the Duke was a feudatory of the Empire. The Duke, not wanting to make anyone unhappy, said that he wanted to invest himself.[11]

Massimiliano slung the white damask robe of Milan's dukes over his own shoulders. The gesture may appear to recall the self-coronations of rulers radically confident in their own might, yet the teenager's solution to the dispute was just the opposite. Nobody invested Massimiliano Sforza with the duchy. He was a prince whose confused installation revealed the absence of the "plenitude of power" (*plenitudo potestatis*) that his ancestors had arrogated to themselves.[12] Massimiliano still employed that magisterial language during his short rule, but the chaos in his reign over the city and duchy belied this discourse of mastery. He needed no reminder of his predicament even on that very day: shelling from the city's still French-held castle cut the festivities short.[13]

Similar disputes over ritual precedence posed Milan's disarray as an urgent question of sovereignty. Almost a year after Massimiliano's investiture, both French and Milanese orators assembled before the newly elected Pope Leo X (r. 1513–1521). In consistory sessions, the two representatives traded loud insults over the tyranny of their respective regimes in Lombardy. The French orator, Claude de Seyssel, argued against the presence of Massimiliano Sforza's envoys. He asserted that "His Sanctity [the pope] should not heed them as orators of the Duke of Milan, because his [Seyssel's] King was the real duke of Milan, invested by Popes Alexander and Julius and by the Emperor himself, and this one is Duke of Milan by force and has no investiture."[14]

Some days later, Marino Caracciolo, Sforza orator, expressed his outrage that the French representatives had listed "Duke of Milan" among Louis XII's official titles, because "he had usurped the duchy of Milan, and the current duke had recovered it with help from the Holy See."[15] Caught in the same bind as Massimiliano at his investiture, Pope Leo could only compromise on both occasions. He simply "sought to assuage and silence them," or guaranteed that the dispute would not engender prejudice against either party (*respondit quod omnia dicta transirent sine praeiudicio*).[16] The pope's prevarication over the politics of lordship exemplified much wider-held worries over an evolving disaster: a vortex of military, legal, political, economic, religious, and cultural disputes that the belligerents had brought to the Milanese duchy. That vortex—and the confusions surrounding it—is what this book interprets. It pursues those spirals as a way to describe an Italian Renaissance polity under almost unbearable pressures. As much as scholars have chased the history of the modern state by asking after its genesis or origins, there has been little talk of its failures, collapses, and stillbirths.[17] The cracking of a state has a history of its own, one that remains largely untold. For understandable reasons of documentation, many histories of Milan in this period end in 1499 with the ouster of the Sforza or commence in 1535 with the

beginnings of centuries of Spanish governance. *Milan Undone* instead fo-
cuses on the years in between; it sees fluctuating regimes as a lens for
interpretation rather than an obstacle to it.

Despite the focus in the foregoing pages on the tensions around
investiture (and we will see much more of it later), the book proposes
an analysis of sovereign power critical of the supposedly legitimating
force of official recognition. Investiture often misleads historians into
seeing it as a conflict-resolving solution, which it rarely proved to be, as
Massimiliano's case reveals. Investiture obsessed these belligerents,
but they also ignored it when it suited them. In other words, the book's
approach takes seriously the evidence that these iron-clad gestures
were always frangible. Formal ratification of rule—perhaps especially
during periods of war, when power structures were in the midst of their
own reformulation—functioned more often as an acknowledgment of realities or wishes (or as a financial exchange) than as a genuinely formative
matrix. Yet the desire for validity animated so much conflict in the Italian
Wars, partly because the sources of validation seemed to diversify and
thus to perpetuate the search for a genuine font of authority: more
rulers declared themselves supreme in contests where a sole authority
used to preside. Among both rulers and subjects, innumerable political
impasses resulted from disagreements over how to recognize and appeal
to superiors.

Sovereignty and Emergency

Such problems invite us to confront the very nature of sovereignty as a
historical concept. This book accepts that a functional European concept of sovereignty existed around 1500, even if it traveled with a slightly
different vocabulary than our current one: *sovranità*, for instance, was not
a commonly employed term in the early sixteenth century.[18] The cluster
of ideas that informed ideological traditions of sovereignty—*potestas*
(power), *auctoritas* (authority), *maiestas* (grandeur), *maioritas* (superiority),
dominium (rule), *imperium* (supreme rule), *iurisdictio* (the right to say what
is law)—actively pertained to the Italian Wars.[19] A crucial additional element that the debates around Massimiliano highlight is the quality of
subjective discernment or recognition (*cognoscere, recognoscere*): namely,
whether or not to acknowledge the claims that others make. Speculation

on this latter legal territory abounded around 1500.[20] Since the era of the Ottonian emperors in the tenth century, it was generally accepted that much of northern Italy, including Lombardy, belonged to the Holy Roman Empire and that Milan's ducal title emanated from a fourteenth-century imperial donation. But even the contours of that relationship remained open to debate.[21] Moreover, French jurists had for more than a century exerted formidable energies to articulate their king's special rights and privileges; increasingly tendentious interpretation of those liberties in the late fifteenth and early sixteenth centuries significantly muddied the waters, even in matters of Italian lordship. *Rex est imperator in regno suo:* the king is emperor in his own kingdom. This notion may explain why, as we will see, French jurists turned to ancient history to prove that northern Italy once belonged to France in a time that was pre-imperial, pre-Christian, and almost pre-Roman. Whether to recognize imperial precedence in Italy then became a much foggier proposition. Moreover, rulers were not alone in adjudicating this genre of argument. Everyone involved in these wars from feudatories to city councils to subjects participated at some point in the process of recognizing (or rejecting) justifications of sovereign sway.

By understanding sovereignty as a malleable construct rather than a concrete fact, we allow ourselves to interpret its historical formulation and manipulation. The more urgent goal then becomes examining how the concept functioned under the pressures that war exerted on it. What is the nature of sovereignty when it undergoes concerted attack? What kind of situation obtains when multiple contenders, sometimes over years, refuse to accept any pretensions other than their own? Who is the real duke of Milan? And how are institutions, territories, and subjects meant to resolve the social confusion that the contest produces? To begin answering such questions, the interpreter must have more than just an appreciation of the abstract Latin nouns listed above. There must also be a capacity to understand how emergency situations such as invasion, war, and domination trouble the concrete application of such ideas. Theoretical concepts need to be complemented by historical frameworks and political realities.

Most useful as a path in this direction are the readings of sovereignty that frame its very definition in terms of emergency. According to these visions, the contours of sovereignty appear most clearly at moments when it appears to dissolve.[22] Only extreme threats and ruptures of lawful norms show nakedly who has the power to act authoritatively.[23] Those moments of legal emptiness open a zone of indistinction where nature and law, outside and inside, interpenetrate.[24] The sovereign power, in such readings, declares itself by deciding where the line between norm and exception resides.[25] In other words, sovereignty arises from acting within the indistinct. The confusion that demands action is itself the matrix of sovereignty; emergency is paradoxically its existential precondition. As he surveyed the predicament of the Duchy of Milan after decades of war in 1522, Emperor Charles V recognized this zone when he described how its residents seemed to turn "to the primeval law of nature when dominion over things was uncertain (*sicut ad primeva naturae iura, quum rerum dominia in incerto erant*)."[26]

The question remains: Who *does* act in this zone of indistinction? To recognize the existence of multiple answers to that question is to apprehend the flickering sovereignty I identified earlier. Sovereigns were pluralized. The struggles they sustained for supremacy determined how long that zone lasted and how deeply it traveled. The force of sovereignty is thus historically contingent, finding moments of strength and weakness according to circumstance. Circumstance also determines whether moments of legal emptiness end with reestablished norms, or whether they become troubling vacuums in which unpunishable crimes and atrocities take place. As the fight for Milan deepened over three decades, the shores of time separating the exit and entrance of antagonistic regimes seemed to widen, as war extended the periods when interim authorities (patrician councils, vice-ducal commissioners, or military lieutenants) nominally oversaw the state. When Ludovico Sforza assumed princely status from his just-dead nephew in 1494, he pointed squarely—and self-consciously, since he had been planning this moment for years—to the "danger that can follow when we leave the state without a definite Lord."[27] Ludovico was clearly self-interested, but he was not wrong; chasms between lords' reigns were genuinely perilous.[28] In 1499, when his rule over Milan seemed doomed, Ludovico sought to preserve some stability by inventing an emergency governing body known as the *Conservatori dello Stato*. Following the Sforza restoration in 1513, Massimiliano reconvened this council. After 1515 we never see it again.[29]

These gaps and stopgaps receive particular attention in the following pages because they created some of the most confounding and durable problems for regimes. It is why so many chapters dwell on these in-betweens: particularly the initial buckling of Sforza rule in 1499–1500, but also 1512–1513 and 1515–1516, and to a lesser extent 1521–1526, 1529–1530, and 1535. One of this book's central aspirations is to contribute a reading of this turbulent time in Milanese history that pays as much attention to the turbulence as to the regimes that have drawn most of the historical analysis so far. To interpret the zones of indistinction cumulatively over time is to identify new territory for understanding the Italian Wars as a sociocultural form. The book documents fissures in the challenged state so as to draw our eye to the politics of failure, to the forces that used the system in order to unmake it, and to the effects that such workings generated. I aim not to defend or reify the state as an entity, but rather to peer inside its wounds in order to see how it was made. In so doing, I highlight the myriad bids for power that have otherwise remained veiled by the opaque skin of the body politic: usurpation, collaboration, defamation, exploitation, resistance, and fraud. In having focused much of our historiography on the fabrication of the state—projects to build civic edifices, urban alliances, and regional consensus—we occasionally overlook these other countervailing forces.

During the early sixteenth century, even after control shifted from one power to another, sovereign contest was not necessarily resolved. Leaving aside that each transfer itself germinated new wars to overturn the settlement, we must recognize how long-lasting sociopolitical disturbance accompanied these shifts. Subject populations and ruling classes were ambivalent about adherence and obedience. Regional divisions and factional constellations—among other factors—fashioned a delicate, changeable latticework of affiliation in the territorial state and its neighbors.[30] Around 1500, enough disenchantment with the Sforza status quo existed that French governance seemed a feasible alternative to some, and many Italian districts welcomed the king as a liberator.[31] Faith in this conceit dwindled as it became clear that structural problems (fiscal mismanagement, disturbances in public order) continued even under new foreign lords. But the fractious power of the idea lasted a long time. That fundamental tension pulled at the Duchy of Milan from within, vitiating its stability.

State structure itself became a victim of these tensions. Historians must not be too quick to trust the efficacy of a polity in crisis. The appearance of institutional norms does not necessarily mean that they exist. That is to say, the mere existence of state structures does not mean that a state actually functions. As we will see, French and Sforza regimes implanted themselves in Milan with vigor and determination; they invested in their rules. They appointed officers, secretaries, castellans; instituted councils and procedures; signed treaties; undertook negotiations; and issued orders. But it does not follow that infrastructure produced functionality, that the state was therefore self-fulfilling. Bureaucracies can be staffed to the hilt and still be radically strained: the workings of sovereignty are unevenly distributed even in the best of times. Apparent progress may seem to be achieved in the halls of princes while all hell breaks loose outside the doors. To boot, in an era when states and the regimes that made them were so closely intertwined, serial regime failures contributed to the decay of the state itself.[32]

Functionality was always a desideratum—sometimes it materialized but other times it evaporated. At their most beleaguered, systems cannibalized themselves. Deputies elected to investigate fraud committed it themselves; term-limited governors claimed perpetual power; rulers serially levied more money than subjects could afford. Compounding these instances of malfeasance was the serious problem of the brevity of regimes. Fleeting duration existentially challenged a culture that valorized continuity. Even functional systems could meet their own demise when replaced or reordered by the next regime. (I will return briefly to this issue in the next section to distinguish this ephemerality from self-selected brevity.) Depending on circumstance, regimes strove vehemently either to uphold an illusion of continuity or to deny it categorically. The reality was complex. Circulation of rulership overwhelmed many of the elements that could guarantee genuinely efficacious links to the past. Nonetheless, individuals and institutions reappeared as conspicuous threads through the warp and weft of decades. Girolamo Morone (1470–1529), the ubiquitous Sforza politico, opens and closes this book because he epitomizes his generation's travails through this labyrinth.

An acknowledgment of these political rotations should not obscure the fact that life carried on for many people in the troubled duchy. We can document remarkable sociocultural continuities that persisted between regimes. Even during abject moments in early sixteenth-century Milan, notaries transacted legal agreements, printers issued books and pamphlets, and painters plied their trade.[33] Artisans worked hard to secure their livelihoods and train their apprentices despite political reversals.[34] Those types of socioeconomic continuities directly served the interests of the government in power. As part of securing its installation, a regime could promote an image of peaceful and normal economic production to cultivate social trust. An economic memorandum penned in 1500, just as the French settled into their rule over Milan, made it very clear that the crown understood the city as a system in which the balance between artisan production and elite consumption needed support to prevent an urban exodus under new lordship.[35] To promote these fiscal continuities—or even the appearance of them—showed an effort to couple subjects' fortunes to the regime's legitimation.

It may be true, as the scholarly consensus suggests, that aspects of the duchy's economic and institutional fortunes eventually emerged from the sovereignty contests in the 1540s strengthened by the trials of the wars.[36] Even the legal articulation of the duchy itself came to be reframed in much simpler terms than had pertained to it before the wars.[37] But it is also true that the wars transformed the duchy from a dynamic, self-governing, court-focused territorial state into a satellite of the global Habsburg Empire. For some of those involved, this rupture opened opportunities inconceivable under continued Sforza rule, while many others perished in the clash.[38] By understanding how the duchy's disaggregation happened through torrents of contest, we can grasp the texture of the transformation. The itineraries—upward, downward, and even circular—of the generation who lived through the wars help us to grasp the challenges and opportunities inherent in the collapse of a major state.

The Double Bind of the Italian Wars

"The Duke has lost his state, his things, and his liberty, and none of his works was finished for him." Leonardo da Vinci, a Sforza factotum for nearly twenty years, scribbled this pithy valediction inside the cover of one of his travel notebooks in 1500.[39] Other voices were less circumspect. "He who wants everything, loses everything," one pamphleteer admonished in a vituperative *ottava rima*.[40] Ludovico Sforza's ouster, failed restoration, and imprisonment shocked observers in Italy, Europe, and beyond.[41] This twist in the geopolitical plot seemed to set everything in a new direction. That was certainly how contemporaries imagined the events that followed 1494, as they borrowed from a repertoire of ancient examples to help frame their own view of the new social and military eversions. Milan's magnitude as both city and duchy made its capture particularly remarkable. In 1499, the Sforza state functionally consisted of ten major cities: Milan, Pavia, Cremona, Como, Lodi, Parma, Piacenza, Novara, Alessandria, and Tortona.[42] Even more cities and districts bound themselves to the dukes by agreement but maintained some nominal autonomy.[43] As one of Europe's grandest metropoles, Milan housed nearly 100,000 people. Its axial location on the Lombard plain and its diversified production lent it a substantial economic prominence in the late fifteenth century.[44] Its court had become one of Italy's hubs of cultural finesse and its feudal lords some of the peninsula's most potent magnates.[45] The successful seizure of such a potent duchy struck many as a profound shock. "The whole state is falling to ruin," one Florentine onlooker observed.[46]

The invasion laid bare the inherent fragility of a seemingly powerful polity such as Milan. Under Sforza rule, the duchy was precocious, robust, and resilient *and* structurally weak, fragmented, and over-extended. Contrasting realities, to be sure, but co-existent ones. The vehement French assault unleashed longstanding internal tensions that should make us question how functional a state fifteenth-century Milan really was. Its "stateness," while discernible, is less self-evident than we often admit. Still, its dissolution was spectacular and troubling. It seemed to be a harbinger—perhaps of divine judgment, but also of new modes of interaction between people. Bewildering novelties appeared to haunt the new century as the shadow of war hovered over Italy. We have come to think of the Italian Wars as a "watershed," a "state of permanent emergency," "a chaotic threat to the good order of the world."[47] The familiar stories about the unprecedented ferocity of French warcraft as a stimulus for Italians to reconsider their cultural agendas do not need to be retold here.[48] This book accepts many of these arguments as foundational— it builds upon the notion that successive years of conflict ignited a slow-burning fire across society. In fact, that very same combustive imagery occurred frequently to writers watching the wars in real time.[49] Those long decades of widening discord occasioned shifts, whether in new political configurations or perceived moral decadence, that contemporaries commented on themselves.[50] Words took on fresh meanings.[51] Things were changing.

And yet, let us also reverse that last sentence to recognize that many things remained unchanged. Italians had already faced similar challenges in the fourteenth and fifteenth centuries. While the dawn of the sixteenth century brought violent new technologies and expanding soldier numbers, the fifteenth century was not as bloodless as we often portray it.[52] The first half of the century had brought Milan decades of war with Venice, which included fractious hostilities on land and water, and the second half drew the duchy into a series of contests with the Swiss cantons involving abject violence.[53] One might say that the Italian Wars, to adapt an adage, were just like every other period but more so. The phrase means to acknowledge how the wars after 1500 triggered a strange dilation of familiar forms into larger, more disruptive versions of themselves. That is the double bind of the Italian Wars: they are both new and not. The early sixteenth-century Italian conflicts push the historian to find the novel in the familiar and vice versa. I take that enigma seriously, and I hope the reader will as well. Throughout, the book examines problems in the war years that were not alien to Italy's fifteenth century. It draws our attention to transalpine interference in Italian affairs, regime change, contest for legitimation, juridical crisis, exile, fraud, confiscation, prophecy, and political domination. Without even casting our eyes outside the Lombard duchy, we can adduce a host of examples of each of those themes from the fifteenth century. Sforza rule in Milan entailed a series of internal contests involving ducal assassination (of Galeazzo Maria, in 1476), banishment (of his brothers and other conspirators by Duchess Bona, in 1477), and usurpation (of Galeazzo Maria's son by Ludovico in 1480). Responses to this complex saga seeped across Europe; its effects were still palpable during the Italian Wars. Giangiacomo Trivulzio (1441–1518), the Milanese Guelf whom Ludovico Sforza had banished in 1495, commanded the French army that captured the duchy in 1499.

The book thus not only uncovers the novelties around 1500, but also traces shifts in the patterns of the familiar or mundane as indices of the way a major state collapses. A central element binding the book's chapters is the problem set out a few pages ago: the effects of the existential challenge of multiple lordships, both concurrently (two or more claimants demanding authority at the same time) and in alternation (antagonists serially toppling each other). Here is where the depth of the intervention by foreign powers also makes a difference during the new century. Regimes across Quattrocento Italy, both republican and princely, had undergone cycles of internal change, both fitful and regular. Factional dissent pushed individuals and families into exile and drew them back; pretenders to sole lordship extinguished each other. Mercenary captains hopped routinely from one side to another. Moreover, many cities designed their governments to resist the accumulation of power by scheduling a rotation of rulers or council members or by dividing power evenly between factions. These traditions struck the French—accustomed to a royal ideology of unbroken male succession—as troublesome during their Italian entrenchment. In 1513 Claude de Seyssel discerned darkly that "Italy is more subject to change (*mutacion*) than any other region of Christendom."[54]

In the same breath, he also recognized a twin truth about war. "War has a long tail: when it vanishes on one side, it ignites on the other."[55] 1499 brought a foreign military coup to the Duchy of Milan that captured, with nearly total success, all the major cities of the state at once. The starkly international character of the new century's contests opened a furious dynamic that diminished the common ground upon which contenders stood. They did not just fight to govern the same state; they fought in large part to replace each other's version of it: new institutions, bureaucratic structures, personnel, elite affiliations, language. France's imperial ambitions in Italy meant that cultural difference became a weapon. Foreign soldiers billeted in Italian homes or sustained themselves on peasant communities; French barons personally assumed lordship of Lombard fiefs; governmentality tilted toward Gallic standards. Such deep efforts to overwrite previous structures made the oscillations between regimes particularly battering. Sforza restorations successively aimed to erase those novelties. In that regard, the state's own knowledge of itself and its hazards suffered. Knowing is abetted by continuity, but continuity was precisely what new regimes wished to deny. That is another double bind of these times. Just how effectively each regime achieved its own vision at the expense of the last varied, but the result was a decadence of the state. The book works to reveal the history of this degenerative dynamic that brought international war to bear upon preexisting tensions, distending them into a double force that gnawed at the state both from inside and outside.

These dynamics did not pertain exclusively to the Lombard dukedom, even if they were particularly striking and long-lasting there. We can observe some version of flickering sovereignty in other polities during the Italian Wars, whether in major war-buffeted centers such as Genoa and Naples or in tiny burgs like Cotignola.[56] Cotignola, the Romagnol town nearly 300 kilometers southwest of Milan, belonged to the Sforza because it was the birthplace of the clan's progenitor, Muzio Attendolo. In 1499, Louis XII sent soldiers to absorb it into French rule; the town then underwent a miniature version of Milan's own travails between rival claimants.[57] To capture the scope of the cracking of a state as sizeable as Milan, the book investigates both the grand scale of the court, city, and ruling classes as well as the diffuse effects that radiated out to populations, subject territories, and adjacent lands.

The Duchy of Milan as a Shatterzone

The Italian Wars unmade the Sforza duchy as an independently governed princely state. Contemporaries framed the process exactly in those same terms, using a common turn of phrase that conveyed abasement and destruction of territories. Francesco Guicciardini described the pressure that France and its ally Venice brought to bear upon Ludovico Sforza in 1499 as "the undoing of the State of Milan (*la disfazione dello Stato di Milano*)."[58] Other cities faced similar crises. When the French army sacked nearby Brescia in 1512, an engineer reported that the city would be "undone, and will not be remade during the lifetime of a man (*si può dire che Bressa sarà desfacta et ad etade de homo vivente non se remetterà*)."[59] In 1515, as French forces threatened Milan, within the city walls the Sforza duke's lieutenant ran a terror campaign hoping to uncover French collaborators. "The citizens stayed submissively in their homes," wrote a chronicler, "awaiting the ruin of the homeland along with its undoing (*aspectando la rovina della patria insieme con la sua disfactione*)."[60] In both Italian and French, the verb *disfare/défaire* coupled ruin with defeat: of course, "defeat" is merely a variant of the same Latin root (*dis* + *facere*) that gives us "undo." To recognize how contemporaries themselves imagined Milan's undoing is to apprehend how their eyes surveyed the myriad damages the wars inflicted.[61]

Since we still often refer to this season in Milanese history as the French occupation, it should not go unsaid that the word "occupation" carried in 1500 same the malevolent ring it does today. An agent wrote to Ludovico Sforza the summer before his ouster that "the King of France is resolved to occupy the state (*di occupare el stato*) of Your Excellency."[62] Louis XII and his secretaries, by the same token, called Sforza the "unjust occupier of our duchy (*injuste occupateur de notre dite duché*)."[63] The notion that the duchy was being preyed upon or held prisoner by an illegitimate lord was a cardinal rhetorical frame for recriminations between both contenders. Beneath these accusations lay the charge that only tyrants committed occupation, because righteous rulers rejected it as unnecessary. Occupation was synonymous with injustice.

As the wars over this territory—occupied then reoccupied, taken then lost—raged on, they produced a shatterzone in and around the Duchy of Milan. "Shatterzone" describes an analytical concept that mid-twentieth-century political scientists coined to explain why certain geographies suffered more conflict than others. Sometimes called a "shatterbelt" or "crush zone," the shatterzone designates an internally weak, immature, or fragmented territory that lies between the geopolitical desires of more substantial powers. When major states contend for these weak areas, the zone of contention finds itself shattered or crushed, and thus further destabilized. When sixteenth-century observers referred to Milan as the "key to Italy," they were articulating, albeit in positive terms, this same strategic reality.[64] Zones of economic and strategic richness could be crushed by the very desire that made them covetable.

The political scientists and geographers who coined the concept of the shatterzone, however, were largely disinterested in thinking about it as an historical phenomenon. They employed it instead as a diagnostic implement for contemporary global policy.[65] By contrast, anthropologists studying colonization and indigenous societies have borrowed the shatterzone as a tool to think through more distant histories of invasion in the sixteenth through eighteenth centuries.[66] In particular, they have used it to replace, and thus reframe, what they see as the problematic concept of the frontier, a word that describes the monolithic advance of colonial power upon new territories and peoples. The idea of the frontier long troubled many anthropologists for its tendency to share an analytical perspective with the advancing colonizer or with an arbitrary political boundary and thus to obliterate the view of the people falling under its hegemony.

Instead, the concept of the shatterzone promised something else: it invokes rupture, crumbling, fragmentation, and, most obviously, percussive impact. Imagine a cracked window with an epicenter radiating asymmetrical shatter-lines, traveling far and having profoundly destabilizing effects. In that sense, the shatterzone model resituated the anthropologist as a more holistic interpreter of conflict's impact and consequences, assessing the complex power dialogues in which both aggressors and victims were imbricated. It also, to my mind, serves as a better way to think about conflicting cultures than the notion of the contact zone, a concept that has become ubiquitous in premodern studies. The fissures of a cracking political or social geography spread much quicker and farther than contact itself does, because disruption—contingent in duration and space—occurs in a wide and irregular starburst around the most contested geographies.

As a framing tool for premodern European historians as well, the shatterzone can prove helpful. Without needing to import all its specific technical appurtenances (which already necessarily differ between disciplines), I see a central contribution of the concept of the shatterzone in how it connects some of the new approaches to studying premodern conflict: a rejection of histories of war as merely political or military histories; a concern to understand and assess displacements, diasporas, informal conflicts, the social effects of military force, and histories of violence; and—as a result of these and other factors—a way to think more ethically about how we write histories of war, that is, to recognize human and environmental consequences with the same clarity that we recognize political change. Perhaps historians can find the shatterzone concept enabling in the way it draws us to follow the cracks rather than the solids, in other words, to tell histories of failure and disaggregation as a way to reimagine our narratives about premodern war and statecraft. Why the shatterzone should matter to premodernist historians, then, is for its invitation to pursue more critically engaged histories of war, to rethink geographies of our analytical gaze beyond the self-evident loci of conflict, and to revise our tendency to focus on war's outcomes before we even consider its processes. Histories of politics and war that smooth over these processes can inadvertently suppress the frictions that we must uncover to reveal the negotiation, production, and application of power. This book thus suggests an alternative to the idea that war-making and state-making are mutually generative historical forces.[67] The large aggressive monarchies—France and the Habsburg Empire—may ultimately have emerged invigorated from the Italian Wars, but Milan's political implosion suggests a more complex history. As the object over which the large powers fought, the duchy's fate has its own lessons to impart. The shatterzone concept acts as the book's governing tool to keep such consequences in view.

Lombardy was a particularly active site for clashes, sacks, and sieges between 1500 and 1530. It was an epicenter of sorts. In a ring around Milan, armies fought the battles of Fornovo (1495), Novara (1500), Agnadello (1509), Ariotta (1513), Marignano (1515), Bicocca (1522), and Pavia (1525). That list accounts only for the best-known events, the most spectacular bolts from the storm clouds. Innumerable other conflicts beset the region, and they are perhaps the hidden story in the wars. They were generated not just by foreign troops but by unpaid mercenaries, vengeful feudal lords, factions, exiles, and bandits in a wide geography destabilized by the shifting claims of power over the duchy. Over the course of the book I select case studies in order to illustrate the geographic and chronological range of the effects of the beleaguered duchy to reveal new or occluded histories of these years of violence. Histories from the shatterzone, in this reading, provide evidence of the chronically irresolvable sovereignty contests unfolding across Lombardy.

The Scope of the Study

Only a handful of historical monographs devoted to Sforza Milan have appeared in English since the end of the Second World War. It is a strange absence in the face of mountains of literature on Florence, Rome, and Venice. Perhaps the Allied bombings of the State Archive in 1943 discouraged a generation of Anglophone historians from Milanese studies; or maybe the swell of postwar interest in the genealogies of republicanism disqualified princely Milan from extended examination. Despite their small number, the existing studies are path-breaking; they have illuminated crucial issues in court life, historiography, law, astrology, politics, and art.[68] Moreover, Milan and its duchy have always remained the subject of an immensely vibrant community of Italians scholars, whose research has recovered Milanese history with perspicacity and imagination. In recent years, Milan's itinerary through the Italian Wars has also experienced renewed attention. We now have not only a number of specialized studies on particular aspects of the period, but also exhaustively researched monographs on the French domination from 1499 to 1522.[69]

I commend these studies to readers interested in a full account of the narrative of the wars in Lombardy at the beginning of the sixteenth century. Moreover, we are now endowed with several fresh synoptic tellings of the Italian Wars in English, Italian, and French.[70] In them readers will find extensive and complementary background for the broader political trials during these years. This book provides the salient context for appreciating the struggles for authority in Milan without, I hope, sacrificing too much of the wider vista. Consequently, the chapters move thematically, rather than chronologically, so as to focus on the problems of sovereign contest in different arenas and to uncover systemic patterns and dispositives.

The study breaks into three parts: Politics, Property, and People. The book's first third examines the challenges that French rule posed to the fundamental components of the Sforza state: time, space, and dynasty. Chapter 1 excavates the layers of legitimizing claims the French crown made in order to secure its domination of Lombardy—for instance, that the region belonged to the ancient settlement of Gallia Cisalpina and that Orléans hegemony, linked by marriage to the Visconti dukes, was more venerable than Sforza lordship. Time was also a technique of lordship for both French and Sforza, a way to designate the *when* of the state. In other words, discourses of time indicated the temporalities that contenders saw as most beneficial to them, periods when they imagined the state to embody signorial fullness or emptiness. If we understand the contest over the duchy according to these conflicting schedules of rulership, we see how the state existed in multiple layered but discontinuous visions, as a palimpsest. Warring narratives about time themselves worked to weaken the cohesion of the state because they refused to acknowledge the zones of time during which they had no functional authority.

How that palimpsest functioned in urban space is the subject of Chapter 2. French rule in Milan wished to cancel Sforza initiatives but also sit atop them. Louis XII and his officers lacked coherent interest in a scheme of architectural implantation other than the reinforcement of walls and fortresses. Control over space did not occur so much through the built environment as in the policing of bodies. Mobility and physical appearance came particularly under the oversight of regimes as a way of making the city transparent to rulers in the midst of self-establishment. The third chapter traces the travails of the Sforza dynasty after it became the object of French delegitimization. On the one hand, it reconstructs the fate of Ludovico Sforza and his family in the years following France's capture of the duchy. On the other, it also examines the cultural apparatus by which the Sforza came to be sidelined (both by French and Italian commentators) as imprudent, degenerate, or unworthy princes. The chapter illustrates the family's disaggregation and isolation, tracing the collapse of Sforza fortunes to the point of near extinction by midcentury.

The book's second part pursues the problem of property, broadly speaking. One of the centrally noteworthy aspects of the Duchy of Milan was the continued presence and power of the landed nobility in both city and country.[71] As a patchwork of longstanding feudal holdings and newly donated fiefs to military and financial elites, the duchy contained a self-important caste of magnates with variable affiliations to the regime. Chapter 4 explores how the Italian Wars' sovereignty battles disrupted the tenuous feudal logics holding the state together. The sense that ownership was no longer a stable category launched many elites into wrathful passions directed against rulers, each other, and populations. The attempts on the part of elites to recoup their losses is the subject of Chapter 5, which traces a burgeoning culture of petition whose ultimate goal was restitution of a vanished *status quo ante*.

Both Chapters 4 and 5 focus on the politics of obscurity, that is, how the nature of these contests—as central authority spun in cycles—could blind rulers and subjects to current or recently past realities. Petitioners could not always see clearly what drove the prince's reasoning or the animus of counterclaimants. Nor could rulers necessarily discern the truth-value of supplicants' cases. Chapter 6 thus addresses the material grounds upon which many of these uncertainties rested: documents, but more often the lack of them. The Milanese duchy had a long history of documentary double-dealing: the Sforza had manipulated histories of succession to their own benefit during their half-century rule. On a much wider level, the war years emptied out many archives, meaning the state's own bureaucratic history was not always accessible. That fact handicapped the state's own ability to see itself, and it thereby opened the door to frauds.

Part III traces histories of different groups of people within the Lombard dukedom and their role in the contests for authority. We first encounter the elite refugees. Groups of Sforza loyalists fled Milan in 1499–1500 for shelter outside the occupied duchy. Chapter 7 follows this diaspora to the sites where exile communities gathered to seek safety and plan their resistance, mostly in Innsbruck, Mantua, and Venice. The chapter also problematizes the category of exile: every regime cast out hundreds of exiles. Subjects expelled by one regime often worked tirelessly to undermine it from outside, whether diplomatically or militarily. Some of these *banniti* found swift reintegration while others remained uprooted indefinitely, becoming agents of destabilization.

Clerics and the battles over holy sovereignty occupy Chapter 8 so as to reveal the interwoven problematics of secular and religious rule. King Louis XII saw the Sforza restoration in 1500 as an ecclesiastical conspiracy with strong links to Rome. The chapter therefore explores the rising tensions between the French crown and the papacy that culminated in the French efforts to depose Pope Julius II. It examines this face-off through prophetic and juridical currents aimed at weakening the position of the papal see. It follows two Milanese prophets embroiled in politics at the nexus of the Fifth Lateran Council and the first stirrings of the Lutheran challenge. Finally, Chapter 9 considers the communities of urban and rural subjects in the Lombard duchy. Focusing mostly on the residents of Milan, it shows the processes by which rulers sought to guarantee loyalty through rituals of consensus. But unanimity, it might be said, is the singularly absent quality of a crumbling state. The chapter suggests how new political opportunities were often matched by bruising restrictions on self-governance and fiscality. Voices of resistance called out in printed libels and satires to critique anonymously the pressures of domination.

Milan's early sixteenth century is replete with frustrations, hesitations, misunderstandings, and overlooked agents such as military laborers, widows, archivists, and rebels. Few of those characters feature centrally in the history of premodern war and politics. Their stories should interest us, however, since they disclose some of the most important work that happened in war: resistance, destruction, restitution, concealment. This book incorporates some of these perspectives into our understanding of the Italian Wars, and I hope that it will encourage others to follow similar lines of inquiry into the sources. The assiduous daily toil of secretaries, ambassadors, notaries, jurists, soldiers, governors, and rulers has bequeathed to us a voluminous record of this period that unveils but simultaneously obscures the era's reversals. There is more to be drawn out of the shadows, especially in the hollows between regimes. The book excavates some of those dark areas in its aspiration to offer a history of political chaos in Renaissance Italy.

Part I

Politics

The Temporality of the State

*K*ing Louis XII entered the newly conquered city of Milan in triumph on 6 October 1499.[1] One week later, Girolamo Morone, a twenty-nine-year-old law graduate and clerk, penned a note to Jacopo Antiquario, almost two decades his senior and a career secretary to Duke Ludovico Sforza. The duke had fled just days earlier; Antiquario was biding his time in nearby Pavia. Morone teased his elder for seeking such an idyllic retreat and regretted the absence of two mutual friends. The young secretary was still in Milan, watching the Sforza state fall apart. He suspected that in Pavia, Antiquario could avoid "the difficulties of revolutions, the whirlwinds (*turbines*) of current times, and the pain of shared defeat" that were inescapable in the capital.[2] Times were circling, politics was rotating. Milan was experiencing what contemporaries called a *mutazione di stato*. Autumn 1499 marked Morone's first use of this turbine locution in his long Milanese career. He remained in Milan as a royal fiscal advocate and senator under the French domination. But he wrote of whirlwinds again in 1512–1513, when Louis XII's government abandoned Milan after the Battle of Ravenna, and once more in 1516, when the French recaptured the city after the slaughter at Marignano.[3]

There may have been other occasions when the term occurred to him: perhaps in 1521 with the second French withdrawal, or in 1525, when Habsburg agents tortured him—by then grand chancellor—to reveal his role in an anti-imperial plot. Morone knew Milan's turbulent vicissitudes in his flesh and bones.

Like many of his contemporaries, Morone felt the peculiarity of his own era.[4] In 1500, after the first of many Milanese uprisings in these years, he remarked how "a great reversal happens every day, and here you can observe the variety of fortune in these incredible times."[5] Such a comment was not mere boilerplate. Fortune's wheel governed time with its unpredictable rotations, and the era's seemingly incessant changes—its spiraling whirlwinds—expressed the workings of those cosmic forces.[6] The state always existed in time, but an apprehension of its temporality erupted into particular prominence during moments of disruption. When one regime replaced another, fissures in the apparent continuity of history revealed themselves. Competing histories overlapped and interpenetrated. Old things became new, and novel things echoed the past. Visions of time thus multiplied in the vortices, fashioning histories and futures that accompanied the political narratives of clashing disputants— here mostly the Sforza and the French. Insofar as it served these calculated agendas, time also functioned as a tool of power, since jostling forces sought endlessly to structure both history and the future in ways beneficial to them. This chapter excavates three particular strata of time that help us understand the quarrels over Milan in the early sixteenth century: the ancient, the dynastic, and the governmental. In analyzing those different contexts, we not only gain purchase on Milanese government and history around 1500, but also see the construction and cultivation of time as an instrument of politics.

The Case for Foreign Indigeneity

The Milanese people are actually French. Such at least is what came to be extrapolated in later centuries from the fifth book of Livy's *Decades*. The ancient historian related how, during the era of Rome's last monarch, Tarquinius Priscus, the kingdom of the Gauls abounded with people. Wishing to unburden the land, King Ambigatus encouraged his two nephews to colonize new territory: Segovesus led his tribe to the Hercynian Forest in

southern Germany, and Bellovesus forged the first road across the Alps
to Italy. After routing Etruscans living near the River Ticino, Bellovesus
founded a city in Insubria called Mediolanum.[7] Through an ancient
Gallic mass migration sealed with a military victory, Milan came into
existence. Machiavelli alluded to this history in his essays on expansion
and migration in the *Discorsi*.[8] Bernardino Corio (1459–1504/5), Duke
Ludovico Sforza's court historiographer, faithfully paraphrased Livy's
words ("*Si lege in Tito Livio . . .,*" he begins) to launch his *Historia Patria*
(1503), a history of Milan from its origins to 1500. But the Livian account had unavoidable contemporaneity in Corio's own day: the last
pages of his book narrated the fall of the Sforza and the installation of
a new French regime in 1499. The Gauls had returned to (re)colonize
the territory by force; time was circling upon itself. Although he evalu-
ated a series of alternative tales of foundation, etymology, and mythic
roots, Corio ultimately accepted Milan's Gaulish foundations proposed by Livy, "in whom I have greater faith."

Corio's predecessors largely shared that faith; details may differ in
histories from earlier centuries, but the Gallic element is always present.
Paul the Deacon's *Historia Langobardorum* (late eighth century) describes
100,000 Gauls who descended into ancient Italy and founded Pavia,
Milan, Bergamo, and Brescia, and called the region Gallia Cisalpina.[9] In
1288, the chronicler Bonvesin de la Riva relied upon Paul's authority for
the city's Gallic origins in his *De Magnalibus Mediolani,* and although Galvano Fiamma's *Cronica Extravagans* (1337) considered a wider array of
sources than Bonvesin, his greatest difficulty lay in deciding which generation of Gauls should be credited with the city's origins.[10] Livy's account was known in France as well; it was catnip to cultural agents of
the crown during the military campaigns of the late fifteenth century
because it amplified historical justifications for French incursions.[11] The
novelty of French domination in the early sixteenth century could thus
be framed as a return, a fruition of ancient seeds. The logics of that
position implied that the French were more indigenous to Milanese
soil than Italians. The Gaulish foundation story externalized the city's
origins in both time and space. The founders were not, as so often happened in Italy, a dead civilization from that same territory. Instead
they were ancestors of modern French culture that in 1500 was still a
living, expanding, and conquering entity. The story's power thus lay in

the ineluctability of French lordship: it was natural because both history and the present authorized it.

In the rhetorical culture of both French and sympathetic Italians, that narrative played an important part in legitimating the new regime.[12] After a Milanese revolt against French domination brought Ludovico Sforza briefly back to power for two months in early 1500, the tenor of reestablished French rule hardened.[13] Milan was no longer imagined simply as a city that Louis XII had liberated from a tyrant; it had become the tyrant's conspirator. The city's second submission to France in April 1500 thus involved a Milanese delegation of good will culminating in a public dialogue between a mouthpiece for the city (Michele Tonso, tasked with voicing the city's apology for its insurrection) and for the crown (the Neapolitan jurist Michele Riccio, absorbed into French service during Charles VIII's conquest of Naples in 1494).[14] Both speakers made recourse to Milan's Gallic origins. Tonso observed that "it is agreed amongst historians that Milan, and all of Insubria, was once a colony of the Gauls."[15] In his responsory oration before the throngs of forcibly penitent Milanese citizens, Riccio scolded them for their infidelity, noting that the city's own orator had just admitted that Milan belonged to the French kings, "legitimate successors in this Duchy."

In a French translation of Riccio's oration that circulated in Lyon and Paris that same year, the translator rendered Riccio's claim about Milan's Gallic past even more insistently. "You have French origins and foundations; the king is your true, indisputable, and natural lord (*naturel seigneur*) to whom—as God commands—you owe love, faith, and obedience." The phrase *naturel seigneur* had emerged in France over the thirteenth and fourteenth centuries to bolster the kings during wars and succession crises, and it bundled together a set of arguments for the monarchy's legitimacy, indigeneity, and stability; the expression reappeared frequently in French vernacular print on Milanese themes around 1500.[16] Francophone readers were thus meant to understand that Valois lordship over Milan functioned according to bonds of affiliation identical to those tying France's own subjects to their crown. In Milan, the oath of fidelity that French agents demanded in 1499 employed this feudal formula as a crutch, requiring the duchy's subjects to swear in Latin legalese to behave as "good, faithful, upright, sincere, and obedient men, citizens, and subjects toward their natural and rightful lords (*naturales*

et directos dominos) and superiors,"[17] meaning the French monarchy and
its operatives.

The union of antique origins with a discourse of natural subjection
proved an effective ideological platform for Milan's French domination.[18] Praise for the city's Gaulish origins became a historical platitude
in the years of French rule. Celebrating the city in a 1518 oration at Santa
Maria delle Grazie, the Francophile Milanese Dominican friar Isidoro
Isolani noted that the ancient Gauls had "called Milan their metropolis,"
and—exalting current French lords through their ancient forebears—he
argued that the city had never been as safe and secure as under Gallic
rule.[19] That same year, the Pavian miniaturist Giovanni Ambrogio Noceto decorated a delicate paper portrait album of twenty-seven Milanese
patrician women to present to King François I. The book closes with a
clear invocation of Gallia Cisalpina in silver ink text on jet paper, addressing the young sovereign in the voice of Milan's elite daughters:
"Under Priscus's reign, fierce Bellovesus first carried the Gallic standards
across the Alps. At that time, Gaulish forebears founded Milan and
birthed our fathers. Thus by rights the strong Gauls hold its walls;
and so by rights do they rule over the ones they generated."[20] For Isolani
and Noceto—Lombards themselves—to voice the atavistic fantasies of
French mastery in Italy reveals both the depth of the idea's success and
the partisan appeal of its logic.

The French desire for Italians always to comport themselves in perfect step with the ideology of domination found its most pervasive articulation in the idea of the good Frenchman (*bon français*), meaning an
Italian whose outlook mirrored and facilitated the transalpine political
ambitions of France.[21] The concept preexisted the Italian Wars, with
roots in the Guelph politics of earlier centuries.[22] It did not depend upon
the deep Gallic past or the seemingly natural lordship of the crown, but
nor did it clash with those notions. It dovetailed with them and constructed an idealized persona, an amenable profile to which Italians
were meant to aspire, a sort of modern subject of Gallia Cisalpina. One
Italian frequently labeled a *bon français* by admirers was Giangiacomo
Trivulzio, the Milanese patrician whose definitive rift with Ludovico
Sforza in the 1490s led him to seek patronage from the French crown
and who became not just marshal of France in the initial invasion of
Milan in 1499, but the very ensign of Francophile collaboration for the

first two decades of the century.[23] The *bon français* became pervasive in those years, a watchword to identify and promote compliant Italians. Not just individuals, but populations—usually those who refused to participate in activities the French considered treasonous—garnered the designation, whether faithful Genoese citizens or the Swiss foot soldiers who refused to join a foiled Milanese uprising against François I in 1516.[24] Truculent Italians, instead, fell on the opposite side of this naming practice. In that same year, Claude de Seyssel concluded that "the subjects and inhabitants of the Duchy are universally bad Frenchmen (*mauuays francoys*), and they hate France more than ever, a hate that grows daily, as much from the ills they suffer because of the war as from French disorder in all things, which is likely to worsen rather than improve."[25]

Italians themselves sometimes employed the label of the *bon français* to signal their willingness to comply with French policy. The bishop of Meaux wrote to Trivulzio in 1516 that Pope Leo X "wishes to live and die a good Frenchman, as he says," implying not only the pontiff's openness to Gallic diplomacy, but also his familiarity with the expression.[26] In 1510, during her husband Francesco Gonzaga's Venetian imprisonment, Isabella d'Este penned a letter to her secretary, assuring him that "we have always known the lord our consort to be a good Frenchman (*bon Francese*) and most inclined toward our Most Christian King, and we know that now in his secret heart he is more thus inclined than ever, prisoner that he is."[27] In 1525, Alberto Pio da Carpi maneuvered to get Pope Clement VII "to declare himself *francese*."[28] The absorption of the phrase into Italians' own lexicon confirms the saturation of political discourse with language that celebrated Italian collusion with the French crown. In so doing, it facilitated a vision of Italy as part of an expanding, even renascent, Gallic empire.[29] The time for Italians to recognize their innate affiliation to France had returned.

Regime Genealogies

Time was a platform of legitimation; duration functioned as a means to justify rule. Arguments invoking the long duration of dynasties undergirded tranquilizing narratives of continuity: serial lifetimes under one rule worked to explain peace, affluence, and good fortune. These qualities in turn helped to naturalize the power of rulers by making the regime appear structurally coterminous with the polity's success. New, untested, or ephemeral political power became precisely the reason to lean upon rhetoric of long duration and to find means of anchoring lordship in deep time. Gaulish origins, stretching back into the mists of antiquity, achieved that on one level. The French kings also pursued it on another level that anchored their power even more conveniently in recent law, politics, and history: the dynastic. In Milan, an essential ancestral timescape belonged to the Visconti family's lordship. Their rule effectively began in 1277 with Archbishop Ottone, achieved political vigor with Azzone in 1329, and found confirmation in 1395–1396, when Emperor Wenceslaus named Giangaleazzo its first duke.[30] The clan's legends became entwined with civic myths. The Visconti ducal legacy in 1499 had particular importance because both of the warring pretenders—Louis XII d'Orléans and Ludovico Sforza—claimed affiliation with it.

Setting aside all other aspects of their remarkable political success in the latter fifteenth century, the Sforza were dynastically impoverished. This fact worked as the primordial weakness in their ambitions of statecraft: Sforza genealogies could trace their roots no deeper than the mercenary captain Muzio Attendolo (1369–1424), who never even settled in Lombardy.[31] By comparison, many of Milan's most illustrious elites figured themselves as descendants of Frankish or Lombard warriors, and about 180 of their family names figured on a 1377 list (Milan's *matricula nobilium*) from which the Sforza were conspicuously absent.[32] Once Francesco Sforza claimed the rank of duke in 1450, his agents—notably the emissary and cultural attaché Nicodemo Tranchedini (1413–1481)—began to compile Sforza genealogies, even if they remained decidedly modest projects.[33] Tranchedini's efforts amounted to only a few notebook pages listing dates and locations of Sforza births from Muzio Attendolo forward.[34] His work consolidated the family's knowledge of its own history and membership, but it was hardly intended for display or celebration. Instead, Tranchedini's research confirmed the dynasty's greenness. Milan's oldest noble families needed no study to know it; from the beginning of Sforza rule, they complained of *gente nuova* surrounding the dukes, pointing to the way that Francesco and his heirs cultivated retainers from outside Milan whose loyalties belonged exclusively to the prince.[35]

Lacking deep embeddedness in Milan's history, the Sforza instead followed an alternate strategy of self-exaltation: the cultivation of a pan-egyric discourse of achievements. Especially during Francesco's rule (1450–1466), a coterie of lettered men erected a princely image in text, highlighting the first Sforza duke's politico-military savvy from the 1420s to the 1450s as a justification for his lordship. Antonio Cornazz-ano's vernacular *Sforziad* (completed 1459) and Francesco Filelfo's Latin verse epic, the *Sphortias* (composed 1451–1472), number as just two of the many projects to celebrate Milan's new duke.[36] By the 1480s and 1490s, the quest to entrench the dynasty in deeper histories led Francesco's son Ludovico to fund further efforts. He commissioned the scholar Giorgio Merula (1430–1494) to research and compose a history of the Visconti family, the *Antiquitatis Vicecomitum*. Francesco Sforza's marriage to Bianca Maria, daughter of the last Visconti prince, authorized their heirs to bind Milan's long Visconti legacy to its recent Sforza history. No longer limited to Tranchedini's notebook genealogies, the dukes of the late fifteenth century could significantly deepen their regime's roots by means of this inheritance. Donato Bossi's Latin *Chronica* (1492) opens with a red-ink Visconti genealogical chart, the last third of which includes their Sforza inheritors.[37] In the 1490s, Ludovico conscripted two other historians to solidify this narrative of continuity: Bernardino Corio and Tristano Calco (1450–1508/16), then prefect of the ducal library at Pavia. The former composed a vernacular history of Milan from its origins to the present day, and the latter assumed oversight of Merula's unfinished Latin account while also undertaking one of his own.[38] The two histo-rians traveled to regional archives together to collect materials in the late 1490s, and their histories came to fruition—it must have seemed per-versely providential to them, not least because it dashed all hope of remuneration—just as their patron was chased from the duchy.[39] Despite this change of fortunes, Calco brought Merula's *Antiquitatis Vicecomitum* to press just months after il Moro's expulsion; Corio published his own *Historia Patria* (a project Ludovico had imagined as "the praises of our most illustrious ancestors, the Visconti princes") in 1503.[40]

Like other compatriots we will encounter in later chapters, Tristano Calco rode the waves of Milan's turbulent regimes in the first uneasy years of the sixteenth century, finding anchorage in the chancery despite the shifting tides of government after 1499. Calco's knowledge of the Visconti patrimony cultivated during research trips and in custodianship of the Visconti library did not go untapped. King Louis XII's claims to Milanese lordship effectively somersaulted those of the Sforza; his case relied upon older, more venerable traditions. In the 1518 inventory of the royal library at Blois, there were at least two books on French claims to Lombardy: one on "how the French kings were lords of Lombardy" and "another book, on parchment, declaring that long ago the Kings of France and the children of their children were kings and lords of Lombardy, beginning with Pepin and concluding with Charles VI—covered with red and yellow patterned damask."[41] To end the lineage with that particular sovereign was no accident. King Charles VI's younger brother, Louis, married Valentina Visconti (1371–1408), Duke Giangaleazzo's only daughter, in 1389.[42] By staking his invasion upon the rights of his grandmother, Valentina, Louis not only tied himself directly to Milan's first titular duke, but also framed the connection squarely as a Visconti privilege, overwriting Sforza efforts to tie themselves to the same history.

After 1499, this dynastic superscription was often literal, as buildings and documents underwent alteration designed to announce the Orléans-Visconti union. Traces still remain of Louis XII's enormous quartered French-Visconti arms, crowned and held aloft by angels flanked by the name "LV REX" painted inside the courtyard at the Sforza pleasure palace at Vigevano (fig. 1.1). French partisans followed decorative suit in their own fortresses in the same years, whether the Pio in Carpi, the Gallarati in Cozzo, the Ghilini in Fontaneto d'Agogna, or the Alberti in Bormio.[43] The quartered arms made their own argument about time: Duke Giangaleazzo had adopted the same shield in the 1390s after his daughter Valentina married into the French royal house; 1500 brought a return to those days of Milanese glory.[44] Likewise, illuminated manuscripts pinched from Pavia's library had Sforza portraits and arms scraped away, to be repainted with those of the French kings.[45] These transformations erased the Sforza while domesticating foreign rule through an argument of native filiation.

Calco brought his experience as a ducal library custodian, researcher, and chancery officer into the politics of the French domination; his

Fig. 1.1 Louis XII's shield in the courtyard of Sforza palace at Vigevano, ca. 1500.
Photo by author.

knowledge of Visconti histories proved newly urgent for an occupying
power that based its rights upon that family's foundations. Tepid toward
Ludovico Sforza, Calco reportedly presented a Visconti genealogy (the
Genealogia Vicecomitum) to Louis XII upon his entry to Milan in 1499 and
made a similar gift (the *De stemmate Vicecomitum*) to the president of
Milan's senate in 1502, Étienne Poncher, bishop of Paris.[46] A manuscript
of Calco's genealogy once belonged to the Biblioteca Trivulziana, but it
vanished in World War II.[47] Another copy, evidently a scroll comprised
of six sheets of parchment, disappeared sometime after the eighteenth
century.[48] Otherwise, the text has been known only in a 1748 transcrip-
tion. It has gone unnoticed that an original scroll of Calco's genealogy—
the only one to survive, apparently—exists at the Bibliothèque Sainte-
Geneviève in Paris (fig. 1.2).[49] Nearly three meters long and formed of
five parchment segments, this 1502 Paris manuscript was addressed
not to Poncher but to Louis II d'Amboise (1477–1510), the twenty-five-
year-old nephew of the king's right-hand man, Cardinal Georges

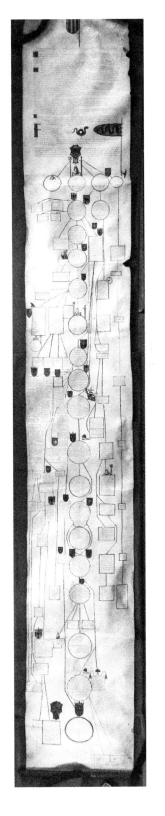

Fig. 1.2 Tristano Calco, *Genealogia Vicecomitum,* 1502.
Bibliothèque Sainte-Geneviève, Paris, MS 864.

Photo by author.

d'Amboise, who was also a brother of Milan's governor, Charles Chaumont d'Amboise.[50] The Amboise family's deep involvement in the highest
administrative ranks of French Lombardy in these years explains the
dedication to Louis II.[51] In rendering the duchy's dynastic history in
graphic form, Calco's genealogical scroll—starting with the earliest Visconti bishops and ending with Louis XII's domination—visualizes
Milan's past as a flow of majesty culminating in French lordship and
renders the argument of succession as an ineluctable victory for the
Orléans king, all while deploying Calco's freshest archival findings.
Grounded in that register of research, it is a vivid departure from an illuminated Visconti genealogy produced a century earlier, in which the
Visconti descend through generations of mythical rulers from the cou-
pling of Venus and Anchises.[52]

Rolling down the center of Calco's parchment, Milan's rulers are represented as large hoops filled with text; the genealogy relegates most
others to secondary status in square or rectangular cartouches on the
margins. In this way, it is not a genealogical tree communicating the dynasty's expansion branch by branch. Instead, its argument is about vertical time: the duchy's succession from the earliest Visconti lords (at top)
to the present (at bottom).[53] While cascading lateral lines indicate the
various offshoots of the clan's descent, the crucial thread here connects
the central circles, binding the most robust rights-inheritances. Giangaleazzo Visconti (1351–1402) plays the scroll's most pivotal part, since in
his person coalesced both an Orléans affiliation (his daughter) and the
ducal investiture (from Emperor Wenceslaus). In following the rulers
after Giangaleazzo's death, Calco's chart captures the complexities of
Milan's fifteenth century. The Visconti lines of descent warp and bow to
avoid touching the free-floating hoop representing the Ambrosian Republic (1447–1450), "thirty months of liberty," before reconnecting with
princely rule in the Sforza era. That new season of lordship begins not
with Francesco Sforza but with his Visconti consort, "Bianca Maria,
daughter of Filippo Maria." The hoops representing the reigns of Francesco Sforza and his heirs are candy-striped, as if to indicate their illegitimacy.[54] Calco's text likewise casts Sforza rule as a mere interlude when
describing the fall of Ludovico, who, "captured by the French," was "led
across the Alps," triggering "the destruction of his entire clan. And all

that his father had acquired in this illustrious realm, he lost."[55] In contrast with the circuitous lines of Sforza filiation, a direct thread descends from Giangaleazzo to Louis XII. It all hangs on that.

Calco's scroll also resituates Visconti heraldry—particularly the viper, or *biscione*—into a context more imperial than mythical (fig. 1.3). Denigrating the Milanese chronicler Galvano Fiamma (1283–1323) for popularizing the story of a Visconti crusader who adopted the arms from a Saracen warrior vanquished at Jerusalem's gates, Calco instead trusts the late antique historian Claudian, who tells of dragon banners in fourth-century Milan under Emperor Honorius.[56] Calco links these imperial dragons with a celebrated Milanese landmark: the bronze snake atop a pillar in the church of Sant'Ambrogio, which others at the same time associated not with imperial military insignia, but with Moses's brazen serpent in the biblical Book of Numbers (fig. 1.4).[57] A contemporaneous painted cabinet in the sacristy of Santa Maria delle Grazie envisions the Milanese serpent as the Mosaic relic; perhaps it is no coincidence that the French president of Milan's senate, Étienne Poncher, probably funded these cabinet decorations in the same period as Calco bestowed the Visconti genealogy on him: the roots of the city's antiquities were under discussion and revision (fig. 1.5).[58] In rejecting this monument's biblical pedigree, Calco instead describes the bronze as a votive offering of "some illustrious prince, following either a miracle or a victory." Here again, Calco prefers to highlight the signorial prerogatives that gave rise to Milan's landmarks and heraldry. Such gentle reorientations of Visconti mythology may have dimmed some of its fantastical luster, but in exchange the family gained ties framed in terms of documentable *translatio imperii* from the Roman emperors to the latter-day Visconti.

Louis XII—long before he became king—had already incorporated the viper into his self-representation. It appeared on his official seals, along with his title of Milan's duke, as early as 1482.[59] In linking or quartering the *biscione* with France's royal lily, as many manuscript illuminations did in the first decade of the sixteenth century, the French requisitioned its civic-dynastic valences from the Sforza and made them speak of a Visconti-Orléans history of Milan.[60] From this vantage, Sforza lineage had little ground for contest: its anchorage in genealogical time was comparably irrelevant.

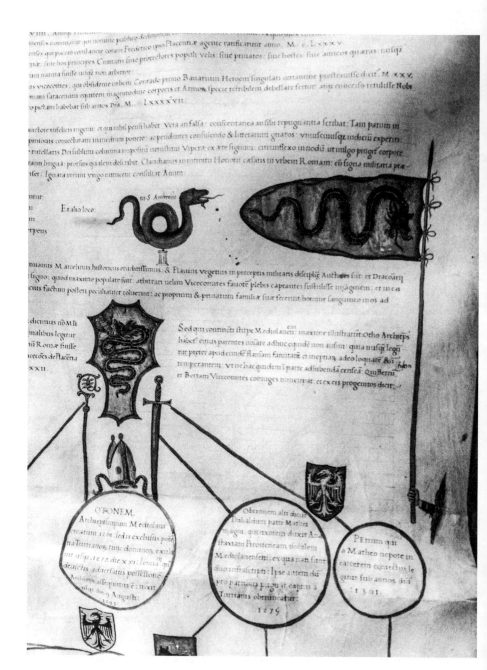

Fig. 1.3 Detail of Calco's *Genealogia Vicecomitum*, 1502.

Photo by author.

Fig. 1.4 Bronze Serpent, before the eleventh century, Basilica of Sant'Ambrogio, Milan. Photo by author.

Future Visions, Former Times, and the Palimpsest State

Five years elapsed between King Charles VIII's extensive military campaign across the peninsula in 1494 and Louis XII's invasion in 1499. Ludovico Sforza had been instrumental in the negotiations that convinced the young monarch to descend into Italy with thousands of troops in order to depose the Aragonese king of Naples and claim its crown for France. When word arrived in June 1493 that Charles VIII had actually committed himself to the idea, it seemed to shock even Ludovico, who declared loudly to the Florentine ambassador that the news "blew his mind."[61] But the invasion did not, as Ludovico expected, work to his favor. The Sforza duke began to fear for the security of his own lordship over Milan. He nervously joined the Holy League that confronted Charles at Fornovo in July 1495 and sent him packing across the Alps.

In the ensuing five years, Ludovico's ducal power reached its zenith, cemented by his nephew's death and by his official imperial investiture with the ducal title. But the experience of the 1494–1495 war had shown

Fig. 1.5 Wooden panel in sacristy of Santa Maria delle Grazie, Milan, ca. 1503–04.
Photo by author.

him that his power was not unshakeable: dark threats from the Duke of
Orléans (the future Louis XII) had already reached him during Charles
VIII's campaign, and it was clear that Ludovico, as much as any other
lord, could become the target of aggressions. Perhaps these fears prompted
the duke to compose, sometime between 1497 and 1499, the exhaustive
will and testament now stored in Paris.[62] In it, he outlined at length
how he wished the duchy to continue after his death under the lordship
of his eldest son, Massimiliano, a boy no older than ten in these years.
Part fatherly advice manual, part government blueprint, and part emergency handbook, Ludovico's testament offers rare evidence of the visions
of futurity embedded in a regime whose days, it turned out, were numbered. Through Ludovico's eyes, we can understand what elements of his
lordship he most insistently wanted to outlast him. That these plans
never unfolded as he imagined them is less important than perceiving
Sforza's political prognosis and his ideal endgame.

The duke ordered that, upon his death, Massimiliano ought first to
confirm the Sforza title to the duchy with the emperor, a command that
acknowledged just how hard it had been to win the privilege, which had
been denied to his nephew Giangaleazzo Sforza (and indeed to all his
kinsmen, including his father Francesco).[63] A trio of governors composed
of Ludovico's first secretary, chamberlain, and the castellan of the Porta
Giovia fortress were to convene in the treasury of the castello to open
the iron-plated, silver-damascened safe containing the prince's instructions and to swear obedience to the child-duke's primary governor. Next,
the duchy's security would be established by notifying regional castellans and requiring them to renew their fealty. Access to the child duke
would be rigorously overseen not just by a cadre of peacetime troops, but
by a double perimeter of guards. (This measure echoed Ludovico's own
active security detail of twenty-five soldiers; by his orders, no one was
meant to approach him or talk to him unless named on a master list.[64])
Ludovico demanded that Massimiliano should live in the keep of Milan's
castle until his fourteenth year, accompanied at all times by the governing council, and he was adamant that the "reputation of government
and administration of the state should remain joined to his person and
to the place he inhabits." The governors would gradually instruct the
boy in rulership by training him to make propositions and to call for a
majority vote. Once aged twenty, Massimiliano, like his father, would

nightly receive the castle's keys from the castellan in his chamber. Until that time, the young Sforza was to curtail any travel and submit his expenditures and largesse to his governing council for ratification.[65] Ludovico's plan protected the core assets he had amassed over his rule: title, land, heir, and riches.

The testament also reveals how he imagined his ideal governing structures. The duke's three elite councils were to become strictly exclusive. The highest council of state (*consiglio del stato,* sometimes also called the *consiglio del castello*) would consist mostly of the above-mentioned officers; Ludovico recommended against visitors and prohibited them from speaking in assembly without written authorization. He also wished to streamline his other major councils, noting that only the "necessity of the times" had led to an inflation of their membership.[66] The secret council (*consiglio secreto*) had proved a fulcrum of power-jostling between internal political factions during the Sforza principate; by Ludovico's day, it was largely excluded from the most important deliberations of state, and many of its appointed members—including Swiss and German foreigners—were purely honorary.[67] He wished for the secret council's membership to be reduced to twenty; in 1488, he had slashed it from sixty officers to a mere eight, but evidently it had quickly grown again.[68] Third was the council of justice (*consiglio de justitia*), a body founded in the Visconti era, staffed with jurists from Milan's elite families and charged with hearing cases and administering justice. Its membership would be restricted to five—numbers comparable to those maintained at the time of Francesco's death in 1466.[69] In finding appropriate officers for the duchy and city's remaining range of treasurers and other magistracies, Ludovico wanted candidates familiar with the traditions of his household: desirable nominees would have been "raised at court" or capable of producing documents "in the style of the court."[70] In the aggregate, il Moro's plan envisioned a leaner, nimbler conciliar class than the one he actually contended with; he wished for one reared at his court and thus less likely to suffer dissension or disloyalty. Faith and loyalty proved a perennial concern for Ludovico. At the testament's end, he warned his son Massimiliano "under punishment of malediction" not to "ride through the land to have himself called Lord, nor make any other show of taking the dominion before our obsequies have been performed and our body has been laid in its place," clothed in ducal robes.[71] Despite the loving provisions Ludovico made for his heir, he feared him as well. Sforza family members who had been excluded, exiled, ousted, or assassinated were too numerous for Ludovico not to recognize his own vulnerability. He wanted to die as Milan's duke.

Ludovico instead died a prisoner, immured in a stone tower in rural France. In place of the carefully choreographed succession that il Moro had projected, an extended contest for authority began within the Milanese state: a sort of slowly-unfurling chaos, still obscured from historical view through years of shifting regimes by a façade of institutional continuity (most notably in the perdurance of civic magistracies, and their regular staffing with officials who upheld the mechanics of quotidian government). Chaos that moves gradually can come to seem ordinary. As we have already seen with Girolamo Morone and Tristano Calco—and still others who will appear in later chapters—several notable high-ranking bureaucrats remained entrenched through successive regimes, as did many personnel in lower magistracies. As governments followed one after another, the work of these officers and their institutions helped to cushion the frequent reversals between (and intermingling of) familiar Visconti-Sforza traditions and novel French and later Spanish forms.[72]

Yet the stabilizing effect of those statesmen went only so far. It was not just that French administrators and their collaborators sometimes ignored—even willfully—the governing commonplaces that had evolved in the Sforza duchy. Instead, the rotation of antagonistic regimes itself eroded confidence in those norms: it became difficult for anyone—ruler, official, jurist, subject—to determine whether old norms pertained or whether new ones needed to be invented. Here is where temporality exerts a central tension. Regimes in this era tended to nurture a retrospective governmental culture, one that valorized former dispensations. That outlook generally functioned well enough to insure some institutional stability, although even Milan's long-standing civic statutes underwent revisions by a team of jurists under both Ludovico in 1498 and Louis in 1502.[73] Moreover, Louis XII often deferred to Visconti traditions as a way to affiliate himself with the authority of their Lombard legacy.[74] But when the past spoke instead of recently ousted lords as usurpers, the question of how to respect precedent became vexed. For instance, part of the French statute revision excised details of historical communal rights agreed with the Holy Roman Empire.[75] Such traditions were dispensable under French domination. Louis XII's conquest launched more than thirty years of contention; it slowly began to reshape the geographical, economic, and political contours of the duchy, beginning with the forms of rule that Ludovico had projected before his ouster. Fundamentally, these contentions were premised upon conflicting temporalities about what signorial and juridical forms should endure.

Ludovico escaped Milan for the imperial court in Innsbruck on 2 September 1499, and the city surrendered to French forces four days later. Louis XII promulgated a vision of his new duchy's administrative contours in the Edict of Vigevano on 11 November 1499. It was a vision transfixed by two traditions: Sforza ducal bureaucracy—about which the drafters of the edict knew a good deal—and French parliamentarianism. Because its injunctions refashioned the essential workings of the state, the decree literally constituted French rule in Italy, making it the regime's foundational charter.[76] Crucially, the edict laid out the new administrative structure of the post-Sforza state. As in a French province, the monarch would rule by means of a governor or lieutenant (Trivulzio was the first of six men to hold the position between 1499 and 1522) whose mission would be primarily military.[77] A civilian counterpart equivalent to the French keeper of the seals would act as president of Milan's senate (its first holder was Pierre de Sacierges, bishop of Luçon, a figure who will reappear in several later chapters). The senate, in turn, became the most durable institutional legacy of French rule in Lombardy, responsible for legislative and judicial administration until its suppression under Austrian domination in 1786.[78] It was an intentionally hybrid institution, staffed by seventeen senators: two prelates, four soldiers, and eleven learned men—five of them French and six of them Italian. The king charged the senators not just with the registration and enforcement of royal decrees, but with a panoply of other duties, including the nomination of officials, the adjudication of civil and criminal trials, and the administration of feudatories. Its hybridity inhered not only in the nationality of the senators, but in its peculiar position astride the duchy's two contending statist timescapes, between the Sforza past and the French future.

Frequently, the Edict of Vigevano invoked the overthrown Sforza regime in order to negate its structures. Certain systems operative in "former times" (*temporibus retroactis*) were meant to cease.[79] The senate, seen from this vantage, was both new and old. The Edict of Vigevano's framers recognized that the Sforza dukes had relied upon the two councils described earlier: one secret, and one of justice. French rule, conversely, would transform these two bodies into a "single supreme council" called the senate, "according to ancient custom." The edict, it appears, strove to alter the structure of these councils for the same reasons that had inspired Ludovico's conciliar contraction in 1488: to disempower or sideline Milanese elites who had become entrenched in the highest levels of the previous regime.[80] The charter claimed its motivation as a desire to limit the number of senators, but in fact it functioned as a politics of exclusion against those who had known power "in former times."[81] It also made certain to uphold the ratios of senatorial nationalities to prevent any future imbalance. Likewise, powers that had once formerly belonged to the duke himself—such as the right to elect at will the city's most prominent officials—now had to pass through the senate and a nominating subcommittee.[82] Certain Sforza prerogatives were a thing of the past.

The edict's language also sutured the Milanese duchy to France's current bureaucratic practices. For instance, Milan's senate bursar would now function with the aid of two specific officers: a scribe and a comptroller whose duties of registering disbursements would transpire "exactly as observed in the chancery of France up to this moment (*hactenus observatum*)."[83] Aside from the obvious goal of standardizing administrative procedure across French regions, this novelty also effectively updated Milan's government to function according to the very latest stroke of French bureaucratic time. In introducing the new chancery habits, the Edict of Vigevano wrenched the Sforza state out of its own schedules and forced it to align with the tempo of royal administration. This was not just a case of Milanese bureaucrats learning new methods. In practice, the only officials conversant with those workings as performed "up to this moment" or "just as the French chancery is accustomed" were men from beyond the Alps. Thus, the edict's insistence upon introducing agents with current knowledge of the royal chancery helped to colonize the remaining administration, substituting many Sforza officials with new, up-to-date French replacements.[84] While the governance of the duchy would necessarily entail a coordination of natives and foreigners, in which their methods would mingle—the regime's first nominated procurator and fiscal advocate were Milanese—the net effect was to banish personnel and procedures too redolent of "former times" under the Sforza by forecasting a rule inflected by current French habits.

Decreeing and erecting a new government on top of another necessarily involved compromise. The layering of administrative cultures—a Sforza bureaucratic substratum partially abraded and overwritten by French scripts of governance—produced a Milanese palimpsest state, in which ghosts of the old government could still be discerned through its replacement. The palimpsest functioned on many levels, as the rest of the book will suggest. In the next chapter, we will see how it even functioned spatially on the level of officers' lodgings, as the rich palaces of Ludovico's fugitive associates soon housed Louis XII's generals.[85] But where this layering phenomenon most notably appeared, and where it articulated itself as something rooted in brackets of conflicting time, was in practices of naming former regimes.

As soon as French rule in Lombardy seemed established—after the Sforza duke's definitive capture in April 1500—Milan's Ludovician era came to be expressed in some variation of a simple phrase: "al tempo del Moro." We read the phrase frequently in Marin Sanudo's Venetian diaries. Sanudo recorded the arrival of news, fugitives, and supplicants into the territory of the Serenissima, not to mention the process of Cremona's absorption into the Venetian terraferma after the French war for Milan. (It remained under Venetian rule until 1509.) In the ensuing months, agents pursued how to administer the new city, asking whether commerce flowing from Comacchio through Cremona had to pay duties "as was customary at the time of the duke of Milan," or whether the Cremonese salt debts due "at the time of signor Ludovico" had been paid.[86] The notion was not unique to Sanudo. The Milanese lord Galeazzo Visconti appeared at the imperial court in 1501 to plead for leniency for his tenants in Cremonese territory, "on account of certain rents from the time of the Illustrious Lord Ludovico Sforza, before the arrival of the French."[87] A Cremonese knight complained to Venetian rectors that Ludovico Sforza had never observed privileges granted to his family by Francesco Sforza in 1450. Would Venice now respect them?[88] Milanese merchants petitioned the Venetian senate in 1503 not to introduce taxes that had not existed "in the time of signor Ludovico."[89] Innumerable new scenarios, in fact, arose from the end of the Sforza regime. Another Visconti, the Milanese condottiere Scaramuccia, "who at the time of il Moro was salaried in the military arts," now offered his services to Venice's *signoria*. Scaramuccia's cousin, Giangiacomo Trivulzio, meanwhile faced reclamations from Swiss mercenaries over "money they were supposed to have at the time of il Moro."[90] French writers employed the phrase as well.[91]

To summon a discrete period in the past by means of a prince's reign was a premodern commonplace that can appear to be a merely convenient, almost thoughtless, gesture. We see it employed frequently, all over Italy. (For instance, Giangiacomo Trivulzio began a confidence to an ambassador in 1506 with: "Let me tell you a story from the time of Duke Francesco."[92]) These formulas concerned a bygone era as a whole entity. The *"tempo del Moro,"* seen from this perspective, is simply an index, an arrow that points backward to easily recognizable intervals. But what is striking about such phrases is the work that they performed for the characters involved. In nearly every case, recourse to describing the *"tempo del Moro"* had to do with former obligations, duties, rights, histories that had been thrown into suspension. Previous dispensations and agreements (often financial ones) had to be confronted and, if possible, set right after their interruption. These zones of past time, users of the phrase implied, were moral vacuums requiring compensation.[93] It should not surprise us that, upon the Sforza restoration that brought Massimiliano to power in early 1513, the young duke faced a torrent of supplications seeking to restore the conditions that had pertained under his father's regime, a phenomenon that Chapter 5 explores in depth.

For the moment, the crucial element to note in these supplications is their description of the intersection of time and power—in other words, how the duration of an unfriendly regime had trapped these petitioners, suspending the justice they expected from the state. We need only a few examples reveal the pattern. Once he became duke in 1513, Massimiliano granted restitution to one of his father's most faithful attendants, citing injustices done at "the time of the unhappy expulsion and capture of our illustrious late father from his own state."[94] Addressed to Milan's captain of justice, the duke's letter describes the plight of Biagino Crivelli, a captain Matteo Bandello later described in his *novelle* as so close to Ludovico that "he seemed more brother than subject."[95] In 1513,

Massimiliano looked back in time. He recounted how—during the violent transition from Sforza to French rule in 1499—a band of siblings from the patrician Malabarba family had insulted Biagino at his own house; they then despoiled him of "all his movable goods inside and outside Milan because Biagino had been a faithful servant of the Lord [Ludovico] our father."[96] Massimiliano now wanted the Malabarba to face justice and Biagino's goods to be restored. After more than a decade of deferral, the wheels of judicial time for Sforza partisans appeared to spin once more.

Count Annibale Bevilacqua, another supplicant to Massimiliano in 1513, reported how his hardships during the French regime had begun on 3 September 1499, or "on the day that your illustrious father of venerable memory left Milan for Germany, or in fact the day following." On that date, French partisans confiscated his family's long-held feudal jurisdictions and possessions. He lamented that the French and their supporters had "kept me oppressed for the space of about fourteen years, alleging no other grounds than I was a staunch Sforzesco and duchesco. Nonetheless I nourished myself with great patience during this period of time while suffering the greatest injuries and insults, miserably hoping that one day the true light of your return would arrive."[97] Despite having meanwhile pursued his case in the French-administered Milanese senate, Bevilacqua found only opposition and cronyism.[98] Similar charges from other voices ("the king's deputies in Italy are ignorant fools") recurred more than once during these years.[99] Bevilacqua's change of fortune in 1499 mirrored the change of state, inaugurating for Sforza partisans a period of trials and frustrations.

By Massimiliano's day, this era—the period 1499–1512—traveled under the name *"il tempo de' francesi."* Many of the Sforza supplicants highlighted in chapter 5 refer to the French domination using some variant of this expression, as did the chancery officers penning Massimiliano's Latin missives (*"tempore gallorum," "sub gallorum iniquo imperio," "tempore occupationis Gallorum"*).[100] It was invoked almost always for contrastive purposes: to cast shade over the former regime and to illuminate more brilliantly the justice of the present. To speak of the *"tempo de' francesi"* was to undo the work of the French regime as a prelude to restorative Sforza justice. Massimiliano Sforza strove to be definitive about that reversion. In March of 1513, his reign still fledgling and tenuous, he issued an edict decrying Milanese subjects who appeared to be "followers and supporters" of Louis XII and who wished to "restore the French to their earlier tyranny" despite the return of a Sforza prince, Milan's "true and legitimate duke."[101] For Massimiliano, the pivotal moment when their allegiance became suspect—in other words, the moment when the Sforza state began to live again in time—was "at the time of the expulsion of the French from the ducal dominion," in June 1512.[102] Nine months had already passed since that time, and the apparent defiance of these agitators galled Massimiliano. Milanese subjects who failed to present themselves personally to the duke in the span of a month would be labeled rebels.

By November 1513, the Sforza deputies on rebels duly recorded, in one single entry spanning thirteen pages, 298 men "condemned for the crime of *lèse majesté* and for rebellion" against Massimiliano, an offense punishable with decapitation and confiscation of goods. The list of dissidents included Giangiacomo Trivulzio and a number of prominent French supporters.[103] But the legal force of this list endured only as long as Massimiliano's brief rule. Within the span of two years, the rebels' juridical status was reversed. After the reconquest by King François I, these partisans would be rewarded and Sforza loyalists, in turn, banished. Despite the clarity with which each regime recorded the date of its own establishment, and despite incessant insistence that subjects should follow schedules and deadlines to obey decrees, such emanations remained wishful. In fact, the transition from one regime to another moved amorphously, all the more so in rural or distant areas at a remove from the center of authority.

Reestablishing the conventions of a ruptured state took a long time, often far too long in the eyes of rulers, a frustration that Massimiliano Sforza faced throughout his reign. Months after he had regained the duchy in 1513, an agent wrote to explain that he had relayed the duke's order for the duchy's towns to remove the public display of French arms. The towns were given "a respectable amount of time" to replace them with Sforza insignia. But some had refused. "Not only did they not want to erase the French insignia," the agent balked, "but nor did they want to paint yours, which to me shows nothing if not the slightest regard for your letters." He then listed the "resistant" towns, most of them north of Milan: Desio, Seregno, Vimercati, Vigevano (where fragments of the painted French arms, illustrated a few pages ago, remain to this day), Gallarate, Varese, Lecco, Mandello, and Bellagio.[104] The towns' resistance to Sforza orders said a good deal about the diffidence of certain communities in face of the restoration, as well as about the geographical distribution of French sympathy. But perhaps most importantly, it testified to their flagrant refusal to recognize the return of the Sforza dispensation in "a respectable amount of time." For these towns, the *"tempo de' francesi"* had not yet ended; the palimpsest state was a physical reality.

Similarly, Ludovico Sforza's rule ended in 1500 not with a blackout, but rather with a sputter. The flickering out of his power took time. Ludovico was not just Duke of Milan, but regent of Bari, in the Kingdom of Naples.[105] After his flight from Milan in 1499, Ludovico gifted the Duchy of Bari to Isabella d'Aragona, the widow of his sidelined nephew Giangaleazzo. In fact, Ludovico offered the gift only insofar as it could exploit Isabella as a legal shell. Should he lose his grasp of power, the reasoning went, he could more easily reclaim Bari from her than from some other claimant.[106] Foreseeing the potential of future litigation, Ludovico appointed a vice-duke of Bari in 1499 to oversee his personal interests when he was expelled from Milan. During his brief restoration in 1500, the city of Bari itself returned to Sforza adherence, though the other cities of the duchy did not.[107] Perhaps because of this resistance he appointed, without dismissing the first one, a second officer to oversee Bari. Now there were two Sforza executives in Bari—doubles, we might call them: each one an echo, a trace, of the two seasons of il Moro's interrupted rule. In February 1501, a year after Ludovico's definitive imprisonment in France, each of his representatives—still acting as if the Sforza duke were in power—maneuvered not just to keep the title of Bari out of Isabella's hands, but to disempower one another, forcing the king of Naples to intervene.[108] Isabella finally gained claim over the duchy only through charters with invented, and in fact impossible, dates: they show that Bari became Isabella's on 10 April 1500, a week before news of Ludovico's capture by French forces had even reached Naples.[109]

The purpose of recounting these examples is to encourage us to dwell analytically on the blurring effect of shifting regimes. The blur is important. Transfers of power are necessarily smudged, imperfect affairs. The dates on charters and edicts would have us think otherwise,

but their specificity can overdetermine our sense of the precision of political change. In the cases offered here, we see the temporal problematics
raised by contests of authority, when sovereign powers overlap and interpenetrate: communities refuse to acknowledge new (or—just as
likely—old) political realities, as if they still lived under a rival dispensation; agents continue to operate in the name of a dispossessed lord, as if
the sovereignty they claimed were not just a relic. Such claims lasted
more than a decade. In 1511, one Milanese petitioner worked to gain
papal privileges for his son by signing his letter with his long-expired
official title under Ludovico Sforza: *Consiliarius Ducis Mediolani.* "The
Duke is dead," scoffed the petitioner's cousin Baldassarre Castiglione,
calling him "madder than a dog."[110] These problems were not unique to
Milan, nor to the period of the Italian Wars. But they proliferated in this
time and place because of the rapid alternation of the disputants' ascen-
dancies, a phenomenon compounded by the wide geographies and cultural frameworks separating the antagonists. Far-flung centers of
authority—Paris, Milan, Bari—exaggerated the political lag, and clashing
ideas of protocol furthered it. These factors facilitated the coexistence
of multiple authorities, affiliations, and visions of the state.

They also made it easier for everyone implicated—subjects, officers,
rulers—to abuse the state. If the duchy's initial resistance to Louis XII's
administration seemed tentative, it was because rumors promised that
the monarch might provide relief from Sforza extortions, which—at
first—it did. But after the 1500 uprising, the French began to levy exactions, beginning as a punitive measure that expanded into a process of
wealth-extraction. Already by 1502, it was baldly evident that Louis's rule
would not restore beneficent justice, as he had promised it would. In that
year, the president of Milan's senate, Pierre de Sacierges, bishop of Luçon,
was forced to withdraw from his office. One chronicler reported that
Sacierges had "done many illicit things"; an audit revealed that he exacted 300,000 ducats from "many gentlemen and people of all ranks"
and had sent the embezzled funds to France.[111] The audit process—the
sindacato—belonged to the traditions inherited from the communal age
and assured that officials conducted themselves according to law.[112]
This review maintained high standards and carried severe penalties:
within the duchy, only this review could ultimately hold Luçon accountable for his embezzlement.[113]

But the crucial procedural check of the *sindacato* seems to have dwindled and vanished soon after. In the same year as Luçon's removal, Milan's citizens submitted petitions to the monarch, one of which requested the fair administration of justice. Milan's supplicants were identifying newly permissive opportunities for corruption, and they fretted that further crimes would be committed with impunity. They were not wrong. In a trio of royal edicts from 1508 and 1509 (the last recently rediscovered), the king addressed several abuses of law in the duchy.[114] Royal finance officers crossed the Alps to examine its administration in 1508, and they reported that the state's "statutes and decrees were not observed, upheld and guarded as they were since time immemorial."[115] If we read the commission's orders for what they sought to reinstate, we can apprehend the magnitude of abuses. Among other misdeeds: city governors and castellans were meddling in civil and criminal cases; officers were claiming perpetual or life-long jurisdiction (instead of respecting their statutory two-year terms); captains and podestàs were not surrendering confiscated funds to the fisc; notaries were failing to keep proper trial records; litigants' goods were being itemized for confiscation before a guilty verdict was rendered; and—crucially—the *sindacato* procedures were in abeyance. The edicts of 1509 confirm it: there were paid substitutes in office who "never undergo the *sindacato* nor swear to undergo it."[116]

Neglect of the *sindacato,* claims of perpetual power, and the litany of other abuses point to the opening of what has been called a "zone of indifference" to the law: in the practice of political power, it is the space in which it becomes immaterial whether actions are undertaken inside or outside frameworks of jurisprudence. In this zone, legal and extralegal powers do not exclude each other, rather they blur together. This state of non-law, known to theorists as the "state of exception," characterizes the exercise of power in polities where war or emergency superimposes the discourse of necessity overtop the discourse of law.[117] In fifteenth-century Florence, the suspension of the *sindacato* in the name of crisis-era executive power produced precisely this sort of outcome: an institutionalized suspension of the statutory regularities of law.[118] In Florence, this suspension served the interests of an oligarchic government's tightening control over the city as the captain of the people came to be replaced by the *Otto di Guardia e Balia.* In wartime Milan, it was the casualty of a process of institutional disintegration.[119] By 1511, the president of the Milanese senate—himself under suspicion of malfeasance—complained to Paris that in Milan "no one wants justice, order, polity, or reform."[120] A central contention of this book is that the undoing of the Sforza state came about through the intersection of two elements traced in this chapter: the practical suspension of accepted conventions that had governed political life in the duchy and the frequency of violent regime change during the first quarter of the century. The first element is a question of habitus, the second of temporality. Norms (of politics, law, government) withstood only so much pressure before splintering. Waves of different regimes—each with its own vision of how and when the state existed—damaged those norms substantially. Despite the claimed intentions of each new government to set right the misdeeds of the past, the very fact of the change undermined the state's structural resilience.

The premodern state always shouldered severe pressures to uphold its own legal and statutory ideals. Often a gulf separated theory of government from its practice. It would be naïve to point to dysfunction in bureaucracies alone as a sign of crisis. We know, for example, that forms of abuse similar to those listed a moment ago lasted well into Milan's sixteenth century, during its administration by the Spanish crown.[121] This is why the cycling interchange of regimes in the early part of the century played such an important role in compounding Milan's existential struggle. The Milanese state became, by and large, a centrifugal rather than a centripetal entity.

Historians understand already that contest was a formative element of political life in this period: numerous studies of factional strife and class conflict have made that clear.[122] The following chapters examine a moment in the life of the state when even these forms of political dynamism become mere tools in strategies of domination. Let us continue to pursue problems at the interstices of power. In so doing, we can grope toward a counter-history of the Renaissance state: fragmentary, imperfect, and volatile.

2

Urban Construction and Social Control as Capture

*S*forza influence had grown brick by brick. When Francesco inaugurated his lordship over the city in 1450, the city's inhabitants had partially dismantled the Visconti castle at Porta Giovia, reducing to meaningful rubble the stronghold of Milan's first dukes.[1] Sforza ambition traveled hand-in-hand with its architecture, and the second half of the fifteenth century witnessed a blossoming of projects in the city and duchy under the supervision of builders such as Filarete, the Solari brothers, and Bramante. Francesco Sforza rebuilt the castle at Porta Giovia; its ornamental and domestic spaces swelled rapidly. Particularly under Galeazzo Maria in the 1470s, it came into its own as the seat of a princely court. When Ludovico Sforza fled in late 1499, he abandoned a sparkling citadel, but one that he once wished always to be "as wild (*salvatica*) as possible"—in other words, more fortress than palace.[2] It had, in fact, become both.[3] But the next decades of foreign rule transformed the castle and the city beyond his wildest imaginings, overwriting Sforza visions of civic space and order with new French fantasies while changing the textures of the built and the lived environment. The city itself evi-

denced the fracturing of the state as centrifugal pressures tugged at social space.

French influence, instead, grew with piles of dirt. In the anxious
summer weeks of 1499, as the French army approached, several of Milan's
citizens dug pits to bury their most precious valuables.[4] The displacement of earth had already been a symptom of Sforza urban projects in
the 1480s and 1490s as Ludovico and his engineers aimed to magnify
the grandeur of the zone around the castle. But these earlier excavations
had civic refreshment and ducal magnificence as their goals. During
the 1490s, Ludovico had purchased several houses facing the castle
with the intention of demolishing them, as a first step in "squaring the
piazza."[5] He had also worked to cultivate and embellish the neighbor-
hood to the castle's west, surrounding the Dominican church of Santa
Maria delle Grazie. With its newly completed tribune (1497–1498)
vaulting outside the gate of Porta Vercellina, the church anchored new
urban projects for Ludovico and his allies. This district—the so-called
Borgo delle Grazie—abutted the ducal gardens surrounding the castle.
Palazzi or yards of Sforza retainers (Sanseverino, Atellani, Castiglioni,
Botta, Stanga, and Leonardo da Vinci) flanked the way.[6] Sforza ambitions were often supersized; Leonardo's colossal equestrian statue, commissioned by Ludovico to adorn the castle piazza, embodied that magnitude. It, like other projects, had to be abandoned when il Moro instead
sent its apportioned bronze to Ferrara in 1494 for cannon-forging. Its
clay model, looming near Porta Vercellina, succumbed to the blows of
Gascon crossbowmen during the first French capture of the city.[7] Despite
efforts of Ferrara's Duke Ercole d'Este to save the model, it ended as
nothing more than debris.

Under the French regime, construction in the city of Milan ceased,
by and large, to serve dynastic visions. Very few French-sponsored interventions in the urban fabric characterize their rule of nearly twenty years.
By contrast, each of the previous Sforza dukes—in shorter reigns—
completed substantial projects. It was in part a symptom of the transformation of Milan from a node of concentrated ducal authority into
violently contested terrain. The Sforza had sought to legitimize their dominion and quell their own fields of contestation (on the part of citizens, local elites, and foreign states) through these building campaigns.

The French hesitated to redeploy that same bold strategy, perhaps fearing reprisals from diverse quarters or perhaps distracted by the contingencies of wars that drained funds, materials, talent, and time.

French authorities instead exchanged architectural magnificence for social control, tightening the perimeters over both space and people. As much as the city continued to transact government and business, the terms of the engagement evolved. Habits unfamiliar to the Milanese—such as billeting soldiers within the city walls—had the effect of militarizing the civic sphere, as the powers usually exerted over troops came to be entangled with those exerted over citizens. These binds allow us to follow two threads in the sources. First, articulations of the built environment testify to its resignification and disaggregation. Eruptions of earth, ephemeral assemblages, and repurposed structures suggest an urban landscape deformed by the impingements of new political frameworks of war in and around the city. Milan was not embellished as a French capital; rather, it was un-built, so to speak, in order to defend against (and as a consequence of conflict with) countervailing forces. While the crown and its agents entertained visions of new monumental construction from walls to palazzi to canals, those visions ultimately remained fantasies. Second, the civic edicts issued by authorities outline programs of social discipline aimed at impeding the threats that a fluid use of civic space by inhabitants, visitors, and undesirables could pose. The French, in collaboration with civic authorities, continued to police concerns that had also bothered the Sforza—blasphemy, the creep of disease, the circulation of stigmatized populations like gypsies and gamblers—but they also introduced forms of oversight particular to a wartime metropole under tenuous administration. Together, these two bodies of sources demonstrate the material and social dimensions of the palimpsest state, as civic erasures and overlays hybridized a city divided between preexisting structures and new realities.

Fraying Milan's Fabric—Castle, Walls, Domiciles

The Sforza castle loomed over Milan; its bulky arsenal could even weaponize it against the town. During the Milanese uprisings of the Cinque Giornate in 1848, the Austrian General Radetzky threatened to turn the castle's firepower upon the city to quell the revolution.[8] That gesture had a tradition. When in 1608 the English wit Thomas Coryate visited Milan, then under Spanish Habsburg governance, he noted that "part of [the castle's heavy guns] are planted Eastward against the towne, to batter it if it should make an insurrection; and part on the contrary side Westward against the country if that should rebell."[9] In a lengthy reflection on the castle's defense system in 1549, the Habsburg governor Ferrante Gonzaga fretted mostly about threats from within the city, not from outside.[10] More than once during the Italian Wars, too, the castle took aim at the city: in 1513, when citizens celebrated England's victory over France at Guinegate by ringing the cathedral bells, the French-held castle pulled shots into the city, hitting the bell-tower.[11] Some years earlier, in 1500, the Sforza castellan—as if to spite both the city and its French invaders— similarly targeted the duomo. The Ferrarese envoy wrote to his duke: "The shot flew just to the Duomo, into the house of a baker, and I saw the damage that it did which, for a cannon-blow, was quite forceful. The shot is iron and weighs 24 pounds. This evening as well they shot at some soldiers crossing the castle piazza, and I understand they killed a French soldier and wounded a boy."[12] When the populace seemed restive, the *campanile* of the duomo was itself fitted with artillery.[13] At times, the Milanese people appeared more resilient than their buildings. In March 1500, the French fired into the city during their campaign to recapture it from Ludovico il Moro. A Mantuan envoy reported: "Every day here there seems to be some miracle of artillery fire, because it seems miraculous that no one is hurt. They say that a mortar fell in the middle of a bed in which five people were sleeping and it touched no-one. [. . .] A cannonball struck a wall and exploded in the face of several men blown down together and they took no grievance. They say that Saint Ambrose watches over this people for the great devotion they always show him."[14] In this telling, human bodies escaped harm while the city's own fabric splintered around them.

For months at a time—sometimes years (1500, 1513, 1521–1523)— during the first quarter of the century, castle and city antagonized each other, especially following changes of lordship.[15] While the town had little recourse in conquest but to surrender, those who held the fortress imagined it not just as a redoubt against surrounding armies, but frequently as a site of implantation and resistance against the city's rulers and inhabitants. As European conflict in the 1490s escalated, the Sforza duke pained himself to protect control of the castle from outsiders. In his apotropaic will and testament, he imagined its castellan as having equal authority to his chief secretary and chamberlain in a crisis.[16] Despite these well-laid disaster plans, after Ludovico fled Milan, his castellan, Bernardino da Corte, ceded the Porta Giovia fortress to the French almost uncoerced on 17 September 1499, "without a single artillery shot."[17] The *castello* seemed suddenly transformed. "The French are dirty people," wrote Marin Sanudo after speaking with a traveler who visited Milan in October 1499. "There is great filth in the castle where Lord Ludovico once wanted never to see even a blade of hay on the ground." Aiming at ostentatious defilement of the Sforza fortress, "the French piss in the chambers and shit in the courts and halls."[18] French debasement of the fortress as a courtly space initiated its transformation into a site of military labor. Now to ward off threats both external *and* internal, French engineers disrupted the interfaces between urban and fortress space that Ludovico Sforza had pursued. In the wake of its rendition, the castle's new Gallic occupants undertook a series of works to ready the castle and its environs for sustained defensive use, effectively cutting it off from the city.

The chronicler Ambrogio da Paullo described ditches dug around the castle's ravelin, a triangular defensive projection facing the city. Over the ditch engineers installed a drawbridge, "where the French guard stands permanently. If the castle had once been strong, from that point it became the strongest [. . .] and many houses were torn down near Porta Comasina, [as was] the Broletto Nuovo (New Assembly) that il Moro had had built, and several other dwellings without any regard, enlarging the castle piazza. Near Porta Vercellina they tore down the Duties House, which used to be on a street near the garden behind the castle near Santo Spirito, and dug the ditch around, locking in the mills beneath the castle, fortifying more than ever."[19] This so-called Broletto Nuovo—not the structure that now carries that name in Piazza dei Mercanti some distance from the castle—seems to have been part of Ludovico Sforza's initiative to solder city to castle. Possibly a public assembly site, it reportedly also served as a food market.[20] In isolating the castle with these new defenses, the French repelled civic gathering and marketing from Milan's castle precinct, carving a literal a divide between military and urban hubs.[21]

In 1507, Venice stewed over France's Italian policies as Genoa boiled over into full revolt. Probably addressing those threats to Milan's east and west, crown agents outlined a plan to extend the ditches from the castle garden around the western flank of the city to the fortified gate of Porta Ticinese. Work orders demanded that "the earth should all be thrown toward Milan, thus making its banks, with the required slope, providing no easy means of ruin."[22] The duty houses at the city's gates would be fitted with bastions, some of earth and wood, other of stone and lime.[23] The bastions would then be topped with parapets prepared for cannons according to military commanders' specifications.[24] Arriving in August, the Mantuan envoy reported that "they do not cease to work continually on the ditches around Milan; they will cost 5,000 scudi and the peasants will pay for them; and they have just finished making seven ravelins, one for each gate. They will cost a good deal, and the priests will pay for them."[25]

Ambrogio's chronicle estimated that over 4,000 people labored on the project that summer, cutting wood and demolishing houses.[26] Similar efforts spread across the entire duchy.[27] At Lodi, forty kilometers southeast of Milan, 1,400 diggers cut trees for half a mile around the city to furnish the ramparts. Ambrogio observed that these works proved to be the unmaking (*desfatione*) of poor gentlemen and peasants: no fortification could ever replace justice. This acerbic utterance seemed to echo Seneca and anticipate Machiavelli: a true leader needs no fortresses because "his one impregnable defense is the love of his countrymen."[28] Instead, Ambrogio critiqued the French king's exactions while also pointing to the environmental and economic hardships that fortification campaigns impressed upon locals. Laborers (*guastadori,* literally "wasters") were regularly coerced; that coercion explains Ambrogio's concern for their unmaking, as does the perennial and disingenuous insistence among captains and recruiters that they travailed willingly, in one case with "more joy and happiness than if they were going to a wedding."[29] *Guastadori* had to be paid through heavy taxes levied upon residents, and once faced with the denuding of the suburban landscape, the chronicler concluded, locals began to ask: "Where can we flee to be safe?"[30] A voice like Ambrogio's explicitly indicted dubious ethics by asking what modes of governance befitted a Renaissance prince. Public works in the name of safety that brought ruin to the public seemed unjust to him. He highlighted the irony of security-propelled building schemes that shored up urban defensibility by leaving inhabitants vulnerable, impoverished, or homeless.

When the French recaptured Milan in 1515, "among the first things" their commander did upon arriving was that he "began to make banks, valleys, and bastions along the trenches of the agitated city, and all the barrels, beams, and other things found in nearby homes were put to that use."[31] Such moves constituted a normal part of fortifying cities for war, but they also entailed a form of architectural cannibalism, as fortifications consumed private property into the substance of their makeshift embankments.[32] Maintaining the integrity of those ephemeral walls perennially vexed authorities, whose decrees from the 1510s to the 1520s, over the course of different regimes, complained to citizens that the urban bastions had been "destroyed and unmade (*destructi et disfacti*) by various people" and prohibited them from "digging wood out" of the bastions or making "passage, access, holes, or any damage to cause deterioration or less security to these ramparts."[33] Officials also regulated shrubbery near the trenches, presumably in an effort to clarify sightlines.[34] Citizens' reclamation of raw materials, as well as their apparent efforts to adapt these hills of earth to their comings and goings, illustrate their quotidian modifications of, or soft forms of resistance to, the military environment erected around them.

Like many fifteenth-century cities, Milan grew beyond its walls, and around 1500 the Borgo delle Grazie was just one of several districts that fanned around the medieval boundaries. These too were susceptible to consumption—flagrantly so in March 1515, when the French commander Trivulzio decided that the best strategy against the enemy imperial troops involved burning parts of the *borghi*, a choice the chronicler Prato vividly lamented: "[Fire] spread and crept into the houses, which sent crackling flames and miserable cries up to the heavens; it made Milan dark with smoke, and with the glimmer of the sparkling sun, everything seemed to burn."[35] Perhaps the fatal consequences of incinerating the suburbs led ultimately to the French plan to encircle Milan with a new wall (developed 1519–1521), encompassing substantially more terrain that the existing one. Engineers undertook a campaign of technical measurements, partly to determine where the new belt of walls would sit on the landscape, but also to assess compensations for owners of private property that would be displaced for construction.[36] With France's ouster from Milan in 1521, the actual building of such walls never came to fruition. Instead, it had to wait until 1529, when the Habsburg governor erected an enclosure, enlarged in 1534, that a successor in turn demolished and replaced in 1552.[37]

The year 1521 was a year of fire. The castle suffered an explosion in June when lightning struck Filarete's tower, the fortress's proudest peak, combusting its powder magazine. It sparked such a blast that "the tower was shattered to its foundation and it threw enormous pieces of stone into the middle of the piazza, and it shook the entire castle." It killed the French castellan and "innumerable other people."[38] Pietro Martire d'Anghiera, a Lombard émigré scholar at the Spanish court, took the explosion as a bad omen for the French, particularly since the tower's monumental marble-sculpted Sforza arms and effigy of Saint Ambrose reportedly survived the detonation and landed intact across the piazza.[39] That year also marked the acceleration of a process that had begun in 1499: the castle's gradual renunciation of its role as a locus of the court as the contingencies of war disqualified it for princely living. Although during their restorations (1513–1515, 1522–1526, and 1531–1535) Ludovico Sforza's two sons sought to inhabit and embellish the fortress in a spirit similar to their father's, the French kings rarely used it during their infrequent stays in Milan, preferring to lodge in suburban villas or in the palazzi of sympathetic local elites.[40] Even in 1531, after Duke Francesco II had been unable to inhabit the city for years, the Sforza castellan claimed to have found the castle "all in disarray."[41]

Across the duchy and throughout the city, residences once opulent were despoiled. Looters may have damaged as many as a hundred urban patrician residences during the Sforza exodus in 1499.[42] From out of the castle's own stronghold in 1500, French-allied Milanese elites shared among each other "the wares and vestments left behind by Ludovico Sforza."[43] The same day that Ludovico fled, the provisional governing council called for the restitution of beds and other fittings that had belonged to the duke but had been "secretly carried away."[44] The furniture was now needed for Louis XII's entourage. As Part II of this book shows, politico-legal contests over ownership of terrain both urban and rural acutely strained relations across the duchy at all levels. During agitated transitions, domiciles of the outgoing regime's elites became the targets of attacks, looting, or appropriation. Even the briefest review of the sacks in 1499–1500 confirms the pattern. Following Ludovico's flight in autumn 1499, the chronicler Prato named the houses of Bergonzio Botta (the ducal treasurer); Galeazzo Sanseverino (Ludovico's son-in-law and captain of his army); Ambrogio da Corte (the duke's steward and financier); Ambrogio Varesi da Rosate (the Sforza astrologer); and the "Ferrarese ambassador," meaning Antonio Costabili, one of il Moro's confidants. After Sforza's fall, Costabili erected one of Ferrara's richest abodes, but as envoy he also sustained a splendid palace in Milan.[45] Crossbowmen broke its windows and carried out wood, planks, beds, ceilings, and food.[46] Most if not all of these residences stood in the castle piazza or the Borgo delle Grazie.[47] The abandoned palace of Sforza retainer Marchesino Stanga, conspicuously comfortable, now served both assembly and court functions, and in turn housed French-appointed chancellors Pierre de Sacierges (1500–1501) and Étienne Poncher (1501–1504).[48] French administrators thus sometimes occupied the very halls that their Sforza forebears had inhabited.

Perhaps because of its constant military investments, the French crown did not pursue major monumental construction in Milan. Even with the continued appointments of engineers and architects, and the forward crawl of a number of religious or private building projects, only a handful of sites advanced. Others remained mere dreams.[49] One figure who devoted some energy to stake French claims upon Milan's landscape was the royal governor, Charles II Chaumont d'Amboise (1473–1511, r. 1500–1511), known in Milan as the *gran maestro* or *gran metro*.[50] The middle of his decade-long residency witnessed a couple of initiatives. First, he lobbied to bring Leonardo da Vinci from Florence back to Milan, remarking that his fame in painting should pale next to "some things we have asked him to do, in drawing and architecture and other things appropriate to our rank."[51] During Leonardo's Milanese sojourn of 1506–1513, he undertook plans to construct a suburban villa for Chaumont for which a few sketches and descriptions remain, outlining its extensive pleasure gardens nourished by waterways coursing toward the city.[52] Ambitiously, Leonardo planned a garden stocked with fragrant citrus trees, hydraulic automata and fountains, and a copper-mesh-covered aviary. It was never built. Second, Chaumont also stimulated the construction of the sanctuary of Santa Maria alla

Fontana outside Porta Comasina, in the open countryside. It too was once proposed as a design by Leonardo.[53] To the waters of the eponymous fountain, the architect and engineer Cesare Cesariano explained, "rich people can be taken who may wish to be cured of every sort of illness."[54] Chaumont himself had been healed there; it is likely that he commissioned the sanctuary in 1507. But it was not his original inspiration, since the shrine in fact replaced a Visconti chapel on the same site, and thus a desire further to enrich the miraculous font may have predated the French arrival.[55] Sources describe two interior fountains near the high altar and a third in the external courtyard. The Lombard sculptor Agostino Busti (called "il Bambaia") left drawings that might correspond to these fountain projects, though it remains improbable that he executed them, given interruptions to the construction.[56] (The church still stands, though it underwent major alterations in the twentieth century.)

Both of Chaumont's projects, tellingly, shared the desire to train waters into prodigious displays. Milan had since the thirteenth century managed an extensive system of canals that tapped the Ticino and Adda Rivers descending from the mountain lakes toward the plain.[57] Canals penetrated the city center as well, permitting the fluid passage of goods and people. Hydraulic engineering formed a normal part of Lombard infrastructural management, but a focus on harnessing waters to act in concert with buildings (a villa, a church) characterize the novelty of Chaumont's commissions. The spread of Leonardo's fascination with water's properties and potentials may account in part for this particularity, though he was not alone. At least one other contemporary Milanese engineer, Bartolomeo della Valle, composed a now-lost treatise on water management, and it remains possible that Leonardo in turn found inspiration in the water features at the royal palace of Blois.[58] French efforts to extort water's forces for making the Adda more navigable resurfaced under François I in 1516.[59] Milan's waters were an asset to its Gallic lords, one they wished to harness for commerce, delight, and therapy. A second feature uniting Chaumont's commissions was their suburban or rural location, an aspect of almost all the major regal or vice-regal commissions, such as the victory chapels on battle sites.[60] The politics and practicalities of new French building in the urban center may have been too delicate to navigate.

Aside from these Chaumont-sponsored ventures, major permanent French implants into Milan's urban landscape were few. Monumental funerary projects arose in specific churches—French collaborator Giangiacomo Trivulzio's tomb at San Nazaro in Brolo with contributions from Leonardo and Bramante (1506–1520); Gaston de Foix's sepulcher first in the Duomo and then at Santa Marta with unfinished marbles by il Bambaia (1512–21)—but they transformed only small quarters of the metropolis and advanced particular family agendas.[61] If anything, the French wished to carry parts of Milan away; one of the kings supposedly wished to detach Leonardo's *Cenacolo* from the walls of the Grazie refectory; failing that, Leonardo's students painted several copies for French patrons to bring across the Alps.[62] French patrons in Milan thus never enunciated a fresh architectural vision of the city as a post-Sforza capital, but rather lay their power atop existing structures through decoration campaigns, ephemeral triumphal structures, and inhabitation of confiscated palazzi.

One still little-known French patron involved in these sorts of decorative campaigns is Nicolas de la Chesnaye, Milan's podestà under François I. Author of vernacular medical literature and moralizing verse (the *Nef de Santé* and *Condampnacion des banquetz* of 1508), his name is carved in marble capitals at Santa Maria alla Fontana, and he commissioned a 1517 votive fresco still today in the apse of Santa Maria delle Grazie (fig. 2.1).[63] Presented by his name-saint, Nicholas, to the Madonna and Child, la Chesnaye kneels devotedly in his voluminous damask robes as a banderole of text curls upward over the Virgin's shoulder. The words belong to a familiar Marian prayer, but may also invoke a motet composed for Milan by the erstwhile Sforza court-chapel composer, Gaspar van Weerbeke.[64] La Chesnaye's investment in embellishing structures new and old probably gives a good sense of the distribution of French patronage across several environments (domestic, monastic, confraternal, and so forth). But the public visibility of his name and likeness remain rare for French elites who implanted themselves in Milan in the early century. Those elites helped to sustain dynamic artistic patronage networks in the duchy despite the fragmentation of previous ones. But the substantial abdication of architecture as a strategy of dynastic establishment, otherwise so common among regimes in this period, suggests that French attention was drawn to other theaters. Those alterna-

Fig. 2.1 Sacra Conversazione with Milan's French podestà, Nicolas de la Chesnaye, 1517. Santa Maria delle Grazie, Milan.

Photo by Timothy McCall.

tive venues were socio-spatial environments—the manifold spheres of urban life, whose instabilities the French often perceived as a threat. Daily passages of inhabitants and visitors, their abilities to gather together, and even their appearance became objects of discipline that struck native observers as severe. Walls were not the only restraints upon civic life; laws and force, too, confined citizens.

Policing Civic Space

King Louis XII made a triumphal entry into Milan after the submission of the Genoese uprising in 1507, the second of three post-conquest visits to his Italian duchy (1502, 1507, 1509). A series of ornate triumphal arches lined his parade route, culminating at the castle piazza. At one of these sites appeared a "representation of Italy, circled by a giant net

(*una gran rete*), meaning to show that it was all under the will of the king"
and by extension under the sway of Mars. As Louis passed by the arches,
a personification of Jove invited the monarch to see how Mars "encircles
and encloses Italy/and no one dares to contradict him!"[65] The net al-
legory unequivocally articulated an idea of domination over the unruly
or unwilling: Leonardo, we just saw, imagined birds at Chaumont's villa
caged by a gauzy copper net (*una sottilissima rete de rame*); Milanese elites of
both sexes tamed their hair with nets of silk or gold (*reticelle*); and patrician hunters ensnared their prey in fatal webs.[66] No escape. The notion
needed no explanation. Milan was entangled and its people subdued.

If the king's will to impose jurisdiction over the city did not trans-
late into stone, it was easier to manage through urban legislation and
its stringent enforcement. The regime did this in collaboration with preexisting structures of local magistracies that oversaw elements of the
city's life (taxes, safety, health, and so forth). As had been the case under
the Sforza, any level of officialdom with the appropriate jurisdiction
could issue decrees (*gride*), from crown agents to municipal government
to special agencies, and these decrees could apply strictly to the city or
broadly to the entire duchy. Criers made the orders public by declaiming
them in central locations identified on the digested copies. Authorities
also disseminated these orders in printed copies; the earliest surviving
impression of a Milanese decree dates to 1495, and at least two rare imprints exist from Louis XII's rule.[67] Transcriptions of decrees survive
plentifully from the first quarter of the sixteenth century (in registers
and loose-leaf), permitting a relatively holistic analysis of the tenor of
the regime's intentions toward Milan's population. It should come as no
surprise that contemporary voices license us to read these decrees not
just as prescriptive emanations but as contingent responses to social conditions. Alighting in Milan from the dependency of Bellinzona in early
1500, that troubled town's official commissioner reported that he had
"understood that the men of the land were armed, [. . . and so] he issued
a decree that everyone should disarm. Once the decree was made the opposite was done, since men ran to arms and seized the commissioner."[68]
In brief, a dialogue existed between authorities' suspicions of civic disruptions, their corpus of decrees, and evolving conditions of urban life.

Consider the strategies of urban discipline following Ludovico Sforza's brief restoration from February to April 1500, ending with his sei-

zure and imprisonment. Perceived by French commanders as an act of Milanese rebellion and disloyalty, the restoration engendered a punitive response once the crown regained the upper hand that spring. Using regulation as a form of retribution, France cast its net over the city. The decrees of spring 1500 reveal a program to tame an agitated city through exacting impingements upon circulation, movement, and bodies. It was, on the one hand, a militarization of public space, insofar as war pressurized that space into a target of unusually tight control. But on the other hand, the word "militarization" perhaps mischaracterizes the nature of that control.[69] The soldiers who composed the military rarely if ever enforced or upheld civic order in this period. In fact, the presence of soldiers—both mercenary and permanent—threatened to compound urban disruption even more than did partisan dissidents. Unruly rather than stabilizing, soldiers did not guarantee public quiescence. The control in question instead presented itself as effortlessly sovereign, legal, and incontrovertible. It continued to issue from sources known to Milanese citizens (the civic criers and their magistracies), but with a newly menacing rigor that bespoke a new font of authority (a conquering power), one pointedly upheld by frameworks of violent castigation (punishment for transgressions). Perhaps what Milan experienced in spring 1500 was a fundamentally troubling political slippage: when a state of emergency presented itself as a new norm, and forms of violence over citizens naturalized themselves as juridical.[70] It was at the very least an aggravated, hyper-vigilant administration in which modes of surveillance familiar to Milanese subjects, such as weapon prohibitions, met new ones, such as enforced shaving of the male population. The following few pages trace such restrictions and the corollary effects upon the citizenry.

Having failed to restore Sforza lordship in the spring rebellion of 1500, a number of conspirators fled the city, as did perhaps as many as 2,000 other elite partisans, "some fleeing one way toward Bergamo, others toward Piacenza, others toward Como to reach Germany, some here, some there, disguised so as not to be identified, suffering hunger and thirst."[71] French officials undertook a remarkable information-gathering campaign to trace these elites and their assets, as Chapter 7 explores in depth. The regime's strategy to reestablish control over the recalcitrant capital involved stanching the flow of people in or out of the

city.[72] Efforts to limit movement are particularly noteworthy. In
May 1500 Cardinal Georges d'Amboise (1460–1510, Chaumont's uncle
and Louis XII's chief counselor) aimed to quell the wave of fugitives by
decreeing "that no person at all should dare from this moment forth to
flee, or bring external items into the city, or otherwise transfer them for
fear of losing them in pillage. Everyone should be ensured that soldiers
will pursue no further harassment."[73] Fearing the spread of false news
by troublesome outsiders, officials demanded notice from innkeepers
and private citizens alike of all guests in the city.[74] Over a year later, concern to maintain a certain civic stasis reappeared in a decree disal-
lowing anyone to change residence within the city, possibly to reassure
the regime that it understood the dynamics of its population distribution.[75] (A similar decree had appeared during the springtime Sforza restoration of 1500 as well.[76]) Officials also forbade traversing the city at
night without a torch, a law often coupled with an interdiction upon
carrying arms.[77]

This last prohibition—motivated by nighttime's ability to veil dangerous weapons and to obscure identification of persons—was not in itself an unusual civic order in this period, regardless of regime.[78] Nonetheless, the threat of unbridled violence in the upturned city was real,
exacerbated by the volatile gangs of mercenary soldiers and their followers (*avventurieri*). Time and again over the first decade of the French
regime, civic officials tried to banish soldiers from the city, particularly
those outside royal employ.[79] They revoked arms permits, prohibited
duels, required the rendition of ammunition, and stipulated the registration of all weapons with the captain of justice.[80] At fairly regular intervals over the course of Louis XII's administration alone, civic officials
issued or reissued such decrees. More than thirty-five weapons prohibitions survive from the first decade alone.[81] Under the Sforza restoration
of 1513–1515—agitated by the same pressures of ongoing conflict—these
measures continued, as they did too through the second French rule of
1515–1521.

In the wake of France's first seizure of Milan, Prato described the
city as *fluctuante* (unquiet); this series of prohibitions purported to impose a program of pacification, though it proved to be a project ineluc-
tably hampered by the conditions of war that the subjection of the duchy
had unleashed. The forces that had disquieted the state were the same

that now wished to stifle its upheavals. Consider the social effects of this program of ostensible pacification that accompanied the French conquest. Lodging the soldiers who so terrified the urban population was particularly contentious. Exemption from housing soldiers within ten miles of the city had been one of the terms of the city's surrender in September 1499.[82] The French ignored those hopeful requests; during preparations for the king's October royal entry, agents had to forbid Milanese citizens from destroying signs naming their houses as billeting sites.[83] At least five major monasteries lodged several thousand foot soldiers. These men "devoted themselves to playing, thieving, blaspheming, and whoring [. . .] and they turned public squares into their tavern."[84]

Even after the majority of soldiers dispersed or left the city in 1500, tensions simmered over the nature of the new civic authorities' vigilance. Ambrogio da Paullo wrote of the "injustices and wicked behaviors" of Milan's first French captain of justice, whose evening patrols struck Ambrogio as an opportunity to molest the citizens. "If they found some poor artisan going home at night, coming from the shop with or without a light, they hunted him down and took him to prison, making him pay—either one *grossone,* or two, or three, or four, as they wished, with or without reason; and lanterns were useless since they took them away [from people] and then said they had been discovered without a torch."[85] Evidence of decree-enforcement remains sparse, but this account suggests that its praxis could surpass both letter and spirit of law to become a malignantly capricious form of discipline. The dangers of traversing the city could arise from law-enforcers themselves.

Ambrogio continued his critique by complaining of a chilling of frank public speech. "There were so many little dogs around, listening and accusing, that one could not speak. When an artisan in the piazza said of the great disorders that occurred every day, 'It is impossible to live like this,' he was accused, costing him 25 gold ducats, such that it was no longer possible to trust anyone."[86] French authorities worried about the proliferation of opposing voices, and prohibited "subjects from holding gatherings of armed men in houses, churches, etc., under the pretext of taking counsel for the common good."[87] In the name of urban renewal in the 1490s, Ludovico Sforza had already licensed the demolition of porticos scattered through the city's neighborhoods, known as *coperti,* where citizens had met to discuss life and share information since the thirteenth century.[88] Restriction of public gathering spaces probably redirected opposition into other venues, such as the dissenting printed pamphlets we will encounter in Chapter 9. These antagonisms moved not just vertically between regime and subjects but laterally between citizens themselves, as partisanship tugged at mechanisms of consensus and encouraged Ambrogio's so-called *cagnetti* (little dogs) to pursue habits of denunciation and to amplify factional stresses.

Fundamental to so many of the French decrees after 1500 was the desire to "see through" their newly conquered population by means of administrative orders designed to produce social translucence. Catalogs of exiles, surveys of visitors, enforced fixity of domicile, limits on mobility, and registers of weapons all advanced that aspiration. Men, too, could potentially become transparent to the eyes of the regime. Impediments to recognizing individuals distressed French administrators, as decrees against unilluminated nighttime circulation indicate. The will for transparency finally made intimate contact with men's bodies in the immediate wake of the French recapture of the city. On Saturday 25 April 1500, the captain of justice issued an edict on behalf of royal authorities *pro barbis* (concerning beards). It ordered that "every person, whoever he may be, who wears a hairy beard, must by the coming Monday have it cut and shaved, under penalty of being imprisoned and paying a fine, without any exceptions."[89] In the very years when a long fifteenth-century trend of clean-shaven Italian faces was slowly ceding to a resurgent beard, this decree raises questions about intentions on both sides of this edict: What had stimulated the beards of Milan's men? And what did French officials hope to achieve in shaving them off?

Some answers to the latter question come in an expanded reissue of the decree in September 1501. After banning offensive weaponry and ordering vagabonds to vacate the city, it addressed clothes and hair: "Because many go about [. . .] disguised in irregular clothing or with counterfeit beards both in the city and in its dominion, which leads us to conclude that they, wishing to do evil, seek not to be recognizable [. . .] it is declared that from this hour, no person should dare [. . .] to disguise himself or be found in disguise, or in any counterfeit or unusual clothing, or with an attached beard (*barba positia*), or a mask or any other thing that would impede easy recognition, on the pain of death and confiscation of all his goods by the royal chamber." Not wishing to let men with real beards off the hook, the order continued: "Because it is understood that many in this city and dominion of Milan allow their beards to grow long and wear beards regardless of the usual habit and practice of men, suggesting sinister intentions and wicked desires, and [because they set] a poor example and sad objective," all men had to shave their beards within twenty-four hours or face four lashes of the whip.[90]

The decree belonged to the project of making citizens legible. By insisting upon identifiable facial features and regular clothing and by emphasizing how unusual it was for Milanese men to wear beards, it aimed to combat wartime irregularities. Milan's is an early appearance of a form of legislation against facial hair that recurred under the French crown during the sixteenth century. Prohibitions against beards appeared in Dijon in 1525 and 1528 and in Paris in 1535 and 1545. Those later orders highlight the violence that authorities expected from beard wearers, citing rogues "who, because of the deeds of war, allow their beards to grow. And after committing murders, homicides, robberies, disturbances and other crimes, grow their beards to prevent their recognition."[91] Carolingian traditions of beard-shaving (*barbatoria*) and hair-cutting (*capillaturia*) had imagined the sacrifice of hair as a gesture of submission to a lord; there is perhaps a deep history at play here, by way of the Frankish kingdoms, that fashioned the uniformly trimmed male population as the ideal form of citizens and subjects.[92]

As far as concerns the intentions of Milan's men in 1500 (that is, to answer the first of our two questions above), the massive Latin history of Milan by the jurist Bernardino Arluno (1478–1535) encourages us to interpret the French order of civic tonsure as a form of submission. Confirming the edicts' claims that beards were uncommon in the city (the bans noted that beards were *ultra el commune rito; fora de la comune consuetudine; ultra comunem aliorum usum*), Arluno relates that many of the city's men had vowed to grow their beards as a way of inscribing mourning for their conquered city upon their bodies—"as a sign of such obstinate grief," he wrote, that it stimulated French officials to issue their edicts "on shaving and cutting hair." Arluno tells us that the audacity of the edict so surprised Milan's citizens that it provoked derision and mockery and that to push back against the new regime the city's men "cherished their beards and fostered the regrowth of their hair." Moreover, it accompanied other changes in men's habits in response to the conquest: some

took up the wearing of shrouds, while others renounced religious observance altogether.[93] While the edicts' language stressed beards as signs
of potential criminality, Arluno instead demonstrates that unshaven
facial hair articulated mourning, that it signaled bodies outside the
norms of regular ablutions marking a state of exception upon the male
populace. In this sense, these beards support the argument proposed in
the last chapter about the state's temporality. Here, citizens marked the
duration of new lordship on their bodies, aligning their appearance with
their sense of displaced time. Such forms of votive hair growth had a long
tradition in ancient and medieval Italy as well,[94] and they point to passive
but demonstrative forms of resistance against the yoke (*jugum* is Arluno's
word) of new lordship that have so far gone unrecognized. Tensions
over this issue evidently continued, since a reissue of the edict appeared in 1505.[95] And as late as 1512, when the irascible Sforza court
poet Lancino Curti died, he reportedly still wore his hair long, contrary
to the "close-to-the-ears" French cut that—along with Gallic fashions in
dress—highlighted what one observer called the "clear admission of
bondage" among Milan's citizens at the twilight of Louis XII's rule.[96]

A coda to this story points to the extent to which Milan's men felt
beset by French shaving orders. Two and half months after the edict's
1501 reissue, the Venetian envoy to the court of Maximilian I, king of
the Romans, mentioned Milan's razor-burn: "I understood that the King
[Maximilian] decided to send to France as his orator Lord Zuan Bon-
temps, and he tells the Milanese that he is sending him to treat his affairs with the Christian King [Louis XII], who commanded them to cut
their beards, so that in a few days everyone will be satisfied. But from
very reliable sources, I understand that the mission of this emissary is
more for things pertinent to the King [Maximilian] than to the Milanese."[97] While the envoy revealed in his last words that Maximilian had
little time for this particular complaint, it nonetheless shows how sol-
emnly Milan's men protected their liberties to fashion their own appearance as a political tool. It drove them to remonstrate with the lord they
considered to be the ultimate arbiter, the king of the Romans, long-
standing sovereign of the Lombard duchy. Maximilian, in turn, paid
enough care to reply that an ambassador had been charged with the case.
Enforced shaving struck the Milanese as a sign of oppression that required sovereign intervention. In impinging upon the skin surfaces of

the citizenry, the edict was a biopolitical gesture directed at controlling the population through a rigorous program of civic tonsure whose goal was identification and submission.

Discipline Makes Disorder

Premodern cities were, it is now a truism, sites of social discipline in which the negotiation of power structures found expression both in consensus and obtrusion, in law and force. What should interest us about Milan's experience in the early sixteenth-century wars is how discipline—despite its drive for order—in fact produced forms of disorder. Newly established authorities pursued classic statist strategies of legitimation by monopolizing violence and employing it as a tool of control. And yet, they struggled mightily to keep their grip. Armed conquest in 1499 launched an era when laws proliferated but force mutated them through abuse or negated them altogether. Rather than consolidating rule, violence directed against landscapes, civic space, and populations instead fragmented the socio-spatial environment. Frequent complaints in a variety of sources—both for and against the French regime—about tumult, disquiet, and disorder attest to the disruption of civic and regional norms.

The French in Milan directed their efforts at spatial control into two related forms of capture: environmental and social. In the first instance, they sacrificed familiar architectural rhetorics of political implantation in favor of fortification, isolating the castle from the city and absorbing urban materials and labor into a defense project that perforce oriented itself toward war's short-term timescapes and away from the long-term ones of monumental establishment. Through artillery fire into the city center from Milan's own castle, through rings of makeshift bastions, earthen walls, and barricades, and through occupation of religious and domestic space by mercenaries and officials, the French overwrote the Sforza legacy with a series of defenses that entrapped the urban population while also unbuilding some of its familiar surrounds. Moreover, most of the plans of the French elite to construct new and ambitious buildings remained mirages.

In the second instance, efforts to tame what seemed to Milan's new lords as a restive population produced thousands of decrees that can be read as an operation to ensure effective implantation of the regime through aggressive social control. Beyond the disciplinary frameworks we would expect in any large sixteenth-century city, the decrees reveal both the ambitions and the limits of the French program of conquest and management. The goal was to foster a workable, peaceful city but one unequivocally enchained to exacting new masters ignorant of local traditions of negotiation. What separated forms of social control once exercised by the Visconti-Sforza dukes from those of the new French lords was the degree of credence that society invested in them. Military invasion entrapped the duchy's people in an untenable situation sustained more through coercion and violence than through means of moral suasion.[98] Subjects needed to be willing to recognize authority as a cultural system practiced by both authorities and people. Few of them saw evidence that any such system existed. Contemporaries described this era as a moment when even lords were forced to heel "with a leash around the neck (*con la choreza al collo*)."[99] Urban populations wore that same leash. Its limits, however, played out in several theaters, whether in the overzealous application of edicts or in the eruptions of both violent and passive resistance from the populace. The conditions for consensual agreement upon just governance had been unsettled. It would take decades to recover them.

3

Delegitimizing the Sforza

*I*n less than a hundred years, the Sforza dynasty's fortunes rose and fell. The Milanese accepted Francesco I as their de facto duke in 1450; by 1535 his grandson Francesco II died without heirs, and the family's role in Italian politics essentially ended. It was not a smooth century. Marked by assassinations, usurpations, and more than three restorations, the Sforza era abounded with efforts to hold onto power. Given that history of tumult, the extent of the family's success is notable. It steered one of Italy's largest and most prosperous realms, establishing a brisk tempo of innovation in state-formation.[1] The dynasty's substantial lordly ambitions manifested in the theaters of bureaucracy, diplomacy, war, law, and culture.

But the juridical foundation of their claim to power remained cloudy. Emperor Wenceslaus elevated Giangaleazzo Visconti to the rank of duke in 1395. Francesco Sforza supposedly absorbed that ducal title by marrying the Visconti heir, Bianca Maria, in 1441. The emperors, however, resisted transferring the Visconti title to the Sforza; this imperial hesitation stimulated a good deal of labor at the Milanese court to justify the regime without the soothing sanction of a higher authority, and

Francesco instead asserted that his ducal title issued from popular ac-
clamation and election.[2] Only in 1495, just four years before Louis XII's
invasion, did Francesco's son Ludovico extract an official investiture
for himself from Maximilian I, king of the Romans and later emperor,
at a substantial price. In so doing, he sidelined the son of his late
nephew Giangaleazzo Sforza, a child primogeniture would have preferred for duke over him. From a purely technical standpoint, Ludovico
thus suffered the knowledge for over half of his reign of double illegitimacy: he was a usurper who, to boot, lacked imperial recognition. The
implications of this fact became blindingly clear only at the sunset of
Ludovico's reign.

When French and imperial contenders for title over Milan supported
their polemics with military force, strong currents of power-justification
pushed against the Sforza dams. These counterclaimants had to support
their efforts to rule not only by performing a suite of legitimizing acts
(for themselves, for subjects, and for observers around Italy and Europe),
but also by extinguishing the validity of competing claims, rendering
them inviable. Machiavelli proposed that a sine qua non in securing a
newly conquered territory was to assure "that the blood of their former
prince is extinguished."[3] This chapter thus traces the intentional and un-
intentional unraveling of Sforza lordship, the mechanics by which the
wars created an environment in which to disassemble the components
of the signorial machine that the Sforza had constructed. This process
of delegitimation was both its own cause and effect: discourses of invali-
dation turned insinuations into reality, gradually smearing the Sforza
out of much of their political and cultural relevance. If we now recognize that signorial regimes built their mastery upon the projection of
aristocratic glamor, we see in the following pages how such forms of
representation could be contested, sullied, or reversed.[4] Real political
might depended upon these optics of power. Deconstruction of Sforza
hegemony proceeded by amplifying preexisting doubts about the house,
notably its inauthenticity and profligacy. "These French gentlemen now
more than ever declare (*publichano*) that Signor Ludovico had little pru-
dence," the Mantuan envoy reported in 1501 as the parlous state of the
finances of Milan's ducal chamber became clear.[5] Sforza's imprudent rulership, they reasoned, brought about his ruin. In the ensuing years, the
family's gradual atomization and isolation supported claims that it was

a dead-end dynasty in several ways: unproductive, unhealthy, unclean, and not even particularly Italian. Accusations of degeneracy became a cudgel that antagonists wielded effectively against the Sforza dynasty. We begin first with an assessment of Ludovico Sforza's strategies of legitimation during his brief restoration before considering how Sforza detractors tarnished those efforts by highlighting the lackluster of Milan's fading rulers. "Now reader," to borrow the words of one Venetian chronicler, "you see how in these times the most worthy house of Sforza lost such a deserving and renowned estate."[6]

The Moor's Last Sigh: Restoration, Capture, Incarceration

On Wednesday, 5 February 1500, Ludovico Sforza needed more than ever to justify himself as lord of Milan. Five months had elapsed since his hasty flight triggered by the French invasion. After months of gathering energy and resources in Austria, he fought his way back to his capital city, scattering resistance and bringing the duchy under his control.[7] ("If the walls, trees, and earth had tongues, they would have cried 'Moro!,'" wrote an ambassador.[8]) That winter morning, in the suburban garden of Gaspare Vimercato near Porta Nuova, he prepared to make a triumphal return.[9] There, he welcomed three diplomats who brought good wishes from their lords. The Mantuan envoy, Francesco Malatesta, assessed the duke's demeanor and appearance, writing that the nearly fifty-year-old duke "had a happy face and looked younger than ever."[10]

What drew Malatesta's longest description was the glittering chain il Moro donned. "He wore around his neck a gold necklace, enameled in the Parisian style with the letter E in the antique fashion of white enamel with a pendant of a mounted diamond, and beneath it a larger emerald, then a very large hanging pearl, which seemed to me a very beautiful lordly thing (*una bellissima etiam signoril chosa*)."[11] One could ignore this detail if it did not reappear later in Malatesta's letter, after Ludovico had paraded through the city. "The necklace was popularly estimated to cost fifty-two thousand ducats," he reported, re-naming each part with its value.[12] Even though Malatesta doubted the amateur appraisal of the crowd, the jewel had evidently dazzled the Milanese. To them, too, it was a very beautiful lordly thing. But that thing, just like the status it represented, was transient. It was probably these very jewels that Ludovico put in hock a month later to help pay for his ongoing war efforts.[13] (Some twenty-two years later, his son Francesco II issued edicts searching for them.[14])

Il Moro continued his plan to re-legitimize, and thereby reinstate, his interrupted rule. Malatesta caught the details of the strategy while also succumbing to it. He was struck by the "humanity the duke showed to everyone of any rank," whether "in extending his hand to anyone who presented himself, in saying humane words, or in making very humane gestures with his lordly cheer."[15] After declining to enter the city beneath a baldachin, an uncharacteristically approachable Ludovico Sforza, hyper-humane, presented himself to his erstwhile subjects. He appeared at court in the city center with elites circled around him and his brother Ascanio at his side. Expressing goodwill toward all (except the ungrateful Trivulzio clan, "men of bad blood"), he repented any offense he may have caused in public or in private. He now desired to reconcile with everyone as "brothers and sons." Addressing one of the deepest problems of his long reign, Ludovico acknowledged that he owed financial debts to many people, and he deputed Ascanio to establish a fiscal commission to put things right.[16] In peroration, he maintained that the common good was also his own good. Applause and jubilation followed. Among those in Milan predisposed to favor their ousted duke, this strategy seems to have worked. Malatesta wrote some two weeks later that citizens who had once complained of the weight of his financial exactions were now "putting hand to purse" in order to support him. Giovanni Antonio della Somaglia, the wealthy son-in-law of Ludovico's recently murdered treasurer—Antonio Landriani, whose assassin we will encounter in Chapter 4—presented the prince with 10,000 ducats, promising 25,000 more.[17] Others offered similar sums; the city raised funds through a system of parish collections, although one chronicler noted that the fundraising campaign "had little effect."[18]

Beyond finances, the duke also had ambitions to reassert his dynastic amplitude. While Ludovico took to the battlefields around Novara, Ascanio was presented with il Moro's three-year-old son, Giovanni Paolo (1497–1535), child of his mistress, Lucrezia Crivelli, a boy "for whom he put on a good deal of celebration."[19] With Ludovico's own legitimate sons in exile at the imperial court, the display of a Sforza scion announced the lineage's potential for extension. Crucially, in his 1495 investiture agreement with Maximilian I, Ludovico had insisted that even his illegitimate children should be considered viable heirs to his ducal title; Giovanni Paolo could thus function as a real successor to his father's title.[20] (In 1535, Giovanni Paolo indeed sought to inherit the duchy after his brother's death, but was possibly poisoned while returning from his Neapolitan interview with Emperor Charles V.[21]) Il Moro had tried a similar tactic of self-display with the children of his house the previous autumn. Just days before his escape, Ludovico paraded through Milan with little Francesco, the eight-year-old son of his late nephew Giangaleazzo, the boy most often called the *duchetto*. He had the youngster, beloved by the duchy's populace but never free to leave the castle, dash before his parading horse. ("Do you have the courage to run?" he reportedly asked the child.[22]) To associate children publicly with the duke produced a spectacle of dynastic futurity; it was a means of welding fecundity to legitimacy. Likewise, pointing backward in time rather than forward, the annual commemorative obsequies for Ludovico and Ascanio's father, Francesco I (held on 5 March during the brief restoration), emphasized the historical duration of Sforza lordship; the ritual brought all the city's magistrates to the cathedral in honor of the ducal house in a bid to consolidate civic affections.[23] It is hard tell whether genuine care for the prince's family or self-preservation from a French sack of Milan is what rallied a citizen army, reputedly numbering 10,000 Milanese, to head toward Novara in April 1500 as reinforcements against the invaders.[24]

Countercurrents, however, were afoot in the divided city. While shouts of "Moro, Moro" could be heard when Ascanio circulated the city with "the usual gentlemen," cries of "Franza, Franza" also filled the air. Barbs aimed at deflating grandeur also flew. Rumor had it that Ludovico "wanted Lord Giangiacomo Trivulzio to be called 'Giacomo the Miller,' just as he called the Lord Duke 'Ludovico from Cotignola.'"[25] These whispers pointed to the Sforza clan's non-Milanese origins, as Romagnol warriors-for-hire less than a century earlier, as if to pose afresh the question of indigeneity in princely rule. The Sforza had always struggled with Milan's nobility over the ruling family's extraction and their supposed importation of *gente nuova*. Language of abasement, projected through exuberant Venetian pamphlet literature celebrating Ludovico's fall, testifies to suspicions at all social levels over the nature of the duke's power.[26] In these very days Marin Sanudo copied a puzzle-poem into his chronicle; once the reader cracks the enigma, the poem describes the serial bad fortune of the Sforza clan.[27]

At Novara, on 10 April 1500, French troops vanquished Ludovico Sforza's army, thick with Swiss fighters. Talk of Sforza mercenary origins may partly explain the contemporary celebrity of the tale of Ludovico's scheme to disguise himself among his own Swiss pikemen.[28] Bearing a halberd and having tucked his long hair under his cap, Ludovico could still not escape detection. Whether because of his princely bearing (and his ill-fitting disguise, as one story had it), or his inability to respond to questions in German, or because his soldiers succumbed to emoluments, the duke was betrayed to the French by his Swiss pikemen—on Good Friday no less, as if providentially.[29] In one account, the treason was sealed with a Judas-like kiss.[30] Ludovico's tactic of disguise was fairly common for entrapped princes: only five years earlier, King Charles VIII had supposedly disguised himself to escape the chaotic battle at Fornovo.[31] When tides turned against them, flamboyant sovereigns had to learn how to vanish; they nonetheless kept certain treasures close at hand. Once they revealed him, Ludovico's mercenaries handed him over to the French captain, Count Ligny, who disarmed him of a sword not unlike the blade, gilded with the ducal *biscione* and topped with a fish-tail pommel, now in Paris's Musée Cluny.[32] Likewise, when Venetian captains ensnared Ascanio on the very same day, he relinquished the sword of King Charles VIII, captured by stradiots at Fornovo in 1495. He may also have surrendered his commander's baton, crowned with a gilded orb and inscribed with his name; he had likely paraded with it during Ludovico's Milanese return in February. His quiet rendition probably never gave him the chance to use the sharp stiletto concealed within the baton's shaft (fig. 3.1).[33]

Disarmed, Ludovico Sforza enjoyed one of his last moments of ostentation during his captivity in Novara, when Ligny presented him and his retinue with outfits made of gold, silver, and silk, "as befitted their station."[34] But thereafter, Ludovico crossed a threshold from prince to prisoner as a process of abasement through isolation began. Accustomed always to a circle of attendants, Ludovico saw his already thin retinue gradually disassembled, beginning with the Sanseverino brothers with whom he had been captured. Louis wished to imprison him in France;

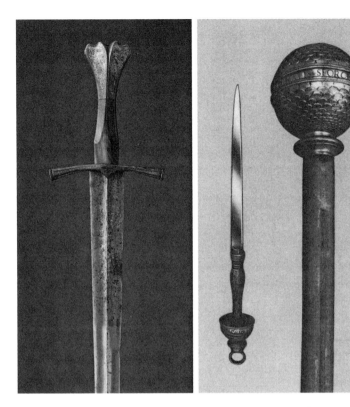

Fig. 3.1 (Left) Sword of Milan's duke, fifteenth-century Italy, Musée Cluny, Paris. Inv. Cl. 11821. (Right) Ascanio Sforza's baton of command with hidden dagger, ca. 1500. Deutsches Historisches Museum, Berlin. Inv. W 1072.

(Left) Photo © RMN-Grand Palais (Musée de Cluny–Musée national du Moyen Âge) / Jean-Gilles Berizzi. (Right) Reproduced from Heinz-Werner Lewerken and Jürgen Karpinski. *Kombinationswaffen des 15.–19. Jahrhunderts/Heinz-Werner Lewerken; Aufnahmen von Jürgen Karpinski.* Militärverlag der Deutschen Demokratischen Republik Berlin, 1989.

Loches was the preferred stronghold deep in the Loire valley, but the king resisted sending Ludovico there at first: Louis liked to hunt on the castle grounds and wanted to avoid seeing the ex-duke. The prisoner would instead go to the dungeon of Lys Saint Georges in Berry, to be overseen by the former captain of Louis's archers. On his way, Ludovico would first pass through Lyon.

Traversing his lost duchy, il Moro reputedly wept when confronted with contemptuous shouts of *"Mora il Moro!"* in Asti, and his health worsened on the trip to the point that he was spitting blood. Upon reaching

Lyon on 2 May 1500, his captors paraded him through the city as a captive on a mule, dressed in black felt from cap to boots: no sign of his gilded silks.[35] (As we will see, Sforza black clothing came to be associated with doleful or priestly sobriety in the new century.[36]) The Venetian emissary in Lyon reported that Ludovico trembled and "forced himself not to show his passions over such a turn of fortune." After his procession, the duke "could not walk a step without help. Everyone says his days are numbered."[37] In Milan, the French publicly exhibited the captive Ascanio in similar fashion, traversing the widest possible breadth of the city. The Venetian chronicler Priuli explained how the French reasoned "that the poor Milanese were reduced to such destruction, calamity, and misery that they could no longer lift their heads, and that with so many Frenchmen in Milan it was impossible for the Milanese, deprived of arms and homes, to buck. Thus the French, to spite the Milanese and to show that they were now lords of Milan, decided to pass with Cardinal Ascanio *per mediam civitatem.*"[38] They detained him in the Porta Giovia castle in a ground-level chamber "of the worst sort," his associates chained at the feet and "treated like dogs."[39] The French killed some members of Ascanio's elite retinue; others were tortured to reveal secrets, fined, or sent to France, "which was then the prison of the Milanese, just as Italy was once the graveyard of the French."[40]

Ludovico became the monarchy's most rigorously confined prisoner of the early sixteenth century. His captors tarried over a week in Lyon as artisans completed the giant cage in which he would sleep on the journey to his dungeon; it was fashioned of a wood-wrapped tempered steel that, if filed or struck, would spark a fire.[41] The duke knew these types of steel cages well. One of them hung in Milan's Broletto to expose convicted blasphemers, and in 1495 he had ordered the city of Piacenza to hang one from its bell-tower, never suspecting he would suffer a similar enclosure.[42] Ludovico's imprisonment at Lys Saint Georges, where he was bereft of all of his retainers, tried his nerves so strongly that the French conceded a small crew of servants, "because they knew his habits."[43] Isolation still gnawed at the man who had been one of the best-informed princes around the Mediterranean.[44] Louis XII knew of his craving for news and kept him selectively informed.[45] When the king's physician, Salomon de Bombelles, passed by Lys Saint Georges in March 1501, he paid a visit to the prisoner and found him "thin, with sunken dark-encircled eyes, complaining that the king held his state." The ex-duke wished to learn the latest intelligence, telling Salomon that negotiations with King Maximilian "cannot go ahead without me." Word of his distress moved Louis enough to grant his prisoner the company of a palace dwarf.[46]

This was, of course, a gesture of empty courtliness. Louis designed Ludovico's isolation specifically to remove him from the information networks that generated political knowledge. In its place, he contented his prisoner with a meager diet of lordly play. Sforza passed his time casting for fish in the moat of his prison; and Venice's orator in France wrote that Ludovico was "in prison, plays with crossbows and cards, and is fatter than ever, as those who have seen him say."[47] King Maximilian worked to extract more comfort for Ludovico, requesting an honorable space in France measuring at least five leagues, where the ex-duke could be together with his retainers, move about freely, and hunt as he wished.[48] Although rumors continued that Louis might grant Ludovico a small state within France, nothing came of these efforts.

What did emerge from the 1501 negotiations, however, was Ascanio's freedom. After nearly eighteen months of keeping the Sforza cardinal in the tower of the castle at Bourges, Louis agreed to release him. To signal his appreciation, Ascanio arranged to retrieve from hock a large pearl once worn around Ludovico's neck and present it to Louis XII.[49] The reward for such favors was a certain level of affection on the part of the French monarch. Writing to his niece Caterina upon his release, Ascanio described himself as "so well regarded and cherished by the King that we are hugely indebted to our Lord God."[50] For a while, the two men hunted together almost daily, and Louis even wrote to the pope to request Ascanio's readmission to the pontifical court.[51] But the king's good faith was mislaid; Ascanio maneuvered against French interests in the two papal conclaves of 1503, aiming either to take the papacy for himself or to support candidates eager to chase the French from Lombardy.[52] By 1504, Louis XII reportedly wanted him to return to imprisonment in France. Unsure where to find safety, he ultimately appealed for asylum in Venice, claiming that he was prepared to lose his annual 17,000-ducat French royal allowance so that he could live free. Whether he settled in Venice or elsewhere, he confided to Venice's representative in Rome: "I do not want to go back to France."[53] Death saved him from having to persuade the Venetian *signoria;* Ascanio died in Rome at age fifty on 28 May 1505. Plague, venom, or French disease numbered among the rumored causes.[54] His most intimate circle was convinced that he had been poisoned, while others blamed plague, tracing its transmission to extended contact during the procession of Corpus Domini with "one of his groomsmen who mingled with whores."[55]

This passing reference to louche grooms was just an echo of a discourse of sexual corruption associated with the Sforza court, and it allows us to assess how whispers of sexual profligacy also came to be linked with regime collapse in the late fifteenth century. Contemporary commentators—either in predicting the fall of a court, or in assessing the causes of its failure—attributed some explicative power to moral decadence: we see it also in contemporaneous assessments of the fall of the Aragonese kings of Naples. Many voices of Ludovico's own era agreed on the destabilizing role played by his political arrogance, isolationism, and temerity. Moral judgments also reverberated in some of these diagnoses. The policing of sexual license belonged to an expanding anti-court tradition whose logic of divine providentialism reasoned that the debauchery staining many courts contributed to their destruction.

Rumors of behavior unbecoming of a lord darkened the twilight of the Sforza dynasty both abroad and in Milan, even if voiced mostly by outsiders. Recent Milanese conflict with the Swiss (at the Battles of Giornico in 1478 and Crevola in 1487) disposed a good deal of Germanophone popular opinion against Milan's dukes; that spite coalesced with already widespread Swiss and German stereotypes framing Italians as sodomites. The discourse evidently contributed to an accusation made at a guesthouse in 1497 by a Lucerne man named Peter Jos, who called Ludovico Sforza an "assfucker" (*arsbrutter*).[56] The specific force of the insult, however, may have related less to Ludovico himself than to strong Swiss suspicions about the sexuality of Lombards and Italians: these types of barbs flew promiscuously in the lexicon of Swiss libels, and sexual smears appeared frequently in efforts to demean politico-economic adversaries.[57] One French chronicle lamented the lordship of Duke Gian Maria Visconti in the early fifteenth century, since it was under his rule that sodomy had flourished first in Lombardy.[58]

A specifically Milanese instance of associating Ludovico's court with sexual license came with an admonishment by the Augustinian *beata,*

Veronica da Binasco (1445–97). Her renown grew locally in the 1490s, notably after her 1495 pilgrimage to Rome to meet Pope Alexander VI. But just a few years earlier, in 1492, she invited Ludovico for an audience at her monastery of Santa Marta in Milan's Porta Ticinese district, as recounted in her *vita* (holy biography). He arrived "in a great cavalcade" at the monastery, entered the enclosure with three of his closest aides, and met with the holy woman in a lengthy secret meeting. She warned him "in the name of God of the great wicked sins committed in his court that provoked God's anger and justice to send retributions upon the world. And in particular, [she spoke of] one stinking sin committed by many, greatly abominable in the eyes of God, who could no longer hold back his justice. And if these abominations did not end swiftly, his Lordship would see tribulations and terrible things sent by God against him and many people." Ludovico thanked Veronica and promised to remedy the sins, at which point she "was lifted into ecstasy," and "the duke touched her hands, and found that they were harder than wood." Then, "well edified, [Ludovico] left the monastery in great happiness." Despite news that Ludovico subsequently attempted to curb some of his court's sins, Veronica's biographer pointed to the "great woes and tribulations" that later followed—an acknowledgment of the insufficiency of the remedies and, so the logic went, the resulting collapse of the duke's rule.[59] Veronica's prophetic warnings shared a disciplining impulse with contemporary Florentine preaching of Savonarola, whose condemnations of luxury and vice even more explicitly threatened divine punishment and political eversion.

The element linking the Swiss man's insult and the mystic's plea was the condemnation of unfruitful sexuality. Complaints over profligate, wasteful sex acts intersected with disapproval of princely courts in the imputation that that they consumed resources and produced nothing. These critiques in turn contributed to the fundamental reality of the Sforza family in the 1490s and after: the ducal house was not a productive—and, according to some polemical extensions of this reasoning that we will encounter shortly, not a viable—princely dynasty. Only Machiavelli's embroidered tale of Caterina Sforza—Ludovico's niece who, in the 1488 siege of Forlì, dramatically and probably spuriously exposed her genitals to her young children's captors to insist that she could bear

Fig. 3.2 Ludovico Sforza's cell at the castle of Loches, France.
Photo by author.

further offspring should they kill her sons—serves as a fecundity-
focused exception to this tendency.[60]

Before exploring the contours of this pessimistic view of the Sforza
around 1500, we must return to the captive Ludovico Sforza, waiting in
his cell. The ex-duke never resigned himself to the imprisonment that
ended his days. One chronicler noted that he "tried hard to escape" from
French custody. He succeeded at least once, when he bribed one of his
French guardsmen, who "covered him in a cartful of straw, and allowed
him to flee. But all for nothing. Ignorant of the road leading toward Germany, he became lost in the nearby groves. The next morning when the
deceit was discovered, everyone went out to look for him, and finally the
dogs found him."[61] He died 17 May 1508. The only material trace of
Ludovico's years in the dungeon of Loches are the chivalric designs—
painted lances, helmets, and letters—decorating the low-hanging vault
of his cell (fig. 3.2). Unlike his brother Ascanio's body, richly entombed

in Andrea Sansovino's marble sepulcher in Santa Maria del Popolo in
Rome, Ludovico's went to its grave with no trace, or at least no record survives of his burial ceremony or location.[62] Even Cristoforo Solari's now-
famous gisant tomb sculptures of Ludovico and his consort Beatrice
d'Este sat moldering in the sculptor's Milanese studio for decades until
their eventual sale to the Certosa di Pavia in 1564, and the duke's remains
never received the honorable interment beneath the dome of Santa Maria
delle Grazie that Ludovico had stipulated in his testament.[63]

Closing Down the Sforza Era: The Problem of Heirs

Voices concerned with court depravity formed just a small part of a much
wider cultural shift that accompanied the decline of the ducal clan's fortunes after 1500. The family's luster as a dynamic, creative force in peninsular politics and culture dimmed. Partly, this was an effect of French
efforts to foreclose Sforza pretensions to rule, and partly it reflected hesitations among allies and enemies alike over the very nature of Sforza
lordship. For the French, a house so recently celebrated as glorious,
worthy, and brilliant had to be positioned in opposing terms in order to
spoil their claims to authority. By dispersing, entrapping, and isolating
the family, Louis XII and François I turned the Sforza into a waning
house with a nonextensible future. During that process, part of which
we have already traced with Ludovico and Ascanio, the family's disgrace
assumed a number of facets. The surviving Sforza faced the dismantling
or contestation of the beauty, splendor, and fecundity once associated
with their rule. (Duke Francesco I had sired at least thirty-five children.[64])
Accordingly, the fabric of their lordliness frayed, and the generation of
Ludovico's sons proved to be the family's last.[65]

The spectacle of dynastic weddings had formed a cornerstone of
Sforza legitimation efforts in the 1490s. The decade sparkled with Sforza
nuptials as Ludovico worked to cement his family's ties with several
ruling dynasties in Italy and beyond. In 1489, Duke Giangaleazzo married Isabella d'Aragona, daughter of the Neapolitan king, a union celebrated the following year with the Bellincioni-Leonardo collaboration
known as the "Festa del Paradiso." In 1491, Ludovico wed Beatrice d'Este
in a double Sforza-Este celebration that also bound Anna Sforza to Beatrice's brother Alfonso. In 1494, Maximilian I Habsburg took Bianca

Maria Sforza (1472–1510), Ludovico's niece, as his bride. The court also marked the birth of Sforza children with sumptuous celebrations, notably Ludovico and Beatrice's sons Massimiliano in 1493 and Francesco in 1495.[66] Accounts of these opulent festivities, traded through ambassadorial networks and celebrated in Latin epithalamia by leading Milanese scholars, publicized the wealth and fertility of Milan's leading house. The court secretary and historiographer Tristano Calco capped his unfinished Milanese history with encomia devoted to these three major Sforza marriages.[67]

All of these marriages fell to pieces even before 1500. Maximilian and his vassals largely disdained Bianca Maria; the young Duke Giangaleazzo died mysteriously in 1494; and Beatrice expired during childbirth in 1497.[68] When the duchess perished, witnesses reported enormous fires in the sky above Milan's castle, "as an omen of the coming calamities of the illustrious Sforza family."[69] In each of these unfortunate weddings, we can see how tides of antagonism turned against the Sforza clan in rhythm with the pressure upon their claims to sovereignty. Bianca Maria Sforza, for instance, suffered from the chilly attitude of the imperial princes and electors toward her family in the German-speaking lands, who resented Maximilian's investiture of Ludovico with Milan's ducal title.[70] Even Maximilian's own resistance to Sforza aspirations softened only when Ludovico funneled him substantial military and financial support packaged with the marriage alliance; in this climate of distrust, Bianca Maria became a fulcrum for disapprobation.[71] Maximilian frequently abandoned her with creditors as a security deposit for unpaid debts.[72] The king complained of her juvenility, inexperience, and barrenness. His concern centered particularly on the latter, and Ludovico's ambassador noted that the king of the Romans worried that she suffered from "indigestion that prohibits conception." He also expressed suspicions, a Milanese agent reported, of her habit of "urinating after coitus: after she got up one night to piss in a chamber, the King followed her in the nude to see where she was going." It was not a hopeful sign for future procreation; Maximilian "never visits the Queen" and only "loves her to honor the matrimonial debt." The couple produced no children.[73] In sum, an impression of disarray in Bianca Maria's household developed in the mid-1490s, and it accompanied "the grief that the Germans gave the Lombards for spending too much."[74]

Laments over Sforza profligacy, as Chapter 7 will show, swelled after 1500 when many of Milan's Ghibelline elites sheltered at the Innsbruck court under Bianca Maria's care.

Isabella d'Aragona, consort of Giangaleazzo and mother of the *duchetto* Francesco, found herself under even greater pressures. Marginalized by Ludovico after her husband's death in 1494, Isabella dressed "in very dark colors with lugubrious fabrics, shabbily (*senza alcuna politezza*)," and she "ate on the ground and showed great sadness." She reasoned that her late spouse, usurped of his duchy, would enjoy the eternal life of a saint, "but," she exhorted, "weep for wretched me, and for my son."[75] As a condition of the city's surrender to Louis XII in 1499, the people of Milan requested that Isabella and her son be allowed to remain as residents.[76] The ex-duchess, however, found no mercy from the French king. Foreseeing the volatility of hosting a pretender to the duchy in the capital, he separated mother and child and sent the boy to France. The young Sforza may have remained some time in Lyon; the tutor his mother appointed to accompany him died there in 1502.[77]

But already by late 1500, news reached Venice that Francesco was "at an abbey, two miles from Tours, in the custody of certain monks with none of his [own company]; the king wants to make him a religious, but it is not [the boy's] intention."[78] At the Benedictine abbey of Marmoutier, some 900 kilometers from Milan, Louis detained the most credible Sforza claimant to the ducal title, isolated even from his preceptor, in a state of enclosed celibacy. At Louis XII's request, Pope Julius II allowed the youngster's appointment to the rank of abbot at age fifteen in 1505, overriding the community's election of one of its own. The monks requested their preferred candidate to be appointed as his vicar, a kind of a shadow authority to perform the spiritual duties the teenager was neither inclined nor equipped to carry out. Francesco served as Marmoutier's titular abbot from 1505 to 1511, but took religious vows only in 1507. His premature death tells volumes about his resistance to the monastic life: he fell from his horse while hunting in the nearby woods of Meslay on Christmas day 1511, having chosen not to assist in the mass.[79]

In the weeks immediately following Francesco's separation from his mother in 1499, Isabella took advantage of the changed regime to pursue further knowledge about her husband's death in 1494. Even though Louis XII's arrival robbed her of her son, it also shattered the power structures that protected arcane details of her consort's mysterious illness and expiry. In an inquest led by two sympathetic Milanese elites, Isabella pursued the role in Giangaleazzo's demise of the astrologer and physician Ambrogio Varesi da Rosate, one of Ludovico's intimates. Captured in flight by French forces, Varesi returned to Milan as a prisoner. He underwent questioning and eventually admitted to administering poison to the young duke "in a syrup" on Ludovico's orders.[80] Varesi's confession supported the widely shared suspicions of many contemporaries against il Moro and finally clarified the enigma of his nephew's end.[81] Isabella apparently intended to launch an official trial against Varesi upon Louis's descent into Lombardy, but no further trace of the accusation has yet surfaced, perhaps because she quit Milan in early February 1500, settling eventually at the Sforza castle in Bari.[82]

Her efforts to recover her son and his rights did not cease with her exile. Before the end of 1500, she prevailed upon Maximilian I to send an agent to the French king requesting her son's installation as rightful Duke of Milan.[83] Perhaps news, a few years later, that Julius II had authorized Francesco's elevation to the abbacy of Marmoutier propelled her next move. In September 1505, Isabella tried to secure the help of an accomplice in a rescue mission. She wrote that her child, the "true duke of Milan, is detained by force in the lands of Gaul by the King of France without reason or cause."[84] To save her son, she wished to procure the services of the Knight Hospitaller Pedro Luis de Borgia Lanzol de Romaní, grand-nephew of Pope Alexander VI. Upon Julius II's election in 1503, Borgia had fled Rome for Naples. Isabella asked Borgia "with all his available industry, diligence, subtlety, and mediation to attempt in every way possible to extract our son from the country, land, and tenement of the King of France and consign him safe and sound into our hands." If successful, Isabella pledged to reward Borgia with 100,000 gold ducats, half paid up front, and half paid "at the time that our son again possesses his state and duchy of Milan." The ex-duchess promised Borgia—whom she imagined would thereafter be persona non grata in France—up to 15,000 ducats further in annual ecclesiastical benefices to find himself an appropriate residence after the covert abduction.

Such an expedition was theoretically feasible. Borgia—a cardinal with military experience and strong Benedictine connections, whose flight to Naples in 1503 reconnected him to the same Aragonese neworks to which Isabella belonged—was perfectly suited to the charge. Nonetheless, this jailbreak operation never materialized. And yet, the ex-duchess's determination to unwind the travails visited upon her family points to the remarkable efficacy of the campaigns against her husband and son. Louis XII succeeded in completing the marginalization that Ludovico Sforza had started. Il Moro wanted only to eclipse his nephew and rule in his place while maintaining a veneer of dynastic stability; Louis, in his push to end the Sforza claim upon Milan altogether, could afford to go farther. He recognized the legal and political threat of the child pretender to Orléans interests, and used distance and monastic isolation as a wedge to frustrate any attempt at restoration or reproduction. Aside from his mother Isabella—who began ostentatiously to sign all her correspondence with the epithet *unica in desgracja* (alone in disgrace)—no one thought of the child duke. The French king had rendered him, like Ludovico in his cell, functionally invisible.

The fate of the *duchetto,* forcibly evacuated from his territories, modeled the kind of reprisals that Sforza adherents could expect from the French. Perhaps anxiety over the potential French response explains why a series of letters flew between Cremona and Venice in April 1506. Lombardy's submission to France led Cremona to exit the duchy and capitulate to Venetian lordship, a loss to the Milanese state that the French resented. A good deal of secrecy thus accompanied the missives exchanged between Cremona's rectors and the doge when they described the arrival in Cremonese territory of a boy "of little beauty, rather of ugly countenance, and in bad estate."[85] This was Cesare (1491–1514), the nearly sixteen-year-old son of Ludovico Sforza and his mistress Cecilia Gallerani.[86] The teenager, whom the rectors estimated to be "about twelve years old, badly dressed, [staying] at a benefice held by Cecilia's brother," had been "seen by many citizens of this land" and had spent two nights in Cremona. Ostensibly on his way to Chiari to lodge with a schoolmaster, the boy was now in the home of a certain Jacomo da Ponte in Soresina, northwest of Cremona.[87] Jacomo reported to the rectors that "Madonna Cecilia had sent him to say that he should keep him in his house until another further notice." The rectors "immediately ordered him to hold this Cesare secretly with him, not releasing him unless by our express license," and requested further advice from Venice on how to proceed.[88]

The rectors' concern over how to manage this troubling visitor testifies to Cremona's delicate balancing act between Venice and French Lombardy in these years. Politically, Cremona functioned as a frontier zone after the fall of the Sforza: ruled by a team of Venetian governors but enmeshed in long-lived Lombard networks, it became a crossroads for French detractors, Venetian sympathizers, counterfeiters, and Sforza partisans. In this position as a hinge between Milan and Venice, Cremona could not afford to attract French ire. Cesare's arrival raised prospects that stirred discomfort among the city's rectors: on one hand, Sforza loyalists who resented the city's recent rendition to Venice might rally around the teenager as a fulcrum of revanchism against the Serenissima; on the other, if French agents learned that Cremona was sheltering a Sforza child, they could mobilize a forceful campaign against the city.[89]

Cremonese rectors had already faced this dilemma in 1502, when Bianca Francesca Sforza (1456–1516), il Moro's half-sister and abbess of the Augustinian convent of Santa Monica in the heart of the city, requested to return to her duties after a period of enforced confinement in Brescia.[90] Venice's rectors in Cremona called the prospect of her return "scandalous and dangerous," because she had already escaped Brescia for Mantua and "never stopped, day or night, to send for citizens and to scheme with them in favor of her brother and write to Germany." Bianca was "a woman of great cunning and heart," who "loves her brother very much." She was the kind of person "whose absence is useful and whose presence is dangerous."[91] It was in Cremona's interests to make the Sforza invisible as well.

Equally arresting in the letters about Cesare in 1506 are the words used to describe the youngster. Ugly, badly dressed, disordered: it is as if the boy manifested his own illegitimacy and his father's fall from power. By contrast, the *duchetto* Francesco—whom contemporaries pitied as a legitimate heir usurped of his title—always attracted praise for his beauty.[92] Even as a captive, Francesco came to Blois at Louis XII's request, since "for his virtue, the king wished to see him."[93] In a period that made tendentious links between physical beauty and moral character, the children of Ludovico Sforza seemed to suffer even greater scorn for their appearance and behavior than their father. Ludovico—called from his youth by the epithet "il Moro" for his swarthy complexion—managed by the 1490s to manipulate his nickname into a visual culture of lordliness.[94] Some elements of that legacy transferred to his sons: Massimiliano occasionally appeared in chronicles as *"il Moretto,"* and the book-illuminator Godefroy le Batave allegorized the Sforza scion as a black African in 1516 in a manuscript for Louise de Savoie, King François I's mother.[95] But the Sforza children also faced freshly unflattering associations with darkness that turned in the direction of dirtiness, disorder, Germanness, dour priestliness, and illness—all forms of representation that fashioned and reinforced images of Sforza decline, even despite the family's return to power in 1512 and 1522.

Massimiliano and Francesco: Less Lordly Lords

Uprooted from their luxurious childhood at Milan's court in 1499, Ludovico and Beatrice's two sons spent their formative years north of the Alps, shuttling between cities in which Habsburg allies gave them shelter (as we will see in Chapter 7). In these years of exile, the young men also became detached from the performative splendors of the Po valley's courts, and particularly from the highly refined Milan-Mantua-Ferrara triangle that defined the most stylish forms of Italian regard at the turn of the century. As much as Milan itself changed during their peregrinations, the Sforza youths transformed as well. Notably, commentators—many of them Italian—drew attention to their lack of suavity, their tendency to be humorless, clerical, Teutonic, or disorderly. Coupled with their failure to produce issue for sustaining their family line, the last two Sforza dukes left a legacy of decadence that mirrored their own duchy's decline.

Massimiliano and Francesco II had already faced inhospitable receptions north of the Alps. For instance, as Francesco matured, his wish to take religious vows induced King Maximilian to support his election as a canon in Cologne. But Sforza blood was not blue enough; despite having a father and grandfather who were dukes of Milan, Francesco's great-grandfather, Muzio Attendolo Sforza, "had no other title than war captain. The [Cologne chapter] took this as insufficiently illustrious and did not wish to elect him to the canonry, and so they rejected him from the chapter."[96] Francesco interrupted his studies in the juridical faculty of the University of Vienna to return to Lombardy when electors named his elder brother, aged nineteen, as duke at the diet of Mantua in August of 1512. When Massimiliano himself returned to Italy following his election, he alighted at the Mantuan court to visit his maternal aunt, Isabella d'Este. Having invested herself substantially in the Sforza cause during the diet that elected him, Isabella traveled to Milan with her nephew in early 1513 as a gesture of dynastic support.[97] Still, she commented frequently in her correspondence on the young Sforza's ultramontane habits, Teutonic wardrobe, and apparent misanthropy; dinner at his table, she thought, "was more German than Lombard."[98]

Statesmen in Milan echoed this concern for the new duke's character. Despite professing his affection for the new duke, Massimiliano's own chancellor, Girolamo Morone, minced no words: "Alas, how dissimilar to his father, how ignoble (*degener*), how negligent, how scornful of his affairs and his own wellbeing, how attentive to his own personal losses!"[99] The prince's failings mattered because of Milan's dire politico-military situation. Massimiliano faced the threat of French troops massing on the duchy's western territories by spring of 1513. It surprised many that he led Milanese and Swiss forces to victory against the French in the Battle of Ariotta in June.[100]

Despite this military success, Massimiliano's triumphal post-battle entry into Milan in July 1513, narrated by the Mantuan envoy Benedetto Capilupi in a pair of letters to Isabella d'Este, captures the failures of the new Sforza prince to stage an appropriate representation of ducal majesty. "Tuesday he will enter Milan on horse, but he will go more unwillingly than can be described because—I think, and so do others—he neither recognizes nor knows how to use his victory."[101] From the letter's start, Capilupi dampened Isabella's hopes. It should have been a beautiful thing to see "entering into Milan a young lord, so victorious, but the opposite happened since few preparations were made and the entry was confused and disorderly." The crowds of cheering Milanese citizens could not hide the meagerness of the displays—a diminution of splendor that bespoke not only the tarnish of the dynasty but the city's own economic fragmentation, as it was unprepared to mount the arms, banners, and triumphal arch that "would have made the entry more honorable." Capilupi later added that there "was no canopy, nor gentleman-footmen as there should be in similar triumphs; the boys and courtiers walked ahead without order," and other ranks of precedence went ignored.[102] Despite his dazzling garments, Massimiliano himself wore "a bit of a beard, and pretty badly combed hair (*cum li capilli assai mal pettenati*). The color of his face was the usual, even a bit thinner from his recent illness." The ambassadors all declined his invitation to dine, because the extraordinary heat had left them dusty and sweaty, and they too feared making a bad impression.[103] Massimiliano's ostensibly victorious moment proved to be a wash, a muddled inversion of the typologies of magnificence that Capilupi—a twenty-five-year veteran of such entries and triumphs—had come to expect. The unflinching critical gaze even of courts friendly to the Sforza captured their struggle to re-legitimize through pomp.

The Mantuan envoy also described his interview with the duke's brother Francesco, so recently returned from Vienna. The younger Sforza spoke with Capilupi "with few words, but good ones. He resembles his father, but is less lordly (*ma non tanto signorile*); he will not be as large a person, but is bulkier than the Duke, with full shoulders, hair similar to the Duke's, and the black clothes of a priest in the German style."[104] (The following year, the Mantuan courtier Mario Equicola echoed this assessment, calling Francesco "very serious, and in public he behaves like a priest and a churchly person."[105]) Capilupi's letter shows the newly restored Sforza court drawn in different directions: on the one hand toward the scintillation associated with the Ludovician 1490s, and on the other toward a sobriety and even coarseness that came to characterize the era of his sons. It is true that, in the spirit of his Este mother and aunt, Massimiliano understood the principles of princely splendor; the budget for ducal attire in 1514 was 30,000 ducats.[106] Yet Massimiliano sometimes struggled with the demands of brilliance that his position required of him; at times, advisers warned him that Italian forms of display required greater investment than German ones.[107] Signaling the éclat of his victory at Ariotta and the traditions of Milanese ducal investiture, Massimiliano wore "all white" from hat to shoes on the day following his Milanese entry, and "he had his brothers Cesare and Giovanni Paolo dressed similarly."[108]

But his habits and demeanor were considerably darker than his wardrobe. Capilupi described how, in a feverish isolation at the castle of

Pavia, Massimiliano had become "so melancholic that everyone is in bad
humor." The Mantuan saw more than just the effects of a recent illness;
from the moment of his return to his duchy, Capilupi had "never seen
him laugh."[109] Massimiliano's tendency toward melancholy formed the
basis for later assessments. In his *Elogi* (composed mostly 1544–1551),
Paolo Giovio assessed Massimiliano's character damningly. Noting that
his face "hardly resembled the noble visages of the Sforza" (Giovio wrote
these essays, after all, to accompany portraits hanging in his gallery), the
Comasque bishop opened by arguing that Massimiliano brought
nothing princely to his reign. Milan's duke expressed the thoughts of a
"sordid soul" in "absurd, often stupid speech," Giovio averred. The young
Sforza appeared to suffer from "a growing insanity" that produced an
uncommon filthiness: "He never changed his undergarments, nor was
he ashamed by the bad odors that emerged from them, nor from the sight
of lice that his very thick and uncombed hair (*impexa coma*) produced."
Despite the "encouragement of valets [and] pleasing urgings of illustrious women," it was only occasionally that his counselors prevailed
upon him to wash well and don fresh clothes. Leaving the heaviest burdens of state to his senators, Massimiliano spent his time hunting and
carousing, a state of affairs that led "most people to believe that his mind
was shattered by toxic potions or some enchantment."[110] Giovio's condemnatory portrait not only echoed—or inflated—observations of contemporaries like Capilupi, but also traced a decline of the image of Sforza
majesty to a nadir of mental and physical degeneracy.[111]

   Even if Giovio noted Massimiliano's pursuit of pleasure with court
women, these dalliances were unlikely to produce a Sforza heir acceptable as a legitimate successor. The absence of a consort—and thus the
threat of dynastic extinction—had posed a problem for the Sforza dukes
since Beatrice d'Este's premature death in 1497. As early as 1498,
Ludovico's emissaries dismissed overtures for him to remarry.[112] As for
Massimiliano, several possible spouses came to be proposed for him,
even at the moment of his surrender to King François I in 1515. Massimiliano instead told the monarch he would retire to France and take holy
vows. With the Sforza duke's abjuration and banishment assured, François offered instead to procure a bride for him, but during Massimiliano's period of French exile (1515–1530), he never wed.[113]

Francesco II faced similar circumstances. His troubled reign as duke—some of the duchy's most turbulent years, during which time the prince was often a fugitive from war-torn Milan for years, and was considered for some time a conspirator against the emperor—scarcely allowed negotiations for a dynastic match. Marriage had not come earlier perhaps because of Francesco's physical stature: the full shoulders that Capilupi noted in 1513 were taken by others as a deformation. Paolo Giovio related fifteen years later that the "military vigor, which shone marvelously in his grandfather, fails to shine forth at all (*nequaquam elucet*)."[114] Venetian observers between 1528 and 1530 witnessed a "melancholic complexion" and "infirm body"—the artist Lomazzo called him "hunchbacked"—and saw that he walked only with difficulty. They assessed his character with greater optimism, but the duke's body drew particular attention as a matrix of Sforza fortunes in Italy. Although the satirist Aretino joked in a comical 1534 astrological send-up that Francesco suffered from "genital impotence" (punning on the prognostic importance of stellar "genitures"), Venice's orator opined just one year earlier that he was lusty enough that "it cannot be doubted that he will have offspring."[115]

Speculation aside, how exactly to orchestrate the politics of Milanese heirs began to concern Emperor Charles V and his ministers in 1525 as they followed Francesco's worsening health and feared his fidelity to the Empire. In agreements settled in 1525 and again in 1529 at Cambrai, Charles maneuvered to regain Milan should Francesco II Sforza die without heir.[116] To clinch that legal devolution, he worked to align a dynastic union that would put the duchy in imperial hands whether the marriage produced children or not. Among Charles's own nieces, the choice fell upon Christina of Denmark (1521–1590), then resident in Ghent under the guardianship of Charles's sister, Mary of Hungary. The proposed union troubled Mary, who wrote to her brother in the summer of 1533 protesting that Christina, at age eleven and a half, had still showed no sign of puberty. Mary worried that the pressure for immediate consummation could endanger Christina; "should she become pregnant before she is fully a woman," she and the child might not survive.[117] The emperor dismissed his sister's scruples, suggesting that the age difference between the couple would more likely bother the duke than his bride.[118] Setting his niece's wellbeing aside, Charles's intuition about the duke's reaction proved true. A Mantuan correspondent at the wedding in May 1534 described the duke seeming "totally dismayed, having to chew such a bitter fruit as belongs to this lady, whom everyone believes will only mature in a few months, since she is in truth only twelve years and two months old."[119] Mary of Hungary's concerns were evident to all.

Yet, the prospect of a sexually immature duchess may actually have suited Charles's designs better than any other option: it prolonged the suspension of Sforza fortunes and left the dynasty without immediate issue, diminishing its likelihood of extension. It also suited François I, who in 1534 wanted Francesco II Sforza to exchange Milan for the Marquisate of Monferrato.[120] When Francesco died of a fever at age forty, just eighteen months after Christina's arrival, the absence of a Sforza heir facilitated Milan's absorption into complete Habsburg control. The young dowager duchess wrote to Charles V that the Porta Giovia castle hoisted imperial standards as soon as mourners carried out the duke's body.[121] Although military contest for Lombardy between France and the Empire continued, the Sforza claims to Milan were spent. Massimiliano Sforza, his hair perhaps still uncombed, had died in exile at Fontainebleau in 1530.[122]

Weeds

After the capture of the elder Sforza brothers in May 1500, one of Louis XII's orators remarked that "his majesty will know just what to do with [Ludovico] and Ascanio, saying that it was necessary to extirpate the bad roots of weeds (*bisognava extirpar le malle radice di le erbe cattive*)."[123] The king's ominous threat neatly expressed the crown's enmity against the Sforza. Louis XII and his agents used metaphors of fruitlessness in other contexts as well, but the language of weeds and roots sprouted promiscuously in the debates over early sixteenth-century Milan.[124] To talk in terms of weeds was to identify an adversary as perennially bothersome but simultaneously unproductive. French discourse, enamored of calling Italy a garden, could thus frame the Sforza as the weeds in Italy's yard: the unwanted plant, the noxious usurper that crowded out the desirable flowers.[125]

The association did not remain the exclusive province of French politicians. Among Lombards, it also came to express a variety of political sentiments grounded in the purgative power of ingesting bitter weeds. For one thing, invoking weeds acknowledged the bittersweet compromises that the Milanese had made with the Swiss Confederation to protect their interests from French encroachments. In 1513, after Swiss forces guaranteed Massimiliano Sforza's victory against the French at Ariotta, Benedetto Capilupi felt it necessary to explain to Isabella d'Este an unusual cry hollered by Massimiliano's guardsmen: Chicory! "When the French were defeated, some Ducheschi [that is, Sforza partisans] said that the Swiss were like chicory taken in syrup to heal people who have ruined their livers. Children cry: 'Chicory is a root that was needed to clean out this country,' and courtiers say to people who are double-crossed: 'you need some chicory.' This name is found as frequently amongst the populace as 'Moro' or 'Duca.'"[126] Capilupi's exegesis helps us makes sense of the cries recorded in a chronicle: "_Duca, duca, Moro, Moro, Maximiano, Maximiano, zuchoria, zuchoria!_ [. . .] Oh, how much Chicory was being eaten in Milan!"[127] The Sforza-Swiss collaboration was a swig of political amaro.

But the joyful children's refrain about the cleansing powers of Swiss allegiance was not reliably stable in its meaning. In the duchy's western reaches—often friendlier to the French because of geographical proximity and signorial bonds to the Orléans family—partisans in Alessandria sang tunes to gratify Louis XII's ears. In 1512, one of Massimiliano's agents wrote to him that anti-Sforza rebels had returned to the area, pronouncing "worse words than before. They sing a song: 'Soon our land will clean away the duke without roots,' crying: 'France, France!'"[128] The rebels had inverted the chicory metaphor as described by Capilupi. Now, accepting French arguments that grounded Lombardy in a deep Gallic past, they positioned Massimiliano Sforza as the rootless duke, ready to be plucked and tossed aside.

Ultimately, residents of the metropolis of Milan, when faced with the prospects of French, Swiss, and Spanish administration, petitioned in their darkest hours for the return of Sforza governance. But that lordship had undergone a fairly thorough dismantling over the first two decades of the century. With the family scattered or deceased, the castle reduced to a besieged redoubt, and the ducal assets all but liquidated, there was great sentiment but little value in Sforza rule by the 1530s. By that point, the Sforza had nearly become the weeds that Louis XII imagined them to be. When, at the century's end the Milanese historian Paolo Morigia (1525–1604) canvassed in his *Nobiltà di Milano* (1595) the city's most illustrious characters, he wrote of its last dukes: "There would also be something to say of Duke Massimiliano and Duke Francesco Sforza, the last of this house, both sons of the great and most unhappy Lodovico; but for now I want to pass over them, to avoid long narrations of their unlucky travails, worthy more of tears than of retelling."[129]

What Morigia construed as a tragedy was also evidence that French strategies of delegitimation had largely succeeded against the Sforza. It was no small thing for such a renowned dynasty to collapse in such a short period of time under the weight of infamy. Beyond the stringent efforts of French agents to ruin the Sforza name, we have also seen how even friendly or neutral observers contributed to the family's deflation, as they recognized how the Sforza sons failed to live up to the grandeur of their father. Legitimation had to be carefully articulated and framed to sustain power.[130] By failing to perform the courtly ostentation and political savvy that Italian states of the early sixteenth century demanded of their princes, the dynasty's listless sons succumbed to a campaign that was as much cultural as military.

Part II

Property

4

Land and Ownership

$\mathcal{C}$onversing with the Venetian envoy Leonardo Blanco in 1504, the Lombard patrician Simone Arrigoni unburdened himself over his turbulent life in recent years, bitterly describing his alienation from familiar modes of politics. When the two men were alone, Arrigoni told Blanco:

> "In the past I have served both Signor Ludovico and the King of France with such faith and goodness that, in the thick of things, both of them wanted me to do whatever they thought to ask. But in the end, they gave and took from me to the point that I could not say with certainty, 'this is mine' (*questo è mio*),"
>
> [Blanco then interjects in his own voice:] and he [Arrigoni] told me many things on this subject which would be long in retelling, such as the origins of his hatred for them. Then he said that although he had achieved things (even though surely he was already respected), he only has two daughters, "my greatest good in the world—one, with God's

grace, married and the other I hope to marry off next week—and I have nothing else besides a wife who makes no sons, a circumstance of little respect. And I will be taken to the point to realize the desire I have always had to make my-self more glorious. To this end I have petitioned for a spot—I want nothing else—which I have begun to build, and I have spent more than 7,000 ducats to make a fortress. More-over, I do not need to buy stones because they can be dug from their own ditches, nor lime, which I am having made, and I have wood too, all without cost. All my thoughts and hopes are vested in this fortress, for I do not enjoy the things of Milan, nor even pay attention to them."

And in fact, my lords, [Blanco concludes] this is true, since I have been at a certain garden and beautiful estate of his outside one of the gates of Milan most delightful in it-self, but I have seen that everything is falling to ruin. His for-tress is said to be called the Rocca of Baiedo, a fortress on an invincible mountain in the Valsassina above the shores of Lake Como.[1]

Torn between service to two warring sovereigns, Arrigoni had reached a point of impasse. His lordly status had become an item of exchange. In cycles, greater princes rewarded and punished him through gifts and confiscations to the point that he no longer felt secure. Piqued and dis-illusioned, he responded by withdrawing from the city and from fa-miliar systems of allegiance to build for himself something he saw as impregnable and inalienable: a mountaintop aerie in the craggy alpine hills. The ability to claim ownership of lands or goods—to say with cer-tainty "this is mine"—fell casualty to the flickering sovereignty of the Italian Wars. Oscillations in princely rule gave each new regime an op-portunity to reward its supporters and punish its detractors; they also opened a space for actors who wielded the greatest amount of force (like Arrigoni, as we will see) to take for themselves what they wished, flying in the face of princely fiat, law, or both. Rights—over goods, dwellings, inheritances, land, titles, and fiefs—changed hands so often between regimes that possession outpaced the deliberate tempo of legal judgment. Confusion and contest reigned not just in the Duchy of Milan but across the entire shatterzone of the wars, spreading across much of northern Italy and beyond. If the decades of the mid-sixteenth century eventually brought settlement to many of these disputes, its early years created a legal haze in which the truth-value of deeds of ownership came into question, fueling the antagonisms at the heart of the conflicts.

Those antagonisms can help us gauge the centrifugal effects of international war in a late-feudal society like Lombardy. The delicate political latticework of the territorial state—erected painstakingly through Visconti and Sforza programs of fourteenth- and fifteenth-century infeudation—required only the slightest wind to come unmoored. France's turbulent arrival blasted at the tenuous anchors of trust, law, and suasion that had helped to balance the duchy under its fifteenth-century dukes. The two decades after 1500 reveal clearly not only the new resentments expressed against transalpine intrusions in Italian affairs but also the longer-lasting dissatisfactions with the power structures of the Milanese state, especially the prerogatives of the prince to expropriate and confiscate at will. War's deprivations moved in myriad directions and stimulated resistance from all quarters. With more than one sovereign often claiming authority, that opposition sometimes pushed in conservative directions to maintain an endangered status quo, sometimes in fresh directions to explode it. Other times, subjects simply complained of losses, seemingly bereft of recourse. Simone Arrigoni was just one of many who felt like he was drowning in the quicksand of territorial redistribution.

Beginning with a survey of the legal tradition surrounding property rights, we will see how laments such as Arrigoni's about extortive princes overturned, probably unwittingly, a longstanding refrain in law commentaries attributing the institution of private ownership to the beneficence of kings. It was an inversion whose corollary implied unjust or even tyrannical lordship. In accompanying Arrigoni and other discontents on their journeys of disillusionment, the chapter traces the contours of a pessimistic vision of the state on the part of its dependents as they groped for more perfect solutions than the ones presented to them. These solutions often took the form of small-scale private resistance to the prince on the part of landed elites, as they struggled to enunciate their own claims in the face of smothering tides.

This Is Mine

At the core of Simone Arrigoni's lament to the Venetian ambassador lay a fundamental issue in Western jurisprudence: the status of private property in relation to the state.[2] In articulating the self-consciously declarative phrase "this is mine," the nobleman worried that his assertion had ceased to matter to authorities stronger than himself and that faith in these princes' laws had been betrayed. That phrase or versions of it had in fact been a central dispositive in framing relations between individuals, community, and sovereign power since antiquity. When Latin translations of Plato's *Republic* began to circulate in fifteenth-century Italy, critics echoed Aristotle in deriding book 5 for its advocacy of radically communal ownership.[3] By sharing everything, Plato's argument went, states might avoid disunion between citizens who could not agree over "mine" and "not mine."[4] At its core, the philosopher's proposal of common ownership posed a fundamental juridical challenge to later centuries: Where was the boundary between state and citizen? As part of his critique of Plato's abolition of any boundary, Aristotle countered that a sense of private ownership "makes an inexpressibly great difference in one's pleasure,"[5] thereby insisting upon borders between common and particular. Alongside these questions of property tracked a set of affiliated concerns about its origin, essentially whether the ultimate source of ownership was nature, man, or (in later Christian commentaries) God, with each possibility corresponding to its own legal tradition.

One of the longest-lived responses to that question came from Augustine, who in his *Tractates* insisted that property rights issued from the law of man, or *ius gentium,* and in particular from kings. "But you say: what is the emperor to me? It is by a right derived from him that you possess the land. Otherwise, if you take away rights created by emperors, who will dare say: 'That estate is mine, or that slave is mine, or this house is mine.'"[6] Augustine's argument inserted the prince squarely into the genealogy of ownership, and his position gained new life when, in the twelfth century, Gratian's *Decretum* amalgamated this language into its opinions on the question of property.[7] The Augustinian position, as diffused through its later reappearance in legal treatises, thus anchored property in the relationship between lords and subjects by insisting on the prince's pivotal role in confirming ownership. Only the good will of rulers entitled subjects to ratify their belongings.

The extent of the prince's powers over his citizens' possessions came into focus in legal commentaries from the twelfth century; in Lombardy, they leapt into further currency following the jurist Baldo degli Ubaldi's ratification of the customary traditions of feudal law in accordance with the power strategies of the Visconti duke in the 1390s.[8] Baldo's endorsement helped to make the common law frameworks of the *Libri Feudorum* an authoritative part of legal operations in the Milanese duchy.[9] Although that corpus—reflecting the broader legal consensus—largely defended feudatories' rights from the sort of princely intervention that Simone Arrigoni was stewing over, it did allow for an important exception: misdeeds on the part of the feudatory. If the landholder could be shown to have committed a fault, his claim upon his land could be challenged. Arguments using landholders' crimes as evidence (especially treason, or *laesa maiestatis*) had been used to disinvest troublesome feudatories throughout the ducal period.[10] At the same time, jurists and officials understood the need to limit princes from capriciously seizing property on flimsy or fraudulent pretenses. Princely ambition often required no crime on the part of subjects to desire exactions from them. Milan's senate had the legal duty to ratify (*interinare*) such royal or ducal rearrangements, but in practice it was far from guaranteed.[11] The tension between the sovereign's self-arrogated authority and the legal tools to restrict it produced a grey zone in theoretical and practical matters alike. In that zone, the discourse of the criminal or rebellious subject chafed against the discourse of the unlawful ruler. In the 1450s, using words that Arrigoni would have recognized, the French statesman Jean Juvénal des Ursins (1388–1473) addressed King Charles VII by rejecting the arguments of certain royal officials who asserted "that everything belongs to the prince, and that no one can say, 'This is mine (*hoc est meum*)' except the prince."[12] The prospect of unchecked royal power led des Ursins directly into an excursus on the slippery slope to tyranny.[13] In Italy, the best-known fourteenth- and fifteenth-century treatises on tyranny (Baldo, Salutati) had rarely mentioned property, but its problematics proliferated in the period's legal commentaries on the prince's rights and jurisdictions. In complaining to the Venetian envoy to Milan in 1504, Simone Arrigoni thus verbalized a classic matrix of contention between rulers and subjects. But his grievance was not formulaic in expressing resentment against his lord. Two sovereigns, not one, had vexed him with their impingements. Both claimed to act as his legitimate superior, and yet he feared his own best interest had vanished between the two of them.

This language of evaporating rights (or their transfer to others) resurfaced frequently during the first decades of the sixteenth century, and not just in the Duchy of Milan. The entire episode we know as the Italian Wars entailed a reconceptualization of Italy's territory that we—still in thrall to narratives of Italian autonomy from Machiavelli through the Risorgimento—have typically framed in terms of political liberty but that even more fundamentally concerned rights to land. The theme of territorial alienation reappeared constantly in far-flung zones beyond Lombardy. We must still grapple historically with the fallout not just of dispute over land, but of the relationship between expressions of entitlement and forms of conflict, since disputes erupted endlessly over this issue. They exploded so often and so vehemently that these conflicts— often small-scale but chronic and recursive—might in fact constitute the hidden substance of the wars, the irritations that perpetuated the destructive slow burn of the initial invasions. While it seems obvious to insist that land disputes are war-matrices, territory infrequently plays a part in analysis of the Italian Wars, which often trains exclusive focus upon politico-cultural effects. And yet, the rapid pace of land's changing hands has helped to conceal it from historians, producing instead a blur that discourages interpretation.[14]

Still, we hear jeremiads for lost property from a range of voices. They do not complain only of the French. When Massimiliano Sforza ascended to his father's ducal throne in 1512, a chronicler described how he "gave fiefs to some, duties to others [. . .] with such little thought" that he seemed to be digging straight into the purses of the Milanese.[15] In 1520, the Venetian orator wrote that as Duke of Milan, François I did not "even have a single tower" since the Sforza dukes and French kings had given away all the duchy's castles to supporters.[16] Laments over the circulation of property could also wear classicizing garb. In dedicating his 1513 edition of Pindar's *Odes* to Andrea Navagero, the printer-scholar Aldo Manuzio explained the delayed edition as an effect of war, noting that "I had to be away from Venice in order to recover land and valuable properties which we had lost, not by our own fault, but because of the current situation." Then, quoting Virgil's *Eclogues*—themselves a reflection on the sociopolitical fallout of ancient Rome's civil wars—he continued: "We too have come to the point in our lives when we have heard the harsh words: 'This is mine (*haec mea sunt*), begone, old tenants!'"[17] The Mantuan secretary Mario Equicola told a similar story about his own family lands.[18] Visiting Peschiera in springtime 1514, Isabella d'Este wrote to her husband that "the names of the king of France and the emperor—who hold this territory with no right to it—were never mentioned without muttered curses."[19]

In such cases of disputed property, at least two forms of contest reveal themselves. On one level, as Arrigoni's case makes clear, the rapid fluctuation of reward and punishment between regimes produced strong antagonisms. Guided by the reasoning that traitors to the prince should lose both movable and immovable goods, Sforza and Valois dukes of Milan during the Italian Wars each in turn targeted for divestiture supporters of their opponents.[20] In 1502, Louis XII confusingly revoked an edict against Ludovico Sforza's concession of lands in Annona and Alessandria, "since our letters contain more latitude than we intend them to have." It was—mind-bendingly—a decree clarifying that an earlier decree should not obstruct the decree against Ludovico's territorial donations, which the king wished to be "null and void."[21] Not only did such moves produce a form of legal chaos in the long term, they also led in the short term to new political formations among those feudatories. Some withdrew themselves from familiar political frameworks in a form of self-imposed isolation, while others discovered new grounds for resistance by inverting the logic that had despoiled them of their lands: if the prince could accuse them of treason, they could resist the prince as a tyrant.

On another level, and here we encounter Manuzio's or Equicola's struggles, arguments erupted between landholders themselves often as a result of clashing donations or confiscations from superior authorities. Land conferred a legal persona upon its holder; thus to be challenged over land-ownership meant also to suffer insult to one's legal personhood.[22] These quarrels also produced lawsuits and, not infrequently, agonistic violence in which disputants decided to circumvent remonstrative channels and settle feuds through a form of private war. Displacement of feudatories into long periods of wandering was not just a problem of direct princely interference but a corollary of these unsettled disputes. Rather than seeing skirmishes and private wars in this period as incidental to the narrative we tell about the Italian Wars, it might be more helpful to describe these endemic irritations over property as a key motor—as conflictual machines in which uncertainties over sovereign status combusted into violence. Before returning to the case of Simone Arrigoni that bears this argument out, we can see some of these problems articulated at both civic and feudal levels upon establishment of French control in 1500.

After France's forces put down the uprising of January to March that briefly restored Ludovico Sforza to power, the entire duchy became culpable of treason in French eyes. Shortly after Sforza's capture at Novara, Louis XII's counselor Cardinal Georges d'Amboise made his way from Vercelli to Vigevano, where he met a delegation of Milanese representatives who had come to sue for royal pity and to promise never again to rise in rebellion against the king. They entreated the cardinal to come to Milan. On Good Friday (17 April 1500), a crucifix-bearing procession of Milanese citizens of all classes—including, one observer estimated, 4,000 children in white robes—appeared before Amboise and his ministers at the old court in Milan's city center. Throngs of Milanese were so numerous that the cardinal descended to the ground floor to receive them all.[23] This is the same event we encountered in Chapter 1, at which Michele Tonso apologized on the city's behalf and Michele Riccio issued the crown's response, chastising the city for its disloyalty but offering clemency in exchange for a hefty levy.

Tonso's oration promised on behalf of the Milanese people never to rise against the king again.[24] They shouldered the blame for their disloyalty, assuring the French that their representatives in the duchy had been caring and faithful. They then make four requests: first, that the king reconsider his imposition of the levy, which would ruin the city's trade and finances; second, that the French prevent the soldiers in Lombardy from ruining the land's harvest; third, that municipal officers might return to their recently stripped offices; and fourth, that the crown prevent the leaders of the coup from further troubling Milan.

Riccio's oration voiced the disappointment of the crown. He accused the Milanese of faithlessness, citing a history of royal and imperial chastisement for the city's disloyalty. The citizens had erred gravely, he continued, in choosing a usurper like Sforza over a great king like Louis. But he promised that if the Milanese entrusted their faith to Louis and his successors, they would undoubtedly enjoy the status of Italy's greatest city.[25] Riccio framed France's arrival in Milan as a liberation: Louis had "brought his army from France to Italy at very great expense neither in pursuit of ambition nor from a desire to expand his rule (which is vast), but so that he might rescue his Milanese subjects from tyranny." While this narrative dismissed the French king's interest in territorial expansion, it highlighted Ludovico Sforza's supposed obsession with controlling the goods of others, specifically his restrictions of "marriages and commercial goods," rights that Louis had returned to each of Milan's citizens, "such that now one can not only say that something is his, but show it." The French translation of this text published in Paris the same year put an even finer point on this passage, insisting to the Milanese that Louis secured "your well-being, honor, and goods, whereas before [under Ludovico] no one could say, 'this is mine' (*cecy est mien*)."[26]

While such accusations of princely encroachment had been made against many forebears and contemporaries, Ludovico had indeed exuberantly interfered in the rights of feudatories whose privileges chafed with his own designs. Best known among these might be the Dal Verme family, whose "state within a state" reached from the Po to the Apennines and whose rights depended upon Milan's dukes.[27] In the 1470s, Pietro Dal Verme clashed with the ducal court over a marriage, leading the chamber to confiscate his goods, which he later regained.[28] He perished in 1485, supposedly poisoned by his wife, Chiara Sforza, at Ludovico il Moro's request. From this moment, the pace of contest over these lands accelerated in rhythm with larger sovereignty conflicts; the point of recounting the following details is to convey some of the attendant disorientation. It could stand in for dozens of other similar contests. Despite immediate reclamations from Pietro's illegitimate sons, within four years Ludovico had bestowed Dal Verme lands upon his own son-in-law, Galeazzo Sanseverino (1458–1525), thereby tightening his power over the vast fief just before his own ouster. Following Milan's uprising against Louis XII in 1500, the French crown redistributed lands of Sforza retainers to its own nobles—a significant act that functioned as a further conflict matrix, and one to which I return in a later chapter; these included Sanseverino's holdings. From Sanseverino the official title of the Dal Verme estate passed to Louis de Ligny, the king's chamberlain.[29]

But from this point, and here is where the story is much less known, a constellation of claimants formed: Sanseverino petitioned the crown for restitution, as did the Dal Verme heirs.[30] When Sanseverino fled in 1499, the Dal Verme took advantage of the chaos to reoccupy their territories. With Sanseverino in exile and thus unavailable to press his claims effectively, the Dal Verme challenged Ligny, and their disagreement escalated to an armed confrontation outside of Bobbio in October 1500.[31] Having cast its lots for the Dal Verme family, Bobbio suffered a French cannonade. Ligny's troops destroyed most of its walls and castle and slayed more than 200 Dal Verme supporters. Twenty more were hanged as traitors to France. By February 1501, proceedings in Milan brought charges against the entire family, alleging that—because the Dal Verme had sworn an oath of loyalty to Louis XII upon his arrival in the duchy—the family had broken faith and acted as rebels.[32] The trial ended in early April with a recommended death sentence, leading the Dal Verme to appeal to Maximilian I, who instead confirmed their legal rights in 1502. Meanwhile Ligny, acting as if France's crown and not the Empire's were the legitimate sovereign, worked to entrench his own claims by confiscating properties from Dal Verme followers to give to his own adherents. When the French abandoned Milan in 1512, the Dal Verme stormed and reoccupied Bobbio. But after François I reconquered the duchy in 1515, he named Sanseverino marquis of Bobbio, since by that date Galeazzo had become a French retainer. In 1517, a French tribunal in Milan sentenced Jacopo Dal Verme and 170 followers to death (a sentence that was never carried out), but in 1521, Emperor Charles V re-confirmed Dal Verme privileges.[33] Even after Galeazzo died at Pavia in 1525, his brothers' heirs pressed his claim against the Dal Verme, who returned to possession of their lands (though only partially) in the early 1530s. It is a dizzying and bloody history.

Similar itineraries of dispute can be traced all over the Duchy of Milan, and elsewhere, during the Italian Wars.[34] These turbines of redistribution had a fogging effect that left many disputants in complete confusion over the status of their holdings. In Galeazzo Sanseverino's petition to Louis XII for his (that is, the Dal Verme) lands in 1500, the language articulated genuine uncertainty. In the list of desired lands, on at least four occasions Galeazzo's advocate concluded: "He does not know who has it." Or even if concessions had been granted in his favor, "the thing had no effect."[35] To burn off the fog and to force effects, some Lombard elites took matters into their own hands.

Simone Arrigoni, Disruptor

One of these elites was Simone Arrigoni (1462–1507). In the last decade of his life, Arrigoni's ambitions for glory ran up against the designs of both his Sforza and his French lords, cornering him into a fatal conflict triggered by the assertion of his own territorial independence. Arrigoni was a courtier and captain whose father had helped Francesco Sforza to secure the Valsassina—and specifically the castle at Baiedo, an improbably imposing crag that acted as a strategic northerly entry point into the Duchy of Milan—against the Venetians in the 1450s.[36] By the 1490s Simone had come to assume significant posts at Ludovico's court.[37] In the summer of 1499, as French armies stirred on the perimeter of the Sforza duchy, Ludovico reportedly levied 10,000 scudi in defense funds from Arrigoni, leading the latter to complain that the exaction would force him to sell all he had.[38] Arrigoni perhaps intuited the coming storm and decided that the first lightning strike would be his.[39] On the last day of August, seven days before the city surrendered and two days before Ludovico Sforza fled, Arrigoni and a band of his men murdered Antonio Landriani, Ludovico Sforza's treasurer and right-hand man, "presuming to do something favorable for the people," Bernardino Corio wrote in 1503. Corio conjectured further "that [Arrigoni's] domain received 800 ducats of income and the Valsassina from the King."[40] Probably that income and territory came after Landriani's death, conceivably as a reward from the French sovereign for helping to precipitate the Sforza fall. But with the French in control of the duchy, the murk over territory formed quickly: just a month after the murder Arrigoni seemed already to be involved in a dispute over "a certain possession taken" from him, by which sovereign remains unclear.[41] Arrigoni's murder of Landriani placed him squarely in the graces of the new ultramontane lord. Even before Louis XII entered the city, Arrigoni had received a gift of water duties in the bishopric of Parma from the French.[42] He was one of four gold-clad Milanese gentlemen to accompany the monarch on his 1499 entry into Milan, and in 1501 he numbered among the retainers of Cardinal d'Amboise.[43]

Under the French, Arrigoni inhabited the skin of the man he murdered. He assumed one of the most important financial posts in the duchy (despite remonstrations from the senate) and received some of Landriani's lands.[44] But, as we saw at the chapter's outset, his relations with the French soured, possibly because of resistance to him inside the new regime, and possibly because he gleaned the long-term opportunities that foreign rule presented for ambitious lords like himself. In his long discussion with Leonardo Blanco in 1504, Arrigoni imagined that that Louis XII's death could not be far away, and he therefore envisioned alternative power constellations emerging in which men like him might find mutual support from Venice or the Swiss. In musing on these prospects, Arrigoni foregrounded his intimacy with another Milanese Guelf he saw as his peer (*suo afectionatissimo*), France's marshal, Giangiacomo Trivulzio.[45] As if to point to the similarly perilous position they both occupied, Arrigoni remarked that Trivulzio also had his own state and had recently become lord of Vigevano, "but which the French have at times said they might take from him, as he himself knows very well." Arrigoni opined that Trivulzio was in a dangerous position with Italians as well, because "almost all Lombards will become his enemy, starting with many of his own company." The only way for Trivulzio to preserve himself was for him to stay in Milan with well-paid armed men at his immediate disposal, since "in Milan, the first to move is the winner." In assessing the state of Milan, Arrigoni described the mutual distrust among the city's Ghibellines (divided into a least three subfactions), and lamented how many had become poor after being "peeled" by the French king. Considering all these dangers to men of his station, Simone offered his services to Venice, noting that he would secure Venetian passage through the Valsassina if the occasion arose.[46]

Most urgently, Arrigoni framed his appeal to Venice as a desire for stable lordship. He insisted: "Do not think that the favor and service that I seek from the most illustrious *Signoria* is out of hope of reward, since I have no heirs and have no need of them, but only to have masters who I can be sure appreciate my service."[47] The words may have been a posture, but they had rhetorical allure. In disavowing his own dynastic perpetuation, Arrigoni here framed his overture purely as a wish for solid anchorage in the flux of sovereign lordship. Blanco advised the *signoria* that Arrigoni would tarry in Milan as he awaited a response. It probably never came. Seeing no support from any quarter, Arrigoni's vestiges of adherence to France slid away, and he quit the city. He was not alone. By 1506, dissent was on the rise across several territories under French sway. The crown invited Milanese exiles to capture or kill fellow *banniti* in exchange for a pardon, and secretive anti-French discussions advanced between Genoese elites and the Spanish crown.[48] Genoa's open rebellion between autumn 1506 and spring 1507 reframed French conceptions of Italian disobedience. When pacts appear to disintegrate, horizons of responsibility tilt. Vertical and horizontal relationships assume new arrangements.

That is how some sources described Arrigoni's detachment. At Baiedo he supposedly welcomed bandits, "damaged all the surrounding country just like an assassin," and raised the imperial flag over his towers, despite having no evident support from the Empire.[49] Whatever form his antagonism took, it functioned to provoke and reprove his estranged lord and more fundamentally to disrupt the fabric of politics. Accordingly, Milan's authorities declared him a rebel in February 1507.[50] Louis XII asked Trivulzio to supervise his capture. Wrested from Baiedo by his own men (a traitorous fate, ironically, he had predicted for Trivulzio), Arrigoni returned as a prisoner to Milan's castle, where he was questioned under torture.[51] In those interrogations he reputedly named Trivulzio and the Venetian *signoria* as conspirators, and by so doing "sought to ingratiate himself and to flee his punishment," one Venetian envoy supposed.[52] Agents sent the transcript of his examination and trial to the king. Less than a month later, Arrigoni—wearing brown velvet and a gold chain, tokens of luxe—was decapitated in the piazza of the castle. His corpse was quartered and his limbs hung at Milan's gates.[53]

Territorial Oscillations and the Production of the Shatterzone

In the sovereign's eyes, Simone Arrigoni had to die. But rather than dwelling here on the exercise of capital punishment as a disciplinary performance, let us return instead to his land, to the castle of Baiedo in Valsassina, a place that might otherwise recede into oblivion. In Milan's chronicles, it recedes from sight as narrations of Louis XII's triumphal entry after suppressing the Genoese revolt eclipse the rebel's fate. But tumult in the vales around Como and Lecco did not end with Arrigoni's life, since the dispute over authority in the Valsassina had in no way been solved in 1507. Instead, one claimant merely extinguished another, and the burdens of territorial uncertainty cascaded down upon the local population. Following Arrigoni's execution, French troops under Trivulzio's authority occupied Baiedo. As one near-contemporary source explains, the inhabitants of the surrounding villages were so angered by the "wickedness and serious extortions French soldiers committed in that castle" that in 1512 delegates from the valley, "alleging the great burdens they suffered because of Trivulzio, succeeded in having it pulled to the ground," leaving nothing but a painted pillar and the cistern.[54] A 1920s photographic postcard of the Valsassina pictures the erasure. The alpine panorama is a nostalgic dreamscape, the Baiedo fortress just a ghostly absence on the peak that looms above the valley town of Pasturo (fig. 4.1).

That absence effaces the history of contest in the region after the demolition of the fortress over the ensuing decades. During the first Sforza restoration in 1513, Duke Massimiliano endowed the pro-Sforza secretary Girolamo Morone with the nearby county of Lecco.[55] Despite Morone's tenaciousness, even his canny trajectory entailed a trail of confiscations and restitutions. Over the course of seventeen years, he lost and regained Lecco a number of times between regimes. Even though evidence shows that King François I confirmed Morone's ownership in 1515, one report of the same year claims that the monarch also gave "4,000 ducats of revenue for some possessions of Lecco" to his marshal in Italy, Jacques Chabannes, sieur de la Palisse.[56] François evidently also gave Lecco to Thomas de Foix, sieur de Lescun, in March 1519.[57] After the second Sforza restoration in 1522, Lecco returned to Morone, who ultimately received a payment from Milan's Hapsburg-administered ducal chamber for its surrender in 1527.[58] This narrative of investiture and divestiture should not license us, however, to render too orderly a process that actually transpired in disorder. Legal maneuvers over disputed feudal land almost always masked violent confrontations or at least attempted to forestall or resolve them. The devolution of privileges in the same territory produced a circle of conflict, in which absence of

Panorama di Pasturo (Valsassina)
Rocca di Baiedo e Chiusa di Introbbio

Fig. 4.1 Rocca di Baiedo e Chiusa d'Introbbio, Valsassina—the site of Simone Arrigoni's castle.

From the author's collection.

certain knowledge of ownership among populations and feudatories alike promised its perpetuation. The example of the Valsassina and Lecco, one of innumerable similar disputes, should make this fact apparent.

Territorial possession was an affair requiring collaboration with, or suasion of, local populations unsettled by political change. Even before Lecco came into Morone's hands, its titular rights circled through several others at the gloaming of Ludovico Sforza's rule. When one of those pro-Sforza feudatories appeared in Lecco in September 1499 to assume possession grounded in il Moro's crumbling authority, he found himself facing 600 armed men of Lecco who refused to swear allegiance to him.[59] Here is the sociopolitical friction that the legal paperwork obscures: recurrent hostility rooted in clashing entitlements authorized by alternating sovereigns who in turn sought to superimpose their own map of privileges upon the territory. We see this dynamic resurface time and again. In the 1510s, Sforza elements continued to battle French ones over Lecco. The Lecchese Francesco Morone (d. 1521) was one of the most active among them, having returned to the region around 1512, following a period of German exile.[60] Critical of the ultramontane regime, Francesco sustained a series of raids against French interests during the ensuing years. Probably a cousin of Girolamo, Francesco shared the political orientation of his much better-known relative and his concern for the Morone claim upon Lecco.[61] In fighting against Gallic incursions, Francesco stepped into the vacuum created by Simone Arrigoni's death by assuming the role of a disruptor.[62] That role grew initially from clan or factional adherence, but often trespassed the limits of partisan action, which classically sought ratification through the support of allies and regional populations. The disruptor, instead, reached for—or merely enacted—a nonpolitics, a sort of nihilism. Destruction became an end in itself, a renunciation of politics that helped to produce the shatterzone.

The fissures of conflict spread rapidly in 1516. At the northernmost reaches of Lake Como, Francesco Morone began sacking and burning villages. A local chronicler supposed that Morone "wanted to put to plunder all the towns of the lake, especially the ones supporting the Guelf faction, since rumor had it that the Guelfs supported the French king."[63] The raids provoked La Palisse who, thanks to King François's donation, now had a vested feudal interest in Lecco and was also serving as governor of Como. La Palisse and his men took to the waters of Lake Como to pacify the region and capture Morone, but the latter escaped through Valsassina, burning the town of Introbio (neighbor to Baiedo) as he fled through the snowy peaks. La Palisse continued his naval campaign to secure the lake's perturbed towns. When he met resistance at the northerly village of Sorico, "knowing the obstinacy of these peasants, [he] ordered the lands of Sorico and Gera to be emptied, sacked, and burned."[64] Other burgs evacuated. In retaliation, the afflicted townspeople allied with 4,000 Swiss soldiers to burn and plunder villages farther down Como's eastern shores (Corenno, Varenna, and other parts of the Valsassina), inching toward Lecco. They then circled over the top of the lake and began assaulting settlements as far east as Lake Lugano.[65]

Further conflict followed, but this brief narrative punctually describes how clashing feudal representatives (Morone / La Palisse) kindled a widening series of conflicts that enflamed the entirety of Lake Como and beyond.[66] Factional suspicions nourished conflicts over feudal rights (and vice versa), as deracinated elites drew each other and regional residents into war. Although Francesco Morone ostensibly saw himself as the region's bulwark against French incursions, and although La Palisse ostensibly represented the region as its governor, neither of them upheld the ethical demands of those positions. Instead, they leveraged populations as tools against each other, ultimately targeting them with larceny, extortion, and arson. Forced to flee flames and assaults, villagers around Lake Como themselves became uprooted raiders. As political regimes alternated in these decades, claimants recovered legitimacy as they forced their opponents out. Then a reversal upturned the power dynamic once again. This process of circulation—a cycle familiar to generations of Italian exiles[67]—found itself further confused by competing sovereigns' insistence upon their rights to authorize political and territorial power. That those sovereigns often misunderstood the history and politics of the lands they gave or seized produced another layer of military or diplomatic labor for claimants as they constructed narratives to support their cases.

Land Grants as Forgetting

Princely largesse was a gesture that wished itself to be limitless, since the performance of unbounded generosity was part of the mystique of monarchy. But a trap in the machinery of such spectacles was the possibility of doubling the same act, gifting something that has already been given away. As the foregoing pages have shown, land rights could be wielded intentionally as a weapon—one that generated fresh conflicts—but they could also circulate almost mindlessly.[68] The sovereign often had the luxury of forgetting what supposedly belonged to whom. But the luxury was illusory, since such lack of concern itself manufactured competition between claimants. One such supplicant in 1516 was the fifteen-year-old Federico Gonzaga, who attended King François I after the French recapture of Milan in late 1515. Federico's father, Francesco, marquis of Mantua, had eschewed taking sides in the war that led to François's victory; to signal his goodwill toward François, he sent his young son to Milan to join his retinue. Soon after his arrival, Federico learned that the territory of Poviglio—a town between Parma and Mantua, which he understood to be his—had been given away.

Mere days after the victory at Marignano that opened the door for a French return to the Duchy of Milan, Federico wrote to his father that a former lord of Poviglio had presented himself. Pier Francesco Noceto, Count of Pontremoli, an erstwhile intimate of Ludovico Sforza and feudatory of Poviglio before 1499, had freshly extracted a promise from the king for its return to him. The perturbed Gonzaga teenager broached the matter with his cousin, and François's constable, Charles de Bourbon. Bourbon reportedly said "that he did not think that the king understood how the matter stood, and that Pier Francesco had done poorly by not telling the king the truth of how things are," but that he was nonetheless certain "that the king will not do this wrong to me [Federico]."[69] A few days later Federico discussed Poviglio with the royal *grand maître*, arguing that François "perhaps did not remember that King Louis of blessed memory had given it to me, and that I could not believe that he would hold Pier Francesco in greater esteem than he did me."[70] The *grand maître* replied that Noceto had in fact possessed privileges to Poviglio under the Sforza. A loyal retainer of il Moro, Noceto had accompanied him to prison in France, a devotion that now struck young François as worthy of reward.[71] Federico conversely had come to own the fief as a child in 1507, when Louis XII rewarded him with it in recognition of his father's military service.[72]

That passage involved a forgetting of its own. In the 1511 war with Pope Julius II, Louis strategically feigned a seizure of Poviglio from the Gonzaga to mask Francesco's covert cooperation in allowing French troops to pass through the land. The maneuver came with a promise to return it after the settlement of the war, a pledge that was swiftly forgotten, to Francesco's displeasure.[73] By 1515, two French kings in a row had lost track—whether intentionally or accidentally—of Gonzaga investment in this key territory. In a bid to secure the land for Federico following Louis XII's loss of Milan in 1512, the boy's mother, Isabella d'Este, petitioned Pope Leo X for his investiture through papal fiat; the pope duly created the Gonzaga heir Count of Poviglio in 1512.[74] Poviglio had thus only newly returned to Gonzaga possession when it appeared to be snatched away again in 1515, this time by an even earlier pretender. When the *grand maître* suggested that Federico would receive compensation for the land, the youngster refused point-blank, saying: "Monsignor, your lordship must make it so that the compensation be given to him and that

this land not be taken from me, since it cannot be done without my dis-
honor."[75] Within a few days, Federico wrote to his father optimistically
that the French would instead offer Noceto compensation in "a very good
castle in the Astigiana" called Cairas.[76] (This was in fact the Rocca
d'Arazzo, one of the first Sforza bulwarks against the French invasion of
1499, and a site of considerable violence. In launching the seizure of the
duchy, Louis XII's troops had captured the castle and "killed all of
Ludovico's soldiers and most of the villagers," before looting and burning
the town.[77]) And yet Noceto's apparent removal from the frame hardly
resolved the issue.

   Proof of investiture had to be produced, as had to be done by a
number of other pretenders seeking the monarch's authorization in their
own separate disputes. "I am told that everyone should now send the con-
firmations of their privileges," Federico wrote to his father, asking him
specifically to send documents showing Louis XII's donation of Poviglio
and seeking clarity on "whether they are to be requested in the same
form, or in another form or manner."[78] While the paperwork arrived by
late December, the Gonzaga privilege was nonetheless "evading ratification in the senate of Milan," and frustrations mounted when the king
departed—with Federico in tow—for France, where the process slowed
considerably.[79] In Lyon the following spring, a brief from Pope Leo X arrived to support Federico's case from the papal vantage. When Gonzaga
agents presented it to the sovereign, François "responded that he wished
to take away everything from my jurisdiction (*si vol tuor in tutto dala iuris-
dition mia*)," and only a clarification on the part of Federico's advocate
insisted that the youth "wishes it to be recognized by Your Majesty," to
which the king acceded (*"e ben farò"*).[80] Once again, the monarch seemed
on the verge of denying ownership; only a sharp interjection reversed the
flow of rights-distribution. But the matter still dragged on for over a year
as it became clear that investiture would necessitate paying an annual
due to the crown. With dwindling funds, Federico sought a remission
of the payment in 1518. King François initially agreed to remit the payment, but "so as to avoid giving occasion to others to ask for similar re-
missions, he wants a false payment of monies that will immediately be
restored."[81]

   In less than a decade, the French crown had conjured a series of ob-
fuscations around Gonzaga ownership of Poviglio. In 1511, it staged an

imaginary military appropriation (promptly forgetting to restore it), and in 1518 it requested a fictive payment of dues. A politics of decorum animated these strategies—a desire on the crown's part to make invisible to observers such as the pope or other courtiers certain machinations of favor—but it also contributed to the cloud of uncertainty that hovered over Poviglio's disputed rights. Part of that uncertainty had to do with funds (the Gonzaga had made substantial loans to the French crown that it could not repay) and with the exigencies of upholding aristocratic honor that a divestiture could sully. Part of it had to do with royal forgetting and the real inability of a newly implanted foreign regime to sustain a practice of omniscience. And part, more fundamentally, had to do with power strategies anchored in territorial redistribution. Property ownership and transfer shaped expressions of faction, patronage, and affiliation, and land became the grounds upon which fidelity and resistance could be tested in times of serial sovereignty claims. In the 1510s, Federico Gonzaga had the advantage of maintaining a close personal proximity to the monarch as he chased his investiture from Milan to Lyon to Paris.

But the threat of losing one's status always loomed when facing kings and emperors. In 1510, Francesco Gonzaga sat imprisoned in Venice following the Battle of Agnadello. The president of Milan's senate, Geoffroy Carles, warned the representative of his wife, Isabella d'Este, "that she must focus her mind on her Mantua and its state [. . .] because otherwise she could wake up one morning and find herself a lady without a state, and I know whereof I speak."[82] The following year, after Francesco's release, Louis XII reportedly mused that, so long as Gonzaga was lord of Mantua, "he would be esteemed and honored by everyone. But when he loses his state he will need to go begging through the world with his sons, and he will find no one to give him bread, and he will become the butt of jokes."[83] Those threats echoed the recent fate of Ludovico Sforza and his heirs.

Unlike Federico Gonzaga, some pretenders remained at a significant remove from court or city and struggled to perceive the logic driving confiscations or donations, or they rejected it outright. For Arrigoni and Morone, such a rejection acted to protect what they framed as their best interests and the source of their own authority. While many of the possessions thrown into question by the Italian Wars involved decades of subsequent litigation, for these men it sparked violent reprisals against sovereigns and their representatives they saw as tyrants or obstacles to be overcome. They were not alone, as a late-1515 letter from Federico Gonzaga testifies:

> Yesterday at the Broletto [in Milan] they cut off the head of one messer Lino [Airoldi] da Imbersago, from Monte Brianza, old and wealthy with 50,000 ducats of capital, who had a great following and took up arms against the king, and it helped very little that the senate of Milan advocated for him because he was a true Sforza man whose services the former dukes had employed, and he was one of the leaders of the men who fought against Giangiacomo [Trivulzio] at San Cristoforo [in the days leading up to the Battle of Marignano in October 1515]. And so they cut off his head. The extortions they commit in this state are innumerable, and by putting [people] in prison, taking money, and consuming everything, [they put] everyone in the worst humor. The Marquis of Monferrato is going home unhappy because the King had given him Valenza and its privileges but then he took it from him and gave it to the *Grand Maître*.[84]

Here again, capital punishment and territorial confiscation coincided as tactics of political containment. These two events in late 1515—Airoldi's execution and the confiscation of Valenza from the marquis of Monferrato—were not causally linked, but in terms of sovereignty strategies they were also not terribly distant. Removal (of freedom, property, or life itself) intended to disempower, but its effects produced fresh energies and antagonisms. While almost all the disruptors we have met in this chapter—Arrigoni, Morone, and now in passing, Airoldi—hailed from the territories north of Milan, similar histories of resistance encircled the French king in Milan in all the duchy's provinces. While discourses of tyranny and resistance framed these territorial disputes, that was not always their ultimate destination. These attempts to delegitimize the current regime accompanied other more orthodox political measures that sought to restore to the duchy's power dynamics a functional system of redress. Accordingly, a culture of petition and request, in which seekers like Federico Gonzaga rehearsed their suffering as a form of entitlement, expanded in both epistolary and legal culture. In fact, in January 1516, shortly after the second French conquest of the duchy, Article 17 of the city's twenty-two requests to the monarch sought an end to seizures of goods without proper legal liquidation.[85] A previous ducal law specifically prohibited abuses of confiscation that caused "everything to be confounded," but it was being ignored. A tide of petitions for some legal recourse was the direct result of inhabiting a world where justice increasingly appeared out of reach.

5

Protecting and Suing

$\mathcal{I}$n his fourth volume of legal opinions, the preeminent Milanese jurist Giason del Maino (1435–1519) acknowledged that sometimes law
cannot keep up with reality. Before him was a case concerning contested
primogeniture in the fief of Savona around 1500.[1] In brief, the patrician
Giovanni Enrico del Carretto faced opposition from his younger brothers
because of a disagreement over whose authority prevailed in their inheritance dispute. Giovanni Enrico argued that his grandmother's feudal
investiture documents, issued in the previous century by Emperor Frederick III, stipulated that the fief would pass to the oldest son. His brothers,
however, preferred the inheritance logic embedded in newer investitures
granted by the dukes of Milan and the French king: namely, that the land
would be divided evenly between the brothers. Del Maino took up
Giovanni Enrico's defense, arguing at length that the Emperor had the
authority to dispense property "above the law, against the law, and outside the law." Not only did this strain of argument seek to legitimate
Giovanni Enrico's imperial investiture documents (and thus his right to
inherit *in toto*), but it also resisted the sovereign ambitions of the contending rights-granters: the Milanese duke and the king of France. Del

Maino's opinion suggested that they were not technically capable of bestowing lands that were the Emperor's to grant.

Certainly, it would have been wise for Giovanni Enrico to secure an imperial confirmation for his claim before pressing it with his siblings. And yet del Maino, who had survived the reigns of five Sforza dukes and two French kings, knew that the military and legal chaos of recent decades could easily obscure such desiderata. He had seen it first-hand. Louis XII gifted del Maino a fief when the French arrived in 1499—Piovera, a castle-town between Tortona and Alessandria—but then confiscated it after Ludovico Sforza's brief restoration in early 1500. "Piovera was taken from me without any real cause or fault," del Maino complained. "I was never cited nor summoned for this case. I have remonstrated several times but it has drawn no more effect than those who lament their calamities to the sun and the moon."[2] Moreover, the town's podestà refused to recognize del Maino's charter from the king, telling the professor "time and time again that I could present those royal letters at the whorehouse."[3] Competing interests and clashing powers left del Maino's case stranded.[4] (In the chapter on verbal frauds in his 1589 *Law of War*, the jurist Alberico Gentili explained how "in our own century" rulers such as Charles V and Louis XII had treated their pacts "in a fashion worthier of shysters than princes."[5]) In a telling argument in his *consilium* on the del Carretto case, del Maino concluded that given "the nature of the times, the array of different dukes and princes who reigned in Lombardy and Liguria who did not recognize the Emperor, at least in practice (*saltem de facto*), Lord Giovanni Enrico and his forebears can be excused if they did not later recognize the sacred Empire and seek investiture as was required."[6]

Contest over Milan, Genoa, and other regions had produced an inescapable complexity in the space between de jure and de facto sovereignty: the wars, at their most fundamental, were *about* deconstructing certain legal arguments about territory through force. During these same years, jurists friendly to the French kings were in the midst of articulating bullish legal frameworks of power designed to remove any impediments posed by traditions of imperial jurisdiction.[7] The most ambitious of them, such as Jean Feu, a law professor at Orléans who served from 1509 to 1512 in Milan's senate, even proposed that the "violent origins" of the ancient Roman Empire—in other words, the construction of a state by conquest of unwilling territories, as Julius Caesar had once captured Gaul—was enough to invalidate any later entitlements of the Holy Roman Empire.[8] Turning for textual support to Livy and Justinus, Feu contended that much of Italy was already Gallic territory in antiquity when Roman expansion began, and he agreed with other Francophiles that the Gauls had founded not only Milan but "also Pavia, Como, Verona, Brescia, Bergamo, Trent, Vicenza, and nearly all the Lombard cities."[9] In his reading, clearly affiliated with the Gallia Cisalpina arguments we encountered in Chapter 1, the roots of French rule in Italy grew far deeper than those of the Empire. What Feu's tendentious account did not perceive was the seeding of new "violent origins" of French empire in his own day. To formulate it instead as a recovery of antique French jurisdiction was more palatable. During these same months in 1509, seeking the alignment of law and fact, Louis XII arranged confirmation of his legal investiture of the Milanese duchy from Maximilian I in the wake of France's military victory at Agnadello.[10] Even given Feu's arguments about the extension of ancient Gaul, the imperially fabricated Visconti duchy gave convenient form and matter to French ambitions. Better to be safe than sorry.

As del Maino's "array of different dukes and princes" asserted their professedly rightful but ultimately transitory control over much of northern Italy, their subsequent reapportionment of territory obscured the mechanics of land-title for more than a generation of Milan's ruling classes. For instance, in July 1500, the French crown reapportioned in one single gesture fifty-three estates from Sforza partisans to the king's own captains and retainers.[11] The previous chapter traced the way that a potent mixture of territorial instability and political alienation contributed to forms of resistance. Violent reprisals on the part of disenfranchised elites against rulers, each other, and subject populations was a hallmark of the duchy's trajectory through the Italian Wars. This chapter illuminates an affiliated and equally revealing facet of the same problem: the campaigns of petition that this class of actors undertook to protect or regain their assets and status.

Some of our best resources for reconstructing the circumstances of these suits are supplication letters in the ducal correspondence.[12] Focusing mostly upon Milanese families who enjoyed close ties to the Sforza in the late fifteenth century (including the Sanseverino, Atellani, and Brivio clans), I show how the petitions they advanced to reclaim their vaporized rights stressed sacrifices and loyalty to sovereigns who, themselves diminished by war's expenses, rarely had means or desire to offer succor. In focusing on their petitions, we thus understand better the obstacles that war-making presented to the workings of normal justice for rulers and seekers alike. But this culture of appeal also demonstrates the resilience of these same families, eager to use the disruptions of war to bring themselves justice or, in some cases, fresh advantage.

The Sanseverino Fight Their Own Demise

The Lombard branch of the Sanseverino clan rose to immeasurable prominence during the Sforza regime but suffered considerable setbacks after its fall. Their itinerary through the French occupations and Sforza restorations reveals how a loyalist family adjusted to life after the ouster of the dynasty that fashioned their ascent. The Sforza and Sanseverino families had intertwined tightly over the second half of the fifteenth century. Not only did both of them manage important lands in Lombardy and the kingdom of Naples (the Sforza held Milan and Bari; this particular branch of the Sanseverino were lords of Colorno and Caiazzo), but they had also expanded their dominions as condottiere clans in the Po Valley.[13] Roberto Sanseverino (1418–1487) never managed to build himself a major state—or capture one—in the same manner as the Sforza, despite his renown as one of the best captains of the central third of the century. Nonetheless, the Sforza built their Milanese power in part through a strategy of mutual consolidation with the Sanseverino. Neither of them members of the established Lombard nobility, the two clans intermarried as a form of politico-territorial legitimation. Despite all the knowledge we now have about the Sforza, the Sanseverino remain in the shadows; notwithstanding his formative role in fifteenth-century warcraft, no study yet exists on Roberto Sanseverino, a political lynchpin of his era.[14] The rest of Roberto's family, so integral to the Sforza era, has all but vanished to the eyes of scholars.[15] Roberto, son of Elisa Sforza, was Duke Francesco I's nephew, making him first cousin or second uncle to all the Sforza dukes before 1500: Galeazzo Maria, Ludovico, and Giangaleazzo. Together, the families shared a military-legal might that helped, in the aggregate, to consolidate the strength of the Sforza regime in the face of enmity from the Lombard elites and the Aragonese kings of Naples. That might also redounded to the benefit of the Lombard branch of the Sanseverino.

Roberto's relationship with his Sforza cousins was both explosive and fortifying—explosive, most importantly, because he was a central suspect in the 1476 assassination of Galeazzo Maria. In its wake he followed his cousin Ludovico into exile; their relationship ran hot and cold to the point of antagonism (one ambassador described them sitting on opposite sides of the same audience chamber, receiving delegations separately because they refused to work together).[16] But in the aggregate, during moments of crisis for Sforza power, the Sanseverino clustered around their Sforza kin as a fortifying force. In the aftermath of their post-assassination exile, in 1479–1482, Ludovico and Roberto essentially co-ruled Milan; and in late 1487, just after Roberto had been killed in battle and Ludovico's health appeared to be failing, many of Roberto's sons rallied at his sickbed to strategize.[17] Finally, when Ludovico failed to recapture Milan from the French in early 1500, it was with three of the Sanseverino that he tried, unsuccessfully, to escape his duchy disguised as a German Landsknecht.[18]

Roberto Sanseverino fathered ten children: three daughters and seven sons. Five of his sons (Gian Francesco, Antonio Maria, Giulio, Galeazzo, and Gaspare, called "Fracasso") pursued their father's métier as a soldier, while two (Federico and Alessandro) became cardinals. His daughters, Giulia, Ginevra, and Sveva, married into the Carafa, Malvezzi, and Anguissola families, respectively.[19] Of his children, Galeazzo enjoyed the position of greatest prestige as both Ludovico il Moro's military captain-general and his son-in-law.[20] In 1490, the thirty-two-year-old Galeazzo wed Ludovico's legitimized eight-year-old daughter Bianca (1482–1496), who has been proposed as the sitter in the drawing known as the "Bella principessa," contentiously attributed to Leonardo.[21] Roberto's other sons also carved out positions of esteem as Lombard military captains. In the years following the breaking of the Sforza duchy in 1500, the Sanseverino family gradually withdrew from the Sforza adherence that had secured their rise. At first they strengthened their bonds with Maximilian I, who had invested Ludovico with his ducal title. (Fracasso, for instance, fought as a captain for Maximilian.[22]) In the autumn of 1501 in Innsbruck, a group of "Ruberteschi"—that is, sons and

followers of Roberto Sanseverino—presented themselves before the king
of the Romans and tried to negotiate their repatriation. A Venetian ambassador, seeing an impasse developing, wrote that "if the exiles think
to return home by means of his Imperial Majesty [Maximilian], they de-
lude themselves, because there is no other way to restitution than the
grace alone of the Most Christian King [Louis XII]."[23] After Maximilian
I invested Louis XII with the duchy of Milan in 1505, the Sanseverino
tilted their allegiance toward France in the hopes of recovering the considerable fortunes they had enjoyed under the Sforza.[24]

As we will see shortly, a number of Roberto's sons negotiated over
decades for their due. But I focus first on a newly married Sanseverino
bride to highlight the often-occluded role of wives, widows, and daughters
in these suits. In this case, it fell to the sixteen-year-old Ippolita Cibo
Sanseverino (1503–1555) to take up the cause of the Cremonese property of Montecollaro. Sometimes called Corte Cavalcabò or Corte
Madama, Montecollaro had once belonged to Bianca Maria Visconti,
whose dotal goods brought vast Cremonese territories, including Cremona itself, into Francesco Sforza's hands in the 1440s. Milan's chancery
endowed Montecollaro to Roberto Sanseverino in 1472, but during his
Milanese exile—including a period when he fought for Venice from 1482
to 1485—his assets, including Montecollaro, devolved to the ducal
chamber. Perhaps with Sanseverino solicitation, the chamber donated
it to Roberto's eldest sons, Gian Francesco and Antonio Maria. The restitution stipulated that they would receive half of its income as a wage
and would rent out the remaining half. The donation of Montecollaro
came into effect once Antonio Maria agreed to serve Ludovico Sforza's
military needs; he would draw 2,000 ducats in annual wages from the
property.[25] This was in 1483.

In 1499, claim to dominate Cremona—a major city of the Lombard
duchy long desired by Venice—passed into Venetian hands as part of an
exchange for Venice's military aid to France against the Sforza.[26] Key in
the rendition to Venice was Pietro Antonio Battaglia, the castellan of Cremona appointed by Ludovico il Moro.[27] In negotiations with the *provveditor* appointed to oversee Cremona for Venice, Battaglia agreed to turn
over the city's Sforza-held castle in exchange for "25 thousand in lands
of which he would see 12 thousand before handing over the fortress, and
many possessions or small castles or other things worth 100 thousand

ducats, and he would be made a Venetian gentleman along with his descendants."[28] Despite some shock in Venice's *collegio* that the *provveditor*
had promised so much, once Battaglia expressed his "desire to die in the
shadow of the State of Venice," the concessions were granted. Among
other gifts, Battaglia received—and here is the crucial connection—a
house on the Grand Canal in the contrada of San Samuele, "which used
to belong to the late Roberto Sanseverino, and because of his death and
his sons' rebellion [it] was confiscated; its value might be about 5,000
ducats."[29] Battaglia was now a direct beneficiary of former Sanseverino
assets.

Evidently among the "small castles or other things" in Venetian
territory that had once belonged to Sanseverino was also Montecollaro.[30] As we have already seen, the fracturing of the Milanese duchy
alienated several holdings that the family saw as their patrimony. Petitions, suits, and trials punctuated the lives of the Sanseverino—as they
did for many others—in an attempt to reclaim enough material resources to sustain themselves through politico-legal battles that often
left them uprooted, financially diminished, or both. By the time that
François I recaptured the duchy in 1515, Roberto's elder sons had already died: Gian Francesco in 1502, and Antonio Maria in 1509. So it
fell to the newest member of the family. In Rome in 1519, Gian Francesco's son—Roberto Ambrogio (1501–1532)—wed Ippolita Cibo, niece
of the late pope, Innocent VIII.[31]

Within days of her wedding, Ippolita advanced a case with the Milanese senate against Battaglia, an alacrity that suggests Montecollaro
may have counted among the assets promised to her by her new clan; or
perhaps she brought the eminence of her maternal family to the negotiations.[32] Since Cremona was once again under French sway in 1519, the
Francophile Sanseverino clan could now reignite its suits with some
chance of success. Ippolita may even have developed a personal rapport
with King François I during his post-conquest stay in Milan in 1515–
1516: she figured among the twenty-seven elite women pictured in a small
manuscript portrait book produced for the monarch.[33] Her mother-
in-law, Barbara Gonzaga Sanseverino (Gian Francesco's widow), numbered among the sovereign's closest acquaintances in that period; her
prominent place in the same portrait book hints at her clout in the king's
circle (fig. 5.1). The two women may even have concerted their efforts to

Fig. 5.1 (Left) Barbara Gonzaga Sanseverino; (right) her daughter-in-law, Ippolita Cibo Sanseverino. Two miniatures by Giovanni Ambrogio Noceto. Biblioteca Trivulziana MS 2159, ff. 3r and 10r. Archivio Storico Civico Biblioteca Trivulziana, Milan.

© Comune di Milano.

inveigh upon key players in the French court to support a prospective case with the senate. Evidence of the contested goods in this case is scanty but clear: Ippolita maintained that Battaglia owed her 9,600 ducats for his usufruct of Montecollaro, thereby framing Battaglia as a mere tenant. Ippolita's pursuit of this case may even have tested the possibility of recovering Roberto the Elder's Grand Canal palace also in Battaglia's possession. Possibly fearing the launch of a series of conflicts—legal or otherwise—Venetian agents in Milan wished to quash her case before it even received a hearing, complaining that the sixteen-year-old Countess of Caiazzo was bothering Battaglia ("*lo molesta*") and requesting that Milan's French governor should intervene to be sure that "these things are not undertaken."[34] Several months later, another letter to the same effect implies that the disagreement had not abated.[35] Only in 1526 did Alfonso d'Avalos—the cousin of Milan's first Spanish governor, and whose mother was a Sanseverino—return Montecollaro to the descendants of Roberto Sanseverino.[36]

Ippolita's suit for Montecollaro, a relatively minor holding among the array of Sanseverino assets, shows the slippage of some Milanese elites into a caste of desperate seekers, appealing to the authority most

favorable to their entreaties, even if those authorities were themselves as
changeable as their sovereign grip on territories. For Ippolita—whose
consort Roberto Ambrogio began his career as a condottiere shortly after
their marriage and who consequently could not always sustain legal pressure for his patrimony—restitution appeals became part of the process
of her integration to the Sanseverino family. During the 1520s and especially after Roberto Ambrogio's death in 1532, Ippolita lived a "vaga-
bond" life, finding little financial support other than through the
graces of her Cibo siblings: her brother Cardinal Innocenzo (1491–1550)
and her sister Caterina Cibo Varano (1501–1557), duchess of Camerino
from 1520.[37]

Ippolita was just one of the Sanseverino clan members to appeal for
favor, restitution, or repatriation. Many of Roberto the Elder's sons continued their efforts for decades. Despite personally disliking Galeazzo
Sanseverino, Louis XII appointed him royal equerry in 1506—in Italy he
was known as the *"Gran Scudier"*—and he maintained military and ceremonial positions under the French kings for the next twenty years. Like
the disruptors we encountered in the last chapter, Galeazzo also pursued
violence against counterclaimants. His disputes with the Dal Verme over
their thorny Sforza-era inheritances rekindled after 1515. He besieged
their fortress stronghold, known as the Rocca d'Olgisio, in the Val Ti-
done southwest of Piacenza in 1516. Righteously immovable, the Dal
Verme held out in the very same fortress where they had resisted the
French since 1500. Despite devastating the countryside (Galeazzo "ruined and sacked everything, and committed greater ills than if he had
been the enemy," one chronicler lamented), Sanseverino failed to van-
quish the fortress in 1516. After an even more devastating siege the following year, Olgisio finally surrendered.[38] (Federico dal Verme in turn
besieged the castle and recaptured it from Sanseverino control in 1520.[39])
Having settled in the Loire valley after 1517 to attend the French court,
in 1521 Galeazzo requested the appointment of a successor so he could
repatriate to Milan (then still in French hands), but he never managed
to extricate himself, and he remained in service until his death at the
Battle of Pavia in 1525.[40] More than two decades spent in search of lost
territory returned almost nothing of what he sought.

Captaining the 1517 Rocca d'Olgisio siege against the Dal Verme
was Thomas de Foix, sieur de Lescun, brother of Odet de Foix, sieur de

Lautrec, Milan's French governor from 1516 to 1521.[41] At Lescun's side was Galeazzo's younger brother, Giulio Sanseverino. He fought in a number of campaigns in the 1510s and 1520s, sometimes assuming captaincies for Galeazzo when he was otherwise engaged. Galeazzo died at Pavia without heirs; as a result, several properties he had always construed as his own would have no Sanseverino claimant against Dal Verme pretensions. To prevent that transfer, Giulio launched a suit against the rival family, which came to nothing.[42] After Galeazzo's death (and certainly after François I's subsequent release from Spanish captivity in March 1526), Giulio addressed a petition to the *grand maître* of France outlining his family's grievances. In French, he wrote:

> I send to you in writing the details about which I should like to speak with the King. To substantiate what I wish to say: it is to remind him [François I] that I have served the late King [Louis XII] and him for twenty-seven years without ever wavering a single day, neither entertaining the notion to leave them, nor thinking of any other thing than serving them. What I gained was having served the flower of my youth, from age nineteen to forty-six. And now moreover, I am poor, having lost 3,000 livres of rents in my Venetian patrimonial territory without ever having learned to recover from those kings any peace or reconciliation as they themselves achieved with the Venetians. This is all in addition to what I already lost in the Duchy of Milan. And finally, I am ill, an illness I acquired by force of work and service.

After outlining payments he had made to his own troops that should have been paid by the king, he continued:

> Right after the death of my late brother the Grand Equerry [Galeazzo] they took away from me all the lands that the [French] King had granted to him and his family, the lands that he had received as recompense for his services, the lands that he held in satisfaction for what the King owed him. What is more, they did not want to repay me what I disbursed at the request of the said lord [François] to sustain his gendarmes in the war. Ultimately, they have taken as little ac-

count of me as if I had just newly come into service. I confess
that I have weak feet and can no longer walk as I am accustomed to do. Nonetheless, thank God, I am not so ill
that I cannot serve in several places just as well as captains
healthier than I am.

He concluded:

Monsieur, I beg you to do this favor: that the King should see
my requests since I do not want to produce any further proof
than through him [that is, by means of his own memory and
recognition]. And if there are unreasonable things in these
demands, let them be stricken. I cannot be importunate
merely by expressing what was due and given to me. It makes
no sense that I should lose what is mine because of it. Here I
have very hefty expenses without having received in three
years more than 2,000 livres. It was said to me at Angoulême
that I would have money soon, but now there is no further
news of it. And if hope cannot come from the grace of the
Lord, I beg you to take me in your protection and favor, as I
have trusted in you. And perhaps Monsieur, even if gouty, I
shall someday do a favor for you.[43]

Giulio Sanseverino's petition spells out how his twenty-seven years of service led him to see war as a machine of consumption; it had devoured
the lives of his brothers, the assets of the family, and even his own youth
and body. To Giulio's mind, that litany of expenses required recompense;
he saw the Sanseverino as the unjust bearers of the costs. The crown coveted land and money, but for its servants the rewards were wholly insufficient. Seen in this light, the monarch's negligence explained why the
Sanseverino had pursued their own family interests through violent
feuds and lawsuits. Despite Giulio's supplicatory language, the letter's
tone indicts the crown. Dressed in the language of gentlemanly persua-
sion, it nevertheless justifies the supplicant's efforts to reveal occluded
or forgotten truths. On one level the letter begs; on another it unveils
the malfeasance of a crown that had forgotten him.

Giulio's request—he may himself have recognized this fact—arrived
at a terrible moment for financial entreaties from Italian retainers. Still

in distress following the king's imprisonment in Madrid after his capture at Pavia, the French monarchy faced a string of widening fiscal troubles that had not abated since the mid-1510s. In 1521, the king's mother had complained of "the significant and almost unbearable expenses that have been made and have still to be made" in the Milanese wars; by 1523 she claimed that the burdens of these problems had ruined her health.[44] After the king's return from captivity in 1526, royal accounts went from bad to worse. The financial crisis—purportedly rooted in royal defaults that triggered desertions of French troops, which in turn contributed to François's loss of Milan—culminated in the trial and execution of Jacques de Beaune, Baron Semblançay (ca. 1452–1527), the king's chief finance minister, along with the imprisonment of more than eight royal finance agents on charges of mismanagement.[45] No evidence of Semblançay's malfeasance remains; the trial may simply have been an expedient for François I to recover his authority after his imprisonment.[46] Thus, around the very same time that Giulio Sanseverino pointed an accusatory finger at the crown in the hopes of receiving some recompense for his Milanese sacrifices, François I himself pointed at Semblançay, exculpating himself from the fiscal shortcomings the Milanese wars had occasioned. It was a gesture of disavowal on the part of the French king that veterans of the Italian Wars knew well. Prior to the siege of the Rocca d'Olgisio in which Giulio participated in 1517, the bishop of Trent wrote to remind the French assailants that according to the terms of an earlier agreement, "the Most Christian King is obliged not to molest [Olgisio]; it is with the Emperor." Rejecting this attempt to forestall France's ambitions, Lautrec responded, "The King promised them nothing," and the siege went ahead.[47]

Royal repudiation of the crown's promises haunted these wars. Contemporaries, even Francophiles, indicted French rule in Italy for its "disorder."[48] Often no specific strategy motivated France's ruptured faith. Expediency overrode pacts, and Giulio Sanseverino was just one of its victims. A French memo dated to 1528, a year after Semblançay's execution, lists all the "demands of the Italians at this court": the litany of requests—nine captains requesting thousands of livres of unsettled pensions, ransoms, or wages—illustrates the trail of unsatisfied debts the crown owed its Italian supporters.[49]

To be sure, the same period abounds with royal graces, pardons, reintegrations, and rewards—all acts that register a desire to fulfil pledges of loyalty. But these measures coincided squarely with the crown's appraisals of its own immediate best interests. The Sanseverino family had invested in the French crown as a way to protect themselves from suffering the fate of the Sforza dynasty, to which they had been so closely tied. Instead, their investment largely replicated that fate because it compelled them to redirect their ambitions from territory to clientage, or put another way, to cede territory as a consequence of their clientage. Land had become a reward for royal service rather than a source of autonomous power. The crown assumed the Sanseverino into prestigious royal appointments (as military or ceremonial agents of the crown) with intentions to reward them with territory, but without the duration of sovereign power in Italy to secure those rewards. The value of their appointments as crown agents lasted, at most, as long as the lifetime of the holders. For that reason, the Sanseverino were left to sue for lost lands in the changing political landscape of the Lombard duchy and beyond.

In sum, French domination left the Sanseverino much reduced. What had been an ascendant dynasty under Francesco and Ludovico Sforza (1450s–1490s) transformed into a struggling one after the turn of the century through a process that swept away much of the clan's ability to occupy, or even to argue for, feudal land. In order to knit the family's dwindling assets together, two cousins married in order to secure Colorno, a territory the Sforza duke granted to Roberto the Elder in 1458. Lavinia (daughter of Roberto Ambrogio and Ippolita Cibo) wed Gianfrancesco (son of Giulio and Ippolita Pallavicino). When he became count of Colorno in 1565, Gianfrancesco launched a lawsuit against the Dal Verme family over the Rocca d'Olgisio and other holdings, perpetuating a legal battle that echoed more than fifty years of military struggle between the families.[50] But French rule in Lombardy accounts for only part of the strain upon the Sanseverino. After the creation in 1545 of the Duchy of Parma, feudal pressures merely transferred to an expanded set of disputants, including the Farnese, Gonzaga, and Vitelli families, the Empire, France, and the papacy.[51] Sanseverino connections to Colorno ended finally in 1612, in the wake of a failed plot of Parmesan feudatories to prevent the Farnese duke from absorbing their lands. The Duke of Parma, Ranuccio Farnese, had the conspirators—including Barbara (1550–1612), the last Sanseverino of Colorno—decapitated and all their goods sequestered.[52] The dispersal of Sanseverino fortunes in Lombardy, so accelerated by the Italian Wars, reached its end.

1513: Sforza Partisans in Search of the Status Quo Ante

Supplicants seeking lost privileges did not address themselves just to the French crown. A similar process during the Sforza restorations—with inverted currencies: pro-Sforza, seeking reparations in light of French misdeeds—mirrored the Sanseverino experience. In 1513, with imperial and Swiss backing, Ludovico's son Massimiliano Sforza returned to Milan for the first time since 1499, now as its duke. In an effort to assume the ducal mantle as if uninterrupted from his father, Massimiliano and his cousin Ottaviano worked to reestablish Ludovico's bureaucracy; it was for many reasons an impossible reconstruction, as the next chapter will show. Almost immediately Sforza partisans, returning to the duchy they had escaped more than a decade earlier, began to present their cases to the newly restored sovereign. Even Isabella d'Este wrote to her nephew Massimiliano: "I am told that many people are running to ask you for offices," before herself asking him to appoint the husband of a friend.[53] These supplications evoked Ludovico's reign with fond reverence, reminding his son—only six years old at the time of his father's ouster and thus in no position to remember—of the privileges the aspirants had once enjoyed and the service they had once paid to the late duke. Isabella made her case by explaining to Milan's new duke that the wife of her preferred appointee was a beloved friend of his late mother and her sister, Beatrice.[54] The aspiring officeholder had been eyeing the position for at least six years under French rule.[55] Isabella and others like her petitioned Massimiliano to untie the knots of perceived injustice that the French had tied. They based these appeals upon a politics of affection that valorized memory, shared suffering, and a commitment to rebuild a shattered world.

On 17 March 1513, just two months after Massimiliano assumed functional control of the duchy by receiving the fealty oaths of Milan's citizens, the heirs of Giacometto della Tella wrote to their duke. Giacometto—whose surname was sometimes also rendered "Atellani"—had been an intimate of Ludovico il Moro. In 1490, Ludovico gave Giacometto two adjoining palaces in the Borgo delle Grazie, immediately opposite the church of Santa Maria delle Grazie.[56] Today refashioned as a museum, the Casa Atellani attracts tourists mainly to see the adjoining vineyard bestowed on Leonardo da Vinci around the same time. During Louis

XII's regime, the Atellani abandoned the home; Leonardo's vineyard
was confiscated and later returned when he alighted again in Milan to
work for Louis XII in 1507.[57] With the first Sforza restoration in 1513,
Giacometto's sons, Carlo, Scipione, and Annibale, addressed Massimiliano in the hopes of regaining some of their erstwhile incomes:

> Most Illustrious Lord: the very happily remembered Lord
> Duke Ludovico your father—for the merits, lengthy atten-
> tions, and burdens borne by the late Sir Giacometto della
> Tella and in repayment for such long-lasting service—gave
> him the fief of Cilavegna [near Pavia] and the duties or tolls
> of the Bridge of Melegnano as is clear from solemn privileges
> which we show here. He remained in peaceful and quiet pos-
> session of these goods so long as the Lord Duke was in the
> Dominion and State of Milan; and Sir Giacometto faithfully
> followed him to Germany at the time of his expulsion from
> his lordship of this state. As a rebel and enemy of the French
> [he] was despoiled and stripped of his possession of the fief
> of Cilavegna and Bridge of Melegnano. They were [then] con-
> ceded to the late Lord Vercellino Visconti without reason or
> summons or request.

The Atellani heirs then came to the heart of their request, aligning themselves with Massimiliano as aggrieved children of unjustly displaced
people.

> And therefore Carlo, Scipione, and Annibale, heirs of the late
> Sir Giacometto, beseech your Most Illustrious Lordship—
> since they were in effect stripped of the possession of the
> aforesaid properties while your father was alive—that you too
> should wish to restore their ownership, as at the time when
> your father went to Germany and was deprived of this Do-
> minion. Moreover, all the remuneration [paid to] Sir Giacom-
> etto by [Ludovico] for such long service consisted in these
> two things, of which he was deprived and stripped, as set out
> above. The heirs of Messer Vercellino seek nothing—since
> they are already in possession—other than to drag us into
> endless arguments, [which is] an intolerable thing. If the

> heirs of Vercellino have any case to argue at all, let them bring
> it before any commissary they wish, and it will be decided in
> court.[58]

The Atellani sons sought to naturalize their rights by positioning the fate of their late father as a tragedy shared with, or even occasioned by, the fate of Massimiliano's father. Both had endured indignities of dispossession that could now be righted by a magnanimous gesture of justice. But whether they knew it or not, they were also overstating the grasping litigiousness of Vercellino Visconti's heirs. It was not just, as the Atellani brothers suggested, French malevolence that had put Cilavegna in Visconti hands. Instead, Visconti was a previous feudatory. In 1477, the fief had devolved to the ducal chamber, which in turn granted it to Vercellino Visconti in 1483. Only after Visconti's disgrace at court—for a serious diplomatic blunder—did Ludovico Sforza transfer it to Giacometto Atellani in 1496.[59] Just two weeks after France captured Milan in September 1499, Giangiacomo Trivulzio, acting in the monarch's name, granted Vercellino Visconti the duties on the bridge at Melegnano and privileges over Cilavegna and framed it as property illegitimately taken from Visconti by Ludovico Sforza.[60] These types of first-order-of-business redistributions typically awarded supporters for their aid after a successful change of regime. With the Atellani in exile at that point, there were no serious counterclaimants, nor would the French have seriously entertained an Atellani suit given their fervent Sforza support. Cilavegna did not remain in Visconti hands for long; the brothers' 1513 petition to Massimiliano clearly effected a transfer back to the Atellani; the family acted as its titular feudatory through the seventeenth century.[61]

What we must see in the saga of this small feudal holding is not just the travails of redistributed property. Although confiscation and concession have escaped broad scholarly interest as strategies of power in themselves—and thus they remain to be theorized as sociopolitical historical problems in premodernity—they were nonetheless, it hardly needs to be said, ubiquitous disciplinary measures around Europe both before and after the period studied in this book.[62] Rather, the tale of the Visconti-Atellani contest over Cilavegna points to the sizeable ambitions of Milanese families on both sides of a state undergoing a sovereignty dispute. Histories could be erased or refashioned. Without Ludovico

Sforza in power to remember the nature of Vercellino's disgrace, his heirs
could advance a reasonable case under the French for their rightful pro-
prietorship; likewise the Atellani could later vilify the Visconti as liti-
gious troublemakers. Petitioners could present themselves as parties
wronged by the last regime, since current rulers could be counted upon
to agree that the ousted rival had miscarried justice.

Less than a week after the Atellani petition, another reached Massimiliano Sforza. The duke had spent the foregoing month at war, trying
to recapture Piacenza for the Milanese duchy: the Sforza nominally surrendered that city, along with Parma and Reggio Emilia, to the papacy
in the same agreement that made Massimiliano duke in 1512.[63] But Pope
Julius had just died in February 1513, and the young Sforza saw an op-
portunity and pounced. Faced with the ducal army and a host of exactions, Piacenza exploded with factional conflict. Many residents fled the
city; nominal papal control resumed only in June of that year. Yet even
amidst the tumult of the duke's military submission of one of his own
towns, recourse to loyalist narratives of displacement *"al tempo de' francesi"* were imagined to function as robust justifications for Sforza petitioners. One of Massimiliano's agents in Piacenza wrote on behalf of a
local citizen, Lazzaro della Porta, claiming that as a "most faithful and
affectionate servant" of the late Ludovico Sforza, della Porta had "suffered for it at the time of the French and he sustained no small inconve-
niences and adversities, and lately in helping and defending Your Illustrious Lordship's faction, he was pursued by agents of the Church and
imprisoned by the Governor of Piacenza."[64] Highlighting della Porta's
history of sacrifices, the petition valorized the duration of his Sforza loyalty as a means of authenticating his good faith in an era of endemic
vacillation.

Finally, the case of Giovanni Francesco Brivio (ca. 1457–1517) illustrates the ways in which petitioners could appeal to the newly restored
Sforza by forecasting Milan's future as a recursive move, a return to a
lost status quo. In other words, by proposing ways to repopulate the new
court and administration with stalwarts of Ludovico's era—or, failing
that, with their descendants—seekers such as Brivio aimed to make
themselves and their families indispensable. Brivio himself had risen to
impressive heights in the early 1480s as a precociously young master of
Ordinary Revenues (*maestro delle intrate ordinarie*), a chief financial officer

of the duchy who belonged to an elite cadre of four financiers who were said "almost to rule the state" in Ludovico's day.[65] Vincenzo Foppa's portrait of him, probably painted in the late 1490s, sets his sharp-eyed aquiline profile against a fur-lined crimson damask robe and red cap: a man of both means and acuity (fig. 5.2).[66] Most notable was his ability during the next fifteen years to retain proximity to his esteemed financial post. After his expulsion in 1500, he regained admission to Milan only in 1504—years after his other siblings had paid 8,000 scudi in atonement fines to the king. Brivio soon served Louis XII in a post nearly identical to his former appointment.[67] Under Massimiliano, he angled to resume his office in Ordinary Revenues.[68] His petition to the young Sforza, however, came very early in the restoration, before it was clear how his fortunes might rise again. He wrote in January, half a year before his reappointment, to Giovanni Colla, preceptor of the exiled Sforza children, whom Brivio must have known before 1500.[69] Colla was now back in Milan as well, overseeing Massimiliano's administration ("once a tutor, now a second duke," one chronicler averred).[70] Because Brivio's affairs still hung in the balance, his appeal betrayed some hunger, as he framed his family's services as a desirable commodity redolent of a bygone age.

Brivio reminded Colla of "my long service, as I wish you to understand that there is no person whatsoever in the Ordinary Magistracy who has been at that position for more time than I was; [it is] 28 years or more since I was made Master of Ordinary Revenues. And therefore I pray that your Lordship might see that I be put in greater esteem than before, since I am now able to serve His Excellency more than ever." Then, in invoking the past service of his two brothers, Alvisio and Alessandro, he positioned his nephews as beneficent shadows of their dead fathers. The late Alvisio had sired "many sons, among whom the first is called Giambattista, a clever youth; for the good service of his father and for the honor of his house, it is wished that he too might be made a magistrate of Ordinary Revenues because he will be a man to bring advantage to his Excellency our Lord." Carlo, the son of "Alessandro my brother who was [once] a groom of Lord Ludovico," could follow his father's footsteps in Massimiliano's court. "It is wished that he might be made a groom in the chamber of his Excellency because he is a gentle youth, and will serve him well and faithfully." Then Brivio concluded by couching these requests

Fig. 5.2 Vincenzo Foppa, *Giovanni Francesco Brivio,* ca. 1495. Museo Poldi Pezzoli, Milan. Inv. 1648.

in terms of his family's sacrifices "in the time when, as I think your Lordship knows, we wagered life and limb to keep [Massimiliano's] father in his state. We suffered imprisonment, exile, pillage, and other great offenses and extortions."[71] Brivio was not exaggerating. Among other trials, his wife Margherita Landriani had been assaulted by soldiers in April 1500 during the French recapture of the duchy.[72] The letter positioned the

return of Brivio men to Sforza service as a solution to the grim shared
memories of the past decade by bridging its shores of time with a familiar
cast of functionaries. Massimiliano, evidently convinced by Brivio's case,
appointed him as regulator of Ordinary Revenues in April 1513.[73]

Brivio's appellate narrative proved so common and effective that
even his detractors used the same tactics against him. Only a few months
after Brivio's reappointment, a Visconti supplicant wrote to ask for the
duke's support against Brivio, a man so "malignant and factious" that
fourteen years earlier his "false testimony" had caused Leonardo Visconti
to suffer imprisonment, exile, and 3,000 ducats of fines.[74] Now they were
in dispute again, and Visconti wanted the duke to punish Brivio. Both
Brivio and Visconti framed their requests as culminations of trials
launched in 1499 and whose consequences they had suffered for (and
because of, and *alongside*) the Sforza. Even when directed against each other,
petitioners framed their own histories as tales of injustice that the prince
could now set right.

The kind of ruptures in political and legal authority that Milan saw
in the early sixteenth century promoted a search for means of self-
authentication among its elites. That process took many forms, including
violent conflict, legal disputes, and petitions, all aimed at restoring them
to an idealized status quo ante. It frequently involved narrating histories
of affiliation with the prince or explaining rights that the circulation of
regimes had obscured. Requests for restoration of a family's goods or
status thus premised themselves upon the intercessory powers of the
prince, that is, upon the notion that wrongs committed by a previous
ruler could finally be righted by fiat of the "true" prince. These petitions
help us to see the thirst for princely intercession, even if that idea nearly
inverts the problem examined in the last chapter, in which sovereign
intrusion functioned as the matrix of conflict rather than as its resolution. But the ideas, of course, did not mutually exclude each other.
The prince as both cause and settler of disputes was a twin belief that
perhaps assumed even greater weight during moments of sovereign contest. Regime fluctuations trained attention upon a sovereign's capaci-
ties (and incapacities) to reorder the world. Both detractors and supporters of the duke exploited uncertainties to develop strategies of
self-preservation.

Whether deployed by allies or opponents, these strategies rooted
themselves in history. The moral authority to petition or resist consisted

in the justification that could be fashioned from competing visions of the past, just as the feuding Sforza and Valois princes found legitimating sustenance in their dynastic stories. Historical precedent had a force that, at times, could equal sharper weapons, and it functioned at all social levels. At the very same time as Lazzaro della Porta—the Sforza partisan imprisoned in Piacenza in 1513—awaited grace from Duke Massimiliano, the duke was himself involved in justifying his own dynastic claim to Parma and Piacenza before Pope Leo X. The young duke wished to avoid losing those two cities, or as he put it, to be "mutilated of these two most honorable limbs."[75] Stuck between pope and emperor, he fretted that any concessions to Leo would leave him "in danger of Imperial anger."[76] Having sent his younger brother Francesco to Rome to "kiss the hand" of the pope and seek a cardinalate, Massimiliano defended his desire to recapture Piacenza by arguing, as one chronicler described the dispute, that it had been "subject to the state of Milan for hundreds of years." The pope countered that "it was found in writings and other histories that no more than 180 years earlier it belonged to the Papal See, but had been usurped." The disagreement spilled into the city itself, where a number of elites, seeing more danger in Sforza than papal domination, "did not cease to search the city for as many of the oldest writings as possible to find histories showing that the Church had been the ruler of the city, in order to produce them and intervene in these negotiations."[77]

Historical documents evidencing rights—charters, donations, notarial acts, letters patent, and state registers—served as potent tools in adjudicating disagreements and remapping power relations at the turn of the sixteenth century. What frustrated so much efficient politico-legal action in contested Milan was the fact that many of those resources had disappeared or no longer existed. The next chapter reconstructs and recounts the challenges of facing the dispersal and haphazard management of records between warring regimes.

6

Document Destruction and Fraud

*O*ne of the deepest questions in grasping the reins of state concerns the fate of a hyper-mundane set of objects: its administrative documents. Past records—of diplomatic agreements, legal decisions, donations, concessions, privileges—both empower and constrain rulers. With access to its own archive, a regime can produce evidence to support claims of its own power, as Duke Massimiliano and Pope Leo each tried to do in Piacenza in 1513. But those same documents can also confound ambitions. They ostensibly limit the bounds of permissible action and bind the powerful to history. In the hands of subjects, an inscribed history is sometimes the only force to hold rulers accountable to their own agreements. The imposition of a new regime in a palimpsest state such as Milan around 1500 only accentuates the convenience and inconvenience of the archive. New rulers can easily confirm privileges granted by former regimes if those concessions appear to be innocuous. Or conversely, they can invent alternative new realities, ignoring the reams of paper and parchment that might contradict their desires, as happened in redistributing lands. Or, to propose another possibility, they may not have the luxury of making such a choice because the archive itself may be gone.

We can no longer reconstruct completely the administrative workings of the Milanese state—under any of its rulers—from 1499 to 1521. Leaving aside the substantial documentary reorganizations of the eighteenth and nineteenth centuries, the Allied bombings of Milan's Archivio di Stato in the Second World War negated any future studies of the whole archive from this period since the attack destroyed, among many other things, all the records of the duchy's senate. As we saw in Chapter 1, Louis XII reorganized two previous Sforza councils into a single senate that oversaw Milanese legislation and adjudication until 1786.[1] During the 1943 bombings, the flames incinerated more than 10,000 boxes of documents covering nearly 300 years of senate deliberations.[2]

But even before twentieth-century depredations, documentary absences bedeviled students of early sixteenth-century Milan. Léon-Gabriel Pélissier, the most assiduous nineteenth-century researcher of Milan's first French domination, considered the archival remains of this period to be mere "debris."[3] To judge by the bulk of material surviving from the earlier Sforza era (1450–99), losses have been considerable: in the ducal letter archive concerning Milanese internal affairs (a series now called *Carteggio Sforzesco—Milano Città e ducato*), five thick boxes of correspondence date to 1494 (a regular year under Ludovico Sforza), but just a single box pertains to the period 1499–1513. Not until 1530 does the stream of letters regain the pace it had during the period prior to the French conquest. Some decades before Pélissier began his Milanese studies, Jules Michelet voiced a similar complaint for the same period in France. Perennially gathering manuscript resources, Michelet noted that the national library had rich collections "for Louis XI, abundant for François I, superabundant—almost overflowing—for the last Valois, [but] lacking for Charles VIII and Louis XII."[4] Michelet could only conclude that Louis XII burned most of his records.

Since, almost by definition, a new regime must attempt at some point to inscribe its own legitimacy through masses of documentation, the absence of records for the French domination of Milan must be explained by some significant but now unidentifiable losses. We cannot know the specific circumstances, but we can trace some of their causes and effects. This chapter explores the phenomenon of dispersion and destruction less as an obstacle to our reconstruction of the past and more as an effect of flickering sovereignty. The instability of the archive is a

symptom of the disruptions of the era.[5] Violent rotation of regimes at-
omizes the archive, which was not just a single site, but a constellation—a
network of castle chambers, administrative offices, and private holdings.
The prince's court as a center of power—already itinerant for both Sforza
dukes and French kings—all but lost any anchorage under a variety of
rulers and governors whose implantations were impermanent or un-
suited to storing and protecting paperwork. Once the archive was imperiled or fragmented, regimes recognized it as a particularly valuable
tool, the "memory of the state."[6] Through it, regimes appreciated how
they could manage self-knowledge and the contesting claims that inundated them from supplicants. In light of the archive's fragmentation,
rulers often sought the expertise of officers who once governed reposi-
tories in an effort to replace missing documents with human memory.
The greatest threat to regimes from the denuding of its own records—
although perhaps even they could not see it clearly as such—was the
specter of deceit and fraud: the possibility that the state could be unmade through pin-pricks, that its inability to corroborate its own past
actions could license innumerable subjects to take fatal advantage of it.
Milan's dukes had been particularly afflicted with these dynamics surrounding the power of the written record, and it is to this history that
we turn first.

Powers and Perils of Document Destruction, 1447–1496

Investitures, charters, letters, and other forms of paperwork obsessed the
Sforza princes.[7] Constantly angling to coopt the international prestige
of their Visconti forerunners, not to mention the official imperial recognition as dukes, they built their regime as much upon the validating
force of documents as upon military and financial power. The union of
the two houses in 1441—when Bianca Maria Visconti wed Francesco
Sforza—facilitated the luster-appropriation that Francesco and his heirs
mobilized after he became duke in 1450. He invoked continuity (with the
traditions of Visconti rule) as a mask for discontinuity (that the Sforza
lacked imperial recognition and thus ruled under a diffuse but impin-
gent pressure to self-justify).

That rhetoric of continuity rested upon a canny confabulation of
documentation from the Visconti archive, which itself had just under-

gone profound trials by the time that Francesco assumed power in 1450, due to the political upheavals following Duke Filippo Maria Visconti's death in 1447. During that three-year interval (1447–1450) a group of oligarchs launched the Golden Ambrosian Republic, figuring it as a recreation of Milan's self-government prior to its submission to Visconti lords in the thirteenth century. The Milanese started to dismantle the Visconti castle at Porta Giovia, Filippo Maria's main residence, using its stones to reinforce the city's breached walls.[8] To reject the Visconti legacy and articulate its independence, the republic's Captains and Defenders of Liberty called in September 1447 for the public burning of books and files of tax inventories as a way to cancel the weight of exactions upon taxpayers.[9] In the meantime, the greatest treasures of the dynastic archive remained unperturbed during this triennium, since they remained protected at Pavia's Visconti castle. Instead, it was the offices of the ex-ducal chancery (in the Porta Giovia castle) and of the republican government itself, working from the old Visconti residence next to the cathedral (the Corte d'Arengo), that faced troubles. Crushed between military threats from both Venetian and Sforza forces, the Ambrosian Republic surrendered to Francesco Sforza in March 1450, and its administrative archive vanished.[10] Surviving republican edicts suggest that document theft had already become a problem for the republic in 1449. Facing the potential of Sforza lordship, citizens may have begun to destroy or hide materials that could bring them misfortune under a new duke.[11] In late 1449, intruders broke into the chancery of the Magistracy of Extraordinary Revenues—the ministry charged with fines, liquidations, and condemnations—and made off with "many books of law, of the oratorical arts, trial records, [and] writings."[12] Just a month before the city's capitulation to Sforza in 1450, the republican government declared that it was searching for "many and infinite writings, books, and accounts transported out of the city of Milan [. . .] of great importance, and many [people] will come to the greatest damage and woe if they are not found."[13] When Francesco Sforza gained control of the city, one of his first orders called for the restitution of books and papers removed from the Corte d'Arengo; other proclamations of the new duke mentioned thefts from the homes of leaders of the fallen republic.[14] The conspicuous lack of documents led him to complain in 1452 of the difficulty of overseeing feudal investitures, "for not being able to find the writings of the late Duke Filippo because they were burned at the time of Milan's liberty."[15]

As much as Francesco Sforza wished to understand the administrative mechanics of government by gathering surviving Milanese records, he himself attempted to craft his rule through the destruction of inconvenient histories. Upon assuming power in 1450, he learned that the Visconti castle at Pavia—where the dynasty had also kept its sumptuous library of over one thousand manuscripts—housed an abundance of historical family charters. With an eye to managing the justification of his new lordship, one of the first things Francesco aimed to find was the testament of Duke Giangaleazzo Visconti, who died in 1402. The testament's importance had partly to do with Giangaleazzo's official investiture as duke by the Holy Roman Emperor: it could clarify some of the outlines of that grant. Moreover, the military struggle that brought Francesco to power in 1450, involving thousands of opposing troops sent by King Charles VII, reminded him of the seriousness of Orléans claims to the lordship of Milan through the inheritance of Giangaleazzo's daughter, Valentina.[16] Those French incursions clarified Francesco's imperative to learn exactly what evidence tended against his claim to ducal power and to confront it.

His suspicions were warranted. It must already have been plain to him that Giangaleazzo's 1388 will dictated that upon extinction of the main Visconti line (as Filippo's death had just fulfilled), the duchy was meant to pass to Valentina's descendants in the house of Orléans. The 1388 testament profoundly threatened Francesco's claim upon the duchy; Sforza interests hinged upon the obliteration of that document. The volatility of this fact pressed Francesco's secretary, Cicco Simonetta, to seek it out. It was not in the Visconti castle archive but instead in the possession of the Pavian notary Andrea Oleari, successor of the official who had solemnized Giangaleazzo's testament some sixty years earlier. Cicco wrote to Oleari explaining that "certain things happening presently [make it] necessary for us to see the original of the testament of the illustrious late lord, our first duke."[17] Oleari must have intuited the new duke's sinister motives, since he offered to send only a copy. In a series of increasingly urgent letters over the week of 19–24 February 1452, Cicco pursued the charter, demanding "the original and not a copy" and calling it "very important to our affairs."[18] When summoned directly,

Oleari temporized further, claiming that he had neither horse nor money for travel. Cicco responded with both threats and encouragement, charging Oleari to appear in Milan under penalty of rebellion and offering him a horse, a servant, and money to make the trip.[19]

The original 1388 testament no longer exists; Cicco seems to have gotten his way. Yet its shadow did not cease in 1452 to stalk the Sforza dynasty. More than forty years later, in 1496, Francesco's son Ludovico il Moro faced it again. The Duke of Orléans (the future Louis XII, Valentina's grandson) had come to Italy in Charles VIII's service in 1494–1495, and Ludovico was anxious to solicit judicial advice, even though he had finally attained the imperial investiture that his father had failed to acquire.

Ludovico asked the law professor Giason del Maino to investigate. Del Maino's probe led him back to the Oleari family of notaries. Evidently unaware of Francesco and Cicco's searches in the 1450s, Giason asked the Oleari notary (a scion of the last one)

> if he had the testament of the first duke, or if he knew who had it. He answered no. Then, investigating day by day with greater diligence I discovered that [Oleari] has a copy of the first duke's testament even though it is neither solemnized nor original. This testament would be of the greatest importance for the Duke of Orléans against your Excellency [Ludovico] because it contains the legal trust (*fideicommisso*) of the state of Milan which—if [Giangaleazzo's sons] Duke Giovanni Maria, Duke Filippo, and sir Gabriello should die without male heirs—dictates that the state of Milan should fall to one of the descendants of Madonna Valentina.[20]

That descendant, of course, was Louis himself. Despite this technically damning conclusion about Sforza lordship, del Maino insisted—without explaining his reasoning—that the testament did not threaten the rule of Ludovico or his sons. Nonetheless, del Maino noted that at least three other copies of the testament probably existed: one with the friars of the Certosa di Pavia, one with a Pavian gentleman, and a third with the Count of Mirandola.[21] Most urgently, del Maino reported that two students currently lodging at the notary's house had recently stayed up all night to transcribe the document. They were sons of Giovanni Giacomo

Ferrari, "doctor and councilor in Asti of the Duke of Orléans." Del Maino urged Ludovico to find all these copies and to make sure that the councilor's sons should be prevented from sending any copy to Asti. Del Maino's insistence on containing the copies of this crucial *fideicommisso* echoed Simonetta's worry that charters damaging to Sforza political power should be concealed or possibly be made to vanish.

Ludovico ordered the Pavian professor to pore over the top-secret documents and report his findings. Del Maino followed up six days later in a much longer letter.[22] Here, he revealed why Ludovico should not fear Orléans pretensions upon the Milanese state. The jurist explained that Louis's claims upon Milan were based upon two legal misprisions. First, the duchy could not pass by way of female inheritance. Giangaleazzo had evidently wished to pass the ducal lineage through Valentina's dowry contract in 1388, but when the emperor created the duchy for him in 1395, the investiture stipulated only male inheritance.[23] Second, imperial fiefs could not be alienated by the feudatory himself, since he did not have the power to alter the terms of the original grant. That fact, del Maino concluded, nullified the potentiality in Giangaleazzo's last will and testament that the duchy could pass to Valentina's heirs.[24] Now confident that his interpretations of the *fideicommisso* would please Ludovico, del Maino urged the duke "to disseminate and publish them at the court of the King of France and other useful locations"; he also drew the prince's attention to the fourth page of the attached copy, where a little manicule pointed to the crucial passage.[25] Ducal histories hidden in the studios of Pavian notaries could be explosive—in turn frightening and emboldening.

As the Sforza dukes came to appreciate, Pavia was a veritable font of historical documents. The castle housed not only the library but more than a dozen cupboards of Visconti charters and registers. For purposes of governance, Francesco had much of the administrative material transferred to Milan, leaving in Pavia the most ancient documentation.[26] In the 1490s, these remaining resources helped to inform Ludovico's historiographers, Giorgio Merula, Tristano Calco, and Bernardino Corio, as they researched their Visconti chronicles and Milanese histories.[27] In Milan, Sforza administrative documentation accrued rapidly in the rebuilt castle thanks to the activities of chancellors and diplomats. On the one hand, Francesco's chancellors undertook a remarkable archival reconstruction effort, searching out notaries who had registered Visconti protocols, interviewing former officials, and transcribing international agreements.[28] On the other, diplomats established new political friendships that Sforza leveraged as tools of legitimation, all the while producing an ocean of ambassadorial correspondence that has been called the largest of its time in Europe.[29] Over the course of the century's second half, the Sforza dukes built a paper dominion serviced by a chancery that was both precocious and disorderly. Inventories appear to have been kept (although they were destroyed in 1943); a locked room above the council chamber housed the most important files; ushers and archivists were appointed. But on the whole the administrative competence of the Sforza archive seems to have paled in comparison to the advanced systems in Savoy or Mantua.[30] One voice complained of chancery officials tossing registers at each other and ruining precious documents by spilling ink over them.[31] If such trivial problems of disorder already plagued the chancery in the Sforza era, it would face a much greater challenge after the French conquest in 1499. Like Francesco in 1450, rulers would need to authorize themselves by invoking the documentary precedent of the former regime while lacking some of its fundamental paperwork.

Government in Search of Paperwork

Some of the patterns we just traced continued into the next century. In 1535, Giovanni Paolo Sforza, Ludovico's son with Lucrezia Crivelli, advanced a claim to inherit the duchy based upon his father's insistence in 1495 that his imperial investiture would legitimize all his male children. Learning of Giovanni Paolo's search for the documentary proof, the castellan of Milan, Massimiliano Stampa, reported to the emperor in 1535 that he had found the original charter "in the archive of writings of this state (*en el archivo de las escripturas deste stado*)."[32] Stampa sent it to Milan's Spanish governor, Antonio de Leyva, for him to burn. Leyva wished to send the original to the emperor, but instead sent a copy for fear that it could fall into the wrong hands.[33] Giovanni Paolo, meanwhile, believed that his late half-brother, Francesco II, had burned it out of spite or had "put it in the hands of someone who would hide it."[34] Sforza history was a long nightmare of suspected incineration.

One reason to rewind, as we have just done, through the histories of Sforza paperwork is to trace precedents and patterns for document loss after the French occupation. Giovanni Paolo's trials aside, evidence of destruction for the period after Ludovico's fall is much harder to trace. But with the foregoing fifty years in mind, we can intuit some of the challenges that administrators faced in 1499–1500. It was not so much that the scribal supports of government disappeared altogether, even if that certainly happened on occasion. It was rather that, over nearly twenty-five years, during waves of rulers with different documentary traditions, structures, and languages, the archive became more of a relic or a ghost than a tool. If the Sforza had found a way to turn their archive into an effective implement of power, that was rarely the case for the duchy's French administrators.[35]

One of the most intractable problems was logistical: the castle at Porta Giovia, repository of the chancery archive, became the city's most contested military site. After its castellan surrendered the stronghold to France on 17 September 1499, its French garrison outlasted Ludovico's nearly two month-long restoration in early 1500, meaning that il Moro ruled Milan essentially blind before his final capture. Itinerant for much of that time (issuing orders from Novara, its suburbs, and his military camp), he still managed to reappoint many of his central chancery officials, to nominate an entirely new fleet of castellans, and to grant a number of patents and safe-conducts.[36] Evidence exists that the Sforza archive still existed within Porta Giovia, though it is unclear exactly what it contained and how long it remained intact.[37] Pavia's castle fell in 1499 as well, and in short order King Louis identified the library as a trophy he wished to export; almost 400 of the collection's 1,000 manuscripts now belong to the national library in Paris, having been carried to Blois by royal agents following the conquest.[38] As early as the first Sforza restoration in 1513, very few treasures remained at Pavia: in explaining why the castle was ill-suited to lodge troops, a correspondent wrote, "In this castle everything has been looted, such that there are neither beds, nor couches, nor desks, nor stools."[39]

In the eddies of changing regimes around 1500, documents that recorded financial obligations were targeted for theft or destruction just as they had been in 1447. First among these were tax records. One chronicler reported that the initial openness of Milan's citizenry to the prospect of Louis XII's rule grew from the rumor that the "French way" involved lower taxes and exemptions from duties and salt levies. Consequently, when Louis's forces entered Milan, the citizens themselves demolished the salt offices and duty houses.[40] Citizens of Milan burned the books cataloguing tax malefactors, and they elected new officials; in the Valsassina region, peasants stormed the house of the deposed Sforza podestà, destroyed his records, and looted 160 ducats.[41] In Pavia citizens broke down the doors of the tribunals, pilfered their paperwork, and burned them in the city's main piazza.[42] While some instances of archive-obliteration may have expressed generic frustrations with the ousted regime, targeting tax records suggests a desire to wipe clean any debts and exactions as a mode of cancelling history and proposing a new dispensation.[43] Records of debts owed to Jewish lenders disappeared when the French took control of Brescia in 1509.[44] A Milanese uprising of 1526 against Spanish military rule included "arsonists of public documents (*congremattori de scripture publice*)."[45]

These were exactly the sorts of records that governments relied upon to stabilize their dominion and assure basic revenues. While on one level new rulers, like their subjects, wished to start from scratch and forge fresh affinities, on another level their role as arbiters depended upon the performance (or even the appearance) of historical omniscience, a genre of knowledge that deep archives helped to generate. Very soon after the disorder that Ludovico's fall precipitated—and in nearly every subsequent transition—regimes called for the recovery of documents. In February 1500, during Ludovico's restoration, his government requested that "anyone who has books or writings of any kind taken out of the ducal court, or from the salt office in the Broletto of Milan [. . .] must return them all to the court's registry office (*officio de la carta*)."[46] Then in mid-April of the same year, less than a week after il Moro's capture, when the duchy came back under French control, the royal government issued its own plea, asking "whoever has or knows others to have any books, registers, documents, or other writings related principally to the Treasury and the Chambers of Ordinary and Extraordinary [Revenues] of the Most Christian King; or trunks, beds, or other things that were inside the Treasury" to notify the government within four days.[47] These were not insignificant records: the instruments of these chambers constituted the chief financial accounts of the duchy.

Over the next few months, a number of edicts highlighted the on-going search for missing paperwork as the regime tried to corral the functioning of the state into some form of normalcy. One of the fore-most concerns was the salt tax. Milan's civic salt commissioners (prob-ably a board of local notables, overseen by the royal agents) issued orders against fraud, insisting that only authorized agents could sell salt.[48] Evi-dently the measures that the agency traditionally used to police the commodity market were unavailable. What the commissioners lacked was their archive; they issued an appeal to anyone who might have "writ-ings, books, files, and instruments of the salt gabelle" to return them within three days.[49] Ultimately their solution may have been simply to recommence from zero, since an order of the following month required citizens to report the amounts of salt they purchased so as to ascertain the size of the market.[50] Around the same time, another edict prohib-ited a form of documentary fraud that raised particular concerns in a regime with little institutional memory: it cautioned notaries against tampering with the written deeds of their deceased colleagues (*esplere atti di notai defunti*), under penalty of nullifying any document they themselves should authenticate.[51] In the invasion's demographic disturbances—notaries surely numbered among the incalculable numbers of Milanese who decamped or died[52]—such interventions loosened links in the chains of legal accountability and permitted enterprising fraudsters, whether notary or client, to seek new advantage. To work toward sta-bility, Louis XII appointed a man named Antoine Cailler as archivist of Milan on 1 July 1500, explaining in his letter of nomination that "nothing could be more profitably established than to restore under good protec-tion the charters and other writings of our records which accrue daily—both ours and those of our subjects—and to appoint someone faithfully to care for, preserve, and deposit them."[53] Cailler's successors or colleagues included native Italians; two Lombards' names also appear as archivists in the first decade of the century.[54]

Still, reverberations of document loss continued for years. We en-counter some of its echoes in 1507, during the administrative stock-taking before Louis XII's personal return to the duchy, his first visit in five years. The French administration was keen to rid itself of some of the overhanging financial obligations of the Sforza era. In the absence of records in the government's own care, the regime relied upon citizens' custodianship of their own paperwork to reconstruct obligations. For instance, the Office of Ordinary Revenues declared that Louis XII wished to settle all Sforza accounts prior to the conquest of 1499, and it invited creditors of the chamber to present themselves, documents in hand, to do so.[55] Likewise, the crown had to cope with what it saw as the financial damages inflicted by Ludovico Sforza during his final days in power. An edict of March 1507 noted that before fleeing to Austria in 1499, il Moro had sold or given away an array of goods, movable and immovable, "which in his final departure could cause him little damage or loss." But the king's government saw his last-minute concessions as a frustrating inheritance of long-duration liabilities, since Ludovico's concessions clouded the ownership of any number of high-value items, even (they are not specified, but we can imagine) urban palazzi or rural lands.[56]

The French wanted to shine light on the matter. The edict declared that the French understood that Ludovico had issued "writings, bills, and warrants" detrimental to state finances. It thus made three injunctions. Anyone who possessed written grants from Ludovico dated up to one month before his flight from the duchy (2 September 1499) had now to present himself for a reckoning to the royal chamber within twenty days. Second, people with knowledge "of the preparation and deceit of these writings" had to make themselves known within the same period. And finally, it summoned anyone who had "writings, records, books, orders, and testimonies" of potential benefit to appear at the royal chamber.[57] Only by compelling the rendition of paperwork from residents could the regime begin to reconstruct the former duke's transactions and obligations as the first step in an attempt to reckon with, or ultimately to cancel, them. At the chapter's end, we will see how Ludovico's debt problem snaked incessantly through this period.

Following France's defeat at Ravenna in the spring of 1512, the French abandoned Milan. It remains unclear whether French officials carried their administrative archive out of the city with them.[58] So few papers remain that one historian wondered whether it had been burned, but traces in Paris suggest that at least some crucial writings (financial as well as administrative) came to the French capital.[59] Before the arrival of Ludovico's son Massimiliano, Milan's governance fell to the new duke's cousin, Ottaviano Maria Sforza, Bishop of Lodi, son of the assassinated Duke Galeazzo Maria and his mistress Lucia Marliani. (Ottaviano

even maneuvered unsuccessfully to assume the ducal title for himself.[60])
Whether the French regime's documents were destroyed or not, one of
Ottaviano's first acts involved a sort of conceptual negation of the
French interlude. He recalled all of Ludovico Sforza's officials, "whether
from the great court itself or from the city" to return "to carry out their
duties with all diligence, faith, and sincerity" until it was decided whether
changes needed to be made.[61] He also called for anyone possessing writings of the deposed (and now dead) Ludovico to restore them to the
government.[62]

In so doing, he aimed to bridge the reigns of father and son as if they
had passed from one to the other unbroken, uninterrupted by the crumbling of the regime. Sforza temporality was to be recommenced. A restorative optimism drove his injunction, since many Sforza officials,
having fled or died in the intervening decade, would never take up their
posts again. Yet, new amnesties for Ludovico's faithful permitted a certain amount of personnel recuperation. We saw in the last chapter that
some former officials, such as Giovanni Francesco Brivio, petitioned to
resume their offices as soon as Massimiliano came to power and managed to maintain or recover a position from one regime to the next.[63] For
those officers who negotiated this transition—and they were almost exclusively Milanese citizens, since no Frenchmen stayed on under the
Sforza—a renewed functional prominence awaited them. Under Louis
XII and François I, ultramontane bureaucratic staff generally pushed
Milan's remaining native administrators to second-string positions,
leaving them as disempowered shadows, or collapsed multiple roles into
fewer positions.[64] The reorganization exemplifies the layered strata of the
palimpsest state, in which a dominant administrative culture worked
atop an abraded one in a single environment. It also had a significant
effect upon the production, oversight, and fate of government paperwork. While political and diplomatic officers had mechanisms for ne-
gotiating the polyglot environment (whether by using Latin or inter-
preters), that was not the case with fiscal reckonings: France's finance
ministers composed all their documents in their own vernacular.[65] It was
a normal habit that nonetheless erected a further barrier to the utility
of these financial records as tool of fiscal authentication by clerks who
knew only Italian language or script. Had the French left their account
books behind in Milan after their withdrawal, language itself might have

hindered those papers from telling their histories of transaction and exaction.

The Sforza restoration under Massimiliano did see some remarkable instances of secretarial continuity—his octogenarian chancellor, Bartolomeo Calco, had been a Sforza secretary since 1472 and served under Louis XII as well; his decades of experience can only have helped the restoration overcome its documentary losses.[66] But the seamless continuation of Sforza rule imagined in the mass-recall of Ludovico's government to Massimiliano's service could never be fully realized. Hundreds of new officers had to be appointed, outnumbering those who resumed positions.[67] Still more telling is the inability of the restored regime to sustain any personnel for very long. In mid-1513, word spread that "all of Milan's officials will be reformed," which probably entailed a purge of bureaucrats sympathetic to the French regime.[68] Was this purge related to the *"mutazione de officiali"* that Massimiliano Sforza undertook in early 1515, perhaps pressed by the anti-imperial politics of Swiss agents in his orbit?[69] Or did the bureaucracy see two transformations in as many years? Despite a certain level of continuity, the archival knowledge vacuum was matched by an administrative one. The same problems faced the regimes of François I in 1515 and Francesco II Sforza in 1521.

Specters of Fraud and the Exploitation of Absence

The culture of official documentation, not just in sixteenth-century Milan but widely across premodern Europe, relied upon the production of multiples. Copies of legal acts—whether in duplicate, triplicate, or some other quantity—guaranteed that all parties involved possessed a version of the terms that cemented their mutual obligations. The copy acted to proliferate and ratify an accepted truth through a network of corroborative versions.[70] In the sixteenth century as before, a panoply of personalities sustained the habit of documentary multiplication: notaries scrawling reams of formulaic Latin, amanuenses reproducing the work of distracted scholars, secretaries transcribing rulers' missives into copybooks (*copialettere*), merchants penning receipts for themselves and for customers. In a sense, this chapter so far has been all about the tension between originals and copies: about the ruler's strong desire to control his own original writings and about the political inconvenience and frustrated ambitions caused by their dispersal or unwanted reproduction.

Now we consider the consequences of all this archival shuffling and blighting. In the conflictual circling of Milan's regimes, the archive's removal or destruction opened doors for malfeasance. As we saw earlier, governments established themselves through public decrees aimed at recovering their important documents and at obviating fraud. Through cases detailed principally in the letters of Massimiliano Sforza—whose correspondence with secretaries and regional governors from 1513 to 1515 survives more abundantly than do similar sources for the French periods—we zero in upon the confusion generated by breaches in the mechanics of trust. We see, in several different permutations, how documentary absence and fraud became bedfellows. When the culture of the copy faltered and ideal procedures of corroboration became impossible, the prince's subjects could subvert the state's ambitions of omniscience with guile. Or, conflicting claims over rights or goods failed to find resolution for want of proper evidence. Or further, when the duke lacked means to verify claims, even the most legitimate request might raise suspicions.

To give a sense of the intricacies of such problems, the first instance I follow is also the most complex: a seemingly innocuous (not to say dull) case of the duties and tariffs of Locarno, a lakeside town on Lago Maggiore, some 120 kilometers north of Milan. Embedded within this contested tax history is a matrix of power relations between elites, cities, and rulers rooted in the questionable validity of official documents. It shows how war layered confusions upon suspicions, producing documentary puzzles that worked in multiple, often contradictory, directions, as frustrations and as opportunities to exploit.

In the foothills of the Alps, mountain-pass cities acted as bulwarks for the Milanese state.[71] Locarno gained fame for its proud fortress, judged second only to Milan's; its fortifications may have been overseen by Leonardo.[72] Locarno and other alpine settlements suffered more than a decade of contention as the Swiss cantons took advantage of buckling Sforza power after 1500 to expand their dominion. Bellinzona offered itself to Swiss dominion upon the first arrival of Louis XII, but other cities surrendered only a decade or so later, following Swiss sieges, sacks, or devastation of the countryside (most significant among them were Lugano, Locarno, and Domodossola).[73] Like many towns in this region, Locarno had come under Milanese sway in the fourteenth century, and the dukes later consolidated Milan's dominion through feudal concessions; the Rusca family of Como held Locarno's feudal title.[74] The Rusca counts collaborated with French forces upon Louis XII's assumption of power. Accordingly, the king almost immediately confirmed Rusca feudal title over Locarno and much of the surrounding area, and the Rusca became allies of Louis de la Trémoille, the captain designated to the area.[75]

But the French invasion also opened up rifts in both the family and the region. The three legitimate Rusca heirs (Counts Eleuterio, Galeazzo, and Franchino) found themselves at odds with their bastard brother, Ercole; during the chaos of the French arrival, Ercole transferred the contents of their Locarno castle to Milan and tried to usurp his brothers by extracting an oath of loyalty from the Locarnese.[76] He continued to rile dissidents against his siblings in the early months of 1500. Meanwhile, Eleuterio pursued strategies to recover Bellinzona from the Swiss. He wrote to his brother Galeazzo in early summer 1500 with a plan. If he could convince the residents of Bellinzona to transfer their allegiance to France, then the Rusca brothers would be able to recover some of their duty-income, which had all but vanished "since commerce cannot run with Bellinzona in such a state of affairs."[77] Knowing that the Swiss strictly policed access to Bellinzona, Eleuterio selected an adherent who could enter the city unsuspected; he "charged him to converse with the men of this land to convert them to the French king."[78] This agent was even studying German in order to make deeper inroads.

Failing that, Eleuterio proposed a diplomatic scam. He suggested "to have a letter in German composed in the name of Bernardino [Morosini, a local notable and negotiator] and the men of the canton Uri with his seal, so that it appears to be addressed to La Trémoille."[79] The letter would outline a peaceful Swiss rendition of Bellinzona to France with Eleuterio and other collaborators as the brokers of the transition. He could then brandish the forged letter to the Swiss: "To make them believe it more, I can have them see the writing in this letter, but not letting it out of my hands so they cannot show it to others, so the affair would not be revealed."[80] This plan seems not to have come to pass, perhaps because rising tensions culminated in a series of Swiss sieges on a number of French-held towns in the spring of 1503. In the subsequent period of détente, Louis XII's agents at Locarno agreed peaceably in 1505 to suspend duties demanded from Bellinzona merchants trafficking there.[81] But by the next year, the French crown complained that duty collectors at Locarno were being "defrauded" by Swiss merchants (probably from locations other than Bellinzona, which now enjoyed exemption), and so the royal chamber nominated a comptroller to oversee the appropriate assessment of duties.[82]

With the end of Louis XII's domination, French troops began to cede the alpine cities to the Swiss. In the summer of 1512, French-held Locarno, Lugano, and Domodossola surrendered to the Swiss; the cities' fortresses gave in by January. By this point, the fogginess of rights and obligations was thick: each town negotiated its own set of rendition terms with the Swiss, while also insisting upon specific preexisting concessions from both the king of France and the dukes of Milan. For its part, the community of Locarno requested exemptions from Milanese duties identical to those that Swiss merchants enjoyed in their trade with the Lombard capital. The Swiss Confederates proposed this item to the newly installed Massimiliano Sforza, who demurred on several occasions.[83]

Then there were also the Rusca counts, whose feudal title over Locarno the French king had so recently confirmed. Technically, it was no longer a Milanese city; Locarno was now Swiss.[84] This transition clearly threatened the Rusca revenues; the loss or diminution of duties had worried them since 1500. Almost immediately after the Sforza restoration, Eleuterio and Galeazzo appear to have launched a suit, stimulating Massimiliano's ducal chamber to investigate their claims in March 1513.[85] Milan's new prince appointed a commissioner to visit the counts to reach the bottom of what they earned from Locarno.[86] The commissioner wrote that the Rusca brothers had produced a list of their Locarno entitlements "in which they demand quite a few things," a copy of which list (now lost) the agent sent to the duke. As proof of their holdings, the brothers produced an agreement—"which is not an original (*quale non è autenticha*)," the commissioner noted—supposedly dating from their father's time and appearing to oblige the Locarnese to certain payments and duties to the counts in exchange for civic rights to the wine retail tax.

The dry details of the tax claims were precisely the feature that raised the commissioner's suspicions over the veracity of the Rusca suit. His doubt over the copied wine tax document had already flagged the possibility of false doubles. He then noted that the counts produced "six witnesses to verify that they earned many other things from the said places. But because one of the witnesses is a cousin, another is [the count's] chancellor [. . .] and some others are their adherents and servants, I thought—to exonerate my conscience and for the sake of truth—to refer what these witnesses say, so that your Excellency can make whatever provision seems appropriate." The witnesses told of the appointment of a comptroller: that claim, at least, seems to be accurate, given the 1506 agreement between the Swiss and Louis XII. But Massimiliano's commissioner had further concerns. More than just seeing the Rusca witnesses as cronies, he doubted the stated value of the family's lost tax income, noting that "it seems a large sum to me in such a country [as Locarno]" and opined that the figures "neither appear nor are proved to be legitimate." To settle his doubts, the duke's agent asked to see their account books, and "Count Galeazzo answered that they did not have them." The agent referred the entire matter back to Massimiliano,

> because the witnesses and documents are of the sort and nature that I described above, and because many times I asked the counts to produce their books of duties and incomes so that it could be calculated how much they earned, each year checked against the next, and so that the fees of officials and other things like restitutions for wars and plagues, and defaulters (*mal paghe*) could be subtracted and we could come to the net figure. But up to the present, they have not wanted to do it."[87]

Lacking further traces of this inquest, we are left with a few possible interpretations. Perhaps in the feud with the troublesome Ercole—in which goods were sacked and dispersed—or in other wartime dislocations, the family's account books went missing. Alternatively, we can see the Rusca clan as consummate fraudsters. Consider Eleuterio's earlier scheme to falsify Bellinzona's submission charter, not to mention another even more intricate deception happening contemporaneously with the tax claim inquest. Around 1514, Eleuterio's wife, the Countess

Eleonora, claimed she had at last given birth to a male heir. A subsequent trial in fact revealed that the Countess Rusca, in concert with her husband, had feigned the pregnancy and instead adopted a child named Girolamo specifically to usurp the inheritance of Eleuterio's nephew.[88] Such tactics suggest it is far from impossible that the Rusca brothers inflated, misstated, or falsified the financial claims they made upon the new Milanese prince. They had, after all, been French partisans; their knowledge of events in the duchy over the past decade far outstripped the duke's. He relied instead upon the document trail that his officers could trace. Further, it is also conceivable that Massimiliano's chamber was not in a position to check any of its own records (specifically any French agreements drawn up with feudatories since 1500), and so the onus fell upon the plaintiffs to present a reasonable case to a prince who had ruled for only a few months. The Rusca suit did not meet that bar. And yet, the suspicions of the ducal agent appear not to have bothered Massimiliano himself: the prince accorded the counts new tax duties in the city of Milan as recompense for the loss of Locarno, and Eleuterio became a (Sforza-appointed) senator in 1515 and a (French-appointed) decurion in 1518.[89] Goodwill of these feudal elites may have been worth the price.

It was not just Massimiliano's government that inherited an atomized archive. Conflicts across the region caused documentary losses and confusions; frauds followed in their wake. We find them in all the regimes of Milan's early sixteenth century. Absent the fastidious bookkeeping of a stable government, a certain bulwark against injustices— even unwitting ones—slipped away. In 1512, when Louis XII's rule began to falter after the French defeat at Ravenna, his government issued an edict against its own grain commissioners, warning citizens that the officials were criminally extorting money for their own private gain.[90] Just a few years later, Massimiliano's deputies charged with liquidating rebels' goods embezzled funds they were meant to deposit in the coffers of the ducal chamber.[91] Officers responsible for upholding the clarity of fiscal accounts instead confounded them.

Beyond bearing the weight of extraordinary war levies, the duchy's subjects resented, as we have seen, the evaporation of privileges granted under former rulers. Several petitions and lawsuits, for instance, concerned the problem of tax doubling. Citizens and feudatories lamented that authorities, lacking knowledge of their appropriate tax bracket, were asking them to pay levies twice.[92] King François's 1515 duchy-wide request for a subsidy entailed years of subsequent recriminations claiming that the regime's demands were built upon misunderstandings. In 1519, the king enjoined a Milanese commission to investigate the allegations "that some are excessively taxed; others separated from obligations; some others exempted who have never paid any burden; others who are not obligated to pay except in their city of residence; and others who are not used to being taxed."[93] In order to thin out the "many pending undecided legal cases," the king's council encouraged the commission to pay a visit to the secretary who supposedly managed "all the books, files, accounts, and writings" documenting current and past tax matters.[94] Only by matching the litigants' claims with archived accounts could some form of settlement be reached. The monarch then challenged the commission to adjudicate appropriate solutions to tax confusions. His agents threatened the duchy's city councils to send their accounts to Milan for vetting; Pavia claimed that it had already paid the levy; that avowal clashed with "the rolls sent from France," which still listed the city as a debtor.[95] Distances—of geography, accounting methods, and cultural understanding—between the French center of authority and the duchy's subject cities prolonged and exacerbated these disputes.

Similar stories of fraud and disorderly documents also emerged from religious communities. In 1512, the abbey of Classe in Ravenna listed all its goods looted by French troops in the sack following the major battle just outside the city: silk hangings, illuminated missals, metalwork, furnishings, food supplies. After enumerating all the items and their value (over 3,000 ducats) the scribe wrote in a note at the foot of the page that although he had compiled the detailed catalog of damages, "hardly a thing is true, since we in fact had little damage," but the abbey along with three other rich congregations had been required to pay 2,000 ducats for the damages done to the city's parish churches, and thus presumably wanted fraudulently to recoup some of those expenses.[96]

During the same year, a series of clashes erupted between the Cistercian communities at the wealthy Lombard abbey of Chiaravalle and at the Milanese monastery of Sant'Ambrogio. The dissention arose in part as a corollary of the French-sponsored church council to depose Pope Julius II, some of whose leading figures stayed at the abbey.

(Chapter 8 treats the wider fallout of this council.) This conflict disrupted Chiaravalle enough that valuables went missing; an edict from Massimiliano's government in 1514 required anyone "who might have goods or writings" taken from Chiaravalle to reveal themselves to two papal deputies within a week.[97] Later that year, the Sforza duke sent a commission to the abbey to compose an inventory of its goods "so that it might be possible to have the full and true information on the revenues of the abbey's possessions."[98] But given years of disruptions (the wars frequently required the monks to pay and house soldiers; the complex would later be sacked in 1528), the abbey itself had difficulty keeping records. At three different occasions in Chiaravalle's account book, its scrivener noted the ledger's total disorder, complaining ultimately in the 1530s that "aside from not being properly balanced, [this book] suffers what the four before it suffered as well: it is lacking a quire, from folio 92 to folio 109."[99] Given the frequent cash exactions that rulers demanded from religious foundations for military support, this kind of fragmentary account book, opaque to ducal commissions of inquiry, may even have helped to protect Chiaravalle's finances. Bad registers protected as much as they revealed.

In a wartime environment of heightened contestation over lands and goods, practices of veiling assets or transactions could be particularly active. Consequently, regular legal channels for the restitution of goods or money brought illusions and delusions. In 1499, Ludovico Sforza escaped Milan owing (among other things) over 70,000 ducats in salt payments to Venice.[100] One of his most faithful finance officers, Ambrogio da Corte, had overseen the debt and acted as its surety. When Milan fell, Ambrogio fled alongside Ludovico's mistress, Lucrezia Crivelli, before landing in snares at Lecco; he was reportedly carrying 150,000 ducats.[101] Once Ambrogio returned to Milan in French custody, Venice began to petition for its salt repayments; the republic's agents entreated the French not to liquidate his goods before the funds could be reimbursed.[102] Venice's debt was substantial, but amounted only to about a tenth of Ludovico's overall obligations.[103] However, Ambrogio—who owed money to Alfonso d'Este as well—died in 1501, and his son Girolamo absorbed his accounts.[104] The matter seemed lost. In 1503, the Venetian agent wrote that the affair "cannot be expedited" and that the French counselor in Milan charged to investigate, Claude de Seyssel, had left the

city.[105] In 1506, Venice's ambassador investigated again, only to find further complexities. He reported that a collaborator had gone to check
"the booklet (*el quaderneto*)"—presumably the auction catalogs—to see if
da Corte had alienated any goods. So far, he had found nothing, but a
sly Milanese auction habit made it difficult to tell for sure:

> The orders of Milan are such that, whoever does not know
> particularly where the goods are, or their extent, cannot see
> the reality at the auctions. [This is] because someone like Gi-
> rolamo da Corte, who wants to sell his goods and hesitates
> to put them at auction, does not have them publicized in his
> own name. [Instead] the buyer goes to a certain magistrate
> and declares his desire to sell his own goods, but gives details
> of what he has bought, and under the guise of selling them,
> the publicity is made. And by that means they free themselves
> and dupe others.[106]

It was possible, in other words, for Girolamo da Corte to game Milan's
auction market and hide the fact that he had already liquidated assets
that could have repaid his father's debt to Venice. This form of fraudulent misregistration for public auctions circumvented their system of
checks and balances: the purpose of declaring the intention to sell and
making that intention public was to allow any counterclaimants upon
the goods (in this case, the *signoria* of Venice) to present themselves and
contest the sale. With that system circumvented, sales could thus happen
far from the scrutiny of interested parties, an obscurity particularly deep
for the vast majority of claimants who lacked the web of agents available to Venice's *signoria*. The occlusion of auction transactions was a long-
standing form of black-market trading.[107] So, my contention is not that
this particular habit is new to the Italian Wars. Tensions in these mar-
kets did, however, tend to peak in moments of civic and military strife.
The salt debt case instead suggests how fraud found energy and license
in a system troubled by war: rotating authorities and mislaid documents
only accentuated confusions produced by malfeasance. If the *signoria* of
Venice could not have a Milanese debt repaid, then other seekers of lesser
stature sailed even stormier waters. An efficient form of erasure, Milan's
auction fraud racket disguised capital transfers and the movement of
valuable goods under a placid veil of normalcy.

Erasure mattered because the absence of clear evidence troubled the workings of a delicate state with serially crumbling regimes. When histories of financial obligations or of patrimonies proved difficult to document, conflict between litigants spooled forward, perennially postponing its own resolution. When the next regime arrived, it rarely had the knowledge to act. If it did, it often tried to cut the thread of discord by serving mere political expediency or financial necessity. Whether it was subjects or rulers who lacked the materials to prove their assertions, the results were similar in that justice became a receding horizon. Many of these suits appeared before Milan's senate for adjudication. As we can gather from the faint echoes of its activities in these years, the senate worked actively to settle such problems, but it often stalled for lack of appropriate substantiating material. How could it resolve a tax contestation without access to precedent? All of Milan's regimes in the early sixteenth century mobilized cadres of deputies, commissions, clerks, and other bureaucrats to help answer these questions and to find "the full and true information" of cases: they left hundreds of letters describing their efforts to fulfil their mandate. Some of these efforts even became commissions of inquiry. In 1509, Louis XII initiated a major Parisian inquest into reports of "abuses, selling of justice, theft, extortion, injustices, and oppression" committed by "feudatories, governors, podestàs, vicars, captains, judges, commissioners, and other officials [. . .] under the cover of their office" in the French-administered Genoese Riviera di Levante.[108] War did not permit complete unaccountability: rather, rulers and subjects habitually compiled writings to obviate it. Nor did it completely disrupt or empty the archive. Some ledgers survived the transitions of governments, registering the daily ebb and flow of Milanese life over the course of several regimes.[109]

But war—and the princely governments that produced it—also opened the door to scriptural obscurity. Despite the remarkable efforts on the part of Milan's regimes to gather information about the state, the shatterzone was rarely governable according to familiar means of documentary accountability. War (and the attendant inflammation of internal conflicts that it licensed) created an environment eminently conducive to misunderstanding, miscommunication, or malfeasance. It also facilitated the destruction or dispersal of writings that carried legal or social force. This vacuum invited the void to be filled. Absence of paperwork offered opportunities for ambitious new claims, but it also smudged the contours of possible action. Work slowed down; or it carried forward uninformed. Without the clarity provided by a functional archive, individuals (as bearers of trust and memory) stepped in to speak in lieu of documents. Yet under the pressures of a crippled state, they too were often transitory. Many of the problems that this chapter has detailed—fraud, interminable legal trials, quarrels over taxes—frequently characterized the dialogues between rulers and subjects in premodern Italy. They were endemic features of city life across this period. But we must not overlook the specific friction that regime change introduced to statist knowledge-production. State knowledge in moments like these became merely an echo of itself. Only through writing did the architecture of sixteenth-century sovereignty find its most durable supports; it was far more delicate than we have realized.

Part III

People

7

Elite Displacements

$\mathcal{B}$etween 1499 and 1500, the Sforza court disintegrated; aulic elites and urban patricians dispersed in every direction. French agents believed that a majority of Sforza partisans fled from Milan to Liguria (the "hills around Genoa"), but many of the most illustrious fugitives imagined three optimal destinations: the Holy Roman Empire's German-speaking lands, Venice, and Mantua. Such were the options Ascanio Sforza considered in April 1500, when a loyal captain suggested either remaining in Milan, "and this on the condition that one might fall into the French king's hands," or fleeing to Germany, "very dangerous, since it means passing through the lands of the Swiss who seized Ludovico" or "go[ing] toward Mantua." If he were caught it would be by Venetians, "and this will be the least evil that I could have," Ascanio figured, even though Venice had allied with the French king.[1] As we have already seen, Ascanio along with five other ecclesiastics surrendered themselves to Venice before Louis XII demanded Ascanio's extradition to France.[2] "*Deus dedit, Deus abstulit,*" Ascanio reportedly sighed, Job-like, upon falling into enemy hands.[3]

During the summer of 1500, as French captains subdued the duchy after Ludovico Sforza's failed restoration, royal officers drew up a catalogue of fugitive rebels, listing men from both the capital and its subject towns.[4] Thorough enough to make one marvel at the reach of French intelligence networks, it collected over two hundred names and each man's supposed location and assets. (One chronicler figured the number of elite refugees to be around 2,000; a French inquisition in the autumn of 1500 named forty-three men as the chief conspirators.[5]) The list's purpose served in part to organize the redistribution of their goods to the king's men, but it probably also helped to consolidate an overview of the potential sites of resistance to French power from outside the duchy. Here is where we learn that many fled to Liguria: Milan's lordship over Genoa allowed easy passage and close ties between the two cities. The catalogue also confirms Ascanio's best options: most of the prominent exiles fled to German lands, Venice, and Mantua (Fig. 7.1).[6]

This chapter maps the Sforza diaspora, focusing particularly on the first and most explosive period that followed in the wake of the initial French conquest and abortive Sforza restoration. Communities of exiles (called variously *fuorusciti, banniti, banditi,* or *ribelli*[7]) slowly agglomerated in new surroundings as they found refuge and began to organize themselves on several overlapping levels: military, legal, financial, social. As much as this chapter reconstructs the nodes that bound excluded partisans together, it also traces the atomization of Milan's elite society. When these wealthy and influential classes retreated to feudal lands to mount opposition or fled the duchy altogether (sometimes never to return), Lombardy's central and regional power structures felt the consequences. The dispersal triggered a gradual redefinition of what it meant to belong to the Milanese duchy's highest social echelons. It entailed a deracination of elite politics as hundreds of families sought to join new power constellations outside the state they knew best. For instance, in 1501, royal orders sent many leading Milanese gentlemen to France, "to remove all the ring-leaders" of factions and pacify the city—a forced evacuation that the "Milanese cannot suffer."[8] This process of flight and removal differed somewhat from what we might call the "normal" exile experience of Italy's fifteenth century, because the end of each regime was coterminous with the moment of exile.[9] Lacking a pardon, one could not return home without facing the hostile powers that had fundamentally

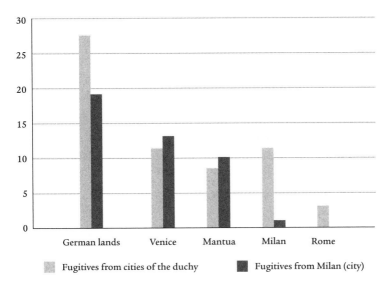

Fig. 7.1 Major destinations of elite Sforzesco refugees from Milan (both the metropole and other cities of the duchy), as registered in the *rotulus* compiled by French agents in 1500. Not shown are (a) several fugitives whose location was unknown, but were suspected to have escaped to Genoa, Monferrato, or Piedmont, and (b) very small numbers of others who fled Milan for smaller cities within the duchy.

transformed the state. The long-term antagonisms and the opportunities built into this phenomenon occupy the closing pages of the chapter. But I devote most of it to explaining what each destination promised for Lombard refugees around 1500.

German Lands: The "Children of Israel"

Tyrol and Bavaria offered security for the highest rank of Sforza refugees. Bianca Maria Sforza had been queen of the Romans for six years at the time of her uncle Ludovico's capture.[10] In the last weeks of his rule in the late summer of 1499, Ludovico grew increasingly panicked as he sent letter after letter across the Alps to secure military help from Bianca Maria's husband, King Maximilian I. (He would not officially become emperor until February 1508.) Maximilian, embroiled in the final stages of the Swabian War between the southern German cities and the Swiss cantons, was so preoccupied that news of Milan's capitulation to France shook him. Refusing food, he took counsel late into the night and slept little, realizing that one of the most prized imperial fiefs in Italy had slipped from his hands.[11] Ludovico Sforza's moneyed clientage had made the Sforza among Maximilian's central politico-financial alliances.[12] Over the next few months, the Innsbruck court became the most redoubtable refuge for the highest circle of Sforza partisans thanks to their affiliation with the queen. As king of the Romans, moreover, Maximilian wielded unique political heft in shielding these fugitives; the imperially affiliated ideology of the Lombard Ghibellines made his support even more attractive. Even before he fled Milan, Ludovico had sent his two sons—and loads of the city's treasure, rumor had it—across the Alps.[13] Escaping up the east flank of Lake Como and bribing his way out of potentially lethal delays with pursuers on his trail, il Moro reached safety when he encountered an imperial escort at Morbegno.[14] Father and sons eventually reunited at Brixen, and the duke continued to Innsbruck to find Maximilian.[15]

While Maximilian's court was even more peripatetic than those of his contemporaries, he embellished Innsbruck in the hopes of endowing it with some imperial grandeur.[16] It housed—on a more permanent basis than his own—his wife's court, and thus proved an obvious destination for Sforza fugitives. Ludovico's flight to Innsbruck in 1499 foreshadowed problems for the exiles who followed him in the coming months: How could imperial lands—or Maximilian himself—afford to support Milan's exiles? Those costs they faced were both political and financial. The burghers of Trent, for instance, resisted requests to house the Sforza family "and part of its court" since it made Trent a target for siege or war.[17] News flowing back to Venice mentioned frequently that Maximilian lacked funds to undertake an Italian campaign—he had cited impecuniousness in his correspondence with Ludovico as a reason not to lend troops to defend Milan; now he fretted over the expenses he knew would issue from its fall. When Ludovico's children arrived in his care, he confiscated over 60,000 ducats' worth of their money and jewels, but also promised them stipends and pledged to support other refugees who began to accumulate in imperial lands.[18]

These exiles unavoidably burdened the king of the Romans' finances. In September 1500 he ordered the queen's majordomo to force all Italians, men and women, to vacate her retinue.[19] His order seems to have had little effect. A year later, Maximilian noted that about forty members of the Sforza family had alighted in Innsbruck, including Ermes,

the queen's brother.[20] Other prominent Sforza partisans also crossed the
Alps: Bianca Maria's half-brothers Galeazzo, Count of Melzo and Otta-
viano, bishop of Lodi (both sons of Duke Galeazzo Maria's mistress,
Lucia Marliani); il Moro's unmarried brothers; his mistress, Lucrezia
Crivelli; the courtiers and captains Galeazzo, Antonio Maria, and Fra-
casso Sanseverino; and Gerolamo Landriani, general of the Umiliati.[21]
These were just a few of the most prominent fugitives. The burden of
Italian hangers-on grew swiftly in Innsbruck. As part of a larger financial plan in 1501, Maximilian contracted the Augsburg financier Jörg
Gossembrot to draw up a budget.[22] It fixed Bianca Maria's allowance and
required her to dismiss a number of household servants including her
Italian chaplains, apothecary, tailor, and her dwarf, Elisa.[23] In total, the
group of exiles Maximilian had to subvent in 1501, perhaps including
other notables and attendants, numbered 180 people.[24] This group came
to be known by the evocative handle "Children of Israel," which drew on
the book of Exodus to describe the beleaguered and impoverished members of the Milanese diaspora.[25]

The ducal children remained in Tyrol during il Moro's restoration.
After his capture and imprisonment, Massimiliano (aged six) and Francesco (aged four) became Maximilian's wards, and they remained in
Habsburg care until the Sforza restoration of 1513. After a brief period
at the court in Innsbruck, Maximilian appointed them a tutor and
housed them at the castle of Steyr with their retinue of twenty-one followers. That entourage—like the larger one at court—grew steadily over
the next couple years. When the boys visited Linz in winter 1501 to attend a play by Conrad Celtis (the newly composed comedy, *Ludus Diane*)
and to reunite with their cousin Bianca Maria, forty-one people accompanied them; by January 1502 there were forty-five.[26] By March of that
year, Maximilian asked the antiquarian scholar Konrad Peutinger (living
in Regensburg, where the Sforza brothers also stayed) to announce the
king's concern that the boys were not living at a standard befitting their
station because of their servants' wasteful habits.[27] Peutinger was to investigate and return their affairs to order.[28] Complaints like these echoed
the recriminations Maximilian and his courtiers had already aimed at
the Sforza queen.

The growth of the youngsters' retinue may have inspired the official
diminution of their stipend: the king reduced their allowance in

June 1504, by which time more than 200 "mouths" surrounded the boys. Maximilian also feared that such expenses diverted funds that he needed to prepare for war.[29] After 1507, the brothers separated as they began to pursue the education appropriate to young princes. Massimiliano traveled north to Brussels and Antwerp to attend the court of Maximilian's daughter Margaret of Austria, regent of the Netherlands.[30] Francesco, for his part, enrolled in law at the Rudolfina in Vienna in 1510.[31] Even though Maximilian would officially invest Louis XII with the Duchy of Milan in 1505—thus robbing the Sforza of the imperial recognition that il Moro had purchased in 1495—the Sforza children were valuable to the king of the Romans not merely as members of his wife's family but as tools to regain imperial control over the Lombard fief. For that reason, Maximilian extended his care especially to his young Sforza namesake Massimiliano, who figured in the emperor's illustrated biography *Weißkunig* (*White King*, 1505–1516) as the *"jungen kunig vom wurm"* (young snake king), a byname that invoked the serpent emblem of the Milanese *biscione* (Fig. 7.2).[32]

Adults of the Sforza clan also sheltered under Maximilian's wing, generally for shorter periods than the ducal children. (Prepare yourself for a welter of Galeazzos.) The queen's brother Ermes and her half-brother Galeazzo both settled in Innsbruck; Maximilian ensured that his tailor provided them with suitable court garb.[33] Both of these Sforza scions served Maximilian in Italian affairs, repaying in fealty what the king had paid in maintaining them. Ermes traveled under the imperial aegis to Florence in early 1502, and for a short while he hoped to govern the turbulent republic for the French king, or at least to captain its militia.[34] But the French disease cut short Ermes' political career, and he died in Innsbruck in 1503.[35] Galeazzo, Count of Melzo, served with greater success over the course of nearly a decade. In late summer 1500, French authorities captured and interrogated him in Milan, where he had been in hiding, probably stirring up Sforza partisans: "It is said there is a whole bunch of plotters," one source reported upon his arrest.[36] Melzo later served as Maximilian's Ottoman envoy before dying of plague during an imperial expedition against the Venetians in 1511.[37]

Many Sforza intimates followed a similar pattern of loyalty. Fracasso Sanseverino, who once served as a Sforza envoy to Maximilian in 1498, fell out with Ludovico and came under the Roman king's protection; he

Fig. 7.2 Woodcut from *Kaiser Maximilians I. Weißkunig*—"Wie der kunig von worm gefangen ward und in der gefangnuß stirbt und sein kinder zway werden dem w. k. presentiert" (How the Snake King was imprisoned and died in prison and his two children were presented to the White King). Massimiliano and Francesco Sforza presented at the court of King Maximilian I Hapsburg. Österreichische Nationalbibliothek, Vienna, Cod. 3033, f. 130ᵛ.

© Österreichische Nationalbibliothek.

acted as Habsburg emissary to Pisa in 1502.[38] Maximilian owned at least two pieces of Fracasso's armor, including his jousting equipment, now in Vienna, forged in the Missaglia workshop and emblazoned in gold with SIGNORE FRACHASSO.[39] (Maximilian esteemed Sanseverino family armor. After the 1487 battle-drowning of Fracasso's father, Roberto, Maximilian paid for his marble tomb in Trent and brought his armor to Innsbruck in 1493.[40]) Many Sforza partisans who did not belong to these princely or military ranks but who soon realized that repatriation was unlikely in the near future settled in German lands for the entirety of Louis XII's reign. Some returned to Milan early under royal grace, but others remained abroad much longer; such at least suggests a 1512 request for safe-passage for Barbara Stampa, a Milanese noblewoman who had spent thirteen years in imperial lands and planned to return home through Cremona.[41]

The exiles of 1499–1500 fled Milan in haste, with little time to set their affairs in order. Galeazzo Visconti (1460–1530), one of Ludovico Sforza's earliest backers in the 1480s and a leading Milanese Ghibelline, was already in Switzerland on missions for il Moro when the French invaded.[42] Louis XII granted him a safe-conduct to return to Milan in May 1500, where he hoped to tell the monarch "the secrets of il Moro," but the king refused to see him.[43] While Visconti was on the lam, his assets were managed by Pietro Carcano, a priest and book-illuminator whom Visconti called "my chaplain and chancellor."[44] Carcano acted in Visconti's stead when French authorities requested an accounting of Visconti's holdings. The magnate's political allegiance revolved over the decades: he "made himself French" and joined the senate in 1505 even while seeming to rally Ghibelline sentiment against being "eaten or devoured" by foreign lordship.[45] He then fought hard on behalf of Massimiliano Sforza, but took refuge in Paris after François I pardoned him.[46] He threw lavish banquets for the kings in Milan (1507) and Paris (1518).[47] Galeazzo's daughter, Clara Pusterla, became a favorite dinner companion of the young François.[48] Visconti soared at particularly lofty altitudes: in 1515, he asked Emperor Maximilian to create him Duke of Milan out of respect for his Sforza-Visconti blood.[49] Few other refugees were fortunate enough to have the kind of asset management or grand self-possession that permitted Visconti to weave between regimes. Even with his good fortune, Galeazzo's Milanese palace was demolished as punishment for his involvement in an anti-French plot in 1516.[50] Because the French stripped many absent elites of their goods, a vast number of fugitives had to seek out largesse and loans, which pushed them to cultivate their connections north of the Alps. (In later years, Isabella d'Este congratulated a Milanese acquaintance of long standing for being "*cossi ricco forauscito*," suggesting the rare union of wealth and exile.[51])

Galeazzo Sanseverino, il Moro's son-in-law, joined this transalpine group of seekers. He played a leading part in the abortive restoration attempt of 1500 and thus figured among the most culpable in the
rebellion against the French; the same Swiss troops who captured il
Moro took Sanseverino alongside him.[52] In June of that year, he entered Pavia in French custody wearing black, "with a long beard and his
face all gaunt with a slightly swollen cheek," and when greeted by ambassadors, he "shrugged with a half-smile."[53] Ransomed by his brothers,
Galeazzo reached German-speaking lands via Mantua; Maximilian
wrote to congratulate him on his freedom and invited him to serve the
Empire as a captain.[54] Galeazzo appeared in Innsbruck by September 1501,
joining the "many Milanese" congregating there to urge Maximilian to
reclaim Milan for the Sforza.[55] While in German lands, Sanseverino
also rekindled a friendship. In a letter to the Nuremberg scholar
Wilibald Pirckheimer, an acquaintance from days of study at Pavia, he
revealed that he owed some debts now that he was a wanderer. Sanseverino wrote from Innsbruck that Maximilian's promised stipend still
had not arrived, but he nonetheless managed (albeit "with great difficulty") to gather 2,000 florins to repay some Nuremberg creditors. He
sent the money by way of Fugger envoys and asked Pirckheimer himself
to pay the debt using these funds. Galeazzo also owed money to
Wilibald himself but delayed sending it, invoking "the fraternal love between us" and promising to refund him in person, since Sanseverino
expected to be in Nuremberg within a short while.[56] And so he was.
Pirckheimer hosted Sanseverino for some time in 1502: the Milanese
guest even summoned his energies to join Nuremberg's Forest Battle
(known as the Schlacht im Walde, 1502) against the Margrave of
Brandenburg. In a chaotic scene of the melée painted by a local artist,
Galeazzo appears at Pirckheimer's side clothed all in black, astride a
dark steed (Fig. 7.3).[57]

The Milanese diaspora activated not only credit networks, but cultural ones as well. During this Nuremberg reunion, Galeazzo perhaps
not only received the book of sports ("*el libro del gioco de arme et bracie*")
he mentioned in one of his letters to Pirckheimer; he may also have shared
his own treasures: tales of and perhaps drawings by Leonardo da Vinci,
whom Sanseverino had probably hosted in Milan. Pirckheimer himself
knew an artistic luminary: Albrecht Dürer. The two Germans had

Fig. 7.3 Anonymous Artist, *Die Schlacht im Walde,* 1502, showing Wilibald Pirckheimer (left) and Galeazzo Sanseverino (right). Germanisches Museum, Nuremberg. Inv. Gm 579.

Photo by author.

recently traveled to Italy together. Sanseverino's visit to Nuremberg thus provided the only link between Dürer and Leonardo.[58] One of Leonardo's students, the Milanese artist Ambrogio Preda, sustained a close relationship with the Innsbruck court both before and after il Moro's ouster. He had painted Bianca Maria's betrothal portrait in 1494 and Maximilian sat for him in 1502; the queen gave him a gift of some clothes in May 1504.[59] He seems to have shuttled between Milan and Innsbruck for over a decade.[60] Despite the Austrians' disdain for the costs incurred by the displaced Milanese court, the traffic in Lombard artistic expertise was itself a commodity with significant prestige for the imperially ambitious dynasty in Tyrol. It sought to extend and absorb the networks of luxury production as the Sforza court dimmed.

From as early as October 1501, the French and German kings were undertaking secret negotiations for peace.[61] French emissaries visited Maximilian's court the following year to discuss the fate of the Milanese diaspora. While the king of the Romans wanted Ludovico and Ascanio freed from captivity and pensioned, the French objected. Even though Maximilian warned that the Milanese exiles would never countenance peace if they remained excluded from their homeland, French reasoning insisted that their rebellion justified punishment and that their antipathy for France had only grown in the intervening time. Maximilian predicated Louis's imperial investiture with Milan upon the reintegration of the exiles, not least because he was now sustaining their costs. Louis wanted to keep part of the confiscated goods for the ducal chamber even if the rebels were to return.[62]

In 1505, Louis and Maximilian reached an agreement in the Alsatian city of Haguenau; Francesco Capello, Venice's orator to the imperial court, conversed with several Milanese *fuorusciti* in Cologne during that summer, suggesting that the peace negotiations had drawn the exiles together in order to exert political pressure during the conference.[63] The Haguenau meeting confirmed Louis XII as duke of Milan, annulling—at least for the time being—the privilege for which the house of Sforza had paid so much.[64] However, some compensation for Sforza backers accompanied this reversal. The peace delegates, perhaps aware that the exiles would only continue to threaten Milan's stability from their perch across the Alps, named thirty-two Milanese men to whom the French monarch offered amnesty. Almost all of them (twenty-eight of the thirty-two) had appeared in the French rebel catalogue of 1500; many were considered intimates of il Moro or instigators ("*principaulx aucteurs*") of the pro-Sforza uprising.[65] This royal gesture of reconciliation had been several years in the making; from as early as 1500, the king had reportedly authorized the return of a trickle of fugitives whom he considered well-behaved.[66]

Whether in fact these exiles took advantage of their right of return remains unclear, as Gerolamo Landriani's case demonstrates. Landriani, general of the Umiliati, had been, according to the French catalogue of rebels *"le chief et le tout de la rebellion"* in 1500.[67] One might not have expected his pardon in 1505, but the Haguenau treaty included his name. After fleeing Milan in 1499 he served the king of the Romans as a vigorous Sforza advocate: he strove in 1501 to have the Venetian orator expelled from Maximilian's court as a spy and a French partisan.[68] After 1505, he led a series of missions to Venice on behalf of the Empire, and he returned finally to Milan in 1512 as envoy of the Holy League against France.[69] Was that visit Landriani's first to home soil in over a decade? If so, repatriation for Sforza intimates may have been easier in principle than in fact. As we have already seen, in 1500 Louis XII had transferred their confiscated goods, especially lands, to his own men.[70]

Because the king had redistributed these assets, exiles' reintegration was often a piecemeal affair. Galeazzo Sanseverino, for instance, received initial support from Maximilian, who negotiated in 1502 with French envoys for the restitution of Galeazzo's goods.[71] But, as we saw in Chapter 5, Sanseverino found greater promise in France's patronage than in the Empire's, since he assumed a post as royal counselor and *écuyer du roy* in 1505. The territories Louis XII bestowed upon him 1506 (at Cusago, in Milan's suburbs) were not the same as those he had left, and were to revert to the crown upon Galeazzo's death.[72] The uprooting of the Sforza partisans in 1499—even when they reconciled with the invaders, as in Sanseverino's case—fractured the patrimonies of a number of prominent families. Even those who stayed in Milan and vowed allegiance to Louis XII petitioned to have their feudal lands confirmed.[73] For the Children of Israel who returned to Milan, the prospects of finding their estates as they had left them were dim.

By the time of Bianca Maria Sforza's death in 1510, Innsbruck no longer exerted the magnetic pull for Milanese exiles that it had over a decade earlier.[74] With the eclipse of the Sforza title to the duchy and many of the key figures of il Moro's era deceased (not just Bianca Maria, but Ludovico and Ascanio), Maximilian was refashioning the political and dynastic ties that had bound Milan to the Empire. Imperial support also explains why Francesco II Sforza and some fellow Milanese exiles rode out parts the second French domination in Tyrol, under the protection of Cardinal Bernardo Cles in Trent.[75] After the death of Maximilian I in 1519, the imperial court vacated Austria to follow Charles V, while his brother Ferdinand I governed Tyrol. The geographic realignment of the Sforza and the relocation of imperial circles to Brussels and Spain meant that Austrian Tyrol waned as a center for Milanese refugees.

Mantua: "Only Mantua Favors Them"

By the time of France's conquest of Milan, Mantua's Marquis Francesco II Gonzaga struggled to discern friends from enemies. Following the first war against France, which culminated in the Battle of Fornovo (1495), he had earned Venetian support until 1497, when he appeared to shift allegiance to the French king.[76] As Ludovico il Moro's brother-in-law, Gonzaga sealed a mutual support agreement, albeit a tenuous one, with Milan just before the French invasion.[77] Once Louis's government established itself in Milan in 1499, Francesco was in the delicate position of maintaining cordial relations with three different political entities: Maximilian I (Mantua was an imperial fief), the growing community of Sforza fugitives in Mantua, and the new French administration in Milan. Francesco assisted at Louis XII's triumphal entry into Pavia in October 1499, and the French king showed his gratitude with a military contract for the marquis.[78] Still, Gonzaga supported Ludovico Sforza's restoration. This balancing act between the major powers became nearly untenable in the wake Ludovico's capture. In April 1500, Gonzaga wrote to Maximilian that he felt himself to be in danger and requested assurances of his support. In the foregoing years, Maximilian had already threatened Mantua's ruler with the revocation of his fief should he devote himself to another power (namely the Venetians).[79] Francesco meanwhile tried to assuage King Louis with an apology worth 50,000 ducats. Despite such gestures of conciliation, the French crown seemed determined in the months following Ludovico's capture to dispossess the Gonzaga lord, or to threaten divestiture as a way to bring him to heel.[80] In the summer of 1501, Maximilian penned a secret set of seventeen articles on the dangers of French machinations in Italy, and he fretted over the wavering imperial allegiances of Ferrara and especially Mantua, whose prince was being "drawn toward him [Louis XII, who was] hoping and desiring to take his lands for himself and to use them according to his will."[81]

Milanese exiles thus posed a problem for the Marquis of Mantua. Bonds between the Gonzaga and Sforza courts had tightened through the 1490s with the sisters Isabella and Beatrice d'Este as marchioness and duchess in these nearby courts. Accordingly, Mantua was an appealing refuge for elite fugitives from Sforza Milan after Ludovico's failed restoration. Mario Equicola, the Mantuan courtier and author, later celebrated Francesco Gonzaga for having sheltered "the greater part of [Milan's] nobles, captains, and lords" at significant expense following il Moro's fall, a sign of the marquis's liberality in times of war.[82] Yet in 1500, Mantua's openness to Sforza partisans only amplified suspicions over the marquis's allegiance. After French officials publicized their *"rotulus"* of Milanese rebels, they soon pressed the marquis over his hospitality to people whom the French saw as criminals.

Pierre de Sacierges, bishop of Luçon and president of the French senate in Milan, pursued the Sforza rebels vigorously, declaring "now is when the King will distinguish his friends from his enemies."[83] He wrote to Francesco in April 1500 urging him to deliver nine Sforza captains and partisans into French hands, fearing that they were plotting in borderlands.[84] Chief among them was Biagino Crivelli, head of Ludovico's crossbowmen, acquaintance of Leonardo da Vinci, and protagonist in one of Matteo Bandello's *novelle,* in which Biagino murders an old priest to steal his benefice. Also listed were the two Gallerani brothers, siblings of Cecilia Gallerani, il Moro's erstwhile mistress.[85] Thus began a long negotiation, lasting more than eighteen months, over the marquis's protection of Milanese dissidents. The Gonzaga envoy in Milan, Francesco Malatesta, warned in December 1500 that Luçon complained of the marquis delivering "good words but bad results" and that he was clearly harboring rebels, naming the Gallerani brothers in particular. Luçon claimed that he heard reports "that all the things that could be said against the King in secret and in public are said in Mantua." Malatesta protested Luçon's accusation and denied the charge, but ended with a further warning for his Gonzaga master: "Speaking faithfully, I remind you that the French are in possession of Italy, and to keep the state of Mantua one must agree with whoever holds Milan."[86] In a postscript, Malatesta named prominent Sforzeschi ("Messer Oldrado Lampugnani,

Cristoforo de Calabria, Count Antonio della Somaglia," all of them men of rank in Ludovico's failed restoration) and suggested to Francesco that if some fugitives asked him for a writ of safe-conduct, "have it done secretly, because these ones here [i.e., the French] have men, and they inform them of what is done there [in Mantua]: and if your Lordship puts on a good face, he might with greater ease obtain every thing."[87]

The recommendation to proceed secretly was important, because the perceived openness of Francesco's welcome to rebels was what galled the French. That he sheltered rebels *"non occulte quidem sed aperte"* threatened to qualify Gonzaga himself as a traitor.[88] Francesco recognized this logic, and he supposedly enjoined his Milanese guests "not to show themselves in public, but he implore[d] them to remain hidden." Many of them in fact temporarily fled Mantua when the French king's herald arrived to survey the city.[89] That same herald requested the immediate surrender of any Milanese rebels, since harboring them "was not the way to preserve friendship," to which the marquis replied, implausibly, that he was unaware that it displeased the king.[90] Diplomatic language in this affair pivoted upon demonstrations of love and friendship and stressed how the marquis's failure to reciprocate facilitated the "plotting and public preaching" against French interests in Italy. When the marquis's brother Sigismondo was in Milan, he wrote of how the French captain La Trémoille "with a gentle motion took me by the hand," just before a meeting with Georges d'Amboise. The French insisted upon friendship not just as a commonplace of diplomacy, but also because it formed part of their strategy to pacify the fractured Milanese duchy and its allies through acts of conciliation.[91] Those gestures balanced the aggressive search for rebels with familial and merciful imagery. Indeed, Luçon had warned Sigismondo that "there are two paths: one of justice, and the other of mercy," in encouraging the Gonzaga to consider their perilous position in regard to royal power.[92]

When Malatesta met with Luçon on 1 January 1501, the bishop again reacted to Gonzaga's equivocations with frustration. The marquis had suggested that rebels who paid a fine and received safe-conducts could be sheltered. "But all the same, they remain rebels against his royal majesty," Luçon protested. It was a point he repeated insistently. Gonzaga's argument, he continued, showed evidence that the marquis "wishes to protect the enemies of the king, because even if they have paid the fine they are still the king's enemies, and if they have a safe-conduct [. . .] it is not so that they can stay in Mantua. All of Italy refuses them, and only Mantua favors them. And if your lordship wishes to say that he is a friend of the king, he must dispel, discard, and abolish the reports that resound in everyone's ears and through all of Milan that your lordship favors the rebels to his majesty." Only by sending the rebels to the French authorities would he "exterminate the root cause of those who speak ill of your lordship, and prove that you are a friend of the king."[93]

Neither Luçon nor the king was unfamiliar with such negotiations over rebellion. Both of them had lived through the so-called *guerre folle* (1485–1488) in France following the death of Louis XI. Luçon was then a royal notary and counselor, and Louis one of the rebels against the Beaujeu regency; the future king in fact stood trial under King Charles VIII for acts of *lèse majesté*.[94] What emerged from that contest in the 1480s were the strengthened authority of the crown and the abasement of the challengers: Louis was imprisoned for three years. In 1505, the king's boon-companion in the conquest of Milan, Pierre de Rohan, marshal of Gié, himself faced trial for treason following a complex quarrel at the French court over Gié's application of his power and influence.[95] Milan's rebels and the royal policy behind their pursuit belong as much in the context of this history of French treason as they do in that of the history of Italian exile. Within that frame, aggressive French efforts to isolate and punish offenders fit into an evolving dispute over the consolidation of royal power and the nature of resistance to it. The "messer Claudio" present for Luçon's conversation with Malatesta was the Milanese senator and political theorist, Claude de Seyssel.[96] He penned a treatise on *lèse majesté*, which remains undated and still unstudied in Paris, but which we might speculatively assign to the first decade of the sixteenth century, when treason became a key discourse on both sides of the Alps.[97] Perhaps even more than Luçon, Seyssel knew the law of treason and feared its destabilizing effects, as the following section of this chapter will show.

In September 1501, the French were still naming men sheltered by the Marquis of Mantua, fearing that at least one of them was counterfeiting money.[98] But correspondence between Milan and Mantua on the question of rebels dried up through 1501 after the French declared the first broad amnesty for rebels. The slackening of French efforts may also have indicated a realignment of French priorities as Cesare Borgia's nearby military campaigns brought France and Mantua into common cause. Moreover, Luçon himself had lost his position. As we saw in Chapter 1, Georges d'Amboise removed him from office and imprisoned him in Milan's castle for fiscal misdeeds.[99] This change of affairs allowed the Gonzaga marquisate to return to a politics of appeasement in regard to both French and imperial patronage. Nonetheless, strong French oversight of passage through Mantuan territory to Venice continued for years.[100] Even before François I's army descended into Italy in 1515, his Milanese detractors began to forward their valuable goods to Mantua, Parma, and Piacenza.[101] After the French victory at Marignano that same autumn, Matteo Bandello wrote that "the city of Mantua served as the safest haven and certain refuge for the exiles of Lombardy."[102]

Venice: "The Greatest Friendship"

Having spent much of the fifteenth century in wars over Venice's expansion into the Lombard plain, the Sforza stance toward Venice—one generally shared by the Milanese citizenry—was suspicious and often hostile.[103] France, however, was cultivating Venetian support at the turn of the century. The two powers had allied against il Moro in preparation for the conquest and maintained what the bishop of Luçon called "the greatest friendship" in 1500, even if France's ambassador claimed that the king felt himself crushed "between two millstones": namely, the papacy and Venice, each demanding French resources.[104] The ties between France and the Serenissima in 1500 should have discouraged rebels' flight into Venetian lands, and in fact the doge and Louis XII had co-issued a "general decree" in which Venice agreed to count Milanese exiles as rebels if they were found in Venetian territory as well.[105] Maximilian countered by requesting from Venice "a general safe-conduct for all the exiles from the state of Milan for the rebellion of Lord Ludovico."[106] Louis's agreement brought its first fruits in May 1500: Venice rendered into French hands—irrespective of imperial safe-conducts—a large number of Milanese gentlemen who had taken refuge in Venetian lands, including Ascanio Sforza.[107] Several were killed or tortured for further information. Many more remained to be discovered in the Veneto over the next few years.

Despite Venice's alliance with France, in reality the Serenissima cooperated only selectively with French measures to seize rebels as part of the republic's strategy to achieve independence from ultramontane demands. On matters of exile rendition, Venice's *signoria* often had to deliberate in council to reach an appropriate legal decision. The mechanics of the Venetian procedural system thus deferred France's hopes to pursue exiles rapidly and by any means possible.

One of the central concerns for French officials was the lands east of Milan into which many of the fugitives fled. From nearby Bergamo and Brescia, to the passes leading Trent-bound and on to Innsbruck, and south toward much-disputed Cremona and the Adda River: all of them belonged to Venice in the century's first decade. And since it was impossible to travel from Mantua to German lands other than by way of Venetian territory, the Serenissima found its *terraferma* among the chief zones for transient Milanese hoping to avoid apprehension. Such, after all, was what Ascanio Sforza had reasoned before his capture in 1500. Thus it was not—as the French suspected of the Gonzaga in Mantua—so much a case of Venice secretly sheltering rebels, as it was that its officials would inevitably find exiles in their custody. French agents pressured Venice's government frequently to surrender these outlaws, especially since they were making seemingly free use of Venetian territory to ferry news and money between Sforzeschi on both sides of the Alps.[108]

In early 1503, the household of Count Gianfrancesco Gambara in the Venetian dependency of Brescia sheltered a number of Milanese fugitives. Venetian officials captured a counterfeiter in Cremona and strung him up to question him. "*Signori,* let me down so I can tell things that will please you," he asked in the torture transcripts.[109] Not only did the forger tell tales of secret negotiations in Trent between Maximilian and Cardinal Amboise, he also revealed a hub of Milanese exiles. This counterfeiter, Orlando de Capilli, had come to Cremona with his patron Vincenzo Atellani to seek a doctor for the latter's *mal francese.* (Vincenzo was a brother of Giacometto Atellani, one of Ludovico's squires, whose sons we met in Chapter 5.) Capilli's testimony revealed that Vincenzo, who once commanded fifty crossbows under Ludovico Sforza, had taken refuge with Gambara, as had many others: Cristoforo da Lavello, a Milanese condottiere's son who was dispossessed in 1500; Dionisio Rotola, one of il Moro's footsoldiers; the military captain Benedetto Crivelli;

Margherita Pio, wife of the exiled Antonio Maria Sanseverino and kins-woman of Countess Alda Gambara; and Morgante Carnevale da Gam-balò, "banished by the French."[110]

This coterie formed an active link between Milan's exiles in Vene-tian and German lands. Vincenzo and Giacometto Atellani had followed Galeazzo Sanseverino to Germany in 1499, and now one of Galeazzo's intimates was traveling "every fifteen days up and down from Germany to Brescia." Asked what he meant when he called the Brescian Count Gambara a partisan ("*tien parte*"), Capilli explained: "All of the banished and exiled people who go up and down frequent his house and lodge there."[111] The revelation of this network must have stirred some censure from the Venetian authorities; the following month, Gambara appeared before the senate to excuse himself for having lodged the Sanseverino in his house, "because they were his relatives. And the count says he will no longer do it."[112]

At least on occasion, Venice did extend succor to elite Milanese fu-gitives. Such was the case of Andrea Borgo, who had served il Moro for seventeen years as a secretary. He lost everything when the French cap-tured Milan, except his life, some credit, and his good name, he told the Venetian ambassador.[113] He eventually made his way into the orbit of the king of the Romans, whom he served for over a decade beginning in 1502, and would later return to Milan as Massimiliano Sforza's chan-cellor in 1512.[114] More frequently, however, Milanese fugitives went to great lengths (such as disguise and self-concealment) in order to escape detection in Venetian lands, a sign of their distrust of their neighbors to the east, particularly given the joint agreement with France on rebels. "Venetians don't look kindly on Milanese": that was the reason two Mil-anese fugitives gave in 1500 when interrogated by Venetian officials in Salò about their disguises as scholars. Several Sforza partisans fled to Bergamo, where the Venetian rectors captured twenty-four of them ranging in age from twelve to sixty. When Bartolomeo Crivelli and his son escaped from captivity in Bergamo's keep, Venetian officials discov-ered the father's abandoned clothes in a monastery: the friars had given him a habit to wear.[115] Crivelli later reported that he had hidden for three days inside a tomb.[116]

Luçon suspected that Milanese rebels were taking advantage of easy transit across Venetian territory. He complained to the *signoria* in late summer 1500 about this promiscuous flow of contacts and concluded that Venice's territories were "full of these sprouts (*talli*), and the rectors [of Venetian dependencies] do not know it." Luçon wanted to send one of his own agents with the authority to arrest these men trafficking to Germany.[117] Wives and children of exiles, Luçon also reported, abounded in the Veneto.[118] When regional Venetian officials did find Milanese exiles, they often did not know how to treat them. The twenty-four fugitives in Bergamo asked the city magistrates if they might leave freely even though they were prisoners: the rectors had to seek advice from the *signoria* for such an unusual request.[119] In these and similar matters, Venice's *signoria* followed legal procedure, much to the frustration of the French. For instance, Luçon appealed in the summer of 1500 to the Venetians on behalf of the castellan of Trezzo whom they had captured and were trying for rebellion.[120] Under French pressure, the Venetian council acquitted the castellan, but when Luçon sued for his immediate release by invoking the language of graces and favors, Venice's agent in Milan replied with a touch of sangfroid: "The affairs of Venice are governed by law."[121]

Less than a decade later, after a reversal that set Venice and France in a conflict culminating in the Serenissima's defeat at Agnadello in 1509, French recollections of Venice's apparently impartial stance toward Milanese refugees was unforgiving. Far from seeing the "greatest friendship" that Luçon had vaunted, his colleague in the Milanese senate Claude de Seyssel instead charged the lagoon city not just with hosting rebels, but with fostering them as well. He claimed that in 1500 Venice had "helped, supported, and defended them [the exiles], hoping to gain more friends in the duchy."[122] Seyssel thus saw Venice working to circumvent the French by nurturing the Milanese resistance. Seyssel described the exiles residing in the cities and towns along the Adda, a borderzone between the two powers. Raiding Milanese territory across the Adda, exiles shouted insults against the French and their king, boasting of their crimes against "the king's subjects"—their Lombard compatriots, in other words. Seyssel believed Venetian authorities dragged their feet in responding to these dissident acts, since the raiders disrupted Louis XII's plans to retake Milanese lands that the Venetians had acquired.

To Seyssel, Venice also exploited its bureaucratic procedures to frustrate French efforts to capture Milan's rebels. When royal officials demanded the surrender of malefactors, Venetian agents "turned the

matter over to their senate," Seyssel complained, "which pretended to observe treaties and alliances. It wrote fine letters to its officers, ordering
them to evacuate or hide the said exiles, rebels, and delinquents for as
long as the king's messengers sought them out."[123] While Venice could
certainly point to certain high-profile captives it had surrendered to the
French, like Ascanio Sforza, the Serenissima "had not done it with a glad
heart, nor of its own desire, but in fear of some greater misfortune,"
namely, the "heat and fury" of Louis XII's military might. Ascanio's surrender was merely a measure to cast off French suspicion; what Seyssel
intuited in the long run, however, was resistance on Venice's part to sat-
isfying its new ultramontane ally.

While Seyssel's invective could be written off as a partisan smear of
the Venetians after their loss at Agnadello, raiders did in fact cross the
Adda or Po to assault territory around Lodi, Piacenza, and Cremona.
When the Adda's waters were low, malefactors ("probably *fuorusciti* from
Lodi," in one case) could wade across the river and attack or kidnap
people and animals on the Milanese banks.[124] Yet even if these assailants relied upon the benign neglect of Venetian authorities, that situation evolved as Venice withdrew from its rule over Cremona in 1509. As
a fulcrum of Franco-Veneto-Milanese tensions, this city's travails from
1509 to 1521 exemplify exiles' role in regional destabilization.[125] Lordship in Cremona shifted four times in twelve years (Sforza to Venice to
France to Sforza to France again). As each regime pushed the last one out,
antagonisms gnawed at the city from inside and outside. Traditional Cremonese factions (Ghibelline, Guelf, and Maltraversi) underlay Venetian,
French, and Sforza adherence. Guelfs suffered the most vicious attacks
for their Venetian or French partisanship, but sometimes it was hard to
discern perpetrators' politics even to those watching the violence happen.

Authorities' impotence filled Cremonese correspondence in these
years. Consider these complexities: in 1513, Massimiliano Sforza's governors oversaw Cremona; French troops still held the city's castle; Venice,
technically allied with France, contested all claims to the city; and
Spanish troops lodged in the region. One local chronicler associated
Massimiliano's assumption of the duchy with a massive wave of factional
murders "because there was no law in Cremona."[126] The Sforza governor
wrote to the new duke that "every hour brings violence, woundings, assassinations in the street, rapes, and other crimes that would be long to

recount," and he was unable "to act opportunely for lack of a strong arm (*per non hauere brazzo potente*)."[127] He addressed the prince a month later "praying on my knees" to be sent military reinforcements to "help your poor subjects: robbed, assassinated, killed, and dragged down worse than dogs."[128] Given exiles' raids and internal friction, it was not impossible that Cremona might capitulate to someone whose arm was stronger than the state's.

In summer 1514, the Ghibelline exile Niccolò Varolo (d. 1527) camped outside the city; citizens feared he might be a new Cabrino Fondulo, the commander who had captured Cremona in 1403 after Duke Giangaleazzo Visconti died.[129] Crumbling authority opened new possibilities for the forceful. Although Varolo did not lay siege, the citizens had good reason to worry. He brought significant disturbance to Cremona, and over the next decade his unpredictability made him a threat to almost every side in the ongoing wars. In 1515–1516, he murdered Massimiliano's captain of justice in Milan, killed Venetian-sympathizing Guelfs in Cremona, and narrowly escaped an imperial ambush in Lodi.[130] Citing Varolo by name, Guicciardini later wondered what was worse, the "bad fortune or the temerity and imprudence of the *fuorusciti* of the duchy of Milan, [...] not just because every one of their efforts failed but because, intent on preying upon the land, they hampered the arrival of victuals."[131] Guicciardini was probably referring here to two foiled plots in 1521, one in Milan and another involving Varolo in Cremona, both of which aimed to foment uprisings across Lombardy against French domination.[132] Milan's French government named two hundred new rebels in September of that year, including the Ghibelline nobleman Giovan Battista Pusterla, who commemorated his escape from French soldiers in a votive panel of the Benedictine mystic Caterina Brugora (1489–1529; Fig. 7.4).[133] Thanks to her prayers, an angel carried Pusterla across a river to safety. The image reimagined the river, often a threshold of exile aggression, as a vehicle of refuge: Pusterla was literally spirited across the waters to liberty.

France and Venice realigned their post-Agnadello collaboration in 1513 and remained allies for the next decade.[134] That bond was important in Cremona, where French anchorage lasted longer than almost anywhere else in Lombardy. Citizens' resentment had turned fervid there, but Venice rarely flagged in its support of French designs. In 1521, as part

Fig. 7.4 Bernardino Luini and Workshop, Votive panel of Giovanni Battista Pusterla for Caterina Brugora, after 1529. The banderole reads: "I, Lord Giovanni Battista Pusterla by your prayers escaped French hands." Collezione Cagnola, Gazzada (Varese), inv. DI.050.

Photo by Vivi Papi, Varese 1995 cod.VP853-95.

of a growing resistance campaign, almost 500 *fuorusciti* unfriendly to France entered Cremona disguised as peasant grocers.[135] Hoping to isolate potentially disruptive forces, the French confined several hundred Cremonese to lands held by the lords of Bozzolo, Ferrara, and Venice in early 1522.[136] A year earlier, after a brief French withdrawal, the city's inhabitants resolved not to allow the foreign regime to reenter. In the vicious confrontation that followed, France prevailed only when Venetian reinforcements arrived. For its part, Cremona's governing council—turning to a fierce native son for aid—entrusted its defense in this assault to none other than the renegade Niccolò Varolo.[137] With France and Venice at the gates, Cremona ultimately opted for one of its own, no matter how feral.

Forgiveness

Exclusion's unavoidable corollary was the question of reintegration. Could rebels be forgiven and returned to obedience? The attractions of home pulled many to seek clemency; others feared the hazards that might await them under unfamiliar lords. Rulers, often hoping to establish an idealized pacific domain, bent more often toward mercy than their flinty counselors did. During the Milanese interregnum between French and Sforza in late 1512, a group of prominent Guelf plotters planned to exact revenge on the resurgent Ghibellines. Sforza agents uncovered the conspiracy and some of the participants fled. When the wife of one intriguer, a senator under French rule, sought her husband's exoneration in mid-1513, the response from the Sforza counselor Andrea Borgo was a categorical dismissal. (Borgo himself had been a possible target in this plot.) Addressing Duke Massimiliano as if to command him, he fumed that "Your Excellency would never pardon them," since there could be no greater treason than their attempt to "overturn this state."[138]

Similarly, in 1522, François I watched from a distance as Lombardy turned against him. The king had charged the smooth Galeazzo Visconti to travel to the duchy and declare a general amnesty in which rebels could return to their former holdings. Lautrec, the king's governor in Lombardy, would have none of it. "Sire, you can pardon whomever you please," he conceded, but Milan's exiles "have so often been traitors and rebels to you, and if you do it, you will always be starting anew and you will never have your state in safety." Lautrec urged the sovereign to listen to the advice of men on the ground "rather than a Galeazzo Visconti, who is such a man as you know yourself." With a general amnesty, Lautrec argued, "you will disappoint all your faithful servants on the other side who abandoned their homes and lost all their goods to serve you."[139] He vowed that he would soon recapture Milan and the monarch could reward the faithful and punish the rebellious. Such was always the promise.

Although the number of Lombard expulsions fluctuated with each regime during the wars, foreign lords tended to eject greater numbers from the duchy than Sforza dukes did. François I condemned about 1,000 people in the late 1510s, and Charles V's agents more than doubled that figure in the late 1520s. Sforza numbers never exceeded 1,000.[140] If panicked missives from regional captains and governors told rulers anything, it was that exiles caused trouble.[141] Disaffected elites instrumentally extended the shatterzone, especially insofar as the wars inflamed internal factional politics and violence in ways that outsiders hardly understood. The role of this caste in hampering ("*difficoltare*," to use Guicciardini's verb) the designs of state-appointed actors made them a strong countervailing force against the (re-)establishment of norms. For this reason, savvy rulers—bidding for good will—eventually matched their proscriptions with absolutions.

Amnesties experimented with consensus; they allowed rulers to bestow paternalistic benevolence. But Milan's case shows how exile policies in the early sixteenth century failed to establish the desired agreement. France's monarchs often showed mercy in person during or shortly after their peninsular campaigns. It is perhaps no coincidence that the readmission of exiles roughly coincided with Italian episodes of healing by royal touch.[142] They were both sanctifications of a sort. Louis XII permitted a trickle to return to the duchy as early as 1500, but the most substantial reprieves occurred in 1502, 1505, and 1511.[143] After François expelled hundreds in 1515, he extended grace in 1516–1517.[144] Yet these general amnesties were not always as generous as they sound. Their terms explicitly excluded those banished for *lèse majesté,* heresy, counterfeiting, or murder: that list would seem to encompass the vast majority of political exiles. Time-sensitive edicts encouraged the forgiven to appear in Milan with copies of their erstwhile privileges; authorities serially reissued these decrees and extended their deadlines—a sure sign of distrust on the part of hesitant *fuorusciti*. When Francesco II Sforza's government began to issue orders in early 1522, it canceled pardons that the French had extended to Lombards who had assassinated Sforza partisans.[145] Within two months, an edict would list 179 new names of men to be killed if they did not leave the city.[146]

Many Milanese elites returned home and recovered their patrimonies in the 1530s, although that process in itself was, as we have seen, often fraught with violence and legal dispute.[147] Key to the phenomenon of Lombard exile in the early Italian Wars was their cumulative, overlapping, and often contradictory waves: the proscription campaigns of warring governments eventually untethered an entire political caste, irrespective—in the long run—of their partisanship. As sovereignty flickered, every partisan, in other words, found himself targeted at some point or another. Unbound, that group not only contributed to the wider military and diplomatic struggles in the region, but also jolted the area's internal dynamics between cities, petty lords, subjects, factions, and networks. Even slipperier than mercenaries, exiles were ubiquitous destabilizers, both cause *and* effect of Milan's implosion.

8

Holy Sovereignties

*L*et us begin with two prophets in two cities. On 13 January 1495, friar Girolamo Savonarola preached a crazy sermon on the Psalms in Florence. He himself described it as "crazy (*pazzo*)," since its central prophetic warning, now infamous, was the destruction of Italy. He had seen a vision of a sword hovering over the peninsula; the blade then turned toward the earth and "with the greatest tempest" scourged it. "The sword which quivered—I must say this to you, Florence—is that of the king of France, which is appearing all over Italy."[1] By that January day, King Charles VIII of France and his army had already left tumultuous Florence; the monarch was now in Rome. Pope Alexander VI had taken shelter in the fortified Castel Sant'Angelo.[2] The scourging of Rome now seemed already to be underway.

Of the second prophet we have fewer details. The report comes to us by way of a chronicler recalling a homily pronounced in Milan perhaps only months before Savonarola's. "I remember, even though I was a child," the chronicler writes, "attending the sermon of a blind friar from the Incoronata, who preached to the duke [Ludovico Sforza] in the piazza del Castello at the time that King Charles was to come to Italy, telling him from the pulpit: SIRE, DO NOT SHOW HIM THE WAY, FOR YOU WILL RE-GRET IT. He regretted it in vain, to all of Italy's detriment."[3] The French intervention proved to be a perfect vehicle for prophetic culture, which connected its apocalyptic traditions to the sinister inversions occasioned by war and upended states. Prophecy was a discourse of sovereignty.[4]

In Florence, Savonarola coupled Charles VIII's arrival to an ambitious politico-religious reform campaign over the next four years, working to refashion the state as a morally purified, populist republic. At the same time, he countered Alexander VI's injunctions against him with fierce challenges to papal authority. Even after his execution in 1498, the radical Dominican's legacy not only burrowed deep into Florentine culture but also seeped across much of Italy and Catholic Europe. In Milan, the unnamed preacher was not a Dominican, nor was he influenced by Savonarola. His house—Santa Maria dell'Incoronata, established in 1445—belonged to the Augustinian Observancy.[5] The Incoronata sustained close ties with the Sforza family, just as the Medici had long patronized Savonarola's San Marco.[6]

This moment around 1500 draws us in two related directions. First, it points to the crucial role that Augustinian prophets played in early sixteenth-century Lombardy, amplified by their intersection with Savonarolism in the 1510s. Augustinians would be particularly active agents in prophetic culture between the 1490s and 1520s, as exemplified in the visionary trances of the nun Arcangela Panigarola and the fiery words of the sermonizer Andrea Baura. Both of these Augustinians took French intervention in Italy as the grounds for religious transformation, albeit from opposite poles: the former authorizing the French and the latter denouncing them. Second, it suggests the power of prophecy to challenge papal authority on moral grounds, particularly when its ideas of a divinely sanctioned French universal monarchy coincided with France's political strategies.[7]

Arguments against the pope's sovereignty—attached to the long tradition of contest between papal and secular lordship, heightened by prophetic antagonisms—lent energy to France's claims in Italy. As the crown strove to secure its peninsular territories, one of the most fruitful avenues was the ideological diminution of papal authority, at the very moment of the pope's most vigorous resistance to the incursion, from 1506 to 1512.[8] Savonarola's briefly blazing moment of prominence had

startlingly redeployed quite traditional tactics: first, a prophetic tradition that mythologized the French crown as divine agent of intervention
in Italian affairs; and second, an invocation of conciliarism, the institutional check on perceived pontifical overreach.

Although the French monarchs had no particular affection for Savonarola, his strategies appealed to them—particularly to Louis XII—in
their attempt to cast a permanent anchor in Italy. One of the corollaries
of that ideological coincidence was the expansion of justifications for
French royal independence from papal oversight. During the first decades of the century, both conciliarism and prophecy acted as shells to
shape and protect French expansionist ambitions by undermining the
pontiff himself. Out of that shell came further justifications for French
authority in Italy, both divine and legal. This chapter investigates how
prophets and ecclesiastical councils addressed divine judgments to the
very core of contested sovereignties. Ostensibly unpolitical because of
their divine origin, their utterances in fact acted as political ballast for
legal arguments over righteous rule. In working through these religious
and legal arguments over the first decades of the century, contenders in
the wars over Milan generated a host of fresh doubts over the foundations and efficacy of traditional authority.

Prophetic Speculations and the *Apocalypsis Nova,* 1502–1503

Currents in politics and prophecy around 1500 explored—and worked
to expand—the remit of French sovereignty in relation to papal authority.
These energies imagined a French empire unchecked by papal dominion,
which in principle enjoyed unique latitude. Arguments against the popes
were layered into constitutional, jurisdictional, and personal arguments.
The constitutional case centered on the conciliar tradition, which argued
that the authority of church councils superseded the Holy Father's. This
longstanding position accrued significant legal heft in the fifteenth
century.[9] The jurisdictional argument (related to the conciliar position)
defended the liberties of the French sovereign to appoint clergy active in
his own kingdom; the Gallican church had seized a pertinent clutch of
privileges during the ecclesiastical disputes at the Council of Basel. In
1438–1439, in the so-called Pragmatic Sanction of Bourges, the king significantly limited papal authority in France.[10] Finally, a pope's personal

character counted for something as well; even the most vigorous theorists of papal power conceded that a bad man sitting on Saint Peter's throne could be removed. These streams flowed into a receptive pool of prophetic culture. A malignant pope was the necessary precursor to the apocalyptic arrival of a holy pastor whose rule would signal the end of time. Savonarola indicted Alexander VI as an unfit shepherd of the church, threatened to convoke a council against him, and promised the advent of an angelic pope.[11] After 1503, Pope Julius II's truculent bellicosity made him an easy target from any one of these directions. Reform became a sovereignty issue; papal resistance to critics became a reason for them to circumvent or undermine the apparently immovable bishop of Rome.

These issues churned within French-dominated Lombardy as well. In October 1499, Cardinal Ascanio Sforza agitated for the massive revolt in favor of his brother, and many of the major co-conspirators across the duchy were churchmen.[12] Once the uprising was quelled, Pope Alexander allowed the victorious French to punish these clerics as they saw fit.[13] Louis XII, seeing these dissidents as evidence of dangerous clerical networks leading to Rome, restricted freedoms of the Lombard church in an edict of October 1500. In it, he instituted a rigorous *placet:* a stipulation that all religious appointments had to please (*placere*) the secular ruler.[14] A *placet* had existed under the Sforza, but Louis tightened it, requiring all papal "letters, bulls, and apostolic provisions" to pass through the Milanese senate for authorization. Professing to be "the most obedient son" of the Roman Church, the king nonetheless fretted that "no provision should tend toward the danger of perturbing all or part of the [Milanese] State, to avoid threats similar to or greater than the recent revolution undertaken by ecclesiastical persons," thereby filtering both clerical liberties and papal dicta through a regime-friendly institution.[15] Using the tradition of the *placet,* the king could not only suppress seditious alliances through ecclesiastical channels; he could also carve out a Gallican legal zone in the Duchy of Milan by requiring papal orders to undergo secular approval according to French political interests. When Lombards directly petitioned Louis to make sure only locals could be invested with church benefices, he gave a nonresponse that effectively barred their access to them.[16]

This zone was augmented by the occasional presence of Cardinal Georges d'Amboise, one of Louis XII's closest advisors, whom critics described as the "true king," a star around which even the sun orbited.[17] He acted as royal proxy on several occasions in Lombardy, including as agent of the duchy's pacification in 1500. As we have seen, his family played a central role in entrenching the domination.[18] With secure mooring in occupied Milan, Amboise could advance his candidacy for the papal see; a successful bid could render Rome, and much of Christian Europe, pliant to French designs.[19] But even with Louis XII's army camped threateningly outside Rome during the conclave of 1503, Amboise's papal ambitions went unrealized. Still, his ecclesiastical authority carried particular weight in Milan. The city's titular archbishop— Cardinal Ippolito d'Este, Isabella's brother—held the position as an absentee sinecure, leaving his pastoral duties in the hands of a vicar. During his extended visits to Milan, Amboise thus embodied a potent intersection of clerical majesty and royal prerogative: a personification of the absorption of Lombardy's ecclesiastical benefices into Gallican interests.

The idea that a French pope might transform the Roman church had a vast cultural significance beyond Amboise's own ambitions. The notion traced its roots to the prophecies of Joachim of Fiore (1135–1202). Subsequent elaborations of his visions placed France at the center of the prophetic program, opening the way to scenarios that made either a French king (a second Charlemagne) or a pope (a so-called angelic pastor)—or both together—the movers of cosmic justice.[20] Savonarola belonged to this long inheritance, as did the Franciscan hermit Amadeo Menez da Silva (ca. 1420–1482), who spent much of his career in Milan.

The conclave of 1503 elected Julius II only fifteen months after the hushed revelation in Rome of a vivid Joachimist prophecy with Milanese connections. The text—known as the *Apocalypsis nova*—had supposedly flowed from the pen of Amadeo. An Iberian transplant to Italy in 1452, Amadeo settled first in Assisi, then in Milan, where his renown as a mystic spread rapidly. With the support of the Sforza dukes, a number of Franciscan "Amadeite" communities expanded across the Lombard duchy.[21] Amadeo served the Sforza on several secret diplomatic missions; Milan's archbishop established the church of Santa Maria della Pace for him. A Sforza envoy to Pope Pius II, Amadeo pursued an eremitic life in

Rome in a grotto near the church of San Pietro in Montorio, serving as one of Pope Sixtus IV's confessors. Near the end of his life, he returned to Milan, where he died.[22]

At San Pietro in Montorio in the spring of 1502, the *Apocalypsis nova* came to light. Its origins remain uncertain and its attribution to Amadeo strongly suspect. On 18 June, the Bosnian Franciscan Juraj Dragisic (1446–1520, known in Italy as Giorgio Benigno Salviati) wrote a letter to a Florentine friend describing it. Amadeo had written a book "as large as Augustine's *City of God*" and had ordered it to be kept sealed until heaven sent someone suitable to open it. Dragisic described how friars had tried on three occasions to open the book but had taken ill and died. Now Dragisic's patron, Bernardino de Carvajal, Cardinal Santa Croce (1456–1521), was urging him to open Amadeo's tome. After singing a mass, the celebrants handed the book to Dragisic, who unsealed it: "It predicts the reformation of the church, the conversion of all infidels, the election of a miraculous new pastor, and the peaceful, pure, and shining kingdom of Christ in our times," he reported, but urged his correspondent to tell no one.[23]

The destabilizing potentials of this prophecy were clear from the outset. Dragisic, who was entrusted with the book and claimed to have copied it, reported in later correspondence that "no living man has read it except the bishop my companion and Cardinal Santa Croce. And now no one can read it except his Lordship; I read it in his chambers, and otherwise it cannot be taken out. His grooms cannot even look at it; he keeps it locked in a box to which he holds the key."[24] Institutional concerns may have motivated this secrecy. Alexander VI—who soon learned about the manuscript's existence—had only just concluded his battle with Savonarola. News of a fresh prophetic text demanded circumspection in Roman circles. Pertinently, both Dragisic and Carvajal—who kept consistent company from 1500 to 1507—differed with the Borgia pope over their Savonarolan sympathies. The Bosnian wrote a treatise favoring the existence of contemporary prophets in 1497, and the Spaniard protected two of Savonarola's adherents after his arrest in 1498.[25] Carvajal, an erstwhile friend of Ludovico and Ascanio Sforza, had already alienated Alexander politically.[26] Like Amboise, Carvajal angled to be elected in the conclave of 1503, perhaps newly fortified by the seemingly providential unsealing of Amadeo's prophecy of an angelic pastor. But the text of the *Apocalypsis nova* presents some complexities. It echoes Dragisic's idiosyncratic technical and conceptual vocabulary too strongly not to belong to his pen, whether in whole or in part.[27] His access to the manuscript for a year prior to its wide circulation also explains its references to current events of Alexander's papacy.[28] A formidable millenarian confection of a new century, the *Apocalypsis*—and its advocates, Dragisic and Carvajal—would (re)appear in Milanese circles before the end of the next decade to fulfil, in some fashion, the prophecy's potential as a tool of political disruption.

Political Speculations and Papal Authority, 1509–1511

If the tides of prophecy augured a new pontifical age, the speculations of politics were not far behind. The age of French transalpine dominance needed its own politico-legal justification. The first step was a flood of arguments outlining the nature of French royalty as minimally constrained by imperial or papal bridles. Insofar as Louis's 1499 seizure of Milan was concerned, French apologists initially fretted little over legitimizing it beyond pointing to the seemingly transparent Orléans heredity; even the Sforza struggled to counter those arguments. But juridical challenges to French intervention across the Alps did accrue, not least in Maximilian I's initial resistance to Louis's Milanese claims. Julius II then began concertedly to agitate against French interests in 1506. After uniting with Louis to defeat Venice at Agnadello in 1509, the pope reversed himself and turned squarely against France. Conflict with both Venice and the pope stimulated a flurry of French writers to sharpen the ambitions of royal power between 1508 and 1511.[29] We know a good deal about the condemnatory rhetoric in Francophile writings by Jean Lemaire de Belges, Symphorien Champier, Jean Saint-Gelais, Pierre Gringore, and countless pamphleteers.[30] However, we know less about the juridical speculations over French power that justified these antipapal conflicts. The cast of advocates was diverse, but many of the voices emerged from communities of lawyers accustomed to the Roman law tradition in Toulouse and Milan-Pavia.[31]

Their writings allow us to trace the conceptual translation of panegyric into legal discourse over the course of a short span of years. Some of these men were both poets and jurists whose verses forecast some of their legal arguments. Christophe de Longueil (1488–1522) was a young scholar in Poitiers when he pronounced a crackling defense of French superiority over Italy in 1508; his quick ascent as a legal prodigy assured him an invitation to join the French *équipe* of lawyers in Italy who worked to support Louis XII's position in the increasingly delicate wrangles with the pope beginning in 1510.[32] Other writers had similar trajectories. In Chapter 5 we met Jean Feu, senator in Milan, who lectured on the defense of royal power in Pavia in 1510.[33] In the same year, Feu's colleague in the senate, Claude de Seyssel, condemned the Venetians in an encomium of Louis that excoriated Venice's disregard for royal majesty.[34] Still other characters, many of them connected to the Milanese regime, became central in the next phases of the dispute.

In the summer of 1509, Julius complained that the kings of France and Spain "are not content with being king, they want to be pope as well, and give benefices and occupy lands and do what they please."[35] Julius's determination to expel the French had congealed. Soon the rift between king and pope seemed to head toward open conflict. One of the routes for Louis—and for Maximilan I, by this point an ally—to obviate outright war appeared to be through a church council. Upon his election, Julius II had sworn to convoke a council within two years; more than seven had already passed. Machiavelli, Florence's envoy to France in these years, wrote to the *signoria* from Blois in summer 1510 that voices at the French court spoke of "withdrawing obedience" from the pope, "holding a council against him, ruining him in temporal and spiritual realms: and these are the mildest threats they make against him."[36] But this prospect required subtler legal maneuvering than the fairly blunt case the crown had mounted against the Sforza; the king faced the juridically dubious venture of waging war against Christ's vicar on earth.

In 1510, a flurry of legal scripts appeared in tempo with the growing enmity. The king's councilor Jehan Ferrault penned a treatise on the *Rights and Primacies of the Crown of France,* in which he laid out twenty of the most significant privileges enjoyed by the French monarchs. The author addressed the monarch in a preface, advertising the work's utility for encouraging subjects to "support your very just and reasonable quarrels."[37] Ferrault's first privilege echoed Feu in restating a fourteenth-century position: that the French king recognized no temporal superior. Rehearsing familiar Gallican cases, Ferrault showed how the popes had granted special rights to the French crown over centuries, rendering its liberties unique in Christendom.

Louis consulted widely on the implications of turning against Julius, beginning with councils of the kingdom's prelates at Orléans and Tours between July and September 1510.[38] Several French jurists provided *consilia* and published opinions on the question. Louis wrote to the universities and regional parlements in August 1510 to explain that the pope "has openly declared war against us and has wanted to trouble and overturn our states in Italy."[39] He requested immediate advice on the legality of war between a pope and a Christian prince. The responses, all supportive, attempted to dissociate Julius II from his divine office and to frame Louis as a victim of unjust aggressions. The lawyer and *parlementaire* Étienne Aufréri (1458–1511), on behalf of the parlement of Toulouse, replied that the pope should not interfere in "that which belongs to the king in Italy," especially since his previous meddling had inspired "seditions, murders, and other great scandals." Should Julius further provoke Louis, "the King will be forced to defend himself with arms not against the vicar of Jesus Christ [. . .] but against the holy father as a private person."[40] Aufréri's decision, grounded in Gallican reasoning already a century old, dissociated the pope from his own grandeur by means of a sort of anticipatory deposition.[41] The pope's personal moral failings impeached him.

Jean Pyrrhus d'Angleberme (1470–1521), a jurist in Orléans who had studied in Paris with Erasmus, composed a brief opinion on the question of oath-taking, using the *Corpus Juris Civilis* as his point of departure.[42] In a dedicatory letter to Étienne Poncher—archbishop of Paris and Milanese chancellor from 1501 to 1504—Angleberme faulted Julius for breaking faith with Louis and offered his legal reasoning as an "antidote to the poison of discord."[43] His short treatise answered two questions. Focusing first on oaths of fidelity, he considered whether fealty sworn to a lord outweighed duty owed to the king. In other words, if a nobleman waged war against the king, presumably in favor of the pope, were the nobleman's subjects required to respect their oath to him over their duties to the king? (As we will see in the next chapter, real juridical confusion over this issue vexed Lombards after 1499: some Milanese understood their preexisting legal oaths as impediments to fighting for their preferred ruler.) Angleberme responded negatively: to wage war against the king was a crime, *tout court,* and fidelity to him overrode other pacts.[44] Angleberme's second opinion concluded that an unjust cause such as Julius's freed Louis from his obedience to the pontiff and permitted him to defend allies against an aggressor who, as a holy pastor, had no right to bear arms.[45] In just two short opinions, the jurist had made the king seem an unassailable assailant.

Angleberme soon found himself enmeshed in the realities of these postulates. He visited Milan in 1515 with François I and joined the Milanese senate in 1519.[46] He dedicated a short epistle "In Praise of Milan" to Jean Barrillon, the secretary of Chancellor Antoine Du Prat. The tribute celebrates Angleberme's fellow French senators in Milan almost more than the city itself.[47]

Other French jurists shared Angleberme's positions on Louis XII's wide liberties. Vincent Cygault (fl. 1491–1523), a judge in Brive, in south-central France, published several opinions on questions of legal jurisdiction, including the French interventions in Italy.[48] He defended the sovereign's Italian rights and assaulted the pontiff's capacity to prosecute a war, notably in his *Allegations on the Italian War* (1513).[49] Cygault brought two legal traditions into heady collaboration. On the one hand, he deployed the fundamental Roman law against treason (the *lex Iulia maiestatis*)—absorbed through Bartolus of Sassoferrato's *On Tyranny*—to indict all claimants against royal power including the Venetians, whom he blamed for souring the relationship between king and pope, and Ludovico Sforza.[50] On the other hand, he mobilized conciliar rhetoric to minimize papal legitimacy, especially given what Cygault took as Julius's weak moral position. He declared the pope subject to the discipline of councils and Louis within his rights to defend his rights against a predatory pontiff, keeper of the sword that "does not kill, but vivifies."[51]

With such legal support, Louis XII challenged Julius II by demanding the convocation of a council.[52] Both king and pope brought material pressures to bear upon their growing antagonism. Exacerbating the jurisdictional dispute over the Gallican zone in the Duchy of Milan, Louis required in September 1510 all holders of Lombard benefices to present themselves to French authorities and confirm their residency in the duchy or face the confiscation of their goods and privileges.[53] Julius issued a bull against Milan's governor, Chaumont d'Amboise, countering that sequestration of ecclesiastical property by lay authorities was illicit and excommunicating him and other French commanders.[54] These hostilities evolved alongside military contest over Bologna, Ferrara, and Mirandola, which, in the latter case, brought Julius himself to the battlefield ("I'll see if I have balls as big as the king of France's," he reportedly remarked as he besieged the city).[55] Louis suffered significant setbacks in both ecclesiastical and military camps with the deaths of Cardinal d'Amboise in May 1510, and of the cardinal's nephew Chaumont in March 1511.[56]

It was in this context that a reform-minded group of French-leaning prelates broke from the pope in 1511. In May of that year, three cardinals led by Bernardino Carvajal met in Milan to initiate the planning for a general council in Pisa that September.[57] Six more joined the movement, but the leadership coalesced around five central figures: Cardinals Carvajal, Borgia, Briçonnet, de Prie, and Sanseverino. Over the summer of 1511, initiatives advanced quickly. Placards announcing the council appeared across Lombardy; the protagonists called the celebrated law professor at Pavia, Filippo Decio (1454–1536), to Milan for consultation.[58]

Perhaps the most remarkable aspect of the conflict was the sovereignty aspirations it triggered for the disputants. Many contemporaries, not without reason, saw the Pisan council as a screen for Louis's aspirations to depose Julius. But the animosities were reciprocal; the rulers resolved to undo or replace each other. Maximilian I, an early advocate of the council, imagined himself assuming both papal and imperial thrones upon Julius's demise, writing to his daughter that he would thereby die a saint.[59] He had news from Giovanni Colla (his envoy in Rome and preceptor of the Sforza sons) that Rome's nobility and populace wanted neither a French nor a Spanish pope; Maximilian asked his Fugger financiers to prepare a 300,000-ducat payment to the voting cardinals to ease his own path to the pontifical see.[60] For his part, Julius had intentions of turning parts of the Milanese duchy into a pontifical state and promised to invest the young Henry VIII with the French title of "most Christian king," should he invade Louis's realm.[61] At the intersection of legal speculation and military action in these years lay a challenge to the traditional boundaries of power transfer: these were threats not just of substitution but often of annihilation. "We will ruin the Church if it cannot be fixed," Milan's finance minister Thomas Bohier mused to the

Florentine envoy, "and without a doubt you will have a long-lasting schism in the Church [. . .] in the end it will all come down to war (*alla fine il tutto si ha a redurre all'arme*)."[62]

Unholy Conflicts, 1511–1512

Bohier probably hoped to shock the envoy with his ominous forecast. But he was not wrong. From the council's first sessions in Pisa until its swift transfer to Milan, the cardinals faced unremitting hostility from suspicious observers and citizens. War followed closely on its heels: before the end of the spring of 1512, French hold on Lombardy crumbled in the wake of the Battle of Ravenna. Enmity hardened against the Pisan gathering as Julius summoned his own council (the Fifth Lateran), intended to undermine the cardinals' moral position.[63] Centrally at stake was the territoriality of sanctity, that is, the extent of religious authority exerted in spaces with loyalties both to Julius as supreme pontiff and to Louis as Duke of Milan and head of the Gallican church. Papal interdicts followed the cardinals from site to site, calling unequivocally for religious services to halt in the host cities. Louis and the cardinals pushed back against these prohibitions, suspending the pope's rights to confer territory and forcing communities to choose between obeying the pope or the king.[64] The most extensive face-offs occurred in Milan, where papal sovereignty and its attendant allegiances came to be layered atop the duchy's already fractured system of loyalties.

Alighting first in Pisa with a substantial military escort, the cardinals found the cathedral already locked to them, so they opened the council at San Michele in Borgo on 2 November 1511.[65] The abbot of San Michele angrily resisted hosting Carvajal in the attached monastery.[66] As Florentine envoy, Niccolò Machiavelli had attempted for months to negotiate the council out of Pisa. (Florence, Pisa's overlord since 1494, itself suffered papal interdict on 28 September for aiding Louis.[67] The Florentine interdict ended in March 1512.) Machiavelli now proposed moving the sessions "either to France or to Germany, where there would be people more apt to obey than the Tuscans are."[68] The Pisans made their arrival quite difficult, refusing to accommodate the cardinals, archbishops, bishops, abbots, and procurators, along with twelve theologians from the Sorbonne and four jurists.[69] The cardinals managed to hold three sessions before a brawl between the churchmen's soldiers and Pisan citizens forced the council to abandon the city for Genoa, the first step of a retreat into lands under French sway.[70]

The cardinals then made for Milan in early December.[71] The second Florentine envoy described how the papal interdict (which would not lift until July 1512) followed them to Lombardy, trapping the Milanese in a choice between pope or king. "There have been a few days without masses, which made such commotion in this city that it is a marvel. On command of the senate, a few unbeneficed priests began to say mass. The canons and other ranks [of clerics] have refused, but the French have gone to find them at their houses. They threaten them with prison and more, so they convene in the church for other divine offices, but it is co-erced, as they say publicly themselves."[72] Some communities, in deference to the pope, refused to break the interdict: the brothers at Sant'Ambrogio (Cistercians), Santa Maria della Passione (Augustinian Canons), and San Pietro in Gessate (Umiliati). "Soldiers were sent to take possession of them," wrote one contemporary.[73] Four days later, Milan's governor or-dered the state treasurer to summon the duchy's clergy to attend the council or face charges of rebellion and confiscation.[74]

Carvajal entered the city to a quiet reception from his fellow cardi-nals and Milan's senators, a handful of young gentlemen (*ma pochi pochi*), and not a single Milanese prelate of rank. Correspondents reported dis-pleasure among the citizens, who knew that the arrival of the concilia-rists increased the likelihood of an attack by the approaching papal army of Swiss mercenaries.[75] The cardinals agreed to delay the Milanese ses-sions until after the new year "on account of the assault of the Swiss and the disturbance of the city."[76] Meanwhile, Zaccaria Ferreri—abbot of Sub-asio and Carvajal's right hand in the Pisan sessions—publicized the council's ideological grounding by issuing selected decrees of the coun-cils of Constance (1414–1418) and Basel (1431–1439)—highpoints of fifteenth-century conciliarism.[77]

By January 1512, even some of the conciliar cardinals began to waver, but Louis XII insisted that the gathering should reach its "desired con-clusion"; he now intended to expend every effort on his Italian wars and supported the cardinals' work "up to the creation of a new pope."[78] Such animus between Louis and Julius heightened concern about conse-quences for participants. Only a single Lombard bishop appeared at the first Milanese session, obeying the monarch's letter threatening him with dispossession.[79] Likewise, the law professor Filippo Decio adjourned to Pavia, claiming that his declining health prevented his continued presence. The cardinals replied that the closer one got to death, the more one needed to work for God's church. Decio then appeared in Milan to quit in person, only to have the conciliarists serve him with a royal writ requiring his continued cooperation.[80] Alongside the opinions of the French lawyers, Decio's earlier 1510 *consilium* on the circumstances obliging a pope to submit to his peers' judgment had substantially undergirded the legal logic for convoking the council. His reticence in 1512 was not mislaid—before the end of the year, he had to flee to France under threat of excommunication. But his reasoning intrigued Julius enough for the pope to offer him and a colleague safe passage to Rome to explain the legal basis of their antipapal arguments. He declined the invitation.[81]

The council's Milanese sessions unfolded at the cathedral over the first four months of 1512, arguing the case for the pope's irresolvable obstinacy (*contumacia*). Military successes may have emboldened the cardinals and their supporters.[82] In February, French forces subdued papal Bologna and sacked Venetian-held Brescia, and on 11 April they defeated a papal-Spanish army at Ravenna. Ten days later, once arguments against the pope had concluded, a conciliar notary strode to each door of Milan's cathedral, calling out: "Who appears here for Pope Julius?" "When no one was found," one witness recalled, "he was charged with obstinacy and his papal authority was suspended."[83] Within a week, the council's decision had been translated into Italian and published as a pamphlet.[84] Circumstances demanded the swift creation of a new pope. Registers from the Lombard abbey of Chiaravalle—whose abbot Agostino Sansoni attended the Milanese sessions—suggest the likely next step. Expenses for 1512 include payments for regalia for Bernardino Carvajal, "made pope in Milan and named Martin VI," and word of his election reappears in other contemporary writings, if not in the dispatches of the lynx-eyed ambassadors.[85]

Carvajal's elevation may not have been trumpeted because the sands continued to shift in the war with the pope: the carnage at Ravenna initiated a slow collapse of Louis XII's estates in Italy. Moreover, two weeks after the Milanese council announced Julius's deposition, the pontiff opened the Fifth Lateran Council in Rome, categorically delegitimizing the dissidents' meetings. The rebel cardinals abandoned Milan for Asti, then Lyon. (Carvajal later claimed that he lost the original *Apocalypsis nova* manuscript in the hasty flight; his title of Pope Martin VI went missing as well.[86]) Louis's ambitions now seemed frustrated. A Mantuan informant at the French court described fears that Julius's Holy League would carve up the French kingdom between the Empire, England, Spain, Swiss cantons, and French nobles: Paris itself would become a territory of the church.[87]

With the French retreat, Sforza agents reentered Milan with Swiss-imperial backing on 20 June 1512. Ottaviano Maria Sforza, bishop of Lodi and interim governor, issued a decree on 6 July announcing the end of the papal interdict and promising to pardon any ecclesiastic "who involuntarily, innocently, and forcibly" celebrated divine offices at the instigation of the "schismatic erstwhile cardinals" and allowed that "corpses of dead Milanese buried openly or secretly during the interdict need not be pulled from their graves." It concluded by warning the city that any lapse of fealty would bring permanent censure.[88] Framed in this way, re-articulation of Sforza sovereignty attached itself to a rhetoric of relief, not just from war, but also from months of religious displacement now soothed by the return of a dynasty in sympathy with the papacy. A Sforza counselor wrote that "the defeat of the French was beneficial not just to us and our state, but also to ecclesiastical liberty and the Apostolic See."[89] Enemies of Julius II were ordered to leave Milan early the following year.[90] "We must be champions and not oppressors of ecclesiastical liberty," the young Sforza duke wrote in 1514; in 1515 he relinquished ducal ratification of ecclesiastical offices (the *placet*).[91] Unsurprisingly, François I reinstated it in 1516, and Francesco II Sforza rescinded it again in 1522.[92]

The exuberant dispute between Louis XII and Julius II did not totally vanish; it simply went underground, as some of the reformist energies of the council planted themselves into Milanese soil, preparing to burgeon anew in the coming years. Carvajal's circle in 1510–1512 consisted of highly educated clerics with a reform agenda that tended toward the occult: this group included not only Juraj Dragisic and Zaccaria Ferreri (a precocious biblical exegete patronized by Giangiacomo Trivulzio), but also the German theologian and magician-alchemist Agrippa von Nettesheim (1486–1535), one of the cardinal's attendants in Pisa who stayed in Pavia until 1515.[93] Considering that Machiavelli also attended the conciliar negotiations, it made for a remarkable cast of some of Europe's least conventional thinkers. Carvajal's own circle of followers made its presence felt at the Milanese convent of Santa Marta, belonging to the Augustinian Observancy. The following section shows how political agendas inherited from Louis XII's domination intertwined with recent prophetic traditions to fashion Santa Marta into a fortress of sanctity to defend French interests in Lombardy.

Arcangela Panigarola and the Politics of French Renewal, 1512–1521

Arcangela Panigarola (1468–1525), an enclosed Milanese mystic, described in her ecstatic visions the contests over authority raging around her. Tensions in her spirituality—between pope and king, between political regimes—make her voice particularly telling evidence of the ideological blur that the Milanese sovereignty disputes produced. Her utterances, inflected and even transformed by contact with the Carvajal circle, show the prophet's impressionability to her interlocutors and to her city's travails. Because the men in her orbit invested so heavily in her speech, they pulled it toward their own agendas.[94] Mirroring her adherents' aspirations and anxieties, she relayed visions of scourge and reform, a potent theme in post-Savonarolan Italy, which accompanied her convent's rise in French Milan.

The church and convent of Santa Marta no longer exist; their remains lie today beneath a high school. But around 1500 this community numbered among Milan's most illustrious, a spiritual refuge for patrician daughters. After joining the Observancy in the 1460s, the nuns expanded their complex in the 1470s. A mystical impulse then took hold of several sisters, and their ranks produced a string of visionaries, including Veronica da Binasco (1445–1497), whose divine trances led her sisters to venerate her as a *beata*. (It was she who reproved Ludovico Sforza for the decadence of his court in 1492.) Her successor in this tradition of ascetic spirituality was a woman who served three terms as the community's prioress between 1500 and 1525: Arcangela Panigarola.[95]

Arcangela's background personified Sforza-era orthodoxies. Her father, Gottardo, had been a key financial official at the court of Duke Galeazzo Maria. Three of her four brothers followed in the paternal footsteps as merchants or tax collectors; the fourth, Ottaviano, was an architectural expert associated with Milan's Fabbrica del Duomo.[96] The nun's actions at the helm of her community also locate her spirituality along familiar axes. A staunch defender of papal authority, Arcangela was prioress of Santa Marta during Julius's 1511 interdict. Like fellow clerics who resisted French orders, Arcangela refused to ignore the interdict and proceed with masses, "even though the Archbishop's vicar went in person with secular authorities to force her to do so with significant threats." But her "virtue and grace" convinced the vicar to leave her in peace: "I would rather fight and dispute with the whole world than the Mother of the Monastery of Santa Marta," he reportedly marveled.[97] Arcangela told Giovanni Antonio Bellotti (d. 1528), a spiritual follower and author of her *vita,* that she believed the anti-Julian council "would go up in smoke" and urged him to avoid the conciliar sessions.[98] Thus on the whole, Arcangela's personal piety up to 1512—including the mystical template modeled by Veronica da Binasco, Panigarola family politics, and her papal partisanship—seems resolutely orthodox.

Yet something changed during the anti-Julian council sessions in Milan. Arcangela began to perform her mysticism differently. She had visions of the papal throne overturned; "new pastors (*novi pastori*)" would soon tend to Christ's flock.[99] These were ideas close to the hearts of the anti-Julian conciliarists. Bellotti himself may have been the prime mover opening this pathway. A native of Ravenna who became confessor of Louis XII's first wife Jeanne, Bellotti served as commendator of the abbey of Saint-Antoine near Grenoble. His career describes the sort of Italian Francophile disposed to join the council gatherings even if he later declared himself "bothered" by the cardinals' urgings to participate.

Arcangela's own writings testify to her links with the highest levels of conciliarists. More than one hundred of her letters survive from the period 1512–1520, many addressed to the Briçonnet brothers: Denis (bishop of Saint-Malo), and after 1515, Guillaume Jr. (bishop of Lodève) as well.[100] Their father, Guillaume Sr., was a leading anti-Julian. Arcangela's first letter dates to the very days in May 1512 that the council began to unwind in Milan. (Julius had officially declared the Briçonnet brothers—along with several other conciliarists—heretics and schismatics in February.[101]) Arcangela recommended the brothers to Bellotti's spiritual care, and they remained attached to Santa Marta even after they departed Milan.

Key in this growing circle of attachments was Juraj Dragisic.[102] He may have been at Carvajal's side during the Milanese sessions; he certainly knew Arcangela well by 1514. Julius II died in 1513, and his successor, Pope Leo X, lifted the censure against the Briçonnets and other collaborators in the council. In a consolatory letter to Denis over his travails, Arcangela mentioned Dragisic as her spiritual beloved (*mio fidele amatore*).[103] Along with Bellotti, he introduced her to radical prophetic currents, including the reformist prophecies of Beato Amadeo and Savonarola. In a letter of August 1514, Arcangela described a vision that narratively echoed the unsealing of the *Apocalypsis nova* in 1502. In it, Amadeo appeared before the Virgin with a book and asked when God wished it to be opened. A voice counseled patience as a toxic illness was purged from the earth. The Virgin placed her hands on the heads of Denis Briçonnet and Bellotti, assuring them of their role in the renovation. An angel would teach them the book's meaning. Bellotti cried out: "Quickly, quickly, let the reform begin!"[104] The promised Amadeite angelic pastor, advocated by Dragisic and filtered through Panigarola's mysticism, soon found embodiment in Denis Briçonnet. In a letter of December 1515 (just two months after the French recaptured Milan), Arcangela wrote that a vision of the Virgin had identified the Briçonnet siblings and Bellotti as her "sweetest sons," whose efforts would launch reform.[105]

During François I's domination, Arcangela's visionary scope continued to widen, as did the networks connecting the French elite to her convent. Denis visited the convent in 1516 to consecrate a chapel.[106] The king appointed Guillaume as his envoy to Rome to consolidate recent settlements with the pope; Denis joined him there and later replaced him in that position.[107] Dragisic settled in Rome during the sessions of the Lateran Council, but Arcangela's visions, as recounted in her letters and in her *vita*, continued to find inspiration in ideas he advocated. She wrote to Denis in 1519 that she and Bellotti had read Savonarola's writings together, and her *vita* describes a vision in which both Amadeo and Savonarola appeared to her. Amadeo applauded the Ferrarese friar as the fulfillment of the *Apocalypsis*. Savonarola, still refulgent from the flames that consumed him, addressed Arcangela and warned that sinful Florence had made itself unworthy of God's grace, and he now foresaw a similar castigation of Arcangela's city:

> "Your city of Milan cannot escape these future calamities; there will be great loss of life." And the frightened virgin [Arcangela] asked: "Might this come about by change of regime?" He responded: "No, it will spring from the envy and pride of those who always destroy mutual fraternal charity and love. They chase these things away, and when they vanish there must necessarily be discord. Faint-heartedness and inveterate faction will be the cause of the effusion of human blood, and there will also be a universal plague such that few will survive."[108]

Arcangela intuitively wondered whether Savonarola's imminent religious renewal might accompany a political reversal. She may well have known of Savonarola's demise in a tumultuous Florence that had recently chased out its Medici rulers; but she herself had recently lived through bloody changes of regime in her own city. Bellotti wrote that Arcangela had foreseen "the tumults of war and change of regime (*tumulti bellici et mutatione del stato*)" in Milan.[109] Her visions had absorbed the political charge of Savonarolism that attached regime shifts and violent suffering to moral renewal. In the same year, a vision of Saint Ambrose warned Arcangela that sinful Milan and all of Lombardy would suffer worse "persecution and tribulation" than even his own time had seen during the Arian heresies; old trees would be uprooted and new ones planted. He described enemies en route, armed to cut down the Milanese. When Arcangela asked the saint to identify the assailants, he replied: "They are the French, who will soon assault and invade Lombardy, devastating and pillaging with no small effusion of human blood, such that many will regret having lived."[110] This bloodshed would achieve God's will, the saint explained. Arcangela's vision of purifying violence turned France's secular armies into divine agents of reform.

Panigarola's renown as a politically relevant visionary attracted French patrons and their supporters to Santa Marta. Giulio Cattaneo, senate secretary and *spenditore,* visited her in 1517. In 1498, Ludovico

Sforza had sent him to Florence to congratulate the city on its execution of Savonarola.[111] Cattaneo now brought alms payments on behalf of King François I to the Savonarolan-inspired prioress of Santa Marta, totaling almost a dozen gifts between 1517 and 1520.[112] Arcangela's influence also touched Milan's French governor, Odet de Foix, sieur de Lautrec.[113] Lautrec's cousin, the young Gaston de Foix, died leading France's army at the Battle of Ravenna. Buried in Milan's cathedral, Gaston's corpse soon fell prey to Swiss soldiers who desecrated his tomb during the French withdrawal. Lautrec hoped to honor his kinsmen with a new sepulcher at Santa Marta sculpted by Agostino Busti (il Bambaia).[114] Unfinished at the time of the French retreat in 1521, the tomb's white marble fragments—monumental and delicate, today preserved in Milan, Turin, and London—testify to the patronal ambitions surrounding the visionary's convent. It is as if the abandoned tomb panels, their glowing filigree scenes of triumph now cracked and abraded, materialized the broken ambitions of French aspirations in the Duchy of Milan. Several other artists contributed to projects connected to Santa Marta and the Carvajal circle, including the painters Bernardino Luini, Bernardo Zenale, and Marco d'Oggiono.[115] A handful of Frenchmen elected Arcangela's convent as their burial site; it had become a magnet for Gallic elites.[116]

But doubts lingered. Not all French adherents found Arcangela's visions equally compelling. Guillaume Briçonnet distanced himself from the prioress in 1517; she wrote that he had "found some great fault in me" and worried that he had become "so angry and harsh" with her.[117] Perhaps the Lateran Council's rigorous new policing of prophets had chilled his ardor.[118] His brother Denis remained in regular contact with Arcangela, but she apologized twice to him in 1519 for "misunderstanding the divine voice."[119] The mystic's sense of ecclesiastical and secular politics had become layered, even unfocused. She sought papal favor but also envisioned the toppling of the papacy; she accepted support from François I but complained of his callow affection for "pomp and womanly conversation"; she always associated French interventions with renewal, but often in its most destructive form.[120] Such ambiguities may belong to prophecy in general: seers always have one foot in the present and another in the future.

Yet in Arcangela Panigarola's case, these ambivalences also echoed her reeducation as a political prophet in the Carvajal circle. When her prophecies articulated notions that her male adherents considered out of step with their own beliefs, they reproved her. Cornered, she then attributed her faulty inspiration to misunderstanding, or even to demonic meddling.[121] News of evolving politics entered the cloister through her followers' report; they provided the secular matter that her visions transformed into spiritual forms. In a political world in which both François I and Charles V contended in 1519 for imperial investiture, it mattered that she confused the two monarchs in a divine vision. "I know well that this brought her great humiliation," Bellotti wrote in her *vita*.[122] Her confusion is the point. Arcangela's prophecy outlines another site where sovereignty flickered in the wars over Milan, where knotty papal polemics and thronging royal armies intertwined even in the spiritual realm. Events in the world outside the convent outpaced reformist apparitions. Panigarola was a political prophet whose politics were out of time.

Despite doubts surrounding Arcangela's prophecies, she never suffered total disgrace as did some of her contemporaries.[123] Bellotti saw to the propagation of her cult in Lombardy; moreover, the French retreat from Milan was soon followed by the death of many of the central players in this circle, including Arcangela in 1525 and Bellotti in 1528.[124] The Panigarola prophetess consolidated a community of followers who tied French fortunes to cosmic reform. One of her successors in Milan, the Augustinian preacher Andrea Baura, instead figured France as the great evil to be extirpated.

Postlude: Sacred and Secular Slippages from Martin Luther to Andrea Baura, 1521–1523

Religious and secular resistance colluded in these years. The energies of conciliarism—reformist, moderative of papal supremacy, and often Francophile—intertwined with the politics of the French military interventions in Italy. It posed afresh the problem of pontifical jurisdiction in temporal and spiritual affairs. Scholars often point to Louis XII's geopolitics as grounds to dismiss this quarrel, as if embarrassed by the material investments in the sovereignty contest.[125] But both the politics and the doctrine were serious. Zones of obedience—doctrinal and political, anchored in deep histories with uncertain futures—were at stake. With its providential import amplified by prophetic voices, the French monarchy

opened space for brutal antipapal critiques that continued to evolve
after Julius II's death. Novel voices appropriated the complaints and
aimed them in new directions.

All the antipapal animosities traced in this chapter were not invisible to Martin Luther. In fact, he walked right through them. In autumn
1511, as the first sessions of the anti-Julian council unfolded in Pisa, Luther stopped in Milan on his way to Rome.[126] On his return voyage in
the spring of 1512, as the conciliarists worked to depose Julius II, he
skirted the Lombard capital in an effort to avoid the Holy League wars
devastating Bologna, Brescia, and Ravenna. During his only trip to Italy,
he witnessed dissention between sacred and secular powers at its most
polemical and violent. Luther also recognized the critiques articulated
by Louis XII's mouthpieces in the early 1510s; he found them intellectu-
ally persuasive.[127] The authority of church councils formed a crucial
node of Luther's 1518 dispute with Cardinal Cajetan at Augsburg over
his perceived unorthodoxies.[128] One church council's ability to overturn
the rulings of another confirmed Luther's view that their decisions belonged to human rather than divine law.[129]

As Luther's challenge to the papacy made waves after 1517, the first
Italian voice to respond in print was a member of Arcangela Panigarola's circle, Isidoro Isolani (ca. 1480–1528). A Francophile Dominican
theologian who made his career at Santa Maria delle Grazie, Isolani
knew Arcangela from publishing the visions of her mystic predecessor,
Veronica da Binasco, in 1518.[130] He knew Cajetan from a jurisdictional
quarrel over the Milanese monastery of Sant'Eustorgio in 1510–1512.[131]
And he knew Luther, at least through his writings, because his 1519 pamphlet upbraided the German for his errant theology.[132] Politically, Isolani supported French rule in Milan through the early 1520s, while other
clerical voices were excoriating it. One such critic was Andrea Baura,
whose disruptive preaching—targeting both the papacy and France in
turn—exemplified the slippage between doctrinal and political discon-
tent in the early 1520s, when the Italian Wars and fledgling Lutheranism
intertwined.

A Ferrarese Augustinian with links to the Este court, Andrea Baura
(fl. 1513–1523) delivered a series of coruscating sermons in Venice from
1517 to 1520.[133] Because he "spoke ill of the pope and of the Roman
curia," critics presumed that he "follow[ed] the doctrine of Fra Martin

Luther."[134] Papal injunctions followed, and Ferrara's episcopal vicar enjoined Baura to retract the lessons of his preaching in 1521.[135] Pressured out of Ferrara and Venice, the preacher eventually found shelter first at the Certosa di Pavia, then in Milan at the Augustinian convent of San Marco in late 1522.[136] In a published attack on Luther (Milan, 1523), Baura clarified his position, claiming divine inspiration and refuting the Saxon friar's arguments against papal power.[137] The Ferrarese hermit found the city in a moment of flux: France's occupying government had retreated in November 1521, and until spring 1522, Milan—nominally under the lordship of Francesco II Sforza—awaited a French siege. Even after the imperial army defeated French forces at Bicocca in April, the Porta Giovia castle refused to submit to the new Sforza duke for another year. The city hovered between regimes, and this was when the preacher mounted the pulpit.

Andrea Baura began to sermonize in Milan in late 1522. The merchant chronicler Burigozzo recorded how "a friar of San Marco preached in this city, and the city held him for a holy man. All the more so because in this time of war he strengthened the Milanese resolve against the French, saying that it was meritorious to Jesus Christ to kill these Frenchmen. He called them swine and cursed them with his maledictions."[138] The friar prepared a banner topped with a crucifix and took it to the cathedral for consecration as Milan's divine standard. In November 1523, the tocsins rang at dawn and Baura appeared in the cathedral square with his banner, mustering residents and allaying their fears by promising victory. He had become a civic prophet, rallying citizens to the cause of urban self-defense.

Burigozzo, however, could not be convinced; he saw a fraud. "He delighted in wishing to seem a prophet," the chronicler wrote. "But truly almost everything was the opposite." He appealed to the lower classes, Burigozzo continued, "because they didn't know what he was. As the psalm says: 'The evil ones tell me lies, but they are not akin to your law, O Lord.' [Psalm 118:85]. And he prattled often of war, loving to please the crowd but not cleaving to the wisdom of God, as was his duty."[139]

Baura's activities did not end here. The unpublished three-volume Milanese history composed by the jurist Bernardino Arluno (1530s) illuminates the environment of suspicion that grew around him in early 1520s Milan.[140] Despite Baura's preaching in favor of Francesco II Sforza and against the return of French rule, unfriendly voices accused the Augustinian of an unspecified crime, possibly incitement. After his denunciation, ducal forces jailed him on suspicion of *"noxium maiestatis,"* and Arluno himself—who portrayed the Ferrarese sympathetically, appreciative of his intellectual brilliance—acted as his legal counsel. Having faced religious censure in Rome, Venice, and Ferrara on suspicion of spreading Lutheran ideas, Baura now caught the attention of civil powers for public disruption in Milan. After lengthy and bitter questioning, authorities found no criminal intent, and the preacher was eventually released. Arluno's history is the last trace we have of Baura's career.

Andrea Baura's case should leave us in a certain state of hesitation, as it clearly did his contemporaries. Chased from several cities for apparent Lutheran tendencies, he also published a treatise against Luther. Welcomed in Milan under the Sforza restoration for his strong anti-French language, he found himself jailed by that same Sforza government on civil charges for his public speeches. A fiery prophet, his prognostications seemed empty to critics. But the hesitation that Baura's case produces should also not incapacitate us; it should instead point us back to the processes by which religious and political sovereignty came under crippling stress in the early sixteenth century. Milan's prophets were indices of intersecting religious histories: the spread of politicized Savonarolism; Gallican disagreements injected into Italian politics; and responses to incipient Lutheranism. When these branches of Catholic conflict intertwined with the territorial wars waged in the same years, the result was a profound and long-lasting amplification of doubt, both secular and sacred.

9

The People

$\mathcal{T}$here had to be a covenant. With the reversals of 1499, the new French lord of Milan needed to secure the good faith of his subjects. Louis XII's subjection of the city and duchy required a pact that certified Lombardy's recognition of its new regime. He wanted not just acknowledgment, but loyalty. Circumstances, it hardly needs to be said, complicated the simple transference of adhesion from one lord to the next. Passion, faction, class, and occasion conditioned the politics of affiliation in the shattered state. So did history, both bygone and recent. Visconti lords first insisted upon an oath of loyalty in 1386, one that appears to have included the entire duchy.[1] Other pledges recurred frequently in the fifteenth century around northern Italy to seal contracts: agreements between rulers and subjects or between feuding factions, whose deliberation process we now understand as the soul of political life.[2] The specific vows of faith that Louis XII sought were perhaps less common.[3] They seemed necessary to rulers as a socio-legal record that subjects respected their authority, and they invoked them at moments of novelty, pressure, or weakness. It figured any future dissent as a contravention of the pact, as treason. From the very beginning of foreign rule

over the duchy, the regime suspected that populations were fickle, luke-
warm, or baldly hostile. Over the first thirty years of the decade, Lombard populations suffered terrible violence as a result of these misgiv-
ings, and not just at French hands. This chapter intends not to chronicle
this suffering, but rather to reveal the circumstances that produced the
conditions for their trials and to trace how the people of the duchy nav-
igated the obstacles that decades of war threw in their path.

Pacts and Fealty

Ludovico Sforza required an oath of fidelity from the Milanese in 1495,
the year his rule as duke received imperial ratification. Before that time,
the Sforza princes based their lordship not upon the ever-elusive imperial election, but upon the popular assent of the citizens.[4] Seeing the
French threat already in 1498, il Moro tried to extract oaths of fidelity
from the duchy's *patres familias* that they would never surrender the
duchy's fortresses to anyone other than him or his heirs.[5] If anything,
that effort instead revealed to him the mixed sentiments about his lordship: over the next several months, he summoned insufficiently faithful
characters from Lodi, Pavia, Alessandria, Bosco, and Tortona to repent
or explain themselves.[6] Ludovico ultimately realized that flight was his
best option when, in late summer 1499, a convocation of Milanese citizens refused to lend him any further support against the French.[7] The
city's representatives made it clear that he, not the populace, had failed
to uphold the pact to protect the city.

From 2 to 6 September 1499, before Milan opened its gates to the
French army, an interim governing council ruled the city.[8] During those
days, about 400 of the city's residents ("high-ranking men, patricians,
and people") gathered at the newly built church of Santa Maria della
Rosa—mere steps from the Broletto, on the site of what is now the Pinacoteca Ambrosiana—to discuss the terms of its surrender (*capitoli di dedizione*), an enumerated set of wishes intended to articulate a desired vision of Milan's future under a new regime. Hastily organized, the
consultation nonetheless debated fundamental civic aspirations. For
days, the city temporized, promising Trivulzio—who captained the
French army outside the gates—that the terms had to be discussed and
the charter signed by leading citizens.[9] The substance of their wishes will

occupy us in the next section of this chapter, but the crucial element to note here is the civic expectations that hung upon those itemized desires. Although they opened by showing deference to the monarch in promising "faith and homage to his Royal Majesty as true, loyal, and faithful servants," the mood was subjunctive.[10] These were, after all, conditions. An oath of civic loyalty would follow only upon agreement of the terms. Because they demanded a response, their delivery to Trivulzio should have launched a dialogue. Instead, he deflected them. The captain made an unofficial entry to the city to take an audience with its people. Seated in the great hall of the old court packed to overflow, Trivulzio listened as an officer read out the terms. The old warrior responded warmly, but, as a Venetian observer bluntly noted, "he said he was not at liberty to grant them."[11] Milan's pact-making process remained incomplete, yet the occupation of the city by thousands of Gascon soldiers—something the *capitoli* expressly wished to avoid—began anyway.

Residents' aggravation with the imposition of French rule grew in these early weeks. Citizens clashed with French representatives over the expected cancelation of Sforza-era taxes. If the Milanese really were French, then they had to be treated as such. One group of men "with great courage" told Trivulzio that "they wished to be either all French or all Lombards: and if French, they wanted to remain exempt and free of [duty] injustices at the gates."[12] Over the next month, royal letters authorized the election of parish syndics to gather opinions from citywide assemblies on the vexed tax question. Notarial records of those meetings reveal how these deliberations over fiscal policy became entangled with the ongoing anxieties over the suspended *capitoli* and the question of swearing the oath to the king—an oath that the citizens postponed in expectation of some kind of royal decision.[13] Once the last of the duchy's Sforza-held castles capitulated on 26 October, the crown announced only limited fiscal relief, prohibited public assemblies across the city and duchy, and required Lombard subjects to swear fidelity to the crown.[14] In response, thousands of Milanese sacked the duty-houses; French forces violently dispersed the agitators.[15]

As Milan's residents faced their bitter disappointment, recriminations mingled with resignation. Girolamo Morone—the scribe at the civic assembly at Santa Maria della Rosa—excoriated his friend Luçon, president of the senate, for the new regime's delay in acknowledging the city's *capitoli.* "To forsake an unfinished project, to disappoint all men's expectations, to dismiss the authority of such a great city: I do not think it flatters the king's glory, much less the strength of the Milanese state."[16] Nonetheless, facing the necessity to submit after the suppression of resistance, citizens had few options.

On 29 October, more than seven weeks after Milan opened its gates to France, the citizens at last swore their oath of fealty to the king. Each parish of the capital named representatives to greet the sovereign, who had arrived in Lombardy only a few weeks earlier. The text of the oath reports that 150 delegates for each of the city's six gate-districts gathered in the castle of Porta Giovia, in the north bay of the courtyard, "under the image of the elephant," a fresco that remains today. Kneeling before the king dressed in regal and ducal attire, and having touched an image of the crucifix and a missal containing the scripture, the Milanese promised "freely, voluntarily, from certain knowledge, led by no error of law or fact, nor by fear, and through mature deliberation" their fealty to the French king and his heirs. It bound them to reveal any dissent against him or his proxies and to halt its spread.[17]

Three days earlier, the citizens of Pavia had gathered in the cathedral to make their own pledge of faith to the king. They too had already submitted a list of unanswered *capitoli,* which they hoped could carve out greater independence for their civic institutions. Pavia, home to the duchy's law school, had made specific requests revealing its inhabitants' juridical savvy. In particular, the city demanded the sweeping cancelation of all decrees of former lords (*quoscumque retroactos principes*), except for a few key protections, including the 1441 ruling known as *de maiori magistratu,* a ducal law that shielded populations against predatory fief holders or officials.[18]

That law empowered civic officials such as podestàs (the "greater magistrate" named in the law's title, representative of the duke) to protect subjects against any act of extortion by feudatories, such as forced vows of fidelity.[19] In so doing, it also arrogated to the duke the ultimate authority in adjudicating questions of politico-legal power in the state, thereby taming the pretensions of regional grandees. It makes sense, then, that the French regime saw value in the law as well. In winter 1501—hoping to dampen the jurisdictional free-for-all that it had created and seeking to reinforce its own juridical weight against the unpredictability of powerful lords across the duchy—the crown threatened to penalize any official who contravened *de maiori magistratu* by issuing unlawful fines, condemnations, or confiscations outside his own area.[20] It may not have escaped the Pavians in October 1499 that, under the vise of their new ultramontane masters, they too could have used the protection of *de maiori magistratu,* but as a wedge against the sovereign himself: they were about to swear a less than voluntary oath to an invading force.

Debates roiled in Pavia about how (and whether) to accept French rule. Some weeks earlier, the rectors of the university wrote to Trivulzio that a scene had unfolded when they called upon students in the faculties of law and arts to swear allegiance to Louis XII. When the university bedel read out Trivulzio's directive to the students, the pupils in law "immediately exited the school and did not want to hear what we had resolved to tell them to convince them to swear the oath." The arts students, by contrast, "immediately swore in the hands of their rector."[21] Disagreements ran deep, not just between faculties but between siblings. The law professor Giason del Maino—who had been on a diplomatic mission for Ludovico il Moro when the city fell—ultimately cast his lot with the French. His brother Ambrogio, Ludovico's governor of Cremona and Piacenza and referendary of Pavia, remained loyal to the Sforza and suffered confiscation of his goods and imprisonment.[22]

Similar fractures characterized the decision to swear oaths across the duchy. Many communities sent delegates to the French camp between August and October 1499 to indicate their submission.[23] Others broke away: Cremona submitted itself instead to Venice in an oath sworn by its citizens in September 1499.[24] Some resisted and wished to escape the necessity.[25] Among the resisters were the Bolognini-Attendolo counts of Sant'Angelo Lodigiano, whose failure to swear loyalty provoked both threats from the French and quarrels among their subjects.[26] Just four days before the Milanese tumult that briefly restored the Sforza duke in 1500, the French regime extracted another oath from sixty-four partisans of leading Milanese families, who swore "with their means and persons" to support the king "in whatever wars, tumults, or commotions might arise against the most serene king or his state."[27] These vows held citizens accountable not just through ritualized holy pledges but through notarized documents; they equipped regimes with legal commitments that, as sovereigns alternated, could prove menacing to the oath-takers.

Confusion arose over the nature of these pledges, particularly the conditions that governed their lawfulness. Could subjects sustain two binding oaths? In 1499, the representative assembly at Milan's Porta Orientale sought a concession from the episcopal vicar to swear to Louis XII, since the citizens recognized that they had a preexisting pact with Ludovico Sforza, which they now believed the vicar could dissolve.[28] Conversely, after swearing the oath to the French, some citizens evidently felt legally bound to fight for France against Ludovico—even against their own preference—during his restoration, as jurists later reported.[29] There was also the question of force and fear. The language of these pacts foresaw these problems and, so went the formula, stressed that they were not taken under duress. Nonetheless, compulsion recurred as a central charge in subsequent efforts to nullify oaths taken by families or communities. In a legal suit over lands in the 1540s, the Malaspina clan alleged that an oath to Louis XII taken by its members decades earlier was invalidated by the fact that he had occupied the duchy "by force and by arms" and thus had no legal right to receive their pledge. Moreover, the Malaspina rendered their pledge "because of fear," and any subsequent acts should thus be voided.[30]

Similarly, in 1515, shortly after François I conquered the duchy, he required oaths of fealty from its citizens.[31] The community of Bobbio, near Piacenza, complained that it had been coerced into its pledge. In a notarized protest, Bobbio's commissioners described how the royal representative, Antonio Assareti, pressed the citizens into professing their loyalty to the king.[32] The Bobbiesi wished to defer the vow, refusing to submit unless the Dal Verme counts, "who until now held this town," legally certified their shift of allegiance.[33] Assareti could not brook the delay and threatened to label the citizens rebels, call soldiers into the town, and imprison its syndics and procurators in the fortress. Making good on his threat, Assareti jailed two civic representatives for the better part of a day, releasing them only at midnight after incessant petitions on the part of the city. Facing this ultimatum, the citizens swore the oath, "by force and fear, and not of their own will," coerced into the ritual to avoid an even worse fate, they complained in a notarized grievance.[34] These dynamics describe an inversion of the scenarios imagined by *de maiori magistratu:* this was not an occasion when the prince or his agents intervened to protect subjects from the overreach of magnates. Instead, Bobbio called for the Dal Verme counts, the city's own fief-holders, as the intercessory broker in an extortionate contest with the prince and his representatives. Still, as part of an effort to centralize and consolidate its position as it had in 1501, the French regime confirmed *de maiori magistratu* in a statewide edict in 1517.[35]

Oaths of fealty concealed their own power negotiations in effusions of affirmative rhetoric and in the projection of a unison voice. Yet even in times of peace, the decision-making process leading to these vows involved contentious collective deliberation. During times of war, we should be even more attentive to both internal community divisions and external pressures. Force and resistance clung to rituals of covenant-making through Milan's early sixteenth century. Domination always carries resistance within it.[36] When Spanish captains demanded a pledge of fidelity from the Milanese following the battle of Pavia in 1525, the parishes simply ignored the order of convocation.[37] It is, moreover, easy to imagine even staunch detractors of a regime submitting grudgingly to such ceremonies for fear of standing out and inviting reprisal. Ludovico Sforza's own court historiographer, Bernardino Corio, quietly swore allegiance to Louis XII in his parish of Santi Nabore e Felice in October 1499.[38] Corio died in 1505, two years after publishing his history of Milan. Unregistered in the city's civic necrologies, he probably expired at one of his rural properties, far from the upturned city he knew better than anyone else.[39] Many of his compatriots decamped as well. Others instead remained in the city—whether hostile, devoted, or diffident to the regime—to work through the challenging politics of upholding civic culture in the face of its gradual deconstruction.

The Politics of Depletion

Displacement of people during the early-century contests over Lombardy involved far more than just the diaspora of elites, although the dispersion of middle and lower classes is nearly impossible to trace. Nonetheless, when we talk of "the people" of a city or district, we should remember first the environmental and physical disturbances that populations faced. With sovereign authority in suspension for long periods, potential for brutal treatment of the populace rarely abated, as enormous battles raged nearby and armies or exiles threatened to pilfer or sack.[40] Plague outbreaks in the years after 1500 compounded these effects.[41] Milan, you will recall the words of one chronicler, was in flux (*fluctuante*), and thus we must think about how depletion became a political problem in these years. People, funds, and forms of civic engagement found themselves emptied out under a cluster of stresses. To say, as civic representatives did frequently in these years, that the duchy had nothing left to give was to articulate depletion as a fundamentally political problem.

At its peak, Sforza Milan was a city of nearly 100,000 souls.[42] While little demographic evidence survives to document the contours of the population, the Italian Wars entailed major shifts: faced with military and economic pressures, elements of the duchy's urban populations decamped.[43] Diplomats referred to civic depletion; chroniclers described it. A memorandum written just after the establishment of French control in 1500 fretted about the demographic hangover from Ludovico Sforza's fiscal debts. Leaving the ex-duke's creditors unpaid would be a recipe for depopulation: artisans (of "wool, silk, cotton, and other crafts") who depended upon these creditors would depart for lack of investment, poor laborers would leave the city, and gentlemen—unable to sustain themselves in an empty city—would retreat to their villas.[44] Incessant conflict was clearly a fiscal problem. Many urbanites evacuated upon the announcement of routine but crushing exactions to pay armies or to placate the sovereign after coming to power (1499, 1500, 1513, 1514, 1515, 1516, and in similar intervals over the next fifteen years). Regime treasurers filled out and distributed preprinted paper slips (*bollettini*) to indicate how much money they expected individual residents to pay. Five rare surviving *bollettini* from the 1510s–1520s addressed to the patrician Federico Panigarola register both the urgency of the demands and the dire consequences of nonpayment ("*per evitare al sacomano de Milano*"; fig. 9.1).[45] In 1513, Massimiliano Sforza closed Milan's gates to prevent urban flight in the face of having to pay a ducal levy; the same happened in Bergamo.[46] By early 1524, Duke Francesco II complained that citizens of Milan had left the city "for the sole reason of avoiding the burdens that war brings," and he demanded their repatriation within two days.[47] The next year, the prince fretted over the exodus of artisans (silk workers

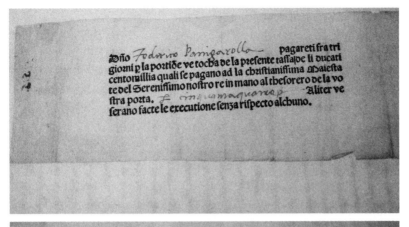

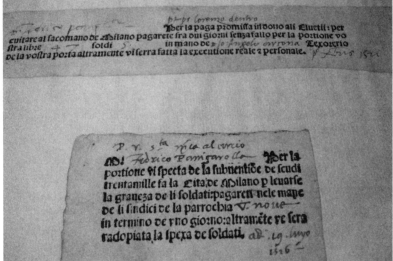

Fig. 9.1 Three of the five surviving *bollettini* for extraordinary wartime levies addressed to
Federico Panigarola, ca. 1513–1526. Tipped into MS Triv. 1342, Biblioteca Trivulziana, Milan.

in particular) and demanded their return to Milan on pain of being declared rebels.[48]

In 1525 under imperial rule, it happened again.[49] In the tense
months after the Spanish entered Milan, "much of Milan escaped," a
chronicler recalled. "Some fled for being unable to pay the fees of the soldiers; many came right back, thinking it could not last long. But as time

went on and the fees increased, gentlemen, merchants, and artisans left their homes and fled."[50] After the famine of 1526, "there were more houses abandoned than inhabited."[51] In 1527, while attempting to keep citizens from fleeing, the Spanish governor deprived those unable to pay a levy of their legal and statutory rights.[52] Only after the governor had allowed German mercenaries to inhabit the city freely for more than a month did he finally allow residents to depart without punishment, by which point "Milan no longer resembled Milan."[53] Fiscal exactions often preluded violent confrontations; to escape was to save both blood and treasure. Here is the nexus between financial and demographic empti-ness—a problem that grew with time, as serial wars consumed the duchy's people, productivity, and riches.[54]

Menaced by armies and rebels, the duchy's rural folk, conversely, sought refuge within city walls. In late August 1499, as French armies descended toward Milan, the chronicler Ambrogio rented a room in nearby Lodi. He witnessed "a multitude of carts and horses loaded with things, women, children" arriving from the suburb of San Grato, a crowd packed "end to end, and so thick that one could only with great effort push through to enter Lodi." In his own rental house "there were eigh-teen marriageable girls and many other women; things were all over the ground because there was no space, and all the houses of Lodi were full of foreigners."[55] In 1516, imperial troops flooded Lombardy to contest the French restoration in Milan. Chaos erupted in the region between the metropole and the Adda River, as weeping peasants flocked toward the city with cattle and children.[56] Consistently during these years, country-folk found themselves pushed to evacuate vulnerable places, leaving a trail of dispersal and depopulation.

Rural land had to be alienated or abandoned. After supporting the Sforza restoration in 1500, the small commune of Voghera faced as pun-ishment an enormous fine levied by its new French feudatory, Count Ligny. In order to meet the payment deadline, the hamlet sold off nearly 250 hectares of municipally owned forest, seeking buyers in Pavia and Milan and dismantling part of its economy in the process.[57] These prob-lems endured. Some rural lands between Milan and Venice lost almost two-thirds of their inhabitants in the first half of the century.[58] In 1529, after some of the worst years of war, English ambassadors reported to King Henry VIII that between Vercelli and Pavia, "for the space of fifty

miles the whole country has been wasted. We saw no man or woman la-
boring in the fields. All the way we found only three women, gathering
wild grapes. The people and children are dying of hunger."[59] Wolves
prowled the countryside "because there were no people in the cities."[60]
In his 1533 report on the state of Milan to the Venetian Senate, the orator Giovanni Basadonna described Lombardy in grim terms, calling it
a "state full of misery and ruin with respect to conditions of times past:
misery and ruin that cannot be overcome in a short span of time, with
workshops ruined and people dead, and this is why industries are lacking,
as are revenues both public and private."[61]

Lombardy's small but active Jewish community also suffered displacement between regimes.[62] Intermittently protected by law under
the fifteenth-century Sforza dukes (Ludovico, however, worked to expel
them in 1490), the Jews met resistance from both Lombard citizens and
their French lords in the first decade of the century, culminating in their
legal expulsion from the duchy in 1503; the displacement was carried out
fitfully over the next few years.[63] Ludovico's sons generally followed a
conciliatory position that the French regimes regularly rolled back.
Jewish communities renewed agreements with Massimiliano Sforza, only
to have pressures (fees, prohibitions against urban settlement, the yellow
badge) rise again under François I, including further rumblings of expulsion.[64] Duke Francesco II settled new pacts with the duchy's Jews in
1522, though cities such as Cremona and Pavia, stimulated by anti-
Semitic preaching, harried the prince to rescind their privileges.[65]

Aside from perennial conflicts over money-lending, dispute circled
around the question of whether the Jews' charters—which bound them
to pay a separate tax—also exempted them from contributing to the exactions, levies, and billeting that accompanied the wars.[66] (Charters ostensibly served to shield them from double taxation, but often, in practice, they did not.) Even supposedly sympathetic regimes targeted the
Jews' assets. Despite Massimiliano's renewal of Jewish privileges in
April 1513, financial strain to his coffers may have encouraged him to
explore a plan to extort the community. One month after the renewal,
the ducal chamber ordered the governors of nine of the duchy's major
cities to undertake a secret census of the Jews and of their financial
standing.[67] While Massimiliano's ouster in 1515 may have scuttled any
long-term strategy associated with this plan, little relief awaited Milan's

Jews through the wars, which compounded their legal and residential uncertainties.

Rural populations and Jews were always already excluded from traditional political subjecthood in the city. But even for urban residents who qualified as members of Milan's *civitas,* forms of civic representation transformed in the wars, blurring traditional modes of participatory engagement. The result of these shifts was complex, bringing both fresh political opportunities and an exhaustion of civic life. Let us examine each in turn, beginning with the glimmers of optimism that accompanied political disruption.

On this first level, the serial uprooting of regimes opened avenues of experimentation in which a greater variety of voices contributed to political dialogue.[68] Forms of representation diversified. To obtain consent for their political or fiscal demands, weak or fledgling rulers frequently summoned parish assemblies such as those convoked to swear oaths. The membership of these consultative groups cut across wide class divisions in the city, allowing an airing of diverse opinions. Wartime disruptions of political norms, in other words, opened venues for the capital's populace to express political desires and to steer crucial decisions about its existence. Some kind of outlet for this type of expression was important: unlike many other Italian cities in this period, Milan had no established citizen assembly.[69] But extraordinary financial demands required some kind of communal sanction. Perhaps because of this fact, Milan's lords consulted parish convocations as the likeliest path toward ratifying their designs.

When no prince ruled, as happened at several key interstitial moments in the early sixteenth century, the populace also assembled independently and ad hoc, of its own accord. These lord-less moments between regimes stimulated citizens to gather and compose the *capitoli* that aimed to articulate visions of the future.[70] In 1499, the terms suggest a radical vision of civic autonomy at the end of the Ludovician era, one that recalled the ambitions of the Ambrosian Republic in midcentury: Milan's citizens requested license to appoint their own state council and assembly to administer statutory reform, criminality, and taxation (thereby leaving crucial fiscal matters out of the sovereign's reach). The *capitoli* asked for the destruction of the Sforza castle at Porta Giovia and civic liberty from French domination should Louis XII die without heirs.[71] These were bold views for a city at the mercy of a foreign army. Their temerity came to be tempered in later submissions.

Outsiders similarly appreciated new opportunities opened during wartime and tried at times to appeal to Milan's citizenry by arguing for its autonomy. In 1511, the Swiss Confederacy, disillusioned by Louis XII's elusive promises to the cantons of trade exemptions and military non-interference, sent a massive army against the French in Lombardy. Upon arriving at Milan's suburban plains, the Swiss captains sent a letter to the city's residents. It informed "the entire populace that we are not seeking your destruction but your liberation from the French," and they requested a parley with Milanese representatives to encourage the citizens to rise up against their domination.[72] It was not an impossible thing. The notion that the capital's citizenry might follow a republican impulse modeled on the Swiss Confederacy became a legitimate prospect over the next five years, as Swiss interests invested heavily in co-administering Massimiliano's restoration in 1512-1515. In 1520, a Venetian ambassador foresaw Milan joining the Swiss Confederacy as the most probable outcome of its existential trials.[73] Despite the fact that this same diplomat insisted that the Milanese wanted an Italian duke, the possibility of total political realignment emerged as one of the most radical scenarios created by the Italian Wars. Disruption of political norms, in sum, created opportunities for rethinking the transaction of politics and who could contribute to it.

On the second level—civic exhaustion—the incessant political experimentation I have just described cast a long, deep shadow. In that pall dwelt frustrations with the torn fabric of political life. Burdensome weights of war, billeting, and tumult compounded dissatisfaction with the multiplicity that the cracking of the state had produced: the chronically changeable ad hoc solutions to the problem of the community's self-representation to the ruler. Barriers of political apprehension between populace and new rulers abounded, as the civic *capitoli* (in 1499, 1502, 1515, and 1516) show. Although Milan's citizens understood their *capitoli* of 1499 in contractual terms, French disregard for them contributed substantially to the uprising that ushered in Ludovico's short restoration in 1500; even after Louis XII's agents regained power, it would take until 1502 for a fresh set of Milanese *capitoli* to reach the sovereign.[74] These new petitions demanded solutions to problems of criminal justice, economic policy, government structure, and exiles. Louis's responses show openness to a certain level of civic self-determination, though he summarily dismissed two demands: to elect six civic officials to oversee the proper management of fiscal affairs, and to reduce merchant duties.[75] By refusing to release fiscal control into the commune's own hands, the sovereign drew a line in the sand. In 1499, the French had imagined that Ludovico Sforza's captured treasures would sufficiently finance the French army for at least three years.[76] But as Louis and his finance ministers soon discovered, and as we have seen throughout this book, they had instead inherited severe credit shortfalls and a fiscal crisis from the Sforza.[77] While the crown wished to set these deficits right, its main objective was still economic extraction.

Citizens recognized this intention. Artisans and shopkeepers expressed their dissatisfaction with political and fiscal policy by literally shutting their doors on the public sphere. Closure to public trade counts as one of the first political responses of the city to French domination.[78] In 1499, a cardinal had to walk from shop to shop to convince merchants to reopen their doors to the city. This type of closure—common enough in conflictual moments of civic life—transformed into a tactic of pure resistance, as merchants responded to unwelcome levies or political duress by bolting their shops and ceasing their trade, rallying to the cry "*serra, serra*! (lock, lock!)."[79]

To illustrate the politics of depletion, let us focus the analysis on one shift between regimes: the months between June 1515 and July 1516. While the first summer appeared to deliver political successes to Milan's artisan class, the next year showed how rotating sovereigns could void this same space of political action. In June 1515, Massimiliano Sforza struggled to sustain his rule. He no longer had any funds at his disposal. On 18 June, pressed for payment by a cadre of Swiss emissaries and aware that King François I was organizing a new invasion, Massimiliano imposed a 300,000-ducat levy upon the exhausted city ("*la exausta città de Milano*").[80] The duke imposed the fine without any prior consultation with residents. In a self-organized assembly, the citizens refused the levy.[81] (They had already paid 200,000 ducats to the Swiss in June, 1513 and had negotiated their way out of another payment in 1514.[82]) The Milanese elected a team of deputies to plead their case to the Swiss ambassadors; in the meantime, "the crowds decided to close their shops, cease any business, and await the end of this affair, promising to help each other out should anything new arise."[83]

The next morning, messengers from the citizen assembly fanned out across the duchy to sound out both Milan's magnates and its other subject cities to see whether united opposition might emerge across the state. Civic representatives put the case to Duke Massimiliano himself, but, unwilling to listen, he had its four members hastily imprisoned. With bells ringing in alarm, the populace gathered in assembly at the cathedral ("*generale unione,*" "*se levorno in comune tutti li homeni Milanexi,*" "*tutto Milano se unitte insema*"[84]), where they raised their standard, a white banner painted with an image of Saint Ambrose. Beneath the patron saint's gaze, the people processed from the duomo to the church of Sant'Ambrogio for a mass.[85] The chronicler Burigozzo, himself a merchant, called the participants "real men (*veri homeni*): not magnates or lesser nobles, but all citizens and merchants."[86] Ducal representatives appeared before the crowd to propose that the city could begin by paying only a fraction of the levy, to which the throng responded: "No more levy! No more levy!"[87] The day ended with a citizen council at the Church of the Rosa.[88] Calls to arms culminated in a skirmish between Milanese citizens and Swiss troops that same day. News reached Venice that Milan was "upside down" and "in great combustion."[89] Following the unrest, Massimiliano allowed its citizens to elect a Council of Twenty-Four representatives (four men from each of the six gates) whose duty would be "to consult and to see to the common good of the homeland."[90] Essentially it functioned as an interim government, since the citizens seemed unwilling to bend to ducal authority.

Cornered, the Sforza prince then made further concessions. First, he revoked his recent levy (on 23 June, five days after its imposition), acknowledging the citizens' complaints that it weighed heavily upon them.[91] Second, he relinquished ducal control over a number of crucial urban privileges (on 11 July). These included the selection of the *vicario di provvisione* (the chief city magistrate), as well as a host of other civic offices.[92] Nomination of these positions had, over time, become a ducal prerogative. In alienating these powers, Sforza traded control over city governance for a sip of fiscal liquidity. The sale brought Massimiliano only 50,000 ducats, a fraction of the sum he had sought.

Historians long assumed that the elected Council of Twenty-Four negotiated this agreement, along with the cancelation of the levy.[93] Recent research has interestingly complicated this picture.[94] Close analysis of the notarial contract of sale between the duke and the city suggests a second body of citizens stepped into the breach: a small group of self-appointed agents working in the name of the city (*agentes nomine comunitatis*) hammered out the terms with Massimiliano, separately from the Council of Twenty-Four. It now appears that the initial political solutions proposed by the Council of Twenty-Four had met with disapproval, and that their authority began quickly to erode. Other citizens—merchant patricians and administrators of holy sites, not popularly elected but self-appointed—reached an agreement with the sovereign, bypassing the elected agents. The notary took pains to disguise the fact that this body had no real juridical authority.[95]

This unbidden intervention raised some central questions: Who was the *comunitas*? Whose actions represented the entire city? An era of evanescent authority provided only foggy answers. Although there would still be occasional recourse over the next decade to parish or elected assemblies like the ad hoc Council of Twenty-Four, this moment in 1515 marked a moment of complex political failure. While this contest between prince and commune appeared primarily to check the Sforza duke's powers, the city lost its prerogatives as well: its elected council was bested by a cadre of patrician and religious elites. This enterprising but legally shady group that negotiated the 1515 concessions with Massimiliano circumvented wide consultation to avoid the socio-political volatility that accompanied genuinely representative negotiation. The French regime that installed itself in late 1515 found similar ways to dampen civic representation. The governorship of Odet de Foix, sieur de Lautrec (1485–1528), exemplified this deepening divide.[96]

The French Return and Lautrec's Government (1516–1521)

In post-conquest *capitoli* submitted to the French in January 1516, followed by a second set in July, Milan's citizens attempted to claw back some autonomy won so recently from Massimiliano, but they faced resistance from a crown eager to reassert itself unequivocally.

Among requests to curb corruption, discipline soldiers, and retain some civic financial management, Milan's representatives also proposed that district electors should directly select its chief urban magistrates (the *vicario* and *XII di Provvisione*), much as had been done with the Council of Twenty-Four. While the crown did not reject the notion of election, it wished to disable communal assent by controlling the process. The king asked for a list of three nominees for each position, from which he or his delegate would select appointees.[97] Once in office, these civic executives would have no right to congregate without direct royal consent.[98] This dictum did more than just reinscribe the pre-1500 ducal habit of appointing civic officials. It signaled the citizens' alienation from their familiar pathways of self-governance, a draining from Milan's politics of a cast of native participants in favor of French ones. (When the citizens asked in person to elect their own *vicario,* the king replied vaguely "that a Frenchman had already been elected, but he would see if he could find some way to gratify them."[99])

This strategy of top-down exclusion found confirmation in Lautrec's own exalted self-image as governor. He deployed richly regal trappings to prop up his lieutenancy, setting himself apart from Milan's political class. An observer in Cremona remarked tartly upon the governor's fondness for making grand civic entries beneath a canopy, which Lautrec "wanted when he came from France to govern the state of Milan, starting from the foot of the Alps. Throughout the whole ducal dominion, he wanted the baldachin carried to all the cities, with processions. Not even the King of France would receive half the honor if he came to Lombardy as Lautrec did."[100] A wide array of voices echoed this withering critique. In mid-July 1518, the Ferrarese envoy to Milan described the duchy's decline, pointing also to the habit of selling offices, a French custom not previously practiced in Lombardy:

> This state is in the worst condition because it is badly governed: there is little justice, and all the offices great and small are given to Frenchmen, and those who do not want them (or cannot serve) sell them, which explains why even justice is for sale; officials' extortions are very cruel and go unpunished; the soldiers behave like devils in the city and

do whatever they like outside; there is neither fear nor obedience. The state has infinite bandits who steal in the streets,
and things are in such dire straits that Milanese gentlemen
dare not stay overnight in the countryside.

A litany of disorders follows: thefts from treasurers, a fear that military
reinforcements might "ruin the people more than they already are," "a
great number of murders," and the inflammation of factional tensions.
He then turns to Lautrec:

The most illustrious Monsignor Lautrec dissatisfies everyone, he looks after nothing, both this side and that are disaffected with him, he does not give even a single finger's breadth
to anyone from the Italian world: as I said, he gives all the
offices to Frenchmen. The French soldiers are led into bad
deeds without letting themselves believe they are doing ill
unless someone quarrels with them; the Italian soldiers are
mistreated.[101]

Just days before this Ferrarese report, Lautrec had substantially reduced
the number of delegates appointed by the city's gate-districts to consult
with the French governor. Noting the diminution of this body of representatives by one hundred heads, the Mantuan envoy wrote:

Here there are 160 gentlemen who govern this city, that is 25
per gate from 6 gates. The illustrious Lautrec, finding the
number too large, appointed 10 men of his choice per gate
who he wants to have all the authority that the 160 had. The
reason for this is not well understood and has led to a great
deal of talk; ultimately it is thought that [the French] will
raise a levy.[102]

The delegate reduction, it seems clear, aimed to narrow the diversity of
voices and render the city pliable to royal demands.[103]

Lautrec demanded a 70,000-scudi levy in November 1518. Foreseeing resistance, he demanded payment within three days, but the silk
and wool merchants decided to close their businesses in protest. When
a French gentleman went to buy some cloth and found no shops open,
news of the strike quickly reached the governor. The members of Milan's

XII di Provvisione met with the city's gentlemen and merchants (*feceno uno gran conseillo per non pagare questo tayono*) in the church of the Benedictine nuns at the Monastero Maggiore, "almost facing Lautrec's residence."[104] They resolved to send negotiators to the governor. But Lautrec, whose palazzo was "stacked at the doors, stairs, and exits with armed men and halberdiers," refused to meet them.[105] He demanded the names of the resistant merchants and had three of them imprisoned in his house. The captain Teodoro Trivulzio, Giangiacomo's nephew, organized a parley between Lautrec and the detained merchants, who insisted that their assembly had confirmed "that his Most Christian Majesty could not impose any levy at all, and they had closed their shops fearing they would be plundered by the crowd."[106] Only when Trivulzio vouched for the good faith of the merchants did Lautrec release them. The city's representatives ultimately offered a fraction of the requested levy, as they would almost every subsequent year in response to crown demands during Lautrec's governorship.[107] Forms of civic consultation, pushed gradually to the margins of Lautrec's vision of politics, came largely to be transacted in opposition to the regime, literally across the street from the center of power. Enforced diminution of representative institutions tightened the channels for political discourse, channels that now served as nodes of resistance to the crown's policies.

Lautrec's season as Milan's governor coupled fiscal exactions with legal interference. These intersections were not new. In the 1490s, Ludovico Sforza had pressed his subjects aggressively on matters of law and money, and complaints over interference in criminal trials had dogged Chaumont d'Amboise, Louis XII's governor of Milan.[108] But by the late 1510s, with the crown's incessant demands, the vise tightened upon the duchy. Even bodies such as the senate, designed to function as an independent judiciary, had its verdicts altered by Lautrec. In 1521, as antiregime configurations expanded across the region, Lautrec charged a senate committee consisting of three French senators to prosecute a trial against the elderly Marquis Cristoforo Pallavicino, member of the powerful feudal clan whose vast territories in the duchy's southeast centered at Busseto.[109] Lautrec's brother Lescun, who counted Pallavicino among his friends, arrested the marquis in Busseto on suspicion of crimes including sheltering exiles; Cristoforo maintained his innocence even under torture. His lengthy Milanese court case, followed closely by observers both inside and outside the duchy, culminated with Lautrec revising the senate's clement decision: rather than face extradition to France, Pallavicino languished in Milan's fortress prison and was decapitated later that year as papal-imperial forces buffeted French sway in Lombardy. The marquis's goods were transferred to Lescun.[110] This "miserable spectacle" affirmed what Francesco Guicciardini—watching events unfold as papal governor of nearby Reggio—described as Lautrec's politics of terror.[111] That politics in turn fed not only the forces of resistance that ended French control; it also stimulated an allied wave of cultural resistance, whose satirical traces serve to end this chapter.

Satire and the Language of Resistance, 1517–1522

Domination stimulates dissident language; a space must exist in which to discuss, assess, and even denounce perceived abuses of power. It was this space that Lautrec worked to eliminate. After 1499, physical environments for convening to share political views became scarcer. The earlier demolition of *coperti* and gathering places in Milan had already removed sites devoted to social and political discourse. Even if citizen assemblies continued to congregate for momentous decisions at the Dominican church of the Rosa or in the garden of the Franciscan church of Santa Maria della Scala, spaces for casual interchange came under strict regulation.[112] As we saw in the book's first part, public speech critical of the regime brought castigation. With François I's accession, surveillance of critique expanded in the French-governed states on both sides of the Alps. Residues of subversive talk instead accrued in cheap pamphlets; they were perfect vehicles for constructing a shared imaginary of resistance that could articulate both elite and popular complaints through performance or reading.[113]

These promiscuously circulating products challenged authorities because they inscribed the destabilizing language of the street-performer, the satirist, and the libeler in a medium that extended audiences for heterodox political discussions without always needing people to gather in real time and space. They were instruments of virtual publics. Moreover, this type of text functioned ideally as an intellectual dagger to eviscerate sovereign power. Sharp words, detached from the person of the offending author, aimed to injure invisibly and to voice the otherwise unspeakable.

Louis XII tolerated satirical jabs at his Italian expansion. He allowed the performance and publication of Parisian farces skewering his campaigns during the first decade of the century and even lent his nominal patronage to a satirist such as Pierre Gringore, author of several cutting send-ups. When Louis died in late 1515, the new young king discarded his predecessor's forbearance.[114] In an order of January 1516—while François was in Milan—the Parisian parlement prohibited the performance of "farces, *sotties,* and other games against the honor of the king" or the rest of the court, on pain of an unspecified punishment.[115] Similar prohibitions reappeared in 1523 and 1525.[116] The 1516 restriction of farce reordered the liberties of Parisian political critiques: in that same year, a well-known *fatiste* was beaten by men rumored to be the king's, and three playwrights were imprisoned for contravening the parlement's order; two years later, Pierre Gringore left Paris for good.[117] Although François nominally tolerated satirical plays, he substantially curtailed their sphere of address.[118]

In the wake of the French loss of Milan in 1521, a series of at least seven libelous pamphlets circulated in Paris. The crown condemned them and ordered them destroyed, though they became well known to Parisian chroniclers, whose transcriptions saved them from utter destruction: *The Painted World, The Bony World, The Frying-Pan World,* and *The Itchy Ones Who Scratch Someone.*[119] The texts elaborate a world-upside-down critique in allegorical scenarios in which "asses make the world perverse." France's people go hungry because "everything has been fried by unbearable severities" brought on by poor leadership and expensive wars. When the authors came to light, they and their printers were sentenced to three years' imprisonment in the Conciergerie.[120]

Evidence from Lautrec's Milan suggests that the Lombard capital, too, produced and consumed an effusion of printed political commentary. In the summer of 1519, Lautrec signed a municipal order condemning what he called "documents" and "defamatory libels" (*cedule, libelli difamatorij*) directed against Milan's senate, the city's captain of justice, and French officials. It challenged the libelers to appear and prove their indictments within fifteen days. Otherwise, the order concluded, "it shall justly be thought that these libels and writings were published and posted (*misse et affixe*) out of malice and not truth."[121] Under Francesco II Sforza in January 1522, Chancellor Girolamo Morone banned the circulation of printed "songs or poems," citing their role in inflaming factional dispute. He ordered all copies of partisan pamphlets to be surrendered to the ducal chamber and prohibited printers from issuing any texts without ducal approval.[122]

The merchant patrician Giovanni Andrea Prato also recorded a list of seventeen pamphlet titles—delightful and puzzling in equal measure—in his Milanese chronicle. Under his comments for the year 1517, Prato, in a moment of uncharacteristic whimsy, frames this list coyly, noting: "Many things remain to be written, but since the chill in these last days of January is so great, my ink has frozen and my frigid fingers prevent me from writing. Nonetheless, wishing to describe a few works newly printed in Milan and elsewhere, and finding myself unable to copy them all, I will only write here their titles, beginning like this."[123] The ensuing list—almost certainly conjured from Prato's imagination—conscripts broadsheet titles to satirize Milan's politics and dozens of its major players.

Alternately cryptic and boisterous, the "newly printed" works deflate well-known figures or parody current affairs. Let us look at just three of the seventeen titles.[124] Take, for instance, the "*Treatise on Blackening Hair,* composed by Sgr. Teodoro Trivulzio, with the glosses of the Grand Squire, and with the Primate's seals, from which book one can expect a marvelous recipe *for dyeing beards.*" It seemingly derides the vanity of two of Milan's great courtier-captains, Trivulzio and Galeazzo Sanseverino (the Grand Squire), both of them nearly sixty in 1517. A "Little work *on inflation, or a dropsy* of the purses of the Milanese, with the remedy *newly* devised and essayed in the recent diet of Fribourg, a Canton of the Swiss," points to the fiscal duress brought upon the Milanese by the exactions to underwrite the king's settlement of the so-called Perpetual Peace with the mercenary-supplying cantons at Fribourg in November 1516. Finally, "Tercets *On the Pimp's Art, and On Overcoming the Modesty of Matrons* to gain favor with the French, compiled by Girolamo Figino and Masino da Lodi, dedicated to Sgr. Antonio Maria Pallavicino, in antique script: *a work most necessary to the present times,*" impugns these three erstwhile stalwarts of Ludovico Sforza's court, who, in collaborating meretriciously with the French, are imagined to be morally as much as politically compromised.[125] The list continues in this spirit, abbreviating to a single page a deft autopsy of the chronicler's beleaguered city. As an imaginary catalog of books, Prato's list predates some of our earliest examples of the genre.[126] As a suggestion of the probably vast ocean of politically en-gaged Lombard cheap print now lost to us, it is tantalizing.[127]

To encourage the vaguest glimmer of likelihood that Prato's catalog might not be so far-fetched, a rare satirical booklet from 1523–1524 has survived: *Il Libro de Lautrecho,* printed in Milan by Agostino da Vimer-cate.[128] Only two full copies exist, in Milan and Nuremberg; another fragmentary copy survives in Florence.[129] The author names himself Francesco Mantovano, a writer often identified as Francesco Vigilio, a comic playwright from Mantua, home to a substantial Milanese exile community.[130] Divided into four books (the last one by far the longest of them), *Lautrecho* narrates Milan's politico-military fortunes from 1521 through the Battle of Bicocca in 1522; its remarkable fourth part aims poisonous satirical darts at Lautrec in the immediate aftermath of his ouster from Milan in 1521, and its title could sit comfortably on Prato's list of publications: *The Fourth book of Lautrec; the description of the whole French war against Milan, and the testament drawn up by Lautrec believing he might die in battle; & the discord born amongst the devils for his soul, thinking he would die in the fighting. And many other things brought about by this war. Com-posed by Francisco Mantuano. Cum Gratia & Privilegio*[131] (fig. 9.2).

The entire poem, sometimes taken to be a farce intended for the stage, centers on Lautrec's arrival at the gates of Hell. It may draw inspi-ration from Seneca's indictments of Emperor Claudius (*Apocolocyntosis Claudii*) or Erasmus's skewering of Pope Julius II (*Julius exclusus*). Having alienated God and the saints through his mistreatment of Milan, Lau-trec descends, still living, to sue for good will from Pluto, though even in Hell he is welcomed icily. The narrative indicts his governorship, fig-uring him as a new Nero who has inflicted "horrific excesses" upon the duchy.[132] The first three books rehearse the unhappy chain of events leading to the conflict at Bicocca. In the fourth, Lautrec foresees his own death in the battle, and he draws up an infernal testament. In it he commends his soul to Pluto, bequeaths his arrogance to the French, his avarice to the Genoese, his fraudulence to the Venetians, his cruelty to his brother, and so forth. A coven of demons dispute which of them will have the pleasure of torturing Lautrec's soul in eternity, and Pluto prom-ises them all a share.[133] In an address to the city's populace, a personi-fied Milan tells of the "sad results" of French rule, cataloguing the "great malice," "evident deceits, and vast injustice." Milan calls upon its people

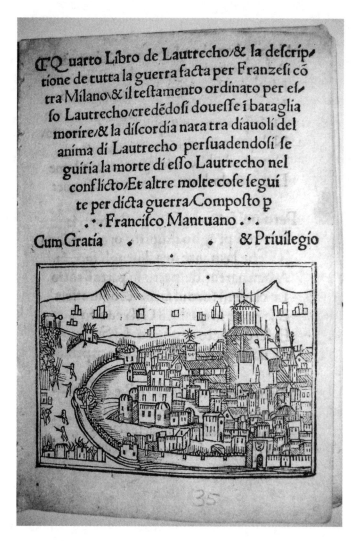

ℭQ uarto Libro de Lautrecho/& la defcrip⸲
tione de tutta la guerra facta per Franzefi có
tra Milano\& il teftamento ordinato per ef⸲
fo Lautrecho/credédofi doueffe i bataglia
morire/& la difcordia nata tra diauoli del
anima di Lautrecho perfuadendofi fe
guiria la morte di effo Lautrecho nel
conflicto/Et altre molte cofe fegui
te per dicta guerra/Compofto p
.∴. Francifco.Mantuano .∴.
Cum Gratia   ·   ·   & Priuilegio

Fig. 9.2 Frontispiece to Book 4 of Francesco Mantuano's *Lautrecho,* ca. 1522. Biblioteca Trivulziana, Milan.

© Comune di Milano.

to "defend our land with arms against the guilty barbarians." Tellingly, given Lautrec's disregard for consultative procedures, Mantovano describes the city's neighborhoods electing leaders and forming bands of "artisans and gentlemen, elders and youths, and every manner of man" to process before the new Sforza chancellor Girolamo Morone, vowing to "halt the Gallic arrogance."[134] While celebrating the restored Sforza regime and its imperial backers, *Il Lautrecho* also forcefully registers complaints stifled over years of contest with the duchy's recalcitrant governor. Near the end, the personified Milan cries out: "I will hear no more: I want Frenchmen out of this land."[135]

Comedy, like the lining of a garment, is the inner side of mourning.[136] The quips that warmed Prato's cold fingers, Lautrec's hellish sojourn: they were necessarily rueful. Outrageous humor carried outrage inside it. As the conflicts over Lombardy lengthened into the 1510s and 1520s, the generation's ambitions to find some kind of social, political, or economic anchorage slackened. The resilience of populations to the rotation of regimes had limits. An eloquent witnesses to this fact is Michel de Montaigne, whose father Pierre Eyquem served François I in occupied Lombardy; Eyquem recounted a tale that identified the burden of constantly shifting politics—in other words, the core problem of Milan's early sixteenth century—as a deadly one. "I have heard my father tell," Montaigne wrote, "how places were taken and retaken so many times in our recent wars in Milan that the people became weary of so many changes of fortune and firmly resolved to die: a tally of at least twenty-five heads of household took their own lives in one single week."[137] Disconsolate echoes in other contemporaneous texts lend strength to this tale that otherwise might seem unlikely. Prato reported that the burden of sustaining foreign armies proved so crushing that some Mantuan householders "died of despair," and Machiavelli noticed that Milan's citizens would "rather die" than face further extortions and sacks.[138] Francesco Guicciardini, watching much of northern and central Italy traverse frightening political territory during these same years, wondered in a short essay "whether killing oneself to avoid the loss of liberty or to avoid seeing one's homeland in servitude proceeds from greatness of soul or from baseness; whether it is laudable or not."[139] Claiming to ground reflections in purely theoretical and historical concerns, Guicciardini's hypothetical circumstances in fact seem firmly anchored in contemporary moral calculus.

Desperation caused by circulating politics can produce fear that nothing is permanent: "We see human affairs and especially states alternating every day: where today there is victory and power, tomorrow there is loss and servitude, and vice versa." Guicciardini figures that "often these revolutions and these tempests" arrive in times when it seems futile to hope. Ultimately, "it cannot be denied that suicide—aside from removing one's chance of ever returning to the desired status—is damaging to others, especially when a man kills himself so as to avoid seeing the servitude of his homeland which he can help much more by living and waiting for some opportunity to restore its liberty and its former estate than by taking his own life."[140] Certain people, he continues, consider it "the greatest insult, by way of iniquitous fortune, to obey, serve, and be subjected to those who by nature and human law are their equals." These men may thus seek to maintain their dignity or glory in self-murder. Guicciardini concludes diffidently that suicide inspired by political domination shows no generosity of soul, "but it could still be disputed whether it is judicious or not."[141] Even if he refused to praise political suicide, he understood why someone would do it.

The covenants that rulers attempted to solder with their new subjects were not just legal agreements; they were moral oaths that placed the people in new configurations of power. At times of growing duress, that new state of affairs could prove existentially insupportable. Reports of householders driven to suicide by the politics of occupation should remind us of this fact, as should incessant civic efforts to negotiate better terms of urban life through *capitoli,* as should growing cultures of political satire. New rulers' first rhetorical gestures upon assuming control—even amidst the vehement articulation of their own rights—always promised better things for subjects and citizens: an end to recent troubles. It was partly upon these grounds of better lordship that populations agreed to submit. But it was also partly upon the grounds of force, which lurked perpetually and unavoidably behind the language of peace. This chapter was not concerned to reveal Lombard populations merely as victims of war, but rather to expose the pathways of action, negotiation, and critique that they pursued in attempting to protect their society from evisceration. The threat of depletion produced certain forms of silence and speech. Satire was not disconnected from the prospect of an emptied civic life. The idea of a communally absent voice, a silent cry, appeared in Burigozzo's description of the anarchy that visited Milan in 1526: "Milan screamed, thinking it was able to scream."[142] Satire vocalized what otherwise had been silenced; it was the voice of mourning.

Conclusion

The Empire Strikes Back

$\mathcal{O}$n 25 October 1525, Habsburg agents interrogated the Sforza chancellor of Milan, Girolamo Morone, under torture.[1] In July, Morone had written a secret and combustive letter to Fernando d'Avalos, the Neapolitan-born marquis of Pescara (1489–1525). Morone worried that the young Emperor Charles V was on the brink of dominating all of Italy and thought that a wide coalition of Italian states should resist him. Morone had already found sympathetic allies in Pope Clement VII and Louise de Savoie, regent of France; the Venetians whispered that the question of Morone's overtures was "inhumed in our Council of Ten, where all the negotiations occur in the most profound silence."[2] If this coalition could push imperial interests from Italy, then the allies would name Pescara king of Naples. This moment in mid-1525 was particularly delicate. Duke Francesco II Sforza, suffering an intractable illness, seemed to be at death's door in Milan. In the event of his demise, one proposed scenario imagined the return of his elder brother, Massimiliano, from French exile to assume the duchy again. The adherents rallied around a rhetoric of Italian liberty from foreign rule; they wished effectively to stitch closed the entire wound in time between 1499 and 1525, to erase the *"tempo de' francesi"* with an Italian geopolitics that could heal with almost no scar.[3]

Pescara instead rubbed salt into the cut. Rather than join the league, he revealed it to the emperor by sending him Morone's letter. The bombshell led to the Sforza statesman's arrest and torture. Charles V insisted at first that he did not suspect the ailing Francesco II's involvement in the plot, although his suspicions darkened as news trickled to him in Madrid.[4] Pescara did not live to see what actions came of his revelations; still suffering from injuries incurred at Pavia, he died in November. The situation in 1525 represented the culmination of new configurations that had already begun to intersect for the Empire, France, and Milan in 1519. In that year, Emperor Maximilian I died. His demise refashioned Habsburg attitudes to the Sforza family and their dynastic claims to the Milanese duchy. In the 1490s, Maximilian's Italian strategy became enmeshed with Sforza interests in ways that pursued him into the new century: he had wed Bianca Maria in 1494, accorded Ludovico the coveted ducal investiture in 1495, acted as the Sforza children's ward after 1499, and facilitated Massimiliano's restoration in 1512–1513. Maximilian's death dissolved those links.

Moreover, the imperial election to name his successor in summer 1519 pitted two contenders for primacy in the Duchy of Milan against each other: Charles V and François I. France mounted an ebullient campaign, and some observers seemed almost certain that the young Valois monarch would win. Writing from Rome, Castiglione described a poor Frenchman living there who wagered all his wealth—300 ducats—on François's victory. When decisive Fugger financing brought Charles the title instead, the man hanged himself.[5] The early 1520s witnessed a crash in the French king's financial credit while the emperor's continued to rise.[6] The young Habsburg emperor, unburdened by a personal history with the Sforza, undertook a slow and steady campaign to absorb the Milanese duchy. At the same time, François's lordship in Italy began to slip. The powerful vassal he appointed as his first Milanese governor in 1515, Charles de Bourbon, later turned his coat and devoted himself to the new emperor.[7] In Lombardy, money problems lay behind resistance campaigns and unresponsive mercenaries. The withdrawal that began in 1521 in fact launched a five-year war of attrition to keep the duchy in French hands. It concluded with the bloody defeat at Pavia, where

Bourbon captured François himself and sent him into imperial custody. The monarch sat in gilded imprisonment in Madrid for a year while his mother, Louise, reigned in his absence.[8] With the king as hostage, the emperor threatened to endow the king's captor, Charles de Bourbon, with title over Milan.[9]

In 1525, hostilities were far from spent. French operatives at the imperial court at Toledo worked not only to hash out terms of the French king's release, but to rescue the monarch's Milanese pretensions. Charles V, exploiting the moment, pressed for the restitution of several other territories including the Duchy of Burgundy, a state with a history just as murky as Milan's: its succession wars had ended in 1482 with its lands divided between France and the Empire. The emperor now wanted it to revert to its former unity under his control. Jean de Selve, ex-vice-chancellor of French Milan, toiled for François in the negotiations at Toledo.[10] He found the juridical disputes dizzying and admitted to the French chancellor that his real strength lay in Burgundian issues; Milan's points of contention flummoxed him. Imperial negotiators dismissed Louis XII's two earlier Milanese investitures in 1505 and 1509 as void because he had not paid homage to the emperor within the stipulated span of one year. When de Selve responded by citing an explicit exemption from that clause in feudal law, he was told "it is observed differently in imperial lands." Each of his arguments met with repudiations, and de Selve wrote after the meeting that he would need further advice and help.[11]

Imperial casuistry created the legal confusions over Sforza inheritance that it claimed to resolve; discomfort with such indeterminacies had in fact been an engine of Morone's conspiracy. In his self-justification to his interrogators, the Sforza chancellor complained that fears in Italy arose after Charles V proved unwilling to confirm the imperial investiture that Francesco II understood as his rightful inheritance. The jurist Giason del Maino's nephew and heir, Tommaso, had made a special mission to Charles's court shortly after the new duke's accession to secure the Sforza privilege, but left empty-handed.[12] Morone's cadre of Italian supporters worried that imperial domination of Milan would crush the peninsula's political independence. If we follow the trajectory of Francesco II's imperial investiture as duke—a process that lasted nearly eight years—we can appreciate how the late Sforza era endured sovereignty contests as confounding as they had been in the 1490s. What had changed over those decades was the meaning of that investment. It no longer merely represented imperial assent of the reigning prince's status: it had instead become a ticket to rule so eminently transferrable that the principality's exchange value now equaled its political value. Networks buzzed with possible alternative contenders for the title of Milan's duke: Charles de Bourbon, George of Austria, Alessandro de'Medici, Federico Gonzaga, Henri of Orléans (future King Henri II).[13] Before the death of Francesco II in 1535, the emperor considered using Milanese investiture to solve intractable disputes over the Hungarian crown between his brother Ferdinand and the Transylvanian voivode János Zápolya.[14] The resident prince was irrelevant; Milan's politics were being sublimated to a higher plane.

Francesco II assumed his ducal title de facto in 1522 after the French withdrew from Milan; he narrowly escaped a French-sponsored assassination attempt in the summer of 1523.[15] In a late-October 1524 charter (*investitura ac infeudatio*), Charles V endowed Francesco II with Ludovico il Moro's fief, canceling any previous stakes held by Louis XII, Massimiliano Sforza, or François I.[16] But whether that document ever came into effect remains unclear.[17] Sforza's envoy, Giovanni Antonio Biglia, arrived in Spain only in early summer 1525 to negotiate the investiture.[18] His work generated another agreement with specific terms (*conventiones*) on 27 July 1525.[19] It highlighted Charles V's expenditures in liberating Milan and demanded 1.2 million ducats.[20] That was nearly ten times the price Louis XII had paid to settle his own investiture in 1509.[21] Biglia managed in his parleys to halve the sum.[22] Then came the twist: just three days later, Pescara wrote to the emperor with news of Morone's anti-imperial league.[23] Biglia had in his hands a freshly sealed parchment to legitimize a Milanese prince who had just been implicated in treason against the Empire.

Suddenly, Francesco II's weak health took second place to his suspect fidelity. Charles mused with trepidation over his Sforza vassal. Having just installed the duke, the emperor wondered how to punish or replace him. Bourbon now seemed not just a threat to the French king, but a feasible substitute for the disgraced Sforza. Over the winter of 1525–1526, imperial forces besieged the duke in Milan's castle. Biglia continued to attend Charles's court as matters worsened. In September 1526 the emperor's secretary asked Biglia to return Sforza's investiture charter. Biglia dug in. "He said he would not part with it and wanted to wait for them to take it from him by force."[24]

Sforza claims to Milan were now severely tarnished, and the imperial jurists composed a narrative of the Milanese fief—sent to the pope to account for the recent wars, and penned just days after Biglia's refusal—that reconstructed the history of its lordship so as to leave it squarely in Charles V's hands.[25] Their account accepted Ludovico's 1495 ducal ascension as legitimate and therefore doubted the validity of the countervailing Orléans-Visconti title; the papacy, they insisted, had erred in confirming that French privilege in times past. That king's failure to observe terms of his two successive imperial investitures in 1505 and 1509 invalidated them both, meaning the duchy technically, and silently, devolved to imperial ownership. Massimiliano Sforza absorbed his father's potential to inherit, but during his rule he controlled the duchy only de facto ("*nullam de eo statu habuit investituram, sed simplicem detentionem nullo jure suffultam*"). That claim was technically false, because the Empire's own electors had authorized Massimiliano for the ducal rank at the diet of Mantua in 1512. In any event, it hardly mattered since Massimiliano forsook his rights to Milan as soon as he "conspired with the French"—a euphemism for his forcible ouster. Following the jurists' logic, François I's treaty with the young Sforza for his submission of the duchy was void from its inception. The Valois king never had licit claim to Milan, their argument held.[26]

The manner in which Massimiliano surrendered the duchy also left the question of Sforza investiture in a legal cloud. He had not technically been fully invested (you may recall from this book's first pages his own self-investiture in 1512), but nor had he renounced his status as Ludovico's named inheritor—he had, in imperial reckoning, simply assumed control. Massimiliano had ruled Milan de facto but not de jure. He bore the potential for investiture but had instead ended his reign by giving the duchy over to an enemy of the Empire. Imperial lawyers argued that in so doing, he vitiated his own ability to transmit the inheritance to family, namely his younger brother, Francesco II. That bind was the Empire's trump card. In this reading, law did not prohibit Francesco from ruling the duchy, but nor could he accept investiture while his elder brother was still alive. Massimiliano was a living, breathing deferral; Francesco, it seemed, a traitorous vassal. Milan was thus Charles V's to dispose as he pleased. As seductively clarifying as this re-constituted narrative appears, the lawyers' smoothly logical retelling of the century's first decades is not the letter's most salient feature. Rather, the very construction of a tendentious narrative and the corollary de-ployment of that history as a tool of disempowerment should strike us as its most significant potential. It was a strategy to intervene in the sovereign contest so as to bring Milan definitively into the Empire's grasp. It constituted a decisive stroke to rescue caesarean sovereignty from its own tangles, to cut the proverbial Gordian knot. Disentangle-ment was, after all, an imperial prerogative: whoever undid the knot in Gordium—as Alexander the Great managed to do—was destined to con-quer the world.

In the midst of these historical rehashings, Massimiliano, exiled in France for a decade, seemed freshly relevant after the French defeat at Pavia. His imagined role in fulfilling Morone's plot and his legal standing as Ludovico's first-born heir returned his name to international conver-sation for the first time in years. That fact engendered unease between the siblings when Francesco II's health stabilized. The brothers corre-sponded in the year following Morone's arrest. Francesco wrote to dis-courage any ambitions his sibling may have harbored to return to the duchy. Massimiliano replied sharply, warning his brother that he would not "take your words as prophecy":

> For you do not wield the power of the words you speak, since you are neither pope nor King of France. You are Francesco Sforza, and I am Massimiliano: you can never force or dupe me, because your person is worth no more than mine (even if you were as healthy as God should wish), nor do you have more friends than I do. I have a good patron and as many friends as you do. But I fear, if you do not change your life, you will lose those friends you have, while I hope to gain more. And if you think that Fortune favors you more than me at present, she could also change things contrariwise, as Your Lordship knows from past experience, when I com-manded and you obeyed me.[27]

Until just before his death in 1530, Massimiliano believed he might be returned to his Milanese command under the aegis of France.[28] As discussions of a criminal trial for Francesco circulated, imperialists lifted the siege of Milan's castle in July 1526, and Francesco II Sforza abandoned Milan for Como, then Crema, Lodi, Cremona, and Vigevano, seeking distance from imperial garrisons. Duke in name but not in law, a fugitive within his own duchy, he would not reenter the castle until April 1531.[29]

In sum, by 1530, the Sforza return to Milan had effectively imploded on an international level. Morone's league of 1525 had thrown enough suspicion upon the dynasty's imperial loyalties that the Sforza family had nearly dropped from the list of Milanese rulers the emperor would countenance. Over these five years—and despite Francesco II Sforza's eventual return to his ancestral castle—the Habsburgs had laid the groundwork to strip the duchy of its Italian lords definitively.

Utterly, Utterly Undone

This situation left Milan hovering in suspension, both legal and existential. During the negotiations in Spain in 1525-1526, Charles V repeated on several occasions that he had no desire to tyrannize Milan or Italy.[30] Indeed, the temporary collapse of French aggressions in Lombardy appeared at first to offer relief from incessant dispute, but François's repudiation of the concessions extracted during his imprisonment promised further hostilities between France and the Empire.[31] Milan had essentially traded one foreign occupation for another. This state of affairs ushered in a period of violence, disease, and famine throughout the capital and the duchy that one historian called "four years of anarchy" (1526-1529).[32] Spanish troops held the city in the emperor's name under a series of military governors (including Pescara until late 1525, Bourbon until mid-1527, Antonio de Leyva until 1530), who exacted increasingly extortive payments in order to support the city's military presence.[33] Reinforced by German mercenaries, the Spanish army preyed upon the city it was meant to protect.

After an urban uprising in April 1526, tensions simmered between the city and the occupying army.[34] Leyva found it increasingly difficult to extract levies to support troops; the burden of such payments led Milan's inhabitants to declare themselves unable to pay "because Milan was utterly, utterly undone (*del tutto del tutto desfatto*)."[35] Frustrated by the city's reluctant disbursals, he allowed soldiers the liberty to inhabit citizens' homes in the summer of 1527.[36] Guicciardini framed Milan's plight in this period as a complete inversion of its former glory. Under combined military-financial pressures, merchants closed all the city's shops and hid their goods underground, burying too the "riches of private homes and church ornaments."[37] Soldiers nonetheless dismantled *palazzi* for firewood and shot the locks off shop doors to get at goods and munitions.[38] Grain shortages brought restrictions on bread-baking, and famine spread through the city.[39] Before the end of the decade, the city may have lost as much as half of its population.[40] The Florentine historian saw Milan's plight as an "incredible example of the reversals of fortune," describing the city "almost without inhabitants because of the terrible damages wrought by plague and because of those who fled and kept fleeing; men and women wore unkempt and very poor clothes; there was no remnant or sign of any workshops or industry that used to bring the greatest wealth to this city; and all the happiness and strength of men transformed into the greatest sadness and fear."[41] News of Milan's suffering traveled far in the late 1520s, and the emperor himself signed a letter to the Milanese entreating them not to despair and abandon what he framed as the imperial defense of Italy.[42]

Only with the 1529 peace between France and the Empire did Milan begin to see relief. Hostilities were not at an end—they continued well into the 1540s, punctuated by devastating raids of mutinous soldiers in the late 1530s and ongoing conflict over military lodging—but the capital itself had by 1531 weathered its worst storms and would avoid the brunt of the next decade's offenses.[43] Helped by papal mediation, Francesco II managed to reconcile with Emperor Charles in late 1529; the duke finally paid the 600,000 ducats to secure the charter that Biglia had defiantly protected in 1526. Francesco called citizens to repopulate the capital and aimed to bring grain and milling back into step with the city's needs.[44] The 1533 report of the Venetian orator, while calling the duchy "full of misery and ruin," also saw how "the abundance that once existed before seven months of famine has returned; the soldiers who consumed the public and the private have been removed, so one might now say that the grace of God has arrived."[45] Over the next decades, many rural communities across the duchy redistributed their collective wealth in order to restimulate their economies, and new money flowed into Lombardy in the form of Habsburg military investments.[46] Despite this gradual urban and rural convalescence, the Sforza duke's fiscality was terminally stressed. Annuities due to Charles V proved crushing, and Francesco demanded loans promiscuously, from Venice to Genoa.[47] In summer 1530, one of the duke's advisors declared the state to be in "total ruin (*ultima ruina*)," and that the duke was prepared "to sell everything except the cities, which he does not wish to sell, because I think he has settled a partition of Tortona with [the Genoese financier] Ansaldo Grimaldi."[48] Not even the duke's wedding to the emperor's niece appeared to bring financial balm.

Milan lurched into the mid-sixteenth century through a joint process of economic recovery and new forms of governance. But it was the combined politico-fiscal pressures of imperial oversight that brought about the extinction of direct princely rule. The state of Milan did not utterly vanish the way that some smaller contemporary principalities did: Cesare Borgia's Duchy of Cesena, the Varano Duchy of Camerino, the Pio lordship of Carpi, to mention just a few cases surrounding Lombardy.[49] It survived as a federation of cities governed from its capital. But through the contests to determine ownership of the state of Milan, the reality of the personal principate itself was utterly undone.

The Alienation of Princely Charisma

Contenders in the early Italian Wars fought fundamentally over the nature of political power in Italy's preeminent states.[50] They grounded their aggression in the proposition that large monarchical powers could accumulate Italian lands and rule them from a distance, thereby transforming princely domination into a specter of itself. In that model—and it is the one that triumphed over Milan—the body of the prince resided outside Italy, but his intentions ostensibly governed in his absence. Conversely, many Italians waged their resistance to defend personal rule anchored in local embodied relationships and the benefits it brought them. In 1520, the Venetian ambassador described how Milan's elites wished not just to have a governor, but to have "a duke, so that offices would remain in their own hands and they could raise their sons at the court of an Italian duke."[51] Likewise, in the wake of the first French domination the lower classes perennially favored Sforza princes.[52] Even those who accepted foreign rule preferred to have proximity to princely charisma—that personal mystique that fashions the allure of sovereignty.[53] In truth, these conflicting visions of the state—that is, locally concentrated versus externally distributed—shared functional structures but they differed profoundly in scale. Monarchies and duchies both sustained courts, oversaw territorial states, and delegated authority outward. But one model was regional and the other international. To resisters, it mattered whether the court's heart beat in Milan, Blois, or Toledo. For external powers to alienate charismatic authority was to crack and export the affiliations that held the state together.

Even though invaders wished in principle to foster the states they captured, they also recognized the necessity to snap apart the most potent existing affinities and practices. This process entailed an effort not just to reformulate ties among elites, but to reformulate the practices of princely rule. Alienation of power was the ultimate purpose of state-breaking. Autonomous political resolve had to be extracted in order to install mouthpieces: governors, viceroys, captains, and other avatars of monarchical fiat. In Milan's past, precisely the force of princely prerogative—the ineffable distinction of command—had played a key role in statecraft. Coupled with their tactics of suasion, that quality brought the dukes power, titles, or both: Giangaleazzo Visconti's charisma helped to confect the duchy in 1395; Francesco Sforza employed what Machiavelli called his "great prowess" to launch himself from private captain to duke in 1450; and Ludovico had played a brilliant but fatal political hand to bring himself rule and then investiture in 1495.[54] However, the wars of the first quarter of the sixteenth century, as this book has suggested, transformed the theater in which these sovereign dramas were performed.

Unlike his ancestors, Francesco II Sforza obtained his 1529 ducal investiture from a position of profound weakness. During his interrupted and fugitive rule, ducal prerogatives that his predecessors had constructed were either given or taken away. In the name of judicial reform in 1522, Francesco II endowed Milan's senate with the "plenitude of power" that the former dukes had jealously guarded because it vastly protected the authority of their dicta; it had been, in times past, the legal container of lordly charisma. Pescara's governorship in 1525 (during which time the duke was besieged in Milan's castle) began to tip the practices of Milan's government toward imperial lordship. Pescara appointed new financial officers to the ducal chamber, now called the "*Cesarea Camera del Stato di Milano,*" thereby claiming the ducal fisc as an imperial organ that remained so for nearly two centuries.[55] In 1529, a newly restored Francesco II ordered the senate to collect the duchy's laws and statutes into a code designed to rationalize the morass of conflicting edicts and rulings that had accrued over time.[56] In 1541 the compilation went to press as the *Constitutiones Dominii Mediolanesis* (*Decrees of the Dominion of Milan*). Authorized by Emperor Charles V, the volume ordered and reconciled the inconsistent sediment of lifetimes of Milan's various rulers.[57] (In the 1530s, Charles sought similar codifications in other contested imperial territories such as the Spanish Netherlands.[58])

The *Constitutiones,* often described as a triumph of legal codification and administrative savvy, certainly attests to the centralizing impulse in Habsburg governance and to the diligence of the duchy's leading jurists. But it was equally another act of alienation, in which the prince relinquished the juridical force of his own living word to the authority of accumulated tradition. Ducal supremacy as a charismatic performance in law and deed was at an end. At its heart, the *Constitutiones*—as a reckoning of the duchy's own legal history—held a mirror up to the state. Like the state, the book was the accumulated residue of regimes. Only through the labor of reconciling texts—which legal historians call "harmonization"—could the confusions of the past begin to assume the clarity desired of the present. Perplexities in the duchy's laws, it is true, would have accumulated even without the wars that beset Italy at the dawn of the sixteenth century; but the proliferation of warring authorities thickened the material to be clarified. It may help us to understand this project of collation if we see it as an institutional component of the effort to recuperate the state from its own contested history. That process of elucidation worked to turn the murk of the past into a code. The necessity for clarity that resulted in the *Constitutiones* suggests that the state essentially needed to be rewritten.

The processes that brought the *Constitutiones* into being between 1529 and 1541 belonged to larger transformations in governance and society that contributed to the stabilization of sovereignty in the Mila-

nese duchy. Legal reform, economic recovery, and the gradual uncou-
pling of dynastic claims from military intervention permitted the
operations of power to level into a new consensus under imperial governance. Domination lived on, to be sure, but fewer contenders asserting
their primal rights through violence meant that the so-called *pax his-
panica* faced less competition than Sforza or French rulers did in the
early part of the century.[59] The Spanish Habsburgs' success in monopolizing the discourse of sovereignty produced a general soothing effect
upon economic, military, political, and legal disputes.

The contested state, this book has proposed, deserves historical
scrutiny for what often goes overlooked in the fissures between regimes.
The fractured polity—just as much as the healthy one in the process of
consolidation—reveals how power relations functioned and what profound social fracas could produce or destroy. Historians interested in
the premodern state have perhaps allowed too much attention to fall exclusively upon the creative, rational impulses of state-building. As a way
to think beyond the legacy of such histories of consolidation and formulation, I have tried to address the book to problems of indistinction:
that is, moments when familiar forms of culture, politics, and life were
blown apart. If the modern state developed through a collaboration of
what one scholar has identified as "legitimacy, discipline, and institutions," we can see in this book how the Italian Wars severely tried those
elements in the Duchy of Milan.[60] To employ concepts like the shatterzone, the blur, and the palimpsest means drawing our analysis toward
issues frequently obscured by war and shifting regimes. This focus is not
intended to reproduce the confusions of war, but rather to identify, trace,
and explain them. For this reason, the book has dwelled upon the manner
in which contest produced opportunities to fashion new narratives and
to overwrite old ones. The sheer proliferation of contending stories—
about politics, history, land, law, prophecy, and community—opened
up times and spaces in which the world seemed to be overturned, or at
least to be transformed. That transformation, forged in the crucible of
war, emerged from chaotic fragmented contingencies, not from rational
strategies and artful designs.

Insofar as this book has advanced an interpretation of what I have
called flickering sovereignty, it has also been in an effort to break apart
the idea of sovereignty. It aimed to employ a methodology that would

reveal new avenues of analysis and new forms of purchase upon the material and ideological bases of power struggles. To trace the buckling, guttering aspirations of sovereignty is to reveal its constituent pieces and its prime manipulators. By doing that, we open it up to critical scrutiny. These kinds of disputes were not unusual in this period; they may even constitute a kind of rule, a fact that should stimulate further interrogations of the friction in what we perhaps too smoothly call "transfers of power." Milan survived the Italian Wars more or less solidly, but in the process its internal workings were liquefied. By seeing the state *as if dissolved,* as Thomas Hobbes imagined, we understand it most penetratingly. The slowly unfolding chaos of war—inferno and matrix in equal parts—reveals Milan's journey from Italy's political behemoth to regional imperial entrepot.

NOTES

INTRODUCTION

1. On the power dynamics between large states and small regional centers, see Hendrik Spruyt, *The Sovereign State and Its Competitors: An Analysis of Systems of Change* (Princeton, NJ: Princeton University Press, 1994); Wim Blockmans, "Voracious States and Obstructing Cities: An Aspect of State Formation in Preindustrial Europe," *Theory and Society* 18 (1989): 733–55.

2. "Et quaxi tutti li nobelli et citadini de Milanno foronno desradichati et malmenati, et questo perché, quando che il s.or Ludovico intrò in Milanno ultimamente, tutti quelli citadini che se dimostroronno favoritti ala corona francese, tutti foronno dal s.or Ludovico prexi, incharzerati et morti et parte malmenati et il loro beni confischatti. Alhora, ritornatto il re di Franza in Milanno, tutti quelli citadini che heranno dimostrati favoriti al s.or Ludovico per Francexi furonno disipatti, incharzerati, malmenati et morti, et li loro beni posti in comun, Siché o per una via, over per l'altra li poveri Milanessi heranno stati malissimo tractadi questo anno et pochi piuj se atrovavanno che havessenno qualche nominanza, over famma, sì quelli dala parta di Franza, chome quelli del s.or Ludovico, et li Francexi principioronno far li mestieri in Milanno et altri che loro non vendevanno, perché li Francexi compravanno dali loro Francexj proprij, sichè li Millanessi non potevanno piuj vender chossa alchuna" (Girolamo Priuli, *I Diarii, 1499–1512,* Arturo Segre, ed. *Rerum Italicarum Scriptores,* vol. 24, part 3 [Città di Castello: Tipi della Casa editrice S. Lapi, 1912–1938], 1: 313).

3. Machiavelli noted the same effect of Louis XII's conquest of Milan in *Il Principe,* Mario Martelli, ed. (Rome: Salerno Editrice, 2006), chap. 3.

4. Patrizia Mainoni, "Alcune osservazioni sulla politica economica di Milano fra Ludovico il Moro e il dominio francese," in Letizia Arcangeli, ed., *Milano e Luigi XII. Ricerche sul primo dominio francese in Lombardia (1499–1512)* (Milan: FrancoAngeli, 2002), 341–52, at 345, citing ASMi, Registri Panigarola, reg. 14, 382–88. Protectionism in the hat trade was a long-standing

posture of northern Italian governments as well. See the laws against foreign hat-trade in Venice in ASV, Compilazione delle leggi 50, Fasc. I, 19–32 (28 May 1475); 57–70 (13 September 1477); 178–79 (25 April 1490), Fasc. II, 37–82 (11 April 1507).

5. For the sailors, millers, and fishermen, see Léon-Gabriel Pélissier, *Documents pour l'histoire de la domination française dans le Milanais (1499–1513)* (Toulouse: Édouard Privat, 1891), doc. 25, 87–88, 25 October 1502; for the merchant corporation, see ASV, Archivio del Senato, Deliberazioni—Terra, reg. 14, cc. 202r–203v, *Capitula Mercatorum Mediolanensium,* 22 May 1503.

6. For a reading of conflicting visions of sovereignty as performed on festive occasions, see George L. Gorse, "A Question of Sovereignty: France and Genoa, 1494–1528," in Christine Shaw, ed., *Italy and the European Powers: The Impact of War, 1500–1530* (Leiden: Brill, 2006), 187–203.

7. For a recent biographical synthesis, see Gino Benzoni, "Massimiliano Sforza," *Dizionario Biografico degli Italiani* 71 (2008): 782–87.

8. On the Milanese resolutions at the Diet of Mantua, see Stephen Kolsky, *Mario Equicola: The Real Courtier* (Geneva: Droz, 1991), 130–33. For Swiss relations with Italy in these years, see Anne Denis, "1513–1515: 'La Nazione svizzera' et les Italiens," *Schweizerische Zeitschrift für Geschichte* 47, no. 2 (1997): 111–28.

9. Marin Sanudo, *I Diarii,* Rinaldo Fulin, ed. (Bologna: Forni, 1969–1979 [1879–1902]), 15: 458–60, Gianiacopo Caroldo in Crema, 1 January 1513.

10. Sanudo, *Diarii,* 15: 460.

11. Sanudo, *Diarii,* 15: 459. On the traditions of Milanese ducal investiture, see Pier Luigi Mulas, "L'Effimero e la memoria. L'Investitura ducale," in Luisa Giordano, ed., *Ludovicus Dux. L'Immagine del potere* (Vigevano: Diakronia, 1995), 172–77; and on the significance of investiture, see the essays in Stewart Gordon, ed., *Robes and Honor: The Medieval World of Investiture* (New York: Palgrave, 2001); Gordon notes in his essay, "A World of Investiture," 1–19, at 13, that secular investiture in which robe-taking indicated a new status was generally rare in the West outside medieval Venice.

12. On this tradition see Jane Black, *Absolutism in Renaissance Milan: Plenitude of Power under the Visconti and Sforza, 1329–1535* (Oxford: Oxford University Press, 2009).

13. Albert Büchi, *Kardinal Matthäus Schiner als Staatsmann und Kirchenfürst* (Zurich: Kommissionsverlag Seldwyla, 1923), 317.

14. Sanudo, *Diarii,* 17: 398–99, Letter of Vetor Lipomano, 13 December 1513.

15. Alberto Caviglia, *Claudio di Seyssel (1450–1520). La Vita nella storia de' suoi tempi* (Turin: Fratelli Bocca Librai, 1928), 285. "Attento quod ipse usurpaverit dictum ducatum mediolanensem, et dictus dux auxilio Sanctae Sedis recuperaverat."

16. Sanudo, *Diarii,* 17: 399 ("Il Papa zercò de mitigarlo e farli tacer"); Cavi-glia, *Claudio di Seyssel,* 285. Alternate phrasing of this same response appears in Paride de Grassi, *Il Diario di Leone X,* Pio Delicati and Mariano Armellini, eds. (Rome: Tipografia della Pace di F. Cuggiani, 1884), 11: "Illud hic non praetermittendum quod cum rex Franciae in suis mandatis nominasset se ducem Mediolani, dominus Martinus Caracciolo orator ducis Mediolani graviter conquestus est, et alte protestatus in forma, cui tamen respondit Papa se admittere quae in mandatis continebantur sine alicuius praeiudicio."

17. Crucial bibliography on the origin of the modern state in Italy appears in the notes of the introduction of Andrea Gamberini and Isabella Lazzarini, eds., *The Italian Renaissance State* (Cambridge: Cambridge University Press, 2009), 1-6.

18. From the vast literature on premodern sovereignty, the most penetrating recent analysis is Francesco Maiolo, *Medieval Sovereignty: Marsilius of Padua and Bartolus of Saxoferrato* (Delft: Eburon, 2007); for discussions of the history of sovereignty as a medieval concept, see 79-86, 286; and the extensive bibliography. For an early social constructionist view from International Relations theorists, see Thomas J. Biersteker and Cynthia Weber, "The Social Construction of State Sovereignty," in Thomas J. Biersteker and Cynthia Weber, eds., *State Sovereignty as a Social Construct* (Cambridge: Cambridge University Press, 1996), 1-21.

19. A comparative legal history of the Italian Wars is still lacking. Such a study would be a useful tool for tracking both legal speculation and theory and for interpreting the application of law in the disputes between European litigants.

20. Jacques Krynen, *L'Empire du roi. Idées et croyances politiques en France, XIIIe–XVe siècle* (Paris: Éditions Gallimard, 1993), 384-414.

21. The imperial affiliation of the city (distinct from the duchy) had its own history going back much farther. Giorgio Chittolini, "Milano 'città imperiale'? Note su due ambascerie di Enea Silvio Piccolomini (1447, 1449)," in his *L'Italia delle* civitates. *Grandi e piccoli centri fra Medioevo e Rinascimento* (Rome: Viella, 2015), 141-64.

22. The observation emerges from Thomas Hobbes's *De Cive* (1651; in the wake of the dissolution of the monarchy during the English Civil Wars), in which he identifies the "state of nature" as the condition that reveals itself when the polity is considered as if it were dissolved, "ut tanquam dissoluta consideretur." See Thomas Hobbes, *On the Citizen,* Richard Tuck, ed. and trans. (Cambridge: Cambridge University Press, 1998), 10, translated there as "to view it [the commonwealth] as taken apart, i.e., to understand correctly what human nature is like."

23. Carl Schmitt, *Political Theology: Four Chapters on the Concept of Sovereignty* (Cambridge, MA: MIT Press, 1985 [1922]), 6-7, 14-15. Schmitt found valu-

able insights not just in readings of Hobbes but also in his engagement with the early nineteenth-century philosopher of war, Karl von Clause-witz. See Raymond Aron, *Clausewitz: Philosopher of War,* Christine Booker and Norman Stone, trans. (London: Routledge & Kegan Paul, 1983), 363–71. The formative nature of war and struggle on sovereignty characterizes not just Schmitt but many of the theorists who responded to his pro-posals, notably Agamben, a close reader of Benjamin. See also the ele-gant essay of Horst Bredekamp, "From Walter Benjamin to Carl Schmitt via Thomas Hobbes," *Critical Inquiry* 25, no. 2 (1999): 247–66, in which he distinguishes between Benjamin and Schmitt by noticing that "while Schmitt views the state of exception as the *conditio sine qua non* for the es-tablishment of sovereignty, Benjamin sees sovereignty as existing in order to avoid the state of exception in the first place" (260).

24. Paraphrased from Giorgio Agamben, *Homo Sacer: Sovereignty and Bare Life,* Daniel Heller-Roazen, trans. (Stanford, CA: Stanford University Press, 1998), 28.

25. Giorgio Agamben, *The State of Exception,* Kevin Attell, trans. (Chicago: Uni-versity of Chicago Press, 2005), 35–40. This work is essentially an expansion and critique of Schmitt. See also Schmitt, *Political Theology,* 15: "The exception is more interesting than the rule. The rule proves nothing; the exception proves everything: It confirms not only the rule but also its ex-istence, which derives only from the exception. In the exception the power of real life breaks through the crust of a mechanism that has be-come torpid by repetition."

26. Imperial edict on the affairs of Milan, 1 February 1522, from Brussels. Giuseppe Müller, ed., *Documenti che concernono la vita pubblica di Gerolamo Morone* (Turin: Stamperia Reale, 1865), doc. 138, 268–70 at 269. After rec-ognizing this situation, Charles V then employed the rhetoric of his own plenitude of power as a remedy to the disease of the state.

27. Ludovico wrote that he "cognoscendo el periculo quale porria seguire quando lassassimo el stato senza certo Signore fin al tempo limitato alla publicatione di privilegii. Essendo el populo de Milano quello che da norma et tira cum se tutti li altri del stato, havemo electo questa via de respondere che acceptamo el peso quale ne proponeno, et per satisfactione del populo, essendo cossì ricercati et instati havemo cavalcato la cità." The phrase appears in Ludovico's instructions (of 22 October 1494) to his em-issary headed for the imperial court to notify Maximilian I of the death of Giangaleazzo Maria on 20 October. Felice Calvi, *Bianca Maria Sforza-Visconti, Regina dei Romani, Imperatrice Germanica* (Milan: Antonio Vallardi, 1888), 74–79, at 76.

28. See Nicole Hochner, "Le Trône vacant du roi Louis XII. Significations poli-tiques de la mise en scène royale en Milanais," in Contamine and Guil-laume, eds., *Louis XII en Milanais,* 227–44.

29. Caterina Santoro, "I Conservatori dello Stato," in *Scritti storici e giuridici in memoria di Alessandro Visconti* (Milan: Istituto editoriale Cisalpino, 1955), 359–66; and Caterina Santoro, *Gli Offici del comune di Milano e del dominio visconteo-sforzesco (1216–1515)* (Milan: Giuffrè, 1968), 377–78.

30. Letizia Arcangeli, "Appunti su guelfi e ghibellini in Lombardia nelle guerre d'Italia (1494-1530)," in Marco Gentile, ed., *Guelfi e ghibellini nell'Italia del Rinascimento* (Rome: Viella, 2005), 391–472.

31. Letizia Arcangeli, "'Les Ytaulx qui désirent franchise'. Invasione francese, permanenze e mutamenti nell'Italia del primo Cinquecento," in *'Terra di mezzo per trattar le regie paci'. Giugno 1507: la grande storia internazionale a Savona*, special issue of *Atti e memorie della società savonese di storia patria* 43 (2007): 137–54, at 138–43.

32. The term "failed state" enjoyed some currency among political scientists in the 2000s; but for a critique and alternative concepts see Charles T. Call, "The Fallacy of the 'Failed State,'" *Third World Quarterly* 29, no. 8 (2008): 1491–1507; Charles T. Call, "Beyond the 'Failed State': Toward Conceptual Alternatives," *European Journal of International Relations* 17, no. 2 (2010): 303–26.

33. See the extensive use of notarial records in Letizia Arcangeli, *Gentiluomini di Lombardia. Ricerche sull'aristocrazia padana nel Rinascimento* (Milan: Edizioni Unicopli, 2003); Stefano Meschini, *La Francia nel Ducato di Milano*, 2 vols. (Milan: FrancoAngeli, 2006); and the description of sources in Matteo di Tullio, *La Ricchezza delle comunità. Guerra, risorse, cooperazione nella Geradadda del Cinquecento* (Venice: Marsilio Editori, 2011), 21–22, 168. For continuities in printing activities, see Sandal's chronological table of Milanese printing from 1501 to 1525 in Ennio Sandal, *Editori e Tipografi a Milano nel Cinquecento* (Baden-Baden: Valentin Koerner, 1977), 3: 123–49; for artists, see the contracts in Janice Shell, *Pittori in Bottega. Milano nel Rinascimento* (Turin: Umberto Allemandi & Co., 1995), 203–300.

34. See, for example, the index of notarial contracts documenting the activities of Milanese wood sculptors from the 1470s to the 1530s by Carlo Cairati and Daniele Cassinelli, "Regesto dei documenti," in *Giovanni Pietro e Giovanni Ambrogio De Donati. Scultori e imprenditori del legno nella Lombardia del Rinascimento*, special issue of *Rassegna di studi e di notizie* 32 (2009): 133–58.

35. ASMi, Registri ducali 26 (1522–35), 185r–186v. Although copied in a later register, the memorandum is dated 1500 and titled "Altri ricordi fideli per conseruatione et mantenimento perpetuo acioche la M.ta regia habij ad dominar per sempre questo foelicissimo stato cum uera et syncera beniuolentia de tutti li populi desso." A key passage appears on 185v. If creditors were to go unpaid, "li exercitij cessariano: li poueri homini non trouando da lauorare se absentariano: li Gentilhomini essendo poche persone in la Cita non poriano sustenere le uictualie sue: lequale non

sostenendosi le Intrate ualeriano poco, per modo sariano necessitati habitare la villa: et a questo modo la Cita remaneria inhabitata da Gentilhomini & Contadini, et li Datij veneriano al basso."

36. On the war as an eventual strengthening agent of the state, see Giorgio Chittolini, "Milan in the Face of the Italian Wars," in David Abulafia, ed., *The French Descent into Renaissance Italy 1494–95: Antecedents and Effects* (Aldershot, UK: Variorum, 1995), 391–404, at 402–03; Guido Alfani, *Calamities and the Economy in Renaissance Italy: The Grand Tour of the Horsemen of the Apocalypse,* Christine Calvert, trans. (New York: Palgrave Macmillan, 2013), 123–24; Séverin Duc, "Il Prezzo delle guerre lombarde. Rovina dello stato, distruzione della richezza e disastro sociale (1515–1535)," *Storia economica* 19 (2016): 219–48, esp. 248.

37. Jane Black, "The Emergence of the Duchy of Milan: Language and the Territorial State," *Reti Medievali Rivista* 14:1 (2013): 197–210, at 209.

38. Massimo Giannini, "Note sulla dialettica politica nel ducato di Milano prima del suo ingresso nell'impero di Carlo V (1499–1535)," *Archivio storico lombardo* 127 (2001): 29–60, especially on Gian Giacomo de' Medici, 55–60.

39. "Il duca perse lo stato e la roba e libertà e nessuna sua opera si finì per lui." For references and further analysis, see Marco Versiero, "'Il Duca [ha] perso lo stato . . .' Niccolò Machiavelli, Leonardo da Vinci e l'idea di stato," *Filosofia politica* 21, no. 1 (2007): 85–105.

40. "El tuto perde quel chel tuto vole." The line comes from one of the sonnets by Panfilo Sasso, the Modenese court poet who published a number of Latin and vernacular works against Ludovico Sforza after his fall. BAM, S.P.XII.164/9, *Capituli e Soneti de miser Pamphilo Saxo Poeta laureato de li diuisione & guerre de Italia & del Moro & del Re di Franza,* n.p.

41. Beyond Europe, Sforza maintained close contact with Ottoman Sultan Bayezid II. See Johann Gröblacher, "König Maximilians I. erste Gesandschaft zum Sultan Baijezid II.," in Alexander Novotny and Othmar Pickl, eds., *Festschrift Hermann Wiesflecker zum 60. Geburtstag* (Graz: Selbstverlag des Historischen Institutes der Universität Graz, 1973), 73–80, at 75 for Sforza's support of imperial summits; see also Giovanni Ricci, *Appello al Turco: I Confini infranti del Rinascimento* (Rome: Viella, 2011), 67–80; Giovanni Ricci, "Lezioni di geopolitica. Ludovico il Moro spiega a Bayezid II la politica italiana di Luigi XII," in Dante Bolognesi, ed., *1512. La Battaglia di Ravenna, l'Italia, l'Europa* (Ravenna: Longo Editore, 2014), 65–73.

42. On the fact that these and other cities had a patchwork of legal relationships to the Sforza dukes, see Jane Black, "Double Duchy: The Sforza Dukes and the Other Lombard Title," in Paola Guglielmotti, Isabella Lazzarini, and Gian Maria Varanini, eds., *Europa e Italia. Studi in onore di Giorgio Chittolini* (Florence: Firenze University Press, 2011), 15–27.

43. Giorgio Chittolini, "Le Terre separate nel ducato di Milano in età sforzesca," in *Milano nell'età di Ludovico il Moro. Atti del convegno internazionale,*

28 febbraio–4 marzo 1983 (Milan: Comune di Milano e Archivio Storico Civico-Biblioteca Trivulziana, 1983), 1: 115–28.

44. Patrizia Mainoni, "The Economy of Renaissance Milan," in Andrea Gamberini, ed., *A Companion to Late Medieval and Early Modern Milan: The Distinctive Features of an Italian State* (Leiden: Brill, 2014), 118–41, esp. 129–30; Patrizia Mainoni, "L'attività mercantile e le casate milanesi nel secondo Quattrocento," in *Milano nell'età di Ludovico,* 2: 575–84.

45. See Giordano, ed., *Ludovicus Dux;* Evelyn Welch, "Patrons, Artists, and Audiences in Renaissance Milan, 1300–1600," in Charles M. Rosenberg, ed., *The Court Cities of Northern Italy* (Cambridge: Cambridge University Press, 2010), 21–70; and the still extremely useful Francesco Malaguzzi Valeri, *La Corte di Lodovico il Moro. La Vita privata e l'arte a Milano nella seconda metà del Quattrocento,* 4 vols. (Milan: Hoepli, 1913). For the nobility after 1500, see Arcangeli, *Gentiluomini di Lombardia;* Federico del Tredici, "Nobility in Lombardy between the Late Middle Ages and the Early Modern Age," in Gamberini, ed., *A Companion,* 477–98.

46. "Li advisi contenuti nelle lectere delli ambasciadori da Milano, contenente in somma che tucto quello stato se ne va in ruina" (4 September 1499; Denis Fachard, ed., *Consulte e pratiche della Repubblica Fiorentina, 1498–1502,* 2 vols. [Geneva: Droz, 1993], 1: 219).

47. Michael Mallett and Christine Shaw, *The Italian Wars, 1494–1559* (New York: Pearson, 2012), 1; Jean-Louis Fournel and Jean-Claude Zancarini, *Les Guerres d'Italie: Des Batailles pour l'Europe, 1494–1559* (Paris: Gallimard, 2003), 114; Marco Pellegrini, *Le Guerre d'Italia, 1494–1530* (Bologna: Il Mulino, 2009), 20.

48. Jean-Louis Fournel, "La 'Brutalisation' de la guerre. Des Guerres d'Italie aux guerres de Religion," *Astérion* 2 (2004): 105–31; Alison Brown, "Rethinking the Renaissance in the Aftermath of Italy's Crisis," in John Najemy, ed., *Italy in the Age of the Renaissance 1300–1500* (Oxford: Oxford University Press, 2004), 246–65.

49. Language of fire and smoke was an ambassadorial commonplace and appears canonically in Guicciardini's characterization of the period; in the first chapter of his history of Italy, he refers to efforts after 1494 "a procurare di spegnere sollecitamente tutte quelle faville che origine di nuovo incendio essere potessino" (Francesco Guicciardini, *Storia d'Italia,* Silvana Seidel Menchi, ed. [Turin: Einaudi, 1971] (I.i) 1: 9). In 1513, the Milanese representative to Pope Leo X was ordered to ask "sua Santità se digna extinguere questo focho, qual se ben a questo principio pare pocho, se dubitamo, lassandosi continuare, non piglia tante forze, che poi brusa tutta Italia," Massimiliano Sforza in Milan giving instructions to Girolamo Morone on his appeal to Leo X, August 1513, in Müller, ed., *Morone,* doc. 43, 76–84, at 84.

50. For comments on moral decay, see Gino Franceschini, "Le Dominazioni francesi," in *Storia di Milano VIII: Tra Francia e Spagna (1500–1530)* (Milan:

Fondazione Treccani degli Alfieri, 1957), 218; Paolo Giovio, *Notable Men and Women of Our Time*, Kenneth Gouwens, ed. and trans. (Cambridge, MA: Harvard University Press, 2013), 379–85.

51. Maurizio Viroli, *From Politics to Reason of State: The Acquisition and Transformation of the Language of Politics, 1250–1600* (Cambridge: Cambridge University Press, 1992); Jean-Louis Fournel and Jean-Claude Zancarini, *La Grammaire de la république* (Geneva: Droz, 2009).

52. Stephen Bowd, *Renaissance Mass Murder: Civilians and Soldiers during the Italian Wars* (Oxford: Oxford University Press, 2018), 11–18; Christophe Masson, *Des Guerres en Italie avant les guerres d'Italie: Les Entreprises militaires françaises dans la péninsule à l'époque du grand schisme d'Occident* (Rome: École française de Rome, 2014).

53. Carlo Alberto Brignoli, *Guerre fluviali. Le Lotte fra Venezia e Milano nel XV secolo* (Milan: Mursia, 2014); Giulia Albini, *Guerra, fame, peste. Crisi di mortalità e sistema sanitario nella Lombardia tardomedievale* (Bologna: Cappelli Editore, 1982); Maria Nadia Covini, *L'Esercito del duca: Organizzazione militare e istituzioni al tempo degli Sforza* (Rome: Istituto storico italiano per il Medio Evo, 1998).

54. Nelson Minnich, "The Healing of the Pisan Schism (1511-13)," in his *The Fifth Lateran Council (1512–17): Studies on Its Membership, Diplomacy and Proposals for Reform* (Aldershot, UK: Ashgate Variorum, 1993), 2: 59–197, appendix 2, 159–61, at 161. "A Justification [by Claude de Seyssel] of Louis XII's Actions Against Julius II, July 1513," from BnF ms. fr. 3087, 101r–102v. On French ideas of Italian mutability, see Jonathan Dumont, *Lilia Florent. L'Imaginaire politique et social à la cour de France durant les Premières Guerres d'Italie (1494–1525)* (Paris: Honoré Champion, 2013), 325–33.

55. Minnich, "The Healing," appendix 2, 161.

56. On Genoa, see Carlo Taviani, *Superba discordia. Guerra, rivolta e pacificazione nella Genova di primo Cinquecento* (Rome: Viella, 2008); Jean Dauvillier, "L'Union réelle de Gênes et du Royaume de France aux XIVe, XVe, et XVIe siècles," *Annales de la Faculté de Droit d'Aix-en-Provence* 43 (1950): 81–112. The Neapolitan case has scant historiography, but see Eleni Sakellariou, "Institutional and Social Continuities in the Kingdom of Naples between 1443 and 1528," in Abulafia, ed., *The French Descent*, 327–53; Renata Pilati, *Officia Principis. Politica e amministrazione a Napoli nel Cinquecento* (Naples: Jovene Editore, 1994).

57. Léon-Gabriel Pélissier, "Notes sur les relations de Louis XII avec Cottignola," *Mélanges d'archéologie et d'histoire* 15 (1895): 77–101. Trivulzio's lieutenant claimed that Cotignola "non è manco del Christianissimo quanto è Milano" (79). See also the letters on the effort of Marcantonio Colonna to take over Cotignola for himself in 1513, in Müller, ed., *Morone*, doc. 22, 34–35, 3 May 1513; doc. 27, 44, 6 May 1513.

58. Francesco Guicciardini, "Le Storie fiorentine," in Giuseppe Canestrini, ed., *Opere inedite di Francesco Guicciardini* (Florence: Barbèra, Bianchi, e Comp., 1859), vol. 3, cap. 19, 205.

59. The author of the account is Alberto Vignati da Lodi. See the full text in Cesare Vignati, "Gaston de Fois e l'esercito francese a Bologna, a Brescia, a Ravenna dal gennaio 1511 all'aprile 1512," *Archivio storico lombardo,* ser. 2, vol. 1, fasc. 4 (1884): 593–622, at 615.

60. Giovanni Andrea Prato, *Storia di Milano,* Cesare Cantù, ed., *Archivio storico italiano* 3 (1842): 216–418, at 339. The events took place in September 1515, just shortly before the battle of Marignano that dislodged the second Sforza restoration.

61. Similar analytical language has recently been used by Séverin Duc, "Les Élites lombardes face à l'effondrement du duché de Milan (ca. 1500-ca. 1540)," in Laurent Coste and Sylvie Guillaume, eds., *Élites et crises du XVIe au XXIe siècle: Europe et Outre-mer* (Paris: Armand Colin, 2014), 101–11.

62. Marchesino Stanga to Ludovico Sforza, 17 May 1499, in Léon-Gabriel Pélissier, *Documents relatifs au règne de Louis XII et à sa politique en Italie* (Montpellier: Imprimerie Générale du Midi, 1912), doc. 17, 164–68 at 165.

63. Letters patent of Louis XII to Nicolas Gaynier of Pavia, giving him goods once owned by Pietro de Vesano, October 1499, in Pélissier, *Documents relatifs,* doc. 6, 94.

64. The phrase is commonly attributed to Margaret of Austria. See Giovanni Vigo, *Fisco e società nella Lombardia del Cinquecento* (Bologna: Il Mulino, 1979), 7–8.

65. Paul R. Hensel and Paul F. Diehl, "Testing Empirical Propositions about Shatterbelts, 1945–76," *Political Geography* 13:1 (1994): 33–51.

66. See in particular the elaborations of the concept by Robbie Ethridge, "Creating the Shatter Zone: Indian Slave Traders and the Collapse of the Southeastern Chiefdoms," in T. J. Pluckhahn and Robbie Ethridge, eds., *Light on the Path: the Anthropology and the History of the Southeastern Indians* (Tuscaloosa: University of Alabama Press, 2006), 207–18; Robbie Ethridge and Sheri M. Shuck-Hall, Introduction, in their *Mapping the Mississippian Shatter Zone: The Colonial Indian Slave Trade and Regional Instability in the American South* (Lincoln: University of Nebraska Press, 2009), 1–62; and a critique of the concept by Denise Ileana Bossy, "Shattering Together, Merging Apart: Colonialism, Violence, and the Remaking of the Native South," *William and Mary Quarterly* 71, no. 4 (2014): 611–31.

67. In this regard, the book shares perspectives with scholars who are trying to rethink the contours both of the Military Revolution debate and the legacy of Charles Tilly. For a sample of recent revisions and further bibliography, see Lars Bo Kaspersen, Jeppe Strandsberg and Benno Teschke, "Introduction—State Formation Theory: Status, Problems, and Prospects," in Lars Bo Kaspersen and Jeppe Stransberg, eds., *Does War Make*

States? Investigations of Charles Tilly's Historical Sociology (Cambridge: Cambridge University Press, 2017), 1–22; J. C. Sharman, "Myths of Military Revolutions: European Expansion and Eurocentrism," *European Journal of International Relations* 24, no. 3 (2018): 491–513.

68. Among this crop of postwar Sforza-era monographs by Anglophone historians (and mostly leaving aside art historical scholarship, which has generally shown more vibrancy): Gary Ianziti, *Humanist Historiography under the Sforzas: Politics and Propaganda in Fifteenth-Century Milan* (Oxford: Oxford University Press, 1988); Gregory Lubkin, *A Renaissance Court: Milan under Galeazzo Maria Sforza* (Berkeley: University of California Press, 1994); Evelyn Welch, *Art and Authority in Renaissance Milan* (New Haven, CT: Yale University Press, 1995); Cynthia Pyle, *Milan and Lombardy in the Renaissance: Essays in Cultural History* (Rome: La Fenice, 1997); Black, *Absolutism;* Monica Azzolini, *The Duke and the Stars: Astrology and Politics in Renaissance Milan* (Cambridge, MA: Harvard University Press, 2013).

69. Arcangeli, *Milano e Luigi XII;* Stefano Meschini, *Luigi XII, Duca di Milano. Gli Uomini e le istituzioni del primo dominio francese (1499–1512)* (Milan: FrancoAngeli, 2004); Meschini, *La Francia nel Ducato di Milano;* Stefano Meschini, *La Seconda dominazione francese nel Ducato di Milano. La politica e gli uomini di Francesco I (1515–1521)* (Varzi: Guardamagna Editore, 2014).

70. Fournel and Zancarini, *Les Guerres d'Italie;* Pellegrini, *Le Guerre d'Italia;* Mallett and Shaw, *The Italian Wars.*

71. Del Tredici, "Nobility in Lombardy," 477–98.

1. THE TEMPORALITY OF THE STATE

1. For the royal entry, see Léon-Gabriel Pélissier, *Les Préparatifs de l'entrée de Louis XII à Milan* (Montpellier: Gustave Firmin et Montane, 1891).

2. Girolamo Morone, *Lettere ed orazioni latine,* Domenico Promis and Giuseppe Müller, eds. (Turin: Stamperia Reale, 1863), letter 3, 9–10 at 9. Girolamo Morone in Milan to Jacopo Antiquario in Pavia, 13 October 1499: "Tu quidem locum philosophanti otio peridoneum studiisque aptissimum Papiam elegisti in qua rerum novarum difficultates praesentesque turbines et communis calamitatis dolorem aut effugere aut sane lenire possis."

3. Morone, *Lettere,* letter 88, Morone to Giason del Maino, 28 June 1512, 198–200 at 199; letter 89, Morone to Matthäus Cardinal Sion, 5 July 1512, 200–201 at 200; letter 123, Morone to Archbishop of Bari & Marino Caracciolo, 14 April 1513, 298–301 at 301; letter 209, Morone to Girolamo Adorno, 12 January 1516, 529–36 at 534.

4. On the concept of political time, see Jean-Claude Zancarini, "Une Philologie politique. Les Temps et les enjeux des mots (Florence, 1494–1530)," *Laboratoire italien* 7 (2007): 61–74 at 63–64.

5. Morone, *Lettere,* letter 22, Girolamo Morone to Girolamo Varadeo, 10 March 1500, 65–71, at 65. "Magna fit in singulos dies rerum commutatio et his temporibus incredibilis fortunae varietas apud nos perspicitur."

6. Jean-Louis Fournel and Jean-Claude Zancarini, *La Grammaire de la république. Langages de la politique chez Francesco Guicciardini (1483–1540)* (Geneva: Droz, 2009), 447–68; R. B. J. Walker, *Inside / Outisde: International Relations as Political Theory* (Cambridge: Cambridge University Press, 1993), 38–40 on Machiavelli and temporality.

7. Livy, *Ab urbe condita,* B. O. Foster, trans. (Cambridge: Harvard University Press, 1924), (V.34), 3: 116–19.

8. Niccolò Machiavelli, *Discorsi sopra la prima deca di Tito Livio,* Francesco Bausi, ed. (Rome: Salerno Editrice, 2001), II.iv (329), II.viii (353).

9. Paulus Diaconus, *Historia Langobardorum,* in G. Waitz, ed., *Scriptores Rerum Germanicum,* vol. 48 (Hanover: Impensis Bibliopolii Hahniani, 1878), lib. 2, cap. 23, 101: "Centum milia quoque Gallorum, quae in Italia remanserunt, Ticinum Mediolanumque, Bergamum Brexiamque construentes, Cisalpinae Galliae regioni nomen dederunt."

10. Bonvesin de la Riva, *Le Meraviglie di Milano,* Angelo Paredi, ed. (Milan: La Vita Felice, 2012), 40–41; Galvano Fiamma, *La Cronaca Estravagante,* eds. Sante Ambrogio Céngarle Parisi and Massimiliano David (Milan: Casa de Manzoni, 2013), cap. 3–6, 216–27. Galvano was not sure whether to count Brennus as the founder, since he reportedly rebuilt Milan some 200 years after Bellovesus's foundation.

11. Robert W. Scheller, "Gallia Cisalpina: Louis XII and Italy 1499–1508," *Simiolus* 15, no. 1 (1985): 5–60, at 6.

12. See Oren J. Margolis, "The Gaulish Past of Milan and the French Invasion of Italy," in Kathleen Christian and Bianca de Divitiis, eds., *Local Antiquities, Local Identities: Art, Literature, and Antiquarianism in Early Modern Europe, c. 1400–1700* (Manchester: University of Manchester Press, 2019), 102–120. I'm grateful to the author for sharing his essay with me before publication.

13. On measures of punishment used against premodern cities, see Letizia Arcangeli, "Città punite tra riforme istituzionali e repressione: casi italiani del Cinque e Seicento," in Patrick Gilli and Jean-Pierre Guilhembert, eds., *Le Châtiment des villes dans les espaces méditerranéens (Antiquité, Moyen Âge, Époque moderne)* (Turnhout: Brepols, 2012), 315–38, esp. 316–22 for Louis XII.

14. When the French captured Milan in 1499, Trivulzio appointed Michele Tonso or Tonsi as *prefetto dell'annona.* See Stefano Meschini, *La Francia nel Ducato di Milano* (Milan: FrancoAngeli, 2006), 1: 77. Riccio, already a royal counselor in Burgundy, became one of Milan's first French senators. See further references in Meschini, *La Francia nel Ducato,* 1: 143, n. 28.

15. The Tonso-Riccio dialogue has been published several times. See Théodore de Godefroy, *Histoire de Louis XII,* (Paris: Abraham Pacard, 1615), 192–204; Louis Legendre, *Vie du cardinal d'Amboise* (Rouen: Robert Machuel, 1726), 405–21; and Johann Christian Lünig, *Codex Italiae Diplomaticus,* vol. 1 (Frankfurt: Impensis Haeredum Lanckisianorum, 1725), cols. 498–504. Here I quote from Godefroy, 196: "Cum inter Historicos constet Mediolanum, omnemque Insubriam, Gallorum vnam penè coloniam fuisse."

16. For the phrase's background, see Jacques Krynen, "Naturel. Essai sur l'argument de la Nature dans la pensée politique à la fin du Moyen Âge," *Journal des savants* 2 (1982): 169–90 at 183–89. "C'est mon seigneur naturel parcial/a qui je doibs tribut fiducial," says the character of Millan in André de la Vigne, *Le Libelle des cinq villes d'Ytallye contre Venise* (Lyon: Noël Abraham, 1509), 7v; and in 1515, upon the recovery of the duchy Pasquier Le Moyne remarked of the Milanese delegation greeting King François I upon his victory at Marignano: "Iceulx millannois ne vindrent point comme lasches & meschans nonobstant les faultes par eulx faictes enuers le roy leur prince & seigneur naturel" (Pasquier Le Moyne, *Le Couronnement du roy Francois premier de ce nom voyages & conqueste de la duche de millan . . .* [Paris: Gilles Couteau, 1519], sig. N v^v). See also Stephen Bowd, *Renaissance Mass Murder: Civilians and Soldiers during the Italian Wars* (Oxford: Oxford University Press, 2018), 130.

17. Léon-Gabriel Pélissier, *Documents pour l'histoire de la domination française dans le Milanais (1499–1513)* (Toulouse: Édouard Privat, 1891), doc. 9, 11–14, at 14: "Agere debent boni, fideles, recti, sinceri et obedientes homines, cives et subdicti erga naturales et directos dominos et superiores suos."

18. See further examples in Jonathan Dumont, *Lilia Florent. L'Imaginaire politique et social à la cour de France durant les Premières Guerres d'Italie (1494–1525)* (Paris: Honoré Champion, 2013), 273–78.

19. Isidoro Isolani, *De Patriae urbis laudibus panegyricus* (Milan: Apud Io. Bap. Bid., 1629), 14–15. "Mediolanum amplissimam quidem, & populosissimam Galliae urbem, quam Galli metropolim appelantes." Isolani drew this phrasing from Plutarch's *Life of Marcellus.* See Plutarch, *Lives,* vol. 5, Bernadotte Perrin, trans. (Cambridge: Harvard University Press, 1917), 452–53.

20. BTM, MS Triv. 2159, 30r. "Bellovesus atrox, Prisco regnante, per Alpes primus in Italiam Gallica signa tulit. Tunc Mediolanum Galli extruxere priores, et nostros ipsi tunc genuere patres iure tenent. Igitur fortes sua maenia [*sic*] Galli iureque quos etiam progenuere regunt." See also John Gagné, "Collecting Women: Three French Kings and Manuscripts of Empire in the Italian Wars," *I Tatti Studies in the Italian Renaissance* 20, no. 1 (2017): 127–84, at 165.

21. Penetrating analysis of the "bon français" appears in Dumont, *Lilia Florent,* 387–97.

22. I am grateful to Oren Margolis for pressing me on this deeper history. See Serena Ferente, "Guelphs! Factions, Liberty, and Sovereignty: Inquiries about the Quattrocento," *History of Political Thought* 28, no. 4 (2007): 571–98.

23. For Trivulzio's split from Ludovico, see Christine Shaw, *The Politics of Exile in Renaissance Italy* (Cambridge: Cambridge University Press, 2000), 81; on Trivulzio, see Dumont, *Lilia Florent,* 392–94. See also Trivulzio's characterization in *Le Journal d'un Bourgeois de Paris sous le Règne de François Ier (1515–1536),* Ludovic Lalanne, ed. (Paris: Chez Jules Renouard, 1854), 78.

24. *La Conqueste et Recouvrance de la Duche de Millan faicte par le Roy nostre sire francoys premier de ce nom . . .* (Paris: Jacques Nyverd, 1518), 29v–30r.

25. Claude de Seyssel, "Certain discours fait par le bon Arceuesque trepassé," in Domenico Cerutti, *Storia della diplomazia della corte di Savoia,* (Rome-Turin-Florence: Fratelli Bocca, 1875), 1: 532–46, at 533.

26. ASV, Capi del Consiglio di Dieci—Lettere di Ambasciatori 15 (Milano 1501–25): Bishop of Meaux in Milan to Giangiacomo Trivulzio, 1 September 1516: "N.re dyt saint pere veult viure et mourir bon francoys comme il dyt."

27. Isabella d'Este to Jacopo Suardo, 28 March 1510; Isabella d'Este, *Selected Letters,* Deanna Shemek, ed. and trans. (Toronto-Tempe: Iter Press & Arizona Center for Medieval and Renaissance Studies, 2017), letter 434, 322–23 at 322. See original Italian phrasing at ASMn, AG 2995, libro 24, 33v. As early as 1500, Francesco himself had written to Clara Gonzaga, duchess of Montpensier, on 6 March 1500: "La certifico, chio sono bon Franzoso e che più presto voria morire che mancare de la fede mia" (Léon-Gabriel Pélissier, *La Politique du marquis de Mantoue pendant la lutte de Louis XII et de Ludovic Sforza, 1498–1500* [Le Puy: Imprimerie Marchessou Fils, 1892], 75, n. 4).

28. Baldassarre Castiglione, *Lettere famigliari e diplomatiche,* Guido La Rocca, Angelo Stello, and Umberto Morando, eds. (Turin: Giulio Einaudi Editore, 2016), 3: #1627, 20–30, Baldassarre Castiglione in Madrid to Giovan Matteo Giberti, 20–26 January 1525: "Dicono ancor ch'el S.r Alberto da Carpi ha cercato de indurre el PP a dechiararse francese."

29. This idea is part of a much larger ideological program that Jonathan Dumont calls "Francogallia." See Dumont, *Lilia Florent.*

30. On the Visconti family before their rise to lordship, see Ambrogio Filippini, *I Visconti di Milano nei secoli XI e XII. Indagini tra le fonti* (Trent: Tangram Edizioni Scientifiche, 2014); Federico Del Tredici, *Un'Altra nobiltà. Storie di (in)distinzione a Milano, secoli XIV–XV* (Milan: FrancoAngeli, 2017), 117–38. On the growth of their state, see Andrea Gamberini, *Lo Stato visconteo. Linguaggi politici e dinamiche costituzionali* (Milan: FrancoAngeli, 2005), 35–67; and Jane Black, "Giangaleazzo Visconti and the Ducal Title," in John E. Law and Bernadette Paton, eds., *Communes and Despots in Medieval and Renaissance Italy* (Farnham, UK: Ashgate, 2010), 119–30.

31. Piero Pieri, "Attendolo, Muzio (Giacomuccio), detto Sforza," *Dizionario biografico degli Italiani* 4 (1962): 543–45.

32. Felice Calvi, *Il Patriziato milanese* (Milan: Andrea Mosconi, 1875), 46–49; Del Tredici, *Un'Altra nobiltà*, 28–36.

33. On Tranchedini, see Paola Sverzellati, "Per la biografia di Nicodemo Tranchedini da Pontremoli, ambasciatore sforzesco," *Aevum* 72, no. 2 (1998): 485–557.

34. Pietro Parodi, "La Genealogia sforzesca in un codice della Laudense," *Archivio storico per la città e i comuni del Circondario e della Diocesi di Lodi*, fasc. 4 (1919): 138–41; Pietro Parodi, "Una Genealogia sforzesca del sec. XV," *Archivio storico per la città e i comuni del Circondario e della Diocesi di Lodi*, fasc. 3 (1920): 87–94; Pietro Parodi, "Nicodemo Tranchedini da Pontremoli genealogista degli Sforza," *Archivio storico lombardo* ser. 5, fasc. 3 (1920): 334–40; Pietro Parodi, *Nicodemo Tranchedini e le genealogie sforzesche del sec. 15* (Abbiategrasso: Tip. Nicora, 1926).

35. Edoardo Rossetti, "'Poi fu la bissa.' Due dinastie, una città e non solo," in Mauro Natale and Serena Romano, eds., *Arte lombarda dai Visconti agli Sforza* (Milan: Skira, 2015), 23–33, at 25.

36. For Filelfo this also included a planned Latin history, *De Vita et rebus gestis Francisci Sphortiae*. See Gary Ianziti, *Humanistic Historiography under the Sforzas: Politics and Propaganda in Fifteenth-Century Milan* (Oxford: Oxford University Press, 1988), esp. 61–70 for Filelfo, and more recently, Gary Ianziti, "Filelfo and the Writing of History," in Jeroen De Keyser, ed., *Francesco Filelfo, Man of Letters* (Leiden-Boston: Brill, 2019), 97–123.

37. Donato Bossi, *Chronica* (Milan: per Antonium Zarotum, 1492), sig. A 1ᵛ. A brief appraisal of Bossi's history appears in Ianziti, *Humanistic Historiography*, 235–36.

38. This is the *Historia Patri,* only published in 1628. Calco's manuscripts are at BAM. See Annalisa Belloni, "L'Historia patria' di Tristano Calco fra gli Sforza e i Francesi: Fonti e strati redazionali," *Italia medioevale e umanistica* 23 (1980): 179–232, at 179, n. 1.

39. See Stefano Meschini, *Uno Storico umanista alla corte sforzesca. Biografia di Bernardino Corio* (Milan: Vita e Pensiero, 1995), 110–17.

40. Meschini, *Uno Storico,* 118, n. 167. In a letter to Busseto in 1499 requesting for Calco to borrow a local manuscript chronicle, Ludovico claimed: "Essendo noi desyderosissimi di vedere una volta reducta insieme la substantia di queste cose, non cessamo de investigarne per tutta Italia dove siano libri apti a questa impresa. Et havuti et adoperati, li facemo restituire liberamente non comportando ne smarischa alcuno" (Emilio Seletti, *La Città di Busseto, capitale un tempo dello Stato Pallavicino* [Milan: Bortolotti, 1883], vol. 3, doc. 91, 100–101, Ludovico Sforza to Raffaele da Busseto, 15 April 1499).

41. Henri Omont, *Anciens inventaires et catalogues de la Bibliothèque nationale* (Paris: Ernest Leroux, 1908), 1: 41, #258.

42. A. Mary F. Robinson, "The Claim of the House of Orleans to Milan," *English Historical Review* 3, no. 9 (1888): 34-62; 3, no. 10 (1888): 270-91.

43. For the Pio decoration of suites of their palace with Louis XII's arms, dated 1506, see Tania Previdi and Manuela Rossi, "Tra 'Le arme del Narbona e del Gran Maestro.' L'Appartamento inferiore del Palazzo dei Pio," in Manuela Rossi, ed., *Alla corte del Re di Francia. Alberto Pio e gli artisti di Carpi nei cantieri del Rinascimento francese* (Carpi: Edizioni APM, 2017), 52-63, and figure 86. In Cozzo, a graffito shows Louis XII embracing Maria di Roero, matron of the Gallarati family. See Luisa Giordano, "Vigevano, terra e dimora signorile," in Luisa Giordano, ed., *Splendori di corte—Gli Sforza, il Rinascimento, la Città* (Milan: Skira, 2009), 19-25, at 25, and figure 6; and Giuseppe Castelli, "Gli Affreschi del castello di Cozzo," *Viglevanum* 10 (2000): 63-65. For the Alberti, see Gianfranco Rocculi, "L'Araldica della dominazione francese nel ducato di Milano," *Archivio araldico svizzera—Archivum araldicum* 128 (2014): 61-75, at 64-66. For the Ghilini: Gianfranco Rocculi, "Sull'Araldica della dominazione francese nel ducato di Milano," *Archivio araldico svizzera—Archivum araldicum* 139 (2016): 25-31, at 25-28.

44. Paolo Zaninetta, *Il Potere raffigurato. Simbolo, mito e propaganda nell'ascesa della signoria viscontea* (Milan: FrancoAngeli, 2013), 166, n. 72.

45. For the repainted manuscripts, see Pier Luigi Mulas, "De Borso d'Este à Geoffroy Carles: L'Illustration de la sphère armillaire dans un exemplaire enluminé de la *Cosmographia* de Ptolémée," *Bulletin du Bibliophile* 1 (2000): 57-72, esp. 61-63 on the alteration of a Pavia copy of Aquinas's *De rege et regno,* in which the president of Milan's senate after 1504, Geoffroy Carles, had roundel portraits of Francesco Sforza and Bianca Maria Visconti replaced with those of Louis XII and Anne de Bretagne to highlight the Visconti-Orléans filiation. See also Pier Luigi Mulas, "Du Pouvoir ducal à la première domination française. La Production de manuscrits enluminés laïcs à Milan," in Silvia Fabrizio-Costa and Jean-Pierre Le Goff, eds., *Léonard de Vinci entre France et Italie, 'miroir profond et sombre'* (Caen: Presses Universitaires de Caen, 1999), 301-11, at 308.

46. Belloni, "Tristano Calco," 296, n. 6, suggests that indications of Calco's gift to Louis XII in 1499 are erroneous, but cites no reason. It seems possible that Calco could have presented the monarch with a copy of Merula's book, printed at this same time. On Étienne Poncher in Milan, see Stefano Meschini, *Luigi XII, Duca di Milano. Gli Uomini e le istituzioni del primo dominio francese (1499–1512)* (Milan: FrancoAngeli, 2004), 124–31.

47. BTM Triv. 1436, now lost. See Giulio Porro, *Catalogo dei codici manoscritti della Trivulziana* (Turin: Stamperia Reale, 1884), 459. Further, see Belloni,

"Tristano Calco," 297. Perhaps because it is a scroll, the manuscript does not appear in Paul Oskar Kristeller, *Iter Italicum* (London: Warburg Institute, 1963–1996).

48. The genealogy was described in the eighteenth century as a "copia cum authographa originali Matrice recitatae Genealogiae Vicecomitum manu & charactere exarata per celebrem Historiographum Tristanum Chalchum, olim Ducalem Secretarium Ducalique Archivo Praefectum, in charta pecudinea sex petiis praegrandibus efformata" (Giuseppe Volpi, *Istoria de' Visconti* [Naples: Mosca, 1748], 2: 279–98, at 298).

49. Bibliothèque Sainte-Geneviève MS 864—"Tableau généalogique des ducs de Milan des premiers Visconti jusqu'à Louis XII," Milan, 1502. The scroll does not appear in Pier Luigi Mulas, "Les Manuscrits lombards enluminés offerts aux français," in Philippe Contamine and Jean Guillaume, eds., *Louis XII en Milanais* (Paris: Honoré Champion, 2003), 305–22.

50. On Louis II d'Amboise, see Meschini, *Luigi XII,* 99, n. 129; Christine Shaw, *Julius II: The Warrior Pope* (Oxford: Blackwell, 1993), 175.

51. Louis II accompanied the monarch on campaign to Lombardy in August–September 1502 and later became a supporter of Lombard artists in Albi. See Claudia Gaggetta, "Louis II d'Amboise et les fresques de la cathédrale Sainte-Cécile d'Albi," in Frédéric Elsig and Mauro Natale, eds., *Le Duché de Milan et les commanditaires français, 1499–1521* (Rome: Viella, 2013), 287–321, at 288.

52. BnF, ms. lat. 5888, with illustrations by Michelino da Besozzo. Annotations in this manuscript indicate it was relocated in 1499 from Pavia to the French royal library. See François Avril and Marie-Thèrese Gousset, *Manuscrits enluminés d'origine italienne,* vol. 3: *XIVe siècle, 1: Lombardie-Ligurie* (Paris: Bibliothèque nationale de France, 2005), cat. 58, 126–28.

53. On the logics of this graphic scheme, see Christiane Klapisch-Zuber, "The Genesis of the Family Tree," *I Tatti Studies in the Italian Renaissance* 4 (1991): 105–29, at 123–24; and Kilian Heck, *Genealogie als Monument und Argument. Der Beitrag dynastischer Wappen zur politischen Raumbildung der Neuzeit* (Munich-Berlin: Deutscher Kunstverlag, 2002), 46–50. For vertical time, see Maurizio Bettini, *Anthropology and Roman Culture* (Baltimore, MD: Johns Hopkins University Press, 1991), 167–83.

54. On the negative connotations of stripes in heraldry (for "princes usurpateurs"), see Michel Pastoureau, *L'Étoffe du diable. Une Histoire des rayures et des tissus rayés* (Paris: Éditions du Seuil, 1991), 56.

55. Bibliothèque Sainte-Geneviève MS 864: "Captus a gallis ex Nouarie die .x. Aprilis 1500 et ductus transalpes uniuerse genti sue exitio fuit: et quod pater acquisiuerat pulcherrimum Regnum amisit."

56. Fiamma, *La Cronaca,* cap. 94, 352–55: "Hoc priuilegium est Vicecomitum, quorum est illud uexillum, quod datum fuit Ottoni uicecomiti, qui super portam ciuitatis Ierusalem singulari duello de capite cuiusdam regis Sar-

acenorum optinuit." Calco, however, called Fiamma an "auctore infelicis ingenii." Ludovico Sforza specifically asked the castellan of Pavia to provide Giorgio Merula, author of the *Antiquitates Vicecomiti*—the book Calco shepherded to press—with access to Fiamma's text, among others. See Ferdinando Gabotto and Angelo Badini Confalonieri, *Vita di Giorgio Merula* (Alessandria: Tipografia Giovanni Jacquemod, 1893), 223–24, n. 5. See also Massimo Carlo Giannini, "Il Biscione," in Francesco Benigno and Luca Scuccimarra, eds., *Simboli della politica* (Rome: Viella, 2010), 137–89, at 152–53.

57. On the snake, located in Sant'Ambrogio since at least the eleventh century, see Marilisa di Giovanni, "Il Serpente di bronzo della Basilica di S. Ambrogio," *Arte lombarda* 11, no. 1 (1966): 3–5; Herbert L. Kessler, "Christ the Magic Dragon," *Gesta* 48:2 (2009): 119–34, at 123–24.

58. For the sacristy painting, see Mario Frassineti, ed., *Santa Maria delle Grazie* (Milan: Federico Motta Editore, 1998), 225; and for Poncher's involvement around 1503–1504, along with Vincenzo Bandello, see Silvia Cocchetti Almasio, "L'Influsso della cultura prospettica bramantesca sui pannelli degli armadi nella sagrestia di Santa Maria delle Grazie," *Arte lombarda* 78, no. 3 (1986): 59–71, at 60. Calco also differs on the origins of the Visconti snake from Merula, whose account follows Fiamma's version. See Giorgio Merula, *Antiquitatis Vicecomitum* (Milan: Minuziano, 1499), 13v–14r.

59. Nicole Hochner, *Louis XII. Les Dérèglements de l'image royal (1498–1515)* (Seyssel: ChampVallon, 2006), 40.

60. Some of the manuscripts are discussed in Hochner, *Louis XII,* 91–92; Scheller, "Gallia Cisalpina," 11.

61. Alison Brown, "Florentine Diplomacy on the Banks of the Po: Bernardo Ricci's Meeting with Lodovico il Moro in June 1493," in Philippa Jackson and Guido Rebecchini, eds., *Mantova e il Rinascimento italiano: Studi in onore di David S. Chambers* (Mantua: Sommetti, 2011), 301–14, at 303 and 310 (in original Italian): "le lettere che haveva di Francia gli rompevano il cervello." I thank Tim McCall for bringing this essay to my attention.

62. BnF ms. ital. 821. Because the opening paragraph acknowledges Ludovico's challenge to raise his sons without his consort, Beatrice, the document must postdate her death in 1497. The testament was published as "Testamento originale ed autentico di Lodovico Maria Sforza, detto il Moro, duca di Milano" (hereafter "Testamento") in Pier Desiderio Pasolini, *Caterina Sforza* (Rome: Ermanno Loescher, 1893), vol. 3, doc. 1114, 413–39, at 413.

63. "Testamento," 414–15.

64. Pélissier, *Documents relatifs,* doc. 1, "Dux Mediolani. Instructio Badini de Papia praefecti custodiae nostrae" 245–47. Pélissier dates the order to 1498.

65. "Testamento," 415–23.

66. "Testamento," 423–27.

67. Daniel M. Bueno de Mesquita, "The Privy Council in the Government of the Dukes of Milan," in Craig Hugh Smyth and Gian Carlo Garfagnini, eds., *Florence and Milan: Comparisons and Relations* (Florence: La Nuova Italia Editrice, 1989), 1: 135–56, at 138; Franca Leverotti, "Gli Officiali del ducato sforzesco," *Annali della Scuola normale superiore di Pisa. Classe di lettere e filosofia,* series 4, 1 (1997): 17–77, at 23.

68. Leverotti, "Gli Officiali," 64, n. 26.

69. On the two councils during the reign of Galeazzo Maria up to 1476, see Franca Leverotti, *'Governare a modo e stillo de' signori . . .' Osservazioni in margine all'amministrazione della giustizia al tempo di Galeazzo Maria Sforza duca di Milano (1466–76)* (Florence: Olschki, 2001), 85–115.

70. "Testamento," 430, 429. On the documentary habits of the Visconti-Sforza chancery, see Alfio Rosario Natale, *Stilus Cancellariae. Formulario Visconteo-sforzesco* (Milan: Giuffrè, 1979), esp. ix–xxv.

71. "Testamento," 438.

72. For useful remarks on continuity and change in the Milanese chancery, see Franca Leverotti, "La Cancelleria dei Visconti e degli Sforza signori di Milano," in Guido Castelnuovo and Olivier Mattéoni, eds., *'De part et d'autre des Alpes' (II): Chancelleries et chanceliers des princes à la fin du Moyen Âge* (Chambéry: Presses de l'Université de Savoie, 2011), 39–52.

73. Some of the jurists participated in both 1498 and 1502 revisions. See Franca Leverotti, "Leggi del principe, leggi della città nel ducato Visconteo-sforzesco," in Rolando Dondarini, Gian Maria Varanini, and Maria Venticelli, eds., *Signori, regimi signorili e statuti nel tardo Medioevo* (Bologna: Pàtron, 2003), 143–88, at 160–62. The royal letters requesting the revision and appointing the jurists appear in *Statuta Mediolani* (Milan: Apud Alexandrum Minutianum, 1502), 19r–v.

74. Meschini, *Luigi XII,* 41.

75. Leverotti, "Leggi del principe," 161, n. 95.

76. Meschini, *Luigi XII,* 25–44, parses the decree *in extenso.*

77. On this position, see Stefano Meschini, "Il Luogotenente del Milanese all'epoca di Luigi XII," in Letizia Arcangeli, ed. *Milano e Luigi XII: Ricerche sul primo dominio francese in Lombardia (1499–1512)* (Milan: FrancoAngeli, 2002), 39–57.

78. Ugo Petronio, *Il Senato di Milano: Istituzioni giuridiche ed esercizio del potere nel ducato di Milano da Carlo V a Giuseppe II* (Milan: Giuffrè 1972), 3–58.

79. The phrase appears at least five times in the edict, always in view of replacing former norms with new habits. Pélissier, *Documents,* doc. 11: 19, 21, 22, 23.

80. Girolamo Morone, in a letter of October 1499, confirms this idea when he describes the sidelining of the Sforza partisans: "Nobiles fere omnes quorum magna pars regnantibus Sfortianis muneribus et honorariis di-

versimode fungebantur, nunc perculsi et attoniti et stomachati videntur, cum perspiciant, magistratuum numerum admodum restringi et ad eos plerosque Gallicae nationis aut Trivultiae factionis etiam indignos promoveri... sed etiam aperte vilipendant" (Girolamo Morone to Girolamo Imperiali, 18 October 1499, in Morone, *Lettere,* doc. 5, 12-15, at 14).

81. Several men named among the first senators belonged to the provisional council that governed Milan after Ludovico's departure; exclusion prevented (or removed) the staunchest Sforza partisans unwilling to collaborate with the French from gaining traction in the senate; indeed two senators appointed in 1499 were dismissed for their alignment with Ludovico Sforza in 1500. For remarks on the continuities in the senate membership between regimes, see Letizia Arcangeli, "'Parlamento' e 'libertà' nell stato di Milano al tempo di Luigi XII (1499-1512)," in Anne Lemonde and Ilaria Taddei, eds., *Circulations des idées et des pratiques politiques. France et Italie (XIIIe-XVIe siècle)* (Rome: École française de Rome, 2013), 209-33, at 215-16; on the two dismissed senators, see 229-30.

82. "Alia officia Judicaturae... prout sunt Capitanei Justitiae, Potestates, Vicarii, Commissarii civitatum et oppidorum, Judices, Consules et alii similes... quae temporibus retroactis per duces Mediolani solebant conferri seu donari... volumus senatores nostros... procedere ad electionem trium virorum, quos in eorum conscientia cognoverint sufficientes ad tale officium obtinendum" (Pélissier, *Documents,* doc. 11, 22).

83. "Prout in cancellaria Franciae fuit hactenus observatum." Changes in documentary habits with the beginning of the French domination are also noted in passing in Natale, *Stilus Cancellariae,* cxxxiii.

84. In this instance, the two officers named to the stipulated positions were not Italians: Pierre de Mansebrey / Manguerey and Pierre Garbot. See Leverotti, "La Cancelleria segreta da Ludovico il Moro a Luigi XII," in Arcangeli, ed., *Milano e Luigi XII,* 224-25, at 250-51.

85. In October 1499, Louis XII gave the Milanese house of Giovanni Sforza, Lord of Pesaro, to Ambrogio da Corte, the Sforza castellan who surrendered the Porta Giovia castle to France; the next month, the king gave the house of Luigi Terzago (executed by Ludovico for a failed coup in 1489) to Catellano Trivulzio, who had helped Louis capture Milan. See the documents in Pélissier, *Documents relatifs,* doc. 8, (96), and 10 (98). In July 1500, Chaumont d'Amboise and Bernard Stuart d'Aubigny found lodging in the palaces of Ludovico's treasurer (Antonio Landriani) and the governor of Lodi (Oldrado Lampugnano), respectively. See Nicola Soldini, "Il Governo francese e la città: imprese edificatorie e politica urbana nella Milano del primo '500," in Arcangeli, ed., *Milano e Luigi XII,* 431-447 at 441, n. 39.

86. Sanudo, *Diarii,* 3: 1077 ("come era assueto a fare a tempo dil ducha di Milam"), 1112 ("debiti cremonesi al tempo dil signor Lodovico").

87. BMV, MS Italiano VII 990 (=9582), 41r. Zaccaria Contarini to Venetian Signoria, 19 October 1501. "Pregando quelle non uoglino molestare alcuno fictuale del p.to m.co M.r Zuan Galeazo [Visconti], habitans su el Cremonese per causa de alcuni ficti del tempo d.l Ill.mo S.or Ludouico Sforza *ante aduentum galorum retro,* et questo per hauer dicti fictuali *usque tunc* facto ad instantia del p.to Zuan Galeazo certo promissione de dinari a certi banchieri per hauer habuto denari dali dicti fictuali dal dicto tempo ut supra."

88. ASV, Capi del Consiglio di Dieci—Lettere di Rettori e di Altre Cariche (Cremona, Casalmaggiore, Soncino, Pizzoleone), 72bis, 69. Petition of Cavaliere Zambaptista di Melli, 25 October 1502. The Cremonese rectors did not know how to respond, "vedendo le rason ad utranque partem."

89. ASV, Archivio del Senato, Deliberazioni—Terra, reg. 14, 202r–203v (22 May 1503): *Capitula Mercatorum Mediolanensium.* The phrase occurs repeatedly. Milan's merchants complained, for instance, of new taxes in Cremona on the sale of German cloth. The Venetians responded: "Respondeatur che cum sit che tal acrescimento sia sta facto per el signor Lodovico Qual era sta deputato per satisfaction de qualunche li haueano impresta danari: che seruarse debi quello che se seruaua al tempo del dicto signor Lodovico."

90. Marin Sanudo, *I Diarii,* Rinaldo Fulin, ed. (Bologna: Forni, 1969-1979 [1879-1902]), 4: 856 ("Item, essi sguizari han fato a missier Zuan Jacomo varie petizione di danari dovevano aver al tempo dil Moro."), and 5: 391 ("Item, che domino Scharamuza Visconte, qual a tempo dil Moro havia stipendiato in arte militari, inteso la Signoria feva zente, si oferiva venirli come bon servitor."

91. Pélissier, *Documents relatifs,* doc. 25, "Donation faite à Angelo Sacco [Giangiacomo Trivulzio's secretary]," 114-15: "donnons . . . le pont, port, et passaige de Gere de la rivière de Adde au droit de Pizzigueton, que a tenu le seigneur Jehan de Ventivolle du temps du seigneur Ludovic, par don de luy."

92. ASV, Capi del Consiglio di Dieci—Lettere di Ambasciatori 15 (Milano 1501-1525), Leonardo Blanco to Leonardo Loredan, 15 March 1506: "Mi ha dicto: voglio contarui quel che interuene a'tempo del Duca Francesco."

93. Compare this critical outlook to the softer forms of past-veneration described in Charles T. Davis, "Il Buon tempo antico," in Nicolai Rubinstein, ed., *Florentine Studies: Politics and Society in Renaissance Florence* (London: Faber and Faber, 1968), 45-69.

94. ASMi, Sforzesco 1418, Massimiliano Sforza in Pavia to Captain of Justice in Milan, 6 May 1513: "Perche ne facto intendere che al tempo de la Infelice expulsione et captura del Ill.mo quondam s.re nostro Patre fora del stato suo."

95. Matteo Bandello, *Tutte le opere,* Francesco Flora, ed. (Verona: Mondadori, 1966) (*Novelle: III.xxvi*), 2: 397–99.

96. ASMi, Sforzesco 1418, as above: "Zoanni Jacomo et li fratelli di Malabarba milanesi feceno Insulto cum le arme alla casa del Nobile Biasino Criuello nostro dilecto aleuo del p.to quondam s.re n.ro patre e li spoliorno de tuti li beni mobili cosi in Milano como de fora ala uilla, per essere dicto Biasino stato fidel seruitore del p.to S.re n.ro Patre."

97. ASMi, Sforzesco 1419, Annibale Bevilacqua in Milan to Massimiliano Sforza, 1 September 1513: "Me hano tenuto oppresso per spacio de quatuordeci anni uel circa, non sapendo addure altro mazore fundamento, saluo chio era gran sforcesco et Duchesco. Tutta uia essendome io nutrito con gran pacientia in questo spacio di tempo con supportare grandissime iniurie et superchiarie miserabilmente expectando che un giorno apparesse la uera luce de la uenuta de ura ex.tia." It is unclear whether the correspondent was Annibale Bevilacqua I, whose family held the feudal county and castle of Macastorna described in the letter; but biographical information suggests Annibale I died in Rome in 1508, aged fifty-five. This letter of 1513 might be evidence that he lived some time longer than previously thought, or the correspondent might be a relative. For reports on Annibale I, see Antonio Frizzi, *Memorie storiche della nobile famiglia Bevilacqua* (Parma: dalla Reale Stamperia, 1779), 86–89; Valerio Seta, *Compendio historico dell'origine, discendenza, attioni et accasamenti della famiglia Bevilacqua* (Ferrara: Per Vittorio Baldini, 1606), 140–41.

98. We know that suspicion of corruption of the *consiglio segreto* (the precursor to the French senate) in civil trials and the agitated interference of litigants was already a problem under Ludovico. See Maria Nadia Covini, *'La Balanza drita.' Pratiche di governo, leggi e ordinamenti nel ducato sforzesco* (Milan: FrancoAngeli, 2007), 37–39.

99. The charge was made by Ottaviano Pallavicino defending his brother-in-law, the senator Francesco Scotti, from accusations of salt fraud in 1503. See Arcangeli, "'Parlamento,'" 231, citing Sanudo, *Diarii,* 7: 671.

100. ASMi, Frammenti Registri Ducali 4b, LXVIII—Patenti (1513-14)—21v (Gratia Thiberii de Robecho, ribellis, 10 December 1513), 169v (Gratia Jo. Francisci de Coyris, 25 April 1514). The third phrase appears in Pierpont Morgan Library, MS M.434, *Litterae ducales donationis ad monasterium Sanctae Mariae Gratiarum,* letter of Milanese senator Alonso de Idiaquez to Emperor Charles V, 7 September 1541, regarding lands near Vigevano, 30v. Other Latin variations in the chancery documents include "post expulsionem gallorum" (in the above-cited ducal register: 26v), "in proximo adventu gallorum" (48r), "novissime invasione facta a gallis" (ASMi, Registri Ducali 64, 30v).

101. ASVr, Fondo Zileri-Dal Verme, 20, fasc. 45. Grida del duca di Milano riguardante li suoi sudditi che se trovano fuori di stato, 18 March 1513.

102. ASVr, Fondo Zileri-Dal Verme, 20, fasc. 45: "Al tempo de la expulsione de francesi fora del stato preditto ducale de milano qual fu del mexe de Junio de l'anno prossimo passato 1512."

103. ASMi, Panigarola, Liber Bannitorum 2/1, (1502–1513): 190v–197v: "Predicti omnes condempnati pro crimine lese M.tis et pro rebelione per eos commissa contra Ill. Et Ex. D.D. Maximilianum Sfortiam Mediolani Ducem in amputatione capitum et confiscatione bonorum et banniti a ducali dominio Mediolani." See also the Sforza edicts against French partisans of 18 September 1512 and 13 March 1513 in Pélissier, *Documents*, docs. 100 and 101, 278–83.

104. ASMi, Sforzesco 1474, Giovanangelo Pietrogallo in Milan to Massimiliano Sforza, 9 March 1513: "In quarum litterarum exequtione pluribus comunitatibus precepi ut infra certum honestum tempus ea insignia depingi facerent et illa gallorum abollerent etiam sub aliqua pena camera d.v. applicate. Nomina locorum quibus precepi et qui renitentes sunt inferius describuntur: Sed videtur quam ipse comunitates et oppida spreto dicto precepto per me facto non solum abradere noluerunt insignia gallorum sed nec etiam insignia v.ra depingi facere, quod iuditio meo nil aliud demonstrat nisi quam paruipendunt litteras d.v." The duke enjoined the painter Giovanni Giacomo da Trezzo and the notary Giovanni Angelo da Pietragalli to undertake the repainting campaign. A contract dated 15 February 1513 records them hiring the painter Giovanni Maria Lampugnano "pro adimplendis et pingendis dictis armis seu insignibus ducalibus" in "tota Martexana cum Seprio et Monte Brianzia; oppidum de Vicomercato cum sua iurisdictione et plebe; oppidum Gallarate cum sua plebe et iurisdictione; Inzinum cum sua iurisdictione." See Janice Shell, *Pittori in Bottega. Milano nel Rinascimento* (Turin: Umberto Allemandi & Co., 1995), doc. 96, 255–56; the men contract the division of their work in doc. 97, 256.

105. Raffaele Licinio, "Bari aragonese e ducale," in Francesco Tateo, ed., *Storia di Bari*, vol 2.: *Dalla Conquista normanna al ducato sforzesco* (Rome: Laterza, 1990), 152–85.

106. The story is far more complex than can be recounted here, in part because Ludovico only held Bari in usufruct for his son Francesco II, whom he had created Duke of Bari. Details of the history are reassembled by Ludovico Pepe, *La Storia della successione degli sforzeschi negli stati di Puglia e Calabria* (Bari-Trani: Vecchi, 1900), 17–74.

107. Pepe, *La Storia*, 60.

108. Pepe, *La Storia*, 82–83.

109. Pepe, *La Storia*, 89.

110. Castiglione, *Lettere* 1: #208, 206–07, Baldassarre Castiglione to Aloisia Gonzaga Castiglione, 27 February 1511.

111. Ambrogio da Paullo, *Cronaca milanese dall'anno 1476 al 1515*, Antonio Ceruti, ed., *Miscellanea di storia italiana* 13 (1871): 91–378, at 172: "Uno certo

monsignor da Lissono era stato governatore in Milano per il passato, et si trovò avere fatte molte cose inlicite, dove fu sendicato, perchè aveva fatte trarre molti gentilhomini et d'ogni conditione gente, in modo fu ditto avere mandato in Franza più de 300,000 ducati, li quali dinari furno robati poi a posta del roy de Franza che li tolse tutti, et poi fu privato del governo." See also Sanudo, *Diarii,* 3: 1637.

112. Gino Masi, "Il Sindacato delle magistrature comunali nel sec. XIV (con speciale riferimento a Firenze)," *Rivista italiana per le scienze giuridiche* 5, no. 1 (1930): 43–115; 5, no. 2 (1930): 331–411; for discussion of the procedure in fifteenth-century Milan, see Covini, *'La Balanza drita,'* 148–52, 269–82.

113. The traditional fourteenth-century Milanese statutes levied a quadruple fine against embezzlement on the part of podestàs. See Antonio Ceruti, ed., *Statuta Iurisdictionum Mediolani, saeculo XIV lata* (Turin: Ex Typis Regiis, 1869), articles XXXVII–XLV, 31–37. Milan's *sindacato* is not listed in the general Italian survey in the appendix to Guy Geltner, "Fighting Corruption in the Italian City-State: Perugian Officers' End of Term Audit (*sindacato*) in the Fourteenth Century," in Ronald Kroeze, André Vitória, and Guy Geltner, eds., *Anticorruption in History: From Antiquity to the Modern Era* (Oxford: Oxford University Press, 2018), 103–21.

114. The first, the Edict of Chinon of 14 August 1508, in French, was published in Pélissier, *Documents,* doc. 65, 187–93; the second, in Italian, was given at Milan and dated 15 July 1509; and the third, in Latin, is dated 18 July 1509. The latter was unearthed by Stefano Meschini in ASMi, Diplomi e Dispacci Sovrani; see Meschini, *Luigi XII,* 340–47. A (fourth?) French version (dated 22 July 1509) was published in Léon-Gabriel Pélissier, "Les Sources milanaises de l'histoire de Louis XII," *Bulletin du Comité des travaux historiques et scientifiques. Section d'histoire et de philologie,* no. 1 (1892): 110–88, doc. 28, 180–82, at 180. Its first item concerns the *sindacato:* "Et premierement volons et ordonnons en ensuyvant nostre dite dernière ordonnance que les offices de cappitaine ordonnes sur le fait de la justice et autres juges officiers de nostre dite duché, soyent mués et sindiqués de deux ans en deux ans, mesmement les cappitaine de Vimerca, Galeras, Marignan, Binasque, Monse, Vaulteline et Lugan, potestatz, de Val de Sesa, Pontremolle et Varese."

115. Pélissier, *Documents,* doc. 65, 189.

116. Meschini, *Luigi XII,* 343–44: the officials should "sindicarentur secundum ordinum antiquorum dispositionem," (343, n. 412), but there were "plerosque eorum esse qui . . . deputant thamen pro eorum arbitrio alias qui capitaneorum et talium officiorum munus gerent et qui numquam sindacantur nec pro sindacatu fideiubent" (344, n. 413).

117. Paraphrased from Giorgio Agamben, *The State of Exception,* Kevin Attell, trans. (Chicago: University of Chicago Press, 2005), 23.

118. Moritz Isenmann, "From Rule of Law to Emergency Rule in Renaissance Florence," in Lawrin Armstrong and Julius Kirshner, eds., *The Politics of Law in Late Medieval and Renaissance Italy: Essays in Honour of Lauro Martines* (Toronto: University of Toronto Press, 2011), 55–76.

119. Compare the evaporation of the *sindacato* here with its forceful support by Francesco Sforza in 1455, in the opening example in Covini, *'La Balanza drita,'* 11–12.

120. "Nul ne veult justice ny ordre ny police ny réformation" (Geoffroy Carles in Milan to Florimond Robertet, 7 July 1511, in Albert Piollet, *Étude historique sur Geoffroy Carles* [Grenoble: Baratier et Dardelet, 1882], 73–76). See also Meschini, *La Francia nel Ducato,* 2: 865.

121. Federico Chabod, "Usi e abusi nell'amministrazione dello Stato di Milano a mezzo '500," in *Studi storici in onore di Gioacchino Volpe per il suo 80. compleanno* (Milano: Sansoni, 1958), 1: 95–191.

122. See most recently Andrea Gamberini, *La Legittimità contesa. Costruzione statale e culture politiche (Lombardia, secoli XII–XV)* (Rome: Viella, 2016).

2. URBAN CONSTRUCTION AND SOCIAL
CONTROL AS CAPTURE

1. Luciano Patetta, "Il Castello nell'età sforzesca (1450-1499)," in Maria Teresa Fiorio, ed., *Il Castello Sforzesco di Milano* (Milan: Skira, 2005), 79–87, at 79; Evelyn Welch, *Art and Authority in Renaissance Milan* (New Haven, CT: Yale University Press, 1995), 176–79; Patrick Boucheron, *Le Pouvoir de bâtir. Urbanisme et politique édilitaire à Milan (XIVe-XVe siècles)* (Rome: École française de Rome, 1998), 208–17.

2. "Testamento originale ed autentico di Lodovico Maria Sforza, detto il Moro, duca di Milano" (hereafter "Testamento") in Pier Desiderio Pasolini, *Caterina Sforza,* vol. 3 (Rome: Ermanno Loescher, 1893), 419: "E volemo che la rocha se servi più salvatica che si può." On Ludovico's projects, see Gigliola Soldi Rondinini, "Le Strutture urbanistiche di Milano durante l'età di Lodovico il Moro," in Gigliola Soldi Rondinini, *Saggi di storia e storiografia visconteo-sforzesco* (Bologna: Cappelli Editore, 1984), 131–58.

3. See the useful reflections in Patrick Boucheron, "Non domus ista sed urbs: Palais princiers et environnement urbain au Quattrocento (Milan, Mantoue, Urbino)," in Patrick Boucheron and Jacques Chiffoleau, eds., *Les Palais dans la ville. Espaces urbains et lieux de puissance publique dans la Méditerranée médiévale* (Lyon: Presses Universitaires de Lyon, 2004), 249–84; and Boucheron, *Le Pouvoir de bâtir,* 556–71.

4. Ambrogio da Paullo, *Cronaca milanese dall'anno 1476 al 1515,* Antonio Ceruti, ed., *Miscellanea di storia italiana* 13 (1871): 91–378, at 118.

5. Ludovico ordered the refashioning of the zone ("squadrare dicta piaza") in July 1492; Luciano Patetta, "Alcune osservazioni su un disegno di Leon-

ardo," *Il Disegno di architettura* 23–24 (2001): 11–18, at 12. See also Richard Schofield, "Ludovico il Moro's Piazzas: New Sources and Observations," *Annali di architettura* 4–5 (1992–1993): 157–67, at 159.

6. Jacopo Ghilardotti, *La Casa degli Atellani e la vigna di Leonardo* (Rome: Rai Eri, 2015), 24–43; Rosa Auletta Marrucci, "Il Borgo delle Grazie fuori di porta Vercellina: Un Incompiuto programma sforzesco," in Mario Frassineti, ed., *Santa Maria delle Grazie* (Milan: Federico Motta, 1998), 24–47. Much more awaits to be learned from Edoardo Rossetti's promised book, *La Città cancellata.*

7. Carlo Pedretti, "The Sforza Horse in Context," in Diane Cole Ahl, ed., *Leonardo da Vinci's Sforza Monument Horse* (Bethlehem, PA: Lehigh University Press, 1995), 27–39. On the reapportioning of the bronze, see Marin Sanudo, *La Spedizione di Carlo VIII in Italia,* Rinaldo Fulin, ed. (Venice: Marco Visentini, 1883), 119.

8. Luchino del Mayno and Luca Beltrami, *Vicende militari del Castello di Milano dal 1706 al 1848* (Milano: Hoepli, 1894), 207.

9. Thomas Coryate, *Coryats Crudities* (London: William Stansby, 1611), 104.

10. Del Mayno and Beltrami, *Vicende militari,* 14–17. See also Marino Viganò, "Du Château-palais de la Renaissance à la citadelle espagnole et autrichienne: Le *Castello Sforzesco* de Milan (XVIe-XVIIIe siècle)," in Gilles Blieck, Philippe Contamine, Nicolas Faucherre, and Jean Mesqui, eds., *Le Château et la ville: Conjonction, opposition, juxtaposition (XIe-XVIIIe siècle)* (Paris: Comité des Travaux Historiques et Scientifiques, 2002), 279–90.

11. Giovanni Andrea Prato, *Storia di Milano,* Cesare Cantù, ed., *Archivio storico italiano* 3 (1842): 216–418, at 320; Gianmarco Burigozzo, *Cronaca Milanese,* Cesare Cantù, ed., *Archivio storico italiano* 3 (1842): 419–552, at 424; Felice Calvi, "Il Castello di Porta Giovia e sue vicende nella storia di Milano," *Archivio storico lombardo,* series 2, vol. 3, fasc. 2 (1886): 229–297 at 265.

12. Ettore Bellingeri to the Duke of Ferrara, 13 September 1499, cited in Nicola Soldini, "Il Governo francese e la città: Imprese edificatorie e politica urbana nella Milano del primo '500," in Arcangeli, ed., *Milano e Luigi XII,* 431–447, at 432.

13. Prato, *Storia,* 237. In 1500, " il Trivulzio se ritirò in Corte, et preso il campanile del Domo, tutto lo fornì de arteglieria."

14. ASMn, AG 1643, unsigned, but probably Francesco Malatesta to Francesco Gonzaga, 2 March 1500: "Ogni di quj se conta qualche miraculo del trar de le arteliarie: perche pare chosa miraculosa che non se faza nocumento ad alchuno. Dichono che uno mortar e chaschato in mezzo uno lecto chel ge era dentro cinque persone et non ha tochato alchuno: [. . .] Vna pietra de uno chanone ha percosso in uno mura et ha imbracato el uolto a molti homeni che erano spesi insieme in uno locho: et non li ha facto dispiacere: Dichono che s.to Ambroso ha cura de questo populo: per le grande deuotione che di continuo se fanno."

15. On the lengthy negotiations over the rendition of the castle in 1513, see Luca Fois, "'Et ledit jour echeu s'ilz ne sont secourriz rendront la place audit seigneur duc . . .' La Resa della guarnigione francese del castello di Porta Giovia di Milano al duca Massimiliano Sforza-Visconti (novembre 1513)," *Annuario dell'archivio di Stato di Milano* (2016): 10-77.

16. "Testamento," 416.

17. Prato, *Storia,* 225.

18. Marin Sanudo, *I Diarii,* Rinaldo Fulin, ed. (Bologna: Forni, 1969-1979 [1879-1902]), 3: 31, 13 October 1499.

19. Ambrogio da Paullo, *Cronaca,* 159. Thomas Coryate later noted that there were two mills at Milan's castle, one for grinding corn, and the other for making gunpowder. Coryate, *Coryats Crudities,* 103.

20. Francesco Muralto, *Annalia,* Pietro Aloisio Donino, ed. (Milan: Cura et Impensis Aloisii Daelli, 1861), 49: Ludovico "voluitque brovetum, ubi cibaria vendebantur; et ut esset in centro civitatis, fabricari fecerat cum magnis expensis super platea castri magni."

21. A similar ditch crawled around the hospital of San Dionigi, to separate residents from diseased patients. Léon-Gabriel Pélissier, *Les Registres Panigarola et le 'Gridario generale' de l'Archivio di Stato' di Milano pendant la domination française (1499-1513)* (Paris: E. Bouillon, 1897), #149, 19, 13 November 1501. On similar strategies of conquest in the fourteenth-century duchy, see Marcello Spigaroli, "La Piazza in ostaggio. Urbanistica e politica militare nello stato visconteo," *Bollettino storico piacentino* 87 (1992): 145-60.

22. Léon-Gabriel Pélissier, *Documents pour l'histoire de la domination française dans le Milanais (1499-1513)* (Toulouse: Édouard Privat, 1891), #57, 158-62, at 159, 30 July; 11 and 16 August 1507.

23. Silvio Leydi notes that the two edicts, one week apart, describe two sets of fortifications with different materials and different measurements. See Leydi, "La Linea esterna di fortificazioni di Milano, 1323-1550," *Storia urbana* 31 (1985): 3-29, at 6-8.

24. Pélissier, *Documents,* 160-61; "signore Theodoro" (Trivulzio?) is named as one of the captains to advise the construction.

25. ASMn, AG 1637, Jacopo Suardo in Milan to Francesco Gonzaga in Mantua, 16 August 1507: "Uero e che non si resta delauorare dicontinuo ali redefossi intorno Milano liquali costano cinque milia scudi eli contadini lipagano edipoi e concluso defare setti reuelini uno per porta quali costarano asai ela spesa lapaga lipreti."

26. Ambrogio da Paullo, *Cronaca,* 205-6.

27. Muralto noted over 1,000 workers upon fortifications at Como, tearing down houses and churches to build them. Muralto, *Annalia,* 100-3.

28. The words belong to Seneca the Younger, "De Clementia," in *Moral Essays 1,* John W. Basore, trans. (Cambridge: Harvard University Press, 1928), 1.19.

412–13; compare to Niccolò Machiavelli, *Il Principe,* Mario Martelli, ed. (Rome: Salerno Editrice, 2006), cap. 20, 269–80. See also Aldo Settia, "Le Fortezze urbani dai Goti a Machiavelli," in his *Proteggere e dominare. Fortificazioni e popolamento nell'Italia medievale* (Rome: Viella, 1999), 149–68, at 162–63.

29. Andrea Gritti in Padua to the Doge in Venice, 26 July 1509: "Prometto a la Serenità Vostra ditti guastadori esser venuti cum tanto iubilo et contenteza che se andissino a noze non poriano dimostrar mazor letitia." Gritti here refers to the laborers preparing Padua against an imperial siege. See Polibio Zanetti, "L'Assedio di Padova del 1509 in correlazione alla guerra combattuta nel Veneto dal maggio all'ottobre," *Nuovo archivio veneto* 2 (1891): 1–168, doc. 18, 135–36. Some background on *guastadori* appears in Richard Trexler, "Correre la terra. Collective Insults in the Late Middle Ages," *Mélanges de l'École française de Rome—Moyen Âge, temps modernes* 96, no. 2 (1984): 845–902, at 850–52.

30. Ambrogio da Paullo, *Cronaca,* 205–7: "Oh! quanto danno se dava a chi toccava il guasto! Et per questo più cressette la paura, et niente altro se diceva, se non: Dove dovemo fugire per star sicuri?"

31. Prato, *Storia,* 352.

32. On the history of the constant process of premodern fortification in Italy, see Daniela Lamberini, "La Politica del guasto. L'Impatto del fronte bastionato sulle preesistenze urbane," in Carlo Cresti, Amelio Fara, and Daniela Lamberini, eds., *Architettura militare nell'Europa del XVI secolo* (Siena: Edizioni Periccioli, 1988), 219–40.

33. Soldini, "Il Governo francese," 436, n. 23, citing edicts in the *Registri Panigarola* of 31 December 1511 and of 12 April 1522. On the prohibition against access holes or damage, see Pélissier, *Les Registres,* #418, 38, n. 8.

34. Soldini, "Il Governo francese," 436, n. 23. On the desire for clearings near city walls during the Italian Wars, see the documents in Lionello Puppi, "Le Mura e il 'guasto.' Nota intorno alle condizioni di sviluppo delle città venete di Terraferma tra XVI e XVIII secolo," in Corrado Maltese, ed., *Centri storici di grandi agglomerati urbani* (Bologna: Editrice Clueb, 1982), 115–21, esp. doc. 3, 18 November 1512, concerning Padua. In Milan, the Spanish governor in 1527 decreed that all obstructions within an arquebus-shot of the city should be razed to prevent cover for enemies. See Marco Formentini, *Il Ducato di Milano. Studi storici documentati* (Milan: Libreria Editrice G. Brignola, 1877), 360–61: decrees of Antonio de Leyva, 14 and 16 August 1527.

35. Prato, *Storia,* 353.

36. G. P. L. & C. E. V., "Progetto per la costruzione di una mura intorno a Milano," *Archivio storico lombardo,* ser. 1, vol. 4, fasc. 2 (1877): 283–94, at 284–85. For the reports of the efforts to raise funds for a new wall as early as 1519, see Sanudo, *Diarii,* 27: 505, Jacopo Caroldo in Milan, September 1519:

"Lautrech vuol fortificar Milano, e per essa ha messo pagar il quinto più di dazio a tutto, che per ducati 20000 et certa quantità paghi il clero; de tutto sarà 50000, e cresce il sal, e vol sia questa imposition per 4 anni."

37. Felice Calvi, *Il Castello Visconteo-sforzesco nella storia di Milano* (Milano: Antonio Vallardi, 1894), 238–39. On the enlargement see Burigozzo, *Cronaca,* 517.

38. Burigozzo, *Cronaca,* 432–33. BnF ms. fr. 26118, 567, lists all the men hired to clean up the damage and bury the bodies.

39. Pietro Martire d'Anghiera, *Opus Epistolarum Petri Martyri Anglerii Mediolanensis* (Amsterdam: Typis Elzeverianis, 1670), letter 733, 421: "In Castelli prima fronte marmorea erant Francisci Sfortiae primi Ducis Mediolani stemmata, portae infixa, cui adhaerebat B. Ambrosii, ejus urbis patroni, marmorea & ipsa ingens imago; labe illa cessante, reperta sunt indemnia integraque, utraque jacentia in platea ipsa opposita Castello, quae jam erat herbida. quid sibi velint haec prodigia, Gallis, ut arbitror, minitantia boni judicent."

40. In 1499, the city wanted the king and his men to stay in public hostels rather than private residences (as the French wished), because "è stato grandissima controversia tra loro [the king's men] e li gentilhomini de Milano per non alogiare ne le case loro." The plan was to lodge the royal party in the Corte Vecchia (the old Visconti palace near the cathedral) and the palaces of Galeazzo Sanseverino, Gianfrancesco Sanseverino, and Marchesino Stanga; Léon-Gabriel Pélissier, *Les Préparatifs de l'entrée de Louis XII à Milan* (Montpellier: Gustave Firmin et Montane, 1891), doc. 1, 29–30; see also docs. 2–4, 30–38.

41. Massimiliano Stampa to Francesco II Sforza, 27 April 1531, quoted in Carlo Catturini, "Dopo Leonardo: La Sala delle Asse al tempo di Francesco II Sforza e Cristina di Danimarca," *Rassegna di studi e di notizie* 38 (2016): 15–30, at 18.

42. Sanudo, *Diarii,* 3: 234: "Hanno esser stà sacomanate in Milano tutti i Crivelli, Landriani et Castioni con soi adherenti, ch'è forsi case 100." (These families were Sforza partisans targeted in April 1500.) Compare to the claim about the number of houses targeted in Roberta Martinis, *L'Architettura contesa. Federico da Montefeltro, Lorenzo de'Medici, gli Sforza e palazzo Salvatico a Milano* (Milano: Mondadori, 2008), 124.

43. Prato, *Storia,* 225. The men were Giangiacomo Trivulzio, Bernardino da Corte, Antonio Maria Pallavicino, and Francesco Bernardino Visconti.

44. Pélissier, *Les Préparatifs de l'entrée,* doc. 7, 42–43, 2 October 1499.

45. Prato, *Storia,* 222. Works on Costabili's Ferrara palace began in 1502. On the Botta palace, see Paolo Merzagora, "Il Palazzo per Bergonzio Botta a Milano," in Christoph Frommel, Luisa Giordano, and Richard Schofield, eds., *Bramante Milanese* (Venice: Marsilio, 2002), 261–80.

46. Martinis, *L'Architettura contesa,* 124: "Il magnifico messer Antonio [. . .] mi fa intendere che la casa nostra è stata molto maltratata da certi balestrieri quali hanno rotte le finestre, li usci, et exportato il ligname, et asse che erano in epsa, cussi le lectiere, come li solari dele camera terrene. Et che ultra questo la Roba de epso messer Antonio cioè frumento, et vini et legnu et altre soe robe, è stata sachegiata" (to Giovanni Giorgio Seregno from Milan, 10 September 1499). Similar problems occurred prior to the Battle of Bicocca in April 1522. The Sforza government under Morone issued an edict against despoiling patrician abodes. See Giuseppe Müller, ed., *Documenti che concernono la vita pubblica di Gerolamo Morone* (Turin: Stamperia Reale, 1865), doc. 154, 291–92, 24 March 1522.

47. Richard Schofield, "Ludovico il Moro and Vigevano," *Arte lombarda,* n.s. 62, no. 2 (1982): 93–140, at 117.

48. On Sacierges and Poncher as successive residents of Stanga's palazzo, see Stefano Meschini, *Luigi XII, Duca di Milano. Gli Uomini e le istituzioni del primo dominio francese (1499–1512)* (Milan: FrancoAngeli, 2004), 117–31, at 125.

49. For the appointments of Milanese architects and engineers under Louis XII, see Bertrand Jestaz, "Les Rapports des français avec l'art et les artistes lombards: Quelques traces," in Contamine and Guillaume, eds., *Louis XII en Milanais,* 273–303, at 274–75. On the ongoing projects, see Francesco Repishti, "La Cultura architettonica milanese negli anni della dominazione francese. Continuità e innovazioni," in Frédéric Elsig and Mauro Natale, eds., *Le Duché de Milan et les commanditaires français (1499–1521)* (Viella: Rome, 2013), 15–29, at 25.

50. Meschini, *Luigi XII,* 67–108.

51. Edoardo Villata, ed., *Leonardo da Vinci. I Documenti e le testimonianze contemporanee* (Milan: Castello Sforzesco, 1999), doc. 237, 204–5, Charles d'Amboise in Milan to Florentine Signoria, 16 December 1506: "Et volemo confessare che in le prove facte de lui de qualche cosa che li havemo domandato, de desegni et architectura, et altre cose pertinente alla condicione nostra, ha satisfacto cum tale modo che non solo siamo restati satisfacti de lui, ma ne havemo preheso admiratione." On the proposal that Chaumont charged Leonardo with defensive constructions at Locarno, see Marino Viganò, "Leonardo in Ticino? Ipotesi sul 'rivellino' del castello di Locarno (1507)," *Arte lombarda* 144, no. 2 (2005): 28–37.

52. Carlo Pedretti, *Leonardo architetto* (Milan: Electa, 1978), 205, 210, citing the *Codice Atlantico* fols. 231r-b, 271v-a, 231r-b.

53. Ferdinando Reggiori, "Il Santuario di Santa Maria alla Fontana di Milano alla luce di recentissime scoperte," *Arte Lombarda* 2 (1956): 51–64.

54. Cesare Cesariano, *De architectura* (Como: Gottardo da Ponte, 1521), 17v.

55. Giovanni Battista Sannazzaro, "L'Amedeo e S. Maria alla Fontana," in Janice Shell and Liana Castelfranchi, eds., *Giovanni Antonio Amadeo: Scultura e architettura del suo tempo* (Milan: Cisalpino, 1993): 297–328, at 298.

The Visconti in question was Giovanni Ambrogio Visconti (who died in 1499), Sforza counselor, soldier, and poet. See documents in Giorgio Galletti, "Precisazioni su Santa Maria alla Fontana a Milano," *Raccolta vinciana*, fasc. 21 (1982): 39–102, at 94–95.

56. On Bambaia's drawings, see Maria Teresa Fiorio, "Due disegni e un possibile intervento del Bambaia in Santa Maria alla Fontana," in Shell and Castelfranchi, eds., *Giovanni Antonio Amadeo*, 589–612.

57. Giuliana Fantoni, *L'Acqua a Milano. Uso e gestione nel basso medioevo (1385–1535)* (Bologna: Cappelli Editore, 1990); Patrick Boucheron, "Water and Power in Milan, c. 1200–1500," *Urban History* 28, no. 2 (2001): 180–93.

58. On Leonardo's hydraulic projects for French patrons, see Sara Taglialagamba, "Leonardo da Vinci's Hydraulic Systems and Fountains for His French Patrons Louis XII, Charles d'Amboise, and Francis I," in Constance Moffatt and Sara Taglialagamba, eds., *Illuminating Leonardo: A Festschrift for Carlo Pedretti Celebrating His 70 Years of Scholarship* (Boston: Brill, 2016), 300–14. On della Valle, see Cesare Maffioli, "Tra Girolamo Cardano e Giacomo Soldati. Il Problema della misura delle acque nella Milano spagnola," in Alessandra Fiocca, Daniela Lamberini, and Cesare Maffioli, *Arte e scienza delle acque nel Rinascimento* (Venice: Marsilio, 2003), 105–36, at 106. On the Blois connection, see Laure Fagnart, *Léonard de Vinci en France* (Rome: L'Erma di Bretschneider, 2009), 28–30.

59. Carlo Pagnani, *Decretum super flumine Abdue reddendo navigabili: La storia del primo Naviglio di Paderno d'Adda (1516–1520),* Gianni Beltrame and Paolo Margaroli, eds. (Milan: Pecorini, 2003). Louis XII also issued decrees governing pre-existing canals. See Pélissier, *Documents,* doc. 76, 226–33, concerning the Martesana canal, and doc. 78, 237–38, regarding blockages.

60. Luisa Giordano, "La Celebrazione della vittoria. L'Esaltazione della storia contemporanea nelle terre della conquista," in Contamine and Guillaume, *Louis XII en Milanais,* 245–71 at 248–54; and John Gagné, "Counting the Dead: Traditions of Enumeration and the Italian Wars," *Renaissance Quarterly* 67, no. 3 (2014): 791–840, at 821–26.

61. Charles Robertson, "The Patronage of Gian Giacomo Trivulzio during the French Domination of Milan," in Guillaume and Contamine, eds., *Louis XII en Milanais,* 323–40, at 334–40; Janice Shell, "Il Problema della ricostruzione del monumento a Gaston de Foix," in *Agostino Busti detto il Bambaia (1483–1548)* (Milan: Finarte and Longanesi & Co., 1990), 32–61.

62. Janice Shell, *Pittori in Bottega. Milano nel Rinascimento* (Turin: Umberto Allemandi & Co., 1995), 119, and related docs. 94–95, 253–55. Bramantino painted a copy for the French treasurer Antoine Turpin, Solario painted one for Georges d'Amboise, and Marco d'Oggiono painted at least two copies for French patrons. Shell suggests that the king who wished to detach the mural was Louis XII, but Vasari says only that "fece venir voglia

al re di Francia di condurla nel regno." See Giorgio Vasari, *Le vite* (Florence: Giuntina, 1568), part 3, vol. 1, 26-27.

63. La Chesnaye has often been misidentified in most of the scholarly literature on Santa Maria delle Grazie as Lachesnave or Lachesnare. See the erroneous reports in Giulio Bora, "La Decorazione pittorica: Sino al Settecento," in *Santa Maria delle Grazie* (Milano: Banca Popolare di Milano, 1983), 140-87, at 147-49; and an image in Frassineti, ed., *Santa Maria delle Grazie,* 234. On La Chesnaye's writings and career, see the introduction in Nicolas de la Chesnaye, *La Condamnation de Banquet,* eds. Jelle Koopmans and Paul Verhuyck (Geneva: Droz, 1991), 27. Fiorio, "Due disegni," 600, mentions the inscription at the Fontana: "Nicolaus a Querceto parisiensis mediolani pretor." See also Jestaz, "Les Rapports des français," 287-92.

64. The text accords with Gaspar's motet *Mater Digna Dei.* On this motet, see Agnese Pavanello, ed., *Gaspar van Weerbeke: Collected Works,* vol. 4: *Motets* (Neuhausen-Stuttgart: American Institute of Musicology, 2010), xlvi-xlix.

65. Prato, *Storia,* 261-62.

66. Pedretti, *Leonardo architetto,* 210 (the words are Leonardo's own). On hair nets, see Elisabetta Gnignera, *I Soperchi ornamenti. Copricapi e acconciature femminili nell'Italia del Quattrocento* (Siena: Protagon, 2010), 123-30; on hunting nets, Giancarlo Malacarne, *Le Cacce del principe. L'Ars venandi nella terra dei Gonzaga* (Modena: Il Bulino, 1998), doc. 38, 204, Francesco Gonzaga on the Ferrarese boar hunt in 1481: "Se metono le rete, le quali sonno state casone de fare morire tuti quelli porci [che] sonno ussiti fora; et benché la piazza sia grande, nondimeno non vedessemo ferire porco alcuno, se non in le rete."

67. I. G., "Una Grida milanese a stampa del XV secolo," *Archivio storico lombardo,* ser. 1 vol. 7, fasc. 2 (1880): 299-302, at 300.

68. "Intese che lj homenj de la terra se erano armati: et come el comissario fu dentro fece far la grida che ognuno deponesse le arme: et facta la grida fu facto el contrario perche lj homenj corseno ale arme et preseno el comissario" (Francesco Malatesta in Milan to Francesco Gonzaga in Mantua. ASMn, AG 1634, 26 January 1500).

69. On the interpenetrations of war and peace in late medieval society, see Giorgio Chittolini, "Il 'Militare' tra tardo medioevo e prima età moderna," in Claudio Donati and Bernhard R. Kroener, eds., *Militari e società civile nell'Europa dell'età moderna (secoli XVI–XVIII)* (Bologna: Il Mulino, 2007), 53-102.

70. Giorgio Agamben, *The State of Exception,* Kevin Attell, trans. (Chicago: University of Chicago Press, 2005), 2-11.

71. Ambrogio da Paullo, *Cronaca,* 153-54.

72. Pélissier, *Documents*, 11, doc. 8, stipulates that Sforza partisans without safe-conducts should be arrested.

73. Pélissier, *Les Registres*, #62, 12 n. 4, 6 May 1500: "Grida che non sia persona alcuna che ardisca da ora in avanti fuggire ne portar robbe che ha di fuori in città, ne altrimenti tramutarle per dubbio di sacchegiamento per cui potessero essergli tolte, ed ognuno stia sicuro che non avrà altra molestia da' soldati."

74. Pélissier, *Les Registres*, appendix, doc. 6, 85–86. 6 July 1500. A later decree demanded that no guests should lodge in the city without a passport; Pélissier, *Les Registres*, #108, 16, 9 March 1501.

75. Pélissier, *Les Registres*, #126, 17, 25–26 June 1501.

76. Pélissier, *Les Registres*, #42, 9, 18 March 1500, issued by Ludovico's brother, Ascanio Sforza.

77. Pélissier, *Les Registres*, #51, 11, 24 April 1500.

78. Similar orders against carrying arms and against masks that hid identities appeared under the Sforza as well. See ASMi, Sforzesco 1496, 12 January 1481, 30 January 1483.

79. Pélissier, *Les Registres* (1500): #70; (1501): #119, 136; (1502): #189; (1506): #291, 305, 330; (1507): #401, 412, 424, 443; (1508): #482; (1509): #559, 617; (1511): #757.

80. Pélissier, *Les Registres*, on arms permit revocation #499, 21 June 1508; on duels #247, 7 December 1505; on surrender of munitions #53, 23 April 1500, and #964, 4 March 1513 (under Massimiliano Sforza); and on the weapons survey #71, 29 May 1500.

81. Pélissier, *Les Registres* (1500): # 34, 51, 59, 71; (1505): #171, 191, 221; (1506): #255, 268; (1507): #342, 356, 398, 435; (1508): #458, 473, 481, 500, 517, 536, 561; (1509): #593; (1510): #635; (1511): #717, 729, 735, 769, 800; (1512): #871, 877, 878, 902, 925; (1513, under Massimiliano Sforza): #949, 978, 989, 995.

82. Pélissier, *Documents*, #2, 2–5, at 5.

83. ASMi, Sforzesco 1141, 2 October 1499. On behalf of the king, "Se fa publica crida et commandamento che non sij persona alcuna che olsa ne presuma sotto pena de rebellione remouere ne descanzellare li segni quali sono o serano facti per li soi foreri o siano seschalchi de lozamenti suso le porte de le case de li citadini designate ad allogiare la compagni & la corte de la sua M.ta in questa sua cita de Milano: anze debiano lassare aperte le porte depse case perche le persone gli allogiarono possano intrare in casa."

84. Prato, *Storia*, 224.

85. Ambrogio da Paullo, *Cronaca*, 160: "Ma se trovavano qualche povero artesco che andasse a casa sua de notte, venendo da la bottega o con lume o senza lume, li predeano et li menavano in presone, et faceano pagare a chi uno grossone, a chi doi, a chi tri, a chi quattro, secondo che poteano a rasone o no, et non bisognavano lanterne, che li tolevano, e poi diceano haverli trovati senza lume."

86. Ambrogio da Paullo, *Cronaca,* 161.
87. Pélissier, *Les Registres,* #76, 13, 13 June 1500: "Si proibisce agli detti sub-diti il far unione d'uomini armati nelle case, chiese, ecc., sotto preteso di tener consiglio per il ben commune."
88. These *coperti* appear originally to have been small covered *piazze* in front of noble houses designed for aristocratic conversation or public use. The chronicler Bonvesin de la Riva claimed there were sixty of them in the late thirteenth century. From the 1470s, advocates of urban renewal described them as havens for thieves and unclean stalls for animals. Defenders described them as locations for public pleasure and passage. See Pietro Ghinzoni, "Di Alcuni antichi coperti ossia portici in Milano," *Archivio storico lombardo* ser. 2, vol. 9, fasc. 1 (1892): 126–40.
89. Pélissier, *Documents relatifs,* appendix doc. 8, 270–72, at 272.
90. ASCM, Registro di Lettere Ducali 16 (1497–1502), 220v–221v: "Item perche si comprehende essere molti in dicta cita et dominio de Milano quali si lassano crescere longhe le barbe et vano barbuti fora de la comune consuetudine et pollicie de li homini: Del che se arguisse sinistra volun-tade et prauo desiderio: Parendo cossa di malo exemplo e trista inten-tione." Attachable 'counterfeit' beards were used in theatrical performances and could have been procured from makers or keepers of costumes. For a Florentine goldsmith who made wigs and beards for the religious plays, see Nerida Newbigin, *Feste d'Oltrarno: Plays in Churches in Fifteenth-Century Florence* (Florence: Olschki, 1996), 1:117; and for further evidence of fifteenth-century theatrical beards, see 1: 72; 1: 171. My thanks go to Nerida Newbigin for these references. For the language of "habit" in rela-tion to beard growth in medieval Italy, see Carol Lansing, *Passion and Order: Restraint of Grief in the Medieval Italian Communes* (Ithaca, NY: Cornell University Press, 2008), 53.
91. Jean-Marie Le Gall, *Un Idéal masculin? Barbes et moustaches (XVe-XVIIIe siè-cles)* (Paris: Payot, 2011), 64–65. Readers may also wish to consult Douglas Biow, *On the Importance of Being an Individual in Renaissance Italy: Men, Their Professions, and Their Beards* (Philadelphia: University of Pennsylvania Press, 2015).
92. Paul Edward Dutton, *Charlemagne's Mustache: And Other Cultural Clusters of a Dark Age* (New York: Palgrave Macmillan, 2004), 18–19.
93. "Nonnulli barbam prolixius enutritam inexpleto luctu promiserunt, hir-sutamque ac rigentiore mento propendentem tam pertinaci moeroris in-dicio demisere, ut edicto publico de cute leviganda, deque pilis tradendis cautum sit; & ne paupertatem aut aeris inopiam excusarent, fisci detri-mento praestaturos impendia praecones admonebant: tanto risu ludibri-oque omnium, ut vix aegreque pauci admodum edicto paruerint. Exinde barbam alere, renascentemque pilum enutrire, tempestas nostra ploratu jugi subtristior induxit: quod deinceps veluti per manus traditum, utentiumque

moribus receptum sic invaluit, ut juvenes juxtaque senes, nullo discrimine ferociter intonsi, fortes sint, & hanc in diem sua tenus barba sapientes. Nonnulli etiam vestem mutaverunt: plures saga sumpserunt: divinorum obliti alii neque vota concipere, neque concepta solvere, aut templa revisere, nimia sui doloris impatientia sustinuerunt" (Bernardino Arluno, *De bello Veneto libri sex,* in J. G. Graevius, ed., *Thesaurus antiquitatum et historiarum Italiae* [Leiden: Petrus Vander, 1722], vol. 5, part 4, 1–306, at 3).

94. David B. Kaufman, "Roman Barbers," *Classical Weekly* 25, no. 19 (1932): 145–48, at 146. For the instance of Julius Caesar not cutting his hair in mourning for a defeated comrade, see Suetonius, *Life of Julius Caesar,* J. C. Rolfe, trans. (Cambridge, MA: Harvard University Press, 1914), 67, 118–19.

95. Pélissier, *Les Registres,* #213, 24 n. 1, 4 July 1505.

96. These phrases appear in Giovio's biography of Curti: "Nihil obiter immutato vetere cultu, quum caeteri cives non obscura confessione servitutis, adventu Gallorum, peregrinam induti vestem, et capillum ad aurem subtondentes, eum pristino more togatum, prolixeque comatum petulanter irriderent" (Paolo Giovio, "Elogia virorum illustrium," in *Pauli Iovii Opera,* Renzo Meregazzi, ed. [Rome: Istituto poligrafico dello stato, 1972], 8: 86–87). I owe this reference to Jill Pederson.

97. BMV, MS Italiano, Classe VII 990 (=9582), Letters of Zaccaria Contarini, 1501–02, 70r–71r, at 71r.

98. On this relationship between force and law, and particularly the way that war conditioned the political relations of the early sixteenth century, see the introductory remarks of Diego Quaglioni and Jean-Claude Zancarini, "Justice et armes au XVIᵉ siècle: Présentation," *Laboratoire italien* 10 (2010): 5–7.

99. ASMn, AG 1634, Francesco Malatesta in Milan to Francesco Gonzaga in Mantua, 9 March 1500.

3. DELEGITIMIZING THE SFORZA

1. See Federico Del Tredici, "Lombardy under the Visconti and the Sforza," in Gamberini and Lazzarini, eds., *The Italian Renaissance State,* 156–76.

2. Jane Black, *Absolutism in Renaissance Milan: Plenitude of Power under the Visconti and Sforza, 1329–1535* (Oxford: Oxford University Press), 2009, 84–92.

3. Niccolò Machiavelli, *Il Principe,* Mario Martelli, ed. (Rome: Salerno Editrice, 2006), cap. 3, 74–75: "E a possederli [i.e., gli stati] securamente basta avere spenta la linea del principe che li dominava" and "e chi le [i.e., gli stati] acquista, volendole tenere, debbe aver dua respetti: l'uno, che il sangue del loro principe antique si spenga; l'altro, di non alterare né loro legge né loro dazi."

4. Fundamental in revealing this fact is Timothy McCall, "Brilliant Bodies: Material Culture and the Adornment of Men in North Italy's Quat-

trocento Courts," *I Tatti Studies in the Italian Renaissance* 16, no. 1/2 (2013): 445-90.

5. ASMn, AG 1634, Francesco Malatesta in Milan to Francesco Gonzaga in Mantua, 3 January 1501: "Questi signori francesi hora piu che maj publichano esser stata pocha prudentia in lo Sig.r Lud.co, dicendo che la masena che pagava S. xij per mozo: etiam de presenti non paga se non S. viij: e cresuta doa milia ducati, per il che concludeno che esso sign.r Ludo .co era inganato da ogniuno et non se ne auedeua, ouera non li sapeua proudere: existimano questi sign.ri francesi esser summa prudentia in quelli principj li quali senza far sinistro alj subditi sanno ben preualerse de le sue intrate, etiam concludeno che uno principe non po longamente durare achi mancha questi duj membri: zoe la beniuolentia de lj subditi etiam la hobedientia de le zente darme: le qual due chose essendone priuato el S. Lud.co hanno chausata la ruina sua—il che dicono el uenire da pocha prudentia."

6. Girolamo Priuli, *I Diarii, 1499–1512,* Arturo Segre, ed. *Rerum Italicarum Scriptores,* vol. 24, part 3 (Città di Castello: Tipi della Casa editrice S. Lapi, 1912–1938), 1: 297: "Or, lector, tu vedi a qual modo in questi tempi ruinò la degnissima caxa sforzescha, che persenno il loro stato, sì degno et sì nominato."

7. Léon-Gabriel Pélissier, "Deux lettres inédites de Louis XII à J. J. Trivulce (28 janvier 1500)," in *Miscellanea Ceriani* (Milan: Hoepli, 1910), 391–402.

8. ASMn, AG 1634, Francesco Malatesta in Milan to Francesco Gonzaga in Mantua, 5 January 1500: "Io credo che se li muri etiam li arbori etiam la terra hauessino habuta lingua che hariano gridato: moro moro."

9. Decades earlier, when Ludovico returned from exile on 7 September 1479, he had also entered the city not in military triumph, but "per la via del giardino." See letter of Zaccaria Saggi to Federico Gonzaga in Marcello Simonetta, ed., *Carteggio degli oratori mantovani alla corte sforzesca,* (Rome: Ministero per i beni e le attività culturali, 2001), vol. 11, letter 219, at 434.

10. ASMn, AG 1634, Francesco Malatesta in Milan to Francesco Gonzaga in Mantua, 5 February 1500: "Alegro in faza e piu zovene che mai."

11. ASMn, AG 1634, Francesco Malatesta in Milan to Francesco Gonzaga in Mantua, 5 February 1500: "Si faceua aconzar al collo un gorzarino doro smaltato a la parisina con questa littera. E. alanticha de smalto biancho con uno pendente de uno diamante in tauola etiam dissotto al diamante uno smiraldo di mazor grandeza chal diamante poi una perla grossisima giu pendente: che mi pareua una bellissima signoril chosa."

12. ASMn, AG 1634, Francesco Malatesta in Milan to Francesco Gonzaga in Mantua, 5 February 1500: "Fu existimato uulgarmente el gorzarino ducati cinquanta doa milia, zoe el gorzarino ducati ~~12000~~ dece milia, el diamante etiam, el smiraldo 7000, la perla 25000: tam io dicho uulgarmente." That popularly estimated value would have placed it in the top

3 percent of all ducal jewels. See Michela Barbot, "Il Valore economico degli oggetti di lusso nella corte viscontea e sforzesca," in Paola Venturelli, ed., *Oro dai Visconti agli Sforza. Smalti e oreficeria nel Ducato di Milano* (Milan: Silvana Editore, 2011), 79–85, at 82, table 1.

13. Gian Giacomo Trivulzio, "Gioje di Lodovico il Moro, duca di Milano, messe a pegno," *Archivio storico lombardo* 3 (1876): 530–34. Consider for instance "El Zoyello cum la insegna de la Moraglia con un smeraldo tavola, un diamante et una perla pendente" (531) or the "Gorzarini dui d'oro smaltati a la Franzese" (532), both valued significantly under 52,000. The date of March 1500 is attached to a number of pearls pawned in the same inventory. For further context on enameled jewels belonging to Ludovico Sforza, see Paola Venturelli, *'Esmaillé à la façon de Milan.' Smalti nel Ducato di Milano da Bernabò Visconti a Ludovico il Moro* (Venice: Marsilio, 2008), 90–107.

14. Edicts from Monza, 28 July 1522, and Milan, 6 August 1522. "Pro Jocalibus Illustrissimi Ducis Ludovici alias in pignore datii notificandis," in Marco Formentini, *Il Ducato di Milano. Studi storici documentati* (Milan: Libreria Editrice G. Brignola, 1877), doc. 35, 432–33, and doc. 37, 435–36. Marin Sanudo, *I Diarii,* Rinaldo Fulin, ed. (Bologna: Forni, 1969–1979 [1879–1902]), 4: 136, reports that Giovanni Antonio della Somaglia put the jewels up for auction in Milan in 1501: they were worth 50,000 ducats, but Ludovico had put them in hock for only 6,000 ducats.

15. ASMn, AG 1634, Francesco Malatesta in Milan to Francesco Gonzaga in Mantua, 5 February 1500: "Prima la humanita che dimostra la S.a del S. ducha ad ogniuno la qual e di tal sorte che la non poria esser piu, si in la sporzere la mano a qualunque li se apresenta, si in dirli humane parole, si in far gesti humanissimi con la sua signoril cera."

16. He also apparently asked Ascanio to have the treasuries of Milan's churches melted down in order to pay his mercenaries. Giovanni Andrea Prato, *Storia di Milano,* Cesare Cantù, ed., *Archivio storico italiano* 3 (1842): 216–418, 243. On Ludovico's debts, see Letizia Arcangeli, "Esperimenti di governo: Politica fiscale e consenso a Milano nell'età di Luigi XII," in Arcangeli, ed., *Milano e Luigi XII,* 255–339.

17. ASMn, AG 1634, Francesco Malatesta in Milano to Francesco Gonzaga in Mantua, 15 February 1500: "De presente [...] ogniuno volontariamente mette man a la borsa propria: ne li graua la spesa: Ne questo procede da altro se non che la experientia demostra che le meglio godere li soi signori cognosciuti cha esser benuisti da quelli che non se congnoschono. Vno come Zohan Antonio de la Somaglia ha portato dece milia ducati a la S.a del S. ducha: etiam li ha ditto chel spenda questi chel ne ha anchora uniticinque milia a sua posta: questo tale fu zenero del tesaurere de chasa landriano."

18. Stefano Meschini, *La Francia nel Ducato di Milano* (Milan: FrancoAngeli, 2006), 1: 104, n. 153 for the parish collections; Prato, *Storia,* 241 for the skeptical remark.

19. ASMn, AG 1634, Francesco Malatesta in Milan to Francesco Gonzaga in Mantua, 27 March 1500: "Mos.r Ascanio ando al perdono a S.to Ambroso, doue li fu portato inanci uno figliolo natural del S. ducha, figliolo de una madona Lucrecia criuella el quale ha nome signor zohan Paulo: al qual fece feste assai: poi more solito chaualcho per la terra." For Giovanni Paolo's youth, see Monica Ferrari, *'Per non manchare in tuto del debito mio.' L'Educazione dei bambini Sforza nel Quattrocento* (Milan: FrancoAngeli, 2000), 251. Lucrezia Crivelli had been captured in September 1499 fleeing Milan with her son, in the company of Ludovico Sforza's treasurer, Ambrogio da Corte; Sanudo, *Diarii,* 2: 1264, 1275. Louis XII gave her Milanese goods to the Francophile Antonio Maria Pallavicino; Crivelli left Milan for Mantua but Pallavicino requested the goods be returned to her. For the donation, see Pélissier, *Documents relatifs,* doc. 23, 112-13, 15 April 1501. For the restitution, see Léon-Gabriel Pélissier, "Les Sources milanaises de l'histoire de Louis XII: Trois registres de lettres ducales aux archives de Milan," *Bulletin du Comité des travaux historiques et scientifiques—section d'histoire et de philologie,* no. 1 (1892): 110-88, at 113, #17 (undated); and for her retreat to Mantua, Alessandro Luzio, "Isabella d'Este e la corte sforzesca," *Archivio storico lombardo* ser. 3, vol. 15, fasc. 29 (1901): 145-76, at 154.

20. Bernardino Corio, *Storia di Milano,* Anna Morisi Guerra, ed. (Turin: Unione Tipografico-Editrice Torinese, 1978), 2: 1562-63.

21. Giovanni Paolo was Marquis of Caravaggio until his death in 1535. See Nicola Ratti, *Della Famiglia Sforza* (Rome: Presso il Salomoni, 1794), 1: 128-30, and more recently Edoardo Rossetti, "Sforza, Giovanni Paolo," *Dizionario biografico degli italiani* 92 (2018): 437-39.

22. Sanudo, *Diarii,* 2: 1044 (for the populace's admiration), 2: 1228 (for the parading). During the September 1499 French invasion, the people of Milan and Cremona even expressed the desire to render their political devotion to this child; Sanudo, *Diarii,* 2: 1217-22. Before fleeing Milan in August 1499, Ludovico had tried to take the Duchetto with him to Germany, but his mother refused. See Corio, *Storia,* 2: 1623; Léon-Gabriel Pélissier, *Recherches dans les archives italiennes. Louis XII et Ludovic Sforza (8 avril 1498–23 juillet 1500)* (Paris: Thorin et Fils, 1896), 2: 204-07.

23. ASMn, AG 1634, Francesco Malatesta in Milano to Francesco Gonzaga in Mantua, 5 March 1500: "Oggi che e sabato se sono celebrati li anuali del quondam s. ducha franceschο: perche ogni anno in tal di se fanno li officij funerali in domo aquello segnore per la chasa sforcescha: doue more solito intraueneno tutti li mazistrati."

24. Meschini, *La Francia nel Ducato,* 1: 104.

25. ASMn, AG 1634, Francesco Malatesta in Milano to Francesco Gonzaga in Mantua, 27 February 1500: "Fu ditto in quello di medesemo vulgarmente chel s. ducha uoleua chel s. Zohan Jacomo Triulcio fusse nominato per Jacomo molinaro, si como lui nominaua el s. ducha per ludouicho da codignola." The tale is also recounted in Giorgio Chittolini, "Milan in the Face of the Italian Wars," in Abulafia, ed., *The French Descent,* 391–404, at 392.

26. Some examples are catalogued in Eleonora Sàita, ed., *'Io son la volpe dolorosa': Il Ducato e la caduta di Ludovico il Moro, settimo duca di Milano (1494–1500)* (Milan: Comune di Milano, 2000), cat. 44, 45, 46.

27. Sanudo, *Diarii,* 3: 361. The poem, "De Sfortia, Francisci, Ludovici et Catharinae Sfortiadum genealogia," by the Ravennan poet Lidio Catto, is solved by reordering the words by snaking vertically through the lines; Catto called it a *carmen anguineum,* perhaps a play on the heraldic biscione. See Rinaldo Fulin, "Difficiles Nugae," *Archivio veneto* 19 (1880): 131–34; see also Stefano Cassini, "Il 'Carmen anguineum' di Lidio Catto," in Stefan Tilg and Benjamin Harter, eds., *Neulateinische Metrik. Formen und Kontexte zwischen Rezeption und Innovation* (Tübingen: Gunter Narr Verlag, 2019), 91–109.

28. The story of Ludovico's capture appeared widely in chronicle sources and correspondence. See Benno Kindt, *Die Katastrophe Ludovico Moros in Novara im April 1500. Eine Quellenkritische Untersuchung* (Greifswald: Julius Abel, 1890).

29. Kindt, *Die Katastrophe,* 71, citing Girolamo Morone: "Infelix Ludovicus, qui non oris, non maiestatis, quam in vultu semper habuit, non proceritatis habitum mutare poterat, licet vestes commutasset agnitus aprehensusque fuerit."

30. Ambrogio da Paullo, *Cronaca milanese dall'anno 1476 al 1515,* Antonio Ceruti ed., *Miscellanea di storia italiana* 13 (1871): 91–378, at 142, makes the Good Friday treason motif explicit; Antonio Grumello, *Cronaca di Antonio Grumello, Pavese,* Giuseppe Müller, ed. (Milan: Francesco Colombo Librajo-Editore, 1856), 55, tells of the kiss.

31. Giovan Pietro Cagnola, *Storia di Milano . . . dal 1023 al 1497,* Cesare Cantù, ed., *Archivio storico italiano* 3 (1842), 1–215, at 200.

32. On the disarming, see Léon-Gabriel Pélissier, *Recherches dans les archives italiennes. Louis XII et Ludovic Sforza (8 avril 1498–23 juillet 1500)* (Paris: Thorin et Fils, 1896), 1: 200; the Milanese ducal sword in Paris cannot be linked definitely to Ludovico, though it is catalogued as an "épée d'un duc de Milan"; see Mario Scalini, ed., *A Bon droit: Spade di uomini liberi, cavalieri e santi* (Milan: Silvana Editoriale, 2007), cat. 54, 223–25; Musée de Cluny, inv. Cl. 11821.

33. On Charles VIII's sword, see Marco Pellegrini, *Ascanio Maria Sforza. La Parabola politica di un cardinale-principe del rinascimento* (Rome: Istituto

storico italiano per il medio evo, 2002), 2: 783; and for a sixteenth-century source, Jean Bouchet, *Les Annales d'Acquitaine* (Poitiers: J. et E. de Marnef, 1557), 186r–v; on the baton, see Boris Koehne, "Des Kardinals Ascanio Maria Sforza Feldherrnstab und Wappen," *Koehne's Zeitschrift für Münz-Siegel- und Wappenkunde* 5, no. 2 (1845): 99–109; Heinz-Werner Gewerken, *Kombinationswaffen des 15.–19. Jahrhunderts* (Berlin: Militärverlag der Deutschen Demokratischen Republik, 1989), 138. Museum für Deutsche Geschichte Berlin, Inv. W 1072 (PC 4493).

34. Prato, *Storia,* 250–51; Sanudo, *Diarii,* 3: 250.

35. Sanudo, *Diarii,* 3: 320–22. Some of these details are also recounted in Eleonora Sàita, "Introduzione," in Sàita, ed., *'Io son la volpe dolorosa',* 9–15.

36. Ludovico had already adopted black clothing and décor during his mourning period for his consort, Beatrice; when he visited Mantua in 1498, a year after her death, his retainers initially requested that all his lodgings were to be prepared in black or *morello*. See Léon-Gabriel Pélissier, *La Politique du marquis de Mantoue pendant la lutte de Louis XII et de Ludovic Sforza, 1498–1500* (Le Puy: Imprimerie Marchessou Fils, 1892), 17, n. 5.

37. Sanudo, *Diarii,* 3: 321. There was later false news that Ludovico had died on 15 May 1500. Sanudo, *Diarii,* 3: 349.

38. Priuli, *Diarii,* 1: 320: "Considerando che li poveri Milanessi heranno reducti a tanta destrutione, calamitade et miseria, che piui non haveanno animo de alzar la testa, et che postea heranno tante gente francesse in Milanno, che non hera possibel che li Milanessi potesseno calzitrar, essendo statti privati il populo de Milanno dele arme loro et de chaxe, donde deliberonno li Francexi, al despecto del populo de Milanno et per dimostrar esser signori di Milanno, de passar cum il cardinal Aschanio per mediam civitatem et andorono ala piuj lontana del chastello che fusse, et comencioronno intrar in la terra."

39. Priuli, *Diarii,* 1: 321.

40. Prato, *Storia,* 252. Prato also lists the names of Ascanio's associates, as does Ambrogio da Paullo, *Cronaca,* 153.

41. Sanudo, *Diarii,* 3: 349; Priuli, *Diarii,* 1: 319.

42. Giuseppe dalla Santa, "Della 'cheba del supplizio' appesa al campanile di San Marco," *Nuovo archivio veneto* 23 (1912): 458–59. Similar cages also hung in Mantua and Venice.

43. Priuli, *Diarii,* 1: 321: "El qual s.or Ludovico, essendo conducto nel sopradicto locho et vedendossi derelicto et abandonato da tutti li soi servitori, che li francessi li haveano licentiatii, se havea posto in grande disperatione. Donde li francessi, avendolli misericordia, li concesseno alchuni deli soi servitori, perché sapevanno li soi chostumi."

44. Giovanni Ricci, *Appello al Turco: I Confini infranti del Rinascimento* (Rome: Viella, 2011), 67–80.

45. Sanudo, *Diarii,* 3: 1619.

46. Sanudo, *Diarii,* 3: 1634–35, from the French orator in Malines, 21 March 1501.

47. Sanudo, *Diarii,* 3: 1619; 4: 333. Both of these reports date to 1501.

48. These are the terms requested in the negotiations at Trent during October 1501; see Sanudo *Diarii,* 4: 155.

49. Sanudo, *Diarii,* 3: 1237.

50. ASF, Mediceo Avanti il Principato, cart. 78, 191. Ascanio Sforza in Paris to Caterina Sforza, 3 March 1502: "Per lauisamo per contenteza sua di essere talmente ben visti & carezati dal X.mo s.or Re, che siamo grandemente obligati a Nro S.or Dio."

51. Sanudo, *Diarii,* 4: 440; Pellegrini, *Ascanio,* 2: 790.

52. Pellegrini, *Ascanio,* 2: 794–825.

53. Antonio Giustinian in Rome to Doge and Council of Ten in Venice, 28 January 1504, in Pasquale Villari, ed., *Dispacci di Antonio Giustinian, ambasicatore veneto in Roma dal 1502 al 1505* (Florence: Successori Le Monnier, 1876): 2: 411–13.

54. Sanudo, *Diarii,* 6: 176.

55. Pellegrini, *Ascanio,* 2: 845: "Alcun suo camerero che haveano pratiche de puctane."

56. Valentin Groebner, "Helden im Sonderangebot: Schweizerische Söldnerbilder zwischen dem 16. und dem 21. Jahrhundert," in Susan Marti, ed., *Söldner, Bilderstürmer, Totentänzer: Mit Niklaus Manuel durch die Zeit der Reformation* (Zürich: Verlag Neue Zürcher Zeitung, 2016), 31–37, at 33. See also Valentin Groeber, *Liquid Assets, Dangerous Gifts: Presents and Politics at the End of the Middle Ages,* Pamela E. Selwyn, trans. (Philadelphia: University of Pennsylvania Press, 2002), 106–9.

57. Helmut Puff, *Sodomy in Reformation Germany and Switzerland, 1400–1600* (Chicago: University of Chicago Press, 2003), 43–44, 116–19.

58. Bouchet, *Les Annales d'Acquitaine,* 183v.

59. BAM MS I 179 inf., *In questo libro se trata de la virtuossa vita de la vergine serore Veronicha del monasterio de Sca Martha de la cita de Milano,* 213v–215r: Ludovico "fu çonto al monasterio con grande caualcharia. Ma desmontando da caualo intro nel monasterio con tri de li piu propinque et mazore de la sua corte. Ela uirgene parlo asua segnoria grande pezo in secreto et per parte de dio gli disse tuti gli grande et celerati pecati gli quale se cometeneno in la sua corte per gli quale molto prouocaueno lira et la iustitia de dio de mandare grande uendete nel mundo. Et maximamente de uno puzolento pecato el quale da molte era cometuto. Et quello grandemente era abominabile nel conspecto de la mayesta de dio. Il quale piu la iustitia sua non lo podeua sostenire. Esse presto non prouedeua che queste grande abominatione cessaseno che sua S.ria uederebe queste tribulatione et grande cosse ad uerse mandarebe dio sopra sua S.ria etiam sopra molti populi pero che la iustitia sua non uoleua piu lassare inpu-

nite tante abomanatione. Etiamdio gli disse la v.ine anchora per parte de dio prometa v.a S.ria se quela prouedara che non se offenda atal modo ala diuina mayestade Ela potentia de la uostra S.ria faça in tuto cessare quisti grandi et norme peccati. Et regere el uostro populo et tuta la v.a S.a drictamente et iustamente faciando la iustitia drieta. Etiam atuto uostra força guardarne da le offesse de dio. Esso dio permete uita longa etiam grande prosperita ala S.ria u.a Et quella sara grandemente amata dal populo vostro. [. . .] Et dopo questo la uergene intesse per diuina gratia chel ducha auea facto prouisione ha una parte deli sopra dicti grande delicti per che piu non se cometesseno. Ma se gli perseuerono in quello dio El sa Ma tanto sono de poy state le guay Et continuamente procedano oltra le grande tribulatione che sono nele creature che glia prouate el sa."

60. For a diagnostic of this famous passage, see Julia Hairston, "Skirting the Issue: Machiavelli's Caterina Sforza," *Renaissance Quarterly* 53, no. 3 (2000): 687-712; Frédérique Verrier, *Caterina Sforza et Machiavel, ou, l'origine d'un monde* (Manziana: Vecchiarelli, 2010).

61. Prato, *Storia,* 266-67.

62. The French chronicler Pasquier le Moyne, visiting Milan in 1515, suggests one possibility: "In the city of Milan in the church of Santa Maria presso San Satiro, Il Moro is buried at the end of the altar in a pillar, and this church is small and very beautiful." See Joanne Snow-Smith, "Pasquier Le Moyne's 1515 Account of Art and War in Northern Italy: A Translation of His Diary from *Le Couronnement,*" *Studies in Iconography* 5 (1979): 173-234, at 233.

63. On Ascanio's tomb, see most recently Jutta Götzmann, *Römische Grabmäler der Hochrenaissance: Typologie, Ikonografie, Stil* (Münster: Rhema, 2010), 57-102; on the fate of Solari's sculptures, see Charles R. Morscheck, Jr., "Grazioso Sironi and the Unfinished Sforza Monument for Santa Maria delle Grazie," in Paola Venturelli, ed., *Arte e storia di Lombardia. Scritti in memoria di Grazioso Sironi* (Rome: Società Editrice Dante Alighieri, 2006), 227-42.

64. Alessandro Giulini, "Di alcuni figli meno noti di Francesco I Sforza, duca di Milano," *Archivio storico lombardo* ser. 5, fasc. 1-2 (1916): 29-53, at 31.

65. The Sforza family was not totally extinguished: it continued in secondary branches, and also had its greatest success outside Italy, when Isabella d'Aragona's daughter Bona Sforza (1494-1557) became queen of Poland and consort of Zygmunt I Jagiellon in 1516. See Henryk Barycz, "Bona Sforza, regina di Polonia," *Dizionario biografico degli italiani* 11 (1969): 430-36; Vito A. Melchiorre, ed., *Documenti baresi su Bona Sforza* (Bari: Mario Adda Editore, 1999), docs. 1-7, 8-26.

66. Attilio Portioli, "La Nascita di Massimiliano Sforza," *Archivio storico lombardo* ser. 1, vol. 9, fasc. 2 (1882): 325-34.

67. The epithalamium for Giangaleazzo Sforza and Isabella d'Aragona, dated February 1489, appears in BAV, Vat. lat. 3923, 42r–65r; see all three of these texts in Pietro Puricelli, *Tristani Chalci Mediolanensis historiographi residua* (Milan: Fratres Malatestas, 1644), 59–120; or a modern edition of the Sforza-Este epithalamium in Guido Lopez, *Festa di nozze per Ludovico il Moro* (Milano: Mursia, 2008), 118–44. For the imperial nuptials: Giasone del Maino, *Epithalamion in nuptiis Maximiliani et Blancae Mariae* (Paris: Antoine Denidel, 1495).

68. On Beatrice's death, see Gabriella Zuccolin, "Gravidanza e parto nel Quattrocento: le morti parallele di Beatrice d'Este e Anna Sforza," in Luisa Giordano, ed., *Beatrice d'Este, 1475–1497* (Pisa: Edizioni ETS, 2008), 111–45.

69. Corio, *Storia di Milano,* 2: 1605 (the year was 1497). During that same period, three of Ludovico's children died: "Biancha, mugliere de Galeazo Sanseverino, e dui figlioli maschii."

70. For the electors' resistance to Maximilian's investiture of Ludovico, see Sanudo, *Diarii,* 3: 682, 880; see also Heinz Angermeier, "Die Sforza und das Reich," in *Gli Sforza a Milano e in Lombardia e i loro rapporti con gli Stati italiani ed Europei (1450–1535)* (Milano: Cisalpino-Goliardica, 1982), 165–91, at 177–86.

71. Some of the very few reports of initial matrimonial affection appear in correspondence unearthed by Christina Antenhofer, "Emotions in the Correspondence of Bianca Maria Sforza," in Heinz Noflatscher, Michael A. Chisholm, and Bertrand Schnerb, eds., *Maximilian I (1459–1519): Wahrnehmung—Übersetzung—Gender,* special issue of *Innsbrucker Historische Studien* 27 (Innsbruck: Studien Verlag, 2011), 267–86, at 277–80.

72. Patrizia Mazzadi, "Bianca Maria Sforza und die Beziehung des Innsbrucker Hofes zu den wichtigen italienischen Höfen der Renaissance," in Sieglinde Hartmann, Freimut Löser, and Robert Steinke, eds., *Kaiser Maximilian I (1459–1519) und die Hofkultur seiner Zeit* (Wiesbaden: Reichert, 2009), 367–81, at 377, n 32. In 1497, Bianca Maria's majordomo, Niklas von Firmian, had to request emergency funds because the queen's household was so poor that stableboys were starving. Inge Wiesflecker-Friedhuber, *Quellen zur Geschichte Maximilians I. und seiner Zeit* (Darmstadt: Wissenschaftliche Buchgesellschaft, 1996), doc. 20, "Brief des Niklas von Firmian, Hofmeisters der Königin Bianca Maria, an Maximilian," 81–82.

73. Sanuto *Diarii,* 11: 733: "in Yspurch era morta; la qual non lassa alcun fiol, nè fiola"; letter of 2 January 1511.

74. Felice Calvi, *Bianca Maria Sforza-Visconti, Regina dei Romani, Imperatrice Germanica* (Milan: Antonio Vallardi, 1888), doc. 6, 155–59, at 157. See also Léon-Gabriel Pélissier, "Les Amies de Ludovic Sforza et leur rôle en 1498–1499," *Revue historique* 48 (January–April 1892): 39–60, at 40, n. 5, a letter from Fribourg, 26 July 1496, concerning an illness from which Bianca

Maria was suffering: "La Ces. M.ta [. . .] ha ordinato oggi se consulti il caso suo, e nel regimento qual sempre ha tenuto inordinato, vole gli sia posto ordine a fine se liberi di questa infirmitate, e poi se disponga a la conceptione, essendo il mal regimento total causa de la privatione di essa." See also Sabine Weiss, *Die Vergessene Kaiserin. Bianca Maria Sforza, Kaiser Maximilians zweite Gemahlin* (Innsbruck-Vienna: Tyrolia Verlag, 2010), 71–84.

75. Marin Sanudo, *La spedizione di Carlo VIII in Italia,* Rinaldo Fulin, ed. (Venice: Marco Visentini, 1883), 200.

76. Pélissier, *Documents,* doc. 2, 3–5, at 5: "Che la illustrissima duchessa Isabella, fiolo e fiole possino star qui in Milano et andar dove li parerà senza che li siano molestati altramente." For Trivulzio's concessions to support her financially until the arrival of Louis XII, see ASMi, Registro delle Missive 213, 4r, 15 September 1499.

77. The tutor was Gregorio da Spoleto. See Emilio Russo, "Gregorio da Spoleto," *Dizionario biografico degli Italiani* 59 (2003): 291–93.

78. Sanudo, *Diarii,* 3: 1237.

79. Paul Delalande, *Histoire de Marmoutier depuis sa fondation par Saint Martin jusqu'à nos jours* (Tours: Imprimerie Barbot-Berruer, 1897), 97–98; Jacques-Xavier Carré de Busserole, *Dictionnaire géographie, historique et biographique d'Indre-et-Loire et de l'ancienne province de Touraine* (Tours: Imprimerie Rouillé-Ladevèze, 1882), 4: 186, #39. See also Isabella d'Este's letter of condolence to his mother in Isabella d'Este, *Selected Letters,* Deanna Shemek, ed. and trans. (Toronto-Tempe: Iter Press & Arizona Center for Medieval and Renaissance Studies, 2017), letter 481, 2 February 1512, 355.

80. Pietro dal Verme and Giovanni Borromeo led the inquest. The report of Varesi's confession appears in the letters of the Mantuan and Ferrarese orators in Milan. Achille Dina, "Isabella d'Aragona, duchessa di Milano e duchessa di Bari," *Archivio storico lombardo* 48 (1921): 269–457, at 385; Pélissier, *Recherches* 1: 206.

81. On the question of Ludovico and the rumors of poisoning, see Felice Fossati, "Lodovico Sforza avvelenatore del nipote? (Testimonianza di Simone Del Pozzo)," *Archivio storico lombardo* ser. 4, vol. 2, fasc. 3 (1904): 162–71, who seems not to know of Varesi's testimony; and Monica Azzolini, *The Duke and the Stars: Astrology and Politics in Renaissance Milan* (Cambridge, MA: Harvard University Press, 2013), 208, with citations from the letter of Ettore Bellingeri to Ercole d'Este, 18 September 1499, 319, n. 168.

82. Dina, "Isabella d'Aragona," 393. Ludovico Pepe, *La storia della successione degli sforzeschi negli stati di Puglia e Calabria* (Bari-Trani: Vecchi, 1900), 75–168. The legal knots surrounding the succession of Bari meant that Isabella did not settle there until at least July 1501 (p. 93), having spent more than eighteen months in Naples trying to wrest its control from agents of Ludovico.

83. Sanudo, *Diarii*, 3: 737.

84. AnF, K 78, n. 8bis, Isabella d'Aragona to Pedro Luis de Borgia Lanzol de Romaní, 8 September 1505.

85. ASV, Capi del Consiglio di Dieci—Lettere di Rettori e di Altre Cariche, 72bis, 84, Rectors of Cremona to Doge Leonardo Loredan and the Council of Ten, undated. Un "puto de pocho aparisentia, immo brutta finosomia, et mal in ordine."

86. On Cecilia, see Carlo Alberto Bucci, "Gallerani, Cecilia" *Dizionario biografico degli Italiani* 51 (1998): 551–53; Maria Nadia Covini, *Donne, emozioni e potere alla corte degli Sforza. Da Bianca Maria a Cecilia Gallerani* (Milan: Unicopli, 2012), 47–60.

87. ASV, Capi del Consiglio di Dieci, 72bis, 88, Rectors of Cremona to Doge Leonardo Loredan and the Council of Ten, 16 April 1506. The letter is labeled "De adventu unus filij D. Lodouici ad Cremonam." "Vene uno fiol del sig.or Ludouico natural nominato Cesar fiolo de vna Madona Cecilia de Milano, che se troua a Milano el qual e stato qui ala porta de ognisanti de fuora giorni doy: che di luy lha ueduto de anni circa dodese mal uestito ad vno benefitio del fratello de ditta Madona Cecilia [. . .] molti cittadini di questa terra lo ha veduto che mai habiamo inteso cosa alcuna saluo da poy partito. [. . .] da Cremona li fece compagna quelli due giorni sete qui et lo fece leuar de qui: et per quello li fa [?] ditto doueua condurlo a Chiari in chamera [?] ad vno maystro de scola."

88. ASV, Capi del Consiglio di Dieci, 72bis, 88, Rectors of Cremona to Doge Leonardo Loredan and the Council of Ten, 20 April 1506: "Hozi ueramente e comparso da noi Jacomo da ponte da sorexina nominato in ditte nre: et hane sponte fatto intendere hauer in casa sua a sorexina el pdto fiolo naturale de sig.r Ludouico nominato Cesar nato de Madona Cicilia al presente moliere del conte Ludouico Bergamino: qual Iacomo dice che ditta madona Cicilia li ha mandato a dire che lo tenga cosi in casa sua fin tanto che altro li mandera dire. Noy immediate hauemoli comandato che esso Cesaro lo tenga secretamente apresso di se non relaxandolo per alcun modo se non expressa licentia et mandato nro."

89. We know Cesare eventually left Cremona, since he appeared at his brother Massimiliano's entry as duke of Milan, described below.

90. For Bianca Francesca, see Giulini, "Di alcuni figli," 53, tav. III; this letter complicates the assertion made in Ferrari, *'Per non manchare,'* 246, that Bianca "trascorre tutta la vita nel monastero cremonese, dove muore nel 1516."

91. ASV, Capi del Consiglio di Dieci—Lettere di Rettori e di Altre Cariche, 72bis, 70, 26 October 1502: "El se pratica che Madonna Biancha sorela natural del Sig.or Ludouico laquale soleua essere Abbatissa de questo Mon.rio habi gratia dala Ill.ma S.a nra de potere ritornare et ha grande Speranza de inpetrare tale gratia. [. . .] Cognoscendo la venuta di quela es-

sere scandolosa et periculosa ho deliberato dirue quelo intendere: che non li sia facto tale gratia che in verita se la ritornasse seria causa de qualche grande inconueniente pero che la faria come la faceua auanti la fusse confinata a Bresa la quale rompete el confine & ando a Mantoa che mai, die noctuque, non cesaua de mandare per i citadini et cum queli praticare in fauore del fratelo et scriuere in alemagna, ne saria posibile la facesse altramente per essere donna de grande inzegno et cuore et ama molto el fratelo et che lei tra alhora vicaria & continue li diceua che la douesse desistere da tale operatione: pero che se el se sapesse seria causa de la destructione del Mon.rio suo et tunc continuaua in le operatione pre-dicte absque vllo timore. Et ben che nui se persaudemo che le S. V. mai non faria tale gratia per essere persona de sorta & conditione che la ab-sentia sua e vtile et la presentia periculosa."

92. Sanudo, *Diarii,* 2: 291, September 1496: "Il fiol dil ducha defonto, di anni 8, bellissimo, savio et astuto garzon, el qual era custodito in castello de Milano, nè non lassava ussir, nè andar per la terra [. . .] stava con la madre et tre bellissime sorelle in habito lugubre, et atendeva a prender virtute, et da tutti li populi era come Idio per ducha desirato."

93. Sanudo, *Diarii,* 3: 1338.

94. Elizabeth McGrath, "Ludovico il Moro and his Moors," *Journal of the War-burg and Courtauld Institutes* 65 (2002): 67–94, at 71.

95. For 'il Moretto,' see Prato, *Storia,* 314. For the moor references, see Giovanni Ricci, "Le Corps du roi et l'Italie," in Bruno Petey-Girard, Gilles Polizzi, and Trung Tran, eds., *François Ier imaginé* (Geneva: Droz, 2016), 61–76, at 69–72; McGrath, "Ludovico," 86.

96. Alvise Mocenigo, "Relazione di me Aluise Mocenigo K. ritornato oratore de la Ces.a M.ta di Carlo V, 1548," in Luigi Firpo, ed., *Relazioni di ambas-ciatori veneti al Senato,* vol. 2: *Germania (1506–1554)* (Turin: Bottega d'Erasmo, 1970), 531–689, at 589. Mocenigo specifies that "tal cosa mi disse il R.mo Sfondrato esserli stata detta dal proprio Duca di Milano [Francesco II]."

97. Stephen Kolsky, *Mario Equicola: The Real Courtier* (Geneva: Droz, 1991), 130–32; Alessandro Luzio, "Isabella di fronte a Giulio II negli ultimi tre anni del suo pontificato," *Archivio storico lombardo* (1912): 17, fasc. 34 (245–344); 18, fasc. 35 (54–144); 19, fasc. 36 (393–456), here in the third part, 407–12; Sarah D. P. Cockram, *Isabella d'Este and Francesco Gonzaga: Power Sharing at the Italian Renaissance Court* (Farnham, UK: Ashgate, 2013), 180–88.

98. ASMn, AG 2120, 63: "hebbi piu del Thodesco che del Lombardo." Isabella d'Este in Milan to Francesco Gonzaga, 18 January 1513, in Luzio, "Isa-bella d'Este e la corte sforzesca," 159–60.

99. Girolamo Morone to the Archbishop of Bari, 11 January 1513: "Heu quam dissimilis est patri, quam degener, quam negligens, quam res suas

et propriam salutem temnens, quam in propria damna studiosus." Morone, *Lettere,* letter 116, 278–82, at 278.

100. Antonio Rusconi, "Massimiliano Sforza e la Battaglia dell'Ariotta (1513, 6 giugno)," *Archivio storico lombardo,* ser. 2, vol. 2, fasc. 1 (1885): 1–16.

101. ASMn, AG 1640, Benedetto Capilupi in Milan to Isabella d'Este in Mantua, 23 July 1513. The letter was also published in Luzio, "Isabella d'Este di fronte a Giulio II (parte terza)," 450–51.

102. ASMn, AG 1640, Benedetto Capilupi in Milan to Isabella d'Este in Mantua, 28 July 1513. See the published version in Luzio, "Isabella d'Este di fronte a Giulio II (parte terza)," 451–55: "Imaginandosi de douere intendere una bella cosa, come era da existimare, intrando in Milano uno giouenetto sig.r tanto uictorioso, ma e seguito il contrario, per essere sta fatto poco apparato, et la Intrata confusa et senza ordine. Dal borgo de la porta Ticinese fina al Domo era coperta la strata de panna de piu colorj et de dui solamente al paro assai mal distesi, le antenne che susteneano le corde doue erano li panni alcuni di loro erano affrascate, alcune no, poche arme et festoni ui erano, et niuno arco, di sorte che senza tal apparato meglio, et piu honoreuole seria stata la Intrata. [. . .] Non ui era pero Baldachino, ne gentilhomini alla staffa come si suol fare in simili Triumphi, Li regaci et cortesani senza ordine precedeano, ma li Conseruatori et Magistrati doppo li si.ri et Ambassiatori seguiuano."

103. Luzio, "Isabella d'Este di fronte a Giulio II (parte terza)," 453: "Et lo s.r Duca inuito m.r Aluyse et me a cena seco, ma per essere strachi puluerenti et sudolenti per essere stato quello giorno il mazor caldo de questo anno non uolessimo cum nro danno quel fauore. Et uenessimo a casa del S.re doue siamo allogiati."

104. Luzio, "Isabella d'Este di fronte a Giulio II (parte terza)," 454: "Mi rispose cum poche ma bone parole. Ha dil aspetto dil padre, ma non tanto signorile, non serra grande di persona, ma piu grosso dil Duca, ha colme le spalle, li capilli simili a quelli del Duca, lo abito negro, et da prete alla Todescha."

105. Domenico Santoro, *Della Vita e delle opere di Mario Equicola* (Chieti: Per tipi di Nicola Jecco, 1906), doc. 14, 257–62, at 259: "Lo S.r Duca de Bari è multo grave, et ben serva in publico il grado di sacerdote et persona ecclesiastica."

106. Cecilia Ady, *A History of Milan under the Sforza* (New York: G. P. Putnam's Sons, 1907), 212.

107. ASMi, Sforzesco 131, Marino Caracciolo to Massimiliano Sforza, 31 July 1513. Caracciolo warned the duke to provide adequate resources for his younger brother's lodging and appearances in Rome, "per ché qua non se fa come in Alamagna che in omne casa se allogia." An excerpt of this letter also appears in Rossana Sacchi, *Il Disegno incompiuto: La Politica artistica di Francesco II Sforza e di Massimiliano Stampa* (Milan: Edizioni Universitarie di Lettere Economia Diritto, 2005), 49.

108. ASMn, AG 1640, Benedetto Capilupi in Milan to Isabella d'Este in Mantua, 28 July 1513: "Era vestito tutto di biancho cioe saio et zupone di raso, rubone, beretta et scarpe di ueluto et similmente ha fatti uestire il s.r Cesare il s.r Zo. Paulo, suoi fratelli." Likewise, during her visit to Milan in January 1513, Isabella d'Este first encountered Massimiliano "vestito duno vestito di damasco bianco alla Todesca sopra uno corsiero bayo guarnato di bianco" (ASMn, AG 2120, 58v, Isabella d'Este in Milan to Francesco Gonzaga in Mantua, 13 January 1513).

109. Luzio, "Isabella d'Este di fronte a Giulio II (parte terza)," 451.

110. Paolo Giovio, "Elogia virorum illustrium," in Renzo Meregazzi, ed., *Pauli Iovii Opera,* vol. 8 (Rome: Istituto poligrafico dello stato, 1972), 8: 438–39.

111. In a similar vein, a Swiss captain in 1515 claimed that Massimiliano slept all day, reveled all night, and lived a disorderly life for a prince, "like a caged bird": "Warum er duot nüt den schlafen den ganzen tag und dienet gott klein und lost kein mes und lebt als hetty er das leben von sim selber. Die nacht duot er nüt den stechen und jubylieren und duot als ob er foegyli gefangen heyg und füret gar ein unordentlich wesen für ein fürsten" (Hermann Specker, ed., "Brief des bernischen Hauptmanns Balthasar Finsternau zu Mailand an die Obrigkeit zu Bern, mit interessanter Charakterisierung des Herzogs Maximilian Sforza, 8. August 1515," *Berner Zeitschrift für Geschichte und Heimatkunde* 18 [1956]: 129–30).

112. Léon-Gabriel Pélissier, *L'Alliance Milano-allemande à la fin du XVe siècle. L'ambassade d'Herasmo Brasca à la cour de l'Empereur Maximilien (Avril–Décembre 1498)* (Turin: Imprimerie Royale de J.-B. Paravia et Comp., 1897), app. 2, doc. 2, Erasmo Brasca in Innsbruck to Ludovico Sforza in Milan, 6 January 1498: King Maximilian "persiste in oppinione e desiderio che V. E. acompagna el suo ill.mo figliol conte Maximiliano con la sorella del duca di Savoya, e lei [i.e., Ludovico] con la figliola del marchese di Brandeburg; et havendogli io mostrato con molti argomenti che V. E. non ha animo de maritarse, ha pocho giovato."

113. BL, MS Harleian 3462, 193r-v, copy of letter of Suardo, Mantuan Ambassador in Milan: Massimiliano "gli fece intendere come lhauea eletto di essere Homo de chiesa per tore ogni suspecto a sua M.ta chel habbi mai piu a pensare al stato de Milano: et che ringratiaua dio che lhauesse leuato de la seruitu de villano e fatto subdito a vn Re tanto nobile quanto era sua M.ta: et lo supplicaua chel non li fosse piu mancato de le promisse, quanto lui era per essere obseruatore de la fede data a sua M.ta: Il Re li rispose fra le altre bone parolle: Mon.s non haueti da dubitare puncto che ui sia mancato: anzi me sono marauigliato che habbiati eletto di essere homo de chiesa, et, et se voleti ue daro moglie: et ui faro qualche honoreuole et bon partito." For royal pressure upon Massimiliano to wed almost two years into his exile, see ASMn, AG 1643, Raphaele Gusperto in Milan to Francesco Gonzaga in Mantua, 15 September 1517: "Item,

che lo Ill. S.re Max.no Sforza de presente debbe togliere per Mogliere una madama Francesa, et che la M.ta Chr.ma li vole dare de presente beni stabili per tanto de intrata quanto porta la pensione sua."

114. "Militaris ille vigor qui in avo mirabiliter enituit in eo nequaquam elucet." The opinion is voiced by Alfonso d'Avalos, who helped Sforza escape from the siege of Milan's castle in 1526; Giovio, *Notable Men and Women*, 140–41.

115. For Aretino's joke, see Alessandro Luzio, ed., *Un Pronostico satirico di Pietro Aretino* (Bergamo: Istituto italiano d'arti grafiche, 1900), 7. For the Venetian orator: Giovanni Basadonna, "Relazione del ducato di Milano," in Eugenio Albèri, ed., *Le Relazioni degli ambasciatori veneti al Senato durante il secolo XVI*, vol. 11 (Cambridge: Cambridge University Press, 2012), 331–347, at 339. Germana Ernst, "Astri e previsioni: Il *Pronostico* di Cardano del 1534," in Marialuisa Baldi and Guido Canziani, eds., *Girolamo Cardano. Le opere, le fonti, la vita* (Milano: FrancoAngeli, 1999), 457–75, at 473–74.

116. In the treaty of the Peace of Cambrai. See Charles Weiss, ed., *Papiers d'État du Cardinal de Granvelle, d'après les manuscrits de la bibliothèque de Besançon* (Paris: Imprimerie Royale, 1841) vol. 1, doc. 97, "Sommaire du traité de Cambrai," 464–70, at 466–67, 29 August 1529.

117. Mary of Hungary in Ghent to Charles V, 25 August 1533: Christina "ny a encores nulle apparence de femme en elle. Et auec ce, Monseigneur, que cest contre dieu, combien que croy, que en ce pays le tout est acceptable, si la metrez vous en hazard, si elle devenoit enchainte devant estre de tout femme, comme a beaucoup on a veu par experience avenir, quelle et lenfant y demouroient" (Karl Lanz, ed., *Correspondenz des Kaisers Karl V (1532–1549)*, (Leipzig: F. A. Brockhaus, 1845), doc. 362, 2: 87–88.

118. Lanz, ed., *Correspondenz*, doc. 363, 2: 89.

119. Luigi Gonzaga in Milan to Isabella d'Este in Mantua, May 4, 1534: "Questa sera si farà la benedictione solita precedente la copula et dormiranno insieme questa notte se non mutano pensiero et mi pare di vedere el S. Duca tutto smarrito, havendo a masticare un frutto così acerbo come è quello di questa S.ra quale a judicio de ognuno non seria da spiccare ancor de qui a qualche mese, non havendo lei per la verità più che 12 anni e 2 mesi" (Luzio, *Un pronostico*, 57).

120. Weiss, ed., *Papiers d'État*, vol. 2, doc. 43, 205–6, 20 or 24 June 1534.

121. Christina of Denmark in Milan to Charles V, 20 November 1535, in Lanz, ed., *Correspondenz*, doc. 414, 2: 206–7. For an elegy to the duke, see Pietro Aretino to the duke's childhood friend and confidant, Massimiliano Stampa, 25 November 1535, in Pietro Aretino, *Lettere*, Francesco Erspamer, ed. (Parma: Ugo Guanda Editore, 1995), doc. 57, 127–30.

122. BnF ms. fr. 17527, Anonymous Parisian Chronicle Miscellany, 191r, describes Massimiliano's funeral in Paris.

123. Sanudo, *Diarii*, 3: 280.

124. For similar charges of fruitlessness made against Pope Julius II, see Robert W. Scheller, "Ung fil tres delicat: Louis XII and Italian Affairs, 1510–11," *Simiolus* 31, no. 1/2 (2004–2005): 4–45, at 12.

125. For this discourse, see Nicole Hochner, "Visions of War in the 'Terrestrial Paradise': Images of Italy in Early Sixteenth-Century French Texts," in Shaw, ed., *Italy and the European Powers,* 239–51.

126. Luzio, "Isabella d'Este di fronte a Giulio II (parte terza)," 453: "Accio che la ex.tia v. intenda quello che significa il cridare Cicorea, Io dico, che rotto che fureno Francesi alcuni Ducheschi dissero che li suyceri seriano la Cicorea, la quale si da in siroppo per guarire quelli che hanno guasto il Figato. Li putti cridano, la Cicorea e una radice che ha falito spaza il paese, Li cortesani uerso quelli che sono mal trauersi dicono: Tu hai bisogno de la Cicorea, et questo nome tanti si frequenta nel populo quanto quello di Moro, o Duca."

127. Ambrogio da Paullo, *Cronaca*, 314, 317.

128. ASMi, Sforzesco 1341, Egidio Bossi in Alessandria to Massimiliano Sforza, 30 September 1512: "Aduiso v. ex.a che quelli rebelli [. . .] son ritornati sopra le terre del Marchese [di Monferrato] a sc.to Saluatore et altri lochi: et ogni giorno piu multiplicano quod dicono pegiore parole che da prima: cantano una canzone: Ducha senza radice spazera presto il nostro paese, cridano Franza, Franza, et simul li Monfarrini. E che venerano dauanti quindeci giorni qua in la cita, e menerano per le ferri tuti li Gebelini."

129. Paolo Morigia, *La nobiltà di Milano* (Milan: Pacifico Pontio, 1595), 311.

130. On this process, see most recently Jean-Philippe Genet, "Pouvoir symbolique, légitimation et genèse de l'État moderne," in Jean-Philippe Genet, ed., *La légimité implicite* (Paris: Publications de la Sorbonne / École française de Rome, 2015), 1: 9–47.

4. LAND AND OWNERSHIP

1. "Mi disse Io ho seruito per el passato el .s. lodouigo et el Re de Franza cum tanta fede et tanto bene che domente eremo in le facende et luno et laltro mi voleano far quello sapea dimandar, et tanden mi hano dato et tolto in modo che non ho possuto dir cum certeza questo e mio et ad questo proposito mi naro molte cosse che longo seria nararle si circa le opera come le cause de lodij cum tuti doi. Poi disse alhora anchora che facesse de le cosse non di meno hauea pur qualche respecto ado fiole sole che altro bene non mi trouo al mondo hora cum da dio gratia vna maritata et laltra spero maridar la settemana future ne mi resto altro che la miglier che non fa fioli et e de poco respecto et sero poi condoto a conditione che potro metter in operatione lanimo che he sempre hauto de operar cosse de

qualche mia Gloria et a questo effecto ho impetrato uno loco ne ho voluto altra cossa el qual mi ho messo a hedificar et ho speso piu di vij M
ducati in far una forteza oltra che non compro piere perche se cauano de
le proprie fosse ne calcine che la fazo far jo et ho legne et tuto senza spesa.
Da questa forteza depende ogni mio pensier et speranza ne godo piu le
Cosse da Milano ne altro per attender a quella (et in effecto Ex.mi S.ri
questo è vero che son stado a certo zardin et bella possession sua fuora
imm.te de vna porta de Millano in suo amenissimo et ho uisto che tuto
va in ruina) Questa rocha disse esser nominata la rocha de Baye forteza
de monte inexpugnabile in val sesena sopra la riua del lago de Como."
ASV, Capi del Consiglio di Dieci—Lettere di Ambasciatori 15 (Milano
1501–1525), Leon Blanco to the Consiglio di Dieci, 19 September 1504.
The letter was also published by Léon-Gabriel Pélissier in *Documents
pour l'histoire de la domination française dans le Milanais (1499–1513)* (Toulouse: Édouard Privat, 1891), doc. 29, 100–06; and in excerpt by Stefano
Meschini, *La Francia nel Ducato di Milano* (Milan: FrancoAngeli, 2006), 1:
387–88, n. 88.

2. For a recent analysis of the conceptual foundations of Western property,
see Christopher Pierson, *Just Property: A History in the Latin West,* vol. 1:
Wealth, Virtue, and the Law (Oxford: Oxford University Press, 2013).

3. James Hankins, *Plato in the Italian Renaissance* (Leiden: Brill, 1991), 1:136.

4. Plato, *Republic,* Christopher Emlyn-Jones and William Preddy, eds. and
trans. (Cambridge, MA: Harvard University Press, 2013), 5.462c.

5. Aristotle, *Politics,* H. Rackham, trans. (Cambridge, MA: Harvard University Press, 1932), 2.2.1263a–b.

6. "Sed quid mihi est imperator? Secundum ius ipsius possides terram. Aut
tolle iura imperatorum, et quis audet dicere: mea est illa villa, aut meus
est ille servus, aut domus haec mea est?" (Augustine, *In Iohannis evangelium tractatus CXXIV,* R. Willems, ed. [vol. 36 of *Corpus Christianorum*]
[Turnhout: Brepols, 1990], 6.25, 66).

7. Gratian, *Decretum,* first recension in progress by Anders Winroth, Dis-
tinctio 8, c. 1, available at http://gratian.org/.

8. On the importance of jurists' opinions on imperial power (and Bulgaro's
possibly spurious opinion to Frederick Barbarossa in 1158 at the Diet of
Roncaglia that he was not lord of private property), see Kenneth Pennington, *The Prince and the Law, 1200–1600* (Berkeley: University of California Press, 1993), 8–34, esp. 16. For Baldus, see Joseph Canning, *The Political Thought of Baldus de Ubaldis* (Cambridge: Cambridge University
Press, 1987), 221–27; see also Cristina Danusso, "Baldo e i *Libri Feudorum,*"
in Carla Frova, Maria Grazia Nico Ottaviani, Stefania Zucchini, eds. *VI
Centenario della morte di Baldo degli Ubaldi, 1400–2000* (Perugia: Università
degli Studi, 2005), 289–311, at 289–90; and Maria Nadia Covini, *'La Bal-*

anza drita.' Pratiche di governo, leggi e ordinamenti nel ducato sforzesco (Milan: FrancoAngeli, 2007), 127, n. 73.

9. Jane Black, "Natura feudi haec est: Lawyers and Feudatories in the Duchy of Milan," *English Historical Review* 109, no. 434 (1994): 1150–73, at 1154.

10. On the crime of *laesa maiestatis* across the communal and early ducal period, see Federica Cengarle, *Lesa maestà all'ombra del biscione: Dalle Città lombarde ad una 'monarchia' europea (1335–1447)* (Rome: Edizioni di storia e letteratura, 2014).

11. Alessandro Visconti, "Note sul diritto di interinazione nel Senato Milanese (con documenti inediti)," *Archivio storico lombardo,* ser. 4, vol. 11, fasc. 21 (1909): 59–96. For an example of the inefficiency of interinazione, see the discussion relating to Poviglio below.

12. Jean Juvénal des Ursins, "Verba auribus percipe, Domine," in P. S. Lewis and Anne-Marie Hayez, eds., *Écrits politiques de Jean Juvénal des Ursins* (Paris: Klincksieck, 1985), 2: 179–405, at 270: "La troisiesme consideracion de ce point principal est de respondre ad ce dient aucuns de vos officiers monstrans selon leur ymaginacion que vous faire le povés et *quod omnia sunt principis* et *quod nullus est qui possit dicere, Hoc est meum, nisi princeps.* Je ne vouldroye deprimer vostre puissance mais l'augmenter de mon petit povoir, et ne fay doubte que ung prince comme vous specialment peut tailler ses subgectz et lever aides en certains cas, et mesmement pour deffendre le royaume et la chose publique."

13. Jean Juvénal des Ursins, "Verba auribus percipe," 271–76. About fifty years later, during the conflict between Louis XII and Pope Julius II (ca. 1510–1512), the Parisian theologian Jacques Almain used similar phrasing to position the prince positively as the arbiter of disputes between subjects: "Orta disputatione inter duos, dicentes, hoc est meum, hoc est tuum, recurritur ad Principem, ut recte sententiet" (Jacques Almain, "Expositio . . . de potestate ecclesiastica & laica," in Louis Ellies du Pin, ed., *Ioannis Gersonii Opera Omnia* [The Hague: Apud Petrum de Hondt, 1728], 2: 1013–1121, at 1028–29).

14. One notable attempt to work through this fog is Daniele Andreozzi, *Nascita di un disordine. Una Famiglia signorile e una valle piacentina tra XV e XVI secolo* (Milan: Edizioni Unicopli, 1993), a book that recreates and explains a chronology of factional shifts. See esp. 177–273.

15. Giovanni Andrea Prato, *Storia di Milano,* Cesare Cantù, ed., *Archivio storico italiano* 3 (1842): 216–418, at 309.

16. Gianiacopo Caroldo, "Relazione del ducato di Milano, 1520," in Arnaldo Segarizzi, ed., *Relazioni degli ambasciatori veneti al senato,* (Bari: Laterza & Figli, 1976 [1912]), 1: 22: "El re, da la cità in fuori, non ha pur una torre: tutte le castelle del ducato sono sta' antiqua e modernamente alienate per li duchi de Milano e re de Franza."

17. Here Manuzio is quoting *Eclogues,* 9.2–4. See Preface to Pindar's *Odes,* in Aldus Manutius, *The Greek Classics,* N. G. Wilson, ed. and trans. (Cambridge, MA: Harvard University Press, 2016), 217. Translation amended in accordance with Loeb edition of *Eclogues.*

18. Carlo Vecce, ed., *Un'Apologia per l'Equicola. Le Due redazioni della* Pro Gallis apologia *di Mario Equicola e la traduzione francese di Michel Roté* (Naples: Istituto Universitario Orientale, 1990), 93.

19. Isabella d'Este in Sirmione to Francesco Gonzaga in Mantua, 21 March 1514, Isabella d'Este, *Selected Letters,* Deanna Shemek, ed. and trans. (Toronto-Tempe: Iter Press & Arizona Center for Medieval and Renaissance Studies, 2017) letter 508, 374–75, at 375.

20. For instance, in September 1499, Louis XII was considering endowing Cesare Borgia with his own Italian state and composed "maxime de li reliquie de' Sforzeschi"—a kind of patchwork of "relics" of Sforza territories. Marin Sanudo, *I Diarii,* Rinaldo Fulin, ed. (Bologna: Forni, 1969–1979 [1879–1902]), 2: 1375.

21. "Littere, in quibus derogatum est decreto edito in anno XXIII incipiendo 'Providere volentes,' de derogatione donationum factarum per Ludovicum Sfortiam de terra Annoni et Alexandrie in fraudem factarum" (Léon-Gabriel Pélissier, "Les sources milanaises de l'histoire de Louis XII," *Bulletin du Comité des travaux historiques et scientifiques. Section d'histoire et de philologie* [1892]: 110–88," doc. 13, 158–59, 28 August 1502).

22. Camilla Boisen and David Boucher, "The Medieval and Early Modern Legacy of Rights: The Rights to Punish and to Property," in William Bain, ed., *Medieval foundations of international relations* (London: Routledge, 2017), 148–65, at 155.

23. Jean d'Auton, *Chroniques de Louis XII,* René de Maulde la Clavière, ed. (Paris: Librairie Renouard, 1889–95), 1: 270–4; Giovanni Andrea Prato, *Storia di Milano,* Cesare Cantù, ed., *Archivio storico italiano* 3 (1842): 216–418, at 250.

24. Théodore de Godefroy, *Histoire de Louis XII* (Paris: Abraham Pacard, 1615), 192–204; Louis, *Vie du cardinal d'Amboise* (Rouen: Robert Machuel, 1726), 405–21; Johann Christian Lünig, *Codex Italiae Diplomaticus* (Frankfurt: Impensis Haeredum Lanckisianorum, 1725), 1: 498–504. See also Jean de Auton, *Chroniques de Louis XII,.* René de Maulde la Clavière, ed. (Paris: Librairie Renouard, 1889–1895), 1: 361.

25. Legendre, *Vie du cardinal,* 420–21.

26. "Il vous asseure de corps, de honneur & de biens que parauant ne estoit personne qui eust peu dire, Cecy est mien" (*Proposition faicte par les nobles, bourgoys, gens de mestiers, manans, et habitans de la ville de millan* [Lyon: Guillaume Balsarin, 1500], B2r). This idea that Ludovico prevented citizens from enjoying their own property was widespread. Four years after Cremona passed from the Milanese state to Venetian lordship in 1499, the Venetian orator reported that the citizens "comenzano a esser contenti

star sotto la Signoria nostra, perchè *godeno el suo* [italics mine] . . . e comenzano a fabrichar caxe e davanti le faze, che prima non osavano al
tempo dil signor Lodovico; e le donne vanno vestite d'oro. El qual signor
Lodovico li angarizava assai, et *ultimamente* volse certo tajon e li messe
pena *ferro* et *igne,* e questo exacerbò li animi loro" (Sanudo, *Diarii* 5:
945–46).

27. Dal Verme lands had in the fourteenth century been appropriated from
other clans in the Piacenza area—namely, the Lazarello, Scotti, and Landi.
See Giorgio Fiori, "Bobbio e i Dal Verme," *Archivio storico per le province parmensi,* ser. 4, vol. 38 (1986): 175–201, at 175, n.1. On the interconnection
of the Dal Verme and Milanese dukes, see Pierre Savy, "Costituzione e fun-
zionamento dello 'Stato vermesco' (fine del XIV-metà del XV sec.)," in
Federica Cengarle, Giorgio Chittolini, and Gian Maria Varanini, eds.,
*Poteri signorili e feudali nelle campagne dell'Italia settentrionale fra Tre e Quat-
trocento* (Florence: Firenze University Press, 2005), 73–81; Pierre Savy, "Les
Feudataires et le contrôle territorial dans le duché de Milan à l'époque des
Sforza," in Marco Gentile and Pierre Savy, eds., *Noblesse et états princiers en
Italie et en France au XVe siècle* (Rome: École française de Rome, 2009), 173–
90; and Pierre Savy, *Seigneurs et Condottières: Les Dal Verme* (Rome: École
française de Rome, 2013), 426–33.

28. Francesca M. Vaglienti, "La Detenzione del conte Pietro dal Verme e la
confisca del suo feudo ad opera di Galeazzo Maria Sforza, duca di Milano," *Nuova rivista storica* 74, nos. 3–4 (1990): 401–16.

29. The transfers were even more complex than this summary allows. For further detail involving Bernardino da Corte's investiture with the Dal
Verme lands, see Giorgio Fiori, *Storia di Bobbio e delle famiglie bobbiesi* (Piacenza: Libreria Internazionale Romagnosi, 2015), 44–47.

30. The Dal Verme began their petition on 19 September 1499; Sanseverino
began his in an undated petition. For the Dal Verme, see Fiori, "Bobbio e
i Dal Verme," 181–86; Christine Shaw, *Barons and Castellans: The Military
Nobility of Renaissance Italy* (Leiden: Brill, 2015), 211. For Sanseverino, see
Auton, *Chroniques,* 1: 378–80, appendix doc. 20.

31. Sanudo, *Diarii,* 3: 805 (17 September 1500) and 880 (3 October 1500); Ambrogio da Paullo, *Cronaca milanese dall'anno 1476 al 1515,* Antonio Ceruti,
ed., *Miscellanea di storia italiana* 13 (1871): 91–378, at 158.

32. ASVr, Fondo Zileri-Dal Verme, 138—Processi, fasc. 396; ASPr, Feudi e
Comunità—Carte feudali 57, 119–31.

33. For details of the death sentence, see Giovanni Crescio, "Un Episodio
storico di giustizia punitiva," *Strenna Piacentina* 18 (1892): 62–67; for the
imperial privilege: ASVr, Fondo Zileri-Dal Verme, 6—Diplomi, Bolle, Privilegi, fasc. 18, "Privilegium Car. V concesssum Co. Federico, & M. Antonio Fratribus de Verme 1521, 25 Martii. Cum insertione Privilegii Maximiliani Imperatoris concessi ipsis Fratribus anno 1502."

34. See the case of Alberto Pio's decades-long struggle between France, the papacy, and the Empire to avoid his family's dispossession in Carpi, which ultimately failed. Shaw, *Barons and Castellans,* 242–43.

35. "Ignorat quis hunc habeat"; "nescit quis hoc teneat"; "nescit quis hoc habeat"; "res effectum non habuit" (Auton, *Chroniques* 1: 379). The document is undated, but the context recommends a date of 1500 or shortly thereafter.

36. Vittorio Adami, "Episodi della guerra tra Milanesi e Veneziani in Val Sassina 1452–1453," *Archivio storico lombardo,* ser. 6, fasc. 2–3 (1926): 309–21.

37. Giuseppe Martini, "Arrigoni, Simone," *Dizionario biografico degli Italiani* 4 (1962): 321–22.

38. Angelo Borghi, ed., *La Rocca di Bajedo in Valsassina* (Missaglia: Bellavite, 2007), 79, citing Paride Cattaneo della Torre's *Cronaca Torriani,* a manuscript now held at the Archivio Pietro Pensa in Esino Lario.

39. Bernardino Corio, *Storia di Milano,* Anna Morisi Guerra, ed. (Turin: Unione Tipografico-Editrice Torinese, 1978), 2: 1621; Felice Calvi, "Antonio Landriani tesoriere generale di Lodovico il Moro," *Rendiconti del reale istituto lombardo di scienze e lettere,* ser. 2, vol. 15 (1882): 681–86, at 685.

40. "Simone Rigone considerando, credendose fare cossa grata al populo et anche asestare il facto [che] suo impero dal re hebbe l'intrata de viii c ducati con Valsasna, uno tanto homo [Landriani] deliberò ocidere" (Corio, *Storia,* 2: 1621). I have removed the accent on *imperò* to make it, more credibly I think, a noun rather than a verb.

41. Sanudo, *Diarii,* 3: 32, October 1499: "Item, di certa possession tolta a Simon Rigone." During his brief restoration, Ludovico Sforza nominated Bartolomeo Mantegazza as castellan of Baiedo; whether Mantegazza ever clashed with Arrigoni over the castle remains unclear. For the nomination, see Lidia Cerioni, "La Cancelleria Sforzesca durante il ritorno del Moro (Gennaio-Aprile 1500)," *Archivio storico lombardo* 93–94 (1966): 140–72, at 156.

42. ASMi, Registri ducali 44, 111, dated 4 September 1499. This donation was confirmed by the king on 11 November 1499. See Pélissier, "Les sources milanaises," 112, #7.

43. Prato, *Storia,* 228; Sanudo, *Diarii,* 4: 136.

44. For the Senate remonstrations, see Stefano Meschini, *Luigi XII, Duca di Milano. Gli Uomini e le istituzioni del primo dominio francese (1499–1512)* (Milan: FrancoAngeli, 2004), 56, n. 92.

45. The esteem seems to have been mutual. In a letter of 1501, Trivulzio claimed: "Io amo molto m.r Jo. Symone per le virtu sue" (ASMn, AG 1634, Giangiacomo Trivulzio to Francesco Gonzaga, 13 August 1501).

46. Pélissier, *Documents,* doc. 51, 103–4.

47. Pélissier, *Documents,* doc. 51, 105.

48. For the exile orders, see Pélissier, *Documents,* doc. 45, 16 May 1506; on the plotting of Genoa's Fregoso family, see Carlo Taviani, *Superba discordia. Guerra, rivolta e pacificazione nella Genova di primo Cinquecento* (Rome: Viella, 2008), 46–50.

49. Prato, *Storia,* 259; Sanudo, *Diarii,* 6: 551, February 1507. ASMn, AG 1637, letter of 16 February 1507, Granges to Francesco Gonzaga: "Non li [i.e., Arrigoni] e rimasto se non el gouerno de vale saxina consorte a venicianj cum una rocha in epsa vale asay forte, et consumptis opibus, se retirato la et ha comenzato a fortifichare poy ad asasinare tuta la vale. Mons.r gran metro [i.e., Chaumont] la mandato [i.e., Trivulzio] a chiamare, non ha voluto venire. Per modo chio credo ruynara."

50. Pélissier, *Documents,* doc. 51, 152–53.

51. Sanudo, *Diarii,* 7: 25, 4 March 1507.

52. ASV, Capi del Consiglio di Dieci—Lettere di Ambasciatori 15 (Milano 1501–25), Nicolò Stella to the Council of Ten, 8 April 1507: "Novamente mi retrouai cum el Signor ZuanJacomo, el qual como deuot.mo de V. S.ta mi disse chel era vera che la Cel. Vra era mixta in lo processo firmato con dicto Arigon perche el meschino per saluarsi non solum nominó quella, ma etiam acusó dicto S.or ZuanJacomo et molti altri á fine di scorrer, zerchar di farsi grato et di fugir la pena." The letter goes on to say that Arrigoni admitted to his confessor that his accusations of Trivulzio and the Signoria had been fabricated.

53. Prato, *Storia,* 259; Sanudo, *Diarii,* 7: 43–44.

54. Paride Cattaneo della Torre's *Cronaca Torriani,* quoted in Giuseppe Arrigoni, *Notizie storiche della Valsássina e delle terre limitrofe* (Milan: Luigi di Giacomo Pirola, 1860), 219.

55. See the donation of 23 November 1513 and the confirmation of 2 October 1514 in Tullio Dandolo, ed., *Ricordi inediti di Girolamo Morone* (Milan: Tipografia e Libreria Arcivescovile, 1855), 43–50. The first donation also elevated Lecco to the status of a county.

56. Sanudo, *Diarii,* 21: 351, 1 December 1515.

57. Pietro Pensa, "Francesco Morone in Lecco: avventuriero o patriota?," *Archivi di Lecco* 5:4 (1982): 577–631, at 613.

58. Letizia Arcangeli, "Morone, Gerolamo," *Dizionario biografico degli Italiani* 77 (2012): 74–78, at 75.

59. Pensa, "Francesco Morone," 597–98. The feudatory was Corradino Vimercati, whose family had once been endowed with Lecco by Duke Filippo Maria Visconti. See the two letters to Lecco (to its podestà and to the men of the city) from Milan's temporary governors, urging them to submit peacefully to Vimercati: ASMi, Feudi Camerali 291, 7 September 1499: (1) Antonio Trivulzio and other governors of Milan to Antonio Villano, podestà of Lecco; (2) Girolamo Landriano and other governors to the men of Lecco.

60. Pensa, "Francesco Morone," 601.

61. Pensa, "Francesco Morone," 580–82; Zanino Volta, "Di Bartolomeo Morone, giureconsulto, maggiorente, cronista milanese e della genealogia moronea," *Archivio storico lombardo,* ser. 2, vol. 3, fasc. 10 (1893): 633–93, at 690–91; for the proposal of Francesco as a cousin of Girolamo, see Felice Calvi, *Famiglie notabili milanesi* (Milan: Antonio Vallardi, 1881), vol. 2, under Moroni, tavola 1.

62. He was among a number of rebels on both sides pursuing this strategy. See Pensa, "Francesco Morone," passim.

63. Francesco Muralto, *Annalia,* Pietro Aloisio Donino, ed. (Milan: Cura et Impensis Aloisii Daelli, 1861), 203–4: "Et nisi aliqui se opposuissent, Moronus volebat omnia Larii lacus oppida in praedam ponere, praecipue eos qui factionem guelpham tuebantur, quia vox erat quod guelphi adhaerebant regi Francorum."

64. Muralto, *Annalia,* 204.

65. Muralto, *Annalia,* 205–6.

66. On some of the later conflicts over Lecco and the Comasco involving the condottiere Gian Giacomo Medici (il Medeghino) in the 1520s, see Rinaldo Beretta, "Gian Giacomo de' Medici in Brianza (1527-1531)," *Archivio storico lombardo,* ser. 5, fasc. 1–2 (1916): 53–120; Roberto Gariboldi, *Il marchese avventuriero* (Milan: Edlin, 2007), 69–87.

67. Christine Shaw, *The Politics of Exile in Renaissance Italy* (Cambridge: Cambridge University Press, 2000).

68. See Christine Shaw's assessment of how Georges d'Amboise adjudicated a land dispute between Francesco Trotti and Antonio Spinola in October 1501. Christine Shaw, "The Role of Milan in the Italian State System," in Arcangeli, ed., *Milano e Luigi XII,* 25–37, at 32.

69. Raffaele Tamalio, *Federico Gonzaga alla corte di Francesco I di Francia nel carteggio privato con Mantova* (Paris: Honoré Champion, 1994), 85–87, at 86: letter of Federico to Francesco Gonzaga, 24 October 1515.

70. Tamalio, *Federico Gonzaga,* 93–96, at 93: letter of Federico to Francesco Gonzaga, 29 October 1515.

71. On Noceto, see Carlo Godi, *Bandello—Narratori e dedicatari della seconda parte delle Novelle* (Rome: Bulzoni, 2001), 2: 104–05.

72. A letter in ASMn, AG 1637, dated 5 March 1507, from Geoffroy Carles to Francesco Gonzaga assures the Marquis that "e stato expedito nel regio senato [milanese] tuto quello era di bisogno sopra la concessione regia facta a lo Ill. S.re frederico figliolo de vra Ex.tia del loco de Pouylio." But conflict between officers in French Milan and Mantua was already evident. See ASMn, AG 1637, Michele Rizzo to Francesco Gonzaga, 14 July 1507.

73. Alessandro Luzio, "Isabella d'Este di fronte a Giulio II negli ultimi tre anni del suo pontificato (parte prima)," *Archivio storico lombardo,* 17, fasc.

34, 245–344, at 282–83. In summer 1512, Isabella wrote a letter to the Governor of Reggio Emilia about confusions over the neighboring holding of Castelnovo: "Siamo auisate che la R.de S.V. con lettera et con ambassiata duno trombetta ha dimandato quel loco alli homini in nome della S.ta de N.S. persuadendosi forsi chel fusse anchora del Ill.mo s.r Duca [Alfonso d'Este] nostro fratello honorando: il quale gia piu de uno anno lo uendette al p.to S. Cardinale et sua S.ria R.ma a nuy, como hauemo ditto. Perho pregamo la s.v. sij contenta non proceder poi ultra in molestarne la possessione della terra nostra" (ASMn, AG 2996, copialettere 30, Isabella d'Este to the Governor of Reggio Emilia, 6 August 1512).

74. Alessandro Luzio, *Isabella d'Este ne' primordi del papato di Leone X e il suo viaggio a Roma nel 1514–1515* (Milan: L. F. Cogliati, 1906), 21–22.

75. Tamalio, *Federico Gonzaga,* 93–96, at 94, Federico to Francesco Gonzaga, 29 October 1515.

76. Tamalio, *Federico Gonzaga,* 128–30, at 129, Federico to Francesco Gonzaga, 20 November 1515.

77. Auton, *Chroniques,* 1: 16–21, at 21. Sanudo *Diarii,* 2: 1104, records that the French "messeno a sacho e usò gran crudeltà amazando homeni, done, puti etc. et quella brusoe," though he earlier suggests the soldiers were released, not killed. Ambrogio da Paullo, *Cronaca,* 354, estimates the dead at 1,200 people.

78. Tamalio, *Federico Gonzaga,* 138–39, at 139, Federico to Francesco Gonzaga, 30 November 1515.

79. Tamalio, *Federico Gonzaga,* 163–64, at 163, Federico to Francesco Gonzaga, 25 December 1515. Federico describes the slow motion of the affair in a letter from Valence: Federico to Francesco Gonzaga, 14 February 1516, 206–10, at 207.

80. Tamalio, *Federico Gonzaga,* 228–29, at 229, Federico to Francesco Gonzaga, 16 March 1516. Federico Gonzaga's claims on Poviglio were also being contested by the city of Parma, whose representatives claimed that it had authority over Poviglio.

81. Quoted in Anthony B. Cashman, "Performance Anxiety: Federico Gonzaga at the Court of Francis I and the Uncertainty of Ritual Action," *Sixteenth Century Journal* 33, no. 2 (2002): 333–52, at 349, n. 60, Francesco Gonzaga to Raphaele Gusperto, 19 June 1518.

82. Isabella d'Este in Mantua to Jacopo Suardo, 13 March 1510, d'Este, *Selected Letters,* letter 431, 319. Shemek identifies "Monsignore Presidente" as the French governor of Milan, Charles d'Amboise, but it was more likely the president of the senate, Carles, who in those same months was experiencing suspicions over his leadership. See Meschini, *Luigi XII,* 132–48, esp. 142–43.

83. Quoted in Luzio, "Isabella d'Este di fronte a Giulio II (parte prima)," 282; reported by Jacopo d'Atri to Francesco Gonzaga, 26 January 1511:

"Da ognuno seria estimato et honorato, ma quando perdesse il stato gli
converia andare per il mondo mendicando cum li figlioli et non trovaria
chi gli desse dil pane et se faria beffe de lui."

84. Tamalio, *Federico Gonzaga,* 161–63, at 162, Federico to Francesco Gonzaga,
23 December 1515. See also Prato, *Storia,* 338.

85. Milanese petitions of January 1516, transcribed in Prato, *Storia,* 359–79.
See article 17, "Bona donata non apprehendantur, nisi liquidatione facta,"
375: "Detestabilem quoque abusum illum tollere dignetur Maiestas Sua,
quo et iura subditorum suorum maxime laeduntur, omniaque confund-
untur; si quidem donatis per Maiestatem Suam aut in feudum, vel aliter
quovis modo concessis aliquibus bonis, statim, nulla facta condemna-
tione, minusque liquidatione, super ipsis bonis, secundum decretorum
formam, donatarii, seu qui concessiones habuerunt, possessiones bonorum apprehendunt, fructusque percipiunt, et omnia devastant." The
monarch acceded to the request for proper legal procedure.

5. PROTECTING AND SUING

1. Giason del Maino, *Consiliorum siue Responsorum d. Iasoni Mayni volumen
quartum* (Venice: Apud Franciscum Zilettum, 1581), 19r–20r, consilium
107. This case has been highlighted in Jane Black, *Absolutism in Renaissance
Milan: Plenitude of Power under the Visconti and Sforza, 1329–1535* (Oxford:
Oxford University Press, 2009), 167.

2. Ferdinando Gabotto, *Giasone del Maino e gli scandali universitari nel Quattrocento* (Turin: La Letteratura, 1888), 219 n. 1: "Locus Pioperae . . . ab-
latus fuit . . . sine ulla vera causa, nec vera culpa, qui nec citatus unquam
fui, nec ad hanc causam vocatus . . . Ego saepissime sum conquaestus, sed
non plus profeci, quam proficiant, qui lunae aut soli calamitates suas
lamentantur."

3. Gabotto, *Giasone,* 218, n. 1: "Impudenter iterum atque iterum respondit
quod literas illas regias ad prostibulum deferrem."

4. By 1510 Piovera belonged to Galeazzo Visconti, senator and leader of Lombardy's Ghibellines, who had nonetheless ingratiated himself with Louis
XII. See Stefano Meschini, *Luigi XII, Duca di Milano. Gli Uomini e le istituzioni del primo dominio francese (1499–1512)* (Milan: FrancoAngeli, 2004) 420,
n. 432.

5. Alberico Gentili, *ll Diritto di guerra* (Milan: Giuffrè Editore, 2008), 2.4, 214:
"Nel nostro secolo, sappiamo che è stato rimproverato a Carlo V e a Luigi
XII di Francia di aver interpretato le parole dei loro patti in maniera degna
più di legulei che di principi."

6. Del Maino, *Consiliorum,* 19v, section 9.

7. Enzo Sciacca, *Le Radici teoriche dell'assolutismo nel pensiero politico francese del
primo Cinquecento (1498–1519)* (Milan: Giuffrè, 1975).

8. See Jean Feu's treatise (probably dated to 1509), "An Rex Franciae recognoscat Imperatorem" (Whether the King of France Should Recognize the Emperor), in his *Commentarii Ioannis Ignei* . . . (Lyon and Orléans: Apud Vincentium de Portonariis, & Apud Franciscum Gueyardum, 1581), 61r–84v (including rebuttals), at 64r, section 18. On Feu's service in Milan's senate, see Meschini, *Luigi XII,* 382–83.

9. Feu, *Commentarii,* 64v, section 22.

10. Stefano Meschini, *La Francia nel Ducato di Milano* (Milan: FrancoAngeli, 2006), 2: 603–05.

11. "Liste des donations faites sur les biens de rebelles confisqués," in Léon-Gabriel Pélissier, *Documents pour l'histoire de la domination française dans le Milanais (1499–1513)* (Toulouse: Édouard Privat, 1891),10 July 1500, doc. 15, 34–39.

12. On the culture of Sforza petitions, see Nadia Covini, "La Trattazione delle suppliche nella cancelleria sforzesca: Da Francesco Sforza a Ludovico il Moro," in Cecilia Nubola and Andreas Würgler, eds., *Suppliche e 'gravamina.' Politica, amministrazione, giustizia in Europa (secoli XIV–XVIII)* (Bologna: il Mulino, 2002), 107–46.

13. For the investiture of Caiazzo in 1461, see Gianluca Battioni, ed., *Carteggio degli oratori mantovani alla corte sforzesca* (Rome: Ministero per i beni e le attività culturali, 1999–2008), vol. 12: 62 n. 3; and for Colorno in 1451, see Giorgio Fiori, "I Sanseverino d'Aragona di Parma e Piacenza," in *Colorno la Versailles dei duchi di Parma* (Parma: La deputazione di storia patria per le province parmensi, 1969), 61–75, at 61–62.

14. The best recent synthesis appears in Alessio Russo, "Sanseverino d'Aragona, Roberto," *Dizionario biografico degli Italiani* 90 (2017): 316–23.

15. Giovanni Azzarà, "I Sanseverino di Lombardia," *Studi meridionali* 9, no. 3 (1976): 228–42, considers the family's history only until the 1480s.

16. Lucia Fontanella, "La Relazione di Roberto Sanseverino sull'assassinio di Galeazzo Maria Sforza," *Pluteus* 6-7 (1988): 67–77; Giovanni Soranzo, "Prefazione a Iohannis Simonettae Rerum Gestarum Francisci Sfortiae Commentarii," in Giosuè Carducci, Vittorio Fiorini, and Pietro Fedele, eds., *Rerum Italicarum Scriptores,* vol. 21, part 2, fasc. 6 (Bologna: N. Zanichelli, 1932), iii–ciii, at xv.

17. On the co-ruling of Milan, see Soranzo, "Prefazione," xvi; on the Sanseverino brothers gathering at Ludovico's side, see Piero Alamanni in Milan to Lorenzo de' Medici in Florence, 13 November 1487, in Melissa Meriam Bullard, ed., *Lettere di Lorenzo de'Medici* (Florence: Giunti-Barbèra, 2004), vol. 9, letter 1104, n. 5, 425–26. Alamanni writes to Lorenzo: "Ora si sono ristrecti insieme questi figli del Signor Roberto col castellano et Piero da Landriano et alcuni altri, pur tucti Ghibellini, et ànno mandato come ho dicto per Monsignor Ascanio, et messer Galeazzo fa testimonantia che'l Signor Ludovico dié quella commissione a Bernardino [da Luna]."

18. Francesco Guicciardini, *Storia d'Italia,* Silvana Seidel Menchi, ed. (Turin: Einaudi, 1971) (IV.xiv) 1: 438–39. The three were Galeazzo, Antonio Maria, and Gaspare (Fracasso).

19. See the genealogical table in Jacob Wilhelm Imhoff, *Genealogiae viginti illustrium in Italia familiarum* (Amsterdam: Ex Officina Fratrum Chatelain, 1710), 292–93.

20. Guillaume Allonge, "Sanseverino, Galeazzo," *Dizionario biografico degli Italiani* 90 (2017): 291–93.

21. Alessandro Giulini, "Bianca Sanseverino Sforza figlia di Lodovico il Moro," *Archivio storico lombardo* 39 (1912): 233–52. For Leonardo's drawing, see Martin Kemp, Pascal Cotte, and Paul Biro, *La Bella Principessa: The Story of the New Masterpiece by Leonardo da Vinci* (London: Hodder & Stoughton, 2010). See also Katarzyna Krzyzagórska-Pisarek, "La Bella Principessa— Arguments against the Attribution to Leonardo," *Artibus et Historiae* 36, no. 71 (2015): 61–89.

22. Vittorio Adami, ed., "Il Carteggio di un capitano di ventura—Gaspare S. Severino d'Aragona detto Fracasso (1475-1518)," *Miscellanea di storia veneta* 4 (1930): 1–162, at 158, letter of 21 May 1502 to Ercole d'Este. See also Guillaume Allonge, "Sanseverino, Gaspare," *Dizionario biografico degli Italiani* 90 (2017): 293–94.

23. BMV, MS Italiano VII 990 (=9582), 105v. Zaccaria Contarini to Venetian Senate, 31 December 1501.

24. Meschini, *La Francia nel Ducato,* 1: 282–83, describes the captaincies granted to certain Sanseverino brothers as early as 1503, thanks to the patronage of their brother, the Cardinal Federico.

25. For summaries of the donation documents, see Riccardo Predelli, ed., *I Libri commemoriali della Repubblica di Venezia: Regesti* (Cambridge: Cambridge University Press, 2012 [1876-1914], 5: 243 (#188); 245 (#192); 246 (#194, #195). See also Andrea Gamberini, "Cremona nel Quattrocento. La Vicenda politica e istituzionale," in Giorgio Chittolini, ed., *Storia di Cremona: Il Quattrocento—Cremona nel Ducato di Milano (1395–1535)* (Cremona: Comune di Cremona, 2008), 2–29, at 24–25, n. 255.

26. Gamberini, "Cremona," 24–30.

27. On Battaglia, see Pietro Bembo, *History of Venice,* Robert W. Ulery Jr., ed. and trans. (Cambridge, MA: Harvard University Press, 2007-09), 1: 324–27; Pietro Giustiniani, *Le Historie Venetiane* (Venice: Appresso Lodovico Avanzo, 1576), 168v–169r; Jacques Gohori, "De Rebus gestis francorum," in Léon-Gabriel Pélissier, *Documents relatifs au règne de Louis XII et à sa politique en Italie* (Montpellier: Imprimerie Générale du Midi, 1912), doc. 1, 1–84, at 24–25; Casimiro Freschot, *La Nobiltà Veneta* (Venice: Appresso Gio. Gabriel Hertz, 1708), 268.

28. Girolamo Priuli, *I Diarii, 1499–1512,* Arturo Segre, ed., *Rerum Italicarum Scriptores,* vol. 24, part 3 (Città di Castello: Tipi della Casa editrice S. Lapi, 1912–1938), 2: 52.

29. Priuli, *Diari,* 2: 52. In addition, the *collegio* endowed Battaglia with Roberto's Veronese pleasure palace of Montorio. See Giovanni Orti, *Memoria storica sul castello di Montorio* (Verona: dalla Società Tipografica, 1824), 31.

30. Although even this fact is uncertain. Massimiliano Sforza's secretary Andrea Borgo was named feudatory of Corte Cavalcabò on 1 February 1513. See Caterina Santoro, *Gli Offici del comune di Milano e del dominio visconteosforzesco (1216–1515)* (Milan: Giuffrè, 1968), 382, n. 18.

31. Ippolita was born in Genoa to Francesco ("Franceschetto") Cibo and Maddalena de'Medici (daughter of Lorenzo il Magnifico). See the annotation of her birth in Franceschetto Cibo's family diary: Luigi Staffetti, ed., "Il Libro di Ricordi della Famiglia Cybo," *Atti della Società ligure di storia patria* 38 (1908): vii–lxvii, 1–615, at 5; and on her death, at 242–43.

32. On counter-dowries of lands and women's management of them, see Evelyn Welch, "Women in Debt: Financing Female Authority in Renaissance Italy," in Letizia Arcangeli and Susanna Peyronel, eds., *Donne di potere nel Rinascimento* (Rome: Viella, 2008), 45–65, at 49–56. Moreover, Milan's French podestà, Nicolas de la Chesnaye, appears to have given Montecollaro / Corte Cavalcabò to Arthus Gouffier, sieur de Boisy, in 1515. See Stefano Meschini, *La Seconda dominazione francese nel Ducato di Milano. La Politica e gli uomini di Francesco I (1515–1521)* (Varzi: Guardamagna Editore, 2014), 37.

33. Gagné, "Collecting Women," 172–73, 182.

34. Marin Sanudo, *I Diarii,* Rinaldo Fulin, ed. (Bologna: Forni, 1969–1979 [1879–1902]), 28: 42 (for the wedding), 591 (for the case against Battaglia).

35. Sanudo, *Diarii,* 29: 46.

36. Giuseppe Molini, ed., *Documenti di storia italiana* (Florence: Tipografia all'insegna di Dante, 1836), doc. 117, 1: 225–27, unnamed Sanseverino to Giulio Sanseverino, 14 August 1526: "El Sign. Marchese del Guasto [Alfonso d'Avalos] restituì al Sign. Conte de Cayazzo mio Sign. et fratelo [Roberto Ambrogio] la corte de li Cavalcabos et il posesso ali giorni passati, con questo che'l mandasse uno homo aposta alo imperatore a solicitar che l'havesse ricompensa, altramente che'l conte li restituisse la corte, non essendo ricompensato."

37. The Cibo chronicle editor Luigi Staffetti wrote that Ippolita "condusse vita randagia perchè ora la troviamo nel Piacentino ora a Roma, sempre bisognosa che i parenti la soccorressero nelle gravi ristrettezze economiche in cui versava, dipendenti dalla poca lieta condizione in cui l'aveva lasciata il marito, che in opere disordinate aveva consumato fin la sua dote" (Staffetti, "Il Libro di Ricordi," 242).

38. The chronicler's assessment is cited in Andrea Corna, *Castelli e Rocche del Piacentino* (Piacenza: Unione Tipografica Piacentina, 1913), 85.

39. ASVr, Fondo Zileri-Dal Verme, 51, fasc. 171—terms for Galeazzo Sanseverino's castellan at Olgisio, Silvestro Martinengo, to capitulate to Federico dal Verme, 14 March 1520.

40. "Solicita la creation dil successor, aziò possi repatriar" (Sanudo, *Diarii,* 30: 374).

41. On the 1517 siege of Olgisio (here called Arzes) led by Lescun, see Sanudo, *Diarii,* 24: 213, 244, 269–70, 307, 307, 312.

42. Fiori, "I Sanseverino," 63, n. 2, refers to the existence of this trial in ASPr, but he gives no specific citation. The acts of the trial remain to be found, despite my searches in ASPr, Feudi e comunità 210 (Sanseverino), Feudi e comunità 111 (dal Verme); Famiglie 481, 482 (Sanseverino) and Famiglie 57 (dal Verme).

43. BL, MS Egerton 26, 22r. David Potter, *Renaissance France at War* (Woodbridge: Boydell Press, 2008), 147, suggested Giulio as the letter's author, since it is signed only "St-Sevryn." Potter's proposal is convincing and matches all the contextual evidence.

44. BnF ms. fr. 2978, 18r, 23 October 1521: "La grande et quasi insupportable despense qui cest faicte et est encores necessaire de fere." François visited his mother at Blois in October of 1523 because she was suffering from "une pluresie qui luy estoit survenue de courroux qu'elle avoit eu à cause de la guerre et des affaires que le Roy avoit en son royaume, en la duché de Milan et ses aultres terres et seigneuries" (Ludovic Lalanne, ed., *Journal d'un bourgeois de Paris sous le Règne de François Ier (1515–1536)* [Paris: Chez Jules Renouard, 1854], 184).

45. Lalanne, ed., *Journal d'un bourgeois,* 307–12. More broadly on the affair, see Alfred Spont, *Semblançay (?–1527): La Bourgeoisie financière au début du XVIe siècle* (Paris: Hachette, 1895).

46. This is the proposal of Philippe Hamon, *L'Argent du roi: Les Finances sous François Ier* (Paris: Comité pour l'histoire économique et financière de la France, 1994), 343–52; see also Philippe Hamon, "Semblançay, homme de finances et de Conseil (v. 1455–1527)," in Cédric Michon, ed., *Les Conseillers de François Ier* (Rennes: Presses Universitaires de Rennes, 2011), 117–30, at 127–30.

47. Sanudo, *Diarii,* 24: 306.

48. See Jean-Louis Fournel, "L'Écriture du gouvernement et de la force en France et en Italie au début du XVIe siècle," in Patricia Eichel-Lojkine, ed., *Claude de Seyssel. Écrire l'histoire, penser le politique en France, à l'aube des temps modernes* (Rennes: Presses Universitaires de Rennes, 2010), 103–20.

49. BnF ms. fr. 3096, 45r–v, letter from Davranches to Villandry, 18 March 1528.

50. Documents of this trial (in 1566–1567) over the rights to the Rocca d'Olgisio and other holdings (by that point under the administration of the Duchy of Parma) can be found in ASVr, Fondo Zileri-Dal Verme—Processi 174—Sanseverino.

51. Ireneo Affò, *Memorie storiche di Colorno* (Parma: Per li Fratelli Gozzi, 1800), 33–60.

52. Alberto Cadoppi, *La Gran congiura: Il Processo di Ranuccio I Farnese contro i feudatari parmensi, 1611–1612* (Parma: Monte Università Parma, 2012).

53. ASMn, AG 2996, copialettere 30, 55r, Isabella d'Este in Mantua to Massimiliano Sforza in Milan (?), November 18, 1512: "Essendomi ditto che molti concorreno a dimandargli officij."

54. Isabella requested the appointment of Francesco Casati (or da Casale), husband of Isabella Trotta, "creata e carissima de la fe. me. de la Ill.ma m.a ura matre" as magistrate of Ordinary Revenues. A letter of 21 November (ASMn, AG 2996, copialettere 30, 55v–56r) suggests that Massimiliano acceded to her request, which ducal registers confirm. See also Franca Petrucci, "Casati, Francesco," *Dizionario biografico degli Italiani* 21 (1978): 235–37, and Santoro, *Gli Offici,* 397.

55. As early as 1507, Francesco and his wife had asked Isabella to help Francesco obtain an official position despite the fact that "molti altri gientilhomini esser amisi in registro a questo offitio auante me"; hey asked Isabella to write letters to Chaumont and Antonio Maria Pallavicino to assure the appointment; ASMn, AG 1637, Francesco and Isabella Casati in Milan to Isabella d'Este in Mantua, 14 June 1507. The effort failed, even after Francesco presented Isabella's letters personally to the king in Asti: "Et poi li diseno che non volendo fare niente ne meterllo alo ofitio de presente nec etiam farlli spectatiua alcuna" (ASMn, AG 1637, Francesco and Isabella Casati to Isabella d'Este, 22 July 1507).

56. Jacopo Ghilardotti, *La Casa degli Atellani e la vigna di Leonardo* (Rome: Rai Eri, 2015), 33.

57. Edoardo Villata, ed., *Leonardo da Vinci. I Documenti e le testimonianze contemporanee* (Milan: Castello Sforzesco, 1999), doc. #244, 211–12.

58. ASMi, Sforzesco 1417, 17 March 1513, supplication on behalf of Carlo, Scipione, and Annibale Atellani, to Massimiliano Sforza. In a letter of the same year, Duke Massimiliano sent Carlo Atellani to Mantua as a messenger to Francesco Gonzaga; ASMn, AG 1616, Massimiliano Sforza in Milan to Francesco Gonzaga in Mantua, 20 November 1513: "Per questo mandamo a v.s. a posta Carlo de Lattella nro camerero, acio che piu extesam.te gli lo narri per parte nra."

59. Nadia Covini, "In Lomellina nel Quattrocento: Il Declino delle stirpi locali e i 'feudi accomprati,'" in Federica Cengarle, Giorgio Chittolini, and Gian Maria Varanini, eds., *Poteri signorili e feudali nelle campagne dell'Italia settentrionale fra Tre e Quattrocento* (Florence: Firenze University Press, 2005), 127–74, in tabella 1: Concessioni feudali in Lomellina nel XV secolo, # 37, 66.

60. BTM, Fondo Belgioioso 306, #18, 21 September 1499. For basic details of the parchment, see also Paolo Margaroli, ed., *Le Pergamene Belgioioso della Biblioteca Trivulziana di Milano (secoli XI–XVIII): Inventari e regesti* (Milan: Comune di Milano, 1997), 1: 308, #874.

61. Covini, "In Lomellina," tabella 1, # 74.

62. See, for instance, the assessments of confiscation throughout the Sforza regime in Letizia Arcangeli, "Ludovico tiranno?," in her *Gentiluomini di Lombardia. Ricerche sull'aristocrazia padana nel Rinascimento* (Milan: Edizioni Unicopli, 2003), 124-48; and Arcangeli, "Gian Giacomo Trivulzio," also in *Gentiluomini di Lombardia,* 58-63.

63. Daniele Andreozzi, "Il Dominio francese e pontificio (1499-1545)," in Piero Castignoli, ed., *Storia di Piacenza,* vol 3: *Dalla Signoria viscontea al principato farnesiano (1313-1545)* (Piacenza: Cassa di Risparmio di Piacenza, 1997), 167-93, at 173-74.

64. ASMi, Sforzesco 1417, 23 March 1513. Alexander Sforza (?) in Piacenza to Massimilano Sforza.

65. On this office see Franca Leverotti, "Gli Officiali del ducato sforzesco," *Annali della Scuola normale superiore di Pisa. Classe di lettere e filosofia,* ser. 4, no. 1 (1997): 17-77, at 24-25. On Brivio's lordly status, see Ambrogio da Paullo, *Cronaca milanese dall'anno 1476 al 1515,* Antonio Ceruti, ed., *Miscellanea di storia italiana,* no. 13 (1871): 91-378, at 105-06.

66. See Mauro Natale's entry in Giovanni Agosti, Mauro Natale, and Giovanni Romano, eds., *Vincenzo Foppa* (Milan: Skira, 2003), 258, cat. no. 79.

67. Letizia Arcangeli, "Esperimenti di governo: Politica fiscale e consenso a Milano nell'età di Luigi XII," in Arcangeli, ed., *Milano e Luigi XII,* 255-339, at 308-9, for his role as *appaltatore* from 1506 to 1509.

68. Franca Petrucci, "Brivio, Giovanni Francesco," *Dizionario biografico degli Italiani* 14 (1972), 354-55; Gianfrancesco Brivio Sforza, ed., *Notizie Storico-Genealogiche della famiglia Brivio* (Milan: Editrice Nuovi Autori, 2000), 98-104; Felice Calvi, *Famiglie notabili milanesi* (Milan: Antonio Vallardi, 1881), vol. 4, Brivio: tavola 9.

69. Franca Petrucci, "Colla, Giovanni," *Dizionario biografico degli Italiani* 26 (1982): 764-66.

70. Giovanni Andrea Prato, *Storia di Milano.* Cesare Cantù, ed., *Archivio storico italiano* 3 (1842): 216-418, at 327: "Già pedante, ma allora un secondo Duca."

71. ASMi, Sforzesco 1417, Giovanni Francesco Brivio to Giovanni Colla in Milan, 1 January 1513.

72. Meschini, *La Francia nel Ducato,* 1: 137; Sanudo, *Diarii,* 3: 262: "La fiola, fo di missier Antonio di Landriano, thesorier, qual fo amazato, et è moglie di missier Francesco da Brevi, et era serata in uno monasterio a Pavia, francesi l'ànno levata per forza de lì, e usato con lei molte desonestà."

73. ASMi, Registri ducali 26, 66r-v. The appointment is undated in the register, but Calvi, *Famiglie,* vol. 4, tavola 9, notes an appointment date of 3 April 1513; cf. Santoro, *Gli Offici,* 397.

74. ASMi, Sforzesco 1411, Leonardo Visconti to Massimiliano Sforza, 26 October 1513: "Ma dicto francesco [da Brippio] como maligno & fac-

tioxo che gia de prima & alora era stato ribelle Poso la captione dil p.to genitore vro. Ala quale epso francesco interuene con testimonij falsi di quali sempre ne fu Copioso: & con fauore de Triuultij & franzoxi opero tanto contro depso supplicante che lo fece incarcerare: et demum mandare in exilio: Et lo pezoroe piu de ducati 3000 doro. Et veramente Ill.mo s.re sono stati pochi de li seruitori di caxa sforzescha che siano stati a tanti periculi et traualie quanto ha facto epso supplicante per sugestione de dicto Francesco." Leonardo Visconti, protonotary and commendatory abbot of San Celso, took part in planning Ludovico Sforza's 1500 restoration and was exiled. His brother, Francesco Bernardino, became a senator under the French. See Meschini, *Luigi XII,* 61, n. 102, 392, n. 262.

75. "Mutilato de questi doi più honorevoli membri, et che in progresso di tempo saria a noi totale iactura dil nostro stato" (Massimiliano Sforza to Marino Caracciolo and Girolamo Morone, 4 May 1513, in Giuseppe Müller, ed., *Documenti che concernono la vita pubblica di Gerolamo Morone.* [Turin: Stamperia Reale, 1865], doc. 24, 37–38 at 38). For political context on Parma and Piacenza in this period, see Letizia Arcangeli, "Tra Milano e Roma: Esperienze politiche nella Parma del primo Cinquecento," in Giancarla Petrini, ed., *Emilia e Marche nel Rinascimento: L'Identità Visiva della 'Periferia'* (Azzano San Paolo: Bolis Edizioni, 2005), 89–118.

76. Massimiliano Sforza to Marino Caracciolo and Girolamo Morone, 4 May 1513, in Müller, ed., *Morone,* doc. 25, 38–42, at 40.

77. Antonio Francesco da Villa, "Cronaca di Anton Francesco da Villa da 1511 al 1556," in A. Bonora and G. Bonora, eds., *Civitatis Placentiae Johannis Agazzari et Antonii Francisci Villa* (Parma: Typis Petri Fiaccadori, 1862), 77–223, at 89. In 1512, it was known to Girolamo Morone that the pontiff claimed Parma and Piacenza through a gift of the twelfth-century Countess Matilda of Canossa. See Girolamo Morone, *Lettere ed orazioni latine,* Domenico Promis and Giuseppe Müller, eds. (Turin: Stamperia Reale, 1863), letter 86, 192–96 at 194, Girolamo Morone to Giason del Maino, 23 June 1512.

6. DOCUMENT DESTRUCTION AND FRAUD

1. Ugo Petronio, *Il Senato di Milano : Istituzioni giuridiche ed esercizio del potere nel ducato di Milano da Carlo V a Giuseppe II* (Milan: Giuffrè 1972), 3–58.

2. On the destruction, see the Ministero dell'Interno, "Archivio di Stato di Milano," in *Notizie degli Archivi di Stato—I danni di guerra subiti dagli archivi italiani* (Rome: Istituto Poligrafico dello Stato, 1950), 13–20, at 15; and Gianfranco Pertot, "Milano e le bombe. Le Distruzioni, le macerie, i primi interventi, la tutela mancata," *Storia urbana* 30, nos. 114–115 (2007): 255–302.

3. Léon-Gabriel Pélissier, *Documents pour l'histoire de la domination française dans le Milanais (1499–1513)* (Toulouse: Édouard Privat, 1891), vi.

4. Jules Michelet, *Histoire de France au seizième siècle: Renaissance* (Paris: Chamerot, 1855), 316.

5. For helpful framing in the problematics of archival disruption and document dispersion, see Filippo de Vivo, Andrea Guidi, Alessandro Silvestri, eds., *Fonti per la storia degli archivi degli antichi Stati italiani* (Rome: Ministero dei beni e delle attività culturali del turismo—direzione generale archivi, 2016), 389–97.

6. The phrase belongs to Philippe Contamine, "La Mémoire de l'état. Les Archives de la Chambre des Comptes du roi de France à Paris, au XVᵉ siècle," in *Media in Francia . . . Recueil de mélanges offert à Karl Ferdinand Werner* (Maulévrier: Hérault-Éditions, 1989), 85–100.

7. On the diplomatic obsession with paperwork, see Francesco Senatore, *'Uno mundo de carta': Forme e strutture della diplomazia sforzesca* (Naples: Liguori Editore, 1998); and on the Sforza regime's use of its own archive for self-regarding history projects, see Gary Ianziti, *Humanist Historiography under the Sforzas: Politics and Propaganda in Fifteenth-Century Milan* (Oxford: Oxford University Press, 1988), especially 162–74.

8. Evelyn Welch, *Art and Authority in Renaissance Milan* (New Haven, CT: Yale University Press, 1995), 176.

9. "Habens libros aliquorum onerum presentet ut debeant publico incendio concremari" (quoted in Cesare Manaresi, ed., *I Registri viscontei* [Milan: Palazzo del Senato, 1915], 1: x). See also the specification of "inventariarum taxarum, talearum, focorum, buccarum, onerisque salis et aliorum quorumvis onerum" (cited in Franca Leverotti, "L'Archivio dei Visconti signori di Milano," in Isabella Lazzarini, ed., *Scritture e potere. Pratiche documentarie e forme di governo nell'Italia tardomedievale [XIV–XV secolo]*, special issue of *Reti Medievali* 9 (2008): 1–22, at 2).

10. Marina Spinelli, "Ricerche per una nuova storia della Repubblica Ambrosiana," *Nuova rivista storica* 70 (1986): 231–52, at 236.

11. The proposal was first made by Gian Piero Bognetti, "Per la storia dello Stato visconteo (Un registro di decreti, della cancelleria di Filippo Maria Visconti, e un trattato segreto con Alfonso d'Aragona)," *Archivio storico lombardo*, ser. 6, fasc. 2–3 (1927): 237–357, at 246.

12. Spinelli, "Ricerche," 237. On the duties of this magistracy (under the Sforza, not the Republic, but we can presume certain similarities), see Franca Leverotti, "Gli Officiali del ducato sforzesco," *Annali della Scuola normale superiore di Pisa. Classe di lettere e filosofia*, ser. 4, no. 1 (1997): 17–77, at 25.

13. "Molte et infinite scripture, libri et rasone esportate da la comunità di Milano . . . de grandissima importantia et molto tornariano a grandissimo danno et sinistro quando non se trovasseno" (BnF, ms. ital. 1546, quoted in Leverotti, "L'Archivio," 2).

14. Spinelli, "Ricerche," 236.

15. "Per non havere possuto trovare le scripture dello ill.mo qd. Sig.re duca Filippo perché furono brusate al tempo della libertà de Milano" (quoted in Manaresi, *I Registri,* 1: xi).

16. Fabio Cusin, "L'Impero e la successione degli Sforza ai Visconti," *Archivio storico lombardo,* fasc. 1–2 (1936): 3–116; Fabio Cusin, "Le Aspirazioni straniere sul ducato di Milano e l'investitura imperiale (1450–54)," *Archivio storico lombardo,* fasc. 3–4 (1936): 277–369.

17. "Perchè alcune cose ne accade presentemente è necessario che vediamo lo originale del testamento che fece lo illustrissimo signore quondam duca primo" (quoted in Pietro Ghinzoni, "Sul Testamento originale di Gian Galeazzo Visconti contenente il fedecommesso a favore dei discendenti della Valentina," *Archivio storico lombardo,* ser. 1, vol. 9, fasc. 2 [1882]: 335–40, at 337).

18. "Te dicemo che noj omnino vogliamo la origine et non la copia [. . .] perché importa molto a facto nostro" (Ghinzoni, "Sul Testamento," 337).

19. Ghinzoni, "Sul Testamento," 339–40.

20. ASMi, Autografi 219, fasc. 20, Giason del Maino in Pavia to Ludovico Sforza in Milan, 10 January 1496: "Domandai ad esso Io. Dominicho [Oleari] sel haueua el testamento del ditto primo ducha o sel sapeua chi lhauesse: me respoxe de non. Da poi de dì in dì inuestigando più oltra diligentemente: ho ritrouato chel dicto Io. Dominicho ha una copia compita del testamento del dicto primo duca benche non sia sollemne ne autenticha. Et questo testamento saria de grande importantia per el duca de Orliens contra V. Ex. Perchè in esso testamento ghe el fideicommisso del stato de Milano, che morando el duca Io. Maria et il duca Filippo et messer Gabriello senza figloli masculi dispone chel stato de Milano peruegna ad uno de figloli de la ill. madona Vallentina"; excerpts from this letter appear in Manaresi, *I Registri,* 1: xv. See also Luigi Osio, ed., *Documenti diplomatici tratti dagli archivj milanesi* (Milan: Tipografia di Giuseppe Bernardoni di Giovanni, 1864), 1: 318–19, n. 1. "Messer Gabriello" (1385–1408) was Giangaleazzo's illegitimate son with Agnese Mantegazzo. On the specific meaning of "solenne" and "autentica" in the context of documentary culture, see Alessandro Pratesi, *Genesi e forme del documento medievale* (Rome: Jouvence, 1999), 34, 105–9.

21. ASMi, Autografi 219, fasc. 20, Giason del Maino in Pavia to Ludovico Sforza in Milan, 10 January 1496.

22. ASMi, Autografi 219, fasc. 20, Giason del Maino in Pavia to Ludovico Sforza in Milan, 16 January 1496.

23. ASMi, Autografi 219, fasc. 20, Giason del Maino in Pavia to Ludovico Sforza in Milan, 16 January 1496: "He da credere chel prelibato Ill. d. Jo Galeazio facesse ogni opera cum lo Imperio per obtenire el priuillegio del ducato de Millano non solum per li figlioli soi masculi ma etiam per le

figliole sue femine. Tutta volta questo penssere et desiderio suo non glie reuscito per che nel anno M.ccclxxxxv quando obtene il naturale titolo et il priuillegio del ducato de Millano et del contado de pauia da Vinceslao Re deli romani: solo obtene il priuillegio per li masculi e non per le figliole sue femine."

24. ASMi, Autografi 219, fasc. 20, Giason del Maino in Pavia to Ludovico Sforza in Milan, 16 January 1496: "Dico che essendo il priuillegio Imperiale concesso al dicto primo duca solum per li figlioli soi masculi e non per le figliole femine che esso primo duco nel suo testamento non ha poduto de rasone fare il dicto fideicomisso per il quale sostituisse alcuna figliola femina ho descendente da lei nel stato suo [. . .] unde la rasone vole chel vassallo nel testamento suo no po fare testamento ne fideicomisso alcuno circa il feudo per che per sua dispositione testamentaria non po immutare la foma et origine et el tenore del priuillegio feudale."

25. ASMi, Autografi 219, fasc. 20, Giason del Maino in Pavia to Ludovico Sforza in Milan, 16 January 1496: "Non saria impertinente cossa che la sublimitate vostra quando meglio hauera facto ordinare questi mei humili ricordi, farli diseminare e diuulgare per la corte del Re de franza et altri lochi expedienti. [. . .] Mando anchora ala Ex.cia v. qui alligata la copia del testamento del primo duca: Et per che e asai longo e proliso quando a v. Ex.a piacesse de trouare subito il capo de dicto fideicomisso il lo signato et he in la quarta carta doue glie per segno una mano."

26. Leverotti, "L'Archivio," 10, 14–20. On similar organizations of documents for the sixteenth-century Este family, see Laura Turchi, "Un Archivio scomparso e il suo creatore? La Grotta di Alfonso II d'Este e Giovan Battista Pigna," in Filippo de Vivo, Andrea Guidi, and Alessandro Silvestri, eds., *Archivi e archivisti in Italia tra medioevo ed età moderna* (Rome: Viella, 2015), 217–37.

27. Annalisa Belloni, "L''Historia patria' di Tristano Calco fra gli Sforza e i Francesi: fonti e strati redazionali," *Italia medioevale e umanistica* 23 (1980): 179–232; Stefano Meschini, *Uno Storico umanista alla corte sforzesca. Biografia di Bernardino Corio* (Milan: Vita e Pensiero, 1995), 112; John Gagné, "After the Sforza: Making History in Milan during the Italian Wars," in Christian Callisen, ed., *Reading and Writing History from Bruni to Windschuttle* (Farnham, UK: Ashgate, 2014), 35–55, at 42–43.

28. Senatore, *Uno mundo de carta*, 90.

29. On Francesco Sforza's diplomats, see Franca Leverotti, *Diplomazia e governo dello stato: I 'Famigli cavalcanti' di Francesco Sforza (1450–1466)* (Pisa: ETS Editrice, 1992), esp. 97–104; on the letters, see Vincent Ilardi, "I Documenti diplomatici del secolo XV negli archivi e biblioteche dell'Europa occidentale (1450–1494)," *Rassegna degli Archivi di Stato* 28 (1968): 349–402, at 353.

30. On the now-lost inventory, see Caterina Santoro, "Notizie su alcuni codici sforzeschi," in *Atti e memorie del terzo congresso storico lombardo, 1938* (Milano:

Giuffrè, 1939), 47–51; for the appointment of ushers and archivists and the location of the archive, see Axel Behne, "Archivordnung und Staatsordnung im Mailand der Sforza-Zeit," *Nuovi annali della Scuola speciale per archivisti e bibliotecari* 2 (1988): 93–102, at 97; on the disorderliness compared to other courts, see Senatore, *Uno mundo de carta,* 101.

31. "Libros seu cancellarie registros alter in alterum per fenestras et scabellas iniicientes, hoc ipsos atramento omnique feditate deturpantes, qui registri ita compti et compositi ac pernitidi servandi sunt, ut nil eis deesse videatur, quod ad commendationem cancellariorum et laudem attingat." (Quoted in Felice Fossati's review of *Inventari e regesti del R. Archivio di Stato di Milano,* in "Bibliografia" section of *Archivio storico lombardo,* ser. 6, fasc. 3 [1931], 364–79, at 368. The text is undated, but refers to the Sforza chancery.)

32. The words are de Leyva's. Massimiliano Stampa to Charles V, 21 November 1535; Antonio de Leyva to Charles V, 27 November 1535, quoted in Federico Chabod, *Storia di Milano nell'epoca di Carlo V* (Turin: Einaudi, 1961), 19, n. 3.

33. Chabod, *Storia di Milano,* 19, n. 4.

34. Chabod, *Storia di Milano,* 19, n. 3.

35. On the strategic use of the Sforza archive to build favorable histories, see Gary Ianziti, "A Humanist Historian and His Documents: Giovanni Simonetta, Secretary to the Sforzas," *Renaissance Quarterly* 34:4 (1981): 491–516, at 502–9.

36. Lidia Cerioni, "La Cancelleria Sforzesca durante il ritorno del Moro (Gennaio–April 1500)," *Archivio storico lombardo* 93–94 (1966): 140–72, esp. 141.

37. Stefano Meschini, *Luigi XII, Duca di Milano. Gli Uomini e le istituzioni del primo dominio francese (1499–1512)* (Milan: FrancoAngeli, 2004), 330, n. 365. A notarial act of 4 August 1503 was drawn up "in camera dicti archivii sita in dicto castro Porte Jovis Mediolani" when some original documents were copied for the two brothers Tommaso and Giovanni Spinetta Malaspina di Villafranca.

38. Élisabeth Pellegrin, *La Bibliothèque des Visconti et des Sforza, ducs de Milan, au XVe siècle* (Paris: Centre national de la recherche scientifique, 1955), 10–11, 71; Ugo Rozzo, "La Biblioteca Visconteo-Sforzesca di Pavia," in *Storia di Pavia: Dal Libero comune alla fine del principato indipendente, 1024–1535* (Milan: Banca del Monte di Lombardia, 1990), 2: 235–326. See also Maria Grazia Albertini Ottolenghi, "La Biblioteca dei Visconti e degli Sforza: Gli Inventari del 1488 e del 1490," *Studi petrarcheschi* 8 (1991): 1–238.

39. Giovanni Maria Sforza, Bishop of Genoa, 29 June 1513, in Carlo Magenta, *I Visconti e gli Sforza nel castello di Pavia,* (Milan: Ulrico Hoepli, 1883), vol. 2, doc. 481, 496–97.

40. Ambrogio da Paullo, *Cronaca milanese dall'anno 1476 al 1515,* Antonio Ceruti, ed., *Miscellanea di storia italiana* 13 (1871): 91–378, at 122–23.

41. Ambrogio da Paullo, *Cronaca,* 125; ASMi, Registro delle Missive 213, 30r, 2 October 1499: Zoanne de Novate, former podestà of Valsassina complained that "essi homeni de dicte commune [Barzia, Concenedo, Cassina, Moggio, Cremeno, Pasturo, Introbio] li siano andati ad la casa et toltoli ducati cento sexanta et rubato et strazato le scripture."

42. Gerolamo Bossi, *Memorie civili di Pavia,* Biblioteca universitaria di Pavia, MS Ticinesi 179, 238, as cited in Letizia Arcangeli, "Cambiamenti di dominio nello stato di Milano durante le prime guerre d'Italia (1495-1516). Dinamiche istituzionali e movimenti collettivi," in Marcello Bonazza and Silvia Seidel Menchi, eds., *Dal Leone all'Aquila. Comunità, territori e cambi di regime nell'età di Massimiliano I* (Rovereto: Edizioni Osiride, 2012), 27-75, at 61.

43. For a similar case from fourteenth-century Ferrara, see Beatrice Saletti, "Registri perduti della Camera Ducale estense: La *Storia della città di Ferrara* del notaio Ugo Caleffini e il suo accesso alla Libraria della Camera," in de Vivo, Guidi, and Silvestri, eds., *Archivi e archivisti,* 285-310, at 299-303.

44. Stephen Bowd, *Venice's Most Loyal City: Civic Identity in Renaissance Brescia* (Cambridge, MA: Harvard University Press, 2010), 199-200.

45. Marco Formentini, *Il Ducato di Milano. Studi storici documentati* (Milan: Libreria Editrice G. Brignola, 1877), 343-44, 27 April 1526; the edict "pardoned" the citizens for an uprising that the Spanish forces were not in a position to quell.

46. Léon-Gabriel Pélissier, "Les Registres Panigarola et le 'Gridario generale' de l'Archivio di Stato' di Milano pendant la domination française (1499-1513)," *Revue des Bibliothèques* (1895), 279 (#37, n. 2): "Chi ha libri ne altre scripture de qualuncha natura exportate fora de la ducale corte, ne de loffitio del sale in Broleto de Milano, li habiano tutti consegnati in dicta corte al officio de la carta."

47. Pélissier, "Les Registres" (1895), 280 (#46, n. 3): "Che chi ha o sappia altri avere alcuni libri, registri, instromenti o altre scritture, spettanti principalmente alla Tesoreria e camera ordinaria e straordinaria della Maestà Christianissima, o casse, letti ed altre robbe che erano in detta tesoreria, le debbe fra quattro giorni aver notificate."

48. Pélissier, "Les Registres" (1895), 282 (#61), 6 May 1500. More generally, focusing mostly on later periods, see Bruno Caizzi, "Sale e fiscalità nel ducato milanese," *Archivio storico lombardo* 118 (1992): 129-81.

49. Pélissier, "Les Registres" (1895), 282 (#65, n. 7), 12 May 1500: "Chi abbia havuto scriture, libri, filze ed utensigli della gabella del sale."

50. Pélissier, "Les Registres" (1895), 283 (#75), 10 June 1500.

51. Pélissier, "Les Registres" (1895), 304 (#132), 21 July 1500. On the oversight of dead notaries' records and the procedures of their transfer to other cus-

todians, see Roissin Cossar, *Clerical Households in Late Medieval Italy* (Cambridge, MA: Harvard University Press, 2017), 35–36.

52. For instance, in September 1499, Ascanio Sforza was said to have fled with 6,000 Milanese (Marin Sanudo, *I Diarii,* Rinaldo Fulin, ed. [Bologna: Forni, 1969–1979 (1879–1902)], 2: 1275), and in April 1500, after Ludovico's failed restoration, the Venetian rectors of Bergamo wrote that "Milan è soto sopra: bia' chi pol fuzir!" (Sanudo, *Diarii,* 3: 220).

53. Léon-Gabriel Pélissier, "Les Sources milanaises de l'histoire de Louis XII," *Bulletin du Comité des travaux historiques et scientifiques. Section d'histoire et de philologie* (1892): 110–88, at 115, #29: "Notum facimus quod nos primo desiderio cupientes ut omnia in hac ditione nostra mature dirigantur, peroptime componantur et in melius reformentur, pro nostra et subditorum nostrorum quiete et commodo cogitavimus id nulla laudabiliora via effici posse quam litterarum nostrarum monumenta et scripturas quae quottidie tam nostris quam subditorum nostrorum negotiis fiunt sub bona custodia reponere et deputare aliquem qui ea fideliter curet, conservet, deponet."

54. Meschini, *Luigi XII,* 330. They are Beltramo Colandis ("regius archiviarius Mediolani residens," 1508) and Giovan Agostino Lavizario (1503, 1510) from Como.

55. Pélissier, *Documents,* doc. 49, 150–51, 2 January 1507.

56. There were at times public calls for citizens with information or documents concerning urban properties to present themselves to the government, as in 1506, when the French demanded any information relating to Ludovico Sforza's pre-1499 purchase of Milan's Dal Verme (or Carmagnola) palace. Pélissier, "Les Registres" (1895), 315 (#277), 6 March 1506.

57. Pélissier, *Documents,* doc. 52, 154–55, 24 March 1507.

58. In Paris, there was no centralized financial archive until 1520; instead, officers maintained their own papers privately, as was typical. See Michel Nortier, "Le Sort des archives dispersées de la Chambre des Comptes de Paris," *Bibliothèque de l'École des chartes* 123, no. 2 (1965): 460–537, at 469.

59. For the suggestion of destruction, see Pélissier, *Documents,* xv; on the traces of the financial documents, see Matteo di Tullio and Luca Fois, *Stati di guerra: I Bilanci della Lombardia francese del primo Cinquecento* (Rome: École française de Rome, 2014), 23.

60. Edoardo Rossetti, "Sforza, Ottaviano Maria," *Dizionario biografico degli Italiani* 92 (2018): 451–54.

61. Pélissier, *Documents,* doc. 98, 276–77, 22 June 1512.

62. ASMi, Atti di governo—Statuti (Registri Panigarola GG) 25, 26 June 1512, 880r–881r: any person "quale al tempo dela bona memoria dil quondam Illustrissimo Signore Duca Ludouico in el suo receso habia hauuto ne sapia che habia hauuto roba alcuna quale era in la Corte sua delarengho de Milano ne habia ne sapia che habia exportato libri, scripture, ne

guastato essa corte debia nel termine de duy giorni proximo aduenire hau-
erli restituite o vero notificato sotto pena dela forcha."

63. Such at least is the evidence from a prosopography of the chancery. See
Franca Leverotti, "La Cancelleria segreta da Ludovico il Moro a Luigi XII,"
in Arcangeli, ed., *Milano e Luigi XII*, 221-53, at 244-50.

64. This is the conclusion (for the era of Louis XII) of both Leverotti, "La Can-
celleria segreta," 252, and Letizia Arcangeli, "Esperimenti di governo:
Politica fiscale e consenso a Milano nell'età di Luigi XII," in Arcangeli, ed.,
Milano e Luigi XII, 255-339, at 295.

65. See the documents edited by di Tullio and Fois, *Stati di guerra*, and the edi-
tors' description of the records, 25-29.

66. Franca Petrucci, "Calco, Bartolomeo," *Dizionario biografico degli Italiani* 16
(1973): 526-30; see also the analysis in Leverotti, "La Cancelleria segreta,"
223-33.

67. The appointments are detailed in ASMi, Registri Ducali 64 (January to
June 1513), and a complete summary of the duke's full appointments appears in Caterina Santoro, *Gli Offici del comune di Milano e del dominio
visconteo-sforzesco (1216–1515)* (Milan: Giuffrè, 1968), 379-435.

68. "Ceterum intendo se hano a reformare tuti li offitiali de Milano, et per
esser mi absente in servitio de la Ex.a del Duca, non voria che l'absentia
mia mi nocesse, zoè che io fusse amosso dal l'offitio mio de advocato
fischale de Milano; però ricorro a la S.a V.a pregandola et suplicandola
la volia far per mi como io spero in operare che io stia fermo al mio offitio" (Alexander Zancha in Tortona to Girolamo Morone in Milan, 5
August 1513, in Giuseppe Müller, ed., *Documenti che concernono la vita
pubblica di Gerolamo Morone* [Turin: Stamperia Reale, 1865], doc. 38,
68-70).

69. Letizia Arcangeli, "Alle origini del consiglio dei sessanta decurioni: Ceti
e rappresentanza a Milano tra Massimiliano Sforza e Francesco I di Valois
(maggio 1515-luglio 1516)," in Stefano Levati and Marco Meriggi, eds.,
Con la ragione e col cuore: Studi dedicati a Carlo Capra (Milan: FrancoAngeli,
2008), 33-75, at 47, quoting a letter of Giovanni Gonzaga, newly appointed
governor of Milan, to his brother Francesco Gonzaga: ASMn, AG 1641,
12 January 1515.

70. Inspired by Hillel Schwartz, *The Culture of the Copy: Striking Likenesses, Unreasonable Facsimiles* (New York: Zone, 1996), 212-16.

71. For an overview, see Andrea Gamberini, "Il Ducato di Milano e gli Svyceri: Uno Sguardo d'insieme," in Rodolfo Huber and Rachele Pollini-
Widmer, eds., *Da Dominio a dominio: Il Locarnese e la Valmaggia all'inizio del
XVI secolo*—special issue of *Bollettino della società storica locarnese* 16 (Locarno: Società Storica Locarnese, 2013), 13-30; Massimiliano Ferri and
Luca Fois, "Le Terre ticinesi tra ducato di Milano, Francia e Svizzeri dalla
caduta di Lugano e Locarno all'alleanza di Lucerna (1513-1521)," *Archivio*

storico lombardo, ser. 12, vol. 18 (2013): 149–82; and Marino Viganò, *Leonardo a Locarno: Documenti per una attribuzione del 'rivellino' del castello, 1507* (Bellinzona: Casagrande, 2008), 137–224.

72. Viganò, *Leonardo a Locarno,* 225–300.

73. On Bellinzona, see Aldo Bassetti and Eligio Pometta, "Gli ultimi anni di Bellinzona ducale e la sua volontaria dedizione agli svizzeri," *Quaderni grigionitaliani* 15, no. 3 (1945–1946): 197–207; 15, no. 4 (1945–1946): 265–76; 16, no. 2 (1946–1947): 126–40; Lidia Cerioni, "Gli ultimi mesi di Bellinzona ducale," *Bollettino storico della svizzera italiana* 26, no. 1 (1951): 1–41; Basilio Biucchi, "Bellinzona nei primi decenni della occupazione svizzera (1500–1555) nella documentazione dei recessi federali," in Giuseppe Chiesi, ed., *Pagine bellinzonesi. Cenni storici, studi e ricerche in occasione del centenario di Bellinzona capitale stabile del Cantone Ticino, 1878–1978* (Bellinzona: Comune di Bellinzona, 1978), 123–52. On the Ticino area generally see Leonardo Broillet, *A Cavallo delle Alpi. Ascese, declini e collocorazioni di ceti dirigenti tra Ticino e Svizzera centrale (1400–1600)* (Milan: FrancoAngeli, 2014), 54–86.

74. On the Rusca clan, see Emilio Motta, "I Rusca di Locarno, Luino, e Val Intelvi," *Bollettino storico della svizzera italiana* 17 (1895) fasc. 1–2 (1–7); 3–4 (33–41); 5–6 (65–70); 7–8 (97–101); 10–12 (153–59).

75. "Terras et loca Locarni cum Castro et tota eius plebe cum vallibus Madiae Lauizariae et Verzaschae cum totam et Jntegram plebem Traualie cum arce ipsius vallis Jtem terram et locum brisaghi lacus maioris, necnon et loca hosteni cum eius vicinantia ac lacunie necnon et loca et Terras vallis Jnteleui comensis diocesis" plus other territories in the val di Lugano. Confirmation privilege of Louis XII to the Rusca counts, 25 October 1499. See Marino Viganò, "Locarno francese (1499–1513): Per i 500 anni del 'rivellino' del Castello visconteo, 1507–2007," *Archivio storico ticinese* 141 (2007): 83–126, appendix 1, 110–13, at 110.

76. The three legitimate brothers appealed to the king in a supplication of January 1500, noting: "Relicto filio vno Jllegiptimo nomine herchules excluso ab huiusmodi sucessione paterna et nihilhominus dictus herchules nititur velle deturbare predictos legiptimos naturales veros et Justos Dominos et possessores in eorum pacifica et quieta possessione sucessionis bonorum tam feudalium quam alodialium: et de facto euacuare fecit et asportare omnia Mobilia et bona exhistentia in domo paterna syta Mediolani. [. . .] Jtem exagitare subditos et vassalos Jurisdictionum feudalium vt eum recognoscerent in Dominum: Et ab eis extorquere Juramentum fidelitatis volendo excludere prenominatos legiptimos: que omnia contra Jus et a Justitia aliena sunt" (Viganò, "Locarno francese," appendix 2, 113–14, at 113).

77. Eleuterio Rusca to Galeazzo Rusca, 4 June 1500, in Viganò, "Locarno francese," appendix 10, 118–20, at 118.

78. Viganò, "Locarno francese," appendix 10, 119.

79. On Morosini's role in these affairs, see Broillet, *A Cavallo delle Alpi,* 62–63; 297–300.

80. Viganò, "Locarno francese," appendix 10, 119.

81. Viganò, "Locarno francese," appendix 14, 123–24.

82. Viganò, "Locarno francese," appendix 15, 124–25.

83. Gianna Ostinelli-Lumia, "'Pro capitulando cum prelibatis dominis nostris': Privilegi, capitoli e concessioni negli anni della conquista confederata (Locarno, Lugano, Mendrisio, 1512–1514)," *Archivio storico ticinese* 141 (2007): 3–28, at 14 n. 87.

84. Gian-Gaspare Nessi, *Memorie storiche di Locarno* (Locarno: Tipografia di Francesco Rusca, 1854), 104–07.

85. Franchino had died aged 26 in 1509. See Motta, "I Rusca," 33–34.

86. See the letter from the agent: ASMi, Sforzesco 1417, 18 March 1513, Bongaleazzo de Castronovate to Massimiliano Sforza, both in Milan. The day before, news came from Lucerne that the Rusca were trying to become citizens of Lucerne and Uri to avoid losing their entitlements. ASMi, Sforzesco 626, 17 March 1513, Giovanni Francesco Stampa in Lucerne to Massimiliano Sforza in Milan: "Ben lauiso che li conti Ruschi de Locarno hanno dato domanda si per li Datij de Locarno como per altro, quanto per farsi Citadini de Lucera et Uria et infino ad hogi non intendo che sianno acceptati."

87. ASMi, Sforzesco 1417, 18 March 1513: "Perche dicti testimonij et instrumenti producti sono de dicta sorte et natura che ho dicto de sopra, et ad benche per mi piu volte ad dicti Conti sia stato domandato che producessino li libri soi et deli datieri et dele loro intrate acio se potesse calchulare per molti anni quanto ne cauauano sotto sopra luno computa cum laltro. Et per potere detraher li carichi de officiali, et altri che vano in simile cose como sa v.s. ac restori de guerre, peste, mal paghe, et altri simili andamenti, per venire poi al neto, che fin al presente non hano voluto fare."

88. This affair, still largely obscure and untraced, happened around 1514–1519; Eleuterio died in 1519. "Verum pretendit prefatus Franchinus, quod ad fraudendum eum adhuc minorem, Magnifica Domina Eleonora Corrigia, Uxor prefati Comiti Eleutherij cum scientia, & consensu praefati Eleutherij finxerit se gravidam, et suposuerit sibi dictum Hieronymum. Et ita videtur esse, quia Comitissia fuerat sterilis usque ad annum 41. Et cum esset Magna Matrona habitans Mediolani, voluit tamen eo die sero, quo dixit peperisse, recedere in Rheda, et ire ad Suburbanum, distans ultra milliare a Civitate, et non praeparatis Obstetricibus, ac Puerperij ornamentis. Recessit etiam associata duabus dumtaxat Ancillis, cum tamen soleret secum multo plures ducere" (cited in Motta, "I Rusca," 36).

89. Massimiliano Sforza granted Eleuterio and Galeazzo Rusca the duty revenue on notarizing civil trials in the city and Duchy of Milan, a conces-

sion registered on 15 April 1514; ASMi, Feudi Camerali—Comuni 297, fasc. 10 (Locarno). See also Motta, "I Rusca," 35.

90. ASMi, Atti di governo—Statuti (Registri Panigarola GG) 25, 18 April 1512. The battle of Ravenna took place six days earlier, on 12 April 1512.

91. ASMi, Sforzesco 628, Deputati rei pecuniarie to Massimiliano Sforza, 23 September 1513.

92. ACPv, Comune—Estimo 249, 364: deputies of the City of Pavia to Giangiacomo Trivulzio, 21 August 1516, concerning the exemption of Angela Georgia. In this case, the city rejected Georgia's exemption request; she had already paid money to the city that it could not afford to return.

93. ASMi, Miscellanea storica 6, fasc. 2 (Censo), François I to Milanese tax commission, 3 April 1519.

94. ASMi, Miscellanea storica 6, fasc. 2 (Censo), François I to Milanese tax commission, 3 April 1519. The secretary was Antonio da Rozasco. He was appointed as a secretary in Massimiliano's *consiglio segreto* on 21 April 1515 and must have found a position under the French restoration. See his 1515 appointment in ASMi, Registri ducali 66, 130v.

95. ACPv, Comune—Estimo 249, 353: Gioffredo Ferrero to the deputies of the City of Pavia, 12 November 1519.

96. Archivio di Stato di Ravenna, Corporazioni religiose, Abbazia di Sant'Apollinare in Classe 239, 42r–43v. I extend thanks to Stephen Bowd for making me aware of this document and sharing his photographs with me. See also Stephen Bowd, *Renaissance Mass Murder: Civilians and Soldiers during the Italian Wars* (Oxford: Oxford University Press, 2018), 75: "Notattj bene benche io habia facto questa notta, che non he vero quasi cossa alcuna, che in facto non hauessemo molto danno, ma quello ho facto, o facto rispectiuo, che hera stato impetracto, che noj insiema con questi altrj trj monasterij richj hauessemo a restaurare et pagar ducatj 2000 ale chiese parochialle & altre in restauratione de li suj danna."

97. Achille Ratti, "Il Secolo XVI nell'abbazia di Chiaravalle di Milano: Notizia di due altri codici manoscritti chiaravallesi," *Archivio storico lombardo* 23, ser. 3, fasc. 9 (1896): 91–161, at 103, and 104–105, n. 4.

98. ASMi, Frammenti Registri Ducali 4b, fasc. 68—Patenti, 109r.

99. Ratti, "Il Secolo XVI," 113; for the earlier complaints, see 106, 109.

100. Domenico Malipiero, *Annali Veneti dall'anno 1457 al 1500,* Francesco Longo, ed. (Florence: Gio. Pietro Vieussieux, 1843), 558; Sanudo, *Diarii,* 2: 876, 975. On modes of salt payments and compensations between Milan and Venice, see Jean-Claude Hocquet, *Le Sel et la fortune de Venise* (Lille: Presses de l'Université de Lille III, 1979), 2: 407–16.

101. Sanudo, *Diarii,* 2: 1255, 1264, 1275.

102. Sanudo, *Diarii,* 2: 1326, 3: 59, 331.

103. Sanudo, *Diarii*, 3: 385–86: "Item, li dacij fonno inchantadi; li ebbe domino Agustim Triulzi, quali li havea prima, zoè li dacij di Milan e lochi per ducati 315 milia a l'anno; di qual, ducati 260 milia dà al roy; 50 milia a pagar debiti fati per il Moro, qualli in anni XV sono pagati; il resto per spexe di dacij." I read this calculus as 50,000 per annum over fifteen years to pay off Ludovico's debts over fifteen years, which would equal about 750,000 ducats.

104. Stefano Meschini, *La Francia nel Ducato di Milano* (Milan: FrancoAngeli, 2006), 1: 152 n. 59.

105. Sanudo, *Diarii,* 5: 191–92, October 1503. The councilor is named as "Claudio Ais," whom Sanudo identifies elsewhere as "Claude Deais" (see Chapter 7, n. 96). For another appearance of this version of Seyssel's name, see Alberto Caviglia, *Claudio di Seyssel (1450–1520). La Vita nella storia de' suoi tempi* (Turin: Fratelli Bocca Librai, 1928), 88.

106. ASV, Capi del Consiglio di Dieci—Lettere di Ambasciatori 15 (Milano 1501-25): Leonardo Blanco to Leonardo Loredan, March 15 1506: "L'ordeni de Millano sono tali, che chi non sa particularmente i beni doue lsono, et li confini, non po veder la veritá á le stride, imperoche un simile ad Hier.o da Corte che voglia vender isui beni, et dubita metterli ále stride, non fa far le cride in nome suo, ma el Compratore va á certo magistrato et denota voler vender sui beni, et da in nota quella che lha comprá, et sotto specie de venderli fa far le cride, et cum tal mezo se liberan loro et gabano altri."

107. Evelyn Welch, *Shopping in the Renaissance: Consumer Cultures in Italy 1400– 1600* (New Haven, CT: Yale University Press, 2005), 187–91.

108. BnF, ms. fr. 2925, *Commission donnéé par le Roy Louis dousiesme a un conseiller de la court de parlement de paris pour aller a genes et y faire au nom dudit Roy duc de Milan et seigneur de genes les perquisitions ordonnéés par ledit Roy comme il est parti par la commission dudit seigneur a la teste de ce liure* (1509): "Hauendo inteso la mayesta del Chr.mo Re nro signore como ne la sua Riperia de Leuante del Genouesato et in le terre de dicta Riperia sono molte subditi oppressi et maltractati per el presente et per el passato cosi per Feudatarij particulari Gouernatori Potestati vicarij capitanei judici commissarij et altri offitiali li quali sotto umbra et auctorita de dicti offitij hano facto piu et diuerse abussione vendicione de justicia pigliarie extorsione in- iustitie et oppressioni et altre diuerse cose indebite con lassare etiam molti deliti impuniti," etc.

109. One example: a register of the tax office from 1492-1512 (thus covering both Ludovico Sforza's and Louis XII's reigns), now lost, survived until the eighteenth century. See Franca Leverotti, "Leggi del principe, leggi della città nel ducato Visconteo-sforzesco," in Rolando Dondarini, Gian Maria Varanini, and Maria Venticelli, eds., *Signori, regimi signorili e statuti nel tardo Medioevo* (Bologna: Pàtron, 2003), 143–88, at 174. The same sur-

vivals can be traced in many of the ducal registers (*registri ducali*) and the copy-book of Milanese edicts (*registri Panigarola*).

7. ELITE DISPLACEMENTS

1. Sanudo, *Diarii,* 3: 229; letter of podestà of Crema, 13 April 1500.

2. Marco Pellegrini, *Ascanio Maria Sforza. La Parabola politica di un cardinale-principe del rinascimento* (Rome: Istituto storico italiano per il medio evo, 2002), 2: 783; Stefano Meschini, *La Francia nel Ducato di Milano* (Milan: FrancoAngeli, 2006), 1: 148.

3. Here, Ascanio quotes from the biblical Book of Job, 1:21. Marin Sanudo, *I Diarii,* Rinaldo Fulin, ed. (Bologna: Forni, 1969-1979 [1879-1902]), 3: 244.

4. Léon-Gabriel Pélissier, *Documents pour l'histoire de la domination française dans le Milanais (1499-1513)* (Toulouse: Édouard Privat, 1891), doc. 16, 39-54.

5. Ambrogio da Paullo, *Cronaca milanese dall'anno 1476 al 1515,* Antonio Ceruti, ed. *Miscellanea di storia italiana* 13 (1871): 91-378, at 153-54; Pélissier, *Documents,* doc. 16bis, 360-66.

6. Bernardino Arluno's Milanese history written in the 1530s confirms these sites, with the addition of Ferrara: "Multi Venetorum fines ingressi, quoniam nobis hostes non erant, nec civibus infensi nostris putabantur, velut securo salubrioreque domicilio diversati sunt: nonnulli praerupta montium superantes, opacacque convallium perniciore cursu transgressi, Germanici recessus abdita penetravere: Mantuam alii, Ferrariamque plures, oras etiam nonnuli maritimas, praecipueque Ligustici maris tractus peragrantes, in alia omnia abiere" (Bernardino Arluno, *De Bello Veneto libri sex,* in J. G. Graevius, ed., *Thesaurus antiquitatum et historiarum Italiae* [Leiden: Petrus Vander, 1722], vol. 5, part 4, 1-306, at 4).

7. For legal categories of exclusion, see Fabrizio Ricciardelli, *The Politics of Exclusion in Early Renaissance Florence* (Turnhout: Brepols, 2007), esp. 7-57.

8. Sanudo, *Diarii,* 3: 1336-37: "Come è stà fato comandameto, per quelli signori francesi, a quelli zentilhomeni de lì vadino in Franza; e questo fano per rimuover tutti quelli capelazi de lì, acciò stagi seguro per queste novità; et di questo quelli milanesi non pono patir, et desiderano ogni mal, *licet* la lhoro speranza de Alemagna vadi di longo."

9. See Christine Shaw, *The Politics of Exile in Renaissance Italy* (Cambridge: Cambridge University Press, 2000); Christine Shaw, "Ce que révèle l'exil politique sur les relations entre les États italiens," *Laboratoire italien* 3 (2002): 13-32.

10. Antonio Ceruti, "Il Corredo nuziale di Bianca M. Sforza-Visconti, sposa dell'imperatore Massimiliano I," *Archivio storico lombardo,* ser. 1, vol. 2, fasc. 1 (1875): 51-75.

11. Hermann Wiesflecker, *Kaiser Maximilian I: Das Reich, Österreich und Europa an der Wende zur Neuzeit* (Vienna: Verlag für Geschichte und Politik, 1971-86), 2: 358-59.

12. Maximilian had several times in the 1490s promised military aid to Ludovico in the event of a French invasion; for the financial supports that Maximilian wanted in recompense, see Léon-Gabriel Pélissier, *L'Alliance Milano-Allemande à la fin du XVe siècle. L'Ambassade d'Herasmo Brasca à la cour de l'Empereur Maximilien (Avril–Décembre 1498)* (Turin: Imprimerie Royale de J.-B. Paravia et Comp., 1897), 16–19.

13. Sanudo, *Diarii*, 3: 176.

14. Léon-Gabriel Pélissier, *Recherches dans les archives italiennes. Louis XII et Ludovic Sforza (8 avril 1498–23 juillet 1500)* (Paris: Thorin et Fils, 1896), 2: 92.

15. Pélissier, *Recherches*, 2: 91.

16. Larry Silver, *Marketing Maximilian: The Visual Ideology of a Holy Roman Emperor* (Princeton, NJ: Princeton University Press, 2008), ix; Inge Wiesflecker-Friedhuber, "Kaiser Maximilian I. und die Stadt Innsbruck," in Heinz Noflatscher and Jan Paul Niederkorn, eds., *Der Innsbrucker Hof: Residenz und höfische Gesellschaft in Tirol vom 15. bis 19. Jahrhundert* (Vienna: Verlag der Österreichischen Akademie der Wissenschaft, 2005), 125–58.

17. Sanudo, *Diarii*, 3: 43.

18. Sanudo, *Diarii*, 3: 348; on the promise of a stipend to the Sforza children and other exiles, see 661. Sanudo reports that Maximilian had promised the ducal children 10,000 florins per annum, and "to the Milanese a thousand [florins], that is, 32 each per year until they return." That would make thirty-one people to whom he promised financial support.

19. J. F. Böhmer, *Regesta Imperii* (hereafter *RI*), vol. 14 (Maximilian I), band (hereafter bd.). 3.2, no. 14365.

20. Ermes Sforza resided in Innsbruck from 1501 until his death there in 1503. See Sabine Weiss, *Die Vergessene Kaiserin. Bianca Maria Sforza, Kaiser Maximilians zweite Gemahlin* (Innsbruck-Vienna: Tyrolia Verlag, 2010), 116, 244–47.

21. For Ermes, Galeazzo, Ottaviano, and the unmarried brothers, see *RI*, 14, bd. 3.1, no. 12443, Zaccaria Contarini to the Doge, 12 September 1501. For Lucrezia Crivelli, see Sanudo, *Diarii*, 3: 511; and for the Sanseverino and Landriano, see 1367: many of the Milanese exiles gathered in February 1501 for the imperial diet in Nuremberg.

22. Wiesflecker-Friedhuber, *Quellen*, doc. 36, "'Niederösterreichischer Vertrag' Maximilians mit Georg Gossembrot (Auszug)," 131–38.

23. Weiss, *Die Vergessene Kaiserin*, 151. An inventory around 1504 showed her household included five cooks and a servant, among them two Italians, "Maister Jacob der alt Welsch koch" and "Maiser Jacob der jüng Welsch koch" (TLA, Cod. 2470, 2, 46r). See also TLA Kunstsachen 1, 534: "Speisung unsere allerg.tn frauwen der Romischen Kunigin," which lists eighty-one people fed by Bianca Maria's household on 25 May 1501 (including a "Zwerg und Narin," the latter probably Elisa). The names listed seem not to include any Milanese refugees, who may not have been con-

sidered part of the accountable household proper. See Daniela Unterholzner, "Essensalltag bei Hof. Zum Frauenzimmer Bianca Maria Sforzas," in Noflatscher, et al., eds., *Maximilian I.,* 287–301.

24. *RI,* 14, bd. 3.1, no. 12243.

25. Wiesflecker, *Kaiser Maximilian I.,* 5: 382, attributes the phrase to Maximilian without citing a source.

26. Weiss, *Die Vergessene Kaiserin,* 262. Sanudo, *Diarii,* 3: 1367, 1374, suggests the boys were on their way to live in Vienna.

27. *RI,* 14, bd. 4.1, no. 16274, Maximilian to Konrad Peutinger, 23 March 1502. Massimiliano Sforza addressed a number of letters to Isabella d'Este from Regensburg between 23 April 1502 and 6 October 1503, in ASMn, AG 1616.

28. *RI,* 14, bd. 4.1, no. 16275, Maximilian to Sigmund von Rohrbach, 23 March 1502.

29. *RI,* 14, bd. 4.1, no. 18848, Francesco Capello to Doge Leonardo Loredan, 9 June 1504.

30. Maximilian referred to Massimiliano in a couple of letters to his daughter: first, asking her and her treasurers to give him a one-time stipend increase because his income was insufficient, and second, asking her to mediate a precedence dispute between Massimiliano and the young Duke of "Zaxssen." See André Joseph Ghislain Le Glay, ed., *Correspondance de l'empereur Maximilien Ier et de Marguerite d'Autriche* (Paris: Jules Renouard, 1839), 1: 197–98, letter 148, Maximilian to Margaret, 13 October 1509, and 460–61, letter 346, Maximilian to Margaret, 16 December 1511.

31. Weiss, *Die Vergessene Kaiserin,* 270.

32. Theodor H. Musper, ed., *Kaiser Maximilians I. Weißkunig* (Stuttgart: Kohlhammer, 1956), 1: 438; Silver, *Marketing Maximilian,* 38.

33. *RI,* 14, bd. 4.1, no. 17540, Maximilian to his tailor, Martin Trumer, 25 August 1503.

34. *RI,* 14, bd. 4.1, no. 15976, Zaccaria Contarini to the Venetian Signoria, 29 January 1502. See also Francesco Guicciardini, "Storia Fiorentina," in Canestrini, ed., *Opere Inedite,* chapter 23, 3: 249.

35. Weiss, *Die Vergessene Kaiserin,* 247.

36. Sanudo, *Diarii,* 3: 715. "Si dice è una gran massa de intrigati."

37. On the Ottoman embassy, see Franz Babinger, "Zwei diplomatische Zwischenspiele im deutsch-osmanischen Staatsverkehr unter Bâjezîd II. (1497 und 1504)," in Fritz Meier, ed., *Westöstliche Abhandlungen: Rudolf Tschudi zum siebzigsten Geburtstag überreicht von Freunden und Schülern* (Wiesbaden: Otto Harrassowitz, 1954), 315–30, at 328–30; Pietro Bembo, *History of Venice,* Robert W. Ulery Jr., ed. and trans. (Cambridge, MA: Harvard University Press, 2007–2009), 3: 263.

38. Ludovico asked his agent Agostino Somenzo at the imperial court "che tu preghi la predicta Maesta [Maximilian] ad esser contenta de non farne

più parlare de luy [Fracasso], perche li deportamenti soi cum nuy ricercano che più non se impazamo de facti soi" (Léon-Gabriel Pélissier, *Documents relatifs au règne de Louis XII et à sa politique en Italie* [Montpellier: Imprimerie Générale du Midi, 1912], doc. 36, 228, 24 June 1499). For Fracasso's 1498 mission, see Walter Höflechner, *Die Gesandten der europäischen Mächte, vornehmlich des Kaisers und des Reiches* (Vienna: Hermann Böhlaus Nachfolge, 1972), 260; *RI*, 14, bd. 4.1, no. 16594, Maximilian to Gonfaloniere of Justice in Florence, 12 June 1502.

39. Sanudo, *Diarii*, 1: 921; *RI*, 14, bd. 4.1, no. 16477. See Pierre Terjanian, ed., *The Last Knight: The Art, Armor, and Ambition of Maximilan I* (New York: Metropolitan Museum of Art, 2019), cat. 38, 116–19. Fracasso's armor is in Vienna, Hofjagd- und Rüstkammer, Inv.-Nr. S I (B 2). Maximilian may also have acquired Ludovico il Moro's armor, now lost, which was listed in the early catalogs of the armory of the Archduke of Tyrol in the late sixteenth century. For references to both Ludovico's and Fracasso's armors in the 1583 inventory, see Laurin Luchner, *Denkmal eines Renaissancefürsten. Versuch einer Reconstruktion des Ambraser Museums von 1583* (Vienna: Verlag Anton Schroll & Co., 1958), 19–20.

40. Francesca de Gramatica, "La Sepoltura 'honoratissima' di Roberto da Sanseverino," in Franco Marzatico and Johannes Ramharter, eds., *I Cavalieri dell'Imperatore. Tornei, battaglie e castelli* (Trent: Castello del Buonconsiglio, 2012), 237–46, at 239. Roberto's armor is in Vienna, Hofjagd- und Rüstkammer, Inv.-Nr. A 3.

41. On the return of several high-ranking Sforza supporters to Milan in 1501, see Sanudo, *Diarii*, 4: 136. These included Giovanni Antonio della Somaglia, Sigerio and Federico Gallerani, Giovanni Francesco Marliani, and others. On Barbara Stampa, see ASMn, AG 1616, Massimiliano Sforza to Francesco Gonzaga, 10 December 1512; she is also listed as the recipient of a gift, presumably in Innsbruck, from Bianca Maria Sforza of a "turcheta di damasco donata a madonna barbara di stampy fatta a 26 di mazo 1502" (TLA Inventar A 1/2, Ausstattungs-Inventar der Bianca Maria Sforza [1493-1508], 22r); and further gifts in April 1502 (23r) and April 1504 (27r).

42. Ernst Gagliardi, *Der Anteil der Schweizer an den italienischen Kriegen, 1494–1516* (Zurich: Verlag von Schulthess & Co., 1919), 315–20, 353–58, 409–10; Höflechner, *Die Gesandten,* 273–75. One of Galeazzo's letters appears in Pélissier, *Documents relatifs,* doc. 28, Galeazzo Visconti in Bern to Ludovico Sforza in Milan, 29 June 1499, 186–89.

43. Sanudo, *Diarii*, 3: 318, 507. Instead, he was seen by Cardinal Amboise. See also his appearance in Milan a month later with Chaumont; Visconti "fo a'sguizari per il Moro, per darli [i.e., Chaumont] information di le cosse di Lombardia."

44. Carcano had served in this capacity since at least the 1480s. Pio Bondioli, "Un Miniatore lombardo ignorato: Pietro Carcano," *La Bibliofilía* 59, no. 1 (1957): 15–22, at 19.

45. Stefano Meschini, *Luigi XII, Duca di Milano. Gli Uomini e le istituzioni del primo dominio francese (1499–1512)* (Milan: FrancoAngeli, 2004), 414–23, see especially his claim on 420, n. 430, that "le cose nostre in questa terra sono in meliori termini non se crede et che non se lassaremo più mangiar ne devorare: io ho levato la cresta et tutti li gebellini et tutti se reducerano a me et etiam qualche guelfi et spero che tutto andara bene."

46. Sanudo, *Diarii,* 3: 515. In July 1500, his goods were returned *"excepto* li feudi, con termine do mexi a star a Milan; tamen la terra non l'à visto volentieri, per esser fato francese." For his partisanship for Massimiliano, see Franceso Guicciardini, *Storia d'Italia,* Silvana Seidel Menchi, ed. (Turin: Einaudi, 1971) (XII.xvi) 2: 1254; on his service with the Milanese-Swiss forces that fought at Marignano against France, see Visconti's letter to King Henry VIII in Pio Bondioli, "La Battaglia di Marignano in una relazione a Enrico VIII d'Inghilterra," *Scritti storici in memoria di Alessandro Visconti* (Milan: Istituto Editoriale Cisalpino, 1955), 169–85.

47. Anne-Marie Lecoq, "Une Fête italienne à la Bastille en 1518," in Giuliano Briganti, ed., *'Il se rendit en Italie': Études offertes à André Chastel* (Paris: Elefante, 1987), 149–68, at 150, 158. For his arrival in Paris with forty Milanese fuorusciti in January 1517, see Sanudo, *Diarii,* 23: 460.

48. John Gagné, "Collecting Women: Three French Kings and Manuscripts of Empire in the Italian Wars," *I Tatti Studies in the Italian Renaissance* 20, no. 1 (2017): 127–84, at 174–77. Some scholars name Clara as daughter of Guido Visconti, but Guido was more likely her grandfather. See the biography of Galeazzo in Giuseppe Volpi, *Istoria de' Visconti* (Naples: Mosca, 1748), 2: 256–64, and specifically 263 for the allusion to Clara and her sister, Veronica Borromeo.

49. Inge Wiesflecker-Friedhuber, ed., *Quellen,* 243, citing Paolo Giovio, *Historiarum sui temporis libri 45* (Basel, 1559–61), bk. 16, 758–71.

50. Giovanni Andrea Prato, *Storia di Milano,* Cesare Cantù, ed., *Archivio storico italiano* 3 (1842): 216–418, at 354; Stefano Meschini, *La Seconda dominazione francese nel Ducato di Milano. La Politica e gli uomini di Francesco I (1515–1521)* (Varzi: Guardamagna Editore, 2014), 52–53, 56. On Galeazzo's pardon and reintegration in December 1516, see Sanudo, *Diarii,* 23: 281.

51. ASMn, AG 2996, copialettere 30, 31v, Isabella d'Este to Galeazzo Pallavicino, 10 August 1512. Galeazzo had collaborated with the French and was thus probably exiled by Massimiliano's government in June or July. He sent Isabella a service of silver plates. She wrote: "De la offerta ni fa de li altri pezi, et max.e di q.l de oro ringra.mo v.s. et congratulamone che la sij cossi ricco forauscito."

52. Antonio Grumello, *Cronaca di Antonio Grumello, Pavese,* Giuseppe Müller, ed. (Milan: Francesco Colombo Librajo-Editore, 1856), 56.

53. Meschini, *La Francia nel Ducato,* 1: 152, n. 61, Giovanni Giorgio Seregno in Pavia to Ercole d'Este in Ferrara, 9 June 1500.

54. Meschini, *La Francia nel Ducato,* I: 152–53; *RI,* 14, bd. 4.3.1, no. 10495, Maximilian to Galeazzo Sanseverino, 9 July 1500, from Augsburg. In January 1501, one of Sanseverino's agents called "el Cingano" had been in Puglia to purchase five horses for him and had delivered them to a location near Mantua; Sanudo, *Diarii,* 3: 1329–30.

55. BMV, MS Italiano VII 990 (=9582), 23v. Galeazzo is mentioned in the company of the Spanish orator in Innsbruck in a letter of Zaccaria Contarini to the Venetian doge, 20 September 1501.

56. Emil Reicke, ed., *Willibald Pirckheimers Briefwechsel* (Munich: Beck, 1940–2009), 1: 124–25, doc. 41, Galeazzo Sanseverino to Wilibald Pirckheimer, 26 July 1501. On the wider context of this link in Milan-Nuremberg relations, see Hermann Kellenbenz, "Augsburg, Nürnberg und Mailand in der Zeit von Ludovico il Moro," in *Milano nell'età di Ludovico,* 1: 67–78, at 75–76.

57. Kurt Löcher, *Die Gemälde des 16. Jahrhunderts: Germanisches Nationalmuseum Nürnberg* (Stuttgart: Verlag Gerd Hatje, 1997), 346–47.

58. See Hans Rupprich, *Wilibald Pirckheimer und die erste Reise Dürers nach Italien* (Vienna: Verlag von Anton Schroll & Co., 1930), 21–24; Franz Winziger, "Dürer und Leonardo," *Pantheon* 29 (1971): 3–21; Giovanni Maria Fara, "Dürer, Leonardo, e la storia dell'arte," in Bernard Aikema and Andrew John Martin, eds., *Dürer e il Rinascimento tra Germania e Italia* (Milan: 24 Ore Cultura, 2018), 81–93, at 86.

59. TLA Inventar A 1/2, 26r: "Vesta di panno contrastino(?) donata Joambrosyo preda da milano 27 di mazo 1504."

60. More on Preda's career appears in Janice Shell, "Ambrogio de Predis," in *The Legacy of Leonardo: Painters in Lombardy 1490–1530* (Milan: Skira, 1998), 123–30.

61. Hermann Wiesflecker, *Österreich im Zeitalter Maximilians I. Der Vereinigung der Länder zum frühmodernen Staat* (Munich: Oldenbourgh, 1999), 369. Maximilian met Georges d'Amboise in Trent for these talks.

62. *RI,* 14, bd. 4.1, no. 16154, Zaccaria Contarini to the Venetian Signoria, 4 March 1502 in Innsbruck.

63. Repatriation had been central to Milanese concerns up to this point. See the observations of the Venetian envoys to Maximilian in 1500: *RI,* 14, bd. 3.2, no. 14336.

64. AnF J 507, n. 31; Meschini, *La Francia nel Ducato,* 1: 334–45.

65. Dietmar Heil, ed., *Deutsche Reichstagsakten unter Maximilian I. (DR)—Achter Band: Das Reichstag zu Köln 1505, teil 1* (Munich: R. Oldenbourg Verlag, 2008), 222–26, Francesco Capello to the Venetian Signoria, 25 June 1505 from Cologne.

66. See Louis XII's order of remission and forgiveness to the city of Pavia (including the return of exiles), dated July 1500, in Pélissier, *Documents relatifs,* doc. 17, 104–06.

67. Pélissier, *Documents,* no. 16, 44.

68. *RI,* 14, bd. 3.1, no. 12484, Zaccaria Contarini to the doge, 19 September 1501, from Innsbruck.

69. Filippo Crucitti, "Landriani, Gerolamo," *Dizionario biografico degli Italiani* 63 (2004): 523–26.

70. Pélissier, *Documents,* doc. 15, 34–39; see the extensive affiliated documents cited in the notes of Meschini, *La Francia nel Ducato di Milano,* 1: 167–72.

71. *RI,* 14, bd. 4.1, no. 15849, Maximilian to Georges d'Amboise, 3 January 1502, in Halle.

72. Pélissier, *Documents,* doc. 16, 39–54, at 39–40. Louis gave Sanseverino's lands away to Ligny, Sampré, and Misocco. For the Cusago gift, see AnF J 507, n. 29. Galeazzo Sanseverino acknowledges receipt of lands of Cusago, 14 December 1506, at Blois.

73. Francesco Somaini, "Le Famiglie milanesi tra gli Sforza e i francesi: Il Caso degli Arcimboldi," in Arcangeli, ed., *Milano e Luigi XII,* 167–220, at 204.

74. On Bianca Maria's death, see Weiss, *Die Vergessene Kaiserin,* 179–86.

75. Sanudo *Diarii,* 22: 128, 24: 356, 28: 522; Gerhard Rill, "Cles, Bernardo," *Dizionario biografico degli Italiani* 26 (1982): 406–12; Renato Tisot, *Ricerche sulla vita e sull'epistolario del Cardinale Bernardo Cles (1485–1539)* (Trent: Società studi trentini di scienze storiche, 1969), docs. 1–9, 165–67, letters from 15 January 1518 to 31 March 1519. See also Giacomo Giudici, "The Writing of Renaissance Politics: Sharing, Appropriating, and Asserting Authorship in the Letters of Francesco II Sforza, Duke of Milan (1522–1535)," *Renaissance Studies* 32, no. 2 (2018): 253–81.

76. Léon-Gabriel Pélissier, *La Politique du marquis de Mantoue pendant la lutte de Louis XII et de Ludovic Sforza, 1498–1500* (Le Puy: Imprimerie Marchessou Fils, 1892), 37.

77. The alliance faltered temporarily as Gonzaga seemed to drift into adherence with Venice. The details are recounted in Pélissier, *La Politique du marquis de Mantoue,* 8, 25–27, 32–34.

78. Pélissier, *La Politique du marquis de Mantoue,* 63–64.

79. For the condotta granted to Francesco, see Laurent Vissière, "Une Amitié hasardeuse: Louis II de la Trémoille et le marquis de Mantoue," in Contamine and Guillaume, eds., *Louis XII en Milanais,* 149–71, at 153; for Gonzaga's fears of his position, see *RI,* 14, bd. 3.2, no. 14063, Francesco Gonzaga to Maximilian, 22 April 1500, from Mantua. For Maximilian's threat about the Mantuan fief, see *RI,* 14, bd. 2, no. 6774, Maximilian to Francesco Gonzaga, 12 November 1498, from Sittard. Pélissier, *La Politique du marquis de Mantoue,* 35–116, narrates and documents the affair from 1498 until late 1500.

80. Sanudo, *Diarii*, 3: 240–41 (April 1500), 3: 369 (early June 1500), 376 (Letter of vicedomino of Ferrara, 5 June 1500).

81. Wiesflecker-Friedhuber, *Quellen*, doc. 33: "Instruktion Maximilians für seinen Statthalter beim Nürnberg Reichsregiment, den Kurfürsten Friedrich von Sachsen [25 August 1501]," 119–26, at 124. Article 11: "Auch haben des kunigs von Franckreich hawptlewt versucht, mit verheyssung grosser provision den marggraven von Mantua zu inen zu ziehen, hoffend und begerend, sein landt auch zu haben und das nach irem willen zu gebrauchen, andere Welische land dadurch zu bezwyngen, in also zu wenden und heben von dem alten schirm und gehorsam des Romischen kunigs und des heiligen reichs, darinn die vorfarn des gemelten marggraven bisher unczerprochenlich beliben sein."

82. Mario Equicola, *Chronica di Mantva*, (Mantua: Francesco Bruschi, 1521), sig. V vi^v: "Poi che la fortuna in potesta del inimico redusse pregione Ludouico Sforza Duca di Milano per diuerse uie, la magior parte de nobili capitanii & signori li quali in tanto naufragio non somerse la horribil tempesta in Mantua fu acceptata & con spesa largamente honorata: Era per tema del Irato Vincitore chiusali Italia tutta: Era parato il magnanimo Marchese sostenere il Danno che di cio aduenire ne potesse per non mancare al debito che a nobili se deue & per non uenir meno al officio de liberalita."

83. Pélissier, *La Politique du marquis de Mantoue*, 75; Meschini, *Luigi XII*, 119.

84. Léon-Gabriel Pélissier, *Documents sur les relations de Louis XII, de Ludovic Sforza et du Marquis de Mantoue de 1498 à 1500, tirés des archives de Mantoue, Modène, Milan et Venise* (Paris: E. Leroux, 1894), doc. 68, 92–93. The Gonzaga archive also houses letters to Francesco from Georges d'Amboise making similar demands: ASMn, AG 1634, Georges d'Amboise to Francesco Gonzaga, 25 and 26 April 1500, from Milan.

85. ASMn, AG 1634, Georges d'Amboise to Francesco Gonzaga, 25 and 26 April 1500, from Milan. All nine names: Blasinus Crivellus, Christoforus de Calabria (another of Ludovico's captains), Marcus Antonius de la Vella, Anthonius Crivellus, Bernardus de Caruciis, duo fratres Sigei Gallerani, frater comitis Ludovici de Rosano D. Bernardus de Anguisolis, Bernardinus (a captain). For Leonardo's note about the wife of Biagino Crivelli, see Irma A. Richter, trans., and Thereza Wells and Martin Kemp, eds., *Leonardo da Vinci, Notebooks* (New York: Oxford University Press, 2008), 346; and for the tale of Crivelli's crime, see Matteo Bandello, *Tutte le opere*, Francesco Flora, ed. (Verona: Mondadori, 1966) (*Novelle: III.xxvi*) 2: 397–99.

86. ASMn, AG 1634, Francesco Malatesta to Francesco Gonzaga, 26 December 1500, from Milan: "Et ben che la s.v. per la prudentia sua non habia bisogno de rechordo alchuno, tamen io fidelmente parlando li rechordo che francesi sono in possessione de italia: & aconseruar el stato de mantua bisogna intendersi con chi possede milano."

87. ASMn, AG 1634, Francesco Malatesta to Francesco Gonzaga—postscript—probably to letter in note above: "Et non saria for di proposito che quelli che desiderano star lj in mantua cerchaseno per qualche uia de farsj aconzar lo suo saluo conducto che poteseno star in lo teritorio de mantua: & se pur la s.v. uol compiacer aqualche uno, fazalo star oculto: per che questi quj hanno zente che li hauisano cio che se fa la: & se la s.v. fa uno pocho de mostra ghagliarda: se pora poj con piu facilita obtegnir ognj chosa."

88. ASMn, AG 1634, Pierre de Sacierges to Francesco Gonzaga, 4 July 1500, from Milan: "Nunc autem ad praefate maiestatem aures delatum est, nonnullos ex dictis rebellibus et alios plerosque qui arma hostilia contra suam Maiestatem pro prefato domino Ludovico nuperrime sumpserunt apud Ex. v. non occulte quidem sed aperte agere multaque in suae maiestatis statum machinari et publice predicare, quod a fidem et amiciciam prelibate Ex. vre in maiestatem suam maxime alienum putat." The phrase "non occulte quidem sed aperte" echoes Bartolo da Sassoferrato's definition of rebellion as "aliquid publice vel occulte machinantur contra principem vel eius officiales." See his *Tractatus de tyranno,* in Diego Quaglioni, ed., *Politica e diritto nel trecento italiano: il 'De tyranno' di Bartolo da Sassoferrato* (Florence: Olschki, 1983), 203–4.

89. Sanudo, *Diarii,* 3: 529, Veronese rectors to Venetian Signoria, 20 July 1500, from Verona.

90. Sanudo, *Diarii,* 3: 529.

91. ASMn, AG 1634, Sigismondo Gonzaga to Francesco Gonzaga, 15 May 1500, from Pavia: "Cum uno gentil atto me prese per mano." On the friendship between Trémoille and Francesco Gonzaga, see Vissière, "Une Amitié hasardeuse."

92. ASMn, AG 1634, Sigismondo Gonzaga to Francesco Gonzaga, 15 May 1500.

93. ASMn, AG 1634, Francesco Malatesta to Francesco Gonzaga, 1 January 1501, from Milan. This passage has also been transcribed in Meschini, *La Francia nel Ducato,* 1: 175, n. 135: "El prefato monsignor [Luçon] per niente non uole acceptar quella parte de lj rebellj: dicendo che ben che habiano pagata la taglia & che habiano lj saluiconducti che *tam aduch restant rebelles m.tis regie* & che questa resone che aduce la s.v. e demostrativa de lo animo de la s.v. per che pare che quella uoglia torre la protectione de lj inimicj del re: per che se bene hanno pagata la taglia sono pero inimicj del re: & se hanno el saluo conducto: per che non stanno achasa sue doue hanno le faculta e mogliere e figliolj: & dice el prefato monsignor che se hanno el saluo conducto non lo hanno de poter star a mantua & che tutta italia li refuta: & sola mantua lj fauorisse: & che se la s.v. uol chel se dicha che la sia amicha del re che la anulla & schomiza e schanzella questa fama che resona in le orechie de ogniuno & per tutto Milano che

la s.v. fauorisse lj rebellj del re: & che la comencj da questo capo che la faza
far uno bando che lj rebelj de la m.ta del re non possano star nel dominio
de la s.v. & che quando qualche uno ge ne capitasse per le manj che la ge
lo mandj: che aquesto modo la extirpara le radice de quellj che dichono
mal de la s.v. & dimostrara de esser amicha del re: Aquesto resonamento
ge e interuenuto el general de sauoia e m.r Claudio & duj altri francesj."

94. On Luçon's position in the French government in the 1480s and '90s, see
Meschini, *Luigi XII,* 117–19; on the *guerre folle* and Louis XII's treason, see
Simon Hirsch Cuttler, *The Law of Treason and Treason Trials in Later Medi-
eval France* (Cambridge: Cambridge University Press, 1978), 234–37; and
also Nicole Hochner, *Louis XII. Les Déréglements de l'image royal (1498–1515)*
(Seyssel: ChampVallon, 2006), 37–39.

95. Frederic J. Baumgartner, *Louis XII* (New York: St. Martin's Press, 1994),
136–39.

96. Malatesta identifies him as "messer Claudio," referred to elsewhere as
"Claude Deais" (Claude de Aix—Seyssel's birthplace), whom Sanudo calls,
along with Michele Rizzo, a royal counselor. See Sanudo, *Diarii,* 3: 1282.

97. BnF, ms. Dupuy 558, 17r–37r.

98. ASMn, AG 1634, 14 September 1501, il Ghivizzano to Francesco Gonzaga,
from Milan. The men were Guido Torello, Oldrado Lampugnano, Gaspar
da Lochio, Christoforo da Calabria, and Biagino [Crivelli?]; the latter was
thought to be falsifying coin.

99. Sanudo, *Diarii,* 3: 1637; Meschini, *Luigi XII,* 123–24.

100. See the letter of Isabella d'Este to Jacopo Suardo of 28 March 1510, in
which Chaumont d'Amboise makes it clear to Isabella that she should
"not let anyone from the duchy of Milano who is headed for Venetian territory pass through our dominion, even if they have written permission
signed by His Lordship" (Isabella d'Este, *Selected Letters,* Deanna Shemek,
ed. and trans. [Toronto-Tempe: Iter Press and Arizona Center for Medieval and Renaissance Studies, 2017], letter 434, at 322).

101. Sanudo, *Diarii,* 20: 237.

102. Bandello, *Tutte le opere* (*Novelle: I.xiv*), 1: 264–380, at 264. Following the
French victory at Marignano, Trivulzio expelled the Ghibellines: "Il perché
in quei dì ai fuoruscti di Lombardia fu la città di Mantova sicurissimo
porto e refugio certo, ove il signor Francesco Gonzaga marchese, uomo
liberalissimo, assai ne raccolse."

103. For a comparative analysis, see John Easton Law, "Un Confronto fra due
stati 'rinascimentali': Venezia e il dominio sforzesco," in *Gli Sforza a Milano,* 397–413.

104. Sanudo, *Diarii,* 3: 857: "optima amicitia"; and 607: "Et l'orator ait: inter
duas molas se ritrova il roy, zoè tra il papa e la Signoria. Et cussì si partì."

105. We learn this in a letter of Zaccaria Contarini to the Venetian Signoria,
18 October 1501, BMV, MS Italiano VII 990 (=9582), 39r–40v, at 40r. Con-

tarini says, regarding the dogal policy, that he answered Maximilian "che lera molti mesi che el X.mo Re et la S.ta vra haueua facto uno Decreto Generale, che tuti li banditi del stato de Milan [. . .] se intendesseno etiam banditi del stato de la S.ta vra."

106. BMV, MS Italiano VII 990 (=9582), 42r-v. Zaccaria Contarini to the Venetian Signoria, 19 October 1501. Maximilian had first promised a list of specific individuals, but he now wanted "el saluo conducto generale del tuti li bandizati de el stato de milano, per la Rebelion de S.or Ludouico."

107. Prato, *Storia*, 252. He notes specifically that the men were handed over "rotto ogni salvo conducto."

108. Sanudo, *Diarii*, 3: 658.

109. ASV, Capi del Consiglio di Dieci—Lettere di Rettori e di Altre Cariche, 72bis, 57: "Exemplum ex constituto suis dicto ad torturam Orlandi in Zampetrj di Capelli de Sto. Columbano, die xviij febr.ij 1502 [*more veneto*, i.e., 1503]." "Et dixit: Signorj, mettime zoso chio ue diro la uerita cose che ue piasera."

110. ASV, Capi del Consiglio di Dieci—Lettere di Rettori e di Altre Cariche, 72bis, 56. This folio is the Cremonese rectors' letter to the Ten with a summary of their entire findings from the interrogation.

111. ASV, Capi del Consiglio di Dieci—Lettere di Rettori e di Altre Cariche, 72bis, 57. The agent crossing the Alps was a man named Pollo Guerra da Voghera.

112. Sanudo, *Diarii*, 4: 869.

113. *RI*, 14, bd. 4.1, no. 16513, Zaccaria Contarini to the Venetian Signoria, 24 May 1502, from Augsburg.

114. Gerhard Rill, "Borgo, Andrea," *Dizionario biografico degli Italiani* 12 (1970): 749–53; he was Bianca Maria Sforza's secretary in 1504. Weiss, *Die Vergessene Kaiserin*, 148.

115. Sanudo, *Diarii*, 3: 273, Alvise di Piero to Cristoforo Moro, 26 April 1500, from Bergamo.

116. Sanudo, *Diarii*, 3: 423.

117. Sanudo, *Diarii*, 3: 737, Vicenzo Guidoto to Signoria, 2 September 1500, from Milan.

118. Sanudo, *Diarii*, 3: 588.

119. Sanudo, *Diarii* 3: 221, Bergamo's rectors to the Signoria, 11 April 1500, from Bergamo.

120. The castellan of Trezzo was Hieronimo da Melzo. See Sanudo, *Diarii*, 3: 226–27, 506, 547, 592, 653–54, 665–66, 684, 754. Trezzo marked the border between the two powers, meaning the castellan's position was delicately divided. He owned lands in Venetian territory, which may explain Venice's jurisdiction over his case. The French had already confiscated his goods because he was a staunch Sforzesco; yet unwilling to see them revert to Venice, they advocated for him.

121. One instance of negotiation between France and Venice over lands can be found in Sanudo, *Diarii*, 3: 246. For this particular episode between Luçon and the secretary, see 665-66, Venetian secretary to Signoria, 20 August 1500, from Milan: "Le cosse di Veniexia si governa per leze." A similar dispute occurred between Ludovico and Venice in 1495 according to Corio, who noted Ludovico's amazement that the Venetians "non volevano procedere al fatto d'arme se prima non era consultato con il senato suo" (Bernardino Corio, *Storia di Milano,* Anna Morisi Guerra, ed. [Turin: Unione Tipografico-Editrice Torinese, 1978], 2: 1598).

122. Claude de Seyssel, "L'Exellence & la Felicité de la Victoire que eut le Treschrestien Roy de France, LOVYS XII, de ce nom, dict Pere du peuple, contre les Venitiens, au lieu appellee Aignadel," in Théodore de Godefroy, *Histoire de Louis XII* (Paris: Abraham Pacard, 1615), 241-336, at 256.

123. Seyssel, "L'Exellence," 257.

124. This evidence comes from the second Sforza restoration. Girolamo Morone to Milan's ducal Conservatori, 2 September 1513. Giuseppe Müller, ed., *Documenti che concernono la vita pubblica di Gerolamo Morone* (Turin: Stamperia Reale, 1865), doc. 46, 87-88. Border raids were a common complaint of exiles; See Shaw, *The Politics of Exile,* 164.

125. Letizia Arcangeli, "La Città nelle guerre d'Italia (1494-1535)," in Giorgio Chittolini, ed., *Storia di Cremona—Il Quattrocento: Cremona nel Ducato di Milano (1395–1535)* (Cremona: Bolis Edizioni, 2008), 40-63.

126. Francesco Robolotti, ed., "Cronaca di Cremona dal MCDXCIV al MDXXV," *Bibliotheca Historica Italica* (Milan: Brigola Bibliopola, 1876), 189-276, at 218: "In dicto anno [1513] per la venuta del dicto duca de Milano se faceva de grandi homicidii perchè non ge era rasone in Cremona."

127. ASMi, Sforzesco 1357, Bernardinus ex Comitibus Patavii in Cremona to Massimiliano Sforza and Andrea Borgo in Milan, 18 July 1513.

128. ASMi, Sforzesco 1357, Bernardinus ex Comitibus Patavii in Cremona to Massimiliano Sforza, 27 August 1513.

129. ASMi, Sforzesco 1357, Piermartire Stampa in Cremona to Massimiliano Sforza, 29 July 1514: "Ill.mo s.re mio, questi sono cose de mala natura, et che mettano questi gentilhomini et citadini in mala dispositione et descontenteza danimo, parendoli che questi siano de li andamenti de Gabrino Fondulo che se insignori di questa cita." On Fondulo, see Nadia Covini, "Fondulo, Cabrino," *Dizionario biografico degli Italiani* 48 (1997): 586-89.

130. Sanudo, *Diarii*, 20: 87; 21: 38; 22: 107-08.

131. Guicciardini, *Storia d'Italia* (XIV.vi) 3: 1423.

132. Meschini, *La Seconda dominazione,* 165; Arcangeli, "La Città durante le guerre d'Italia," 56.

133. Pusterla, Massimiliano Sforza's governor of Como, was exiled in both 1515 and 1521: the miraculous escape could attach to either year. On his readmission in 1516, see Gino Franceschini, "Le Dominazioni francesi," in *Storia di Milano VIII: Tra Francia e Spagna (1500–1530),* 82–333 (Milan: Fondazione Treccani degli Alfieri, 1957), 212, and for his 1521 exile, see Meschini, *La Seconda dominazione,* 165, n. 102. If we take the palm in Brugora's hand as a sign of posthumous veneration, the panel would be dated sometime after 1529. On Brugora, see Giovanna della Croce, "Maria Caterina Brugora (1489–1529) una mistica milanese sconosciuta," *Mediaevistik* 7 (1994): 71–91; and on the panel, see Miklós Boskovits and Giorgio Fossaluzza, eds., *La Collezione Cagnola* (Busto Arsizio: Nomos Edizioni, 1998), 1: 174–75.

134. For the diplomatic background focusing on the French ambassador in Venice, see Jean de Pins, "Autour des Guerres d'Italie," *Revue d'histoire diplomatique* 61 (1947): 215–46; and 62 (1948): 88–113.

135. BnF, ms. fr. 2992, 15r–16v, Thomas de Foix outside Reggio Emilia to François I, 25 June 1521: "Sire a ceste heure ay eu aduis quilz ont mis secretement dedans cremonne quatre ou cinq cens hommes, et y sont entrez desguisez et vestuz en paysans faignans y aller vendres des uiures et auecques le nombre de gens de cheual quilz on, sont deliberez de mectre ceste nuyt leur entreprinse a execucion."

136. Antonio Campi, *Cremona Fedelissima Città* (Milan: Filippo Ghisolfi, 1645), bk 3, 14; Robolotti, ed., "Cronaca di Cremona," 240, 242, 246.

137. Biblioteca statale di Cremona, MS. Bib. Gov. 264, Domenico Bordigallo, *Cronaca,* 326r.

138. Müller, ed., *Morone,* doc. 32, 53–55, Andrea Borgo to Massimiliano Sforza, 15 June 1513.

139. BnF, ms. fr. 2978, 84r, Lautrec in Cremona to François I, 5 January 1522.

140. Séverin Duc, "Il Prezzo delle guerre lombarde. Rovina dello stato, distruzione della ricchezza e disastro sociale (1515–1535)," *Storia economica* 19 (2016): 219–48, at 226.

141. Meschini, *La Seconda dominazione,* 135–41, offers an overview.

142. For the French kings' healing in Italy, see Noémi Rubello, "Una Bella et caritativa cosa. Épisodes de thaumaturgie royale pendant la période des guerres d'Italie," *Le Moyen Âge* 120, no.1 (2014): 53–77.

143. On the 1502 amnesty, see Meschini, *La Francia nel Ducato,* 1: 246–29; for 1511 see Pélissier, *Documents,* doc. 91, 266–68.

144. Prato, *Storia,* 397–401, royal remission dated the penultimate day of November 1516, and listing the chief nobles forgiven; see also the extensions and clarifications in ASMi, Sforzesco 1499, 13 February 1517 and 17 April 1517; Sanudo, *Diarii,* 23: 284.

145. Müller, ed., *Morone,* doc. 134, 263–64, 6 January 1522: "Gratie tempore gallorum facte sine pace sub pretextu, quod occidissent bannitos, non valent."

146. Müller, ed., *Morone,* doc. 150, 286–87, 6 and 7 March 1522.

147. Emperor Charles V issued an edict of forgiveness on 9 December 1529 to all *banniti* who had agitated against Spanish and imperial governance. Marco Formentini, *Il ducato di Milano. Studi storici documentati* (Milan: Libreria Editrice G. Brignola, 1877), doc. 85, 491–95.

8. HOLY SOVEREIGNTIES

1. Girolamo Savonarola, "Psalms, Sermon III," in Anne Borelli and Maria Pastore Passaro, eds. and trans., *Selected Writings of Girolamo Savonarola* (New Haven, CT: Yale University Press, 2006), 59–76, at 69, 74.

2. Silvio Biancardi, *La Chimera di Carlo VIII (1492–1495)* (Novara: Interlinea Edizioni, 2011), 459, 495.

3. Giovanni Andrea Prato, *Storia di Milano,* Cesare Cantù, ed., *Archivio storico italiano* 3 (1842): 216–418, at 251.

4. Jean-Marie Le Gall has recently advanced an entirely religious reading of the Italian Wars: Jean-Marie Le Gall, *Les Guerres d'Italie (1494–1559). Une lecture religieuse* (Geneva: Droz, 2017).

5. A survey around 1500 numbered Milan's religious institutions at around 235. BAM MS H 87 sup., 45r–49r, published in Guglielmo Beretta, *Elenco delle Parrocchie, Chiese, Abbazie, Conventi, Monasteri, e Ospedali verso la fine del XV secolo* (Milano: Scuola Tipografia Artigianelli, 1939). There were fifteen Milanese Augustinian communities: one house of Canons Regular, four houses of Conventuals (three of which were female), and nine houses of Observants (seven of which were female)—including the Incoronata and Santa Marta, to be discussed later. See also Mario Sensi, "Osservanza agostiniana. Origini e sviluppi," in Alessandra Bartolomei Romagnoli, Emore Paoli, and Pierantonio Piatti, eds., *Angeliche visioni. Veronica da Binasco nella Milano del Rinascimento* (Florence: Edizioni del Galluzzo, 2016), 71–139.

6. Maria Luisa Gatti Perer, *"Umanesimo a Milano: L'Osservanza Agostiniana all'Incoronata,"* special monographic issue of *Arte Lombarda* n.s. 53 / 54 (1980): 3–141, at 3–6; Federico Gallo, "L'Osservanza agostiniana a Milano nel secolo XV: Il Convento di S. Maria Incoronata," in Bartolomei Romagnoli, Paoli, and Piatti, eds., *Angeliche visioni,* 141–72. On text production at the Incoronata, see Mirella Ferrari, "Per la fioritura di S. Ambrogio nel Quattrocento Milanese. Appunti su umanisti e codici," *Archivio ambrosiano* 26 (1973–1974): 132–147, at 142.

7. On this tradition, see Jean-François Maillard, "Empire universel et monarchie gallique: Héritages italiens et aspects de l'illuminisme politique chez les kabbalistes chrétiens français de la Renaissance," in Françoise

Crémoux and Jean-Louis Fournel, eds., *Idées d'empire en Italie et en Espagne (XVIe–XVIIe siècle)* (Mont-Saint-Aignan: Publications des universités de Rouen et du Havre, 2010), 193-216.

8. In 1506 Julius II's anti-French alignments began to accrue as he supported the uprising in Genoa and his submission of Bologna. See Carlo Taviani, "Testimonianze e memorie di una rivolta: Genova 1506-1507," in Gian Mario Anselmi and Angela De Benedictis, eds., *Città in guerra. Esperienze e riflessioni nel primo '500. Bologna nelle "Guerre d'Italia"* (Bologna: Minerva Edizioni, 2008), 179-96; Angela De Benedictis, *Una Guerra d'Italia, una resistenza di popolo. Bologna 1506* (Bologna: Il Mulino, 2004).

9. Antony Black, *Council and Commune: The Conciliar Movement and the Fifteenth-Century Heritage* (London: Burns and Oates, 1979); Francis Oakley, *The Conciliarist Tradition: Constitutionalism in the Catholic Church, 1300–1870* (Oxford: Oxford University Press, 2008). For the period examined in this chapter, see Jotham Parsons, *The Church in the Republic: Gallicanism and Political Ideology in Renaissance France* (Washington, DC: Catholic University of America Press, 2004), 25-37; Tyler Lange, *The First French Reformation: Church Reform and the Origins of the Old Regime* (Cambridge: Cambridge University Press, 2014), 78-132.

10. Gallicanism was commonly defended by the third estate, the university, and the parlements, sometimes even against the political wishes of the high clergy and kings. For an analysis of the state of affairs at the Estates General of 1484, see Jean-Louis Gazzaniga, "Les États généraux de Tours de 1484 et les affaires de l'Église," *Revue historique du droit français et étranger,* ser. 4, vol. 62, no. 1 (1984): 31-45, at 38-39.

11. Donald Weinstein, "Savonarola, Florence, and the Millenarian Tradition," *Church History* 27, no. 4 (1958): 291-305, at 298-99.

12. Carlo Marcora, "Il Cardinal Ippolito d'Este, Arcivescovo di Milano (1497-1519)," *Memorie storiche della diocesi di Milano* 5 (1958): 325-520, at 367.

13. Stefano Meschini, *Luigi XII, Duca di Milano. Gli Uomini e le istituzioni del primo dominio francese (1499–1512)* (Milan: FrancoAngeli, 2004), 60.

14. On the history of this institution and its political manipulation, see Andrea Galante, *Il Diritto di placitazione e l'economato dei benefici vacanti in Lombardia* (Milan: Tip. Bernardoni di C. Rebeschini e C., 1893), especially in the Lombard duchy, 41-67.

15. Marcora, "Il Cardinal," doc. 9, 78-79: "Promulgazione della necessità del regio *exequatur* per le bolle pontificie" (3 October 1500). On the Sforza *placet* and Louis's alterations, see Luigi Prosdocimi, *Il Diritto ecclesiastico dello Stato di Milano dall'inizio della signoria viscontea al periodo tridentino (sec. XII–XVI)* (Milan: Edizioni de 'L'Arte,' 1941), 64-75, esp. 68-69; see also Isabella Orefice, "Libertà ecclesiastica e dominio del principe, in Milano, durante Ludovico il Moro," in Archivio di Stato di Milano, *Ludovico il Moro. La sua città e la sua corte (1480–1499)* (Como: New Press, 1983), 129-45.

16. Meschini, *Luigi XII,* 64–65, n. 115. These requests emerged from the civic *capitoli* of 1502 and 1507; Louis also exercised powers over Genoese and Cremasco ecclesiastical benefices in the same way. See Luigi Tommaso Belgrano, "Della dedizione dei Genovesi a Luigi XII re di Francia," *Miscellanea di Storia Italiana* 1 (1862): 559–659, doc. 13 (submission terms of 1499), 634–58, at 653, cap. 30, "de beneficiis ecclesiasticis." On Crema: Léon-Gabriel Pélissier, *Documents pour l'histoire de la domination française dans le Milanais (1499–1513)* (Toulouse: Édouard Privat, 1891), doc. 74 (27 July 1509), 208–20, at 217 (article 22). In the long run, Rome seems to have exerted efficient control over benefices, since in 1520 the Venetian orator noted that the duchy's benefices were "de' forestieri, né vi è alcuno francese che abia episcopato o beneficio che vaglia." Gianiacopo Caroldo, "Relazione del ducato di Milano, 1520," in Arnaldo Segarizzi, ed., *Relazioni degli ambasciatori veneti al senato* (Bari: Laterza & Figli, 1976 [1912]), 1: 1–29, at 28.

17. Nicole Hochner, "Le Portrait satirique du cardinal d'Amboise," in Jonathan Dumont and Laure Fagnart, eds., *Georges Ier d'Amboise 1460–1510. Une Figure plurielle de la Renaissance* (Rennes: Presses universitaires de Rennes, 2013), 95–111.

18. See Cédric Michon, "Georges d'Amboise, principal conseiller de Louis XII," in Dumont and Fagnart, eds., *Georges Ier,* 17–30; Laurent Vissière, "Georges d'Amboise, le rêve de l'équilibre," in Dumont and Fagnart, eds., *Georges Ier,* 49–64, at 51; Benoist Pierre, "Le Cardinal Georges d'Amboise et les prélats de son clan. Le Salut par le service royal et la cour," in Alain Marchandisse, Monique Maillard-Luypaert, and Bertrand Schnerb, eds., *Évêques et cardinaux princiers et curiaux (XIVe–début XVIe siècle): Des Acteurs du pouvoir* (Turnhout: Brepols, 2017), 49–79.

19. On the election of 1503, see Christine Shaw, *Julius II: Warrior Pope* (Oxford: Blackwell, 1993), 117–21; Frederic J. Baumgartner, *Behind Locked Doors: A History of the Papal Elections* (New York: Palgrave Macmillan, 2003), 87–90.

20. Marjorie Reeves, *The Influence of Prophecy in the Later Middle Ages* (Oxford: Oxford University Press, 1969), 320–31. These later expansions of Joachimist thought occurred mostly in the fourteenth century, though with thirteenth-century foundations. See also Cesare Vasoli, "Il Mito della monarchia francese nelle profezie fra 1490 e 1510," in Dario Cecchetti, Lionello Sozzi, and Louis Terreaux, eds., *L'Aube de la Renaissance* (Geneva: Éditions Slatkine, 1991), 149–65; Anne Denis, *Charles VIII et les Italiens. Histoire et mythe* (Geneva: Droz, 1979), 19–30.

21. Gabriella Ferri Piccaluga, "Economia, devozione e politica: Immagini di francescani, amadeiti ed ebrei nel secolo XV," in *Il Francescanesimo in Lombardia: storia e arte* (Milan: Silvana Editoriale, 1983), 107–22.

22. Anna Morisi Guerra, "The Apocalypsis Nova: A Plan for Reform," in Marjorie Reeves, ed., *Prophetic Rome in the High Renaissance Period* (Oxford: Oxford University Press, 1992), 27–50, at 28.

23. BTM, MS Triv. 402, *Apocalypsis nova,* 127r, Juraj Dragisic in Rome to Ubertino Risaliti in Florence, 18 June 1502. The letter has been published in Anna Morisi Guerra, *Apocalypsis nova. Ricerche sull'origine e la formazione del testo del pseudo-Amadeo* (Rome: Istituto storico italiano per il medio evo, 1970), 28–29. On Dragisic, see Cesare Vasoli, "Giorgio Benigno Salviati (Dragisic)," in Reeves, *Prophetic Rome,* 121–56.

24. BTM, MS 402, *Apocalypsis nova,* 127v, Dragisic to Risaliti, undated. Also published in Morisi Guerra, *Apocalypsis nova,* 31 n. 56.

25. Dragisic was part of Carvajal's équipe on diplomatic missions. See Gigliola Fragnito, "Carvajal, Bernardino Lopez de," *Dizionario biografico degli Italiani* 21 (1978): 28–34; Gian Carlo Garfagnini, "Giorgio Benigno Salviati e Girolamo Savonarola. Note per una lettura delle 'Propheticae solutiones,'" *Rinascimento* 29 (1989): 81–123; Nelson H. Minnich, "The Role of Prophecy in the Career of the Enigmatic Bernardino López de Carvajal," in Reeves, ed., *Prophetic Rome,* 111–20, at 113.

26. Marin Sanudo, *I Diarii,* Rinaldo Fulin, ed. (Bologna: Forni, 1969–1979 [1879–1902]), 3: 844, September 1500: "El reverendissimo Santa Croxe è catholico, savio, e à cuor l'impresa contra infideli; *tamen* è amico dil signor Lodovico e di Ascanio; e il papa ha ditto: À preso la conza quando fo legato a Milan; *in reliquis* è nimicho nostro."

27. Cesare Vasoli, "Sul probabile autore di una 'profezia' cinquecentesca," *Il Pensiero Politico* 2, no. 3 (1969): 464–72; Cesare Vasoli, "Ancora su Giorgio Benigno Salviati (Juraj Dragisic) e la 'profezia' dello pseudo Amadeo," *Il Pensiero Politico* 3, no. 3 (1970): 417–21; Cesare Vasoli, "Notizie su Giorgio Benigno Salviati (Juraj Dragisic)," in his *Profezia e Ragione: Studi sulla cultura del Cinquecento e del Seicento* (Naples: Morano, 1974), 17–127.

28. Morisi Guerra, "The Apocalypsis Nova," 33–35.

29. Florence Alazard, *Agnadel, 1509—La Bataille oubliée. Louis XII contre les Vénitiens* (Rennes: Presses universitaires de Rennes, 2017), 91–191; Françoise Bonali-Fiquet, "La Bataille d'Agnadel dans la poésie populaire italienne du début du XVIe siècle," in Jean Balsamo, ed., *Passer les Monts: Français en Italie—l'Italie en France (1494–1525)* (Paris: Honoré Champion, 1998), 227–43.

30. Pierre Gringore, *Oeuvres polémiques rédigées sous le règne de Louis XII,* Cynthia J. Brown, ed. (Geneva: Droz, 2003); Jennifer Britnell, *Le Roi très chrétien contre le pape. Écrits antipapaux en français sous le règne de Louis XII* (Paris: Garnier Classiques, 2011), 19–83; Nicole Hochner, *Louis XII. Les Déréglements de l'image royal (1498–1515)* (Seyssel: ChampVallon, 2006), 153–75; Massimo Rospocher, *Il Papa guerriero. Giulio II nello spazio pubblico europeo* (Bologna: Il Mulino, 2015), 263–91.

31. A concise overview of the events in these years appears in Frederic J. Baumgartner, "Louis XII's Gallican Crisis of 1510–1513," in Adrianna E. Bakos, ed., *Politics, Ideology and the Law in Early Modern Europe* (Rochester, NY: University of Rochester Press, 1994), 55–72.

32. Théophile Simar, *Christophe Longueil, humaniste (1488–1522)* (Louvain: Bureau de Recueil, 1911), 15–41. Over a decade later, Longueil's oration was well enough known in Italy that a Roman teenager defended his city against its argument in an address before the pope in the days that Longueil was in Rome to receive honorary citizenship. See Baldassarre Castiglione, *Lettere famigliari e diplomatiche,* Guido La Rocca, Angelo Stello, and Umberto Morando, eds. (Turin: Giulio Einaudi Editore, 2016), 1: #336, 321–22, Baldassarre Castiglione in Rome to Isabella d'Este in Mantua, 16 June 1519.

33. Feu called his treatise *An rex Franciae* "nonnullae conclusiones . . . secutus potius ordinem conclusionum publicatarum Papiae"; see Jean Feu, *Commentarii Ioannis Ignei . . .* (Lyon & Orléans: Apud Vincentium de Portonariis, & Apud Franciscum Gueyardum, 1581), 62r. The lecture is also mentioned in Jacques Poujol, "Jean Ferrault on the King's Privileges: A Study of the Medieval Sources of Renaissance Political Theory in France," *Studies in the Renaissance* 5 (1958): 15–26, at 21 n. 21.

34. Claude de Seyssel, *La Victoire du roy contre les veniciens* (Paris: Anthoine Verard, 1510).

35. Shaw, *Julius II,* 249, citing Cessi, *Dispacci,* 12 October 1509.

36. Niccolò Machiavelli in Blois to Dieci di Balìa in Florence, 10 July 1510, cited in Augustin Renaudet, ed., *Le Concile gallican de Pise-Milan: Documents florentins (1510–1512)* (Paris: Edouard Champion, 1922), 4.

37. BNF, ms. fr. 5208, Jehan Ferrault, *Le Traite de maistre Jehan Ferrault . . . des excellans et souuerains droitz et preheminences duy lis et de la couronne de France* (1510), 1v; a more extensive Latin version—a presentation copy for the king via the chancellor—is BnF ms. lat. 4777. See also Poujol, "Jean Ferrault." Poujol dismisses the possibility that the timing of Ferrault's treatise may relate to the contest with Julius II, seemingly unaware of the monarch's wide consultations to solidify a legal basis for his policies.

38. Frederic J. Baumgartner, *Louis XII* (New York: St. Martin's Press, 1994), 212–13.

39. Louis XII to the Parlement of Toulouse, 12 August 1510, in Jean-Louis Gazzaniga, "Le Conflit de Louis XII et de Jules II devant le Parlement de Toulouse (1510–1512)," *Revue historique du droit français et étranger,* ser. 4, vol. 57 (1979): 623–30, appendix 1, 629.

40. Étienne Aufréri on behalf of the Parlement of Toulouse to Louis XII, 22 August 1510, in Gazzaniga, "Le Conflit," appendix 2, 630.

41. Both Pierre d'Ailly (1351–1420) and Jean Gerson (1363–1429) left commentaries on the juridical separation of the pope as a person from his plenipotentiary office. See Victor Martin, *Les Origines du gallicanisme* (Geneva: Megariotis Reprints, 1978 [1939]), 2: 135–36.

42. Pyrrhus's inspiration was *Codex* 4.1.2. See BnF, ms. lat. 4712, Jean Pyrrhus d'Angleberme, *Repetitio L.z. C. de Jureiu. In qua Jurisurandi & confoederationis*

materia examussim tractatus & potissimum tres questiones (1510). See also Marguerite Boulet, "Une 'Repetitio' de Pierre d'Angleberme sur la loi 'Jurisjurandi' (C., IV, .1, fr. 2.)," *Revue historique de droit français et étranger,* ser. 4, vol. 25 (1948): 323-34.

43. BnF, ms. lat. 4712, 4r-7r, at 6v-7r.

44. BnF, ms. lat. 4712, 10v-11r; Boulet, "Une 'Repetitio,'" 327-29.

45. BnF, ms. lat. 4712, 11r-14v, Boulet, "Une 'Repetitio,'" 329-33. Here Angleberme essentially reverses the logic of the first argument. While the first opinion prohibits subjects (the weak party) from battling against the king (the strong party), the second opinion allows the king to wage war against the pope because in Roman law sons (weak, here taken as Louis) can kill fathers (strong, taken as Julius) but not vice versa.

46. Stefano Meschini, *La Seconda dominazione francese nel Ducato di Milano. La Politica e gli uomini di Francesco I (1515–1521)* (Varzi: Guardamagna Editore, 2014), 202-3. Perhaps he was encouraged into his senate position by Poncher, the dedicatee of his treatise.

47. François Secret, "Une Lettre oubliée de Jean Pyrrhus d'Angleberme," *Bibliothèque d'Humanisme et Renaissance* 35:1 (1973): 79-84.

48. Patrick Arabeyre, "Cigauld, Vincent," in Jean-Louis Halpérin, Jacques Krynen, and Patrick Arabeyre, eds., *Dictionnaire des juristes français, XIIe–XXe siècle* (Paris: Presses universitaires de France, 2007), 192. See also Elizabeth Armstrong, *Before Copyright: The French Book Privilege System 1498–1526* (Cambridge: Cambridge University Press, 1990), ad indicem.

49. Vincent Cygault, *Allegationes Vincentii . . . super bello ytalico* (Lyon: In calcographia Jacobi Rolant, 1513).

50. Cygault, *Allegationes,* sig. C ii^{r-v}; sig. E iii^v–iv^r.

51. Cygault, *Allegationes,* sig. C iv^v–D v^r. "Et sancta ecclesia gladium non habet nisi spiritualem qui non occidit sed viuificat" (C v^r). This formula of the sword that "does not kill but vivifies"—which appears frequently in the debates over Julius II—has a long exegetical tradition, part of which emerges from the ninth-century letters of Pope Nicholas I. See Gerard E. Caspary, *Politics and Exegesis: Origen and the Two Swords* (Berkeley: University of California Press, 1979), 186.

52. "Lettres qui défendent aux sujets du roi de se pourvoir en cour de Rome pour quelque suject que ce soit," given by Louis XII at Blois, 16 August 1510, in J. M. Pardessus, ed., *Ordonnances des roys de France de la troisième race* (Paris: Imprimerie Nationale, 1723-1849), 21: 436-39; Jean Caulier to Margaret of Austria, 1 October 1510, *Lettres du Roy Louis XII* (Brussels: Chez François Foppens, 1712), 2: 39-48, at 46-47.

53. For background to this dispute, see Shaw, *Julius II,* 245-52. On Louis's order, see Marcora, "Il Cardinal," 386.

54. Marcora, "Il Cardinal," doc. 14, 505-10, 7 October 1510. Cf. Sanudo, *Diarii,* 11: 456: "la bolla di la scomunicha contra il gran maestro e Milan è

expedita, ma non publichata" (24 September 1510). For the publication
of this order in French and vernacular, see Rosa Salzberg, *Ephemeral City:
Cheap Print and Urban Culture in Renaissance Venice* (Manchester: University
of Manchester Press, 2014), 5, 14, n. 28.

55. Baumgartner, *Louis XII,* 213–15; Sanudo, *Diarii,* 11: 722: "Vederò, sì averò
sì grossi li coglioni, come ha il re di Franza."

56. Chaumont's death was hastened after being struck in the face by a snow-
ball containing a rock during a 400-person snowball fight in Correggio.
See Robert Goubaux and Pierre-André Lemoisne, eds., *Mémoires du
Maréchal de Florange* (Paris: Renouard, 1913), 1: 63.

57. Shaw, *Julius II,* 284; Sanudo, *Diarii,* 12: 250–54 (16 May 1511); Giovan
Domenico Mansi, *Sacrorum conciliorum nova et amplissima collectio* (Paris:
H. Welter, 1901–27), 34: 157–61.

58. For the placards, see Francesco Pandolfini in Pontealovino to Dieci di
Balìa in Florence, 21 May 1511, Renaudet, *Le Concile,* doc. 45, 32–33, at 33,
and Sanudo, *Diarii,* 12: 218, 253; for the summoning of Decio, see Francesco Pandolfini in Milan to Dieci di Balìa in Florence, 28 June 1511, Renaudet, *Le Concile,* doc. 84, 60–61.

59. Christine Shaw, "Julius II and Maximilian I," in Michael Matheus, Arnold
Nesselrath, and Martin Wallraff, eds., *Martin Luther in Rom. Die Ewige Stadt
als kosmopolitisches Zentrum und ihre Wahrnehmung* (Berlin: De Gruyter,
2017), 155–68.

60. Maximilian I in Brixen to Paul von Liechtenstein, September 16 1511. Appendix to Hermann Wiesflecker, "Neue Beiträge zur Frage des Kaiser-
Papstplanes Maximilians I. im Jahre 1511," *Mitteilungen des Instituts für österreichische Geschichtsforschung* 71 (1963): 311–32: "Und versprechen den
cardinaln und etlichen andern personnen in dissen sachen zuverhelfen
bis in dreymal hundert tausent ducaten zugebrauchen und das solches
alles allain dur der Fukher pankh daselbs zue Rom endtlichen gehandelt"
(330). "Wier füegen dir auch zu wissen, das uns unsser secretari Jan Colla
auf heut geschriben hat bey ainer aignen posst, das die Vrsiner, Colloneser
und das populus Romanus gentzlichen geschlossen sein und fiergenomben
haben, kainen bapst, der francösich oder hispanisch sey oder durch dissen
gemacht werde, zu haben oder anzunemen" (332).

61. On Julius's intentions in Lombardy see Marco Pellegrini, "'Lombardia
pontificia.' I Disegni del papato sul ducato di Milano nell'età delle guerre
d'Italia," in Alberto Rocca and Paola Vismara, eds., *Prima di Carlo Borromeo: Istituzioni, religione e società agli inizi del Cinquecento* (Rome: Bulzoni
Editore, 2012), 69–106, at 88–91. For the English king, see Sanudo, *Diarii,*
14: 202: "È da saper, il Papa in concistorio à privo il Roy di Franza dil titolo di Christianissimo, e promesso darlo al re di Ingaltera, si con effeto
el romperà a Franza; e questo breve l'à dato in man di do cardinali, et è
secretissimo."

62. Francesco Pandolfini in Milan to Dieci di Balìa in Florence, 11 September 1511, Renaudet, *Le Concile,* doc. 216, 211.

63. Julius issued the summons on 25 July 1511 for the Fifth Lateran to convene in Rome on 19 April 1512. See Walter Ullmann, "Julius II and the Schismatic Cardinals," in Derek Baker, ed., *Schism, Heresy and Religious Protest* (Cambridge: Cambridge University Press, 1972), 177–93, at 187.

64. In the Pisan sessions of the council, the participants declared "durante dicto Concilio, el Papa non possa creare cardinali, nè creare, publicare, nè dare in feudo terra, città, nè castello alcuno ad persona alcuna, si non vol Concilio" (Sanudo, *Diarii,* 13: 330–32, at 331).

65. Rosso Ridolfi and Antonio Portinari in Pisa to Dieci di Balìa in Florence, 2 November 1511, Renaudet, *Le Concile,* doc. 398, 448–52, at 450. Thanks to Florentine intervention, the Pisans opened the cathedral to the council. See Nelson Minnich, *"Rite Convocare ac Congregare Procedereque:* The Struggle between the Councils of Pisa-Milan-Asti-Lyons and Lateran V," in Nelson Minnich, *Councils of the Catholic Reformation* (Aldershot, UK: Ashgate, 2008), 9: 1–54, at 20.

66. Antonio Portinari in Pisa to Dieci di Balìa in Florence, 11 October 1511, Renaudet, *Le Concile,* doc. 318 [mislabeled 218], 361–62.

67. On the observance of the interdict, see Dieci di Balìa in Florence to Pierfrancesco Tosinghi, 28 September 1511, Renaudet, *Le Concile,* doc. 269, 291–92.

68. Niccolò Machiavelli in Pisa to Dieci di Balìa in Florence, 6 November 1511, Renaudet, *Le Concile,* doc. 413, 470–71.

69. For the participants, see the list of prelates who assembled first at Piacenza in letter of Rosso Ridolfi in Sarzana to Dieci di Balìa in Florence, 13 October 1511, Renaudet, *Le Concile,* doc. 327, 371–75, esp. 374, n. 86.

70. "On account of these cardinals," a Florentine reported from Fivizzano, "the city is under interdict, and the citizens are ill-disposed and in very bad humor" (Giovanni Barducci in Fivizzano to Dieci di Balìa in Florence, 22 November 1511, Renaudet, *Le Concile,* doc. 483, 544).

71. Enrico Cattaneo, "La Condotta dei milanesi durante il concilio di Pisa-Milano, 155–1512," *Ricerche storiche sulla Chiesa Ambrosiana* 2 (1971): 245–79.

72. Francesco Pandolfini in Milan to Dieci di Balìa in Florence, 1 December 1511, Renaudet, *Le Concile,* doc. 497, 558–59.

73. Prato, *Storia,* 285.

74. Francesco Pandolfini in Milan to Dieci di Balìa in Florence, 4 December 1511, Renaudet, *Le Concile,* doc. 500, 560–61; Prato, *Storia,* 286.

75. Francesco Pandolfini in Milan to Dieci di Balìa in Florence, 7 December 1511, Renaudet, *Le Concile,* doc. 503, 563; Sanudo, *Diarii,* 13: 350. For the mercenaries, see Pandolfini's letter of December 10, Renaudet, *Le Concile,* doc. 507, 565–66, and Prato, *Storia,* 286–87.

76. Cattaneo, "La Condotta," 255, n. 37.

77. Zaccaria Ferreri, ed., *Acta Scitu dignissima docteque concinnata Constantiensis concilii celebratissimi* (Milan: Gotardo de Ponte, 1511); Zaccaria Ferreri, ed., *Decreta & acta Concilii Basiliensis nuper Impressa Cum gratia & priuilegio* (Milan: Gotardo de Ponte, 1511).

78. Roberto Acciaiuoli in Blois to Dieci di Balìa in Florence, 17 January 1512: "Sua Maesta si è resoluta di fare tutto lo sforzo che sia necessario per offendere l'inimici et fare la guerra in ogni luogo et dovunque possiamo senza respecto; et mandare inantii el concilio insino alla creatione d'un altro Pontefice" (Renaudet, *Le Concile,* doc. 539, 598–99).

79. The bishop was Antonio IV Trivulzio, bishop of Asti. Francesco Pandolfini in Milan to Dieci di Balìa in Florence, 4 January 1512, Renaudet, *Le Concile,* doc. 526, 584–86: "Tra li vescovi non vene fu che uno di questo Stato cioè Monsignor d'Asti: il quale fino ad qui non ha mai voluto intervenire in alchuno luogo con questi del concilio, non sanza qualche indignatione et querela di questi cardinali; pure stamattina è concorso, strecto et dalle lectere comandatorie del Re e da comandamenti factili qui sotto varie pene et privationi."

80. See Decio's resignation letter and the cardinals' reply in Cattaneo, "La Condotta," 271–72.

81. Myron P. Gilmore, *Humanists and Jurists: Six Studies in the Renaissance* (Cambridge, MA: Harvard University Press, 1963), 74–78. See Decio's opinion in Filippo Decio, *Consilia sive responsa* (Frankfurt: Feyrabend, 1588), 163–69.

82. In January, Jean Lemaire de Belges republished his treatise in Paris on councils and schisms, adding a valedictory prophecy of the imminent election of an angelic French pope. Jean Lemaire de Belges, *Traicté de la différence des schismes et des conseils de l'église,* Jennifer Britnell ed. (Geneva: Droz, 1997), 275, n. 441.

83. 21 April 1512. Prato, *Storia,* 295. See also Minnich, *"Rite Convocare,"* 50–51.

84. *Suspension del .S. nro Julio pappa / .ij. da ogni administratione cosi ne le / cose spirituale come ne le temporale.* (Milan: Giovanni Antonio Zaita da Monza, 1512). BTM Inc C 259 / 35. The pamphlet is dated 8 April 1512, but is hand-corrected in contemporary script to 28 April 1512; see Ennio Sandal, *Editori e tipografi a Milano nel Cinquecento* (Baden-Baden: Valentin Koerner, 1977), 3: 93, 97.

85. Achille Ratti, "Il Secolo XVI nell'abbazia di Chiaravalle, di Milano: Notizia di due altri codici manoscritti chiaravallesi," *Archivio storico lombardo* 23, ser. 3, fasc. 9 (1896): 91–161, at 101, with Ratti's commentary on 100–103 n. 1; Cattaneo, "La Condotta," 262–63; Antonio Grumello, *Cronaca di Antonio Grumello, Pavese,* Giuseppe Müller, ed. (Milan: Francesco Colombo Librajo-Editore, 1856), 138; Luigi da Porto, *Lettere storiche,* Bar-

tolommeo Bressan, ed. (Florence: Le Monnier, 1857), doc. 60, 247–49 (as "papa Evardino"); Stefano Meschini, *La Francia nel Ducato di Milano* (Milan: FrancoAngeli, 2006), 2: 1017, n. 453, sees Carvajal's election only as an "anecdotal tradition."

86. Fragnito, "Carvajal," 31. An illuminated Lombard copy of the *Apocalypsis* produced for Cardinal François Tournon sometime during the second French domination survives in BnF, ms lat. 9587. Pier Luigi Mulas, "I Francesi nel Ducato: Riflessi nei libri miniati," in Frédéric Elsig and Mauro Natale, eds., *Le Duché de Milan et les commanditaires français (1499–1521)* (Rome: Viella, 2013), 79–106, at 88–90, 103.

87. Alessandro Luzio, "Isabella d'Este di fronte a Giulio II negli ultimi tre anni del suo pontificato (parte seconda)," *Archivio storico lombardo* (1912): 18, fasc. 35, 54–144, at 87: "Qui se è inteso che la Lega se hanno divisa la Franza in questa forma: la cità de Parise sia de la Ecclesia."

88. See the text of the edict in Cattaneo, "La Condotta," 273–74.

89. See the first few pages of Paolo Prodi, "Relazioni diplomatiche fra il ducato di Milano e Roma sotto il duca Massimiliano Sforza (1512–1513)," *Aevum* 30 (1956): 437–493. The words on ecclesiastical liberty belong to Girolamo Morone; see Giuseppe Müller, ed., *Documenti che concernono la vita pubblica di Gerolamo Morone* (Turin: Stamperia Reale, 1865), doc. 33, 56–62, at 57. 21 June 1513.

90. ASMi, Sforzesco 1499, 25 January 1513.

91. Cited from a letter in which Massimiliano Sforza adjudicated a dispute between the Canons Regular of Bernate and the Crivelli family, in Marcora, "Il Cardinal," 411; on the relinquishment see Formentini, *Il Ducato di Milano. Studi storici documentati* (Milan: Libreria Editrice G. Brignola, 1877), doc. 5, "Pro Libertate Ecclesiae," 393–94.

92. For François I see Galante, *Il Diritto di placitazione,* 62; for Francesco II see Prosdocimi, *Il Diritto,* 71–72.

93. Eckehart Stöve, "Ferreri, Zaccaria," *Dizionario biografico degli Italiani* 46 (1996): 808–11; Bernardo Morsolin, *Zaccaria Ferreri: Episodio biografico del secolo decimosesto* (Vicenza: Tip. Reale–Gir. Burato, 1877), 43–60; Joseph Orsier, *Henri Cornélis Agrippa: Sa Vie et son oeuvre d'après sa correspondance* (Paris: Bibliothèque Chacornac, 1911), 15; Charles Nauert Jr., "Agrippa in Renaissance Italy: The Esoteric Tradition," *Studies in the Renaissance* 6 (1959): 195–222, at 198–202.

94. On this tendency, see John Coakley, *Women, Men, and Spiritual Power: Female Saints and Their Male Collaborators* (New York: Columbia University Press, 2006), 211–27, esp. 221.

95. A recent synoptic analysis of the prophetesses of Santa Marta appears in Gabriella Zarri, "Profezia, politica e santità femminile in Santa Marta: Un Modello," in Rocca and Vismara, eds., *Prima di Carlo Borromeo,* 187–202.

NOTES TO PAGES 217-219

96. Gino Barbieri, "Gottardo Panigarola, mercante e spenditore sforzesco alla luce di nuovi documenti," *Atti e memorie del terzo congresso storico lombardo, 1938* (1939): 311-26, at 316. On Ottaviano, see Cristina Quattrini, "Artisti e committenti a S. Marta al tempo di Arcangela Panigarola," in Bartolomei Romagnoli, Paoli, and Piatti, eds., *Angeliche visioni,* 481-502, at 498-501.

97. BAM, MS O 165 sup., Giovanni Antonio Bellotti, *Incomincia la legenda dela Ven.da Vergine suora Archangela Panigarola priora et Matre nel sacro monasterio de sancta Martha de Milano, del ordine de santo Augustino sotto regulare obseruantia* (hereafter *Legenda*), 21r-v.

98. BAM, *Legenda,* 21r-v.

99. BAM, *Legenda,* 110r; 120v.

100. BAM, MS E 56 suss., *Coppie de lettere de la R.da matre del Mon.io de S.ta Martha de Milano, scripte in nome de la S.ta Matre allo Veschouo di Tholone* (hereafter *Lettere*).

101. Nelson Minnich, "The Healing of the Pisan Schism (1511-13)," in Nelson H. Minnich, *The Fifth Lateran Council (1512–17): Studies on Its Membership, Diplomacy and Proposals for Reform* (Aldershot, UK: Ashgate Variorum, 1993), 2: 59-197, at 82, n. 47.

102. On Dragisic's role in Arcangela's spirituality, see Tamar Herzig, *Savonarola's Women: Visions and Reform in Renaissance Italy* (Chicago: University of Chicago Press, 2008), 157-64.

103. BAM, *Lettere,* 6r-7r, Arcangela Panigarola to Denis Briçonnet, 11 March 1514.

104. BAM, *Lettere,* 9r-v, Arcangela Panigarola to Denis Briçonnet, 10 August 1514.

105. BAM, *Lettere,* 14r, Arcangela Panigarola to Denis and Guillaume Briçonnet, 21 December 1515.

106. For Guillaume's visit, see BAM, *Lettere,* 15v, Arcangela Panigarola to Denis Briçonnet, 12 June 1516; for Denis's arrival and consecration of Santa Marta's new chapel, see BAM, *Lettere,* 20v-21v, Arcangela Panigarola to Guillaume Briçonnet (date not recorded).

107. On the Briçonnets in Rome, see Minnich, "The Healing." Guillaume was traveling on this trip with the scholars Jacques Lefèvre d'Étaples and Christophe de Longueil. See Jean de Pins, *Letters and Letter Fragments,* Jan Pendergrass, ed. (Geneva: Droz, 2007), doc. 66, 202-4, Jean de Pins to Johannes Jacobonus (?) late April-early May 1516.

108. BAM, *Legenda,* chap. 97, visions of 23 and 24 May 1518, 173v-174v: "La cita tua Milano non fugira anchora queste future calamitate. Sara in quella grande mortalitate Alhora questa vergine spauentata disse, sara forse questo per mutatione de stato. Rispose non, Ma sera per inuidia et per la superbia loro, quale sempre nocceno ala mutua et fraterna charitate et amore, et queli cazano e doue non sono e necessario li sia discordia, ig-

nauia de animo et inueterate factione serano causa dela effulsione de lhu-
mano sangue, sera anchora peste vniuersale in modo che poche ne resta-
rano." Compare the citation in Herzig, *Savonarola's Women,* 163, which is
slightly truncated.

109. BAM, *Legenda,* chap. 18, "Del spirito della prophetia," 15r–v: "Predisse anchora questi tumulti bellici et mutatione del stato talmente che ueddo
ogni cosa virificarsi secondo che lei predisse, et maxime che Regnando la-
quila in Milano el Mozzo del frumento valerebbe vinti libre preparo el
molino et forno nel Monasterio de alchuni anni inanci che fusse la ne-
cessita de adoperarli."

110. BAM, *Legenda,* 202r: "Cosi contra li impij e rectissimo judice e per uenire
ali Milanesi e a tuta la lombardia tale persecutione et tribulatione quale
non e occorsa a mei tempi. Assai veramente assai lo indugentissimo patre
ha expectato fin qui e stato tempo de misericordia: da qua inante non sera
se non de vindicta et ira se non ho perdonato ali Arriani: como perdonaro
ali mei fioli Milanesi: le fetidissime et puzolente sceleragine le quale sono
peruenute fin al sedente in Throno. Non voglij fiola da qui inante doman-
dare misericordia ne inducie ma piu presto domanda che queste plante
siano fine ala radice strepate et noui arbori siano insediti. Gia li vostri inimici sono inuiati al camino. Gia hano parechiato le saete et tuti li arma-
menti acio ve assaltino et prosternino in terra. Alhora questa vergine
spauentata de queste parolle lo interrogo, chi erano quelli, quali pen-
sauano tale cose contra milanesi et luy rispose sono Francesi, quali
presto assaltarano et inuaderano la lombardia la vastarano et depreda-
rano et sara non picola effusione de sangue humano talmente che a molti
rincrescera el viuere et alhora la vergine disse, Non cognosco li Francesi
piu justi ne meliori deli Insubri et non posso capire in che modo ne possano in pena de nostri peccati farne tanti mali, et esso rispose: cosi como
Dio vole essere seruito nel proximo."

111. Giulio Cattaneo (like Girolamo Morone, Tristano Calco, and Giovan
Francesco Brivio) served both Sforza and French lords between the 1490s
and 1520s. See Franca Petrucci, "Cattaneo, Giulio," *Dizionario biografico
degli Italiani* 22 (1979): 473–74; for Ludovico's instruction to Cattaneo of
24 April 1498, see Isidoro del Lungo, "Fra' Girolamo Savonarola," *Archivio
storico italiano,* n.s., 18 (1863): 3–41, doc. 44, 37–38. On Cattaneo's role
under the French, see Franca Leverotti, "La Cancelleria segreta," in Arcangeli, ed., *Milano e Luigi XII,* 221–53, at 244–45; Meschini, *La seconda
dominazione,* 226.

112. BAM, *Lettere,* 33v, Arcangela Panigarola to Denis and Guillaume Briçonnet,
4 March 1517. A payment appears in BAM *Lettere,* 68r: "1521 die 20
martij—jo Suor Archangela di panigaroli madre del mon.rio de s.ta
martha confesso hauere hauto dal Mag.co d. Julio cathaneo spenditore
del li Ill.mo Monsig.re presidente 40 siue XL lire imperiali qualli sono

per la elimosina regia." Nearly a dozen more contributions of the same amount appear in BAM MS C 75 sup., Giovanni Pietro Puricelli, *Chronica del monastero delle monache di sancta Martha dell'Ordine di sant'Agostino in Milano:* gifts of François Ier (69r), and larger amounts from Denis Briçonnet (58v, 65r).

113. BAM *Lettere,* 33v (4 March 1517); 38v (2 October 1517); 53v (2 November 1518).

114. Janice Shell, "Il Problema della ricostruzione del monumento a Gaston de Foix," in *Agostino Busti detto il Bambaia (1483–1548)* (Milan: Finarte and Longanesi & Co., 1990), 32–61; Silvio Leydi, "'Con pompa más triunfante que fúnebre.' I Funerali milanesi di Gaston de Foix (25 aprile 1512)," in Arcangeli, ed., *Luigi XII,* 59–73.

115. Maria Teresa Binaghi Olivari, "L'Immagine sacra in Luini e il circolo di Santa Marta," in Piero Chiara, ed., *Sacro e profano nella pittura di Bernardino Luini* (Milan: Silvana Editoriale d'Arte, 1976), 49–76; Quattrini, "Artisti e committenti," 481–502.

116. BAM, MS A 198 suss., *Notta di quelli sepolti nella nostra Chiesa esteriore,* 11v–14v.

117. BAM, *Lettere,* 34r, Arcangela Panigarola to Guillaume Briçonnet (date not recorded); Michel Veissière, "Guillaume Briçonnet et les courants spirituels italiens au début du XVIe siècle," in Michele Maccarone and André Vauchez, eds., *Échanges religieux entre la France et l'Italie du Moyen Âge à l'époque moderne* (Geneva: Slatkine, 1987), 215–28, at 220.

118. Joachim Stieber, ed., *Conciliorum Oecumenicorum Generaliumque Decreta* II/2 (Turnhout: Brepols, 2013), sessio XI, 19 December 1516, "Circa modum praedicandi," 1403–8.

119. BAM, *Lettere,* 63v–64r, Arcangela Panigarola to Denis Briçonnet, 11 September 1519, and 18 September 1519.

120. BAM, *Legenda,* 191v–192r. The critique of young François I appears in a vision of Saint Louis, in which Arcangela asks the saint about François. Saint Louis promises her "vederai che Dio comutara queste sue legiereze in grauissime cogitatione, et le veste ornate in corace et arme per che sara constructo attendere ad altre cose che ad pompa e conuersatione muliebre."

121. BAM, *Lettere,* 47r–v, Arcangela Panigarola to Denis Briçonnet, 24 April 1518.

122. BAM, *Legenda,* 15r–v.

123. Adriana Valerio, "Domenica da Paradiso e Dorotea di Lanciuola: un caso toscano di simulata santità degli inizi del '500," in Gabriella Zarri ed., *Finzione e santità tra medioevo ed età moderna* (Turin: Rosenberg & Sellier, 1991), 129–144; Lorenzo Polizzotto, "When Saints Fall Out: Women and the Savonarolan Reform in Early Sixteenth-Century Florence," *Renaissance Quarterly* 46, no. 3 (1993): 486–525.

124. On Bellotti's role in Arcangela's legacy, see Herzig, *Savonarola's Women,* 164-66.

125. Ullmann, "Julius II"; J. H. Burns, "Conciliarism, Papalism, and Power, 1511-1518," in Diana Wood, ed., *The Church and Sovereignty, c. 590–1918: Essays in Honour of Michael Wilks* (Oxford: Basil Blackwell, 1991), 409-28.

126. The chronology of Martin Luther's voyage to Rome has recently been re-dated from 1510-1511 to 1511-1512. For the traditional timing, see Martin Brecht, *Martin Luther* (Stuttgart: Calwer Verlag, 1983), 1: 104–09; for the updated chronology, see Hans Schneider, "Martin Luthers Reise nach Rom: Neu datiert und neu gedeutet," in Werner Lehfeldt, ed., *Studien zur Wissenschafts- und zur Religionsgeschichte* (Berlin: De Gruyter, 2011), 1-157, esp. 114-27.

127. Luther probably read about the Council of Basel in Zaccaria Ferreri's 1511 Milanese edition; see Nelson Minnich, "The First Printed Editions of the Modern Councils: From Konstanz to Lateran V (1499-1526)," *Annali dell'Istituto storico italo-germanico in Trento / Jahrbuch des italienisch-deutschen historischen Instituts in Trient* 29 (2003): 447-68, at 448.

128. Nelson Minnich, "Luther, Cajetan, and Pastor Aeternus (1516) of Lateran V on Conciliar Authority," in Matheus, Nesselrath, and Wallraff, eds., *Martin Luther in Rom,* 187-204, at 200-04.

129. Minnich, "Luther, Cajetan," 203, esp. n. 52.

130. For the links between Panigarola and Isolani, see John Gagné, "Fixing Texts and Changing Regimes: Two Holy Lives in French-Occupied Milan," in Alison K. Frazier, ed., *The Saint Between Manuscript and Print: Italy 1400–1600* (Toronto: Centre for Reformation and Renaissance Studies, 2015), 379-420, esp. 386-97.

131. Michael Tavuzzi, *Prierias: The Life and Works of Silvestro Mazzolini da Prierio, 1456-1527* (Durham, NC: Duke University Press, 1997), 60-66.

132. Nansen Defendi, "La 'Revocatio M. Lutherii ad Sanctam Sedem' nella polemica antiluterana in Italia," *Archivio storico lombardo,* ser. 8, vol. 4 (1953): 67-153.

133. Ottavia Niccoli, *Prophecy and People in Renaissance Italy* (Princeton, NJ: Princeton University Press, 1990), 89-91, 105-08, 111-13; Daniel Gutiérrez, "I Primi agostiniani italiani che scrissero contro Lutero," *Analecta Augustiniana* 39 (1976): 7-74, at 19-38.

134. Sanudo, *Diarii,* 29: 495, 24 December 1520. See also Fedele Lampertico, "Di Frate Andrea da Ferrara," appendix 1 to "Atto di Adunanza," *Nuovo archivio veneto* 5 (1893): 249-55, at 250. Floriano Montino to Sigismondo d'Este, 15 January 1521: "Si è detto che costì havete ancor uuj un nouo affectatore de la doctrina soa [i.e., Martin Luther] el quale in publici sermoni et dispute, sostenta o tenta di sostentare alcune sentencie et opinioni erronee et dannate, et dicono che è quel nostro da Baura de l'ordine medesimo."

135. Lampertico, "Di Frate Andrea," 252, excerpt from letter of 18 March 1521.
136. Antonio Samaritani, "La 'Defensio' di Pietro Scazano in favore di Andrea Baura contro Lorenzo Castrofranco (a. 1520) ai podromi della polemica antiluterana in Italia," *Analecta Augustiniana* 47 (1984): 5-42, at 19.
137. Andrea Baura, *Apostlicae potestatis defensio. Reuerendi patris fratris Andree Baurie ordinis Eremitarum Sancti Augustini sacre Theologie Doctoris eximii ac verbi diuini predicatoris Celeberrimi. In Lutherum.* (Milan, 1523), sig. ii^v.
138. Giovanni Marco Burigozzo, *Cronaca di Milano*, Cesare Cantù, ed., *Archivio storico italiano* 3 (1842): 419-552, at 443.
139. Burigozzo, *Cronaca*, 444.
140. BAM, MS A 140 inf., *Bernardini Arluni Historia Mediolanensis a Gallorum Victoria ad Marignanum usque ad Francisci I Gallorum Regis captiuitatem,* 122v-126r. I extend my thanks to Frances Muecke for her help with Arluno's tortuous Latin. On Arluno, see Nicola Raponi, "Arluno, Bernardino," *Dizionario biografico degli Italiani* 4 (1962): 217-18.

9. THE PEOPLE

1. Andrea Gamberini, *La Città assediata. Poteri e identità politica a Reggio in età viscontea* (Rome: Viella, 2003), 268-69.
2. Massimo della Misericordia, "'Per non privarci de nostre raxone, li siamo stati desobidienti.' Patto, giustizia e resistenza nella cultura politica delle comunità alpine nello stato di Milano (XV secolo)," in Cecilia Nubola and Andreas Würgler, eds., *Operare la resistenza: suppliche, gravamina e rivolte in Europa (secoli XV-XIX)* (Bologna: Il Mulino, 2006): 147-215; Massimo della Misericordia, "'Como se tuta questa universitade parlasse.' La Rappresentanza politica delle comunità nello stato di Milano (XV secolo)," in François Faronda, ed., *Avant le contrat social. Le Contrat politique dans l'Occident médiéval (XIIIe-XVe siècle)* (Paris: Publications de la Sorbonne, 2011), 117-70; Paolo Prodi, *Il Sacramento di potere: Il Giuramento politico nella storia costituzionale dell'Occidente* (Bologna: Il Mulino, 1992); Carlo Taviani, "Peace and Revolt: Oath-Taking Rituals in Early Sixteenth-Century Italy," in Samuel Cohn Jr., Marcello Fantoni, Franco Franceschi, and Fabrizio Ricciardelli, eds., *Late Medieval and Early Modern Ritual: Studies in Urban Culture* (Turnhout: Brepols, 2013), 119-36.
3. A useful study of an earlier fidelity oath is Isabella Lazzarini, *Il Linguaggio del territorio fra principe e comunità. Il Giuramento di fedeltà a Federico Gonzaga (Mantova 1479)* (Florence: Firenze University Press, 2009).
4. No documentation survives for this 1495 oath beyond an early twentieth-century reference by Ettore Verga. See Letizia Arcangeli, "Milano durante le guerre d'Italia: Esperimenti di rappresentanza e identità cittadina," *Società e storia* 104 (2004): 225-63, at 233, n. 34; Jane Black, *Absolutism in Renaissance Milan: Plenitude of Power under the Visconti and Sforza, 1329-1535* (Oxford: Oxford University Press, 2009), 84-92.

5. Marin Sanudo, *I Diarii,* Rinaldo Fulin, ed. (Bologna: Forni, 1969–1979 [1879–1902]), 1: 995, letter from Brescia, 18 June 1498.

6. Léon-Gabriel Pélissier, *Recherches dans les archives italiennes. Louis XII et Ludovic Sforza (8 avril 1498–23 juillet 1500)* (Paris: Thorin et Fils, 1896), 1: 455–56.

7. Sanudo, *Diarii,* 2: 1210.

8. Stefano Meschini, *La Francia nel Ducato di Milano* (Milan: FrancoAngeli, 2006), 1: 62–66; Sanudo, *Diarii,* 2: 1256.

9. ASMi, Sforzesco 1143, letter of Governors of Milan to Giangiacomo Trivulzio (n.d., but probably 4 September 1499) and letter of Governors of Milan to Giovanni Marco della Croce (5 September 1499).

10. Léon-Gabriel Pélissier, *Documents pour l'histoire de la domination française dans le Milanais (1499–1513)* (Toulouse: Édouard Privat, 1891), doc. 9, 11–14, at 12.

11. Sanudo, *Diarii,* 2: 1289. The observer was Zuam Antonio Dandolo, Venetian provveditore in Caravaggio: "Li à risposto non haver libertà a conciederli."

12. Letter of the Florentine envoy Vespucci in Milan, 14 September 1499, quoted in Letizia Arcangeli, "Esperimenti di governo: Politica fiscale e consenso a Milano nell'età di Luigi XII," in Arcangeli, ed., *Milano e Luigi XII,* 255–339, at 277.

13. Letizia Arcangeli surveyed more than seventy notarial deeds dating from 16 to 18 October 1499 in all the city's parishes. See Arcangeli, "Esperimenti di governo," 278–82, especially 281.

14. ASCMi, Registri ducali 16 (1497–1502), 158v.

15. Arcangeli, "Esperimenti di governo," 281–82.

16. Girolamo Morone, *Lettere ed orazioni latine,* Domenico Promis and Giuseppe Müller, eds. (Turin: Stamperia Reale, 1863), doc. 8, 20–22. Girolamo Morone to Pierre de Sacierges, bishop of Luçon, 25 October 1499. This letter is dated one day prior to the tax uprising on 26 October.

17. Pélissier, *Documents,* doc. 9, 11–14.

18. Claudia Storti Storchi, "'Acciò che le cause passino più consultamente e con minor rechiamo.' Nodi della giustizia nei primi anni del dominio di Luigi XII sul Ducato di Milano," in Letizia Arcangeli, ed., *Milano e Luigi XII. Ricerche sul primo dominio francese in Lombardia (1499–1512)* (Milan: FrancoAngeli, 2002), 147–65, at 156–57, esp. n. 48; Maria Nadia Covini, *'La Balanza drita.' Pratiche di governo, leggi e ordinamenti nel ducato sforzesco* (Milan: FrancoAngeli, 2007), 132, says that Pavians "considervano questa legge uno dei fondamenti rocciosi della preponderanza giurisdizionale della città."

19. Emilio Nasalli-Rocca, "Il Decreto del 'Maggior Magistrato' e la sua giurisdizione," *Bollettino storico piacentino* 29 (1934): 107–17; 30 (1935): 3–10, 71–80; Ugo Petronio, "Giurisdizioni feudali e ideologia giuridica nel ducato di Milano," *Quaderni storici* 26, anno 9, fasc. 2 (1974): 351–402, at 357; Black, *Absolutism,* 141.

20. Pélissier, *Documents,* doc. 20, 63–64, 23 December 1501.

21. Léon-Gabriel Pélissier, "Textes et fragments inédits relatifs à l'histoire des moeurs italiennes (1498–1500), tirés des archives italiennes," *Revue des langues romanes* 40 (1897): 516–51, at 549–50.

22. Ferdinando Gabotto, *Giason del Maino e gli scandali universitari nel Quattrocento* (Turin: La Letteratura, 1888), 214, 217.

23. Among others, delegations came from Voghera, Castelleone, Casalmaggiore, Pizzighettone, Parma, and Bormio. See Pélissier, *Recherches,* 2: 9, 58, 268–70. These also included city-states not subject to the Lombard duchy but touched by the new lordship. For the Sienese case, see Léon-Gabriel Pélissier, "Documents sur l'ambassade Siennoise envoyée à Milan en Octobre 1499," *Bullettino senese di storia patria* 3 (1896): 43–66.

24. Guido Sommi Picenardi, *Cremona durante il dominio de' veneziani (1499–1509)* (Milan: Tipografia di Francesco Albertari, 1866), 30–37, for the notarial act of Cremona's oath to Venice.

25. We saw in Chapter 4 the case of the subjects of Lecco who refused to swear an oath to the Sforza feudatory Corradino Vimercati at the moment of the French arrival in 1499.

26. Pélissier, *Recherches,* 2: 271.

27. "Istituzione per una società per la conservazione della Città di Milano nella fedeltà e devozione verso il Re di Franca, duca di Milano," 1 February 1500, in appendix to Ambrogio da Paullo, *Cronaca milanese dall'anno 1476 al 1515,* Antonio Ceruti, ed., *Miscellanea di storia italiana* 13 (1871): 91–378, at 362–69.

28. Acangeli, "Esperimenti di governo," 282, n. 99.

29. Alberico Gentili, *Il Diritto di guerra* (Milan: Giuffrè Editore, 2008), 2.18, 349–50. See also Letizia Arcangeli, "Cambiamenti di dominio nello stato di Milano durante le prime guerre d'Italia (1495–1516). Dinamiche istituzionali e movimenti collettivi," in Marcello Bonazza and Silvia Seidel Menchi, eds., *Dal Leone all'Aquila. Comunità, territori e cambi di regime nell'età di Massimiliano I,* 27–75 (Roverto: Edizioni Osiride, 2012), 27–75, at 47.

30. ASF, Mediceo del Principato, 2728, 4: "Al giuramento prestato al Re di Francia è breve la risposta, perche detto Re all'hora haveva il Titolo nel Ducato di Milano, nè riconosceva dall'Imperatore ma lo occupava con la forza e con l'Armi, perciò non puo dirsi che ricevette il Giuramento in virtù de' Privilegij concessi dalli Imperatori Romani ò da Re; quali Privilegij esso Re impugnava [. . .] e così non opera tal Giuram.to nè li Atti indi seguiti, perseverando il medesimo e non cessando per causa di timore, sono fatti come spontanei e non nuocono a successori che non giurono nè perciò si poter far' pregiuditio a S. Maestà Cesarea il dicui consento non ci intevenne, e tali che così spontaneam.te giuranti dovevano esser più tosto privati." This case was highlighted by Jane Black, "Natura feudi

haec est: Lawyers and Feudatories in the Duchy of Milan," *English Historical Review* 109, no. 434 (1994): 1150-73, at 1161.

31. Sanudo, *Diarii,* 21: 446. The oaths in Milan proper took place in January of the following year. Letter of 7 January 1516 from Milan: François "era in la sala di Corte vechia sopra uno tribunal con li sui baroni atorno [...] et ha dato el giuramento di fedeltà a tuta questa città, et domino Ambrosio di Fiorenza dotor eloquente fece una oration vulgar laudando esso Re. Da poi fu chiamati a venir davanti Soa Maestà tutti li feudatarii dil duchato, et li deputati di le 9 porte quali ripresentano tutto il popolo, li collegi de li doctori e tutti li magistrati, a li quali fu dato uno juramento sopra uno messal."

32. Biblioteca Comunale di Piacenza, MS Com. 474, vol. 2, doc. 150, 16 December 1515. On Assareti, see the brief mention in Stefano Meschini, *La Seconda dominazione francese nel Ducato di Milano. La Politica e gli uomini di Francesco I (1515–1521)* (Varzi: Guardamagna Editore, 2014), 283-84. He may also be the "Assareto" Morone called "fratello carnale de uno deli principali forausciti et fautori del S. Zoan Iacobo Trivultio, et de la parte francesca" (Girlamo Morone to Cardinal of Ferrara, 25 July 1514, in Giuseppe Müller, ed., *Documenti che concernono la vita pubblica di Gerolamo Morone* (Turin: Stamperia Reale, 1865), doc. 114, 198-99.

33. Biblioteca Comunale di Piacenza, MS Com. 474, vol. 2, doc. 150, 16 December 1515. "Habuerunt et habent in comissione speciali a p.tis d. presidentibus Bobij de non prestando dict. Jur.to nisi prius certificatis Ill.ribus d.mnis comittibus de verme qui hactenus dictam ciuitatem Bobij tenuerent."

34. Biblioteca Comunale di Piacenza, MS Com. 474, vol. 2, doc. 150, 16 December 1515. "Dict. Jur.tum per fidelitatis prestabunt per vim et metum & tanquam coacti & per conseruari indemnitate dicte ciuitate non autem ex eorum propria voluntate et mero abitrio."

35. ASMi, Sforzesco 1499, 4 March 1517, "Confirmatio decreti de mayori magistrati & pro denuntijs & querellis."

36. Paraphrased from James C. Scott, *Domination and the Arts of Resistance. Hidden Transcripts* (New Haven, CT: Yale University Press, 1992), 45: "Relations of domination are, at the same time, relations of resistance."

37. Arcangeli, "Milano durante le guerre," 262.

38. Stefano Meschini, *Uno Storico umanista alla corte sforzesca. Biografia di Bernardino Corio* (Milan: Vita e Pensiero, 1995), 123, 284-85.

39. Meschini, *Uno Storico,* 164, 209-10.

40. An array of violent acts in 1500 across the duchy appear in Pélissier, *Recherches,* 2: 263-65.

41. Franceso Muralto, *Annalia,* Pietro Aloisio Donino, ed. (Milan: Cura et Impensis Aloisii Daelli, 1861), 76-77; Giovanni Andrew Prato, *Storia di Milano,* Cesare Cantù, ed., *Archivio storico italiano* 3 (1842): 216-418, at 255;

Francesco Robolotti, ed., "Cronaca di Cremona dal MCDXCIV al MDXXV," in *Bibliotheca Historica Italica,* (Milan: Brigola Bibliopola, 1876), 189–276 at 202.

42. See references in Giovanna Tonelli, "The Economy in the Sixteenth and Seventeenth Centuries," in Gamberini, ed., *A Companion,* 142–65, at 143–45; see also Beatrice Besta, "La Popolazione di Milano nel periodo della dominazione Spagnola," in Corrado Gini, ed., *Atti del congresso internazionale per lo studio dei problemi della popolazione* (Rome: Istituto poligrafico dello stato, 1932), 1, 593–610.

43. Some scholars have explored demographic questions outside the scope of the Italian Wars in Francesca Vaglienti and Cristina Cattaneo, eds., *La Popolazione di Milano dal Rinascimento: Fonti documentarie e fonti materiali per un nuovo umanesimo scientifico* (Milan: Biblioteca francescana, 2013). See also more generally Stephen Bowd, "Mass Murder in Sacks during the Italian Wars, 1494–1559," in Trevor Dean and K. J. P. Lowe, eds., *Murder in Renaissance Italy* (Cambridge: Cambridge University Press, 2017), 249–68.

44. ASMi, Registri Ducali 26 (1522–1535), 185r–86v, at 185v. The memorandum is dated 1500 but was evidently transcribed into a later ducal register. On the document's dating, see Arcangeli, "Esperimenti di governo," 268.

45. BTM, MS Triv. 1342, *Chronica Prati de rebus Mediolanensibus,* 5 *bollettini* (tipped in between folios 174–75, 299–300, 303–4, and at end of manuscript), addressed to Federico Panigarola of the parish of San Lorenzo dentro, and later Santa Maria Maddalena al Cerchio. For mention of the distribution of *bollettini,* see Prato, *Storia,* 317 (June 1513); and Giovanni Marco Burigozzo, *Cronaca di Milano,* Cesare Cantù, ed., *Archivio storico italiano* 3 (1842): 419–552, at 396 (22 December 1516).

46. Prato, *Storia,* 317; for Bergamo, see ASMi, Sforzesco 1411, 18 October 1514.

47. ASMi, Sforzesco 1422, 21 January 1524. The crida is titled "Quod solita habitare ciuitatis MLI & absentati a principio belli termino bidui reuertantur & quod nulli se absentent."

48. Angelo Pavesi, *Memorie per servire alla storia del commercio dello Stato di Milano* (Como: Staurenghi, 1778), 41–42.

49. Burigozzo, *Cronaca,* 450.

50. Burigozzo, *Cronaca,* 458–59.

51. Burigozzo, *Cronaca,* 462.

52. Marco Formentini, *Il Ducato di Milano. Studi storici documentati* (Milan: Libreria Editrice G. Brignola, 1877), 348–49, decrees dated 14 August 1526, 15 October 1526, 27 January 1527, and 11 February 1527. In the first decree, the governor declared the legal nullity of non-payers. See also docs. 68–72, 470–76.

53. Formentini, *Il Ducato di Milano,* doc. 73, 476–77, 16 September 1527; on the lodging and emptiness, see Burigozzo, *Cronaca,* 472–74: "Milano non pa-

reva più Milano, e le botteghe erano quasi tutte serrate" (473); "Milano non era più Milano, ma mezzano e manco" (474).

54. Visconti and Sforza dukes had worried about depopulation as well, though their concerns were largely about economic protectionism. See Amintore Fanfani, "Aspetti demografici della politica economica nel ducato di Milano (1386-1535)," in his *Saggi di storia economica italiana* (Milan: Vita e Pensiero, 1936), 123-57.

55. Ambrogio da Paullo, *Cronaca,* 116. At the same time, Milan closed its gates to prevent suburban dwellers from entering the city; Prato, *Storia,* 224. In May 1500, a Venetian agent encountered a carriage of women fleeing from Cassano to Milan, "per dubito de francesi" (Sanudo, *Diarii,* 3: 306.)

56. Prato, *Storia,* 351: "Chi avesse veduto, come io viddi, i poveri contadini, affanati e ansii condurre le loro mandrie alla Città, et le povere villanelle con li figlioletti a mano venirsene tutte piangenti, et quasi semimorte sotto il grave peso! Veramente era una pietà, una calamita, proprio a vedere loro."

57. Enrico Roveda, "Un Generale francese al governo di un feudo lombardo: Ligny e Voghera," in Arcangeli, ed., *Milano e Luigi XII,* 107-40, at 132-37.

58. See the demographic figures in Matteo di Tullio, *La Richezza delle comunità. Guerra, risorse, cooperazione nella Geradadda del Cinquecento* (Venice: Marsilio Editori, 2011), 38.

59. Carew and Sampson to Henry VIII, 12 September 1529, J. S. Brewer, ed., *Letters and Papers, Foreign and Domestic, Henry VIII,* vol. 4, 1524-1530 (London: Eyre and Strahan, 1875), #6092, 2719.

60. Burigozzo, *Cronaca,* 504.

61. Giovanni Basadonna, "Relazione del ducato di Milano," in Eugenio Albèri, ed., *Le relazioni degli ambasciatori veneti al Senato durante il secolo XVI* (Cambridge: Cambridge University Press, 2012), 11: 331-47, at 333.

62. Emanuele Artom, "Gli Ebrei in Italia nell'età delle dominazioni straniere e della controriforma," *La Rassegna Mensile di Israel,* ser. 3, vol. 15, no. 10 (1949): 456-67; Anna Antoniazzi Villa, "Gli Ebrei dei domini sforzeschi negli ultimi decenni del Quattrocento," in *Milano nell'età di Ludovico il Moro,* 1: 179-84; Pierre Savy, "Convertire gli ebrei? I doveri del principe tra imperativi religiosi e necessità politica (Lombardia, XV secolo)," *Reti Medievali Rivista* 18, no. 2 (2017): 189-218.

63. Schlomo Simonsohn, *The Jews in the Duchy of Milan,* (Jerusalem: Israel Academy of Sciences, 1982), vol. 2, docs. 2303, 2304, 2305, 2308 for the cases of Piacenza and Cremona in 1504-1506. In 1519, a Venetian knight named Ludovico's tolerance of Jews as the reason he was ousted: "Il ducha di Milan per aver favorido zudei e tenirli, fo cazado dil Stado" (Sanudo, *Diarii,* 28: 63).

64. Simonsohn, *The Jews,* vol. 2, docs. 2322 (the renewal under Massimiliano, 8 April 1513); 2355 (Massimiliano extends the Jews' privileges for five more

years, 14 May 1515); 2357 (levy raised to pay King François I even from those usually exempt, including the Jews, 12 August 1515); 2365 (Cremona requests the banishment of the Jews, invoking the order issued under Louis XII, 21–25 March 1518); 2379 (François I orders Jews to wear the yellow badge, 4 May 1520); 2382 (Milanese representative in Cremona threatens that Jews will be banished from the duchy, 9 November 1520). On the badge during the wars, see Flora Cassen, *Marking the Jews in Renaissance Italy* (Cambridge: Cambridge University Press, 2017), 76–77, 84–86.

65. Simonsohn, *The Jews,* vol. 2, docs. 2383 (Pavia requests banishment of Jews after Franciscan sermons, 1521); 2394 (indicates new charters with Duke Francesco II, but prohibiting Jews from living in cities unless they wear the badge, 9 December 1522); 2397 (temporary extension of Jewish charters, 7 January 1523).

66. Simonsohn, *The Jews,* vol. 2, docs. 2339 (Pavia's Jews complain of lodging and extraordinary tax burdens, 8 February 1514); 2342 (further complaints about wartime burdens, 8 March 1514); 2349 (Pavia's Jews reiterate their exempt status, 7 November 1514); 2381 (Lautrec orders Cremona's Jews to pay for army provisions like other citizens have done, 20 July–15 December 1520).

67. Simonsohn, *The Jews,* vol. 2, doc. 2326, 2 May 1513. The cities were Cremona, Parma, Piacenza, Novara, Alessandria, Tortona, Pavia, Como, and Lodi. See the responses from Lodi (doc. 2327) and Como (doc. 2328).

68. This argument is a central contention of Arcangeli, "Esperimenti di governo," and Arcangeli, "Milano durante le guerre."

69. Arcangeli, "Milano durante le guerre," 244; Arcangeli, "Cambiamenti," 49; Letizia Arcangeli, "Alle origini del consiglio dei sessanta decurioni: Ceti e rappresentanza a Milano tra Massimiliano Sforza e Francesco I di Valois (Maggio 1515–luglio 1516)," in Stefano Levati and Marco Meriggi, eds., *Con la ragione e col cuore: Studi dedicati a Carlo Capra* (Milan: FrancoAngeli, 2008), 33–75, at 47; Letizia Arcangeli, "Marignano, una svolta? Governare Milano dopo la 'Battaglia dei giganti' (1515–1521). Note a margine di studi recenti," *Archivio storico lombardo* 141 (2015): 223–63, at 249.

70. John Gagné, "Crisis Redux: The View from Milan, 1499," in Nicholas Scott Baker and Brian Jeffrey Maxson, eds., *After Civic Humanism: Learning and Politics in Renaissance Italy* (Toronto: Centre for Reformation and Renaissance Studies, 2015), 215–40.

71. Pélissier, *Documents,* doc. 2, 3–5.

72. Charles Kohler, *Les Suisses dans les guerres d'Italie de 1506 à 1512* (Paris: Picard, 1897), doc. 23, 612–13, at 613.

73. "È opinion de molti che a la fine Milano si farà canton de' sguizari," and further along: "Concludo e replico che, expulsi francesi e barbari de Italia, facilmente Milano potria farse canton de'sguizari" (Gianiacopo Caroldo, "Relazione del ducato di Milano, 1520," in Arnaldo Segarizzi, ed., *Re-*

lazioni degli ambasciatori veneti al senato [Bari: Laterza & Figli, 1976], 1: 1–29, at 29). See the same opinion expressed by the French chronicler Pasquier Le Moyne in Joanne Snow-Smith, "Pasquier Le Moyne's 1515 Account of Art and War in Northern Italy: A Translation of His Diary from *Le Couronnement*," *Studies in Iconography* 5 (1979): 173–234, at 220.

74. AnF J 507, n. 25. These petitions were subsequently printed in Pélissier, *Documents*, doc. 22, 66–82.

75. Pélissier, *Documents*, doc. 22, requests 21 (77–78) and 29 (81).

76. Sanudo, *Diarii*, 2: 1209, letter from podestà of Crema, 2 September 1499.

77. Franca Leverotti, "La Crisi finanziaria del ducato di Milano alla fine del Quattrocento," in *Milano nell'età di Ludovico*, 2: 585–632; Pierre Hamon, "L'Italie finance-t-elle les guerres d'Italie?," in Jean Balsamo, ed., *Passer les monts: Français en Italie, L'Italie en France (1494–1525)* (Paris: Honoré Champion, 1998), 25–37. After an evening-out period under Louis XII's regime, fiscal matters worsened with the Sforza restoration and the second French domination; see Matteo di Tullio and Luca Fois, *Stati di guerra: I Bilanci della Lombardia francese del primo Cinquecento* (Rome: École française de Rome, 2014), 69–79.

78. Arcangeli, "Cambiamenti," 54.

79. Burigozzo, *Cronaca*, 453.

80. The phrase belongs to Prato, *Storia*, 328, but others also used it in the same year. Sanudo, *Diarii*, 21: 448, after the French conquest, the city's representatives asked the king (12 January 1516): "Che essendo la terra di Milan, et la prima di Lombardia et una de le prime in Italia, per la acerbità de tempi depauperata et exausta, et che del publico et in comuni non hanno redito alcun, piacesse a Sua Maestà darle qualche ragione nel reddito." See also Ambrogio da Paullo, *Cronaca*, 352. See the edict announcing the levy in Formentini, ed., *Il Ducato di Milano*, lib. 3, doc. 11, 656–58.

81. Sanudo, *Diarii*, 20: 256. The citizens claimed that exactions had become so frequent that only resistance would force them to cease.

82. Letizia Arcangeli, "'Essendo tempo de pagare ad signori helvetii.' Resistenza fiscale e problemi costituzionali nella Milano del 1514," *Archivio storico ticinese* 156 (2014): 34–56, at 46.

83. Prato, *Storia*, 328.

84. Prato, *Storia*, 329; Burigozzo, *Cronaca*, 425; Ambrogio da Paullo, *Cronaca*, 353.

85. Prato, *Storia*, 329. On the mobilization of Ambrosian solidarity in times of struggle, see Patrick Boucheron, "Les Combattants d'Ambroise. Commémorations et luttes politiques à la fin du Moyen Âge," in Patrick Boucheron and Stéphane Gioanni, eds., *La Mémoire d'Ambroise. Usages politiques et sociaux d'une autorité patristique en Italie (Ve–XVIIIe siècle)* (Paris: Éditions de la Sorbonne-École française de Rome, 2015), 484–98.

86. Burigozzo, *Cronaca,* 425.

87. Prato, *Storia,* 330.

88. Burigozzo, *Cronaca,* 425. Prato instead describes this event taking place at the "Rocca"; see Prato, *Storia,* 330–31. During that meeting, the drums of a passing Swiss guard agitated the assembly to the point of chaos, and many people were crushed to death in the panicked flight.

89. Sanudo, *Diarii,* 20: 329, Letter from Bartolomeo Contarini, provveditor at Crema.

90. Prato, *Storia,* 332.

91. See the document revoking the duke's required levy (23 June 1515), in Formentini, ed., *Il Ducato di Milano,* lib. 3, doc. 12, 659; see also the grida urging the payment of the reduced fees (12 and 14 July 1515), lib. 3, docs. 9–10, 654–56.

92. These positions included the ministers of streets, of victuals, and of the commune's treasury, along with rights over the weighing of flour and wheat, and the administration of waters; Prato, *Storia,* 331. See also Ettore Verga, "Delle Concessioni fatte da Massimiliano Sforza alla città di Milano (11 luglio 1515)," *Archivio storico lombardo* 21 (1894): 331–349, at 333–338.

93. Verga, "Delle Concessioni."

94. Arcangeli, "Alle origini," 35ff, in a new reading of ASCMi, Lettere ducali 1512–1522, 96v–106.

95. Arcangeli, "Alle origini," 49–53.

96. On Lautrec, see Bertrand de Chantérac, *Odet de Foix, Vicomte de Lautrec, Maréchal de France (1483–1528)* (Paris: Librairie Historique A. Margraff, 1930).

97. Prato, *Storia,* 367–71, article 9 (January *capitoli*), "De Officiis Civitatis."

98. Prato, *Storia,* 370, response to article 9 (January *capitoli*): "Attamen prohibetur, sub poena emendae arbitrariae, ne dicti eligentes se habeant aliquomodo congregare sine licentia Principis, seu Senatus; nec pariter dictus Vicarius et duodecim provisionum, sub poena perditionis officiorum, et nisi vocato in eorum congregatione Locum Tenente Regis, ad cuius officium spectat praedictis interesse congregationibus."

99. Sanudo, *Diarii,* 21: 448–50, 7 January 1516: "Del Vicario de li provision, rispose che l'era stà fato eletion di uno zentilhomo francese, *tamen* ch'el se vederia s'el si potea trovar modo di gratificarli."

100. Robolotti, ed., "Cronaca di Cremona," 231. See also Philippa Woodcock, "Living Like a King? The Entourage of Odet de Foix, Vicomte de Lautrec, Governor of Milan," *Royal Studies Journal* 2 (2015): 1–25.

101. Giovanni da Fino in Milan to Alfonso d'Este in Ferrara, 21 July 1518, quoted in Meschini, *La Seconda dominazione,* 89–90.

102. Raffaele Gusperto in Milan to Francesco Gonzaga in Mantua, 11 July 1518, quoted in Meschini, *La Seconda dominazione,* 97, n. 133.

103. Arcangeli, "Marignano," 253, reaches a similar conclusion.

104. Raffaele Gusperto in Milano to Francesco Gonzaga in Mantua, 24 December 1518, quoted in Meschini, *La Seconda dominazione,* 96, n 131. This church, San Maurizio, would soon be transformed by Bernardino Luini's fresco campaign of the early 1520s. See Edoardo Rossetti, "'Chi bramasse di veder il volto suo ritratto dal vivo.' Ermes Visconti, Matteo Bandello e Bernardino Luini. Appunti sulla committenza artistica al Monastero Maggiore," *Archivio storico lombardo* 138 (2012): 127-65.

105. Meschini, *La Seconda dominazione,* 96, n. 131.

106. Meschini, *La Seconda dominazione,* 96, n. 131.

107. For the resolution of the 1518 dispute, see Prato, *Storia,* 412; for the regularity of the levies, see Arcangeli, "Marignano," 260.

108. See the letter of Girolamo Morone in Milan to Étienne Poncher in Paris, 23 January 1508: "Operam navamus recte procederetur, si Carolus de Ambasia prorex noster ita abstineret, sicuti et debet et pollicitus est, a confusione iudiciorum maxime criminalium quae omnia solitis ministris, solitaque avaritia corrumpit et foedat" (Morone, *Lettere,* 161).

109. Emilio Seletti, *La Città di Busseto, capitale un tempo dello Stato Pallavicino* (Milan: Bortolotti, 1883), 1: 317-21, for Cristoforo's death. On the family's politics during the early Italian Wars, see 1: 293-301, 309-15; Meschini, *La Seconda dominazione,* 152-56.

110. Meschini, *La Seconda dominazione,* 156.

111. Lautrec "o per non perdere l'occasione di saziare l'odio prima conceputo o per mettere con l'acerbità di questo spettacolo terrore negli animi degli uomini, fece decapitare publicamente Cristoforo Pallavicino: spettacolo miserabile, per la nobiltà della casa e per la grandezza della persona e per la età, e per averlo messo in carcere molti mesi innanzi alla guerra" (Guicciardini, *Storia d'Italia* [XIV.viii] 3: 1436). On Guicciardini's governorship, see Letizia Arcangeli, "Tracce delle esperienze di Guicciardini governatore nella *Storia d'Italia,*" in Claudia Berra and Anna Maria Cabrini, eds., *La* Storia d'Italia *di Guicciardini e la sua fortuna* (Milan: Cisalpino, 2012), 89-118.

112. For mention of these gathering sites, see ASMn, AG 1634, Francesco Malatesta in Milan to Francesco Gonzaga in Mantua, 9 March 1500: "Qui hozi se e comenzo apredichare: in corte predicha uno frate charmilitano: se predicha al zardino, et ala rosa, ogniuno ha gran concorso." And later, under Massimiliano, "Fu fatto uno sermone in nome del ducha Maximiano al populo milanexe al giardino presso a santa Maria de la Scala, per uno m. Filipo da Sormano, exortando il populo esser fidele al duca, et laudando Dio havere liberato Milano fora de le mane de francexi" (Ambrogio da Paullo, *Cronaca,* 278). In the 1523 French siege of Milan, grain mills were set up "nella Roxa, et nel Zardino, et in Brovetto novo, et in tutte le Parochie" (Burigozzo, *Cronaca,* 442).

113. See Massimo Rospocher, "Versi pericolosi? Controllo delle opinioni e ricerca del consenso durante le guerre d'Italia," in Diogo Ramada Curto, Julius Kirshner, Eric R. Dursteller, and Francesca Trivellato, eds., *From Florence to the Mediterranean and Beyond: Essays in Honour of Tony Molho* (Florence: Olschki, 2009), 381–408; Massimo Rospocher and Rosa Salzberg, "'El Vulgo zanza': Spazi, pubblici, voci a Venezia durante le guerre d'Italia," *Storica* 48 (2010): 83–120; Rosa Salzberg, *Ephemeral City: Cheap Print and Urban Culture in Renaissance Venice* (Manchester: University of Manchester Press, 2014).

114. Denis Crouzet, "From Christ-Like King to Antichristian Tyrant: A First Crisis of the Monarchical Image at the Time of Francis I," *Past and Present* 214 (Supplement 7) (2012): 220–40.

115. AnF, X1a, Parlement de Paris: Conseil—register 1517 (5 January [1515 old style] 1516), 44r–v. Published summaries can be found in Michel Félibien, *Histoire de la Ville de Paris* (Paris: Chez Guillaume Desprez, 1725), 4: 634, 637, 645, 674.

116. ANF, X1a, Parlement de Paris: Conseil—register 1526 (December 23, 1523), 26r; register 1529 (December 29, 1525), 66r.

117. For the beating of the *fatiste* monsieur Cruche, see Ludovic Lalanne, ed., *Le Journal d'un bourgeois de Paris sous le Règne de François Ier (1515–1536)* (Paris: Chez Jules Renouard, 1854), 14–15. For the imprisonment of Jacques le Bazochin, Jehan Serre, and Jehan du Pontalais, see 39–40. The foremost *fatiste* of Louis XII's reign was Pierre Gringore. On his departure from Paris, see Cynthia J. Brown, Introduction to Pierre Gringore, *Oeuvres polémiques rédigés sous le règne de Louis XII* (Geneva: Droz, 2003), 9–61, at 24; and Charles Oulmont, *La Poésie morale, politique et dramatique à la veille de la Renaissance: Pierre Gringore* (Geneva: Slatkine Reprints, 1976 [1911]), 17–20.

118. On François's attitudes to farce, see Sara Beam, *Laughing Matters: Farce and the Making of Absolutism in France* (Ithaca, NY: Cornell University Press, 2007), 45–46.

119. BNF ms. fr. 17527, 9v; 15r–19v; 28v–30r; 37r–38v; 51v–53v; 63r–64r; 78v–79v. The texts were published by Anatole de Montaiglon, ed., *Recueil de poésies françoises des XVe et XVIe siècles: Morales, facétieuses, historiques* (Paris: P. Jannet, 1855), 12: 193–237. See also the commentary of Jonathan Dumont, *Lilia florent. L'Imaginaire politique et social à la cour de France durant les Premières Guerres d'Italie (1494–1525)* (Paris: Honoré Champion, 2013), 141–44.

120. Lalanne, ed., *Bourgeois de Paris*, 133.

121. ASMi, Sforzesco 1500, 6 August 1519: "Et perche sua ex.tia de voluta del p.to senato iudica expediente al bene publico et al interesse del Re Chr. mo Duca de milano per la cui M.ta dicti officiali sonno deputati, che se intenda la uerita di quanto in epse cedule et libelli difamatorij si contene.

Per questa causa se fa publica crida per parte del prelibato, illustrissimo et ex.mo mons.re lo locotenente generale in Italia, che essendo alchuno di quale grado et condicione voglia si sia, che pretenda per via alchuna essere vero quanto se narra in dicto libello, o sia cedule, contra li nominati in quelle o alchuno di loro, et lo voglia verificare, compara arditamente nante sua ex.tia in termino de giorni quindeci proximi auenire, che sara admisso ad verificare circa cio quello vorra verificare come e dicto et per premio di tale verificatione guadagnara et li sarano dati scutti ducento doro. Et passando li dicti giorni quindeci non comparendo alchuno che voglia fare dicta verificatione, meritamente se pensara che tali libelli et cedule siano misse et affixe per malignita et non per verita."

122. Edict of 25 January 1522, Müller, ed., *Morone*, doc. 136, 266-67.
123. Prato, *Storia*, 402-04; Emilio Motta, "Pasquinate e censura a Milano nel '500," *Archivio storico lombardo* 38 (1911): 305-315. See also *Storia di Milano* (Milan: Fondazione Treccani degli Alfieri, 1957), 8: 213-15. Letizia Arcangeli, "Appunti su guelfi e ghibellini in Lombardia nelle guerre d'Italia (1494-1530)," in Marco Gentile, ed., *Guelfi e ghibellini nell'Italia del Rinascimento* (Rome: Viella, 2005), 391-472, at 408, n. 55, refers to the list in passing.
124. Latin text is indicated with italics; nonitalicized text indicates Italian.
125. Girolamo Figino served the French as royal grain deputy from 1505; see Stefano Meschini, *Luigi XII, Duca di Milano. Gli Uomini e le istituzioni del primo dominio francese (1499-1512)* (Milan: FrancoAngeli, 2004), 240. Masino da Lodi worked for senator Galeazzo Visconti and was appointed *"capitaneus devetus"* by Massimiliano Sforza in 1514; see Meschini, *Luigi XII*, 146; ASMi, Registri ducali 66, 56v-57r, 18 September 1514. Pallavicino, nephew of Giangiacomo Trivulzio, served as French-appointed governor of Bergamo after 1509; see Meschini, *La Francia nel Ducato*, 2: 590.
126. Dirk Werle, *Copia librorum: Problemgeschichte imaginierter Bibliotheken, 1580-1630* (Tübingen: Max Niemeyer Verlag, 2007), 95-110.
127. Ugo Rozzo, *La Strage ignorata. I Fogli volanti a stampa nell'Italia dei secoli XV e XVI* (Udine: Forum, 2008). Rozzo makes brief reference to Prato's catalog, 134.
128. Ennio Sandal, *Editori e Tipografi a Milano nel Cinquecento* (Baden-Baden: Valentin Koerner, 1977), 1: 77, #137.
129. BTM, Triv. M 34, Francesco Mantovano, *Libro de Lautrecho* (Milan: Agostino da Vimercate, 1523?); Germanisches Nationalmuseum, [part of the Scheurl-Bibliothek collection], old #557=new #437; BNCF, MAGL.19.6.147. The Florence copy lacks the fourth and final book.
130. Alessandro d'Ancona, *Origini del teatro in Italia: Studj sulle sacre rappresentazioni* (Florence: Successori Le Monnier, 1877), 2: 159, n. 2. The full text was published in Hermann Varnhagen, ed., *Lautrecho, eine italienische Dichtung aus dem Jahren 1521-23* (Erlangen: F. Junge, 1896); see also Antonio

Medin, "Il Quarto libro del poemetto drammatico sul Lautrec," *Rassegna Bibliografica della Letteratura Italiana* 1 (1893): 214–18.

131.   *Quarto Libro de Lautrecho & la descriptione de tutta la guerra facta per Franzesi contra Milano & il testamento ordinato per esso Lautrecho credendosi douesse in battaglia morire & la discordia nata tra diauoli del anima di Lautrecho persuadendosi seguiria la morte di esso Lautrecho nel conflicto. Et altre molte cose seguite per dicta guerra. Composto per Francisco Mantuano. Cum Gratia & Priuilegio.* Also circulating at this time was the "Lamento di Lautrech," a reworking of a fourteenth-century Milanese lament on the fall of Bernabò Visconti. See Antonio Medin and Ludovico Frati, eds., *Lamenti storici dei secoli XIV, XV e XVI.* (Bologna: Commissione per i testi di lingua, 1969 [1890]), 3: 301–319.

132.   *Libro de Lautrecho,* 31v.

133.   *Libro de Lautrecho,* 60v–65v.

134.   *Libro de Lautrecho,* 20r–21v.

135.   See, for instance, *Libro de Lautrecho,* 43v–45v; the quotation appears on 70v.

136.   The phrase belongs to Walter Benjamin, "Ursprung des deutschen Trauerspiels," in Rolf Tiedemann and Hermann Schweppenhäuser, eds., *Walter Benjamin: Gesammelte Schriften 1* (Frankfurt: Suhrkamp, 1974), 203–430, at 304. See also Judith Butler, "Afterword: After Loss, What Then?," in David L. Eng and David Kazanjian, eds., *Loss: The Politics of Mourning* (Berkeley: University of California Press, 2003), 467–73, at 470.

137.   Michel de Montaigne, *The Complete Essays,* M. A. Screech, ed. and trans. (New York: Penguin, 2003 [1987]), 1.14, 55.

138.   Prato, *Storia,* 355; Niccolò Machiavelli, 14 February 1526, quoted in Séverin Duc, "Il Prezzo delle guerre lombarde. Rovina dello stato, distruzione della richezza e disastro sociale (1515–1535)," *Storia economica* 19 (2016): 219–48, at 229. Machiavelli suggests Tuscany's people faced the same problems for being even less able to sustain the costs of war than was Lombardy.

139.   Francesco Guicciardini, "Del suicidio per ragione di libertà o di servitù," in Giuseppe Canestrini, ed., *Opere inedite* (Florence: Cellini, 1857-67), 10: 382–88. See also K. J. P. Lowe, "Redrawing the Line Between Murder and Suicide in Renaissance Italy," in Dean and Lowe, *Murder,* 189–210.

140.   Guicciardini, "Del suicidio," 385.

141.   Guicciardini, "Del suicidio," 388.

142.   Burigozzo, *Cronaca,* 450: "Milano cridava pensando di poter cridare."

CONCLUSION

1.   See Morone's self-defense document: "Examen Hieronymi Moroni detenti in carceribus marchionis Pischariae" in Giuseppe Müller, ed., *Documenti che concernono la vita pubblica di Gerolamo Morone* (Turin: Stamperia Reale, 1865), doc. 231, 474–97.

2. Venetian Council of Ten to the Venetian Ambassador in Milan, 17 May 1525, Müller, ed., *Morone,* doc. 177, 342–44, at 343.

3. On the restorative politics of many early sixteenth-century conspiracies, see K. J. P. Lowe, "Conspiracy and its Prosecution in Italy, 1500–1550: Violent Responses to Violent Solutions," in Barry Coward and Julian Swann, eds., *Conspiracies and Conspiracy Theory in Early Modern Europe* (Aldershot, UK: Ashgate, 2004), 35–53, at 43–46. For more general examinations of anti-tyrannical conspiracies, see Renaud Villard, *Du bien commun au mal nécessaire. Tyrannies, assassinats et souveraineté en Italie vers 1470-ver 1600* (Rome: École française de Rome, 2008).

4. Baldassarre Castiglione, *Lettere famigliari e diplomatiche* (Guido La Rocca, Angelo Stello, and Umberto Morando, eds. Turin: Giulio Einaudi Editore, 2016), 3: #1684, Baldassarre Castiglione to Nikolaus von Schönberg, 15 November 1525, 172–76, at 174; #1686, Baldassarre Castiglione to Nikolaus von Schönberg, 2 December 1525, 177–81, at 179–80; #1687, same correspondents, 9 December 1525, 181–86, at 182.

5. For the Fugger role in the election, see Mark Häberlein, "Jakob Fugger und die Kaiserwahl Karls V. 1519," in Johannes Burkhardt, ed., *Die Fugger und das Reich. Eine Neue Forschungsperspektive zum fünfhundertjährigen Jubiläum der ersten Fuggerherrschaft Kirchberg-Weißhorn* (Augsburg: Wißner Verlag, 2008), 65–81; for the suicide see Castiglione, *Lettere,* 1: #258, 343–45, at 344.

6. Séverin Duc, "Il Prezzo delle guerre lombarde. Rovina dello stato, distruzione della richezza e disastro sociale (1515–1535)," *Storia economica* 19 (2016): 219–48, at 237–41.

7. Philippe Hamon, "Charles de Bourbon, connétable de France (1490–1527)," in Michon, ed., *Les Conseillers de François Ier,* 95–97; Denis Crouzet, "Le Connétable de Bourbon entre 'pratique,' 'machination,' 'conjuration' et 'trahison,'" in Yves-Marie Bercé and Elena Fasano Guarini, eds., *Complots et conjurations dans l'Europe moderne* (Rome: École française de Rome, 1996), 253–69.

8. Aimé Champollion Figeac, *Captivité du roi François Ier* (Paris: Imprimerie Royale, 1847); Jean-Marie Le Gall, "François Ier—roi-chevalier vaincu et captif. Ou de l'usage de l'éthique chevaleresque pendant l'année de Pavie, 1525–1526," in Martin Wrede, ed., *Die Inszenierung der heroischen Monarchie: Frühneuzeitliches Königtum zwischen ritterlichem Erbe und militärischer Herausforderung* (Munich: De Gruyter, 2014), 128–51.

9. Baldassarre Castiglione to Mercurino Gattinara, October 1525, Castiglione, *Lettere,* 3: #1678, 160–62, at 160. The prospect of Bourbon pleased Clement VII as well: "Quando seguisse la morte del D.ca di Milano, el PP estima necessarijssimo che Sua M.ta provegga subito de novo D.ca prima che nascesse altro tumulto, il che sarrebbe periculosissimo. El parere di Sua S. ta sarrebbe il D.ca di Borbon, el quale è tanto intimo di Sua M.ta e mezzo italiano, overo D. Georgio d'Haustria, benché piú gli piaccia Borbone."

10. G. Clément-Simon, "Un conseiller du roi François Ier, Jean de Selve premier président du Parlement de Paris, négociateur du traité de Madrid," *Revue des questions historiques* 37, tom. 29 (1903): 45–120.

11. Jean de Selve in Toledo to Antoine du Prat, 12 August 1525, Champollion Figeac, *Captivité du roi*, doc. 131, 295–98.

12. Müller, ed., *Morone*, 475; Castiglione, *Lettere*, 3: #1694, 198–205, at 200, Baldassarre Castiglione to Nikolaus von Schönberg, 18 December 1525–19 January 1526.

13. Gino Franceschini, "Le Dominazioni francesi," in *Storia di Milano VIII: Tra Francia e Spagna (1500–1530)* (Milan: Fondazione Treccani degli Alfieri, 1957), 82–333, at 305; see also above, n. 9, Baldassarre Castiglione to Mercurino Gattinara, October 1525.

14. Renato Tisot, *Ricerche sulla vita e sull'epistolario del Cardinale Bernardo Cles (1485–1539)* (Trent: Società studi trentini di scienze storiche, 1969), 101, 106, 115, 138–40; Rill, "Cles, Bernardo," *Dizionario biografico degli Italiani* 26 (1982): 406–12; Paula Sutter Fichtner, *Ferdinand I of Austria: The Politics of Dynasticism in the Age of the Reformation* (New York: Columbia University Press, 1982), 58–65, 103.

15. The would-be assassin was Bonifazio Visconti. Francesco II Sforza to Margaret of Austria, 30 August 1523, Müller, ed., *Morone*, doc. 168, 310–12; Giovanni Marco Burigozzo, *Cronaca di Milano*, Cesare Cantù, ed., *Archivio storico italiano* 3 (1842): 419–552, at 440.

16. Jean Dumont, *Corps universel diplomatique du droit des gens* (Amsterdam: Brunel & Wetstein, 1726), tome 4, part 1, doc. 177, 198–99.

17. Castiglione noted (see my italics ahead) that the Emperor "inanti la battaglia [di Pavia] havea data *una forma della investitura* de Milano, nella quale erano condicioni molto piú dure che quelle che ha voluto poi in questa ultima fatta dopo la vittoria" (Castiglione, *Lettere*, 3: #1687, 181–186, at 183, Baldassarre Castiglione to Nikolaus von Schönberg, 9 December 1525).

18. Roberto Zapperi, "Biglia, Giovanni Antonio," *Dizionario biografico degli Italiani* 10 (1968): 415–17.

19. Dumont, *Corps universel*, tome 4, part 1, doc. 187, 434–35.

20. Francesco Guicciardini, *Storia d'Italia*, Silvana Seidel Menchi, ed. (Turin: Einaudi, 1971) (XVI.viii) 3: 1645.

21. Marco Formentini, *Il Ducato di Milano. Studi storici documentati* (Milan: Libreria Editrice G. Brignola, 1877), 337.

22. Marin Sanudo, *I Diarii*, Rinaldo Fulin, ed. (Bologna: Forni, 1969–1979 [1879–1902]), 39: 304; Castiglione, *Lettere*, 3: #1663, 127–34 at 130, Baldassarre Castiglione in Toledo to Nikolaus von Schönberg, 26 July 1525.

23. Müller, ed., *Morone*, doc. 184, 358–67, Pescara in Milan to Charles V in Toledo, 30 July 1525.

24. Castiglione, *Lettere,* 3: #1725, 265-79, at 276, Baldassarre Castiglione to Nikolaus von Schönberg, 8 September 1526: "Io. Alemanno ha dimandato all'ambasciator de Milano la investitura del stato, la quale li fu data già molti mesi. Esso ha detto non volergela dare, et voler aspettare che ge la levino per forza."

25. The document, dated 17 September 1526 is reproduced in Odorico Raynaldi, *Annales Ecclesiastici* (Paris: Bloud et Barral, 1877), "Caroli V Apologeticae litterae quibus ad Pontificem remittit bellorum causas," 31: 526-35, para. 22-43.

26. Raynaldi, *Annales Ecclesiastici,* 31: 530, para. 33.

27. ASMi, Sforzesco 1474, Massimiliano Sforza in Amboise to Francesco Sforza, 16 August 1526: "Ne si pensi pero V. S. che io tenghi il suo dire per profezia et che non sapia che in lei non he potere de cio che dice perche non he papa ne re di Franza, et lei como Francesco Sforza et io como Maximiliano non mi potra sforzare ne inganare mai, perche la persona sua non uale piu de la mia ancora fusse sana che Dio il uolesse, ne ha piu amici de mi. Jo ho bon patrone et ho tanti amici come lei ma dubito bene se non muta uita perdera quelli ha et io spero acquistarne de li altri. Et se li pare che la Fortuna al presente ladiuti piu di me quella medesima si potrebbe mutare et fare in contrario como altre uolte V. S. ne ha uisto experientia che io comandaua et lei mi ubidiua."

28. Giuseppe Molini, ed., *Documenti di storia italiana* (Florence: Tipografia all'insegna di Dante, 1836), 2: #256, 147-48, Anonymous correspondent in Lodi to Massimiliano Sforza in Paris, 13 March 1529.

29. Burigozzo, *Cronaca,* 505-07.

30. Castiglione, *Lettere,* 3: #1687, 181-186, at 183, Baldassarre Castiglione to Nikolaus von Schönberg, 9 December 1525.

31. See François's protest in Champollion Figeac, *Capitivité du roi,* doc. 222, 466-78, 13 January 1526.

32. Franceschini, *Le Dominazioni francesi,* 277-307.

33. Antonio Álvarez-Ossorio Alvariño, "*La Cucagna o Spagna:* Los Orígines de la dominación española en Lombardía," in Giuseppe Galasso and Carlos José Hernando Sánchez, eds., *El Reino de Nápoles y la Monarquía de España entre agregación y conquista* (Rome: Real Academia de España en Roma, 2004), 401-52.

34. Burigozzo, *Cronaca,* 450-59.

35. Burigozzo, *Cronaca,* 480: "Non poter più cavar contribuzione da Milano per essere del tutto del tutto desfatto."

36. See Leyva's orders dated 3 August and 18 August 1527 in Formentini, *Il Ducato di Milano,* 359-61; Idan Sherer, *Warriors for a Living: The Experience of the Spanish Infantry in the Italian Wars, 1494-1559* (Leiden: Brill, 2017), 87-88.

37. Guicciardini, *Storia d'Italia* (XVII.viii) 3: 1750.

38. Burigozzo, *Cronaca*, 475, 495.

39. Burigozzo, *Cronaca*, 480, 483, 494, 496.

40. Stefano d'Amico, *Spanish Milan: A City within the Empire, 1535–1706* (New York: Palgrave Macmillan, 2012), 11.

41. Guicciardini, *Storia d'Italia* (XVII.viii) 3: 1750.

42. ASCMi, Cimeli 3, 39, Charles V in Burgos to the Notables of Milan, 15 January 1528; reproduced in Franceschini, *Le Dominazioni francesi*, 298.

43. Michael Mallett and Christine Shaw, *The Italian Wars, 1494–1559* (New York: Pearson, 2012), 232–42; Sherer, *Warriors for a Living*, 132–36; Mario Rizzo, *Alloggiamenti militari e riforme fiscali nella Lombardia Spagnola fra Cinque e Seicento* (Milan: Unicopli, 2001).

44. Formentini, *Il Ducato di Milano*, 374–76, decree of 22 January 1530.

45. Giovanni Basadonna, "Relazione del ducato di Milano," in Eugenio Albèri, ed., *Le relazioni degli ambasciatori veneti al Senato durante il secolo XVI* (Cambridge: Cambridge University Press, 2012), 11: 331–47, at 341.

46. Matteo Di Tullio, *La Richezza delle comunità. Guerra, risorse, cooperazione nella Geradadda del Cinquecento* (Venice: Marsilio Editori, 2011); Matteo di Tullio, "Cooperating in Time of Crisis: War, Commons, and Inequality in Renaissance Lombardy," *Economic History Review* 71, no. 1 (2018): 82–105; Guido Alfani, *Calamities and the Economy in Renaissance Italy: The Grand Tour of the Horsemen of the Apocalypse*, Christine Calvert, trans. (New York: Palgrave Macmillan, 2013), 123–27, 137.

47. Duc, "Il Prezzo delle guerre," 243–45.

48. Marino Caracciolo to Charles V, 2 July 1530, cited in Federico Chabod, *Storia di Milano nell'epoca di Carlo V* (Turin: Einaudi, 1961), 240–41: "Il Duca ha facto un precone che e contento vendere ogni cosa excepto le cita, le quale non vorria vendere, perche penso che trovaria partito de Tertona con Ansaldo Grimaldo."

49. Pier Giovanni Fabbri, "Il governo e la caduta di Cesare Borgia a Cesena (1500-1504) nella cronaca di Giuliano Fantaguzzi," *Nuova rivista storica* 72, nos. 3-4 (1988): 341–88; John E. Law, "The Ending of the Duchy of Camerino," in Shaw, ed., *Italy and the European Powers*, 78–90; Alberto Sabattini, *Alberto III Pio. Politica, diplomazia e guerra del conte di Carpi. Corrispondenza con la corte di Mantova, 1506–1511* (Carpi: Danae, 1994), 87–91.

50. The schematic distinctions between dynastic and "total" wars drawn in Vivek Swaroop Sharma, "War, Conflict and the State Reconsidered," in Kaspersen and Strandsbjerg, eds., *Does War Make States?*, 181–217, are too pat to be helpful in their partitioning of dynastic wars and total wars.

51. Gianiacopo Caroldo, "Relazione del ducato di Milano, 1520," in Arnaldo Segarizzi, ed., *Relazioni degli ambasciatori veneti al senato* (Bari: Laterza & Figli, 1976 [1912]), 1: 1–29, at 29: "Milanesi voriano aver uno duca, azò li offici remanissero in loro e che potesseno nutrir li fioli sui a la corte de uno duca italiano; ma questo è verissimo: che, dovendo aver oltramontani, affirmano che francesi sono megliori de li altri, adducendo molte evidente ragione; e questo ho inteso da li maior ducheschi."

52. Note the popular support in 1523 for Francesco II: "Quando esso illustrissimo signor Ducha cavalcha per la città, tutto el populo li grida dietro: 'Ducha, ducha, non temer, stà di bon animo.' Et così anchora tutto el populo stà di perfetto core melio che mai" (Sanudo, *Diarii,* 34: 450, 22 September 1523).

53. Charisma was what Max Weber described as a means to legitimize domination ("resting on devotion to the exceptional sanctity, heroism or exemplary character of an individual person, and of the normative patterns or order revealed or ordained by him") and named it as one of the "three pure types of authority"; see Max Weber, *Economy and Society: An Outline of Interpretive Sociology,* Ephraim Fischoff, trans. (Berkeley: University of California Press, 1978 [1922]), 212–16, 241–53. See also Alain Boureau, "How Christian Was the Sacralization of Monarchy in Western Europe (Twelfth–Fifteenth Centuries)?," in Jeroen Deploige and Gita Deneckere, eds., *Mystifying the Monarch: Studies on Discourse, Power, and History* (Amsterdam: Amsterdam University Press, 2006), 25–34, 235–37.

54. Niccolò Machiavelli, *Il Principe,* Mario Martelli, ed. (Rome: Salerno Editrice, 2006), cap. 7, 126–27: "Francesco, per li debiti mezzi e con una sua gran virtú, di privato diventò duca di Milano, e quello che con mille affanni aveva acquistato con poca fatica mantenne." See also Georges Peyronnet, "François Sforza: De Condottiere à Duc de Milan," in *Gli Sforza* (1982), 7–25.

55. Formentini, *Il Ducato di Milano,* docs. 59, 60, 61: 462–64, edicts of 14, 22, 27 November 1525. See the use of the term by regional officials in di Tullio, *La Richezza delle comunità,* 81.

56. Maria Gigliola di Renzo Villata, "Sulle trace di un diritto 'patrio' nel ducato di Milano a metà Cinquecento: Tra *Novae Constitutiones* (1541) e fonti del diritto antiche e recenti," *Studia borromaica* 26 (2012): 121–56, at 121–32; Jane Black, "The Politics of Law," in Gamberini, ed., *A Companion,* 432–53, at 446–52.

57. On the first and second printings, see Kevin Stevens, "Publishing the *Constitutiones Dominii Mediolanensis* (1541–1552): New Revelations," *La Bibliofilía* 116, nos. 1–3 (2014): 215–30.

58. See Charles V's 1531 codification efforts in the Spanish Netherlands outlined in Willem Jans Zwalve, "Codificatie in Nederland," in W. J. Zwalve

and J. H. A. Lokin, *Hoofdstukken uit de Europese codificatiegeschiedenis* (Groningen: Wolters-Noordhoff, 1992), 243–309, at 243–45.

59. Most recently, see Alfani, *Calamities,* 37–41; Mario Rizzo, "Sticks, Carrots and all the Rest: Lombardy and the Spanish Strategy in Northern Italy between Europe and the Mediterranean," *Cahiers de la Méditerranée* 71 (2005): 145–84.

60. Pierangelo Schiera, "Legitimacy, Discipline, and Institutions: Three Necessary Conditions for the Birth of the Modern State," *Journal of Modern History* 67, Supplement: *The Origins of the State in Italy, 1300–1600* (1995): S11–S33.

BIBLIOGRAPHY

MANUSCRIPT SOURCES

Austria

Tiroler Landesarchiv, Innsbruck (TLA)
    Cod. 2470, II
    Inventar A 1/2
    Kunstsachen, I, 534

France

Archives nationales de France, Paris (AnF)
    J 507
    K 78
    X1a, Parlement de Paris: Conseil—reg. 1517, 1526
Bibliothèque nationale de France, Paris (BnF)
    Fr. 2925, 2978, 3087, 3096, 5208, 17527, 26118
    Ital. 821
    Lat. 4712, 4777, 5888
    Dupuy 558
Bibliothèque Sainte-Geneviève, Paris
    MS 864

Great Britain

British Library, London (BL)
    MS Harleian 3462
    MS Egerton 26

Italy

Cremona
Biblioteca Statale di Cremona
   MS Bib. Gov. 264

Florence
Archivio di Stato di Firenze (ASF)
   Mediceo Avanti il Principato, 78
   Mediceo del Principato, 2728

Mantua
Archivio di Stato (ASMn)
   Archivio Gonzaga (AG) 1616, 1634, 1637, 1640, 1643, copialettere 2120, 2995, 2996

Milan
Archivio di Stato (ASMi)
   Atti di governo—Statuti (Registri Panigarola GG) 25
   Autografi 219
   Carteggio Sforzesco 131, 626, 628, 1141, 1143, 1341, 1357, 1411, 1417, 1418, 1419, 1422, 1474, 1496, 1499, 1500
   Feudi Camerali 291, 297
   Frammenti Registri Ducali 4b, LXVIII
   Miscellanea storica 6
   Panigarola, Liber Bannitorum 2 / 1
   Registro delle Missive 213
   Registri ducali 26, 44, 64, 66

Archivio Storico Civico (ASCM)
   Registro di Lettere Ducali 16

Biblioteca Ambrosiana (BAM)
   MS A 140 inf.
   MS A 198 suss.
   MS C 75 sup.
   MS E 56 suss. (*Lettere*)
   MS I 179 inf.
   MS O 165 sup. (*Legenda*)

Biblioteca Trivulziana (BTM)
   Fondo Belgioioso 306
   MS Triv. 402, 1342, 2159

Parma
Archivio di Stato (ASPr)
   Feudi e Comunità - Carte feudali 57, 210, 211
   Famiglie 57, 481, 482

Pavia
Archivio Civico di Pavia (ACPv)
   Comune—Estimo 249

Piacenza
Biblioteca Comunale
   MS Com. 474

Ravenna
Archivio di Stato di Ravenna
   Corporazioni religiose—Abbazia di Sant'Apollinare in Classe 239

Venice
Archivio di Stato (ASV)
   Capi del Consiglio di Dieci—Lettere di Ambasciatori, 15
   Capi del Consiglio di Dieci—Lettere di Rettori e di Altre Cariche, 72bis
   Compilazione delle leggi 50, Fasc. I & II
   Archivio del Senato, Deliberazioni—Terra, reg. 14

Biblioteca Marciana (BMV)
   MS Italiano VII 990 (=9582)

Verona
Archivio di Stato (ASVr)
   Zileri-Dal Verme 6, 20, 51, 138, 174

United States

New York
Pierpont Morgan Library
   MS M.434

Vatican City

Biblioteca Apostolica Vaticana (BAV)
   Vat. lat. 3923

PRINTED SOURCES

Adami, Vittorio, ed. "Il Carteggio di un capitano di ventura—Gaspare S. Severino d'Aragona detto Fracasso (1475–1518)." *Miscellanea di storia veneta* 4 (1930): 1–162.

Almain, Jacques. "Expositio . . . de potestate ecclesiastica & laica." In Louis Ellies du Pin, ed., *Ioannis Gersonii Opera Omnia*, 2: 1013–21. The Hague: Apud Petrum de Hondt, 1728.

Ambrogio da Paullo. *Cronaca milanese dall'anno 1476 al 1515,* Antonio Ceruti, ed. *Miscellanea di storia italiana* 13 (1871): 91–378.

Aretino, Pietro. *Lettere*. Francesco Erspamer, ed. Parma: Ugo Guanda Editore, 1995.

Aristotle. *Politics*. H. Rackham, trans. Cambridge, MA: Harvard University Press, 1932.

Arluno, Bernardino. *De Bello Veneto libri sex*. In J. G. Graevius, ed., *Thesaurus antiquitatum et historiarum Italiae*, vol. 5, part 4, 1–306. Leiden: Petrus Vander, 1722.

Augustine. *In Iohannis evangelium tractatus CXXIV*. R. Willems, ed. Vol. 36 of *Corpus Christianorum*. Turnhout: Brepols, 1990.

Auton, Jean de. *Chroniques de Louis XII*. René de Maulde la Clavière, ed. 4 vols. Paris: Librairie Renouard, 1889–1895.

Bandello, Matteo. *Tutte le opere*. Francesco Flora, ed. 2 vols. Verona: Mondadori, 1966.

Basadonna, Giovanni. "Relazione del ducato di Milano." In Eugenio Albèri, ed., *Le relazioni degli ambasciatori veneti al Senato durante il secolo XVI*, 11: 331–47. Cambridge: Cambridge University Press, 2012.

Baura, Andrea. *Apostlicae potestatis defensio. Reuerendi patris fratris Andree Baurie ordinis Eremitarum Sancti Augustini sacre Theologie Doctoris eximii ac verbi diuini predicatoris Celeberrimi. In Lutherum*. Milan, 1523.

Bembo, Pietro. *History of Venice*, 3 vols. Robert W. Ulery Jr., ed. and trans. Cambridge, MA: Harvard University Press, 2007–2009.

Beretta, Guglielmo. *Elenco delle Parrocchie, Chiese, Abbazie, Conventi, Monasteri, e Ospedali verso la fine del XV secolo*. Milano: Scuola Tipografia Artigianelli, 1939.

Bonvesin de la Riva. *Le Meraviglie di Milano*. Angelo Paredi, ed. Milan: La Vita Felice, 2012.

Borelli, Anne, and Maria Pastore Passaro, eds. & trans. *Selected Writings of Girolamo Savonarola*. New Haven: Yale University Press, 2006.

Bossi, Donato. *Chronica*. Milan: per Antonium Zarotum, 1492.

Bouchet, Jean. *Les Annales d'Acquitaine*. Poitiers: J. et E. de Marnef, 1557.

Brewer, J. S., ed. *Letters and Papers, Foreign and Domestic, Henry VIII*, v. 4: 1524–30. London: Eyre and Strahan, 1875.

Burigozzo, Giovanni Marco. *Cronaca di Milano*. Cesare Cantù, ed., *Archivio storico italiano* 3 (1842): 419–552.

Cagnola, Giovan Pietro. *Storia di Milano . . . dal 1023 al 1497*. Cesare Cantù, ed. *Archivio storico italiano* 3 (1842): 1–215.

Campi, Antonio. *Cremona Fedelissima Città*. Milan: Filippo Ghisolfi, 1645.

Caroldo, Gianiacopo. "Relazione del ducato di Milano, 1520." In Arnaldo Segarizzi, ed., *Relazioni degli ambasciatori veneti al senato*, 1: 1–29. Bari: Laterza & Figli, 1976 [1912].

Carteggio degli oratori mantovani alla corte sforzesca. 15 vols. Rome: Ministero per i beni e le attività culturali, 1999–2008.

Castiglione, Baldassarre. *Lettere famigliari e diplomatiche*, 3 vols. Guido La Rocca, Angelo Stello, and Umberto Morando, eds. Turin: Giulio Einaudi Editore, 2016.

Ceruti, Antonio, ed. *Statuta Iurisdictionum Mediolani, saeculo XIV lata.* Turin: Ex Typis Regiis, 1869.

Cesariano, Cesare. *De Architectura.* Como: Gottardo da Ponte, 1521.

Champollion Figeac, Aimé. *Captivité du roi François Ier.* Paris: Imprimerie Royale, 1847.

Corio, Bernardino. *Storia di Milano,* 2 vols. Anna Morisi Guerra, ed. Turin: Unione Tipografico-Editrice Torinese, 1978.

Coryate, Thomas. *Coryats Crudities.* London: William Stansby, 1611.

Cygault, Vincent. *Allegationes Vincentii . . . super bello ytalico.* Lyon: In calcographia Jacobi Rolant, 1513.

D'Ancona, Alessandro. *Origini del teatro in Italia: studj sulle sacre rappresentazioni,* vol. 2. Florence: Successori Le Monnier, 1877.

Dandolo, Tullio, ed. *Ricordi inediti di Girolamo Morone.* Milan: Tipografia e Libreria Arcivescovile, 1855.

D'Anghiera, Pietro Martire. *Opus Epistolarum Petri Martyri Anglerii Mediolanensis.* Amsterdam: Typis Elzeverianis, 1670.

Da Porto, Luigi. *Lettere storiche.* Bartolommeo Bressan, ed. Florence: Le Monnier, 1857.

Decio, Filippo. *Consilia sive response.* Frankfurt: Feyrabend, 1588.

De la Vigne, André. *Le Libelle des cinq villes d'Ytallye contre Venise.* Lyon: Noël Abraham, 1509.

Del Maino, Giasone. *Epithalamion in nuptiis Maximiliani et Blancae Mariae.* Paris: Antoine Denidel, 1495.

——. *Consiliorum siue Responsorum d. Iasoni Mayni volumen quartum.* Venice: Apud Franciscum Zilettum, 1581.

D'Este, Isabella. *Selected Letters.* Deanna Shemek, ed. and trans. Toronto-Tempe: Iter Press & Arizona Center for Medieval and Renaissance Studies, 2017.

De Pins, Jean. *Letters and Letter Fragments.* Jan Pendergrass, ed. Geneva: Droz, 2007.

Dumont, Jean. *Corps universel diplomatique du droit des gens.* Amsterdam: Brunel & Wetstein, 1726.

Equicola, Mario. *Chronica di Mantva.* Mantua: Francesco Bruschi, 1521.

Fachard, Denis, ed. *Consulte e pratiche della Repubblica Fiorentina, 1498–1502,* 2 vols. Geneva: Droz, 1993.

Ferreri, Zaccaria, ed. *Acta Scitu dignissima docteque concinnata Constantiensis concilii celebratissimi.* Milan: Gotardo de Ponte, 1511.

——. *Decreta & acta Concilii Basiliensis nuper Impressa Cum gratia & priuilegio.* Milan: Gotardo de Ponte, 1511.

Feu, Jean. *Commentarii Ioannis Ignei . . .* Lyon & Orléans: Apud Vincentium de Portonariis, & Apud Franciscum Gueyardum, 1581.

Fiamma, Galvano. *La Cronaca Estravagante.* Sante Ambrogio Céngarle Parisi and Massimiliano David, eds. Milan: Casa de Manzoni, 2013.

Firpo, Luigi, ed. *Relazioni di ambasciatori veneti al Senato,* vol. 2: *Germania (1506–1554).* Turin: Bottega d'Erasmo, 1970.

Formentini, Marco. *Il Ducato di Milano. Studi storici documentati.* Milan: Libreria Editrice G. Brignola, 1877.

Gentili, Alberico. *ll Diritto di guerra.* Milan: Giuffrè Editore, 2008.

Giovio, Paolo. "Elogia virorum illustrium." In Renzo Meregazzi, ed., *Pauli Iovii Opera,* vol. 8. Rome: Istituto poligrafico dello stato, 1972.

———. *Notable Men and Women of Our Time.* Kenneth Gouwens, ed. and trans. Cambridge, MA: Harvard University Press, 2013.

Giustiniani, Pietro. *Le Historie Venetiane.* Venice: Appresso Lodovico Avanzo, 1576.

Goubaux, Robert, and Pierre-André Lemoisne, eds. *Mémoires du Maréchal de Florange,* 2 vols. Paris: Renouard, 1913.

Grassi, Paride de. *Il Diario di Leone X.* Pio Delicati and Mariano Armellini, eds. Rome: Tipografia della Pace di F. Cuggiani, 1884.

Gratian. *Decretum.* First recension in progress by Anders Winroth: http://gratian.org/.

Gringore, Pierre. *Oeuvres polémiques rédigées sous le règne de Louis XII.* Cynthia J. Brown, ed. Geneva: Droz, 2003.

Grumello, Antonio. *Cronaca di Antonio Grumello, Pavese.* Giuseppe Müller, ed. Milan: Francesco Colombo Librajo-Editore, 1856.

Guicciardini, Francesco. *Opere inedite di Francesco Guicciardini,* 10 vols. Giuseppe Canestrini, ed. Florence: Barbèra, Bianchi, e Comp., 1859–1867.

———. "Storia Fiorentina." In Giuseppe Canestrini, ed., *Opere inedite,* 3. Florence: Barbèra, Bianchi, e Comp., 1859.

———. "Del suicidio per ragione di libertà o di servitù." In Giuseppe Canestrini, ed., *Opere inedite,* 10: 382–88. Florence: Cellini, 1867.

———. *Storia d'Italia.* 3 vols. Silvana Seidel Menchi, ed. Turin: Einaudi, 1971.

Heil, Dietmar, ed. *Deutsche Reichstagsakten unter Maximilian I.—Achter Band: Das Reichstag zu Köln 1505, teil 1.* Munich: R. Oldenbourg Verlag, 2008.

Hobbes, Thomas. *On the Citizen.* Richard Tuck, ed. and trans. Cambridge: Cambridge University Press, 1998.

Isolani, Isidoro. *De Patriae urbis laudibus panegyricus.* Milan: Apud Io. Bap. Bid., 1629.

Juvénal des Ursins, Jean. "Verba auribus percipe, Domine." In P. S. Lewis and Anne-Marie Hayez, eds., *Écrits politiques de Jean Juvénal des Ursins,* 2: 179–405. Paris: Klincksieck, 1985.

La Chesnaye, Nicolas de. *La Condamnation de Banquet.* Jelle Koopmans and Paul Verhuyck, eds. Geneva: Droz, 1991.

La Conqueste et Recouvrance de la Duche de Millan faicte par le Roy nostre sire francoys premier de ce nom . . . Paris: Jacques Nyverd, 1518.

Lalanne, Ludovic, ed. *Le Journal d'un bourgeois de Paris sous le Règne de François Ier (1515–1536).* Paris: Chez Jules Renouard, 1854.

Lanz, Karl, ed., *Correspondenz des Kaisers Karl V,* vol. 2 (1532–1549). Leipzig: F. A. Brockhaus, 1845.

Le Glay, André Joseph Ghislain, ed. *Correspondance de l'empereur Maximilien Ier et de Marguerite d'Autriche,* 2 vols. Paris: Jules Renouard, 1839.

Lemaire de Belges, Jean. *Traicté de la différence des schismes et des conseils de l'église.* Jennifer Britnell, ed. Geneva: Droz, 1997.

Leonardo da Vinci. *Notebooks.* Irma A. Richter, trans., and Thereza Wells and Martin Kemp, eds. New York: Oxford University Press, 2008.

Lettres du Roy Louis XII, 4 vols. Brussels: Chez François Foppens, 1712.

Livy. *Ab urbe condita,* 11 vols. B. O. Foster, trans. Cambridge, MA: Harvard University Press, 1924.

Lünig, Johann Christian. *Codex Italiae Diplomaticus,* vol. 1. Frankfurt: Impensis Haeredum Lanckisianorum, 1725.

Luzio, Alessandro, ed. *Un Pronostico satirico di Pietro Aretino.* Bergamo: Istituto italiano d'arti grafiche, 1900.

Machiavelli, Niccolò. *Discorsi sopra la prima deca di Tito Livio.* Francesco Bausi, ed. Rome: Salerno Editrice, 2001.

——. *Il Principe.* Mario Martelli, ed. Rome: Salerno Editrice, 2006.

Malipiero, Domenico. *Annali Veneti dall'anno 1457 al 1500.* Francesco Longo, ed. Florence: Gio. Pietro Vieussieux, 1843.

Manaresi, Cesare, ed. *I Registri viscontei,* vol. 1. Milan: Palazzo del Senato, 1915.

Mantovano, Francesco. *Libro de Lautrecho.* Milan: Agostino da Vimercate, 1523?.

Mansi, Giovan Domenico. *Sacrorum conciliorum nova et amplissima collectio,* 54 vols. Paris: H. Welter, 1901–1927.

Manutius, Aldus. *The Greek Classics.* N. G. Wilson, ed. and trans. Cambridge, MA: Harvard University Press, 2016.

Medici, Lorenzo de'. *Lettere di Lorenzo de'Medici,* vol 11. Melissa Merriam Bullard, ed. Florence: Giunti-Barbèra, 2004.

Medin, Antonio, and Ludovico Frati, eds. *Lamenti storici dei secoli XIV, XV e XVI,* 3 vols. Bologna: Commissione per i testi di lingua, 1969 [1890].

Melchiorre, Vito A., ed. *Documenti baresi su Bona Sforza.* Bari: Mario Adda Editore, 1999.

Merula, Giorgio. *Antiquitatis Vicecomitum.* Milan: Minuziano, 1499.

Molini, Giuseppe, ed. *Documenti di storia italiana,* 2 vols. Florence: Tipografia all'insegna di Dante, 1836–1837.

Montaiglon, Anatole de, ed. *Recueil de poésies françoises des XVe et XVIe siècles: morales, facétieuses, historiques,* vol. 12. Paris: P. Jannet, 1855.

Montaigne, Michel de. *The Complete Essays.* M. A. Screech, ed. and trans. New York: Penguin, 2003 [1987].

Morigia, Paolo. *La Nobiltà di Milano.* Milan: Pacifico Pontio, 1595.

Morone, Girolamo. *Lettere ed orazioni latine.* Domenico Promis and Giuseppe Müller, eds. Turin: Stamperia Reale, 1863.

Müller, Giuseppe, ed. *Documenti che concernono la vita pubblica di Gerolamo Morone.* Turin: Stamperia Reale, 1865.

Muralto, Francesco. *Annalia.* Pietro Aloisio Donino, ed. Milan: Cura et Impensis Aloisii Daelli, 1861.

Musper, Theodor H., ed. *Kaiser Maximilians I. Weißkunig,* 2 vols. Stuttgart: Kohlhammer, 1956.

Osio, Luigi, ed. *Documenti diplomatici tratti dagli archivj milanesi,* vol. 1. Milan: Tipografia di Giuseppe Bernardoni di Giovanni, 1864.

Pagnani, Carlo. *Decretum super flumine Abdue reddendo navigabili: La Storia del primo Naviglio di Paderno d'Adda (1516–1520).* Gianni Beltrame and Paolo Margaroli, eds. Milan: Pecorini, 2003.

Pardessus, J. M., ed. *Ordonnances des roys de France de la troisième race,* 23 vols. Paris: Imprimerie Nationale, 1723-1849.

Pasquier Le Moyne. *Le Couronnement du roy Francois premier de ce nom voyages & conqueste de la duche de millan* . . . Paris: Gilles Couteau, 1519.

Paulus Diaconus. *Historia Langobardorum.* In G. Waitz, ed., *Scriptores Rerum Germanicum,* vol. 48. Hanover: Impensis Bibliopolii Hahniani, 1878.

Pélissier, Léon-Gabriel. *Documents pour l'histoire de la domination française dans le Milanais (1499–1513).* Toulouse: Édouard Privat, 1891.

——. "Les Sources milanaises de l'histoire de Louis XII: Trois registres de lettres ducales aux archives de Milan." *Bulletin du Comité des travaux historiques et scientifiques—section d'histoire et de philologie,* no. 1 (1892): 110-88.

——. *Documents sur les relations de Louis XII, de Ludovic Sforza et du Marquis de Mantoue de 1498 à 1500, tirés des archives de Mantoue, Modène, Milan et Venise.* Paris: E. Leroux, 1894.

——. "Documents sur l'ambassade Siennoise envoyée à Milan en Octobre 1499." *Bullettino senese di storia patria* 3 (1896): 43-66.

——. "Textes et fragments inédits relatifs à l'histoire des moeurs italiennes (1498-1500), tirés des archives italiennes." *Revue des langues romanes* 40 (1897): 516-51.

——. "Deux lettres inédites de Louis XII à J. J. Trivulce (28 janvier 1500)." In *Miscellanea Ceriani,* 391-402. Milan: Hoepli, 1910.

——. *Documents relatifs au règne de Louis XII et à sa politique en Italie.* Montpellier: Imprimerie Générale du Midi, 1912.

Plato. *Republic.* Christopher Emlyn-Jones and William Preddy, eds. and trans. Cambridge, MA: Harvard University Press, 2013.

Plutarch. *Lives,* vol. 5. Bernadotte Perrin, trans. Cambridge, MA: Harvard University Press, 1917.

Prato, Giovanni Andrea, *Storia di Milano.* Cesare Cantù, ed. *Archivio storico italiano* 3 (1842): 216-418.

Priuli, Girolamo. *I Diarii, 1499–1512,* Arturo Segre, ed. 3 vols. *Rerum Italicarum Scriptores,* vol. 24, part 3. Città di Castello: Tipi della Casa editrice S. Lapi, 1912-1938.

Proposition faicte par les nobles, bourgoys, gens de mestiers, manans, et habitans de la ville de millan. Lyon: Guillaume Balsarin, 1500.

Puricelli, Pietro. *Tristani Chalci Mediolanensis historiographi residua.* Milan: Fratres Malatestas, 1644.

Quaglioni, Diego, ed. *Politica e diritto nel trecento italiano: Il 'De tyranno' di Bartolo da Sassoferrato.* Florence: Olschki, 1983.

Raynaldi, Odorico. *Annales Ecclesiastici,* vol. 31 (1513–1526). Paris: Bloud et Barral, 1877.

Renaudet, Augustin, ed. *Le Concile gallican de Pise-Milan: Documents florentins (1510–1512).* Paris: Edouard Champion, 1922.

Robolotti, Francesco, ed. "Cronaca di Cremona dal MCDXCIV al MDXXV." In *Bibliotheca Historica Italica,* 189–276. Milan: Brigola Bibliopola, 1876.

Sanudo, Marin. *I Diarii.* Rinaldo Fulin, ed. 58 vols. Bologna: Forni, 1969–1979 [1879-1902].

Sanudo, Marin. *La Spedizione di Carlo VIII in Italia.* Rinaldo Fulin, ed. Venice: Marco Visentini, 1883.

Sasso, Panfilo. *Capituli e Soneti de miser Pamphilo Saxo Poeta laureato de li diuisione & guerre de Italia & del Moro & del Re di Franza.* BAM, S.P.XII.164/9.

Seneca the Younger. "De Clementia." In *Moral Essays,* John W. Basore, trans., 1: 356–447. Cambridge, MA: Harvard University Press, 1928.

Seyssel, Claude de. *La Victoire du roy contre les veniciens.* Paris: Anthoine Verard, 1510.

———. "L'Excellence & la Felicité de la Victoire que eut le Treschrestien Roy de France, LOVYS XII, de ce nom, dict Pere du peuple, contre les Venitiens, au lieu appellee Aignadel." In Théodore de Godefroy, *Histoire de Louis XII,* 241–336. Paris: Abraham Pacard, 1615.

———. "Certain discours fait par le bon Arceuesque trepassé." In Domenico Cerutti, ed., *Storia della diplomazia della corte di Savoia,* 1: 532–46. Rome-Turin-Florence: Fratelli Bocca, 1875.

Specker, Hermann, ed. "Brief des bernischen Hauptmanns Balthasar Finsternau zu Mailand an die Obrigkeit zu Bern, mit interessanter Charakterisierung des Herzogs Maximilian Sforza, 8. August 1515." *Berner Zeitschrift für Geschichte und Heimatkunde* 18 (1956): 129–30.

Statuta Mediolani. Milan: Apud Alexandrum Minutianum, 1502.

Stieber, Joachim, ed. *Conciliorum Oecumenicorum Generaliumque Decreta* II/2. Turnhout: Brepols, 2013.

Suetonius. *Life of Julius Caesar.* J. C. Rolfe, trans. Cambridge, MA: Harvard University Press, 1914.

Suspension del .S. nro Julio pappa/.ij. da ogni administratione cosi ne le/cose spirituale come ne le temporale. Milan: Giovanni Antonio Zaita da Monza, 1512. BTM Inc C 259/35.

Tamalio, Raffaele. *Federico Gonzaga alla corte di Francesco I di Francia nel carteggio privato con Mantova.* Paris: Honoré Champion, 1994.

Vasari, Giorgio. *Le Vite.* Florence: Giuntina, 1568.

Vecce, Carlo, ed. *Un'Apologia per l'Equicola. Le Due redazioni della* Pro Gallis apologia *di Mario Equicola e la traduzione francese di Michel Roté.* Naples: Istituto Universitario Orientale, 1990.

Villa, Antonio Francesco da. "Cronaca di Anton Francesco da Villa da 1511 al
1556." In A. Bonora and G. Bonora, eds., *Civitatis Placentiae Johannis Agazzari
et Antonii Francisci Villa,* 77–223. Parma: Typis Petri Fiaccadori, 1862.

Villari, Pasquale, ed. *Dispacci di Antonio Giustinian, ambasicatore veneto in Roma dal
1502 al 1505,* 3 vols. Florence: Successori Le Monnier, 1876.

Villata, Edoardo ed., *Leonardo da Vinci. I Documenti e le testimonianze contemporanee.*
Milan: Castello Sforzesco, 1999.

Weiss, Charles, ed. *Papiers d'État du Cardinal de Granvelle, d'après les manuscrits de
la bibliothèque de Besançon,* 2 vols. Paris: Imprimerie Royale, 1841.

Wiesflecker-Friedhuber, Inge. *Quellen zur Geschichte Maximilians I. und seiner Zeit.*
Darmstadt: Wissenschaftliche Buchgesellschaft, 1996.

SECONDARY SOURCES

Abulafia, David, ed. *The French Descent into Renaissance Italy 1494–95: Antecedents
and Effects.* Aldershot: Variorum, 1995.

Adami, Vittorio. "Episodi della guerra tra Milanesi e Veneziani in Val Sassina
1452–1453." *Archivio storico lombardo,* ser. 6, fasc. 2–3 (1926): 309–21.

Ady, Cecilia. *A History of Milan under the Sforza.* New York: G. P. Putnam's Sons,
1907.

Affò, Ireneo. *Memorie storiche di Colorno.* Parma: Per li Fratelli Gozzi, 1800.

Agamben, Giorgio. *Homo Sacer: Sovereignty and Bare Life.* Daniel Heller-Roazen,
trans. Stanford, CA: Stanford University Press, 1998.

——. *The State of Exception.* Kevin Attell, trans. Chicago: University of Chicago
Press, 2005.

Agosti, Giovanni, Mauro Natale, and Giovanni Romano, eds. *Vincenzo Foppa.*
Milan: Skira, 2003.

Alazard, Florence. *Agnadel, 1509—La bataille oubliée. Louis XII contre les Vénitiens.*
Rennes: Presses universitaires de Rennes, 2017.

Albertini Ottolenghi, Maria Grazia. "La Biblioteca dei Visconti e degli Sforza:
Gli Inventari del 1488 e del 1490." *Studi petrarcheschi* 8 (1991): 1–238.

Albini, Giulia. *Guerra, fame, peste. Crisi di mortalità e sistema sanitario nella Lombardia tardomedievale.* Bologna: Cappelli Editore, 1982.

Alfani, Guido. *Calamities and the Economy in Renaissance Italy: The Grand Tour of the
Horsemen of the Apocalypse.* Christine Calvert, trans. New York: Palgrave Macmillan, 2013.

Allonge, Guillaume. "Sanseverino, Galeazzo." *Dizionario biografico degli Italiani* 90
(2017): 291–93.

——. "Sanseverino, Gaspare." *Dizionario biografico degli Italiani* 90 (2017): 293–94.

Álvarez-Ossorio Alvariño, Antonio. "*La Cucagna o Spagna:* Los Orígines de la
dominación española en Lombardía." In Giuseppe Galasso and Carlos José

Hernando Sánchez, eds., *El Reino de Nápoles y la Monarquía de España entre agregación y conquista,* 401–52. Rome: Real Academia de España en Roma, 2004.

Andreozzi, Daniele. *Nascita di un disordine. Una Famiglia signorile e una valle piacentina tra XV e XVI secolo.* Milan: Edizioni Unicopli, 1993.

———. "Il Dominio francese e pontificio (1499–1545)." In Piero Castagnoli, ed., *Storia di Piacenza, vol 3: Dalla Signoria viscontea al principato farnesiano (1313–1545),* 167–93. Piacenza: Cassa di Risparmio di Piacenza, 1997.

Angermeier, Heinz. "Die Sforza und das Reich." In *Gli Sforza,* 165–91.

Antenhofer, Christina. "Emotions in the Correspondence of Bianca Maria Sforza." In Noflatscher, Chisholm, and Schnerb, eds., *Maximilian I,* 267–86.

Antoniazzi Villa, Anna. "Gli Ebrei dei domini sforzeschi negli ultimi decenni del Quattrocento." In *Milano nell'età di Ludovico il Moro,* 1: 179–84.

Arabeyre, Patrick. "Cigauld, Vincent." In Jean-Louis Halpérin, Jacques Krynen, and Patrick Arabeyre, eds., *Dictionnaire des juristes français, XIIe-XXe siècle,* 192. Paris: Presses universitaires de France, 2007.

Arcangeli, Letizia, ed. Milano e Luigi XII. Ricerche sul primo dominio francese in Lombardia (1499–1512). Milan: FrancoAngeli, 2002.

———. "Esperimenti di governo: Politica fiscale e consenso a Milano nell'età di Luigi XII." In Arcangeli, ed., *Milano e Luigi XII,* 255–339.

———. *Gentiluomini di Lombardia. Ricerche sull'aristocrazia padana nel Rinascimento.* Milan: Edizioni Unicopli, 2003.

———. "Milano durante le guerre d'Italia: Esperimenti di rappresentanza e identità cittadina." *Società e storia* 104 (2004): 225–63.

———. "Appunti su guelfi e ghibellini in Lombardia nelle guerre d'Italia (1494–1530)." In Marco Gentile, ed., *Guelfi e ghibellini nell'Italia del Rinascimento,* 391–472. Rome: Viella, 2005.

———. "Tra Milano e Roma: Esperienze politiche nella Parma del primo Cinquecento." In Giancarla Petrini, ed., *Emilia e Marche nel Rinascimento: L'identità Visiva della 'Periferia',* 89–118. Azzano San Paolo: Bolis Edizioni, 2005.

———. "'Les Ytaulx qui désirent franchise.' Invasione francese, permanenze e mutamenti nell'Italia del primo Cinquecento." In *'Terra di mezzo per trattar le regie paci.' Giugno 1507: La grande storia internazionale a Savona,* special issue of *Atti e memorie della società savonese di storia patria* 43 (2007): 137–54.

———. "Alle origini del consiglio dei sessanta decurioni: Ceti e rappresentanza a Milano tra Massimiliano Sforza e Francesco I di Valois (Maggio 1515–luglio 1516)." In Stefano Levati and Marco Meriggi, eds., *Con la ragione e col cuore: Studi dedicati a Carlo Capra,* 33–75. Milan: FrancoAngeli, 2008.

———. "La Città nelle guerre d'Italia (1494–1535)." In Giorgio Chittolini, ed., *Storia di Cremona—Il Quattrocento: Cremona nel Ducato di Milano (1395–1535),* 40–63. Cremona: Bolis Edizioni, 2008.

———. "Cambiamenti di dominio nello stato di Milano durante le prime guerre d'Italia (1495–1516). Dinamiche istituzionali e movimenti collettivi." In

Marcello Bonazza and Silvia Seidel Menchi, eds., *Dal Leone all'Aquila. Comunità, territori e cambi di regime nell'età di Massimiliano I,* 27–75. Rovereto: Edizioni Osiride, 2012.

———. "Città punite tra riforme istituzionali e repressione: Casi italiani del Cinque e Seicento." In Patrick Gilli and Jean-Pierre Guilhembert, eds., *Le Châtiment des villes dans les espaces méditerranéens (Antiquité, Moyen Âge, Époque moderne),* 315–38. Turnhout: Brepols, 2012.

———. "Morone, Gerolamo." *Dizionario biografico degli Italiani* 77 (2012): 74–78.

———. "Tracce delle esperienze di Guicciardini governatore nella *Storia d'Italia*." In Claudia Berra and Anna Maria Cabrini, eds., *La* Storia d'Italia *di Guicciardini e la sua fortuna,* 89–118. Milan: Cisalpino, 2012.

———. "'Parlamento' e 'libertà' nello stato di Milano al tempo di Luigi XII (1499–1512)." In Anne Lemonde and Ilaria Taddei, eds., *Circulations des idées et des pratiques politiques. France et Italie (XIIIe-XVIe siècle),* 209–33. Rome: École française de Rome, 2013.

———. "'Essendo tempo de pagare ad signori helvetii.' Resistenza fiscale e problemi costituzionali nella Milano del 1514." *Archivio storico ticinese* 156 (2014): 34–56.

———. "Marignano, una svolta? Governare Milano dopo la 'Battaglia dei giganti' (1515–1521). Note a margine di studi recenti." *Archivio storico lombardo* 141 (2015): 223–63.

Armstrong, Elizabeth. *Before Copyright: The French Book Privilege System 1498–1526.* Cambridge: Cambridge University Press, 1990.

Aron, Raymond. *Clausewitz: Philosopher of War.* Christine Booker and Norman Stone, trans. London: Routledge & Kegan Paul, 1983.

Arrigoni, Giuseppe. *Notizie storiche della Valsássina e delle terre limitrofe.* Milan: Luigi di Giacomo Pirola, 1860.

Artom, Emanuele. "Gli Ebrei in Italia nell'età delle dominazioni straniere e della controriforma." *La Rassegna Mensile di Israel,* ser. 3, vol. 15, no. 10 (1949): 456–67.

Auletta Marrucci, Rosa. "Il Borgo delle Grazie fuori di porta Vercellina: Un Incompiuto programma sforzesco." In Mario Frassineti, ed., *Santa Maria delle Grazie,* 24–47. Milan: Federico Motta, 1998.

Avril, François, and Marie-Thèrese Gousset. *Manuscrits enluminés d'origine italienne,* vol. 3: *XIVe siècle, 1: Lombardie-Ligurie.* Paris: Bibliothèque nationale de France, 2005.

Azzarà, Giovanni. "I Sanseverino di Lombardia." *Studi meridionali* 9, no. 3 (1976): 228–42.

Azzolini, Monica. *The Duke and the Stars: Astrology and Politics in Renaissance Milan.* Cambridge, MA: Harvard University Press, 2013.

Babinger, Franz. "Zwei diplomatische Zwischenspiele im deutsch-osmanischen Staatsverkehr unter Bâjezîd II. (1497 und 1504)." In Fritz Meier, ed., *Westöstliche Abhandlungen: Rudolf Tschudi zum siebzigsten Geburtstag überreicht von Freunden und Schülern,* 315–30. Wiesbaden: Otto Harrassowitz, 1954.

Balsamo, Jean, ed. *Passer les monts: Français en Italie, L'Italie en France (1494–1525)*. Paris: Honoré Champion, 1998.

Barbieri, Gino. "Gottardo Panigarola, mercante e spenditore sforzesco alla luce di nuovi documenti." *Atti e memorie del terzo congresso storico lombardo, 1938* (1939): 311–26.

Barbot, Michela. "Il Valore economico degli oggetti di lusso nella corte viscontea e sforzesca." In Paola Venturelli, ed., *Oro dai Visconti agli Sforza. Smalti e oreficeria nel Ducato di Milano*, 79–85. Milan: Silvana Editore, 2011.

Bartolomei Romagnoli, Alessandra, Emore Paoli, and Pierantonio Piatti, eds. *Angeliche visioni. Veronica da Binasco nella Milano del Rinascimento*. Florence: Edizioni del Galluzzo, 2016.

Barycz, Henryk. "Bona Sforza, regina di Polonia." *Dizionario biografico degli Italiani* 11 (1969): 430–36.

Bassetti, Aldo, and Eligio Pometta. "Gli ultimi anni di Bellinzona ducale e la sua volontaria dedizione agli svizzeri." *Quaderni grigionitaliani* 15, no. 3 (1945–1946): 197–207; 15, no. 4 (1945–1946): 265–76; 16, no. 2 (1946–1947): 126–40.

Baumgartner, Frederic J. *Louis XII*. New York: St. Martin's Press, 1994.

——. "Louis XII's Gallican Crisis of 1510-1513." In Adrianna E. Bakos, ed., *Politics, Ideology and the Law in Early Modern Europe*, 55–72. Rochester, NY: University of Rochester Press, 1994.

——. *Behind Locked Doors: A History of the Papal Elections*. New York: Palgrave Macmillan, 2003.

Beam, Sara. *Laughing Matters: Farce and the Making of Absolutism in France*. Ithaca, NY: Cornell University Press, 2007.

Behne, Axel. "Archivordnung und Staatsordnung im Mailand der Sforza-Zeit." *Nuovi annali della Scuola speciale per archivisti e bibliotecari* 2 (1988): 93–102.

Belgrano, Luigi Tommaso. "Della dedizione dei Genovesi a Luigi XII re di Francia." *Miscellanea di Storia Italiana* 1 (1862): 559–659.

Belloni, Annalisa. "L''Historia patria' di Tristano Calco fra gli Sforza e i Francesi: Fonti e strati redazionali." *Italia medioevale e umanistica* 23 (1980): 179–232.

Benjamin, Walter. "Ursprung des deutschen Trauerspiels." In Rolf Tiedemann and Hermann Schweppenhäuser, eds., *Walter Benjamin: Gesammelte Schriften 1*, 203–430. Frankfurt: Suhrkamp, 1974.

Benzoni, Gino. "Massimiliano Sforza." *Dizionario biografico degli Italiani* 71 (2008): 782–87.

Beretta, Rinaldo. "Gian Giacomo de' Medici in Brianza (1527-1531)." *Archivio storico lombardo* ser. 5, fasc. 1–2 (1916): 53–120.

Besta, Beatrice. "La Popolazione di Milano nel periodo della dominazione Spagnola." In Corrado Gini, ed., *Atti del congresso internazionale per lo studio dei problemi della popolazione*, 1: 593–610. Rome: Istituto poligrafico dello stato, 1932.

Bettini, Maurizio. *Anthropology and Roman Culture*. Baltimore, MD: Johns Hopkins University Press, 1991.

Biancardi, Silvio. *La chimera di Carlo VIII (1492–1495)*. Novara: Interlinea Edizioni, 2011.

Biersteker, Thomas J., and Cynthia Weber, "The Social Construction of State Sovereignty." In Thomas J. Biersteker and Cynthia Weber, eds., *State Sovereignty as a Social Construct*, 1–21. Cambridge: Cambridge University Press, 1996.

Binaghi Olivari, Maria Teresa. "L'Immagine sacra in Luini e il circolo di Santa Marta." In Piero Chiara, ed., *Sacro e profano nella pittura di Bernardino Luini*, 49–76. Milan: Silvana Editoriale d'Arte, 1976.

Biow, Douglas. *On the Importance of Being an Individual in Renaissance Italy: Men, Their Professions, and Their Beards*. Philadelphia: University of Pennsylvania Press, 2015.

Biucchi, Basilio. "Bellinzona nei primi decenni della occupazione svizzera (1500–1555) nella documentazione dei recessi federali." In Giuseppe Chiesi, ed., *Pagine bellinzonesi. Cenni storici, studi e ricerche in occasione del centenario di Bellinzona capitale stabile del Cantone Ticino, 1878–1978*, 123–52. Bellinzona: Comune di Bellinzona, 1978.

Black, Antony. *Council and Commune: The Conciliar Movement and the Fifteenth-Century Heritage*. London: Burns and Oates, 1979.

Black, Jane. "Natura feudi haec est: Lawyers and Feudatories in the Duchy of Milan." *English Historical Review* 109, no. 434 (1994): 1150–73.

———. *Absolutism in Renaissance Milan: Plenitude of Power under the Visconti and Sforza, 1329–1535*. Oxford: Oxford University Press, 2009.

———. "Giangaleazzo Visconti and the Ducal Title." In John E. Law and Bernadette Paton, eds., *Communes and Despots in Medieval and Renaissance Italy*, 119–30. Farnham, UK: Ashgate, 2010.

———. "Double Duchy: the Sforza dukes and the other Lombard title." In Paola Guglielmotti, Isabella Lazzarini, and Gian Maria Varanini, eds., *Europa e Italia. Studi in onore di Giorgio Chittolini*, 15–27. Florence: Firenze University Press, 2011.

———. "The Emergence of the Duchy of Milan: Language and the Territorial State." *Reti Medievali Rivista* 14, no. 1 (2013): 197–210.

———. "The Politics of Law." In Gamberini, ed., *A Companion to Late Medieval and Early Modern Milan*, 432–53.

Blockmans, Wim. "Voracious States and Obstructing Cities: An Aspect of State Formation in Preindustrial Europe." *Theory and Society* 18 (1989): 733–55.

Bognetti, Gian Piero. "Per la storia dello Stato visconteo (Un registro di decreti, della cancelleria di Filippo Maria Visconti, e un trattato segreto con Alfonso d'Aragona)." *Archivio storico lombardo*, ser. 6, fasc. 2–3 (1927): 237–357.

Boisen, Camilla, and David Boucher. "The Medieval and Early Modern Legacy of Rights: The Rights to Punish and to Property." In William Bain, ed., *Medieval Foundations of International Relations*, 148–65. London: Routledge, 2017.

Bonali-Fiquet, Françoise. "La Bataille d'Agnadel dans la poésie populaire italienne du début du XVIe siècle." In Balsamo, ed., *Passer les monts,* 227–43.

Bondioli, Pio. "La Battaglia di Marignano in una relazione a Enrico VIII d'Inghilterra." In *Scritti storici in memoria di Alessandro Visconti,* 169–85. Milan: Istituto Editoriale Cisalpino, 1955.

———. "Un Miniatore lombardo ignorato: Pietro Carcano." *La Bibliofilía* 59, no. 1 (1957): 15–22.

Bora, Giulio. "La Decorazione pittorica: Sino al Settecento." In *Santa Maria delle Grazie,* 140–87. Milano: Banca Popolare di Milano, 1983.

Borghi, Angelo, ed. *La Rocca di Bajedo in Valsassina.* Missaglia: Bellavite, 2007.

Boskovits, Miklós, and Giorgio Fossaluzza, eds. *La Collezione Cagnola,* 2 vols. Busto Arsizio: Nomos Edizioni, 1998.

Bossy, Denise Ileana. "Shattering Together, Merging Apart: Colonialism, Violence, and the Remaking of the Native South." *William and Mary Quarterly* 71, no. 4 (2014): 611–31.

Boucheron, Patrick. *Le Pouvoir de bâtir. Urbanisme et politique édilitaire à Milan (XIVe-XVe siècles).* Rome: École française de Rome, 1998.

———. "Water and Power in Milan, c. 1200-1500." *Urban History* 28, no. 2 (2001): 180–93.

———. "Non domus ista sed urbs: Palais princiers et environnement urbain au Quattrocento (Milan, Mantoue, Urbino)." In Patrick Boucheron and Jacques Chiffoleau, eds., *Les Palais dans la ville. Espaces urbains et lieux de puissance publique dans la Méditerranée médiévale,* 249–84. Lyon: Presses Universitaires de Lyon, 2004.

———. "Les Combattants d'Ambroise. Commémorations et luttes politiques à la fin du Moyen Âge." In Patrick Boucheron and Stéphane Gioanni, eds., *La mémoire d'Ambroise. Usages politiques et sociaux d'une autorité patristique en Italie (Ve-XVIIIe siècle),* 484–98. Paris: Éditions de la Sorbonne-École française de Rome, 2015.

Boulet, Marguerite. "Une 'Repetitio' de Pierre d'Angleberme sur la loi 'Jurisjurandi' (C., IV, .1, fr. 2.)." *Revue historique de droit français et étranger,* ser. 4, vol. 25 (1948): 323–34.

Boureau, Alain. "How Christian Was the Sacralization of Monarchy in Western Europe (Twelfth–Fifteenth Centuries)?" In Jeroen Deploige and Gita Deneckere, eds., *Mystifying the Monarch: Studies on Discourse, Power, and History,* 25–34, 235–37. Amsterdam: Amsterdam University Press, 2006.

Bowd, Stephen. *Venice's Most Loyal City: Civic Identity in Renaissance Brescia.* Cambridge, MA: Harvard University Press, 2010.

———. "Mass Murder in Sacks during the Italian Wars, 1494-1559." In Dean and Lowe, eds., *Murder,* 249–68.

———. *Renaissance Mass Murder: Civilians and Soldiers during the Italian Wars.* Oxford: Oxford University Press, 2018.

Brecht, Martin. *Martin Luther,* 3 vols. Stuttgart: Calwer Verlag, 1983.

Bredekamp, Horst. "From Walter Benjamin to Carl Schmitt via Thomas Hobbes." *Critical Inquiry* 25, no. 2 (1999): 247–66.

Brignoli, Carlo Alberto. *Guerre fluviali. Le Lotte fra Venezia e Milano nel XV secolo.* Milan: Mursia, 2014.

Britnell, Jennifer. *Le Roi très chrétien contre le pape. Écrits antipapaux en français sous le règne de Louis XII.* Paris: Garnier Classiques, 2011.

Brivio Sforza, Gianfrancesco, ed. *Notizie Storico-Genealogiche della famiglia Brivio.* Milan: Editrice Nuovi Autori, 2000.

Broillet, Leonardo. *A Cavallo delle Alpi. Ascese, declini e colloborazioni di ceti dirigenti tra Ticino e Svizzera centrale (1400–1600).* Milan: FrancoAngeli, 2014.

Brown, Alison. "Rethinking the Renaissance in the Aftermath of Italy's Crisis." In John Najemy, ed., *Italy in the Age of the Renaissance, 1300–1500,* 246–65. Oxford: Oxford University Press, 2004.

———. "Florentine Diplomacy on the Banks of the Po: Bernardo Ricci's Meeting with Lodovico il Moro in June 1493." In Philippa Jackson and Guido Rebecchini, eds., *Mantova e il Rinascimento italiano: Studi in onore di David S. Chambers,* 301–14. Mantua: Sommetti, 2011.

Brown, Cynthia J. "Introduction" to Pierre Gringore, *Oeuvres polémiques rédigés sous le règne de Louis XII,* 9–61. Geneva: Droz, 2003.

Bucci, Carlo Alberto. "Gallerani, Cecilia." *Dizionario biografico degli Italiani* 51 (1998): 551–53.

Büchi, Albert. *Kardinal Matthäus Schiner als Staatsmann und Kirchenfürst.* Zurich: Kommissionsverlag Seldwyla, 1923.

Bueno de Mesquita, Daniel M. "The Privy Council in the Government of the Dukes of Milan." In Craig Hugh Smyth and Gian Carlo Garfagnini, eds., *Florence and Milan: Comparisons and Relations,* 1: 135–56. Florence: La Nuova Italia Editrice.

Burns, J. H. "Conciliarism, Papalism, and Power, 1511–1518." In Diana Wood, ed., *The Church and Sovereignty, c. 590–1918: Essays in Honour of Michael Wilks,* 409–28. Oxford: Basil Blackwell, 1991.

Butler, Judith. "Afterword: After Loss, What Then?" In David L. Eng and David Kazanjian, eds., *Loss: The Politics of Mourning,* 467–73. Berkeley: University of California Press, 2003.

Cadoppi, Alberto. *La Gran congiura: Il Processo di Ranuccio I Farnese contro i feudatari parmensi, 1611–1612.* Parma: Monte Università Parma, 2012.

Cairati, Carlo, and Daniele Cassinelli, "Regesto dei documenti." In *Giovanni Pietro e Giovanni Ambrogio De Donati. Scultori e imprenditori del legno nella Lombardia del Rinascimento,* special issue of *Rassegna di studi e di notizie* 32 (2009): 133–58.

Call, Charles T. "The Fallacy of the 'Failed State.'" *Third World Quarterly* 29, no. 8 (2008): 1491–1507.

———. "Beyond the 'Failed State': Toward Conceptual Alternatives." *European Journal of International Relations* 17, no. 2 (2010): 303–26.

Calvi, Felice. *Il Patriziato milanese*. Milan: Andrea Mosconi, 1875.

——. *Famiglie notabili milanesi*, 4 vols. Milan: Antonio Vallardi, 1881.

——. "Antonio Landriani tesoriere generale di Lodovico il Moro." *Rendiconti del reale istituto lombardo di scienze e lettere*, ser. 2, vol. 15 (1882): 681–86.

——. "Il Castello di Porta Giovia e sue vicende nella storia di Milano." *Archivio storico lombardo*, series 2, vol. 3, fasc. 2 (1886): 229–97.

——. *Bianca Maria Sforza-Visconti, Regina dei Romani, Imperatrice Germanica.* Milan: Antonio Vallardi, 1888.

——. *Il Castello Visconteo-sforzesco nella storia di Milano*. Milano: Antonio Vallardi, 1894.

Canning, Joseph. *The Political Thought of Baldus de Ubaldis*. Cambridge: Cambridge University Press, 1987.

Carré de Busserole, Jacques-Xavier. *Dictionnaire géographie, historique et biographique d'Indre-et-Loire et de l'ancienne province de Touraine*, 6 vols. Tours: Imprimerie Rouillé-Ladevèze, 1878–1884.

Cashman, Anthony B. "Performance Anxiety: Federico Gonzaga at the Court of Francis I and the Uncertainty of Ritual Action." *Sixteenth Century Journal* 33, no. 2 (2002): 333–52.

Caspary, Gerard E. *Politics and Exegesis: Origen and the Two Swords*. Berkeley: University of California Press, 1979.

Cassen, Flora. *Marking the Jews in Renaissance Italy*. Cambridge: Cambridge University Press, 2017.

Cassini, Stefano. "Il 'Carmen anguineum' di Lidio Catto." In Stefan Tilg and Benjamin Harter, eds., *Neulateinische Metrik. Formen und Kontexte zwischen Rezeption und Innovation*, 91–109. Tübingen: Gunter Narr Verlag, 2019.

Castelli, Giuseppe. "Gli Affreschi del castello di Cozzo." *Viglevanum* 10 (2000): 63–65.

Cattaneo, Enrico. "La Condotta dei milanesi durante il concilio di Pisa-Milano, 155–1512." *Ricerche storiche sulla Chiesa Ambrosiana* 2 (1971): 245–79.

Catturini, Carlo. "Dopo Leonardo: La Sala delle Asse al tempo di Francesco II Sforza e Cristina di Danimarca." *Rassegna di studi e di notizie* 38 (2016): 15–30.

Caviglia, Alberto. *Claudio di Seyssel (1450–1520). La Vita nella storia de' suoi tempi*. Turin: Fratelli Bocca Librai, 1928.

Cengarle, Federica. *Lesa maestà all'ombra del biscione: Dalle Città lombarde ad una 'monarchia' europea (1335–1447)*. Rome: Edizioni di storia e letteratura, 2014.

Cerioni, Lidia. "Gli ultimi mesi di Bellinzona ducale." *Bollettino storico della svizzera italiana* 26, no. 1 (1951): 1–41.

——. "La Cancelleria Sforzesca durante il ritorno del Moro (Gennaio–Aprile 1500)." *Archivio storico lombardo* 93–94 (1966): 140–72.

Ceruti, Antonio. "Il Corredo nuziale di Bianca M. Sforza-Visconti, sposa dell'imperatore Massimiliano I." *Archivio storico lombardo*, ser. 1, vol. 2, fasc. 1 (1875): 51–75.

Chabod, Federico. "Usi e abusi nell'amministrazione dello Stato di Milano a mezzo '500." In *Studi storici in onore di Gioacchino Volpe per il suo 80. compleanno,* 1: 95–191. Milano: Sansoni, 1958.

———. *Storia di Milano nell'epoca di Carlo V.* Turin: Einaudi, 1961.

Chantérac, Bertrand de. *Odet de Foix, Vicomte de Lautrec, Maréchal de France (1483–1528).* Paris: Librairie Historique A. Margraff, 1930.

Chittolini, Giorgio. "Le Terre separate nel ducato di Milano in età sforzesca." In *Milano nell'età di Ludovico,* 1: 115–28.

———. "Milan in the Face of the Italian Wars." In Abulafia, ed., *The French Descent,* 391–404.

———. "Il 'Militare' tra tardo medioevo e prima età moderna." In Claudio Donati and Bernhard R. Kroener, eds., *Militari e società civile nell'Europa dell'età moderna (secoli XVI–XVIII),* 53–102. Bologna: Il Mulino, 2007.

———. "Milano 'città imperiale'? Note su due ambascerie di Enea Silvio Piccolomini (1447, 1449)." In Claudio Donati and Bernhard R. Kroener, eds., *L'Italia delle* civitates. *Grandi e piccoli centri fra Medioevo e Rinascimento,* 141–64. Rome: Viella, 2015.

Clément-Simon, G. "Un Conseiller du roi François Ier, Jean de Selve premier président du Parlement de Paris, négociateur du traité de Madrid." *Revue des questions historiques* 37, no. 29 (1903): 45–120.

Coakley, John. *Women, Men, and Spiritual Power: Female Saints and Their Male Collaborators.* New York: Columbia University Press, 2006.

Cocchetti Almasio, Silvia. "L'Influsso della cultura prospettica bramantesca sui pannelli degli armadi nella sagrestia di Santa Maria delle Grazie." *Arte lombarda* 78, no. 3 (1986): 59–71.

Cockram, Sarah D. P. *Isabella d'Este and Francesco Gonzaga: Power Sharing at the Italian Renaissance Court.* Farnham, UK: Ashgate, 2013.

Contamine, Philippe. "La Mémoire de l'état. Les Archives de la Chambre des Comptes du roi de France à Paris, au XVᵉ siècle." In *Media in Francia . . . Recueil de mélanges offert à Karl Ferdinand Werner,* 85–100. Maulévrier: Hérault-Éditions, 1989.

Contamine, Philippe, and Jean Guillaume, eds. *Louis XII en Milanais.* Paris: Honoré Champion, 2003.

Corna, Andrea. *Castelli e Rocche del Piacentino.* Piacenza: Unione Tipografica Piacentina, 1913.

Cossar, Roissin. *Clerical Households in Late Medieval Italy.* Cambridge, MA: Harvard University Press, 2017.

Covini, Maria Nadia. "Fondulo, Cabrino." *Dizionario biografico degli Italiani* 48 (1997): 586–89.

———. *L'Esercito del duca: Organizzazione militare e istituzioni al tempo degli Sforza.* Rome: Istituto storico italiano per il Medio Evo, 1998.

———. "La Trattazione delle suppliche nella cancelleria sforzesca: Da Francesco Sforza a Ludovico il Moro." In Cecilia Nubola and Andreas Würgler, eds., *Sup-*

pliche e 'gravamina.' Politica, amministrazione, giustizia in Europa (secoli XIV–XVIII), 107–46. Bologna: il Mulino, 2002.

——. "In Lomellina nel Quattrocento: Il declino delle stirpi locali e i 'feudi accomprati.'" In Federica Cengarle, Giorgio Chittolini, and Gian Maria Varanini, eds., *Poteri signorili e feudali nelle campagne dell'Italia settentrionale fra Tre e Quattrocento*, 127–74. Florence: Firenze University Press, 2005.

——. *'La Balanza drita.' Pratiche di governo, leggi e ordinamenti nel ducato sforzesco.* Milan: FrancoAngeli, 2007.

——. *Donne, emozioni e potere alla corte degli Sforza. Da Bianca Maria a Cecilia Gallerani.* Milan: Unicopli, 2012.

Crescio, Giovanni. "Un Episodio storico di giustizia punitiva." *Strenna Piacentina* 18 (1892): 62–67.

Crouzet, Denis. "Le Connétable de Bourbon entre 'pratique,' 'machination,' 'conjuration' et 'trahison'." In Yves-Marie Bercé and Elena Fasano Guarini, eds., *Complots et conjurations dans l'Europe moderne*, 253–69. Rome: École française de Rome, 1996.

——. "From Christ-Like King to Antichristian Tyrant: A First Crisis of the Monarchical Image at the Time of Francis I." *Past and Present* 214, suppl. 7 (2012): 220–40.

Crucitti, Filippo. "Landriani, Gerolamo." *Dizionario biografico degli Italiani* 63 (2004): 523–26.

Cusin, Fabio. "L'Impero e la successione degli Sforza ai Visconti." *Archivio storico lombardo*, fasc. 1–2 (1936): 3–116.

——. "Le Aspirazioni straniere sul ducato di Milano e l'investitura imperiale (1450–54)." *Archivio storico lombardo*, fasc. 3–4 (1936): 277–369.

Cuttler, Simon Hirsch. *The Law of Treason and Treason Trials in Later Medieval France.* Cambridge: Cambridge University Press, 1978.

Dalla Santa, Giuseppe. "Della 'cheba del supplizio' appesa al campanile di San Marco." *Nuovo archivio veneto* 23 (1912): 458–59.

D'Amico, Stefano. *Spanish Milan: A City within the Empire, 1535–1706.* New York: Palgrave Macmillan, 2012.

Danusso, Cristina. "Baldo e i *Libri Feudorum.*" In Carla Frova, Maria Grazia Nico Ottaviani, and Stefania Zucchini, eds. *VI Centenario della morte di Baldo degli Ubaldi, 1400–2000*, 289–311. Perugia: Università degli Studi, 2005.

Dauvillier, Jean. "L'Union réelle de Gênes et du Royaume de France aux XIVᵉ, XVᵉ, et XVIᵉ siècles." *Annales de la Faculté de Droit d'Aix-en-Provence* 43 (1950): 81–112.

Davis, Charles T. "Il Buon tempo antico." In Nicolai Rubinstein, ed., *Florentine Studies: Politics and Society in Renaissance Florence*, 45–69. London: Faber and Faber, 1968.

Dean, Trevor, and K. J. P. Lowe, eds. *Murder in Renaissance Italy.* Cambridge: Cambridge University Press, 2017.

De Benedictis, Angela. *Una Guerra d'Italia, una resistenza di popolo. Bologna 1506.* Bologna: Il Mulino, 2004.

Defendi, Nansen. "La 'Revocatio M. Lutherii ad Sanctam Sedem' nella polemica antiluterana in Italia." *Archivio storico lombardo,* ser. 8, vol. 4 (1953): 67–153.

De Gramatica, Francesca. "La sepoltura 'honoratissima' di Roberto da Sanseverino." In Franco Marzatico and Johannes Ramharter, eds., *I Cavalieri dell'Imperatore. Tornei, battaglie e castelli,* 237–46. Trent: Castello del Buonconsiglio, 2012.

Delalande, Paul. *Histoire de Marmoutier depuis sa fondation par Saint Martin jusqu'à nos jours.* Tours: Imprimerie Barbot-Berruer, 1897.

Della Croce, Giovanna. "Maria Caterina Brugora (1489–1529) una mistica milanese sconosciuta." *Mediaevistik* 7 (1994): 71–91.

Della Misericordia, Massimo. "'Per non privarci de nostre raxone, li siamo stati desobidienti.' Patto, giustizia e resistenza nella cultura politica delle comunità alpine nello stato di Milano (XV secolo)." In Cecilia Nubola and Andreas Würgler, eds., *Operare la resistenza: Suppliche, gravamina e rivolte in Europa (secoli XV–XIX),* 147–215. Bologna: Il Mulino, 2006.

——. "'Como se tuta questa universitade parlasse.' La Rappresentanza politica delle comunità nello stato di Milano (XV secolo)." In François Faronda, ed., *Avant le contrat social. Le Contrat politique dans l'Occident médiéval (XIIIe–XVe siècle),* 117–70. Paris: Publications de la Sorbonne, 2011.

Del Lungo, Isidoro. "Fra' Girolamo Savonarola." *Archivio storico italiano,* nuova serie, 18 (1863): 3–41.

Del Mayno, Luchino, and Luca Beltrami. *Vicende militari del Castello di Milano dal 1706 al 1848.* Milano: Hoepli, 1894.

De Pins, Jean. "Autour des Guerres d'Italie." *Revue d'histoire diplomatique* 61 (1947): 215–46; 62 (1948): 88–113.

Del Tredici, Federico. "Lombardy under the Visconti and the Sforza." In Gamberini and Lazzarini, eds., *The Italian Renaissance State,* 156–76.

——. "Nobility in Lombardy between the Late Middle Ages and the Early Modern Age." In Gamberini, ed., *A Companion to Late Medieval and Early Modern Milan,* 477–98.

——. *Un'Altra nobiltà. Storie di (in)distinzione a Milano, secoli XIV–XV.* Milan: FrancoAngeli, 2017.

Denis, Anne. *Charles VIII et les Italiens. Histoire et mythe.* Geneva: Droz, 1979.

——. "1513–1515: 'La Nazione svizzera' et les Italiens." *Schweizerische Zeitschrift für Geschichte* 47, no. 2 (1997): 111–28.

De Vivo, Filippo, Andrea Guidi, and Alessandro Silvestri, eds., *Archivi e archivisti in Italia tra medioevo ed età moderna.* Rome: Viella, 2015.

——, eds. *Fonti per la storia degli archivi degli antichi Stati italiani.* Rome: Ministero dei beni e delle attività culturali del turismo—direzione generale archivi, 2016.

Di Giovanni, Marilisa. "Il Serpente di bronzo della Basilica di S. Ambrogio." *Arte lombarda* 11, no. 1 (1966): 3–5.

Dina, Achille. "Isabella d'Aragona, duchessa di Milano e duchessa di Bari." *Archivio storico lombardo* 48 (1921): 269–457.

Di Renzo Villata, Maria Gigliola. "Sulle trace di un diritto 'patrio' nel ducato di Milano a metà Cinquecento: Tra *Novae Constitutiones* (1541) e fonti del diritto antiche e recenti." *Studia borromaica* 26 (2012): 121–56.

Di Tullio, Matteo. *La Richezza delle comunità. Guerra, risorse, cooperazione nella Geradadda del Cinquecento.* Venice: Marsilio Editori, 2011.

———. "Cooperating in Time of Crisis: War, Commons, and Inequality in Renaissance Lombardy." *Economic History Review* 71, no. 1 (2018): 82–105.

Di Tullio, Matteo, and Luca Fois. *Stati di guerra: I Bilanci della Lombardia francese del primo Cinquecento.* Rome: École française de Rome, 2014.

Duc, Séverin. "Les Élites lombardes face à l'effondrement du duché de Milan (ca. 1500–ca. 1540)." In Laurent Coste and Sylvie Guillaume, eds., *Élites et crises du XVIe au XXIe siècle: Europe et Outre-mer,* 101–11. Paris: Armand Colin, 2014.

———. "Il Prezzo delle guerre lombarde. Rovina dello stato, distruzione della ricchezza e disastro sociale (1515–1535)." *Storia economica* 19 (2016): 219–48.

Dumont, Jonathan. *Lilia Florent. L'Imaginaire politique et social à la cour de France durant les Premières Guerres d'Italie (1494–1525).* Paris: Honoré Champion, 2013.

Dumont, Jonathan, and Laure Fagnart, eds. *Georges Ier d'Amboise 1460–1510. Une figure plurielle de la Renaissance.* Rennes: Presses universitaires de Rennes, 2013.

Dutton, Paul Edward. *Charlemagne's Mustache: And Other Cultural Clusters of a Dark Age.* New York: Palgrave Macmillan, 2004.

Elsig, Frédéric, and Mauro Natale, eds. *Le Duché de Milan et les commanditaires français (1499–1521).* Viella: Rome, 2013.

Ernst, Germana. "Astri e previsioni: Il *Pronostico* di Cardano del 1534." In Marialuisa Baldi and Guido Canziani, eds., *Girolamo Cardano. Le opere, le fonti, la vita,* 457–75. Milano: FrancoAngeli, 1999.

Ethridge, Robbie. "Creating the Shatter Zone: Indian Slave Traders and the Collapse of the Southeastern Chiefdoms." In T. J. Pluckhahn and Robbie Ethridge, eds., *Light on the Path: the Anthropology and the History of the Southeastern Indians,* 207–18. Tuscaloosa: University of Alabama Press, 2006.

Ethridge, Robbie, and Sheri M. Shuck-Hall. "Introduction." In Robbie Ethridge and Sheri M. Shuck-Hall, eds., *Mapping the Mississippian Shatter Zone: The Colonial Indian Slave Trade and Regional Instability in the American South,* 1–62. Lincoln: University of Nebraska Press, 2009.

Fabbri, Pier Giovanni. "Il Governo e la caduta di Cesare Borgia a Cesena (1500–1504) nella cronaca di Giuliano Fantaguzzi." *Nuova rivista storica* 72, nos. 3–4 (1988): 341–88.

Fagnart, Laure. *Léonard de Vinci en France.* Rome: L'Erma di Bretschneider, 2009.

Fanfani, Amintore. "Aspetti demografici della politica economica nel ducato di Milano (1386-1535)." In Amintore Fanfani, *Saggi di storia economica italiana,* 123–57. Milan: Vita e Pensiero, 1936.

Fantoni, Giuliana. *L'Acqua a Milano. Uso e gestione nel basso medioevo (1385–1535).* Bologna: Cappelli Editore, 1990.

Fara, Giovanni Maria. "Dürer, Leonardo, e la storia dell'arte." In Bernard Aikema and Andrew John Martin, eds., *Dürer e il Rinascimento tra Germania e Italia,* 81–93. Milan: 24 Ore Cultura, 2018.

Félibien, Michel. *Histoire de la Ville de Paris,* 5 vols. Paris: Chez Guillaume Desprez, 1725.

Ferente, Serena. "Guelphs! Factions, Liberty, and Sovereignty: Inquiries about the Quattrocento." *History of Political Thought* 28, no. 4 (2007): 571–98.

Ferrari, Mirella. "Per la fioritura di S. Ambrogio nel Quattrocento Milanese. Appunti su umanisti e codici." *Archivio ambrosiano* 26 (1973–1974): 132–47.

Ferrari, Monica. *'Per non manchare in tuto del debito mio.' L'Educazione dei bambini Sforza nel Quattrocento.* Milan: FrancoAngeli, 2000.

Ferri, Massimiliano, and Luca Fois. "Le Terre ticinesi tra ducato di Milano, Francia e Svizzeri dalla caduta di Lugano e Locarno all'alleanza di Lucerna (1513–1521)." *Archivio storico lombardo,* ser. 12, vol. 18 (2013): 149–82.

Ferri Piccaluga, Gabriella. "Economia, devozione e politica: immagini di francescani, amadeiti ed ebrei nel secolo XV." In *Il Francescanesimo in Lombardia: Storia e arte,* 107–22. Milan: Silvana Editoriale, 1983.

Fichtner, Paula Sutter. *Ferdinand I of Austria: The Politics of Dynasticism in the Age of the Reformation.* New York: Columbia University Press, 1982.

Filippini, Ambrogio. *I Visconti di Milano nei secoli XI e XII. Indagini tra le fonti.* Trent: Tangram Edizioni Scientifiche, 2014.

Fiori, Giorgio. "I Sanseverino d'Aragona di Parma e Piacenza." In *Colorno la Versailles dei duchi di Parma,* 61–75. Parma: La deputazione di storia patria per le province parmensi, 1969.

——. "Bobbio e i Dal Verme." *Archivio storico per le province parmensi,* ser. 4, vol. 38 (1986): 175–201.

——. *Storia di Bobbio e delle famiglie bobbiesi.* Piacenza: Libreria Internazionale Romagnosi, 2015.

Fiorio, Maria Teresa. "Due disegni e un possibile intervento del Bambaia in Santa Maria alla Fontana." In Shell and Castelfranchi, eds., *Giovanni Antonio Amadeo,* 589–612.

Fois, Luca. "'Et ledit jour echeu s'ilz ne sont secourriz rendront la place audit seigneur duc . . .' La Resa della guarnigione francese del castello di Porta Giovia di Milano al duca Massimiliano Sforza-Visconti (novembre 1513)." *Annuario dell'archivio di Stato di Milano* (2016): 10–77.

Fontanella, Lucia. "La Relazione di Roberto Sanseverino sull'assassinio di Galeazzo Maria Sforza." *Pluteus* 6–7 (1988): 67–77.

Fossati, Felice. "Lodovico Sforza avvelenatore del nipote? (Testimonianza di Simone Del Pozzo)." *Archivio storico lombardo,* ser. 4, vol. 2, fasc. 3 (1904): 162–71.

——. Review of *Inventari e regesti del R. Archivio di Stato di Milano. Archivio storico lombardo,* ser. 6, fasc. 3 (1931): 364–79.

Fournel, Jean-Louis. "La 'Brutalisation' de la guerre. Des Guerres d'Italie aux guerres de Religion." *Astérion* 2 (2004): 105–31.

Fournel, Jean-Louis, and Jean-Claude Zancarini. *Les Guerres d'Italie: Des Batailles pour l'Europe, 1494–1559.* Paris: Gallimard, 2003.

——. *La Grammaire de la république. Langages de la politique chez Francesco Guicciardini (1483–1540).* Geneva: Droz, 2009.

——. "L'Écriture du gouvernement et de la force en France et en Italie au début du XVIe siècle." In Patricia Eichel-Lojkine, ed., *Claude de Seyssel. Écrire l'histoire, penser le politique en France, à l'aube des temps modernes,* 102–20. Rennes: Presses Universitaires de Rennes, 2010.

Fragnito, Gigliola. "Carvajal, Bernardino Lopez de." *Dizionario biografico degli Italiani* 21 (1978): 28–34.

Franceschini, Gino. "Le Dominazioni francesi." In *Storia di Milano VIII: Tra Francia e Spagna (1500–1530),* 82–333. Milan: Fondazione Treccani degli Alfieri, 1957.

Frassineti, Mario, ed. *Santa Maria delle Grazie.* Milan: Federico Motta Editore, 1998.

Freschot, Casimiro. *La Nobiltà Veneta.* Venice: Appresso Gio. Gabriel Hertz, 1708.

Frizzi, Antonio. *Memorie storiche della nobile famiglia Bevilacqua.* Parma: dalla Reale Stamperia, 1779.

Fulin, Rinaldo. "Difficiles Nugae." *Archivio veneto* 19 (1880): 131–34.

Gabotto, Ferdinando. *Giasone del Maino e gli scandali universitari nel Quattrocento.* Turin: La Letteratura, 1888.

Gabotto, Ferdinando, and Angelo Badini Confalonieri. *Vita di Giorgio Merula.* Alessandria: Tipografia Giovanni Jacquemod, 1893.

Gaggetta, Claudia. "Louis II d'Amboise et les fresques de la cathédrale Sainte-Cécile d'Albi." In Elsig and Natale, eds., *Le Duché de Milan,* 287–321.

Gagliardi, Ernst. *Der Anteil der Schweizer an den italienischen Kriegen, 1494–1516.* Zurich: Verlag von Schulthess & Co., 1919.

Gagné, John. "After the Sforza: Making History in Milan during the Italian Wars." In Christian Callisen, ed., *Reading and Writing History from Bruni to Windschuttle,* 35–55. Farnham, UK: Ashgate, 2014.

——. "Counting the Dead: Traditions of Enumeration and the Italian Wars." *Renaissance Quarterly* 67, no. 3 (2014): 791–840.

——. "Crisis Redux: The View from Milan, 1499." In Nicholas Scott Baker and Brian Jeffrey Maxson, eds., *After Civic Humanism: Learning and Politics in Renaissance Italy,* 215–40. Toronto: Centre for Reformation and Renaissance Studies, 2015.

——. "Fixing Texts and Changing Regimes: Two Holy Lives in French-Occupied Milan." In Alison K. Frazier, ed., *The Saint between Manuscript and Print: Italy 1400–1600,* 379–420. Toronto: Centre for Reformation and Renaissance Studies, 2015.

——. "Collecting Women: Three French Kings and Manuscripts of Empire in the Italian Wars." *I Tatti Studies in the Italian Renaissance* 20, no. 1 (2017): 127–84.

Galante, Andrea. *Il Diritto di placitazione e l'economato dei benefici vacanti in Lombardia*. Milan: Tip. Bernardoni di C. Rebeschini e C., 1893.

Galletti, Giorgio. "Precisazioni su Santa Maria alla Fontana a Milano." *Raccolta vinciana*, fasc. 21 (1982): 39–102.

Gallo, Federico. "L'Osservanza agostiniana a Milano nel secolo XV: il convento di S. Maria Incoronata." In Bartolomei Romagnoli, Paoli, and Piatti, eds. *Angeliche visioni*, 141–72.

Gamberini, Andrea. *La Città assediata. Poteri e identità politica a Reggio in età viscontea*. Rome: Viella, 2003.

——. *Lo Stato visconteo. Linguaggi politici e dinamiche constituzionali*. Milan: FrancoAngeli, 2005.

——. "Cremona nel Quattrocento. La Vicenda politica e istituzionale." In Giorgio Chittolini, ed., *Storia di Cremona: Il Quattrocento—Cremona nel Ducato di Milano (1395–1535)*, 2–29. Cremona: Comune di Cremona, 2008.

——. "Il Ducato di Milano e gli Svyceri: Uno Sguardo d'insieme." In Rodolfo Huber and Rachele Pollini-Widmer, eds., *Da Dominio a dominio: Il Locarnese e la Valmaggia all'inizio del XVI secolo*—special issue of *Bollettino della società storica locarnese* 16 (Locarno: Società Storica Locarnese, 2013), 13–30.

——, ed., *A Companion to Late Medieval and Early Modern Milan: The Distinctive Features of and Italian State*. Leiden: Brill, 2014.

——. *La Legittimità contesa. Costruzione statale e culture politiche (Lombardia, secoli XII-XV)*. Rome: Viella, 2016.

Gamberini, Andrea, and Isabella Lazzarini, eds., *The Italian Renaissance State*. Cambridge: Cambridge University Press, 2009.

Garfagnini, Gian Carlo. "Giorgio Benigno Salviati e Girolamo Savonarola. Note per una lettura delle 'Propheticae solutiones.'" *Rinascimento* 29 (1989): 81–123.

Gariboldi, Roberto. *Il Marchese avventuriero*. Milan: Edlin, 2007.

Gatti Perer, Maria Luisa. "*Umanesimo a Milano: L'Osservanza Agostiniana all'Incoronata*." Special issue of *Arte Lombarda*, n.s. 53 / 54 (1980): 3–141.

Gazzaniga, Jean-Louis. "Le Conflit de Louis XII et de Jules II devant le Parlement de Toulouse (1510–1512)." *Revue historique du droit français et étranger*, ser. 4, vol. 57 (1979): 623–30.

——. "Les États généraux de Tours de 1484 et les affaires de l'Église." *Revue historique du droit français et étranger*, ser. 4, vol. 62, no. 1 (1984): 31–45.

Geltner, Guy. "Fighting Corruption in the Italian City-State: Perugian Officers' End of Term Audit (*sindacato*) in the Fourteenth Century." In Ronald Kroeze, André Vitória, and Guy Geltner, eds., *Anticorruption in History: From Antiquity to the Modern Era*, 103–21. Oxford: Oxford University Press, 2018.

Genet, Jean-Philippe. "Pouvoir symbolique, légitimation et genèse de l'État moderne." In Jean-Philippe Genet, ed., *La Légitimé implicite*, 1: 9–47. Paris: Publications de la Sorbonne / École française de Rome, 2015.

Gewerken, Heinz-Werner. *Kombinationswaffen des 15.–19. Jahrhunderts.* Berlin: Militärverlag der Deutschen Demokratischen Republik, 1989.

Ghilardotti, Jacopo. *La Casa degli Atellani e la vigna di Leonardo.* Rome: Rai Eri, 2015.

Ghinzoni, Pietro. "Sul Testamento originale di Gian Galeazzo Visconti contenente il fedecommesso a favore dei discendenti della Valentina." *Archivio storico lombardo,* ser.1, vol. 9, fasc. 2 (1882): 335–40.

———. "Di Alcuni antichi coperti ossia portici in Milano." *Archivio storico lombardo,* ser. 2, vol. 9, fasc. 1 (1892): 126–40.

Giannini, Massimo Carlo. "Note sulla dialettica politica nel ducato di Milano prima del suo ingresso nell'impero di Carlo V (1499–1535)." *Archivio storico lombardo,* 127 (2001): 29–60.

———. "Il Biscione." In Francesco Benigno and Luca Scuccimarra, eds., *Simboli della politica,* 137–89. Rome: Viella, 2010.

Gilmore, Myron P. *Humanists and Jurists: Six Studies in the Renaissance.* Cambridge, MA: Harvard University Press, 1963.

Giordano, Luisa, ed., *Ludovicus Dux. L'Immagine del potere.* Vigevano: Diakronia, 1995.

———. "La Celebrazione della vittoria. L'Esaltazione della storia contemporanea nelle terre della conquista." In Contamine and Guillaume, *Louis XII en Milanais,* 245–71.

———. "Vigevano, terra e dimora signorile." In Luisa Giordano, ed., *Splendori di corte—Gli Sforza, il Rinascimento, la Città,* 19–25. Milan: Skira, 2009.

Giudici, Giacomo. "The Writing of Renaissance Politics: Sharing, Appropriating, and Asserting Authorship in the Letters of Francesco II Sforza, Duke of Milan (1522–1535)." *Renaissance Studies* 32, no. 2 (2018): 253–81.

Giulini, Alessandro. "Bianca Sanseverino Sforza figlia di Lodovico il Moro." *Archivio storico lombardo* 39 (1912): 233–52.

———. "Di Alcuni figli meno noti di Francesco I Sforza, duca di Milano." *Archivio storico lombardo,* ser. 5, fasc. 1–2 (1916): 29–53.

Gli Sforza a Milano e in Lombardia e i loro rapporti con gli Stati italiani ed Europei (1450–1535). Milano: Cisalpino-Goliardica, 1982.

Gnignera, Elisabetta. *I Soperchi ornamenti. Copricapi e acconciature femminili nell'Italia del Quattrocento.* Siena: Protagon, 2010.

Godefroy, Théodore de. *Histoire de Louis XII.* Paris: Abraham Pacard, 1615.

Godi, Carlo. *Bandello—Narratori e dedicatari della seconda parte delle Novelle,* 2 vols. Rome: Bulzoni, 2001.

Gordon, Stewart, "A World of Investiture." In Stewart Gordon, ed., *Robes and Honor: The Medieval World of Investiture,* 1–19. New York: Palgrave, 2001.

Gorse, George L. "A Question of Sovereignty: France and Genoa, 1494–1528." In Shaw, ed., *Italy and the European Powers,* 187–203.

Götzmann, Jutta. *Römische Grabmäler der Hochrenaissance: Typologie, Ikonografie, Stil.* Münster: Rhema, 2010.

G. P. L. and C. E. V. "Progetto per la costruzione di una mura intorno a Milano." *Archivio storico lombardo,* ser. 1, vol. 4, fasc. 2 (1877): 283–94.

Gröblacher, Johann. "König Maximilians I. erste Gesandschaft zum Sultan Baijezid II." In Alexander Novotny and Othmar Pickl, eds., *Festschrift Hermann Wiesflecker zum 60. Geburtstag,* 73–80. Graz: Selbstverlag des Historischen Institutes der Universität Graz, 1973.

Groebner, Valentin. *Liquid Assets, Dangerous Gifts: Presents and Politics at the End of the Middle Ages.* Pamela E. Selwyn, trans. Philadelphia: University of Pennsylvania Press, 2002.

——. "Helden im Sonderangebot: Schweizerische Söldnerbilder zwischen dem 16. und dem 21. Jahrhundert." In Susan Marti, ed., *Söldner, Bilderstürmer, Totentänzer: Mit Niklaus Manuel durch die Zeit der Reformation,* 31–37. Zürich: Verlag Neue Zürcher Zeitung, 2016.

Gutiérrez, Daniel. "I Primi agostiniani italiani che scrissero contro Lutero." *Analecta Augustiniana* 39 (1976): 7–74.

Häberlein, Mark. "Jakob Fugger und die Kaiserwahl Karls V. 1519." In Johannes Burkhardt, ed., *Die Fugger und das Reich. Eine Neue Forschungsperspektive zum fünfhundertjährigen Jubiläum der ersten Fuggerherrschaft Kirchberg-Weißhorn,* 65–81. Augsburg: Wißner Verlag, 2008.

Hairston, Julia. "Skirting the Issue: Machiavelli's Caterina Sforza." *Renaissance Quarterly* 53, no. 3 (2000): 687–712.

Hamon, Philippe. *L'Argent du roi: Les Finances sous François Ier.* Paris: Comité pour l'histoire économique et financière de la France, 1994.

——. "L'Italie finance-t-elle les guerres d'Italie?" In Balsamo, ed., *Passer les monts,* 25–37.

——. "Charles de Bourbon, connétable de France (1490–1527)." In Michon, ed., *Les Conseillers,* 95–97.

——. "Semblançay, homme de finances et de Conseil (v. 1455–1527)." In Michon, ed., *Les Conseillers,* 117–30.

Hankins, James. *Plato in the Italian Renaissance,* 2 vols. Leiden: Brill, 1991.

Heck, Kilian. *Genealogie als Monument und Argument. Der Beitrag dynastischer Wappen zur politischen Raumbildung der Neuzeit.* Munich-Berlin: Deutscher Kunstverlag, 2002.

Hensel, Paul R., and Paul F. Diehl. "Testing Empirical Propositions about Shatterbelts, 1945–76." *Political Geography* 13, no. 1 (1994): 33–51.

Herzig, Tamar. *Savonarola's Women: Visions and Reform in Renaissance Italy.* Chicago: University of Chicago Press, 2008.

Hochner, Nicole. "Le Trône vacant du roi Louis XII. Significations politiques de la mise en scène royale en Milanais." In Contamine and Guillaume, eds., *Louis XII en Milanais,* 227–44.

——. *Louis XII. Les Dérèglements de l'image royal (1498–1515).* Seyssel: ChampVallon, 2006.

———. "Visions of War in the 'Terrestrial Paradise': Images of Italy in Early Sixteenth-Century French Texts." In Shaw, ed., *Italy and the European Powers,* 239-51.

———. "Le Portrait satirique du cardinal d'Amboise." In Dumont and Fagnart, eds., *Georges Ier,* 95-111.

Hocquet, Jean-Claude. *Le Sel et la fortune de Venise,* 2 vols. Lille: Presses de l'Université de Lille III, 1979.

Höflechner, Walter. *Die Gesandten der europäischen Mächte, vornehmlich des Kaisers und des Reiches.* Vienna: Hermann Böhlaus Nachfolge, 1972.

Ianziti, Gary. "A Humanist Historian and His Documents: Giovanni Simonetta, Secretary to the Sforzas." *Renaissance Quarterly* 34, no. 4 (1981): 491-516.

———. *Humanist Historiography under the Sforzas: Politics and Propaganda in Fifteenth-Century Milan.* Oxford: Oxford University Press, 1988.

———. "Filelfo and the Writing of History." In Jeroen De Keyser, ed., *Francesco Filelfo, Man of Letters,* 97-123. Leiden-Boston: Brill, 2019.

I. G. "Una Grida milanese a stampa del XV secolo." *Archivio storico lombardo,* ser. 1 vol. 7, fasc. 2 (1880): 299-302.

Ilardi, Vincent. "I Documenti diplomatici del secolo XV negli archivi e biblioteche dell'Europa occidentale (1450-1494)." *Rassegna degli Archivi di Stato* 28 (1968): 349-402.

Imhoff, Jacob Wilhelm. *Genealogiae viginti illustrium in Italia familiarum.* Amsterdam: Ex Officina Fratrum Chatelain, 1710.

Isenmann, Moritz. "From Rule of Law to Emergency Rule in Renaissance Florence." In Lawrin Armstrong and Julius Kirshner, eds., *The Politics of Law in Late Medieval and Renaissance Italy: Essays in Honour of Lauro Martines,* 55-76. Toronto: University of Toronto Press, 2011.

Jestaz, Bertrand. "Les Rapports des français avec l'art et les artistes lombards: Quelques traces." In Contamine and Guillaume, eds., *Louis XII en Milanais,* 273-303.

Kaspersen, Lars Bo, and Jeppe Strandsbjerg, eds., *Does War Make States? Investigations of Charles Tilly's Historical Sociology.* Cambridge: Cambridge University Press, 2017.

Kaspersen, Lars Bo, Jeppe Strandsbjerg, and Benno Teschke, "Introduction—State Formation Theory: Status, Problems, and Prospects." In Kaspersen and Strandsbjerg, eds., *Does War Make States?,* 1-22.

Kaufman, David B. "Roman Barbers." *Classical Weekly* 25, no. 19 (1932): 145-48.

Kellenbenz, Hermann. "Augsburg, Nürnberg und Mailand in der Zeit von Ludovico il Moro." In *Milano nell'età di Ludovico,* 1: 67-78.

Kemp, Martin, Pascal Cotte, and Paul Biro. *La Bella Principessa: The Story of the New Masterpiece by Leonardo da Vinci.* London: Hodder & Stoughton, 2010.

Kessler, Herbert L. "Christ the Magic Dragon." *Gesta* 48, no. 2 (2009): 119-34.

Kindt, Benno. *Die Katastrophe Ludovico Moros in Novara im April 1500. Eine Quellen-kritische Untersuchung.* Greifswald: Julius Abel, 1890.

Klapisch-Zuber, Christiane. "The Genesis of the Family Tree." *I Tatti Studies in the Italian Renaissance* 4 (1991): 105–29.

Koehne, Boris. "Des Kardinals Ascanio Maria Sforza Feldherrnstab und Wappen." *Koehne's Zeitschrift für Münz- Siegel- und Wappenkunde* 5, no. 2 (1845): 99–109.

Kohler, Charles. *Les Suisses dans les guerres d'Italie de 1506 à 1512.* Paris: Picard, 1897.

Kolsky, Stephen. *Mario Equicola: The Real Courtier.* Geneva: Droz, 1991.

Kristeller, Paul Oskar. *Iter Italicum,* 6 vols. London: Warburg Institute, 1963–96.

Krynen, Jacques. "Naturel. Essai sur l'argument de la Nature dans la pensée politique à la fin du Moyen Âge." *Journal des savants* 2 (1982): 169–90.

———. *L'Empire du roi. Idées et croyances politiques en France, XIIIe-XVe siècle.* Paris: Éditions Gallimard, 1993.

Krzyzagórska-Pisarek, Katarzyna. "La Bella Principessa—Arguments against the Attribution to Leonardo." *Artibus et Historiae* 36, no. 71 (2015): 61–89.

Lamberini, Daniela. "La Politica del guasto. L'Impatto del fronte bastionato sulle preesistenze urbane." In Carlo Cresti, Amelio Fara, and Daniela Lamberini, eds., *Architettura militare nell'Europa del XVI secolo,* 219–40. Siena: Edizioni Periccioli, 1988.

Lampertico, Fedele. "Atto di Adunanza." *Nuovo archivio veneto* 5 (1893): 213–85.

Lange, Tyler. *The First French Reformation: Church Reform and the Origins of the Old Regime.* Cambridge: Cambridge University Press, 2014.

Lansing, Carol. *Passion and Order: Restraint of Grief in the Medieval Italian Communes.* Ithaca, NY: Cornell University Press, 2008.

Law, John Easton. "Un Confronto fra due stati 'rinascimentali': Venezia e il dominio sforzesco." In *Gli Sforza,* 397–413.

———. "The Ending of the Duchy of Camerino." In Shaw, ed., *Italy and the European Powers,* 78–90.

Lazzarini, Isabella. *Il Linguaggio del territorio fra principe e comunità. Il Giuramento di fedeltà a Federico Gonzaga (Mantova 1479).* Florence: Firenze University Press, 2009.

Lecoq, Anne-Marie. "Une Fête italienne à la Bastille en 1518." In Giuliano Briganti, ed., *'Il se rendit en Italie': Études offertes à André Chastel,* 149–68. Paris: Elefante, 1987.

Le Gall, Jean-Marie. *Un Idéal masculin? Barbes et moustaches (XVe-XVIIIe siècles).* Paris: Payot, 2011.

———. "François Ier—Roi-chevalier vaincu et captif. Ou de l'usage de l'éthique chevaleresque pendant l'année de Pavie, 1525–1526." In Martin Wrede, ed., *Die Inszenierung der heroischen Monarchie: Frühneuzeitliches Königtum zwischen ritterlichem Erbe und militärischer Herausforderung,* 128–51. Munich: De Gruyter, 2014.

———. *Les Guerres d'Italie (1494–1559). Une Lecture religieuse.* Geneva: Droz, 2017.

Legendre, Louis. *Vie du cardinal d'Amboise.* Rouen: Robert Machuel, 1726.

Leverotti, Franca. "La Crisi finanziaria del ducato di Milano alla fine del Quattrocento." In *Milano nell'età di Ludovico,* 2: 585–632.

——. *Diplomazia e governo dello stato: I 'Famigli cavalcanti' di Francesco Sforza (1450–1466).* Pisa: ETS Editrice, 1992.

——. "Gli officiali del ducato sforzesco." *Annali della Scuola normale superiore di Pisa. Classe di lettere e filosofia,* ser. 4, 1 (1997): 17–77.

——. '*Governare a modo e stillo de' signori . . .' Osservazioni in margine all'amministrazione della giustizia al tempo di Galeazzo Maria Sforza duca di Milano (1466–76).* Florence: Olschki, 2001.

——. "La Cancelleria segreta da Ludovico il Moro a Luigi XII." In Arcangeli, ed., *Milano e Luigi XII,* 221–53.

——. "Leggi del principe, leggi della città nel ducato Visconteo-sforzesco." In Rolando Dondarini, Gian Maria Varanini, and Maria Venticelli, eds., *Signori, regimi signorili e statuti nel tardo Medioevo,* 143–88. Bologna: Pàtron, 2003.

——. "L'Archivio dei Visconti signori di Milano." In Isabella Lazzarini, ed., *Scritture e potere. Pratiche documentarie e forme di governo nell'Italia tardomedievale (XIV–XV secolo),* special issue of *Reti Medievali* 9 (2008): 1–22.

——. "La Cancelleria dei Visconti e degli Sforza signori di Milano." In Guido Castelnuovo and Olivier Mattéoni, eds., *'De part et d'autre des Alpes' (II): Chancelleries et chanceliers des princes à la fin du Moyen Âge,* 39–52. Chambéry: Presses de l'Université de Savoie, 2011.

Leydi, Silvio. "La Linea esterna di fortificazioni di Milano, 1323–1550." *Storia urbana* 31 (1985): 3–29.

——. "'Con Pompa más triunfante que fúnebre'. I Funerali milanesi di Gaston de Foix (25 aprile 1512)." In Arcangeli, ed., *Luigi XII,* 59–73.

Licinio, Raffaele. "Bari aragonese e ducale." In Francesco Tateo, ed., *Storia di Bari,* vol 2. *Dalla Conquista normanna al ducato sforzesco,* 152–85. Rome: Laterza, 1990.

Löcher, Kurt. *Die Gemälde des 16. Jahrhunderts: Germanisches Nationalmuseum Nürnberg.* Stuttgart: Verlag Gerd Hatje, 1997.

Lopez, Guido. *Festa di nozze per Ludovico il Moro.* Milano: Mursia, 2008.

Lowe, K. J. P. "Conspiracy and Its Prosecution in Italy, 1500–1550: Violent Responses to Violent Solutions." In Barry Coward and Julian Swann, eds., *Conspiracies and Conspiracy Theory in Early Modern Europe,* 35–53. Aldershot, UK: Ashgate, 2004.

——. "Redrawing the Line between Murder and Suicide in Renaissance Italy." In Dean and Lowe, eds., *Murder,* 189–210.

Lubkin, Gregory. *A Renaissance Court: Milan under Galeazzo Maria Sforza.* Berkeley: University of California Press, 1994.

Luchner, Laurin. *Denkmal eines Renaissancefürsten. Versuch einer Reconstruktion des Ambraser Museums von 1583.* Vienna: Verlag Anton Schroll & Co., 1958.

Luzio, Alessandro. "Isabella d'Este e la corte sforzesca." *Archivio storico lombardo,* ser. 3, vol. 15, fasc. 29 (1901): 145–76.

——. *Isabella d'Este ne' primordi del papato di Leone X e il suo viaggio a Roma nel 1514–1515.* Milan: L. F. Cogliati, 1906.

——. "Isabella di fronte a Giulio II negli ultimi tre anni del suo pontificato." *Archivio storico lombardo* (1912): (parte prima) 17, fasc. 34, 245–344; (parte seconda) 18, fasc. 35, 54–144; (parte terza) 19, fasc. 36, 393–456.

Maffioli, Cesare. "Tra Girolamo Cardano e Giacomo Soldati. Il Problema della misura delle acque nella Milano Spagnola." In Alessandra Fiocca, Daniela Lamberini, and Cesare Maffioli, eds., *Arte e scienza delle acque nel Rinascimento,* 105–36. Venice: Marsilio, 2003.

Magenta, Carlo. *I Visconti e gli Sforza nel castello di Pavia,* 2 vols. Milan: Ulrico Hoepli, 1883.

Maillard, Jean-François. "Empire universel et monarchie gallique: Héritages italiens et aspects de l'illuminisme politique chez les kabbalistes chrétiens français de la Renaissance." In Françoise Crémoux and Jean-Louis Fournel, eds., *Idées d'empire en Italie et en Espagne (XVIᵉ-XVIIᵉ siècle),* 193–216. Mont-Saint-Aignan: Publications des universités de Rouen et du Havre, 2010.

Mainoni, Patrizia. "L'Attività mercantile e le casate milanesi nel secondo Quattrocento." In *Milano nell'età di Ludovico,* 2: 575–84.

——. "Alcune osservazioni sulla politica economica di Milano fra Ludovico il Moro e il dominio francese." In Letizia Arcangeli, ed., *Milano e Luigi XII. Ricerche sul primo dominio francese in Lombardia (1499–1512).* Milan: FrancoAngeli, 2002.

——. "The Economy of Renaissance Milan." In Gamberini, ed., *A Companion to Late Medieval and Early Modern Milan,* 118–41.

Maiolo, Francesco. *Medieval Sovereignty: Marsilius of Padua and Bartolus of Saxoferrato.* Delft: Eburon, 2007.

Malacarne, Giancarlo. *Le Cacce del principe. L'Ars venandi nella terra dei Gonzaga.* Modena: Il Bulino, 1998.

Malaguzzi Valeri, Francesco. *La Corte di Lodovico il Moro. La Vita privata e l'arte a Milano nella seconda metà del Quattrocento,* 4 vols. Milan: Hoepli, 1913.

Mallett, Michael, and Christine Shaw. *The Italian Wars, 1494–1559.* New York: Pearson, 2012.

Marcora, Carlo. "Il Cardinal Ippolito d'Este, Arcivescovo di Milano (1497–1519)." *Memorie storiche della diocesi di Milano* 5 (1958): 325–520.

Margaroli, Paolo, ed. *Le Pergamene Belgioioso della Biblioteca Trivulziana di Milano (secoli XI-XVIII): Inventari e regesti.* Milan: Comune di Milano, 1997.

Margolis, Oren J. "The Gaulish Past of Milan and the French Invasion of Italy." In Kathleen Christian and Bianca de Divitiis, eds., *Local Antiquities, Local Identities: Art, Literature, and Antiquarianism in Early Modern Europe, c. 1400–1700,* 102–20. Manchester: University of Manchester Press, 2019.

Martin, Victor. *Les Origines du gallicanisme,* 2 vols. Geneva: Megariotis Reprints, 1978 [1939].

Martini, Giuseppe. "Arrigoni, Simone." *Dizionario biografico degli Italiani* 4 (1962): 321–22.

Martinis, Roberta. *L'Architettura contesa. Federico da Montefeltro, Lorenzo de'Medici, gli Sforza e palazzo Salvatico a Milano.* Milano: Mondadori, 2008.

Masi, Gino. "Il Sindacato delle magistrature comunali nel sec. XIV (con speciale riferimento a Firenze)." *Rivista italiana per le scienze giuridiche* 5, no. 1 (1930): 43–115; 5, no. 2 (1930): 331–411.

Masson, Christophe. *Des Guerres en Italie avant les guerres d'Italie: Les Entreprises militaires françaises dans la péninsule à l'époque du grand schisme d'Occident.* Rome: École française de Rome, 2014.

Matheus, Michael, Arnold Nesselrath, and Martin Wallraff, eds., *Martin Luther in Rom. Die Ewige Stadt als kosmopolitisches Zentrum und ihre Wahrnehmung.* Berlin: De Gruyter, 2017.

Mazzadi, Patrizia. "Bianca Maria Sforza und die Beziehung des Innsbrucker Hofes zu den wichtigen italienischen Höfen der Renaissance." In Sieglinde Hartmann, Freimut Löser, and Robert Steinke, eds., *Kaiser Maximilian I. (1459–1519) und die Hofkultur seiner Zeit,* 367–81. Wiesbaden: Reichert, 2009.

McCall, Timothy. "Brilliant Bodies: Material Culture and the Adornment of Men in North Italy's Quattrocento Courts." *I Tatti Studies in the Italian Renaissance* 16, no. 1/2 (2013): 445–90.

McGrath, Elizabeth. "Ludovico il Moro and his Moors." *Journal of the Warburg and Courtauld Institutes* 65 (2002): 67–94.

Medin, Antonio. "Il Quarto libro del poemetto drammatico sul Lautrec." *Rassegna Bibliografica della Letteratura Italiana* 1 (1893): 214–18.

Merzagora, Paolo. "Il Palazzo per Bergonzio Botta a Milano." In Christoph Frommel, Luisa Giordano, and Richard Schofield, eds., *Bramante Milanese,* 261–80. Venice: Marsilio, 2002.

Meschini, Stefano. *Uno Storico umanista alla corte sforzesca. Biografia di Bernardino Corio.* Milan: Vita e Pensiero, 1995.

———. "Il Luogotenente del Milanese all'epoca di Luigi XII." In Arcangeli, ed., *Milano e Luigi XII,* 39–57.

———. *Luigi XII, Duca di Milano. Gli Uomini e le istituzioni del primo dominio francese (1499–1512).* Milan: FrancoAngeli, 2004.

———. *La Francia nel Ducato di Milano,* 2 vols. Milan: FrancoAngeli, 2006.

———. *La Seconda dominazione francese nel Ducato di Milano. La Politica e gli uomini di Francesco I (1515–1521).* Varzi: Guardamagna Editore, 2014.

Michelet, Jules. *Histoire de France au seizième siècle: Renaissance.* Paris: Chamerot, 1855.

Michon, Cédric. "Georges d'Amboise, principal conseiller de Louis XII." In Dumont and Fagnart, eds., *Georges Ier,* 17–30.

———, ed., *Les Conseillers de François Ier.* Rennes: Presses Universitaires de Rennes, 2011.

Milano nell'età di Ludovico il Moro. Atti del convegno internazionale, 28 febbraio–4 marzo 1983, 2 vols. Milan: Comune di Milano e Archivio Storico Civico-Biblioteca Trivulziana, 1983.

Ministero dell'Interno. "Archivio di Stato di Milano." In *Notizie degli Archivi di Stato—i danni di guerra subiti dagli archivi italiani*, 13–20. Rome: Istituto Poligrafico dello Stato, 1950.

Minnich, Nelson H. "The Role of Prophecy in the Career of the Enigmatic Bernardino López de Carvajal." In Reeves, ed., *Prophetic Rome*, 111–20.

——. "The Healing of the Pisan Schism (1511–13)." In Nelson H. Minnich, *The Fifth Lateran Council (1512–17): Studies on Its Membership, Diplomacy and Proposals for Reform*, 2: 59–197. Aldershot, UK: Ashgate Variorum, 1993.

——. "The First Printed Editions of the Modern Councils: From Konstanz to Lateran V (1499–1526)." *Annali dell'Istituto storico italo-germanico in Trento / Jahrbuch des italienisch-deutschen historischen Instituts in Trient* 29 (2003): 447–68.

——. *"Rite Convocare ac Congregare Procedereque:* The Struggle between the Councils of Pisa-Milan-Asti-Lyons and Lateran V." In Nelson Minnich, *Councils of the Catholic Reformation*, 9: 1–54. Aldershot, UK: Ashgate, 2008.

——. "Luther, Cajetan, and Pastor Aeternus (1516) of Lateran V on Conciliar Authority." In Matheus, Nesselrath, and Wallraff, eds., *Martin Luther in Rom*, 187–204.

Morisi Guerra, Anna. *Apocalypsis nova. Ricerche sull'origine e la formazione del testo del pseudo-Amadeo*. Rome: Istituto storico italiano per il medio evo, 1970.

——. "The Apocalypsis Nova: A Plan for Reform." In Reeves, ed., *Prophetic Rome*, 27–50.

Morscheck, Charles R., Jr. "Grazioso Sironi and the Unfinished Sforza Monument for Santa Maria delle Grazie." In Paola Venturelli, ed., *Arte e storia di Lombardia. Scritti in memoria di Grazioso Sironi*, 227–42. Rome: Società Editrice Dante Alighieri, 2006.

Morsolin, Bernardo. *Zaccaria Ferreri: Episodio biografico del secolo decimosesto*. Vicenza: Tip. Reale—Gir. Burato, 1877.

Motta, Emilio. "I Rusca di Locarno, Luino, e Val Intelvi." *Bollettino storico della svizzera italiana* 17 (1895) fasc. 1–2 (1–7); 3–4 (33–41); 5–6 (65–70); 7–8 (97–101); 10–12 (153–59).

——. "Pasquinate e censura a Milano nel '500." *Archivio storico lombardo* 38 (1911): 305–315.

Mulas, Pier Luigi. "L'Effimero e la memoria. L'Investitura ducale." In Giordano, ed., *Ludovicus Dux*, 172–77.

——. "Du Pouvoir ducal à la première domination française. La Production de manuscrits enluminés laïcs à Milan." In Silvia Fabrizio-Costa and Jean-Pierre Le Goff, eds., *Léonard de Vinci entre France et Italie, 'miroir profond et sombre,'* 301–11. Caen: Presses Universitaires de Caen, 1999.

——. "De Borso d'Este à Geoffroy Carles: L'Illustration de la sphère armillaire dans un exemplaire enluminé de la *Cosmographia* de Ptolémée." *Bulletin du Bibliophile* 1 (2000): 57–72.

——. "Les Manuscrits lombards enluminés offerts aux français." In Philippe Contamine and Jean Guillaume, eds., *Louis XII en Milanais,* 305–22.

——. "I Francesi nel Ducato: Riflessi nei libri miniate." In Elsig and Natale, eds., *Le Duché de Milan,* 79–106.

Nasalli-Rocca, Emilio. "Il Decreto del 'Maggior Magistrato' e la sua giurisdizione." *Bollettino storico piacentino* 29 (1934): 107–17; 30 (1935): 3–10, 71–80.

Natale, Alfio Rosario. *Stilus Cancellariae. Formulario Visconteo-sforzesco.* Milan: Giuffrè, 1979.

Nauert, Charles, Jr. "Agrippa in Renaissance Italy: The Esoteric Tradition." *Studies in the Renaissance* 6 (1959): 195–222.

Nessi, Gian-Gaspare. *Memorie storiche di Locarno.* Locarno: Tipografia di Francesco Rusca, 1854.

Newbigin, Nerida. *Feste d'Oltrarno: Plays in Churches in Fifteenth-Century Florence,* 2 vols. Florence: Olschki, 1996.

Niccoli, Ottavia. *Prophecy and People in Renaissance Italy.* Princeton, NJ: Princeton University Press, 1990.

Noflatscher, Heinz, Michael A. Chisholm, and Bertrand Schnerb, eds., *Maximilian I. (1459–1519): Wahrnehmung—Übersetzung—Gender,* special issue of *Innsbrucker Historische Studien* 27 (2011).

Nortier, Michel. "Le Sort des archives dispersées de la Chambre des Comptes de Paris." *Bibliothèque de l'École des chartes* 123, no. 2 (1965): 460–537.

Oakley, Francis. *The Conciliarist Tradition: Constitutionalism in the Catholic Church, 1300–1870.* Oxford: Oxford University Press, 2008.

Omont, Henri. *Anciens inventaires et catalogues de la Bibliothèque nationale,* 5 vols. Paris: Ernest Leroux, 1908–21.

Orefice, Isabella. "Libertà ecclesiastica e dominio del principe, in Milano, durante Ludovico il Moro." In Archivio di Stato di Milano, *Ludovico il Moro. La sua città e la sua corte (1480–1499),* 129–45. Como: New Press, 1983.

Orsier, Joseph. *Henri Cornélis Agrippa: Sa Vie et son oeuvre d'après sa correspondance.* Paris: Bibliothèque Chacornac, 1911.

Orti, Giovanni. *Memoria storica sul castello di Montorio.* Verona: dalla Società Tipografica, 1824.

Ostinelli-Lumia, Gianna. "'Pro Capitulando cum prelibatis dominis nostris': Privilegi, capitoli e concessioni negli anni della conquista confederata (Locarno, Lugano, Mendrisio, 1512-1514)." *Archivio storico ticinese* 141 (2007): 3–28.

Oulmont, Charles. *La Poésie morale, politique et dramatique à la veille de la Renaissance: Pierre Gringore.* Geneva: Slatkine Reprints, 1976 [1911].

Parodi, Pietro. "La Genealogia sforzesca in un codice della Laudense." *Archivio storico per la città e i comuni del Circondario e della Diocesi di Lodi,* fasc. 4 (1919): 138–41.

——. "Una Genealogia sforzesca del sec. XV." *Archivio storico per la città e i comuni del Circondario e della Diocesi di Lodi,* fasc. 3 (1920): 87–94.

——. "Nicodemo Tranchedini da Pontremoli genealogista degli Sforza." *Archivio storico lombardo,* ser. 5, fasc. 3 (1920): 334–40.

——. *Nicodemo Tranchedini e le genealogie sforzesche del sec. 15.* Abbiategrasso: Tip. Nicora, 1926.

Parsons, Jotham. *The Church in the Republic: Gallicanism and Political Ideology in Renaissance France.* Washington, DC: Catholic University of America Press, 2004.

Pasolini, Pier Desiderio. *Caterina Sforza,* 3 vols. Rome: Ermanno Loescher, 1893.

Pastoureau, Michel. *L'Étoffe du diable. Une Histoire des rayures et des tissus rayés.* Paris: Éditions du Seuil, 1991.

Patetta, Luciano. "Alcune osservazioni su un disegno di Leonardo." *Il Disegno di architettura* 23–24 (2001): 11–18.

——. "Il Castello nell'età sforzesca (1450–1499)." In Maria Teresa Fiorio, ed., *Il Castello Sforzesco di Milano,* 79–87. Milan: Skira, 2005.

Pavesi, Angelo. *Memorie per servire alla storia del commercio dello Stato di Milano.* Como: Staurenghi, 1778.

Pavanello, Agnese, ed. *Gaspar van Weerbeke: Collected Works,* vol. 4: *Motets.* Neuhausen-Stuttgart: American Institute of Musicology, 2010.

Pedretti, Carlo. *Leonardo architetto.* Milan: Electa, 1978.

——. "The Sforza Horse in Context." In Diane Cole Ahl, ed., *Leonardo da Vinci's Sforza Monument Horse,* 27–39. Bethlehem, PA: Lehigh University Press, 1995.

Pellegrin, Élisabeth. *La Bibliothèque des Visconti et des Sforza, ducs de Milan, au XVe siècle.* Paris: Centre National de la Recherche Scientifique, 1955.

Pellegrini, Marco. *Ascanio Maria Sforza. La Parabola politica di un cardinale-principe del rinascimento,* 2 vols. Rome: Istituto storico italiano per il medio evo, 2002.

——. *Le Guerre d'Italia, 1494–1530.* Bologna: Il Mulino, 2009.

——. "'Lombardia pontificia.' I Disegni del papato sul ducato di Milano nell'età delle guerre d'Italia." In Rocca and Vismara, eds., *Prima di Carlo Borromeo,* 69–106.

Pélissier, Léon-Gabriel. Les Préparatifs de l'entrée de Louis XII à Milan. Montpellier: Gustave Firmin et Montane, 1891.

——. *La Politique du marquis de Mantoue pendant la lutte de Louis XII et de Ludovic Sforza, 1498–1500.* Le Puy: Imprimerie Marchessou Fils, 1892.

——. "Les Amies de Ludovic Sforza et leur rôle en 1498–1499." *Revue historique* 48 (January–April 1892): 39–60.

——. "Les Sources milanaises de l'histoire de Louis XII." *Bulletin du Comité des travaux historiques et scientifiques. Section d'histoire et de philologie,* no. 1 (1892): 110–88.

——. "Notes sur les relations de Louis XII avec Cottignola." *Mélanges d'archéologie et d'histoire* 15 (1895): 77–101.

——. "Les Registres Panigarola et le 'Gridario generale' de l''Archivio di Stato' di Milano pendant la domination française (1499–1513)." *Revue des Bibliothèques* (1895): 271–351; (1896): 177–224; (1897): 46–70.

——. *Recherches dans les archives italiennes. Louis XII et Ludovic Sforza (8 avril 1498–23 juillet 1500),* 2 vols. Paris: Thorin et Fils, 1896.

——. *L'Alliance Milano-Allemande à la fin du XVe siècle. L'Ambassade d'Herasmo Brasca à la cour de l'Empereur Maximilien (Avril–Décembre 1498).* Turin: Imprimerie Royale de J.-B. Paravia et Comp., 1897.

——. *Les Registres Panigarola et le 'Gridario generale' de l''Archivio di Stato' di Milano pendant la domination française (1499–1513).* Paris: E. Bouillon, 1897.

Pennington, Kenneth. *The Prince and the Law, 1200–1600.* Berkeley: University of California Press, 1993.

Pensa, Pietro. "Francesco Morone in Lecco: Avventuriero o patriota?" *Archivi di Lecco* 5, no. 4 (1982): 577–631.

Pepe, Ludovico. *La Storia della successione degli sforzeschi negli stati di Puglia e Calabria.* Bari-Trani: Vecchi, 1900.

Pertot, Gianfranco. "Milano e le bombe. Le Distruzioni, le macerie, i primi interventi, la tutela mancata." *Storia urbana* 30, nos. 114–115 (2007): 255–302.

Petronio, Ugo. *Il Senato di Milano: Istituzioni giuridiche ed esercizio del potere nel ducato di Milano da Carlo V a Giuseppe II.* Milan: Giuffrè 1972.

——. "Giurisdizioni feudali e ideologia giuridica nel ducato di Milano." *Quaderni storici* 26, anno 9, fasc. 2I (1974): 351–402.

Petrucci, Franca. "Brivio, Giovanni Francesco." *Dizionario biografico degli Italiani* 14 (1972): 354–55.

——. "Calco, Bartolomeo." *Dizionario biografico degli Italiani* 16 (1973): 526–30.

——. "Casati, Francesco." *Dizionario biografico degli Italiani* 21 (1978): 235–37.

——. "Cattaneo, Giulio." *Dizionario biografico degli Italiani* 22 (1979): 473–74.

——. "Colla, Giovanni." *Dizionario biografico degli Italiani* 26 (1982): 764–66.

Peyronnet, Georges. "François Sforza: De Condottiere à Duc de Milan." In *Gli Sforza,* 7–25.

Pieri, Piero. "Attendolo, Muzio (Giacomuccio), detto Sforza." *Dizionario biografico degli Italiani* 4 (1962): 543–45.

Pierre, Benoist. "Le Cardinal Georges d'Amboise et les prélats de son clan. Le Salut par le service royal et la cour." In Alain Marchandisse, Monique Maillard-Luypaert, and Bertrand Schnerb, eds., *Évêques et cardinaux princiers et curiaux (XIVe–début XVIe siècle): Des Acteurs du pouvoir,* 49–79. Turnhout: Brepols, 2017.

Pierson, Christopher. *Just Property: A History in the Latin West,* vol. 1: *Wealth, Virtue, and the Law.* Oxford: Oxford University Press, 2013.

Pilati, Renata. *Officia Principis. Politica e amministrazione a Napoli nel Cinquecento.* Naples: Jovene Editore, 1994.

Piollet, Albert. *Étude historique sur Geoffroy Carles.* Grenoble: Baratier et Dardelet, 1882.

Polizzotto, Lorenzo. "When Saints Fall Out: Women and the Savonarolan Reform in Early Sixteenth-Century Florence." *Renaissance Quarterly* 46, no. 3 (1993): 486–525.

Portioli, Attilio. "La Nascita di Massimiliano Sforza." *Archivio storico lombardo,* ser. 1, vol. 9, fasc. 2 (1882): 325–34.

Poujol, Jacques. "Jean Ferrault on the King's Privileges: A Study of the Medieval Sources of Renaissance Political Theory in France." *Studies in the Renaissance* 5 (1958): 15–26.

Pratesi, Alessandro. *Genesi e forme del documento medievale.* Rome: Jouvence, 1999.

Predelli, Riccardo, ed. *I Libri commemoriali della Repubblica di Venezia: Regesti,* 8 vols. Cambridge: Cambridge University Press, 2012 repr. [Venezia: A spese della Società, 1876–1914].

Previdi, Tania, and Manuela Rossi. "Tra 'Le arme del Narbona e del Gran Maestro.' L'Appartamento inferiore del Palazzo dei Pio." In Manuela Rossi, ed., *Alla corte del Re di Francia. Alberto Pio e gli artisti di Carpi nei cantieri del Rinascimento francese,* 52–63. Carpi: Edizioni APM, 2017.

Prodi, Paolo. "Relazioni diplomatiche fra il ducato di Milano e Roma sotto il duca Massimiliano Sforza (1512–1513)." *Aevum* 30 (1956): 437–493.

———. *Il Sacramento di potere: Il Giuramento politico nella storia costituzionale dell'Occidente.* Bologna: Il Mulino, 1992.

Prosdocimi, Luigi. *Il Diritto ecclesiastico dello Stato di Milano dall'inizio della signoria viscontea al periodo tridentino (sec. XII–XVI).* Milan: Edizioni de 'L'Arte,' 1941.

Puff, Helmut. *Sodomy in Reformation Germany and Switzerland, 1400–1600.* Chicago: University of Chicago Press, 2003.

Puppi, Lionello. "Le Mura e il 'guasto.' Nota intorno alle condizioni di sviluppo delle città venete di Terraferma tra XVI e XVIII secolo." In Corrado Maltese, ed., *Centri storici di grandi agglomerate urbani,* 115–21. Bologna: Editrice Clueb, 1982.

Pyle, Cynthia. *Milan and Lombardy in the Renaissance: Essays in Cultural History.* Rome: La Fenice, 1997.

Quaglioni, Diego, and Jean-Claude Zancarini. "Justice et armes au XVIᵉ siècle: Présentation." *Laboratoire italien* 10 (2010): 5–7.

Quattrini, Cristina. "Artisti e committenti a S. Marta al tempo di Arcangela Panigarola." In Bartolomei Romagnoli, Paoli, and Piatti, eds., *Angeliche visioni,* 481–502.

Raponi, Nicola. "Arluno, Bernardino." *Dizionario biografico degli Italiani* 4 (1962): 217–18.

Ratti, Achille. "Il Secolo XVI nell'abbazia di Chiaravalle di Milano: Notizia di due altri codici manoscritti chiaravallesi." *Archivio storico lombardo* 23, ser. 3, fasc. 9 (1896): 91–161.

Ratti, Nicola. *Della Famiglia Sforza,* 2 vols. Rome: Presso il Salomoni, 1794.

Reeves, Marjorie. *The Influence of Prophecy in the Later Middle Ages.* Oxford: Oxford University Press, 1969.

——, ed. *Prophetic Rome in the High Renaissance Period.* Oxford: Oxford University Press, 1992.

Reggiori, Ferdinando. "Il Santuario di Santa Maria alla Fontana di Milano alla luce di recentissime scoperte." *Arte Lombarda* 2 (1956): 51–64.

Repishti, Francesco. "La Cultura architettonica milanese negli anni della dominazione francese. Continuità e innovazioni." In Elsig and Natale, eds., *Le Duché de Milan,* 15–29.

Ricci, Giovanni. *Appello al Turco: I Confini infranti del Rinascimento.* Rome: Viella, 2011.

——. "Lezioni di geopolitica. Ludovico il Moro spiega a Bayezid II la politica italiana di Luigi XII." In Dante Bolognesi, ed., *1512. La Battaglia di Ravenna, l'Italia, l'Europa,* 65–73. Ravenna: Longo Editore, 2014.

——. "Le Corps du roi et l'Italie." In Bruno Petey-Girard, Gilles Polizzi, and Trung Tran, eds., *François Ier imaginé,* 61–76. Geneva: Droz, 2016.

Ricciardelli, Fabrizio. *The Politics of Exclusion in Early Renaissance Florence.* Turnhout: Brepols, 2007.

Rill, Gerhard. "Borgo, Andrea." *Dizionario biografico degli Italiani* 12 (1970): 749–53.

——. "Cles, Bernardo." *Dizionario biografico degli Italiani* 26 (1982): 406–12.

Rizzo, Mario. *Alloggiamenti militari e riforme fiscali nella Lombardia Spagnola fra Cinque e Seicento.* Milan: Unicopli, 2001.

——. "Sticks, Carrots and All the Rest: Lombardy and the Spanish Strategy in Northern Italy between Europe and the Mediterranean." *Cahiers de la Méditerranée* 71 (2005): 145–84.

Robertson, Charles. "The Patronage of Gian Giacomo Trivulzio during the French Domination of Milan." In Guillaume and Contamine, eds., *Louis XII en Milanais,* 323–40.

Robinson, A. Mary F. "The Claim of the House of Orleans to Milan." *English Historical Review* 3, no. 9 (1888): 34–62; 3, no. 10 (1888): 270–91.

Rocca, Alberto, and Paola Vismara, eds. *Prima di Carlo Borromeo: Istituzioni, religione e società agli inizi del Cinquecento.* Rome: Bulzoni Editore, 2012.

Rocculi, Gianfranco. "L'Araldica della dominazione francese nel ducato di Milano." *Archivio araldico svizzera—Archivum araldicum* 128 (2014): 61–75.

——. "Sull'Araldica della dominazione francese nel ducato di Milano." *Archivio araldico svizzera—Archivum araldicum* 139 (2016): 25–31.

Rospocher, Massimo. "Versi pericolosi? Controllo delle opinioni e ricerca del consenso durante le guerre d'Italia." In Diogo Ramada Curto, Julius Kirshner, Eric R. Dursteller, and Francesca Trivellato, eds., *From Florence to the Mediterranean and Beyond: Essays in Honour of Tony Molho,* 381–408. Florence: Olschki, 2009.

———. *Il Papa guerriero. Giulio II nello spazio pubblico europeo*. Bologna: Il Mulino, 2015.

Rospocher, Massimo, and Rosa Salzberg. "'El Vulgo zanza': Spazi, pubblici, voci a Venezia durante le guerre d'Italia." *Storica* 48 (2010): 83–120.

Rossetti, Edoardo. "'Chi bramasse di veder il volto suo ritratto dal vivo.' Ermes Visconti, Matteo Bandello e Bernardino Luini. Appunti sulla committenza artistica al Monastero Maggiore." *Archivio storico lombardo* 138 (2012): 127–65.

———. "'Poi fu la bissa.' Due dinastie, una città e non solo." In Mauro Natale and Serena Romano, eds., *Arte lombarda dai Visconti agli Sforza*, 23–33. Milan: Skira, 2015.

———. "Sforza, Giovanni Paolo." *Dizionario biografico degli Italiani* 92 (2018): 437–39.

———. "Sforza, Ottaviano Maria." *Dizionario biografico degli Italiani* 92 (2018): 451–54.

Roveda, Enrico. "Un Generale francese al governo di un feudo lombardo: Ligny e Voghera." In Arcangeli, ed., *Milano e Luigi XII*, 107–40.

Rozzo, Ugo. "La Biblioteca Visconteo-Sforzesca di Pavia." In *Storia di Pavia: Dal Libero comune alla fine del principato indipendente, 1024–1535*, 2: 235–326. Milan: Banca del Monte di Lombardia, 1990.

———. *La Strage ignorata. I Fogli volanti a stampa nell'Italia dei secoli XV e XVI*. Udine: Forum, 2008.

Rubello, Noémi. "Una Bella et caritativa cosa. Épisodes de thaumaturgie royale pendant la période des guerres d'Italie." *Le Moyen Âge* 120, no. 1 (2014): 53–77.

Rupprich, Hans. *Wilibald Pirckheimer und die erste Reise Dürers nach Italien*. Vienna: Verlag von Anton Schroll & Co., 1930.

Rusconi, Antonio. "Massimiliano Sforza e la Battaglia dell'Ariotta (1513, 6 giugno)." *Archivio storico lombardo* ser. 2, vol. 2, fasc. 1 (1885): 1–16.

Russo, Alessio. "Sanseverino d'Aragona, Roberto." *Dizionario biografico degli Italiani* 90 (2017): 316–23.

Russo, Emilio. "Gregorio da Spoleto." *Dizionario biografico degli Italiani* 59 (2003): 291–93.

Sabattini, Alberto. *Alberto III Pio. Politica, diplomazia e guerra del conte di Carpi. Corrispondenza con la corte di Mantova, 1506–1511*. Carpi: Danae, 1994.

Sacchi, Rossana. *Il Disegno incompiuto: La Politica artistica di Francesco II Sforza e di Massimiliano Stampa*. Milan: Edizioni Lettere Economia Diritto, 2005.

Sàita, Eleonora, ed. *'Io son la volpe dolorosa': Il Ducato e la caduta di Ludovico il Moro, settimo duca di Milano (1494–1500)*. Milan: Comune di Milano, 2000.

Sakellariou, Eleni. "Institutional and Social Continuities in the Kingdom of Naples between 1443 and 1528." In Abulafia, ed., *The French Descent*, 327–53.

Saletti, Beatrice. "Registri perduti della Camera Ducale estense: La *Storia della città di Ferrara* del notaio Ugo Caleffini e il suo accesso alla Libraria della Camera." In De Vivo, Guidi, and Silvestri, eds., *Archivi e archivisti*, 285–310.

Salzberg, Rosa. *Ephemeral City: Cheap Print and Urban Culture in Renaissance Venice.* Manchester: Manchester University Press, 2014.

Samaritani, Antonio. "La 'Defensio' di Pietro Scazano in favore di Andrea Baura contro Lorenzo Castrofranco (a. 1520) ai podromi della polemica anti-luterana in Italia." *Analecta Augustiniana* 47 (1984): 5–42.

Sandal, Ennio. *Editori e tipografi a Milano nel Cinquecento,* 3 vols. Baden-Baden: Valentin Koerner, 1977.

Sannazzaro, Giovanni Battista. "L'Amedeo e S. Maria alla Fontana." In Shell and Castelfranchi, eds., *Giovanni Antonio Amadeo,* 297–328.

Santoro, Caterina. "Notizie su alcuni codici sforzeschi." In *Atti e memorie del terzo congresso storico lombardo, 1938,* 47–51. Milano: Giuffrè, 1939.

———. "I Conservatori dello Stato." In *Scritti storici e giuridici in memoria di Alessandro Visconti,* 359–66. Milan: Istituto editoriale Cisalpino, 1955.

———. *Gli Offici del comune di Milano e del dominio visconteo-sforzesco (1216–1515).* Milan: Giuffrè, 1968.

Santoro, Domenico. *Della vita e delle opere di Mario Equicola.* Chieti: Per tipi di Nicola Jecco, 1906.

Savy, Pierre. "Costituzione e funzionamento dello 'Stato vermesco' (fine del XIV-metà del XV sec.)." In Federica Cengarle, Giorgio Chittolini, and Gian Maria Varanini, eds., *Poteri signorili e feudali nelle campagne dell'Italia settentrionale fra Tre e Quattrocento,* 73–81. Florence: Firenze University Press, 2005.

———. "Les Feudataires et le contrôle territorial dans le duché de Milan à l'époque des Sforza." In Marco Gentile and Pierre Savy, eds., *Noblesse et états princiers en Italie et en France au XVe siècle,* 173–90. Rome: École française de Rome, 2009.

———. *Seigneurs et Condottières: Les Dal Verme.* Rome: École française de Rome, 2013.

———. "Convertire gli ebrei? I doveri del principe tra imperativi religiosi e necessità politica (Lombardia, XV secolo)." *Reti Medievali Rivista* 18:2 (2017): 189–218.

Scalini, Mario, ed. *A Bon droit: Spade di uomini liberi, cavalieri e santi.* Milan: Silvana Editoriale, 2007.

Scheller, Robert W. "Gallia Cisalpina: Louis XII and Italy 1499-1508." *Simiolus* 15, no. 1 (1985): 5–60.

———. "Ung fil tres delicat: Louis XII and Italian Affairs, 1510-11." *Simiolus* 31, no. 1/2 (2004-2005): 4–45.

Schiera, Pierangelo. "Legitimacy, Discipline, and Institutions: Three Necessary Conditions for the Birth of the Modern State." *Journal of Modern History* 67, suppl.: *The Origins of the State in Italy, 1300–1600* (1995): S11–S33.

Schmitt, Carl. *Political Theology: Four Chapters on the Concept of Sovereignty.* Cambridge, MA: MIT Press, 1985 [1922].

Schneider, Hans. "Martin Luthers Reise nach Rom: Neu datiert und neu gedeutet." In Werner Lehfeldt, ed., *Studien zur Wissenschafts- und zur Religionsgeschichte,* 1–157. Berlin: De Gruyter, 2011.

Schofield, Richard. "Ludovico il Moro and Vigevano." *Arte lombarda,* n.s. 62, no. 2 (1982): 93–140.

———. "Ludovico il Moro's Piazzas: New Sources and Observations." *Annali di architettura* 4–5 (1992–1993): 157–67.

Schwartz, Hillel. *The Culture of the Copy: Striking Likenesses, Unreasonable Facsimiles.* New York: Zone, 1996.

Sciacca, Enzo. *Le Radici teoriche dell'assolutismo nel pensiero politico francese del primo Cinquecento (1498–1519).* Milan: Giuffrè, 1975.

Scott, James C. *Domination and the Arts of Resistance. Hidden Transcripts.* New Haven, CT: Yale University Press, 1992.

Secret, François. "Une Lettre oubliée de Jean Pyrrhus d'Angleberme." *Bibliothèque d'Humanisme et Renaissance* 35, no. 1 (1973): 79–84.

Seletti, Emilio. *La Città di Busseto, capitale un tempo dello Stato Pallavicino,* 3 vols. Milan: Bortolotti, 1883.

Senatore, Francesco. *'Uno mundo de carta': Forme e strutture della diplomazia sforzesca.* Naples: Liguori Editore, 1998.

Sensi, Mario. "Osservanza agostiniana. Origini e sviluppi." In Bartolomei Romagnoli, Paoli, and Piatti, eds., *Angeliche visioni,* 71–139.

Seta, Valerio. *Compendio historico dell'origine, discendenza, attioni et accasamenti della famiglia Bevilacqua.* Ferrara: Per Vittorio Baldini, 1606.

Settia, Aldo. "Le Fortezze urbani dai Goti a Machiavelli." In Aldo Settia, *Proteggere e dominare. Fortificazioni e popolamento nell'Italia medievale,* 149–68. Rome: Viella, 1999.

Sharma, Vivek Swaroop. "War, Conflict and the State Reconsidered." In Kaspersen and Strandsbjerg, eds., *Does War Make States?,* 181–217.

Sharman, J. C. "Myths of Military Revolutions: European Expansion and Eurocentrism." *European Journal of International Relations* 24, no. 3 (2018): 491–513.

Shaw, Christine. *Julius II: Warrior Pope.* Oxford: Blackwell, 1993.

———. *The Politics of Exile in Renaissance Italy.* Cambridge: Cambridge University Press, 2000.

———. "Ce que révèle l'exil politique sur les relations entre les États italiens." *Laboratoire italien* 3 (2002): 13–32.

———. "The Role of Milan in the Italian State System." In Arcangeli, ed., *Milano e Luigi XII,* 25–37.

———, ed. *Italy and the European Powers: The Impact of War, 1500–1530.* Leiden: Brill, 2006.

———. *Barons and Castellans: The Military Nobility of Renaissance Italy.* Leiden: Brill, 2015.

———. "Julius II and Maximilian I." In Matheus, Nesselrath, and Wallraff, eds., *Martin Luther in Rom,* 155–68.

Shell, Janice. "Il Problema della ricostruzione del monumento a Gaston de Foix." In *Agostino Busti detto il Bambaia (1483–1548),* 32–61. Milan: Finarte and Longanesi & Co., 1990.

——. *Pittori in Bottega. Milano nel Rinascimento.* Turin: Umberto Allemandi & Co., 1995.

——. "Ambrogio de Predis." In *The Legacy of Leonardo: Painters in Lombardy, 1490–1530,* 123–30. Milan: Skira, 1998.

Shell, Janice, and Liana Castelfranchi, eds. *Giovanni Antonio Amadeo: Scultura e architettura del suo tempo.* Milan: Cisalpino, 1993.

Sherer, Idan. *Warriors for a Living: The Experience of the Spanish Infantry in the Italian Wars, 1494–1559.* Leiden: Brill, 2017.

Silver, Larry. *Marketing Maximilian: The Visual Ideology of a Holy Roman Emperor.* Princeton, NJ: Princeton University Press, 2008.

Simar, Théophile. *Christophe Longueil, humaniste (1488–1522).* Louvain: Bureau de Recueil, 1911.

Simonsohn, Schlomo. *The Jews in the Duchy of Milan,* 2 vols. Jerusalem: Israel Academy of Sciences, 1982.

Snow-Smith, Joanne. "Pasquier Le Moyne's 1515 Account of Art and War in Northern Italy: A Translation of His Diary from *Le Couronnement.*" *Studies in Iconography* 5 (1979): 173–234.

Soldi Rondinini, Gigliola. "Le Strutture urbanistiche di Milano durante l'età di Lodovico il Moro." In Gigliola Soldi Rondinini, *Saggi di storia e storiografia visconteo-sforzesco,* 131–58. Bologna: Cappelli Editore, 1984.

Soldini, Nicola. "Il Governo francese e la città: Imprese edificatorie e politica urbana nella Milano del primo '500." In Arcangeli, ed., *Milano e Luigi XII,* 431–447.

Somaini, Francesco. "Le Famiglie milanesi tra gli Sforza e i francesi: Il Caso degli Arcimboldi." In Arcangeli, ed., *Milano e Luigi XII,* 167–220.

Sommi Picenardi, Guido. *Cremona durante il dominio de' veneziani (1499–1509).* Milan: Tipografia di Francesco Albertari, 1866.

Soranzo, Giovanni. "Prefazione a Iohannis Simonettae Rerum Gestarum Francisci Sfortiae Commentarii." In Giosuè Carducci, Vittorio Fiorini, and Pietro Fedele, eds., *Rerum Italicarum Scriptores,* vol. 21, part 2, fasc. 6, iii–ciii. Bologna: N. Zanichelli, 1932.

Spigaroli, Marcello. "La Piazza in ostaggio. Urbanistica e politica militare nello stato visconteo." *Bollettino storico piacentino* 87 (1992): 145–60.

Spinelli, Marina. "Ricerche per una nuova storia della Repubblica Ambrosiana." *Nuova rivista storica* 70 (1986): 231–52.

Spont, Alfred. *Semblançay (?–1527): La Bourgeoisie financière au début du XVIe siècle.* Paris: Hachette, 1895.

Spruyt, Hendrik. *The Sovereign State and Its Competitors: An Analysis of Systems of Change.* Princeton, NJ: Princeton University Press, 1994.

Staffetti, Luigi, ed. "Il Libro di Ricordi della Famiglia Cybo." *Atti della Società ligure di storia patria* 38 (1908): vii–lxvii, 1–615.

Stevens, Kevin. "Publishing the *Constitutiones Dominii Mediolanensis* (1541–1552): New Revelations." *La Bibliofilía* 116, nos. 1–3 (2014): 215–30.

Storia di Milano, vol. 8. Milan: Fondazione Treccani degli Alfieri, 1957.

Storti Storchi, Claudia. "'Acciò che le cause passino più consultamente e con minor rechiamo'. Nodi della giustizia nei primi anni del dominio di Luigi XII sul Ducato di Milano." In Arcangeli, ed., *Milano e Luigi XII,* 147-65

Stöve, Eckehart. "Ferreri, Zaccaria." *Dizionario biografico degli Italiani* 46 (1996): 808-11.

Sverzellati, Paola. "Per la biografia di Nicodemo Tranchedini da Pontremoli, ambasciatore sforzesco." *Aevum* 72, no. 2 (1998): 485-557.

Taglialagamba, Sara. "Leonardo da Vinci's Hydraulic Systems and Fountains for His French Patrons Louis XII, Charles d'Amboise, and Francis I." In Constance Moffatt and Sara Taglialagamba, eds., *Illuminating Leonardo: A Festchrift for Carlo Pedretti Celebrating His 70 Years of Scholarship,* 300-14. Boston: Brill, 2016.

Taviani, Carlo. *Superba discordia. Guerra, rivolta e pacificazione nella Genova di primo Cinquecento.* Rome: Viella, 2008.

——. "Testimonianze e memorie di una rivolta: Genova 1506-1507." In Gian Mario Anselmi and Angela De Benedictis, eds., *Città in guerra. Esperienze e riflessioni nel primo '500. Bologna nelle "Guerre d'Italia,"* 179-96. Bologna: Minerva Edizioni, 2008.

——. "Peace and Revolt: Oath-Taking Rituals in Early Sixteenth-Century Italy." In Samuel Cohn Jr., Marcello Fantoni, Franco Franceschi, and Fabrizio Ricciardelli, eds., *Late Medieval and Early Modern Ritual: Studies in Urban Culture,* 119-36. Turnhout: Brepols, 2013.

Tavuzzi, Michael. *Prierias: The Life and Works of Silvestro Mazzolini da Prierio, 1456-1527.* Durham, NC: Duke University Press, 1997.

Terjanian, Pierre, ed. *The Last Knight: The Art, Armor, and Ambition of Maximilian I.* New York: Metropolitan Museum of Art, 2019.

Tisot, Renato. *Ricerche sulla vita e sull'epistolario del Cardinale Bernardo Cles (1485-1539).* Trent: Società studi trentini di scienze storiche, 1969.

Tonelli, Giovanna. "The Economy in the Sixteenth and Seventeenth Centuries." In Gamberini, ed., *A Companion to Late Medieval and Early Modern Milan,* 142-65.

Trexler, Richard. "Correre la terra. Collective Insults in the Late Middle Ages." *Mélanges de l'École française de Rome—Moyen Âge, temps modernes* 96, no. 2 (1984): 845-902.

Trivulzio, Gian Giacomo. "Gioje di Lodovico il Moro, duca di Milano, messe a pegno." *Archivio storico lombardo* 3 (1876): 530-34.

Turchi, Laura. "Un Archivio scomparso e il suo creatore? La Grotta di Alfonso II d'Este e Giovan Battista Pigna." In De Vivo, Guidi, and Silvestri, eds., *Archivi e archivisti,* 217-37.

Ullmann, Walter. "Julius II and the Schismatic Cardinals." In Derek Baker, ed., *Schism, Heresy and Religious Protest,* 177-93. Cambridge: Cambridge University Press, 1972.

Unterholzner, Daniela. "Essensalltag bei Hof. Zum Frauenzimmer Bianca Maria Sforzas." In Noflatscher, Chisholm, and Schnerb, eds., *Maximilian I,* 287–301.

Vaglienti, Francesca M. "La Detenzione del conte Pietro dal Verme e la confisca del suo feudo ad opera di Galeazzo Maria Sforza, duca di Milano." *Nuova rivista storica* 74, nos. 3–4 (1990): 401–16.

Vaglienti, Francesca M., and Cristina Cattaneo, eds. *La Popolazione di Milano dal Rinascimento: Fonti documentarie e fonti materiali per un nuovo umanesimo scientifico.* Milan: Biblioteca francescana, 2013.

Valerio, Adriana. "Domenica da Paradiso e Dorotea di Lanciuola: Un Caso toscano di simulata santità degli inizi del '500." In Gabriella Zarri ed., *Finzione e santità tra medioevo ed età moderna,* 129–44. Turin: Rosenberg & Sellier, 1991.

Varnhagen, Hermann, ed. *Lautrecho, eine italienische Dichtung aus dem Jahren 1521–23.* Erlangen: F. Junge, 1896.

Vasoli, Cesare. "Sul probabile autore di una 'profezia' cinquecentesca." *Il Pensiero Politico* 2, no. 3 (1969): 464–72.

———. "Ancora su Giorgio Benigno Salviati (Juraj Dragisic) e la 'profezia' dello pseudo Amadeo." *Il Pensiero Politico* 3, no. 3 (1970): 417–21.

———. "Notizie su Giorgio Benigno Salviati (Juraj Dragisic)." In Cesare Vasoli, *Profezia e Ragione: Studi sulla cultura del Cinqucento e del Seicento,* 17–127. Naples: Morano, 1974.

———. "Il Mito della monarchia francese nelle profezie fra 1490 e 1510." In Dario Cecchetti, Lionello Sozzi, and Louis Terreaux, eds., *L'Aube de la Renaissance,* 149–65. Geneva: Éditions Slatkine, 1991.

———. "Giorgio Benigno Salviati (Dragisic)." In Reeves, ed., *Prophetic Rome,* 121–56.

Veissière, Michel. "Guillaume Briçonnet et les courants spirituels italiens au début du XVIe siècle." In Michele Maccarone and André Vauchez, eds., *Échanges religieux entre la France et l'Italie du Moyen Âge à l'époque moderne,* 215–28. Geneva: Slatkine, 1987.

Venturelli, Paola. *'Esmaillé à la façon de Milan.' Smalti nel Ducato di Milano da Bernabò Visconti a Ludovico il Moro.* Venice: Marsilio, 2008.

Verga, Ettore. "Delle Concessioni fatte da Massimiliano Sforza alla città di Milano (11 luglio 1515)." *Archivio storico lombardo* 21 (1894): 331–349.

Verrier, Frédérique. *Caterina Sforza et Machiavel, ou, l'origine d'un monde.* Manziana: Vecchiarelli, 2010.

Versiero, Marco. "'Il Duca [ha] perso lo stato . . .' Niccolò Machiavelli, Leonardo da Vinci e l'idea di stato." *Filosofia politica* 21, no. 1 (2007): 85–105.

Viganò, Marino. "Du Château-palais de la Renaissance à la citadelle espagnole et autrichienne: le *Castello Sforzesco* de Milan (XVIe-XVIIIe siècle)." In Gilles Blieck, Philippe Contamine, Nicolas Faucherre, and Jean Mesqui, eds., *Le Château et la ville: Conjonction, opposition, juxtaposition (XIe–XVIIIe siècle),* 279–90. Paris: Comité des Travaux Historiques et Scientifiques, 2002.

——. "Leonardo in Ticino? Ipotesi sul 'rivellino' del castello di Locarno (1507)." *Arte lombarda* 144, no. 2 (2005): 28–37.

——. "Locarno francese (1499–1513): Per i 500 anni del 'rivellino' del Castello visconteo, 1507–2007." *Archivio storico ticinese* 141 (2007): 83–126.

——. *Leonardo a Locarno: Documenti per una attribuzione del 'rivellino' del castello, 1507.* Bellinzona: Casagrande, 2008.

Vignati, Cesare. "Gaston de Fois e l'esercito francese a Bologna, a Brescia, a Ravenna dal gennaio 1511 all'aprile 1512." *Archivio storico lombardo,* ser. 2, vol. 1, fasc. 4 (1884): 593–622.

Vigo, Giovanni. *Fisco e società nella Lombardia del Cinquecento.* Bologna: Il Mulino, 1979.

Villard, Renaud. *Du Bien commun au mal nécessaire. Tyrannies, assassinats et souveraineté en Italie vers 1470-ver 1600.* Rome: École française de Rome, 2008.

Viroli, Maurizio. *From Politics to Reason of State: The Acquisition and Transformation of the Language of Politics, 1250–1600.* Cambridge: Cambridge University Press, 1992.

Visconti, Alessandro. "Note sul diritto di interinazione nel Senato Milanese (con documenti inediti)." *Archivio storico lombardo,* ser. 4, vol. 11, fasc. 21 (1909): 59–96.

Vissière, Laurent. "Une Amitié hasardeuse: Louis II de la Trémoille et le marquis de Mantoue." In Contamine and Guillaume, eds., *Louis XII en Milanais,* 149–71.

——. "Georges d'Amboise, le rêve de l'équilibre." In Dumont and Fagnart, eds., *Georges Ier,* 49–64.

Volpi, Giuseppe. *Istoria de' Visconti,* 2 vols. Naples: Mosca, 1748.

Volta, Zanino. "Di Bartolomeo Morone, giureconsulto, maggiorente, cronista milanese e della genealogia moronea." *Archivio storico lombardo,* ser. 2, vol. 3, fasc. 10 (1893): 633–93.

Walker, R. B. J. *Inside / Outside: International Relations as Political Theory.* Cambridge: Cambridge University Press, 1993.

Weber, Max. *Economy and Society: An Outline of Interpretive Sociology.* Ephraim Fischoff, trans. Berkeley: University of California Press, 1978 [1922].

Weinstein, Donald. "Savonarola, Florence, and the Millenarian Tradition." *Church History* 27, no. 4 (1958): 291–305.

Weiss, Sabine. *Die Vergessene Kaiserin. Bianca Maria Sforza, Kaiser Maximilians zweite Gemahlin.* Innsbruck-Vienna: Tyrolia Verlag, 2010.

Welch, Evelyn. *Art and Authority in Renaissance Milan.* New Haven, CT: Yale University Press, 1995.

——. *Shopping in the Renaissance: Consumer Cultures in Italy 1400–1600.* New Haven, CT: Yale University Press, 2005.

——. "Women in Debt: Financing Female Authority in Renaissance Italy." In Letizia Arcangeli and Susanna Peyronel, eds., *Donne di potere nel Rinascimento,* 45–65. Rome: Viella, 2008.

——. "Patrons, Artists, and Audiences in Renaissance Milan, 1300–1600." In Charles M. Rosenberg, ed., *The Court Cities of Northern Italy,* 21–70. Cambridge: Cambridge University Press, 2010.

Werle, Dirk. *Copia librorum: Problemgeschichte imaginierter Bibliotheken, 1580–1630.* Tübingen: Max Niemeyer Verlag, 2007.

Wiesflecker, Hermann. "Neue Beiträge zur Frage des Kaiser-Papstplanes Maximilians I. im Jahre 1511." *Mitteilungen des Instituts für österreichische Geschichtsforschung* 71 (1963): 311–32.

——. *Kaiser Maximilian I: Das Reich, Österreich und Europa an der Wende zur Neuzeit,* 5 vols. Vienna: Verlag für Geschichte und Politik, 1971–1986.

——. *Österreich im Zeitalter Maximilians I. Der Vereinigung der Länder zum frühmodernen Staat.* Munich: Oldenbourgh, 1999.

Wiesflecker-Friedhuber, Inge. "Kaiser Maximilian I. und die Stadt Innsbruck." In Heinz Noflatscher and Jan Paul Niederkorn, eds., *Der Innsbrucker Hof: Residenz und höfische Gesellschaft in Tirol vom 15. bis 19. Jahrhundert,* 125–58. Vienna: Verlag der Österreichischen Akademie der Wissenschaft, 2005.

Winziger, Franz. "Dürer und Leonardo." *Pantheon* 29 (1971): 3–21.

Woodcock, Philippa. "Living like a King? The Entourage of Odet de Foix, Vicomte de Lautrec, Governor of Milan." *Royal Studies Journal* 2 (2015): 1–25.

Zancarini, Jean-Claude. "Une Philologie politique. Les Temps et les enjeux des mots (Florence, 1494–1530)." *Laboratoire italien* 7 (2007): 61–74.

Zanetti, Polibio. "L'Assedio di Padova del 1509 in correlazione alla guerra combattuta nel Veneto dal maggio all'ottobre." *Nuovo archivio veneto* 2 (1891): 1–168.

Zaninetta, Paolo. *Il Potere raffigurato. Simbolo, mito e propaganda nell'ascesa della signoria viscontea.* Milan: FrancoAngeli, 2013.

Zapperi, Roberto. "Biglia, Giovanni Antonio." *Dizionario biografico degli Italiani* 10 (1968): 415–17.

Zarri, Gabriella. "Profezia, politica e santità femminile in Santa Marta: Un Modello." In Rocca and Vismara, eds., *Prima di Carlo Borromeo,* 187–202.

Zuccolin, Gabriella. "Gravidanza e parto nel Quattrocento: Le Morti parallele di Beatrice d'Este e Anna Sforza." In Luisa Giordano, ed., *Beatrice d'Este, 1475–1497,* 111–45. Pisa: Edizioni ETS, 2008.

Zwalve, Willem Jans. "Codificatie in Nederland." In W. J. Zwalve and J. H. A. Lokin, *Hoofdstukken uit de Europese codificatiegeschiedenis,* 243–309. Groningen: Wolters-Noordhoff, 1992.

ACKNOWLEDGMENTS

For more than a decade, my life has run a circle around the globe between North America, Europe, and Australia. But the point of departure and return for this project was in the Tuscan hills, at the Villa I Tatti in Florence. As a graduate student reader in 2006, I arrived there after my first extended trip to the Milanese archives. At I Tatti I found a remarkable community of scholars who took my research seriously and helped me ask better questions. I am grateful to Joe and Françoise Connors and all the 2005–2006 fellows and visiting professors, especially David Gentilcore, Luke Syson, Stefanie Walker, and the late Brian Curran. What cosmic luck to return as a fellow myself in 2016–2017, where—a decade later—I found a new cast of characters but the same venerable theater. I could not have asked for a more stimulating and productive fellowship: it left me refreshed and optimistic about the richness of our field and its potentials. I thank Alina Payne as well as the wonderful staff of Biblioteca Berenson, particularly Michael Rocke, Jocelyn Karlan, Angela Dressen, as well as Lukas Klic, Andrea Caselli, Gennaro Giustino, Patrizia Carella, and Amanda Smith.

At Harvard University I am deeply indebted to Ann Blair, James Hankins, and Katharine Park. Since 2010, I have thrived in the effervescent History Department at the University of Sydney. The support of my wonderful colleagues, in particular Penny Russell and Frances Clarke, has kept me sane. Both of them shouldered extra work in 2016 to allow me to take up my fellowship in Florence. Nick Eckstein, Hélène Sirantoine, Andrew Fitzmaurice, Francesco Borghesi, Nerida Newbigin, Anne Rogerson, Dan Anlezark, and Frances Muecke always make me happy to return to Sydney's sunshine. I'm also delighted to join an inexplicable trend: most of the books on Sforza Milan published in English since the

1980s have been written by scholars who have worked, at some point or another, in Australia.

An array of libraries, archives, and scholarly institutions in France and Italy have made my work not just possible but enjoyable. For special help in Italy, I'd like to thank Andrea Bardelli at the Collezione Cagnola in Gazzada, and Massimo Baucia at the Biblioteca Comunale Passerini-Landi in Piacenza. Much of my Venetian research unfolded while I was in residence at the Centro Vittore Branca at the Fondazione Cini, where the hospitality of Marta Zoppetti and Massimo Busetto made me never want to leave. The staff of the Archivio di Stato di Milano has seen me at my weary worst, and they still continue to welcome me with warmth and collegiality each time I return. In Paris, Nathalie Rollet-Bricklin and her brilliant colleagues at the Bibliothèque Sainte-Geneviève gave me plenty of space and time to unfurl the Visconti-Sforza genealogy. The staff at Widener Library (Harvard) and Fisher Library (Sydney) have unfailingly located even the rarest imprints.

So many colleagues and friends have supported me during the long years I've worked on this project; each name in this list could expand into pages of gratitude. Let me recognize in particular Albert Ascoli, Niall Atkinson, Monica Azzolini, Nic Baker, Susanna Berger, Jane Black, Alastair Blanshard, Francesca Borgo, Stephen Bowd, Thomas A. Brady, Susanna Burghartz, Angela De Benedictis, Mark De Vitis, Jonathan Dumont, Konrad Eisenbichler, Marco Faini, Jean-Louis Fournel, Alison Frazier, Jeanette Fregulia, Marco Gentile, Giacomo Giudici, Ken Gouwens, Ingrid Greenfield, Ken Hammond, Gary Ianziti, Nicole Hochner, Catherine Kovesi, Sara McDougall, Oren Margolis, Starleen Meyer, Hannah Murphy, Antonio Musarra, Alexander Nagel, Jill Pederson, Massimo Petta, Nimrod Reitman, Brian Richardson, Andrea Rizzi, Massimo Rospocher, Rosa Salzberg, Monika Schmitter, Martin Schwarz, Deanna Shemek, Eve Straussman-Pflanzer, Carlo Taviani, Nick Terpstra, Evelyn Welch, Ed Wouk, and Cristiano Zanetti. I regret that this book went to press before I was able to read Séverin Duc's *La guerre de Milan: Conquérir, gouverner, resister dans l'Europe de la Renaissance* (Champ Vallon, 2019).

Tim McCall and Liz Horodowich, both fierce readers, scrutinized the full typescript and heaped it with thoughtful suggestions, as did the reviewers for Harvard University Press; as a group, they gave me some of the most productive commentary I've ever received. The book responds to as many of their ideas as possible; much still remains to be thought and rethought. Series editor Kate Lowe's humor and incisiveness betray her genuine care for our field; my editor Andrew Kinney's optimism and precision have been immensely fortifying. Aileen Feng and Emanuele Lugli became a second family for me in Florence, a reminder of the incessant pleasures of great company. My parents, Frank and Stephanie, and my brother James make me wish I could spend more than just two weeks a year in Canada.

More than a century ago, the scholar who first began systematically to publish documents from the French domination of Milan was Léon-Gabriel Pélissier (1863–1912). He used to study and write into the early hours, until he heard the night train passing behind the gardens of his home in Montpellier at 3:30 am. Two Milanese historians remind me of Pélissier's unflagging energy and devotion to scholarship: Letizia Arcangeli and Elena Brambilla. No other scholar knows Milan's political history in the early sixteenth century as vividly and profoundly as does Letizia Arcangeli. I doubt there is a document in this book that she has not already examined, and her rich essays always push me to think again. Her generosity and expertise have inspired me to be as considered as possible with the sources. The late Elena Brambilla, too, seemed always to be at work: she was a force of nature and a historian of remarkable breadth. She hosted me on several lengthy research trips to Milan from my student days onward—over fifteen years of acquaintance. Elena helped to make Milan a second home for me, a gift I could scarcely repay. Without her support and encouragement, it is safe to say, this book would never have been written. It is to her memory, with affection and esteem, that I dedicate it.

INDEX

Adda River, 65, 192, 194, 195

Agnadello, battle of, 20, 124, 129, 194, 195, 196, 207

Agostino da Vimercate, 247

Agrippa von Nettesheim, 216

Airoldi, Lino, da Imbersago, 125

Alberti family, 35

Alessandria (Italy), 14, 101, 111, 128, 226

Alexander the Great, 256

Alexander VI, Pope (Rodrigo Borgia), 7, 87, 92, 201–204, 206–207

Alps: cities in, 162; correspondence over, 177, 192; cultural differences across, 47, 190; French invasion across, 1, 41, 207, 241, 244; Gaulish invasion across, 29, 31; Italians crossing, 38, 95, 178–179, 182, 185, 192; traversing, 54, 66

Alsace (France), 185

Amadeites, 205

Amadeo Menez da Silva, 205–206, 218

Ambassadors, 90, 131, 155, 214; English, 234; Ferrarese, 64, 241–242; Florentine, 41, 208, 211, 212–213; French, 7, 185; Imperial, 180–181, 211; Mantuan, 59, 61, 78, 79, 96–98, 100, 188–190, 215, 242; Milanese, 7, 90, 98, 254; Spanish, 6; Swiss, 238; Venetian, 6, 84, 85, 99, 105, 108–109, 110, 116–117, 185–186, 226, 235, 237, 258–259

Ambigatus, King of Gaul, 28

Amboise, Charles II Chaumont d', 38, 64, 65, 68, 70, 210–211, 243

Amboise, Georges, Cardinal of Rouen, 36–38, 70, 112, 116, 189, 191, 205, 206, 211

Amboise, Louis II d', 36, 38

Amboise family, 36–38

Ambrogio da Paullo, 60, 61, 71, 234

Ambrose, Saint, 59, 63, 239

Ambrosiana, Pinacoteca (Milan), 226

Ambrosian Republic (1447–1450), 38, 151, 236

Anchises, 38

Angleberme, Jean Pyrrhus d', 209

Angoulême (France), 137

Anguissola family, 131

Annona (Italy), 111

Antiquario, Jacopo, 27

Antwerp (Belgium), 180

Apennines, 113

Aragona, Isabella d', 52, 89, 91–93

Aragonese rulers of Naples, 41, 86, 89, 93, 131

Arazzo, Rocca di. *See* Cairas

Architecture, 22, 56–64, 66

Archives: Ambrosian Republic, 151–152; Archivio di Stato di Milano, 20, 149; in Castello Sforzesco (Porta Giovia), 155–156, 158–159; visited by Ludovico's historians, 34; Visconti archive at Pavia, 150–151; and war, 23, 162–171

Aretino, Pietro, 99

Arians, 219

Ariotta, battle of, 20, 96, 97